William N. Dember • Joel S. Warm
University of Cincinnati

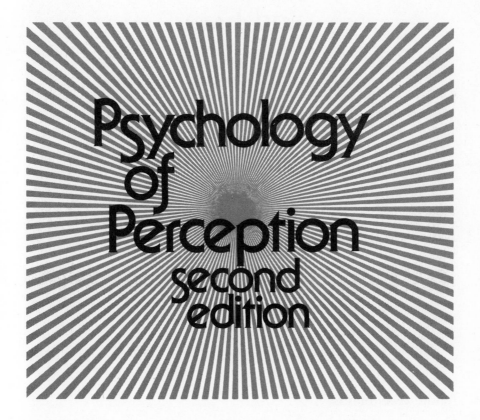

Psychology
of
Perception
second
edition

Holt, Rinehart and Winston
New York Chicago San Francisco Dallas
Montreal Toronto London Sydney

To Cynthia and Fran

Library of Congress Cataloging in Publication Data

Dember, William Norton, 1928-
Psychology of perception.

Bibliography: p. 458
Includes index.
1. Perception. I. Warm, Joel S., joint
author. II. Title.
BF311.D44 1979 152 78-16099
ISBN 0-03-006426-0

Printed in the United States of America

9 0 1 2 038 9 8 7 6 5 4 3 2

Acknowledgments

Cover figure from MacKay, D.M. "Interactive processes in visual perception." in W.A. Rosenblith (Ed.) *Sensory communication.* Reprinted by permission M.I.T. Press, Cambridge, Massachusetts. Figure 1.2—Harmon, L.D., & Julesz, B. "Masking in visual recognition: Effects of two-dimensional filtered noise." *Science, 180*:1194–1197, 1973. Copyright © 1973 by the American Association for the Advancement of Science. Figures 1.5 and 1.6—Biederman, I. "Perceiving real-world scenes." *Science, 177*:77–80, 1972. Copyright © 1972 by the American Association for the Advancement of Science.

Figure 2.1—Corso, J.F. *The experimental psychology of sensory behavior.* Copyright © 1967 by Holt, Rinehart and Winston. Reprinted by permission of Holt, Rinehart and Winston. Figure 2.2—Arand, D. By permission of the author. Table 2.3—Galanter, E. "Contemporary psychophysics." In R. Brown, E. Galanter, E. Hess, and G. Mandler, *New directions in psychology.* Copyright © 1962 by Holt, Rinehart and Winston. Reprinted by permission of Holt, Rinehart and Winston. Table 2.5—Boring, E.G., Langfeld, H.S., & Weld, H.P. *Introduction to psychology.* Copyright © 1939 by John Wiley & Sons, Inc. Reprinted by permission. Figure 2.5—Detwiler, S.R. "Some biological aspects of vision." *Sigma Xi Quarterly. 29:*112–129, 1941. Figure 2.6—

Preface

Since the first edition of *Psychology of Perception* was published in 1960, there has been a vast increase in the amount of research on perception as well as in its technical and theoretical quality. For example, what seemed a promising new development two decades ago—the theory of signal detection—is now so firmly established and so fully elaborated that it cannot properly be presented in much less than a total chapter. Similar developments have occurred in many other aspects of the study of perception, perhaps most notably in regard to neurophysiological mechanisms underlying the perception of form and contour. In preparing this revised edition we have tried to take account of the many new ideas, methods, and findings; at the same time, we have felt it important to maintain continuity with the past, so that the reader can better place recently acquired information in its historical context. In short, we have tried to balance the new with the old. For the most part, it is the methods and results which are new; the questions have been around for a long, long time.

In addition to the difficult task of selecting what to include, and of that, what to present in some detail and what merely to mention, we have had to face another formidable problem: To what extent can we simply assert the "truth" about some perceptual phenomenon, and omit qualifications and alternative interpretations; and to what extent are we obligated to reflect the reality that in this enterprise, as in much of science, answers are often tentative and research often raises as many issues as it settles? Again, we have tried to maintain a balance between the simplicity which might be most comfortable for the reader and the complexity which typically represents the current state of knowledge. Our motivation here is not just to be accurate reporters. We have in mind two main purposes for this book, the same two which guided the first edition: (1) to impart factual information about perception and (2) to carry students through the process of generating, conducting, and evaluating research in psychology, using perception as the medium through which the research process is exemplified. That is, we want our readers to come away not only knowing a great deal about perception, but also understanding how such knowledge can be acquired. Our hope is that some of today's readers of this book will be tomorrow's researchers.

As in its first edition, this book heavily emphasizes visual perception. We are not blind to the other sense modalities, and indeed make cross-modal comparisons and references to research on the other modalities, especially audition and touch, where pertinent. Nevertheless, our main interest happens to lie with vision, and that is what we are best prepared to write about. This is not pure idiosyncrasy: People are mainly visual animals, and the principles of perception are largely based on research conducted on the visual system. Moreover, we assume that most readers will already have been introduced to the other sense modalities in previous courses, such as introductory psychology, biology, and physics. Our intent is to build on that foundation, but we do so chiefly by concentrating on visual perception. As before, we also are concerned mainly with perception as it is investigated by psychologists. We certainly acknowledge the contributions of other disciplines—for example, philosophy, art, physics, biology, and physiology. And again, we try to bring in such material where pertinent. However, this is a book written by two psychologists, addressed primarily to advanced psychology students. Others, of course, are more than welcome to join us.

We were greatly aided in our work by many people to whom we would like to offer our thanks: Karen Wall and Kristine Gundrum for typing the manuscript; Kristine Gundrum for generating the data we used for illustrating the psychophysical methods described in Chapter 2; Eve Lackritz and Marjorie Bagwell for their invaluable help with the figures and references; the anonymous reviewers, who made numerous useful suggestions about style and content; Glen Rand and Diane Kopriwa for preparing original illustrations; and Roger Williams, Joan Greene, Fran Bartlett, and Arlene Katz of Holt, Rinehart and Winston, who combined patience, support, and judicious prodding in just the right doses to see us to completion through a most demanding, but most rewarding task.

Cincinnati, Ohio   William N. Dember
                                                      Joel S. Warm

Contents

1
Introduction

THE PROBLEM OF PERCEPTION

The Psychological Approach

It seems a human characteristic to take our assets for granted until they are lost or threatened. This has certainly been so in the case of our life-supporting physical environment: only recently has the general public been concerned over the fragility of the quality of such physical resources as air or water. We often treat our human resources and abilities in the same casual fashion.

To most people, the fact that we are consciously aware of features and events in our surrounding environment is not very startling; it is a familiar, natural, and obvious aspect of living which, for the most part, is largely accepted without question. Consider for example, the photograph in Figure 1.1 of a university campus in the evening. Imagine yourself positioned in the location of the camera that took this picture. Surely you would be aware of a cluster of buildings, with windows differing in amount of illumination; you would notice that the buildings were of varying sizes and that access to them could be gained from a walkway that extends below and away from the place where you are stationed. Yet if you stop to consider this for a moment, there is a problem to be solved, one which has occupied the thoughts of philoso-

1

FIGURE 1.1   A photograph of the campus of the University of Cincinnati in the evening.

phers and scientists at least since the days of ancient Greece. The problem stems from the fact that you need not actually come in direct physical contact with the elements of such a scene to appreciate their nature. Just how is it, then, that we make contact with the realities of our surrounding environment? Precisely how do we form the impressions of the qualitative and quantitative aspects of external objects, of their spatial positions and movements, which guide our commerce with the world in which we live? That problem is the central concern of the area of psychological inquiry known as perception.

Psychology and philosophy   Historically, systematic thought about perceiving was the province of philosophy. More specifically, it emerged from that branch of philosophy known as epistemology, which asks whether a real, physical world actually does exist independently of our experience and if so, how we can come to know its properties, and how the truth or accuracy of that knowledge can be determined. The psychological approach to perception takes a somewhat different task. Psychologists do not agonize over the existence or nonexistence of a physical world; by and large, they simply take a physical world for granted, particularly as it is described in those branches of physics concerned with electromagnetic and acoustic energy, optics, acoustics, and mechanics. The problem for psychologists takes the form of finding out how percepts are constructed from the interaction of physical energy (for example, light) and the perceiving organism.

Distal and proximal stimuli   The nature of this problem may become clearer if posed in terms of the concepts of distal and proximal stimuli. The term *distal stimulus* refers to a physical aspect of the external environment or, more precisely, to the physical energy which emanates from an external stimulus source. The term *proximal stimulus* refers to this physical energy as it impinges on a sensory receptor. In the scene depicted in Figure 1.1, for example, the pattern of light reflected from the buildings represents distal stimuli, whereas the image produced in the eye by this pattern of light is the proximal stimulus. It is important to realize that the proximal stimulus differs considerably from the distal stimulus which it supposedly reflects. First of all, much of the light which emanates from a distal source is lost before it even reaches the receptor surface of the eye (the retina); it is scattered by molecules in the air and by structures in the eye itself. Second, the resulting proximal image is usually much smaller than the distal object, and, as Kepler demonstrated long ago, the spatial orientation of the image on the retina is inverted relative to the distal stimulus. Third, the proximal stimulus unlike the distal stimulus is partly under the control of the observer through head and eye movements. Finally, while information about an external object or event reaches the eye in the form of electromagnetic energy, it is transmitted to the brain of the observer in quite a different form through electrochemical changes in the vast network of neural circuitry that mediates between eye and brain. Given these drastic differences between distal stimuli and their proximal representations, the fact that our perceptions are generally accurate or *veridical* enough to permit adequate adjustment to our environment is quite remarkable. Indeed, as you will see, the process of perception calls upon an impressive array of skills and sensitivities with which people are endowed.

The Meaning of Perception

Before proceeding with a description of the problems, methods, and empirical facts of perception which have been uncovered through psychological research, we want to indicate more specifically what we mean by the term "perception." Language can often be a barrier as well as an aid to communication, and the word "perception" is a case in point. The fact is that perception is one of those words that serves better as the title of a book, or book chapter, or a unit of an academic curriculum, than it does as a precise functional term with an exact scientific meaning. We get closer to the latter with the word "perceiving." That is, perceiving connotes activity, or process; by contrast "perception" seems to connote a thing or state. It is the *process* of perceiving, not some static entity, with which we are primarily concerned.

Now, organic processes take place continuously in time; they rarely occur in discrete units, with clearly delimited beginnings and endings. And yet, the investigation of a process may be quite difficult, if not impossible, without the introduction of artifical temporal "slices" into the ongoing process. Such slices in the perceptual process are analogous to "still" photos extracted from a TV or motion picture. It is these stills that we have in mind when we use the word "percept." For convenience, we may need to study percepts, but what we are after is an understanding of the total process of which percepts represent temporal samples.

Agreed, then, that our interest is in a process we call perceiving, which we hope to be able to investigate by studying percepts, we still need further to specify what that process is. To this end, we might begin by considering the notion of input-output relations.

Input and output   It is one characteristic of living things that they are sensitive to physical energy impinging on them. This sensitivity may be manifested in a simple way, such as a paramecium's swimming away from a region of low acidity. The manifestation may be more complex, such as a baby's crying when stuck with a pin. It may be even more complex, but exhibiting the same basic phenomenon, such as an outfielder's running exactly to the right place to catch a fly ball.

In all of these cases, some aspect of the *output,* or, in psychological language, the *behavior* of the organism, is related to some aspect of the input, or *stimulation* impinging on the organism. Differences in complexity arise from differences in the range and pattern of relevant aspects of input capable of influencing the organism's behavior, as well as from differences in types and patterns of potential output. Thus, it would be relatively easy to specify the stimulation and the behavior involved in the baby's crying, while to do the same for the outfielder would be an enormously difficult task. Nevertheless, the behavior of both the baby and the outfielder clearly are influenced by impinging stimulation.

Now, think of a machine which is entirely insensitive to input. We might call it a pure "emitting" machine. Its output can be complexly patterned, systematic, and even very useful, but it would be uninfluenced by external physical conditions. Its output, in short, would be invariant under variable environments. Given sufficient knowledge about its output patterns, you could predict its "behavior" without reference to stimulus conditions. In contrast, to predict the behavior of a living organism it is almost always necessary to have thorough knowledge about the organism's immediate environment.

The example above had better be qualified somewhat. Our emitting machine might drastically alter its output after being pounded with a sledgehammer or dropped into a blast furnace. In that sense, it obviously is not entirely uninfluenced by the physical energies surrounding it. But as long as these energies do not rise above certain limits, the machine's output is unaffected by them. If these limits are exceeded, then the machine's physical structure is modified; it becomes a different machine, and a different behavior pattern, if any at all, will be emitted. Once again, however, given that modified structure, the output is predictable independently of knowledge about the machine's environment.

Energy, then, has two aspects. It can permanently, or for significant lengths of time, change the physical structure of a machine, or an organism, and in this way indirectly influence behavior. This is its purely *physical* aspect.

An impingement of energy, within "limits," may also influence behavior, but not necessarily through a lasting change in structure. Its influence may be effective only during the course of its own duration; once gone, it might as well not have happened, at least as far as the machine's gross structure is concerned. Energy in this sense is a carrier of signals or messages. This is its *informational* aspect. Though both aspects are relevant to behavior, it is the informational which is of basic interest to the psychologist.

The machine described above emitted behavior without regard to environmental conditions. For many purposes this is an ideal arrangement. It is often extremely desirable to have machines that are self-sufficient, machines from which a fixed output can be expected under wide variations of environmental conditions. On the other hand, the usefulness of certain machines is markedly enhanced by making them sensitive to certain aspects of their surroundings and, perhaps also, of their own outputs.

To make this discussion a little more concrete, suppose that our emitting machine above is a new kind of subway train, designed to eliminate the necessity of a human operator. A variety of requirements must be met in the construction of such a train. It must, for example, stop at specific stations. The train must somehow "know where it is." One way of providing this information might be something like the following:

Coupled to the train's wheels is a device that measures the number of revolutions the wheels make by having the wheels generate an electric charge which is then stored in a condenser. The amount of voltage built up would be a function of the number of revolutions made by the wheels. When the amount stored reaches a certain preset critical value, the voltage is discharged, providing a signal that disengages the driving mechanism of the train and engages its brakes. The critical value is preset, of course, according to the distance from the train's starting point to its desired stopping point.

Another requirement might involve regulation of the train's speed. As passengers alight and depart, the load carried by the train varies. This variation in the load would be reflected in its speed, unless the power delivered to the wheels were correspondingly varied. How might the train "know" how heavy the load, and thus how much power to deliver? Again, a device might be attached to the train's wheels to measure their speed of revolution. If the speed deviates from a preset value, this information is *fed back* to the train's driving mechanism in such a way as to increase or decrease power output.

The point of this rather elaborate example is to illustrate the way in which an emitting machine can be made more flexible, and hence more useful, by equipping it with devices sensitive to certain aspects of the machine's own output. The behavior of the machine is no longer independent of environmental conditions. In this case the "environment" is provided by the machine's own output. An emitting machine with *feedback* has the rudiments of a *perceptual system*.

The feedback device suggested above for stopping the train seems rather cumbersome. Furthermore, station stops are rarely equidistant; a different critical value might be needed for each pair of starting and stopping points. This could be built into the system, but there should certainly be an easier way to accomplish the same function.

One such way, though not necessarily the simplest, would involve providing the train with a photoelectric cell, which, when stimulated, would give the signal to disengage the engine and apply the brakes. It would then only be necessary to install in each station an appropriate source of light to stimulate the photocell.

The train's behavior, in this case, is also influenced by conditions in its environment; this time the environment is, physically, exterior to it. The influence is exerted through the mediation of a device—the photocell—which is both sensitive to a specific source of energy emanating from the environment—the light—and capable of delivering a signal that modifies the train's output. This machine, also, has the rudiments of a perceptual system.

What is it about these two subway trains that makes it appropriate to attribute to them "the rudiments of a perceptual system"? It is simply that they are equipped with devices that simultaneously have two properties: (1) they are sensitive to certain types of physical energy, or information; and (2) they are capable, when properly stimulated, of delivering messages that modify the machines' output.

A perceptual system, then, is one which relates input to output, a system which receives various kinds of sensory input, processes this input, and thereby leads to the production of a particular response. Such a system is one which mediates or intervenes between stimuli and responses. The study of perception is the study of such systems as they occur in living organisms. The perceptual systems of organisms, of course, are tremendously more complex than those of the hypothetical subway trains discussed above. It is the assumption of the psychologist, however, that even in this complexity certain basic principles are operative. It is the hope of the psychologist that through a combination of imagination—that is, theory construction—and patient research, these principles will be revealed.

Sensation and perception   It is generally agreed by psychologists of diverse theoretical orientations that perceiving, as it occurs in people, is a process whereby stimulus information is elaborated and interpreted so as to yield organization and meaning. Look at Figure 1.2.

At first glance, this figure may appear to be nothing more than a mosaic of black, gray, and white patches. However, if you examine it for a while (preferably at arm's distance), something different will emerge—a familiar face that on subsequent viewing will reappear without difficulty.[1] In terms of our

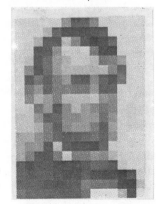

FIGURE 1.2 A computer-processed block portrait. Increased viewing distance permits more precise perception.
(From Harmon and Julesz, 1973)

definition of perception, the quiltwork of elements of varying brightness represents basic input information; the familiar face which emerges after some
study is the product of a perceptual system which actively organizes, interprets, or "makes sense" out of this basic input.

In arriving at a definition of perception, we need to face a difficult problem around the use of the terms *sensation* and *perception*. Whether intended
or not, these terms suggest a theoretical bias on the part of the writer, since
in the long historical development of psychology, careful distinctions have often been drawn between phenomena to be called "perceptual" and those
more properly classed as "sensory" (Boring, 1942). Early writers conceived
of sensations as irreducible elements from which perceptions are formed, as
experiences which are simpler and less meaningful than perceptions and uninfluenced by learning and other psychological processes such as motivation
and emotion. Such distinctions are still made by some psychologists (for example, Hebb, 1972; Scharf, 1975). By contrast, others favor a position in
which no important distinction is made between sensory and perceptual systems (for example, Gibson, 1966; Graham, 1951).

Our own position is that of the latter camp—that sensation and perception do not reflect fundamentally different modes of psychological functioning. First of all, it seems doubtful that we ever experience a "pure" or
meaningless sensation. Our awareness of the environment is most often organized in terms of meaningful objects; trees, faces, books, tables, and dogs are
normally seen rather than the dots, lines, colors, and other stimulus elements
of which they are composed. Osgood has articulated this point very cogently:

Anything even approaching a pure sensation is a traumatic experience to the adult:
sometimes the slight movements of one's ear against the pillow produce a roaring
sound, like coal sliding into the cellar or a flight of bombers approaching. Until, by

[1] This figure is commonly seen by most people as the face of President Abraham Lincoln.

immediate experiment, the source of this experience is localized—and the sensation "put in its place" so to speak—one feels a mounting anxiety. This datum fits into no frame of reference. (Osgood, 1953, p. 193.)

Return for a moment to our illustration in Figure 1.2. The patches of varying brightness that we termed "basic visual information" are not pure sensations by any means. It is difficult if not impossible to describe this mosaic of stimulation without saying anything about the fact that there are sharp boundaries and discontinuities in the scene where one aspect of the surface of the figure appears to stop and another begins. In short, there is organization among the elements of the figure even prior to their appearing as a familiar face.

Still another reason for not making a fundamental distinction between sensation and perception comes from the fact the sensory receptors do not act as mere transmission channels to higher cortical centers. In vision, for example, a great deal of organizing and patterning of stimulus information takes place in the eye itself even before neural impulses leave the retina on their way to the brain. Specific synaptic mechanisms have been identified which sharpen up the visual message in terms of intensity and spatiotemporal contrast and which serve to reduce the amount of information that is fed to higher neural centers (Geldard, 1972; Uttal, 1973; Werblin, 1972).

We elect, therefore, not to make any fundamental distinction between sensation and perception; both terms are considered to refer to a complex but continuous process by which the organism searches for and extracts information about its environment in order to facilitate adaptive responding. For pedagogical reasons, however, one can focus arbitrarily upon different parts or levels of the total perceptual process. In this book, we will be concerned less with events occurring at or immediately beyond peripheral sensory organs ("sensation") than with those more central events which presumably take place farther "upstream" in the nervous system ("perception").

PERCEIVING: A COMPLEX PROBLEM

Koffka's Question

Scientific inquiry is often advanced by a good question. Such a question was phrased in relation to perception by the Gestalt psychologist Kurt Koffka (1935) when he asked, "Why do things look as they do?" An immediate response to this question might be, "Because they are what they are," or more generally, "Because the proximal stimulation is what it is." Indeed, this form of an answer to Koffka's question was originally formulated by Greek philosophers who proposed that our perceptions of the world were due to miniature copies (eidola) of external objects that entered the mind through the senses. As Koffka recognized, such an answer is inadequate. It does not specify exactly how proximal stimuli are projected to the "mind," and it is also wrong; not only do proximal stimuli differ considerably from the distal stimuli that they represent, but the resulting percepts often have properties considerably different from these of the proximal stimuli.

Ambiguous figures   Consider the forms presented in Figure 1.3. In your initial glance at the form in the far left, either the black or the white cross will stand out as the predominant percept or "figure," with the other serving as background. Upon repeated inspection, however, the two crosses will appear to switch roles, with the original figure becoming background and vice versa. The middle figure is called a Necker cube. This cube may be seen in either of two ways: the nearest surface is either the quadrilateral *ABCD,* or *EFGH,* and these two orientations will replace each other if you continue to look at the cube for a while. The remaining illustration appears to be a three-pronged figure. But, if you inspect it carefully, you will see that it really is an "impossible figure" — one in which your experience does not accord with the physical nature of the drawing. All of these examples illustrate a common point — your perceptual experience arising from them has characteristics that are not *in* the physical stimulus per se. While these stimuli permit such experience, they do not demand it; the perceptual system itself must be contributing to the way these stimuli (and hence presumably all stimuli) are perceived.

Random-dot stereogram   A more dramatic example of this effect can be seen in Plate 1 (taken from Julesz, 1971). If you examine this figure with the naked eye, it has the appearance of a meaningless array of red and blue elements. However, if you view the figure with a red filter over the right eye and a green filter over the left (Kodak Wratten gelatin filters No. 58 red, and No. 25 green), a striking effect will occur. A spiral surface will appear to come forward off the page. Since this effect may take some time to emerge, the figure should be examined until depth is perceived. As will be described in Chapter 8, this effect is the result of presenting the eyes with different views of the same scene, a result that cannot be attributed solely to the nature of the proximal stimulation but, instead, represents a reconstruction or interpretation by the perceptual system of that stimulation.

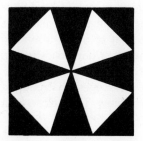
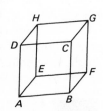
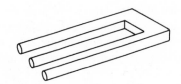

FIGURE 1.3   Ambiguous figures. See text for explanation.

Amodal properties   Relations between sense modalities provide still another means for indicating that the answer to Koffka's question does not reside in the concept of *eidola*. A large number of investigations have demonstrated that if human observers are allowed to inspect stimuli in one sense modality (visual forms, for example), they can later identify or recognize these stimuli when presented through a different sensory channel (by touch, for example). Further, training for perceptual discriminations in one sensory channel can enhance subsequent performance on a similar task in another sensory mode (Clark, Warm, and Schumsky, 1972; Freides, 1974; Gibson, 1969; Shaffer and Ellis, 1974; Warm, Stutz, and Vassolo, 1975). The interesting aspect of these effects is that the different sensory channels are receptive to different forms of physical input. The eye, for example, is stimulated by electromagnetic radiation, whereas touch experiences arise from gradients of mechanical deformation in the skin. As Gibson (1969) puts it, the phenomena of intersensory matching and transfer imply that some invariant stimulus relations or "amodal" properties must be abstracted from different forms of proximal input—an achievement which implies that perception is an active process, not simply a passive recorder of stimulus input.

Clearly, then, the answer to Koffka's question is not simply that things appear as they do because they are what they are. In order to provide an answer to Koffka's query, we must reject the concept of *eidola* in favor of a view which considers perception as an active, dynamic process rather than as a structureless medium for handling inputs received from the environment. Evidently our awareness of the world is somehow developed by a process which seeks and extracts information from the ambient flow of energy surrounding us and imposes complex transformations and syntheses upon this incoming information.

Context Effects

Brightness contrast   Related to the active nature of perceptual processing is the fact that it does not occur in a vacuum. Every bit of perceptual activity occurs in a context. That is, it occurs together with other activity, and the effect of a particular stimulus depends upon the context in which it is embedded (Helson, 1964). Hence, perception is relativistic rather than absolute. One of the simplest instances of relativity in perception is that of brightness contrast. As is illustrated in Figure 1.4, the apparent brightness of a stimulus depends not only on its own luminance but also on that of the surrounding stimulation. The same gray circle looks brighter against a dark background and darker when placed against a white surround.

For another demonstration of brightness contrast we suggest that you fixate steadily for about one minute on the black square below. Then close your

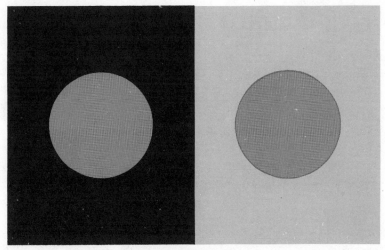

FIGURE 1.4   An illustration of brightness contrast. The two circles are physically equal in brightness, but the circle on the dark field appears brighter than the one on the light field.

eyes, and you will see a "negative afterimage" of the square: the square looks light. Now pick out two walls, preferably adjacent, one fairly well lighted and the other dark. If you change fixation back and forth between the walls, the square will change in brightness, appearing the darker against the lighter wall. These demonstrations reveal, then, that the value of a stimulus attribute can be increased or decreased depending on the context in which it occurs.

Real-world scenes   The importance of context effects in perception is underscored by the fact that their influence is demonstrable not only under isolated conditions in which stimuli are surrounded by homogeneous space or unrelated entities, but under "real-world" conditions as well. Creatures and objects in our environment almost always occur in predictable relation to other things — that is, in some situation or context. A clever study by Biederman (1972) has shown dramatically that if this normal context is altered, people's ability to identify familiar objects is severely impaired.

In this study, subjects briefly viewed photographs of many varied scenes such as streets, kitchens, desk tops, and so forth, which were presented in a *tachistoscope,* a device which permits the controlled exposure of stimuli for precise periods of time. The task of the subjects was simply to identify a familiar object which occupied a particular position in a given scene. Two versions of each scene were shown, one in which the scene was coherent and one in which it was jumbled — rearranged so as to destroy the normal spatial relations of the components. An example of a coherent and a jumbled scene is given in Figure 1.5.

Within each scene, the position of the critical stimulus object was cued by

FIGURE 1.5 Sample scenes from Biederman, 1972. (a) coherent (b) jumbled. Note that the lower-left section in both scenes is the same. The bicycle would have been the cued object.

an arrow which appeared in the appropriate location. Some of the time (cue before condition) the arrow was presented immediately before the presentation of a scene, while at other times (cue after condition) it was presented immediately after the scene had been flashed. The subjects identified the cued object on each trial by selecting it from a group of four alternatives displayed in a photo album. On half of the trials (alternative before condition) they were permitted to inspect the alternatives before the scene was shown, while on the remaining trials (alternative after condition) they viewed the alternatives only after viewing the scene.

The results of this experiment are plotted in Figure 1.6. They show that the context in which a familiar object was presented exerted a profound effect upon the accuracy of its identification. The percentage of correct identifications was poorer when the scene was jumbled than when it was coherent, and this held true whether or not the subjects knew where to look and what to look for.

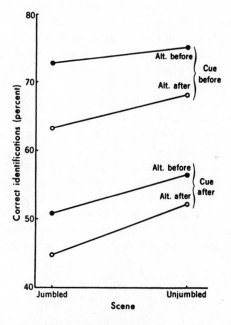

FIGURE 1.6 The percentage of correct identifications of familiar target objects presented within the context of jumbled and unjumbled (coherent) scenes. On some trials (cue before) the location of the target object was specified prior to the presentation of the scene, while on the remaining trials (cue after) target location was specified after the scene was presented. Similarly, on some trials (alternatives before) the nature of the target object was specified prior to exposure of the scene, while in the remaining trials (alternatives after) the nature of the target was not indicated until after the scene was presented. (From Biederman, 1972)

The theme of contextual constraint will appear frequently in the problems of perception that are discussed in this text. It is context which introduces into perception the complexity that often makes it a bewildering, but also a fascinating, area of study.

THE THEORETICAL STATUS OF PERCEPTION: SOME EXPLICIT BIASES

Perception as a Psychological Construct

Percepts as inferences   An important aspect of the scientific study of perception is the realization that we are dealing with the private experience of individuals. Percepts are not overt events; they are covert events, and thus not amenable to direct observation by psychologists. By way of illustration, let us perform a hypothetical experiment suggested by Allport (1955), who addressed this issue in great detail. Suppose that you are interested in exploring the effects of context on perception for yourself by determining if the background upon which stimuli are presented influences the way in which they appear. You show the lines in the left panel of Figure 1.7 to a friend, who reports that they seem to be "straight and parallel," as indeed they physically are (a point which can be easily verified by the use of a ruler). Next, you present the lines in the right panel, which are also straight and parallel but, in this case, your friend reports that the lines appear to be curved or bent. On the basis of these observations, you conclude that your friend's perceptual system can sometimes be "fooled" with regard to the physical nature of the lines by contextual conditions.

But have you actually observed the operation of your friend's perceptual process? Certainly not. You, yourself, have not come in direct physical contact with that process, nor have you observed it with an elaborate piece of scientific equipment, as, for example, a biologist might observe chromosomes through a microscope. In fact, you really have no *direct* knowledge about how the lines appeared to your friend, nor can you ever have such knowl-

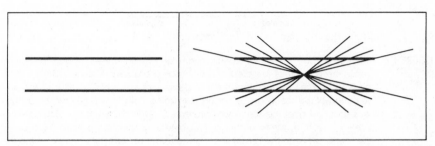

FIGURE 1.7   The Hering illusion. The two horizontal lines in each panel are straight and parallel, but appear to be bowed in opposite directions in the panel at the right.

edge. What you have done is to make an inference about a property of your friend's perceptual system, an inference based upon known stimulus input— the lines in Figure 1.7—and observed response output—the statements that the lines appeared straight and parallel in one case and bent in another. In this sense, the concept "perception" has the logical status of a psychological construct—a hypothetical mechanism which is invoked to account for certain relations between stimulus input and overt behavior.

Access to perception   The trick in doing research on perception, or any other covert process, is to develop techniques which will provide access to this hypothetical process indirectly by means of inferences drawn from objective data. Lest this logic seem perverse or peculiar to psychology, we should point out that much that is interesting in the physical sciences proceeds according to the same strategy. For example, the particles and the interactions among them in subatomic physics are known to physicists not through direct observation, but by tracks on a photographic plate.

A crucial difficulty inherent in this endeavor centers on the fact that the behavioral responses from which inferences are to be made about perception are ordinarily multiply determined. That is, they are the end product of a multiplicity of factors—in effect, all of the other processes that determine behavior, for example, learning, memory, motivation, emotion, and so on. Therefore, rules and methods need to be developed for separating the perceptual from other sources of influence on behavior.

Fortunately, some progress toward this end has been made. For example, it is generally agreed that in order to infer that perception is mediating some response, the investigator has to be able to identify a relevant stimulus which accompanies that response. If the response in question occurs in the complete absence of the stimulus, we are probably dealing with memory, hallucinations, or some form of bias in response selection, but not with perception itself (Hochberg, 1956; Natsoulas, 1967; Solley and Murphy, 1960).

Converging operations   Another means for deciding whether to attribute the outcome of some experimental procedure to perception rather than to some other process is to employ *converging operations*. This refers to the use of two or more experimental manipulations (or measures), so chosen as to allow for the elimination of alternative hypotheses about the process which mediates an observed stimulus-response relationship (Garner, Hake, and Eriksen, 1956). Frequently, *bias in response selection* is implicated as an alternative to a perceptual interpretation.

An elegant example of the use of converging operations to separate response from perceptual processes comes from an experiment by Neisser (1954) on the well-established finding that people given prior instructions which set them to attend to a particular stimulus are able to respond to that stimulus more efficiently than otherwise. Two basic interpretations have been suggested to account for this effect. One argues that the instruction-induced set serves to "tune" the perceptual system to the stimulus in question, enabling it to be perceived more clearly or more vividly than usual. An alternative hypothesis places the locus of this effect outside the perceptual system, arguing that set simply serves to raise the probability of certain critical responses and has nothing to do directly with perceptual organization.

Neisser investigated the effects of set by determining the speed at which observers could accurately recognize tachistoscopically presented words that were exposed for very brief periods of time. The observers were first presented with a list of words to study and were informed that some of them would later be presented for tachistoscopic recognition. The important feature of the experiment was the type of words used for presentation in the tachistoscope. Some of the words were control words that the observers had not seen before; others were from the original set-inducing list, and the remainder were homonyms of the set words — words which are spelled differently yet are pronounced alike (for example, NO and KNOW, RAIN and REIN, COLONEL and KERNEL). The same verbal response would be employed in responding to the set words and their homonyms. Therefore, relative to the control words, recognition of the set words and their homonyms would be expected to be facilitated if set operated on response probabilities, but recognition of the homonyms should not be facilitated if set affects the perceptual process. Neisser found that the set words could be recognized at faster exposure speeds than both their homonyms and the control words and that there was no evidence for enhanced recognition of the homonyms relative to the control stimuli. In this case, then, set facilitated seeing, but not saying — the experimental procedure of set induction tapped into a function of the perceptual system rather than a response selection process.

An experiment by Keele (1972) on the Stroop effect provides another example of the use of converging operations. The Stroop effect is one in which reaction time to name a color increases when the color prints out an irrelevant color word, for example, BLUE printed in red ink (the correct response being "red"). Obviously, the Stroop effect reflects interference in the handling of stimulus information. But what is the source of this interference? One possibility is that the lengthening of reaction time stems from the additional time it takes for the perceptual system to process divergent sources of information: color and form. An alternative interpretation is that the two sources of information lead to different responses and that response conflict is the source of the Stroop phenomenon.

In order to answer these questions, Keele obtained reaction times for naming the color of ink when the ink printed out color and noncolor words and scrambled letters. The noncolor-word condition presented divergent sources of input with respect to color and form, but would not require divergent responses in eliciting *color* names. Keele's results indicated that reaction times for color naming were almost identical in the noncolor-word and scrambled-letter conditions and that they were much slower in the color-word condition — the condition which allowed for conflict in terms of both input information and response selection. These results led Keele to conclude that the source of interference lay not in the perceptual processing of divergent sources of stimulus information but rather in the selection of appropriate responses once this information had been processed.

The experiments by Neisser and by Keele illustrate how it may be possible to determine experimentally the boundaries between perception and other processes which affect overt behavior. Through clever experiments like these, psychologists who study perception are able to perform a systems analysis upon unseen mental processes or, as Julesz (1971) has described it, to do "mental anatomy without a knife."

Explanatory Frameworks

Molecular versus molar approaches   In thinking about the nature of perception, psychologists have been plagued by the problem of *reductionism,* or more generally by the problem of level of explanation. Some students of perception seek to account for perceptual phenomena by trying to reduce them to physiological events. For this approach, a knowledge of the physiochemical composition of the proximal stimuli which trigger particular perceptual experiences and of the anatomical and physiological systems which subserve these experiences constitutes the appropriate level of explanation. Granted that physiological processes must underlie psychological processes, it seems to us and to others as well (for example, Kaufman, 1974; Neisser, 1967; Uttal, 1973) that current knowledge in physiology is not sufficiently developed to account fully for perception. If we want to understand how the perceptual system works, we may need to appeal to nonphysiological sources of explanation. Moreover, even if we did have complete knowledge of the physiological factors involved, there remains the question of whether a reductionist explanation would be entirely satisfactory: can we ever really account for behavior at the molar level when we reduce it to a molecular level (Anokhin, 1961; Woodworth, 1958; Woodworth and Sheehan, 1964)? An alternative approach to understanding perception, then, is to seek theoretical explanations which remain at the purely psychological level.

The position taken here is of the latter sort. The orientation of this book is to search for an understanding of perceptual processes in terms of the kinds of psychological operations which may be inherent in these processes. We will deal mainly with questions about how the perceptual system functions and less so with the properties of the "hardware" of which it is composed. Of course, physiological factors can and do impose limitations on perceptual organization. Therefore, we will not entirely neglect physiological mechanisms; they will be brought in where especially pertinent.

Structuralism, Gestalt psychology, and behaviorism   Workers in the philosophy of science have made the interesting observation that the growth of a particular field of science does not come solely from the gradual accumulation of empirical facts; it comes also from periodic changes in the ways of looking at or approaching the phenomena of interest (Conant, 1947; Kuhn, 1962; Leeper, 1972). This point is nowhere more evident than in the historical development of the study of perception (Boring, 1942; Pastore, 1971; Woodworth and Sheehan, 1964).

Psychology was founded as an experimental science in the late 19th century, and it took on the structuralist flavor of the prevailing physical sciences. Structuralism, as formulated by Wilhelm Wundt, posed psychology's task as discovering the elements of conscious experience (e.g., sensations, feelings and images) and their modes of combination. This was to be accomplished by the method of *introspection,* a technique of analytic self-observation, in which emphasis is placed upon teasing out the components of immediate experience. In the early part of the present century, the structuralist approach was challenged both by *Gestalt* psychology and by *behaviorism,* though for quite different reasons.

The Gestaltists elected to study perception in terms of inherent organization and configurational properties, and they built up a formidable array of evidence to suggest that psychological events in general, and perceptual events in particular, must be understood in terms of their holistic nature; breaking them down into elements destroys their essential meaning. "The whole is greater than the sum of its parts" is a phrase which epitomizes this conceptual approach toward the investigation of perceptual processes. Like the structuralists, Gestalt psychologists made use of subjective report, but in the form of *phenomenological observation,* which focuses on how things appear rather than on how they are composed.

Both of these approaches were indicted on methodological grounds by John Watson, the founder of behaviorism. Watson argued that introspection and phenomenological observation were mentalistic and therefore unscientific. That is, the data of psychology, as in all sciences, must be objective, not subjective, so that they can be open to public scrutiny and verification. Consequently, the methodological emphasis in all branches of psychology was to be on observable stimuli and observable responses. This position became the dominant theme in American psychology. In the early days of the behavioristic tradition, emphasis was placed on an "empty organism" view, in which the focus of consideration was only upon observable events and not upon mediational activities between these events. Later, however, neo-behavioristic psychologists began to use observable stimulus-response relations to draw inferences about covert processes within the organism.

Information processing   Recently, a vigorous new approach has evolved within experimental psychology known as the information-processing approach. It, too, makes use of objective stimulus-response relations to draw inferences about mediational mechanisms, but its view of the processes that intervene between stimuli and responses is more dynamic than the one which characterized the earlier behavioristic tradition. The information-processing approach has its origins in the need to understand the complex perceptual skills involved in operating complex man-machine systems and in the development of communication engineering and the general-purpose computer. It owes its present form to the seminal work of psychologists such as Broadbent (1965; 1971), Garner (1962), Fitts and Posner (1967), Neisser (1967), and Simon (1967). A good review of the genesis of this approach can be found in Leeper (1972).

The information-processing approach to perception stresses a limited-capacity system which processes stimulus input in terms of a sequence of operations taking place in several stages over time. It emphasizes how stimulus input is coded, stored, and utilized, and it seeks to examine the interactions between subsystems of the perceptual process as well as those between perception and other processes (e.g., learning and memory). Our treatment of perception in this book broadly follows the information-processing approach. It is essential to note that we are referring not to a particular theory of perception in the formal sense but only to a general point of view which provides a convenient framework within which to study the complex, often elusive phenomena known collectively as perception.

2
Basic Psychophysics

PSYCHOPHYSICAL QUESTIONS

Input and Output

In the first chapter, a perceptual system was defined as one that relates input to output. There is a wide variety of questions that one can ask about the operation of such a system.

On the input side, such questions as these are important: (1) What general types of information or energy can the system receive? (2) For a given type of energy, what is the least amount of energy required for the system to be activated? (3) For a given type of energy, what is the smallest difference in amount of energy to which the system can react? (4) How does the system respond to variations in amount of energy? These questions represent basic queries into the manner in which the perceptual system handles information regarding the internal and external environment of the perceiver provided by the eye, the ear, the skin, and other sensory organs. To answer such questions empirically, however, one must consult not only the input side but also the output side of the system. Here the important issues are mainly methodological. They seem to boil down to one general question: What aspects of output best reveal the information processing properties of the system? The nature of these issues may perhaps be best considered initially in terms of a practical example.

An Illustrative Example

In the late 1950s, a great deal of concern was expressed over the claim that a method had been developed for presenting advertising matter without the viewers' knowing that they had been stimulated. The message presumably reached the viewers in a form that was effective in modifying one aspect of their behavior without modifying another. For example, in response to the message "Buy popcorn," they would do so, but without having been aware that the message had been presented. The message was said to be subliminal, in the sense that the viewers were unaware of it.

It is easy to see why some people would find such an advertising technique ethically questionable. But for the purposes of the present chapter, "subliminal advertising" provides an excellent vehicle for introducing some of the basic perceptual questions and the kinds of tasks used to study them.

As indicated above, the subliminal advertising technique, to be effective, must fulfill two requirements: (1) the viewers must not be aware of any stimulation from the message; (2) the viewers' behavior must be influenced in a very particular, and very gross, way—they must buy popcorn. The technique, as was claimed by its developers, involves repeatedly flashing the message on a screen (e.g., of a movie theater). In order that the veiwers not be aware of the message (since this would detract from their enjoyment of the movie, and might therefore have the undesired effect of decreasing popcorn sales), it is flashed on the screen for very brief durations. Also, it is of a very low brightness level compared with the part of the screen on which it is flashed.

Note again that the point of this procedure is to get the message "through" without the viewers' being aware that anything is happening on the screen other than the movie they are watching. Thus, not only is the message unreadable, but its very presence must go unnoticed.

The distinction between "unreadable" and "unnoticed" is a very useful one. It should be obvious that for a stimulus to be noticed requires much less information than for it to be readable. Indeed, noticing the presence of a stimulus seems to require just about the least information of any perceptual task a person might be asked to perform. On the other hand, being able to read a message seems to require a great deal more information.

The first point to be made, then, is that there is a variety of perceptual tasks, and that these tasks may be ordered according to the amount of information required to perform them successfully.

The concept of a threshold The word "subliminal" is synonymous with the phrase "below threshold." From the discussion above, it should be apparent that a stimulus which is below threshold is one containing insufficient information for a particular perceptual task to be successfully accomplished. In contrast, an above-threshold stimulus does contain the necessary amount of information. Obviously, there must be some particular amount of information which characterizes the point separating below-threshold from above-threshold stimulation. It is this point of transition which is called the threshold. In general, a threshold is defined as the minimal amount of information required for the accomplishment of a task. Note that in the definition of a threshold, the input-receiving properties of the system are determined by reference to the system's output—that is, task accomplishment. The individual must do something to reveal that the threshold value of stimulation has been reached. In this case, the measure of accomplishment may be an increase in popcorn sales following the "subliminal" advertisement.

Detection of a change   What was referred to above as "noticing the presence of" a stimulus will hereafter be called detection. A detection task requires nothing more than indicating that some predefined event has occurred. No other information about the event is called for, and therefore the stimulus need not convey information beyond what is enough to establish its existence.

The detection threshold will be at a minimum when the perceptual task is the most general. In the example above, assume for now that the screen was blank except when "Buy popcorn" was projected on it. The viewers' task was to indicate "whether or not they had noticed a flash of light on the screen." This task is more general than one requiring the viewers to indicate, for example, "whether or not they had noticed some letters flashed on the screen." The latter task would probably yield a higher threshold value than the former.

The task might have been phrased so as to be even more general than the original one. For example, the viewers might have been asked to indicate "whether or not something happened on the screen." This form of the detection task has been found empirically to yield the lowest threshold, at least with experienced subjects.

The point here is that even within the category of detection there are tasks that differ in their generality, and hence differ in the threshold values they yield.

What seems psychologically basic to the most general form of the detection task is a reaction to change or rate of change. "Did something happen on the screen?" psychologically means, "Did anything about the screen change in any way?" An immediate response to change seems to be one of the fundamental properties of the perceptual system.

This idea is one of those which have a long history in psychological thought. It is clearly expressed by William James in his *Principles of Psychology:*

There is a real sensation of difference, aroused by the shock of transition from one perception to another which is unlike the first. This sensation of difference has its own peculiar quality, as difference, which remains sensible, no matter of what sort the terms may be, between which it obtains. (James, 1890, pt. I, p. 495.)

One of the most fascinating aspects of this primitive reaction to change is that the individual may be aware of change, but not necessarily aware of what has changed, in what manner it has changed, or how much it has changed. Again, James has nicely stated this idea:

The difference, thus immediately felt between two terms, is independent of our ability to identify either of the terms by itself. I can feel two distinct spots to be touched on my skin, yet not know which is above and which is below. I can observe two neighboring musical tones to differ, and still not know which of the two is the higher in pitch. Similarly I may discriminate two neighboring tints, whilst remaining uncertain which is the bluer or the yellower, or how either differs from its mate. (James, 1890, Pt. I, p. 496.)

In summary, then, the detection task requires reporting the occurrence of this "shock of transition." There are a number of special methods that have been developed for measuring detection thresholds. These will be described in detail later in the chapter. At this point, however, it will be useful to indicate one important aspect of these methods.

It is conventional to speak of two kinds of detection thresholds: *absolute* and *difference*. The *absolute threshold* refers to the least amount of energy that a system can respond to when the stimulus to be detected is imposed on a "zero background." That is, the system is unstimulated except for the presentation of the to-be-detected, or "target," stimulus. For example, the absolute detection threshold for the stimulus "Buy popcorn" would be obtained if the screen and the rest of the theater were completely dark, except for those times when the message was flashed.

A *difference threshold* refers to the least change in stimulation that can be detected when the system is already being stimulated. Here, for example, "Buy popcorn" would be imposed on an already illuminated screen, and the experimental problem would be to find out how much brighter than the screen the message must be in order to be detected at threshold level. The illustrations in the James quotation above are also examples of the detection of a difference.

In the sense that detection, in essence, involves a reaction to change, the distinction between absolute and difference thresholds may be a trivial one. The absolute threshold involves detecting a change from zero to some finite value; the difference threshold involves detecting a change from one finite value to another. In both cases it is the change which is basic. Whether this is a change from zero or from some other value is probably not of fundamental importance so far as the perceptual process itself is concerned.

It should be pointed out that the perceptual system is responsive not only to change but also to the opposite of change — that is, constancy or equality. The response to equality does not necessarily represent merely the failure to notice a change. Under many conditions the "sensation" of equality, to borrow from James, is just as positive, just as "shocking," as the "sensation of difference." For example, while one is rarely struck by the difference between the faces of two people, the near identity of the faces of twins is often extremely compelling.

Recognition thresholds   Consider once again the subliminal advertising example. When the concept of a detection threshold was being discussed, it was pointed out that in the measurement of such a threshold the subject's task was merely to report the existence, or occurrence, of an event. It was not necessary to say, for example, what it was that had occurred.

Suppose, however, that the task is different; the subject must report what the message was. To make the task easier, the instructions specify that two words will be flashed on the screen, and these words will be one of the following phrases: (1) "Buy popcorn," (2) "Drink Coke," (3) "Almond Joy," (4) "Coffee time."

In order to perform this task, subjects must go through something like the following process. They must compare the perceived message ("Buy popcorn") with each of the four possible messages, and select the one that is the least different from it. In actuality, this process may involve using a number of features of the message; in the present case, any one of several features would suffice. For example, subjects might concentrate only on first letters or on last letters, or they might consider only the location of the gap between the two words. Whatever features the subjects use, their report can be conceived of as depending ultimately on the extent to which the presented target matches some aspect or aspects of the members of the set of possible targets.

A task such as the one above is called a *recognition task*. A recognition threshold can be obtained in the same manner as the detection threshold — that is, by finding the minimal amount of information necessary for correct recognition at some arbitrary level of probability. In the illustration above, "information" could be varied, for example, by changing the brightness of the message or by changing its duration. Again, it should be obvious that a recognition threshold for a given stimulus will be higher than a detection threshold for that stimulus.

Identification thresholds   In the recognition task described above, the subjects are provided with a set of possible stimuli that they must match with a target stimulus. For some purposes, it may be necessary to omit the set of possible stimuli. The subjects are simply asked to identify the target stimulus. They may be told that it consists of two English words and must report what the words are.

The basic process underlying the identification task is probably the same as that for the recognition task. The difference is that in the identification task the subjects must provide their own comparison stimuli against which to match the perceived stimulus. Knowing that the target is "two English words" does somewhat narrow the range of possible alternatives, though it still leaves the range enormous compared with that in the recognition task. For this reason, identification thresholds ordinarily would be expected to be, or seem to be, higher than recognition thresholds.

To return to the subliminal advertising situation, the viewers are being asked, in a sense, to perform a kind of identification task. That is, they must make one particular response—buying popcorn—out of a very large number of possible responses, including doing nothing. The popcorn-buying response indicates that they have "identified" the message.

Indeed, the buying requirement seems even more stringent than an accurate verbal report might be. To satisfy the buying requirement, a viewer must, after all, get up, walk to the popcorn counter, fight through the rest of the crowd that is presumably doing the same thing, get the attention of the harried salesperson, ask for popcorn, and put up fifty cents—all this without being aware that anything unusual has happened on the screen.

Incidentally, it is such considerations as these that make one so skeptical about the claims of the subliminal advertisers. Of course, the general scheme out of which these doubts arise may be wrong, at least in some respects. Verification of the advertising claims would definitely force some revision of the ideas presented in this section. Regardless of whether or not this is necessary, however, these ideas should prove useful as a preliminary framework for understanding the kinds of methodology utilized in much perceptual research.

BASIC CONCEPTS IN PSYCHOPHYSICS

Objective Measurement

Definition of psychophysics   Thus far, in the questions we have posed regarding a perceptual task, and in our subliminal advertising example, we have implied the existence of quantitative relations between changes in physical stimulation and concomitant changes in the reported aspects of sensory experience. Such relations, and methods for investigating them, comprise an important part of the study of perception known as *psychophysics*. Familiarity with psychophysics is essential for an understanding of research in perception, since much of the work in perception employs some variety of what are called psychophysical methods. Indeed, much of the language of perception is the language of psychophysics! Many of the psychophysical methods are as old as experimental psychology itself, whereas others are of more recent origin. All, however, have as their purpose the precise, reliable, and efficient assessment of lawful relationships between the physical characteristics of stimuli and the reportable aspects of sensory experience.

The problem of phenomenalism   The phrase "reportable aspects of sensory experience," used in describing the purpose of psychophysical methods, is important and merits closer examination. Recall from our discussion in

Chapter 1 that perception is a covert process. As such, it represents the private experiences of the observer—experiences which are not open to direct observation by the psychophysical investigator. Instead, the nature of these experiences is known by inferences made from the relation between stimulus input and overt responses. What kinds of responses should we use in making such inferences? We could, of course, ask for a detailed description of the observer's impressions of the stimulus. Such a report represents a self-observation and is termed a *phenomenal report.* Undoubtedly, a report of this sort could reveal a great deal about the observer's experience, but reliance upon phenomenal reports poses substantial methodological problems for the study of perception.

Attneave (1962) has made the point that the observer's response system can be considered as a set of instruments by which we can make observations of subjective experience. As in physical measurement, care must be taken to ensure precision. Elaborate verbal utterances, however, constitute reports on "private" data—their accuracy cannot be checked against those of other observers and comparisons between observers cannot be made except in the grossest way. Phenomenological reports, then, are too closely tied to the observer's own act of observing to meet the rigorous standards of objectivity and public verifiability that are characteristic of modern science (Allport, 1955; Natsoulas, 1967). The psychophysical methods represent an alternative approach to the problem of probing the observer's experience—an approach which emphasizes objective and quantitative measurement.

Psychophysical Assumptions

Three continua   Before describing the technical details of the classical psychophysical methods, we want first to consider some of the basic concepts involved in their use. Implicit in any psychophysical investigation is the assumption of three continua involving physical, subjective, and judgmental relations (Corso, 1967; Guilford, 1954). The three continua are outlined in Figure 2.1.

The physical continuum represents a graded series of changes in some physical property of a stimulus such as the intensity of a light source, the amplitude or frequency of a sound wave, or the weight of an object. The subjective continuum corresponds to such familiar aspects of sensory experience as brightness, loudness, pitch, and heaviness and reflects a graded series of "private" responses to changes in the physical properties of stimuli. The last continuum, the judgment continuum, signifies overt responses by the observer, often taking the form of simple verbal reports, such as "I see a flash of light." The data on which psychophysical measures are based derive from overt judgments; it is from these data that we *infer* the nature of the subjective experiences which accompany variations in the physical nature of the stimuli. Researchers in psychophysics often assume that a perfect linear corre-

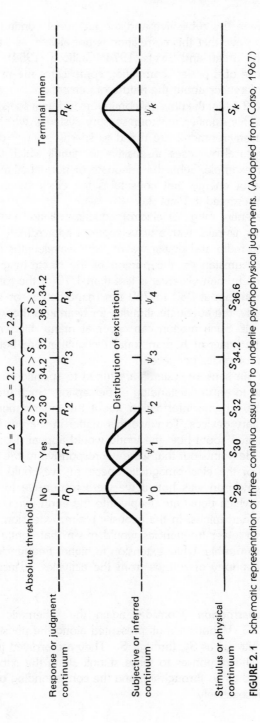

FIGURE 2.1 Schematic representation of three continua assumed to underlie psychophysical judgments. (Adapted from Corso, 1967)

lation exists between the subjective and the judgment continua, but there is good reason to believe that this correlation is not always as neat and simple as we might wish (Green and Swets, 1974; Guilford, 1954). As you might expect, the absence of a perfect correlation complicates the process of drawing appropriate inferences about the nature of perception.

Note in Figure 2.1 that the physical continuum is drawn so as to be the longest of the three. This signifies that our sensory systems, which gather information about the environment, are tuned to specific ranges of energy, and we are, for all practical purposes, insensitive to stimuli which fall outside the critical range. For example, light, the adequate or normal stimulus for vision, represents a class of energy that constitutes the electromagnetic spectrum. This spectrum is presented in Plate 2.

Note that the entire range of electromagnetic radiation extends from the extremely short cosmic rays, with a wavelength of approximately 10 trillionths of an inch, to long radio and power waves, with wavelengths of many miles. Under ordinary circumstances, the portion of the electromagnetic spectrum that is visible to the human observer is less than 1/70 of the total range—that is, wavelengths from about 380 to 760 nm (nanometers, or millionths of a millimeter). Similarly, the adequate stimulus for hearing is the wave motion of molecules in the air. Such motion can occur at many different frequencies, but in general, the limits of human tonal recognition are between 20 and 20,000 Hz (Hertz, or cycles per second).

The fact that our sensory systems are tuned to specific ranges of energy is vitally important to an understanding of perception. Such tuning sets basic limits on our ability to gain information about the environment without the use of supplementary devices. To place this matter in sharper focus, Geldard (1962) has speculated about how the world would appear if our senses were tuned differently. He points out that were we responsive to the long waves of the infrared part of the electromagnetic spectrum, we could tell by merely looking if an electric iron was hot; if we were responsive to the extremely short cosmic rays which penetrate deeply into the earth, we could "see" the presence of caves and mines. In the acoustic realm, extension of the audible range of sounds to lower frequencies would mean that gently swaying trees would be heard to rumble, while extension to higher frequencies would bring with it a new cacophony of sounds from the activities of insects and small marine animals.

Statistical abstraction Consider again the schematic diagram presented in Figure 2.1. Various stimuli presented along the physical continuum are designated arbitrarily as S_{29} through S_k. They are arrayed in terms of energy magnitude. The responses to these stimuli along the subjective continuum are designated as ψ_o through ψ_k, and the corresponding overt responses as R_o through R_k respectively.

A major assumption of psychophysics is that at any brief moment in time a particular amount of energy is required for accomplishing a given perceptual task. Nevertheless, this value may fluctuate from time to time for the individual observer. Thus, whereas at a given moment the threshold value for a stimulus may be fixed, over time it will be variable. What is below threshold at one point in time may be above at another; what is above at one moment may be below at the next. The further assumption is often made that these momentary fluctuations in the value of the threshold are randomly distributed and that this distribution can be described by a normal curve such that its mean, median, and mode are equal. Thus, the mean of the hypothetical distribution of momentary thresholds is the point above and below which 50 percent of the momentary threshold values fall.

The implication of all this is that the amount of energy needed to accomplish a perceptual task is not an all-or-nothing affair. Clearly, a particular task will generally be accomplished with increasing success as the amount of relevant energy increases. However, the determination of the minimal amount of energy needed, the threshold value, becomes a matter of statistical abstraction and, to some degree, of arbitrary definition. Operationally, a threshold is the amount of energy needed for task accomplishment at some arbitrary criterion of response probability, usually 0.50. In this sense, the psychophysical threshold corresponds to the mean of a hypothetical distribution of momentary thresholds.

Psychophysical landmarks   Given these assumptions regarding stimulus effectiveness, it is possible to identify several important psychophysical landmarks. Note in Figure 2.1 that stimulus S_{29} produces a distribution of excitation along the subjective continuum whose mean (or mode) lies along the dotted portion of the line representing this continuum. Stimulus S_{29} falls predominantly outside the observer's range of awareness, and effectively it would be nondetectable, as would all stimuli of lesser magnitude. By contrast, stimulus S_{30} results in a distribution of excitation whose mean just coincides with the solid portion of the line representing the subjective continuum. It is just detectable on the basis of a 0.50 criterion, or, to express this another way, it is the stimulus quantity whose probability of arousing a positive detection response is 0.50. Stimulus S_{30} represents the stimulus value for what we have called the absolute threshold. Customarily, it is designated by the abbreviation RL after the German term *Reiz* meaning "stimulus" and the Latin term *limen* meaning "threshold" or "doorway." The absolute threshold, then, can be considered as "a doorway to awareness."

The stimulus quantity S_{30} on the physical scale represents the effective origin of the subjective scale. What physical stimulus would be judged as stronger than S_{30} just half of the time and, therefore, be the next step on the subjective continuum? That question relates to what we have called a difference threshold, for we are interested in determining the least amount of stimulation necessary for the observer to detect a change in stimulus input. Suppose we find that S_{32} meets the criterion of being judged as greater than S_{30} 50 percent of the time. The difference in magnitude between S_{30} and S_{32} represents the difference threshold or *difference limen (DL)*. In this case, $DL = 2$, and S_{32} represents one "just noticeable difference" (jnd) above S_{30}. Similarly, $S_{34.2}$ represents one jnd above S_{32} and $S_{36.6}$ one jnd above $S_{34.2}$. The point made previously about the somewhat arbitrary nature of thresholds is nicely illustrated in our description of the RL and the jnd. Think about what would happen if we had adopted a higher criterion of response probability, say, 0.75, or a lower criterion, such as 0.25. The stimulus quantities accepted as reaching the absolute or difference thresholds would necessarily have to be higher in the former case and lower in the latter.

It should be evident that we could continue to mark off the subjective continuum of Figure 2.1 in successive jnd steps until we reach stimulus value S_k. At this point, at least half of the distribution of excitation falls in the dotted region of the continuum. Consequently, all stimuli above S_k would essentially be nondiscriminable. This occurs for two reasons. Stimuli above S_k would either be outside the range of stimulus values to which the sensory system is receptive, as for example tones above 20,000 Hz, or they would be of such magnitude as to injure sensory tissue, as is the case when one looks directly at the sun for more than a brief glance. Stimulus S_k represents the upper bound of the effective range of stimulation and is designated as the *terminal limen* (TL).

CLASSICAL PSYCHOPHYSICAL METHODS

Historical Foundation

Gustav Fechner A German physicist-philosopher, Gustav Theodor Fechner (1801–1887), is regarded as the founder of the formal study of psychophysics. As a philosopher, he was concerned with the mind-body problem and took the position that mind and matter are one; they represent alternate ways of viewing a single reality (Boring, 1950). In view of his training in physics, is it not surprising that Fechner attacked this problem experimentally by trying to relate "physical energy" to "mental energy." That is, he sought to work out definite quantitative relations between physical stimulation and resulting conscious sensations. In pursuit of this aim, Fechner developed several techniques for psychophysical measurement. He published his work in a treatise, *Elemente der Psychophysik* (1860), which has been profoundly influential—not, as he had hoped, for its philosophical significance, but for the research methods it made available. Though serious doubt has arisen over the past few decades about Fechner's methods (see Chapter 3), they are worth reviewing here for two reasons. First, it is hard to understand the newer methods without knowing what they were designed to replace. Second, Fechner's methods were used in the collection of most of the data found in the literature on psychophysics. In the following section, we present in considerable detail two of the most widely used psychophysical methods.

The Method of Limits

Absolute thresholds Also known as the method of minimal change, just noticeable differences, and serial exploration, the method of limits is most often employed in the determination of absolute and terminal limens. The distinguishing feature of the method of limits is that the experimenter presents stimuli for judgment in small steps involving an ascending or descending order. As an illustrative example, assume that we are interested in determining the stimulus intensity necessary for a very brief flash of light to be just detectable. An observer is seated in a dimly illuminated room facing a 6 by 6-centimeter dark screen. On each trial, a circular spot of light, 5 millimeters in diameter, is presented for 10 milliseconds in the center of the otherwise dark screen. The experimenter signals each trial by saying "Ready," and the observer is instructed to report "Yes" if the spot of light was detected and "No" if not. The calculations involved in determining the RL in this case are presented in Table 2.1.

One question which comes to mind with the method of limits is how many alternating ascending and descending series to run. Usually, the experimenter uses as many alternating series as are practicable or at least until the data seem stable. Ten alternating series were employed in our illustrative example. A second important question involves the range of stimulus values to present. This range is established by roughly approximating the observer's RL through exploratory trials. The range is then set so that the highest and lowest stimulus values are clearly above and below the estimated threshold. In our illustration, the stimulus values covered a range of 18 to 32 units of intensity in 1-unit steps. These values are given in arbitrary units of intensity for ease of discussion.

As can be seen in Table 2.1, the experiment was initiated with a descending series and used a flash of light that was clearly detectable. The observer's affirmative response to this stimulus is indicated by a + on the record sheet. The intensity of the light flash was lowered by 1-unit steps on each succeeding trial of the initial descending series, and the observer continued to report affirmatively until stimulus value 21 was reached; to that stimulus the observer said "No," as is indicated by a − on the record sheet. Thus, in the initial descending series, the observer's RL lay somewhere between stimulus values 21 and 22. The RL on any series is taken as the midpoint of the two values where a change of response occurs. In this case, the midpoint was 21.5, and the value was entered as the threshold value (T) for the initial descending series. Next, an ascending series was run beginning at stimulus value 12, well below the observer's threshold, and continuing in increments

TABLE 2.1   Calculations for the Detection
            Threshold by the Method of Limits

Intensity Values (Arbitrary Units)	Alternate Descending and Ascending Series									
	D	A	D	A	D	A	D	A	D	A
30	+									
29	+						+			
28	+						+		+	
27	+		+				+		+	
26	+		+				+		+	
25	+		+		+		+		+	
24	+		+		+		+		+	
23	+	+	+		+	+	+		+	
22	+	−	+		+	−	+	+	+	
21	−	−	+		−	−	−	−	+	
20	−	−	−		−		−	−	−	+
19	−		−		−		−			−
18	−		−		−		−			−
17	−		−	+	−					−
16	−		−	−	−					−
15	−		−		−					−
14			−		−					−
13			−							
12			−							

$T=$ 21.5 22.5 20.5 16.5 21.5 22.5 21.5 21.5 20.5 19.5
$RL = 208/10 = 20.8$ intensity units; $SD = 1.77$ intensity units.
MEAN descending $= 105.5/5 = 21.1$; MEAN ascending $= 102.5/5 = 20.5$.

of 1 unit until an affirmative report was obtained at stimulus value 23. The threshold value of 22.5 was entered on the record sheet for this series. Five ascending and five descending series were completed in this manner.

The absolute threshold can be computed from these data simply by averaging all of the T values. The resulting mean value, 20.8, is the RL. Inspection of Table 2.1 will reveal some variability among the T values. Observers typically vary like this over repeated series, and different observers can be expected to differ from one another, not only with respect to their RLs but also with respect to the relative stability of their judgments. The standard deviation (SD) of the distribution of T values is used to measure the instability or variability in an observer's performance.

In addition to averaging across all T values, it is also possible to compute means for the ascending and descending series separately and obtain ascending and descending RLs. These values are presented in the bottom row of Table 2.1. Note that in our example the ascending threshold is smaller than the descending threshold. Such a result is not uncommon with the method of limits. It was reported, for example, in a study of the detection of a brief flash of light by Brackmann and Collier (1958), who also noted that differences between ascending and descending RLs are amplified by increasing the size of the step-intervals that are used.

Sources of error   Inequalities between the results of ascending and descending series often occur because of two response tendencies that appear in the course of judgments. One of these, called the *error of habituation,* is the tendency to keep reporting "Yes" in a descending series and "No" in an ascending series. Because the observers necessarily make the same response in successive trials in a given series, they become accustomed to it and may continue to make this response even after the threshold is reached. The other tendency is known as the *error of anticipation.* Within any series of judgments, observers are aware that their responses must eventually shift from one category to the other. Consequently, they may anticipate such change and alter their responses prematurely. The errors of habituation and anticipation are functionally opposite. When the ascending RL is smaller than the descending RL the error of anticipation may be greater than the error of habituation. These types of errors can be satisfactorily controlled through the use of alternating ascending and descending sequences of judgments.

Another type of response error that enters into the method of limits stems from the point of origin of each series. If, for example, all of the ascending sequences were initiated at the same stimulus value, observers could come to realize that the same number of "No" responses always occurs between the start of the series and the point of transition to an affirmative response and could use this information as an incidental cue to judgment. The same possibility arises if all of the descending series were started at an identical stimulus value. To overcome such errors, each ascending and each descending sequence is begun at a different starting point, as is illustrated in Table 2.1.

The method of limits is open to still another subtle source of error. This involves what is referred to generally as a *context effect* and specifically as an *adaptation-level effect.* Essentially, the point is this: The perceived value of a particular stimulus is influenced by the values of the other stimuli presented in the same context. In establishing a detection criterion, subjects use as context all the stimuli with which they have been presented. Thus, if the arbitrary starting point of the limits method is high, the criterion level, and hence the threshold, will tend to be high. If the starting point and the remaining stimuli are lower, the criterion level and the estimated threshold may be lower.

Now, this influence of context is not peculiar to the method of limits, but it is likely to pose a problem for that method for the very reason that makes the method of limits so popular—that is, its flexibility. As it becomes apparent to the experimenter about where the threshold value falls, it becomes tempting to short-circuit the full limits procedure by leaving out extreme stimulus values. Why bother to present a stimulus that the subject is sure to detect every time? The experimenter, concerned about saving precious time, begins to present only the stimuli close to where the threshold is believed to lie. And the threshold will indeed be located there, but partly because of the context effect and the other related influences. The very flexibility of the method of limits thus leaves it open to systematic distortion on the part of the experimenter.

Such distortions become extremely important if the hypothesis being tested is that the threshold will vary as a result of certain experimental manipulations. The experimenter, expecting the hypothesis to be verified, innocently chooses the values of the stimuli to be presented in accordance with the expectation of about where the threshold values should fall. For the condition expected to yield the lower threshold, a lower set of stimulus values is employed than for the other condition. Sure enough, the two thresholds do differ, but not necessarily as a result of the intended experimental manipulation.

That such a possibility is not merely fanciful is illustrated in some research by Riggs, Cornsweet, and Lewis (1957). Their failure to replicate some very impressive and theoretically significant findings on the electrophysiology of color vision led them to examine closely the psychophysical method used in the original experiments. They discovered that procedural inadequacies of the sort described above could probably account for the reported but unreplicable results. What looked like neat and orderly relations turned out to be mainly artifacts of a naive, but common, use of the method of limits.

Note should be taken that the data gathered by the method of limits are not always as regular as those in our illustration. For example, observers may often be unsure of the appropriate response on a given trial and indicate their indecision to the experimenter. Uncertain responses are usually treated in two ways. The experimenter may run that particular trial again, or else may count "doubtful responses" as constituting a shift in judgment from the previous trial. Usually, it is best to instruct the observer to guess when not certain and thereby avoid the doubtful category (Engen, 1971a).

Difference thresholds   To illustrate the computation of a difference threshold by the method of limits, assume that stimulus value 25 is employed as a standard or point of reference. Our task is to determine the intensity of a flash of light that appears to be just noticeably brighter or dimmer than the standard stimulus. The experimental arrangement and general procedure remain the same. This time, however, two stimuli are presented on each trial: the standard and a comparison stimulus. The observer is instructed to say whether the apparent brightness of the comparison stimulus is "greater than" (+), "equal to" (=), or "less than" (−) that of the standard. The observer is also instructed to guess, when uncertain, which category is applicable. Table 2.2 presents the necessary calculations.

Once again, alternating descending and ascending series are run. The serial order in which the standard and comparison stimuli are presented is also alternated from trial to trial. Two threshold values are determined for each se-

TABLE 2.2   Calculations for the Difference
Threshold by the Method of Limits

Intensity Values (Arbitrary Units)	Alternate Descending and Ascending Series									
	D	A	D	A	D	A	D	A	D	A
32	+								+	
31	+						+		+	
30	+		+				+		+	
29	+		+	+	+		+		+	
28	+		+	=	+		+		+	
27	=	+	+	=	+	+	+		+	+
26	=	=	=	=	+	=	=	+	+	=
ST=25	=	=	-	-	=	=	=	=	=	=
24	-	-		-	-	-	=	=	=	=
23		-		-		-	-	-	-	-
22		-		-		-		-		-
21		-		-		-		-		-
20		-		-		-		-		-
19		-		-						-
18		-								-
$T(+)=$	27.5	26.5	26.5	28.5	25.5	26.5	26.5	25.5	25.5	26.5
$T(-)=$	24.5	24.5	25.5	25.5	24.5	24.5	23.5	23.5	23.5	23.5

MEAN $T(+) = 265.0/10 = 26.5$.
MEAN $T(-) = 243.0/10 = 24.3$.
IU = Interval of uncertainty = MEAN $(T+)$ − MEAN $(T-) = 26.5 − 24.3 = 2.2$ intensity units.
DL = Difference threshold = $IU/2 = 2.2/2 = 1.1$ intensity units.

ries. The upper threshold $(T+)$ represents the point of transition from "greater than" to "equal to," while the lower threshold $(T-)$ represents the point of transition from "equal to" to "less than." If, in a given series, a reversal in response occurs without an "equal" judgment—that is, a reversal from $T+$ to $T-$ or $T-$ to $T+$ —then the upper and lower thresholds are identical. In our illustrative case, the experiment was initiated with a descending series. A transition in responding occurred between stimulus valued 28 and 27. Thus, the upper threshold lay at the midpoint of these two values, and 27.5 was entered as the estimate of $T+$ for this series. The intensity of the comparison stimulus was decreased until stimulus value 24 was reached, where a transition form "equal to" to "less than" occurred. The threshold value of 24.5 was then entered on the record sheet. A similar procedure was followed for the remaining descending and ascending series.

The difference limen (DL) is determined by dividing the range of responses into three parts: (1) an upper portion representing stimulus values for which the apparent brightness of the comparison stimulus is greater than that of the standard, (2) a lower portion representing comparison stimulus values consistently judged to be dimmer than that of the standard, and (3) a midportion where neither $T+$ nor $T-$ responses predominate and equal judgments are most frequent. This third portion is known as the *interval of uncertainty* (IU). The lower limit of the upper portion is taken as the mean of the $T+$ values, while the upper limit of the lower portion is taken as the mean of the $T-$ values. The IU is determined by subtracting the average value of $T-$ from the average value of $T+$. If you think about this for a moment, you will see that in effect the IU spans a range of two DLs, from "greater than" to "equal to" and from "equal to" to "less than." The average DL is taken as one-half of the IU, which in our example is 1.1 units. Thus, stimulus value 25 must be increased by 1.1 units to 26.1 in order to appear just noticeably brighter. Conversely, it must be decreased by a similar amount to 23.9 in order to appear just noticeably dimmer.

Point of subjective equality and constant errors   Two additional indices may be computed from the data. One of these is the *point of subjective equality* (PSE) — that is, the comparison stimulus value most likely to be judged equal to the standard. It is defined as the midpoint of the IU. If an observer acts as a perfect measuring instrument, the PSE should be identical to the standard. This, however, is rarely the case. Usually, there is some systematic error in judgment, termed the *constant error* (CE). The magnitude of the constant error is the difference between a standard and the stimulus judged equal to it. In our illustrative case, the PSE was above the standard. By convention, a difference in that direction is considered to yield a *positive* constant error. If the PSE lies below the standard, the CE is considered to be *negative*. The term "constant error" itself is an unfortunate one, because it may connote carelessness or sloppiness on the part of the observer. On the contrary, the systematic response tendencies which yield a constant error may allow important inferences to be drawn about the nature of perceptual processes. A detailed consideration of the implications of these so-called "errors" may be found in Underwood (1966) and Woodworth and Schlosberg (1954).

Variations of the method of limits   The method of limits is quite flexible and, in actual practice, may be used with several variations. For example, in determining thresholds, it may sometimes be advisable to check on the observer's tendency to guess. Consequently, the stimulus may be omitted on certain trials. Such check trials are termed *vexier-versuche*. Still another variation is the so-called modified method of limits in which only ascending trials are given. This technique is employed in cases where presenting stimulus values well above threshold might directly affect the observer's RL. This is known to happen, for example, in the measurement of thresholds for olfactory and electrical stimulation, where intense stimuli tend to elevate the RL (Engen, 1971a; Hawkes and Warm, 1960a).

A more substantial variation on the classical method of limits is referred to as the "up-and-down" or the "staircase" method (Guilford, 1954; Cornsweet, 1962). This method typically requires less time than the standard method of limits and therefore is especially useful for tracking temporal changes in the observer's threshold. To measure the RL with this method, the investigator begins as in the usual method of limits, but changes direction after each change in the observer's response. If the observer responds "Yes" to a stimulus, the next stimulus is made weaker; if the response is "No," the next stimulus is made stronger. The stimulus is increased or decreased in constant steps from trial to trial, and the procedure is continued until a predetermined number of trials is reached.

As an illustration of the staircase method, we will consider a study by Arand and Dember (1976) which was concerned in part with determining the shortest exposure duration necessary for an observer to detect the presence of a small black disk in the visual field. The stimuli were presented in a tachistoscope. On each trial, the observer gazed at a point in the center of the visual field and was asked to report whether a solid black disk, 8mm (millimeters) in diameter, appeared to the right or to the left of the fixation point. In this illustration, a correct response is analogous to an affirmative report and an incorrect response to a negative report. The data from one observer are presented in Figure 2.2. Correct detections are labeled "right" and incorrect detections are labeled "wrong."

Preliminary trials indicated the observer's threshold was approximately 13

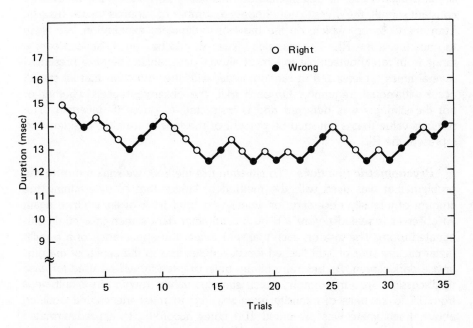

FIGURE 2.2 Illustration of the staircase method. (After Arand, 1974)

msec (milliseconds), and the session was initiated slightly above this point at 15 msec. As indicated in the figure, the observer detected the target on the first trial (in this experiment detection was defined as *two* successive correct responses), and the stimulus duration was lowered by 0.5 msec to 14.5 msec for the next trial. The exposure time was again lowered by 0.5 msec for the third trial, at which point the first incorrect response occurred. Consequently, exposure time was increased by 0.5 msec for trial number four. This procedure was continued until a total of 35 trials had been completed. A simple way to compute the value that represents the exposure duration threshold from this technique is to determine the mean duration of correct judgments and the mean duration of incorrect judgments. The difference between these scores is the interval of uncertainty, and the midpoint of this interval is the threshold. For the present data, the duration threshold was computed to be 13.4 msec. A further refinement of the staircase method, called the "double staircase," and more complete techniques for the statistical treatment of the results can be found in Cornsweet (1962) and Dixon and Massey (1957).

The Method of Constant Stimuli

Absolute thresholds   Like the method of limits, the method of constant stimuli is also known by several other names. These include the *method of right and wrong cases,* the *frequency method,* and the *method of constant stimulus differences.* In determining the absolute threshold by the method of constant stimuli, the investigator chooses a number of stimulus values (usually from five to seven) which, on the basis of preliminary exploration, are likely to encompass the RL. The stimulus values should be equally spaced over a range from rarely detectable to almost always detectable. They are presented several times (at least 20) in random order with the restriction that all stimuli occur with equal frequency. On each trial, the observer reports whether or not the stimulus was detected and is instructed to guess if uncertain. The stimulus value that is detected 50 percent of the time is usually considered to represent the RL.

Psychometric functions   To illustrate this method, we shall return to the problem that was used with the method of limits—that of determining the amount of intensity necessary for detecting a brief flash of light. Once again an observer is seated before a 6 by 6-centimeter dark screen in a dimly illuminated room. The task on each trial is to detect the appearance of a 5-millimeter circular spot of light flashed for 10 milliseconds in the center of the otherwise dark screen. As before, arbitrary units of intensity will be used for ease of discussion. In our example, seven stimulus values ranging in 2-unit steps from 14 to 26 units of intensity were selected to meet the criteria outlined above. Each value was presented 100 times according to a predetermined random order for a total of 700 trials. With the method of constant stimuli, an observer's responses can be displayed as a *psychometric* function, a graph in which response probability, in this case the probability (or the proportion) of detections, is plotted for each stimulus value. Such a function for one observer is presented in Figure 2.3.

With a reasonably large number of responses, data based upon the constant-stimuli technique usually reveal an S-shaped relation, in which lower values of stimulus magnitude are detected only occasionally, whereas higher values almost always elicit an affirmative response. Notice that in our data no stimulus was detected exactly 50 percent of the time. Stimulus intensity 18 was detected on 29 percent of the trials, and stimulus intensity 20 was detected 58 percent of the time. Consequently, the RL must lie between these

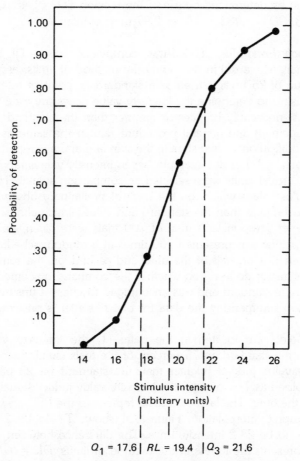

$Q_1 = 17.6 \mid RL = 19.4 \mid Q_3 = 21.6$

FIGURE 2.3 Detection probability as a function of stimulus intensity obtained by the method of constant stimuli. Intensity values are in arbitrary units.

two points. If we assume that the percentage of trials in which the light flash is detected increases linearly between intensity values 18 to 20, we can determine the intensity value with a detection probability of 0.50 by graphic linear interpolation, as shown in the figure. In the example, the RL is 19.4 units of intensity.

The variability of the observer's responses can also be determined through graphic interpolation by locating stimulus values with detection probabilities of 0.25 (symbolized as Q_1) and 0.75 (symbolized as Q_3), respectively, and by calculating the semi-interquartile range *(Q)* according to the formula $Q = \frac{1}{2} (Q_3 - Q_1)$. In terms of Q, response variability in this example was 2.0 intensity units. If the assumption is made that the observer's judgments are normally distributed, the standard deviation of this distribution of responses can be determined by use of the relation $SD = 1.483Q$. According to Figure 2.3, $SD = 1.483 \times 2.0$, or 2.97 units of intensity.

Difference thresholds   To illustrate computation of the DL by this technique, we shall, as we did in describing the method of limits, assume that an intensity value of 25 units is used as a standard or point of reference. Once again, our task is to determine the intensity value necessary for a flash of light to appear just noticeably brighter or dimmer than the standard. The experimental arrangement and general procedure remain the same as before with one basic modification — two stimuli, the standard and a comparison, are presented on each trial. For our example, seven intensity values ranging in 2-unit steps from 19 to 31 units were selected as comparison stimuli. This range included stimulus values which, on the basis of preliminary observations, were rarely judged brighter than the standard and values which almost always elicited a "brighter" response. A total of 700 trials were given. Each standard-comparison pairing was presented 100 times in a random schedule; the standard appeared first on half of the trials and second on the remainder. The observer was instructed to report whether the comparison seemed brighter or dimmer than the standard and was encouraged to guess if unsure. A psychometric function summarizing the data for one observer is presented in Figure 2.4.

Three points are located in the data: (1) the intensity value judged brighter than the standard on 75 percent of the trials (symbolized as $T+$), (2) the intensity value judged brighter than the standard on 25 percent of the trials (symbolized as $T-$), and (3) the intensity value judged equal to the standard half of the time. The last, of course, represents the PSE.

Using graphic interpolation, Figure 2.4 shows $T+$ to be 26.6 intensity units and $T-$ to be 23.2 intensity units. The difference between $T+$ and $T-$, 3.4 units, represents the IU. As in the method of limits, $DL = IU/2$ or, in this case, 1.7 intensity units. Thus, for this observer, an intensity of 26.7 units was

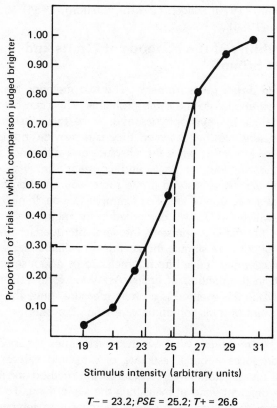

FIGURE 2.4 Proportion of comparison brighter judgments obtained by the method of constant stimuli. Stimulus intensity values are in arbitrary units. The standard stimulus was an intensity value of 25.

just noticeably brighter than the standard and a value of 23.3 units was just noticeably dimmer. Figure 2.4 also shows that the PSE was located at 25.2 units. Consequently, the observer's constant error, defined as PSE-standard, was +0.2 units of intensity.

The use of graphic linear interpolation to determine threshold values with the method of constant stimuli is the simplest procedure to follow, especially when the data are as regular as those employed in our illustration. It is open to the criticism, however, that it does not use all of the data in locating liminal values; in both illustrative examples only two of the seven proportions were used. Furthermore, graphic interpolation may fail to yield accurate values when data are less regular than those in our illustrations. Several more sophisticated techniques are available for handling data obtained by the method of constant stimuli. Cogent descriptions of these alternate procedures can be found in D'Amato (1970), Engen (1971a), Guilford (1954), and Woodworth and Schlosberg (1954).

Comparability of the Methods of Limits and Constant Stimuli

Indirect and direct measurement   The two methods that we have just described can be applied to the same problems. They can be used to determine liminal values in psychophysics and, since the smaller the threshold value the more sensitive the observer, they can provide indices of keenness of discrimination. However, while the absolute and difference thresholds determined by the methods of limits and constant stimuli are conceptually equivalent, they are not measured in the same way and hence may not turn out to be numerically equivalent. For example, if you think carefully about the manner in which the DL was computed in the method of constant stimuli, you will realize that the DL represents the semi-interquartile range. Therefore, in the method of constant stimuli, the keenness of differential sensitivity is not determined directly; it is derived from a measure of response variability. Such is not the case in the method of limits. As Woodworth (1938) pointed out long ago, the DL in this method is a direct measure, since the observer is on the alert for a point of transition and aware when it occurs.

A choice of methods   We have two techniques for measuring thresholds. Which produces a better estimate of threshold values? Traditionally, psychophysical investigators have considered the methods of limits and constant stimuli as different ways of measuring the same thing. To strike an analogy with physics, the situation is similar to measuring temperature through the expansion of a liquid in glass as in a thermometer, or electrically as in a thermocouple. The choice of whether to employ the method of limits or constant stimuli in a given experiment depends more upon practical than upon theoretical considerations. Among the practical considerations are the time available for experimentation, whether stimuli can be presented continuously or only in discrete steps, and whether simultaneous or successive pairs of presentations are possible (Engen, 1971a).

A mark of methodological sophistication in any scientific enterprise is the degree to which disparities between alternate techniques of measurement can be understood. Our prior analogy with physics is not completely accurate because physicists have found ways of equating temperature measures made through different means. Recently, Herrick (1967, 1973) has offered ways to place the data from the methods of limits and constant stimuli into the same computational format. While the technical details of these procedures exceed the scope of this chapter, the inquisitive reader might find in Herrick's work an interesting approach toward the development of more direct comparisons between these two traditional methods for investigating thresholds.

Indicator Responses

Thus far in our discussion of ways to answer psychophysical questions, we have focused primarily on techniques of stimulus presentation. However, from what was said in the previous section concerning the observer's response system as a measuring instrument, one might conclude that the type of response involved might also be an important element in psychophysical methodology. This is indeed the case; the value of a psychophysical measure often depends in part upon the indicator response that has been selected for observation. In this section, we shall examine two general categories of indicator response that are commonly employed in psychophysical measurement. The discussion that follows will use illustrations from the case of detection, but it should be noted that the ideas are also applicable to other types of perceptual tasks — for example, discrimination, recognition, and identification.

Two kinds of indicator responses One obvious way of finding out whether or not a subject has detected a stimulus is to ask: "Did you see that stimulus?" The response called for is a simple yes or no, or some equivalent. We shall refer to this kind of indicator as a *yes-no response*. Our illustrations involving absolute thresholds determined by the methods of limits and constant stimuli employed a yes-no response.

The second type of indicator response will be referred to as a *forced-choice response*. Here the subject must respond in such a way as to *demonstrate* stimulus detection. In interpreting the yes-no response, the experimenter takes the subject's report at face value. In the forced-choice situation the experimenter must be "convinced" that the task has really been accomplished. For example, the situation might be arranged so that the stimulus occurs in one of several alternative locations (*spatial* forced-choice), or during one of several time intervals (*temporal* forced-choice). On each trial the subject must report which one of the alternatives contained the stimulus. It is not enough simply to assert that the stimulus was detected; detection must be proved by indicating where or when it occurred. The Arand and Dember (1976) experiment, which we used earlier to illustrate the staircase method, employed a spatial forced-choice response.

A rough analogy may clarify the difference between yes-no and forced-choice indicator responses. Suppose that you were giving an arithmetic test to a group of children. Under some circumstances it might be appropriate simply to have them indicate for each problem whether or not they knew the answer. "Do you know the sum of 14 and 17?" you might ask. Ordinarily, however, in giving a test, you would want more than a yes-no answer. The more convincing answer would be given to the question: "What is the sum of 14 and 17?" The latter question does not call for the children's own evaluation of their knowledge; the examiner can tell from the replies whether or not the children know the answer. For those who said "31," the chances are very high that they did indeed know it; for those who said any other number, it would be safe to infer that they did not know the answer.

The forced-choice situation thus demands that subjects provide evidence of task accomplishment. They are not asked for an introspective report. Indeed, subjects may demonstrate, by making the appropriate indicator response, that they can detect a stimulus which they themselves are unaware of perceiving. Continuing the analogy, students are often encouraged to guess in a multiple-choice exam because they very often "know" more than they realize; their "guesses" score better than chance.

Empirical comparisons Because of considerations of the kind suggested above, the two forms of indicator response may be expected to yield different threshold estimates. An extensive set of experiments by Blackwell (1953) has borne out this contention. Visual-detection thresholds were measured under a variety of conditions, with both yes-no and forced-choice responses. The forced-choice response was found to yield generally lower thresholds than the yes-no response. The former was also found to be less easily influenced by other variables such as the spacing and ordering of the stimuli. In general, both within a day's session and between daily sessions, thresholds were more reliable when estimated from forced-choice than from yes-no data.

In addition to Blackwell's experiments, Green and Swets (1974) and Viemeister (1970) present data from detection studies which confirm the advantages of the forced-choice response. Why, then, ever use a yes-no response? One reason is that the yes-no procedure typically is easier to set up and is less time-consuming than the forced-choice. Now, this latter is not only a practical advantage; it also gives the yes-no response superiority over the forced-choice response on theoretical grounds. For one thing, the more rapid the measurements from which the threshold is estimated, the less influential will be any systematic changes in sensitivity that might occur over time. In general, the threshold estimated from a brief series of measures should more closely approximate the hypothetical momentary threshold than does one estimated from a temporally extended series of measures.

Another important advantage of the yes-no indicator follows from the above considerations. That is, the ability to measure the threshold quickly provides an opportunity to track the course of systematic changes in the threshold. Suppose, for example, that you are interested in studying the effect of a drug on the visual-detection threshold. You know that, pharmacologically, the effect of the drug varies over time, being weak soon after administration, increasing to a maximum, and then declining. You would like to be able to follow the changes in visual threshold that may accompany these temporal changes in the action of the drug. Obviously you would like a way of measuring the threshold that is able to pick up short-term changes. A method that requires 30 minutes to obtain a single threshold estimate would not be suitable if the interesting threshold variations all occurred within that time. The quick method may, therefore, also be the only useful one.

It is for reasons such as these that the yes-no indicator response is for many purposes superior to the forced-choice response. Which of the two types of responses to use in any specific context requires a decision on the part of the experimenter that takes account of the advantages and disadvantages of each. In general, the most widely used combinations of method of stimulus presentation and type of indicator response are the forced-choice indicator in conjunction with the method of constant stimuli and the yes-no indicator in conjunction with the method of limits.

BASIC SENSITIVITY OF THE PERCEPTUAL SYSTEM

Absolute Sensitivity and the Effective Range of Stimulation

The classical psychophysical methods are tools for gaining knowledge about the operation of a perceptual system. We have illustrated their use in the measurement of thresholds in order to prepare you for problems that we will encounter in the remainder of this book. However, given an introduction to such "tools," you might reasonably ask at this point whether any answers can be given to the questions posed at the outset of this chapter regarding the nature of a perceptual system. In the section that follows, we will deal with general answers to two of these questions: (1) In relation to the absolute threshold, what is the least amount of energy required for the system to be activated? (2) In relation to the difference threshold, what is the smallest difference in amount of energy to which the system can react?

Use of the classical psychophysical methods to study absolute thresholds has led to the discovery that the human observer is strikingly sensitive to certain forms of energy variations. These kinds of determinations can be quite complex, and they require detailed control and precision in the specification of stimuli, because absolute thresholds depend upon many stimulus factors.

Retinal structure and function Let us consider the question of the smallest amount of light or electromagnetic radiation that can be detected. We need, first, to indicate some basic facts about the major structural components of the eye (see Figure 2.5).

The inner portion of the back of the eye is lined with a surface known as the *retina,* which contains approximately 130.5 million light-sensitive cells. As shown in the figure, these are known as rods and cones after the manner in which they are shaped. Cone cells are specialized for color discrimination, whereas rods are specialized for detecting low-intensity illumination. Indeed, in regard to the detection of light, rods are approximately a thousand times

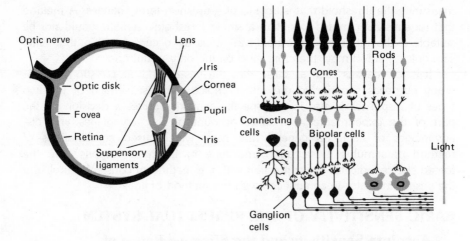

FIGURE 2.5   Sketch of right eyeball, top view; simplified schematic illustration of the nerve-cell network in a vertebrate retina. (Network adapted from Detwiler, 1941, after Dember and Jenkins, 1970)

more sensitive than cones (Geldard, 1972). The *fovea,* a depression in the center of the retina, contains only cones, and the concentration of cones falls off rapidly just outside the fovea, reaching a low value at about 20° in the periphery of the eye. Rods appear just outside the fovea and reach maximum density at about 20° in the periphery. These structural and functional characteristics imply that the eye is in reality not one sense organ, but two — an implication often expressed as the "duplicity" theory of vision. Given these structural and functional characteristics, it is evident that in order to gain the best estimate of the minimum amount of light required for a detection threshold, stimuli should be presented in the periphery of the eye, where rod density is greatest.

Incidentally, a convincing demonstration of the greater sensitivity of the rods to small amounts of light can be performed very easily on a starry night. Find a star, which, when viewed directly, is very dim and seems to disappear every so often. The same star will appear much brighter if you direct your fixation a little bit away from it. Instead of falling on the fovea, the image of the star is now in the periphery.

Visibility curves   To complicate the matter of visual-detection thresholds still further, the maximum sensitivity of both the rods and the cones is related to the wavelength of light used. This effect is revealed by photopic and scotopic visibility curves such as those shown in Figure 2.6.

Photopic and scotopic visibility curves plot the relative amount of energy needed to reach absolute threshold as a function of wavelength. The curve

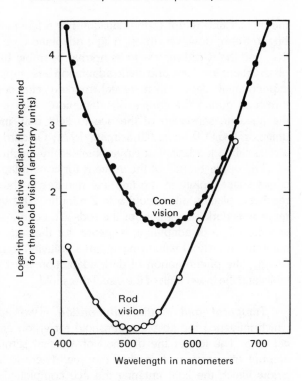

FIGURE 2.6 Photopic (cone) and scotopic (rod) visibility curves. The curves illustrate the relative amounts of energy needed to reach threshold as a function of wavelength. (After Chapanis, 1949, and Corso, 1967))

labeled scotopic (twilight or dim illumination) represents rod functions; that labeled photopic (daylight vision) represents cone functions. Note that rod thresholds reach their lowest value (greatest sensitivity) at about 505 nm (green), whereas cones are maximally sensitive to a wavelength of about 550 nm (yellow-green). This difference in sensitivity under dim and high illumination is known as the *Purkinje shift,* and is of obvious significance in determining the minimum absolute visual detection threshold.

State of adaptation Sensitivity to light is not an invariant quality of the rods and cones; it also depends upon prior activity of the visual system. Thus, under stimulation by light, the visual system progressively loses its sensitivity, while sensitivity is restored during periods of nonstimulation. The decrease in sensitivity is known as *light adaptation;* the increase in sensitivity following nonstimulation is called *dark adaptation.*

Both light and dark adaptation are familiar phenomena outside the laboratory. When you first enter a movie theater from the bright sunlight, you can barely see your way to a seat. The theater seems exceedingly dark: your eyes are light-adapted. Gradually, it becomes possible to see things that were at first invisible: your eyes are now dark-adapted. The extreme sensitivity of your dark-adapted eyes often becomes painfully apparent when you leave the theater and return to the daylight. For a few minutes, it seems unbearably bright. Soon, however, through light adaptation, your eyes become less sensitive, and the world returns to its normal bearable brightness. These anecdotal observations on light and dark adaptation are supported by a great mass of experimental data which reveal marked changes in the visual-detection threshold during the course of adaptation. With a suitable adaptation time, the absolute sensitivity of the eye to light may increase as much as 5 log units, or 100,000 times (Christman, 1971; Geldard, 1972). Figure 2.7 shows a classical dark-adaptation curve obtained by Hecht and Shlaer (1938).

The upper branch of the curve is for cone adaptation. It indicates that the cones adapt rapidly in the first few minutes in the dark and that adaptation reaches a plateau after about 5 to 7 minutes. The second branch of the curve represents dark adaptation for the rods. The curve shows that the time course and the range of adaptation is greater for the rods and that the rods reach a minimum threshold value (maximum sensitivity) in approximately 30 minutes. Clearly, the phenomenon of dark adaptation must also be considered in establishing the lower limit of the visual threshold.

Temporal and spatial summation Two additional stimulus factors which influence the absolute threshold for vision are target duration and target area. The longer the duration of a visual stimulus, the greater the total amount of energy that reaches the eye. There is, in fact, a critical duration below which the light entering the eye completely summates in its effect. It does not matter how this light is distributed over time within that interval. Thus, if within the interval a target having an intensity I were presented for a duration x, it would have the same visual effect as an intensity of $I/2$ and a duration of 2x. Below this critical duration, time and intensity are reciprocal. This relationship is expressed as $It = k$, where I is the target intensity, t is the

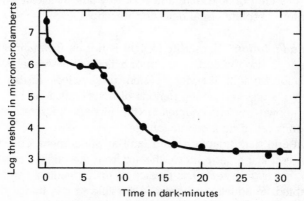

FIGURE 2.7 The course of dark adaptation following exposure to light. The first section of the curve is for cones, the second is for rods. (From Hecht and Shlaer, 1938)

duration, and k is a constant. This relation is known as *Bloch's Law*. The reciprocity between time and intensity for the absolute threshold for vision holds for durations up to about 0.1 second. At slightly longer durations, there is less than perfect reciprocity and finally, at approximately 0.5 second and longer, the intensity of light needed for the threshold becomes independent of stimulus duration.

Target area is also one of the primary stimulus determinants of the detection threshold. In general, the greater the area, the lower the threshold. Over very small target areas, usually 10 minutes of arc or less, there exists a perfect reciprocal relation between area and intensity: decreases in target intensity can be compensated for by increases in target area. The reciprocity between target area and intensity is known as *Ricco's Law*. Symbolically, Ricco's Law reads $Ia = k$, where I is the target intensity, a is the area, and k is a constant. At somewhat larger areas beyond the region in which Ricco's Law holds, a second formulation obtains, known as *Piper's Law*, $I \sqrt{a} = k$. Finally, when target area is increased still further, the threshold becomes a direct function of intensity alone.

Bloch's Law and Ricco's Law are similar in that they both express an integrative function of the perceptual system. The former states that the perceptual system integrates energy over time while the latter reflects the integration of energy over space. These laws also imply that both target duration and target area must be specified in determining the smallest amount of light that can be detected.

Absolute threshold values   From the facts just presented, it is apparent that an attempt to gain an estimate of the minimum amount of light required for visual detection is a complex affair indeed. However, a very careful experiment by Hecht, Shlaer, and Pirenne (1942) provided an elegant answer to this question. These investigators presented their stimulus to the portion of the retina of maximal rod density and used completely dark-adapted observers. The stimulus consisted of a very small patch (10 minutes of arc) of greenish light (510 nm) presented monocularly (that is, to one eye) for 1/1000 second (one millisecond). By means of the method of constant stimuli, they determined the minimum amount of light necessary for a detection probability of 0.60.

A light beam may be described physically in terms of packets of energy called *quanta*. On the basis of their results, Hecht, Shlaer, and Pirenne concluded that a single quantum of light is sufficient to activate a rod cell and that only about 10 quanta are necessary to reach detection threshold. While there is some disagreement among other investigators as to the exact number of quanta needed for threshold, they have generally confirmed the basic findings of Hecht and his co-workers that the estimated threshold value is exquisitely small (Bartlett, 1965; Cornsweet, 1970). As Geldard describes it:

The visual apparatus is apparently tuned to the highest possible degree consistent with the nature of light energy. If man's eyes were much more sensitive to light than they are, the "shot effect" in photon emission would be perceived and "steady" light would no longer appear steady! (Geldard, 1972, p. 39.)

Human hearing rivals vision as a detector of stimulation. Like visual thresholds, acoustic thresholds are dependent upon a variety of factors. However, in regions of greatest sensitivity, one estimate suggests that a tone may be audible when the movement of air particles initiates a displacement of the eardrum that is considerably less than the diameter of a hydrogen molecule (Thurlow, 1971). If the ear were any more sensitive, its usefulness as a detector of acoustic stimulation would be limited, for it would respond to the random movement of molecules in the air. Other sensory channels also exhibit extraordinarily low detection thresholds. Further impressions of this level of sensitivity can be gained by considering some approximate detection-threshold values in commonplace terms such as those presented in Table 2.3.

Effective range of stimulation   The range of energy values between the absolute limen (RL) and the terminal limen (TL), the "effective range" of stimulation, provides still another way to gauge the sensitivity of a perceptual system. The wider this range, the greater the receptive capacity of the system. The effective ranges of stimulation for visual and acoustic stimuli are very broad indeed. The terminal limen for vision, roughly the brightness of snow in the midday sun, is approximately 10^9 times the absolute visual threshold. In hearing, the terminal limen approximates the sound level of a jet plane afterburner, a value 10^{14} times the absolute threshold intensity (Mowbray and Gebhard, 1961).

TABLE 2.3   Approximate Detection Threshold Values in Representative Terms (after Galanter, 1962)

Sense modality	Detection threshold
Light	A candle flame seen at 30 miles on a dark clear night (about 10 quanta).
Sound	The tick of a watch under quiet conditions at 20 feet (about 0.0002 dynes/cm²).
Taste	1 teaspoon of sugar in 2 gallons of water.
Smell	1 drop of perfume diffused into the entire volume of a 3-room apartment.
Touch	The wing of a bee falling on the cheek from a distance of 1 cm.

Differential Sensitivity

Weber's Law   In addition to absolute thresholds and the RL–TL range, the sensitivity of a perceptual system can be examined in terms of difference thresholds. The smaller an increment in energy necessary for a difference to be perceived, the greater the sensitivity of the system. In the earlier part of this chapter, we pointed out that the size of a stimulus increment (ΔI) necessary to attain a difference threshold grows with increasing values of the referent or standard stimulus. That statement expresses what is a fairly common experience. For example, if a room were illuminated by a single flashlight, adding a second flashlight would alter the apparent illumination noticeably. However, if a room were illuminated by a thousand flashlights, the light added by one more flashlight would probably not even be noticed. Yet, in both cases, the physical illumination changed by an equal physical unit (one flashlight's worth). This relation between the size of the difference threshold and the magnitude of the referent stimulus suggests that on an *absolute* basis perceptual sensitivity declines as stimulus magnitude increases. On the other hand, if we consider the size of the jnd *relative* to that of the standard, then a different conclusion emerges.

In a series of experiments, conducted over 140 years ago, on people's ability to discriminate weight, pressure, and the length of lines, E. H. Weber noted an important regularity in the relation between the jnd and standard stimulus magnitude. He reported that the ratio of the value of a jnd to the magnitude of the standard stimulus is invariant over different levels of the standard stimulus. This proportionality is known as *Weber's Law;* symbolically, it reads:

$$\Delta I/I = k$$

where I is the magnitude or intensity of the standard stimulus, ΔI the threshold increment, or the jnd, and k is some constant (in this case a fraction, or proportion).

To illustrate Weber's Law, suppose we use a 100-gram weight as a standard and find that we must add 2 grams to reach a just noticeable difference in heaviness. If we now use a 500-gram standard we might need to add 10 grams before a difference is noticed. In both cases, however, the incremental value was in the ratio of 2/100 of the standard weight.

Weber's Law furnishes us with a valuable index of the discriminatory power of any sensory modality: the smaller the Weber fraction, the keener the discrimination. The idea is shown graphically in Figure 2.8.

Over the years, many determinations of Weber fractions have been made in a variety of sense modalities. These values are scattered in handbooks of sensory functions and in chapters on hearing, vision, tactual sensitivity, etc. (Christman, 1971; Corso, 1967; Geldard, 1972; Stevens, 1951a). Some illustrative values are presented in Table 2.4.

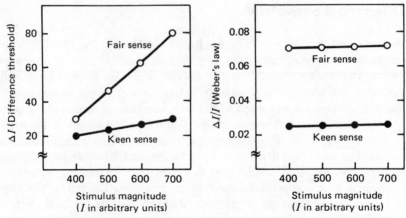

FIGURE 2.8   Weber's law in two hypothetical sense modalities. The abscissa in both panels represents the magnitude of the standard stimulus. In the left panel, the ordinate represents the absolute change (ΔI) necessary for a difference threshold in each modality. In the right panel, the ordinate represents Δl/l, the Weber fraction, or the relative change necessary for a difference threshold in each modality. (After Woodworth and Schlosberg, 1954)

TABLE 2.4   Weber Fractions for Various Sensory Discriminations (after Boring, Langfeld, and Weld, 1939)

	Weber Fraction
Deep pressure, from skin and subcutaneous tissue, at about 400 gm	1/77
Visual brightness, at about 1000 photons	1/62
Lifted weights, at about 300 gm	1/53
Tone, for 1000 cycles per second, at about 100 db above the absolute threshold	1/11
Smell, for rubber, at about 200 olfacties	1/10
Cutaneous pressure, on an isolated spot, at about 5 gm per mm	1/7
Taste, for saline solution, at about 3 moles per liter concentration	1/5

The validity of Weber's Law   In addition to providing an index of sensitivity, Weber's ratio can potentially serve as a powerful vehicle for prediction. If the ratio of the size of the jnd to the standard is indeed a constant, then by knowing one jnd within the effective range of stimulation for a given sensory dimension, we know them all! The prospect of such predictive power explains why so much research has been done to test the validity and generality of Weber's Law. Unfortunately, it turns out that Weber's Law does not universally hold. The failure of the Weber ratio to be constant over all values

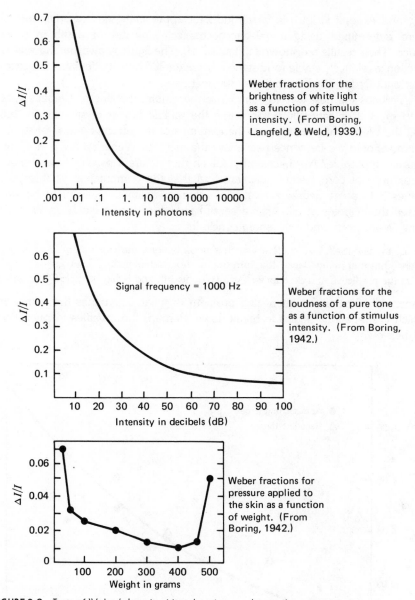

Weber fractions for the brightness of white light as a function of stimulus intensity. (From Boring, Langfeld, & Weld, 1939.)

Weber fractions for the loudness of a pure tone as a function of stimulus intensity. (From Boring, 1942.)

Weber fractions for pressure applied to the skin as a function of weight. (From Boring, 1942.)

FIGURE 2.9   Tests of Weber's Law in vision, hearing, and tactual sensitivity.

within a sensory dimension is illustrated in Figure 2.9. Classic curves for brightness, loudness, and pressure are plotted in each panel of the figure.

In order to convey the variety of conditions under which Weber's Law has been tested it is interesting to consider a study by Vincent, Brown, Markley, and Arnoult (1969), in which jnd's for approaching and receding targets were determined using an electromechanical simulator of depth in outer space. Their results are shown in Figure 2.10. The figure shows that the Weber fraction is relatively stable for distances between 200 and 800 feet, but increases precipitously for distances beyond 800 feet.

Perhaps the best way to summarize the empirical status of Weber's Law is to say that it generally holds within the middle ranges of stimulation, but that the Weber ratio increases at the extremes of the effective range of stimulation. Should we be concerned about the fact that Weber's Law is not universally applicable? Not necessarily. Given that different psychophysical measures are not completely equivalent and that the computation of threshold values is to some degree a matter of arbitrary definition, we might be surprised that it holds at all! After a careful review of the research on Weber's Law, Woodworth and Schlosberg concluded:

As for the law itself, any student who has gone beyond the elementary level in any science has met many "laws" that turn out to "hold within limits." They are very useful at the predictive and descriptive level. (Woodworth and Schlosberg, 1954, p. 225.)

There still remains the interesting problem of what determines the points at which Weber's Law begins to break down. Perhaps those values follow a law of their own.

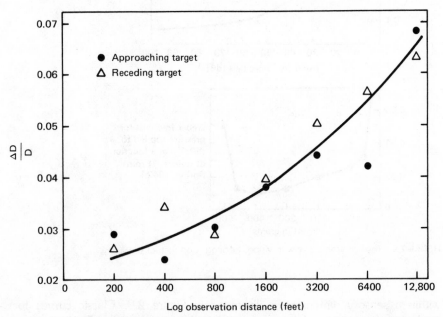

FIGURE 2.10 Weber fractions for the distances of approaching and receding targets in a simulated outer-space environment. (From Vincent, Brown, Markley, and Arnoult, 1969)

3
Theory and Measurement of Psychophysical Discrimination

The previous chapter provided a working description of techniques for threshold measurement and some fundamental psychophysical data. The study of psychophysics has also led to some interesting theoretical questions regarding the mechanisms which may underlie threshold measurements. We will consider some of these issues in the present chapter.

THE CONTINUITY-NONCONTINUITY ISSUE

The concept of an observer's threshold in the detection and discrimination of stimuli is basic to classical psychophysics. Fechner (1860) conceived of a threshold as an approximately constant point above which stimulus differences were detectable and below which they were not. He viewed the brain as a physiologically active organ in which there was spontaneous neural activity. Consequently, in order to be detected, incoming stimuli had to generate a level of neural excitation that was larger than the spontaneous activity already present within the brain. For Fechner, a stimulus which reached an absolute or difference threshold was one which lifted neural activity over this "neural barrier." The notion of a threshold as a barrier that had to be breached has also been expressed by Titchener (1905), who argued that the "frictional resistance" of a sense organ had to be overcome before a stimulus would produce a change in perceptual awareness, and more recently by Krantz (1969), who speaks of a threshold as a barrier separating internal sensory states.

Characterizing thresholds as barriers implies that perceptual experience is discontinuous, shifting in a stepwise fashion from a state of no awareness to awareness. This notion has given rise to a theoretical issue which can be termed the phi-gamma–neural-quantum controversy regarding the "true" nature of thresholds. Specifically, does our awareness of the presence of stimuli or of changes in stimulation contain abrupt discontinuities imposed by the proposed "neural barrier," or does psychophysical discrimination actually vary in a smooth, continuous manner corresponding to continuous changes in stimulation?

The Phi-gamma Hypothesis

Numerous psychophysical studies which followed Fechner's pioneering work provided data which challenged the validity of the barrier approach to the nature of thresholds. First of all, these studies made it evident that the threshold may not be the relatively fixed point that Fechner had postulated. The same stimulus was not equally effective for different individuals or even for the same individual from one time to another (Corso, 1963; Swets, 1961). Furthermore, psychometric functions relating probability of detecting a stimulus to stimulus magnitude did not typically reveal a stepwise characteristic. Instead, response probability tended to vary in a continuous, though nonlinear, manner with changes in stimulus magnitude. We observed this relation in Chapter 2 in our consideration of the method of constant stimuli (see Figures 2.3 and 2.4). As a further example, Figure 3.1 presents some data from an experiment by Mueller (1951) on the difference threshold for the brightness of a visual target. In this study, observers were required to detect the brightening of an illuminated target under various conditions of ongoing illumination of the target.

The figure shows that the amount of light, ΔI, that had to be added to the target to achieve a 50 percent difference threshold depended upon the ongoing level of target illumination. More to the point of this discussion is the fact that in all cases the probability of detecting a brightness increment increased from 0 to 1.00 as a continuous, sigmoidal (S-shaped) function of ongoing target illumination.

Results such as these led several investigators to deny the existence of thresholds in perceptual experience. As early as 1888, Jastrow argued that there was no threshold in any true sense of the term and that perceptual awareness is best characterized as a continuum varying smoothly in degree of clearness of experience. From this point of view, threshold values resulted from intrinsic variability in the observer and from extrinsic variability in the source of stimulation. Among the intrinsic factors that have been identified are variations in fatigue and inhibition, fluctuations in the physiological state of sensory receptors, lapses in attention and memory, changes in the ob-

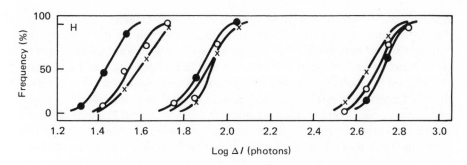

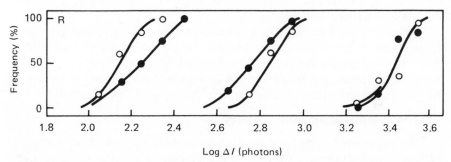

FIGURE 3.1 Percentage of positive responses in a visual-detection experiment as a function of the increment in retinal illuminance. (After Mueller, 1951)

server's willingness to make positive or negative responses (fluctuations in observational attitude), variations in the observer's expectancies based upon experience in the experimental situation, and practice in making psychophysical judgments (Cornsweet, 1970; Corso, 1963; Swets, 1961). Extrinsic sources of variability refer to uncontrolled fluctuations in the intensity or quality of the stimuli that are presented for judgment.

Apparently, the answer to the puzzle of why the same stimulus was not equally effective for different observers or for the same observer from time to time lay in the fact that there are numerous sources of error in psychophysical judgments which render them subject to variations from trial to trial. This line of reasoning led to the development of the *phi-gamma hypothesis* — a position which emphasizes the notion of random variation and probability in judgments.

The phi-gamma hypothesis assumes that the sources of error in psychophysical judgments are independent (random), and hence their effects are distributed according to the normal curve of probability. According to the phi-gamma hypothesis, a psychophysical judgment made in relation to a given stimulus does not depend solely upon the physical characteristics of the stimulus. It also depends upon a large number of uncontrolled factors, whose effects approximate the normal laws of chance and which act to aid or hinder judgment on any given trial. In addition, more of these factors must be favorable for the detection of stimuli of weak magnitude than for the detection of stimuli of strong magnitude. This accounts for the typical form of the psychometric function and provides the basis for a statistical definition of the threshold. Viewed in another way, the phi-gamma hypothesis asserts that psychophysical discriminations proceed by infinitely small increments which can best be described by a continuous mathematical function and that these discriminations are subject to fluctuations through uncontrolled random influences during the course of an experimental session or from one session to another. Thus, as Corso (1967) has pointed out, this position implies that perceptual sensitivity, as reflected in the absolute or difference threshold, is a variable and not a constant affair.

Because of its emphasis upon the concept of random errors in judgment, the phi-gamma hypothesis also asserts that the integral of the normal probability curve, or the normal *ogive,* best describes the psychometric function. In mathematical terms, the integral of the normal probability curve is known as the phi-function of gamma, hence the term "phi-gamma hypothesis."

The Neural Quantum Theory

The approach to psychophysical discrimination just described maintains that perceptual awareness is a continuous function of physical stimulus magnitude. This position was generally acceptable as long as psychologists thought that the neural structures which mediated perceptual experience simply increased or decreased the intensity of their output in order to reflect stimulus changes. A basic principle of neurophysiology states, however, that information transmission in the axons of nerve cells follows what is known as the all-or-none law. That is, impulses in the axons are ungraded in magnitude — they either occur with the largest magnitude possible under the circumstances or they do not occur at all. This implies that information transmission within the nervous system is functionally organized on a "go–no go" basis. Here, then, is a theoretical paradox. How can a continuous change in the physical nature of a stimulus give rise to an apparently continuous change in perceptual awareness when the neural mechanisms which underlie such change are composed of units which behave according to the all-or-none law? *The neural quantum theory* of perceptual discrimination initially formalized by Stevens, Morgan, and Volkmann (1941), and recently restated by Stevens (1972), was designed to accommodate the all-or-none principle of neurophysiology.

This position asserts that perceptual thresholds exist and that we do indeed perceive an all-or-none increase or decrease in stimulus magnitude. In other words, a continuous change in the stimulus produces finite jumps in perception. The reason for the sigmoidal form of the typical psychometric function is that sources of variability in the psychophysical experiment distort the truly quantal nature of perceptual experience. Aside from variations in the presentation of stimuli, there are intrinsic variations in the observer. As Stevens explains, "the problem with the human observer is that he is human—at any moment he may not keep his mind on his work and, thereby, spoil the experiment" (1961a, p. 813). It is important to note that within the framework of this position, the term "quantum" is not synonymous with physical units of energy such as in the quantum theory of light proposed in physics. The term "quantum" refers to the assumption that somewhere in the nervous system there are functional gates or neural units that operate in an all-or-none fashion once a threshold is crossed (Stevens, 1972).

The neural quantum theory pictures the process underlying threshold determinations in the following way. At any particular instant, a stimulus of a given magnitude will excite a certain number of neural units or neural quanta. In addition, there will also be a surplus or residue of excitation which will be insufficient to excite additional neural units, but which remains available to combine with an increment in the physical magnitude of the stimulus and, thereby, excite one or more additional neural units. These ideas are illustrated in Figure 3.2.

From what has been said so far, the simplest assumption one could make would be that an observer will detect a change in stimulus magnitude whenever one additional neural quantum has been excited. The theory does not view the matter so simply, however. It also assumes that the overall sensitivity of the observer fluctuates in a random manner on a moment-to-moment basis and that this fluctuation causes the value of residual excitation at any point in time to fall with equal likelihood at values between the quantal boundaries, that is, between the last neural unit excited and the next in line. These fluctuations in sensitivity may exceed the size of a single quantum, and, therefore, the observer cannot reliably determine when a single addi-

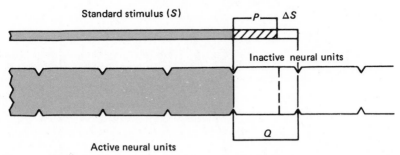

FIGURE 3.2 Schematic illustration of the neural quantum theory. A standard stimulus (S) is strong enough to excite the neural units indicated by the shaded area. It also leaves a surplus of excitation (P) which is insufficient to excite the next unit in line. However, the surplus remains available to combine with an increment (ΔS), which might be added to the standard and thereby excite one or more additional units. Q represents one additional neural quantum. (After Bekesy, 1960)

tional quantum is excited. Accordingly, the neural quantum position assumes that the observer adopts a "two-quantum" criterion for response. Under this assumption, a stimulus increment which energizes one additional quantum unit or less has a zero probability of being detected, whereas an increment which excites two additional quantal units or more has a 100 percent probability of being detected. As described by Stevens (1972), the neural quantum theory applies primarily to difference thresholds; the overall fluctuations in the observer's sensitivity make it difficult to isolate quantal functions in relation to the absolute threshold. Figure 3.3 presents a schematic representation of the stepwise psychometric function predicted by the neural quantum theory.

Given the assumptions of this position and a two-quantum criterion of response, the neural quantum theory predicts that the psychometric function will have three characteristics: (1) the smallest stimulus increment that elicits a detection response 100 percent of the time will be twice as large as the largest increment that is not detected, (2) the psychometric function will be linear between the points of zero and 100 percent detection, and (3) the slope of the psychometric function will be inversely proportional to its intercept on the x-axis.

Stevens and Volkmann (1940) performed an experiment on difference thresholds for the loudness of a pure tone which provided data in line with

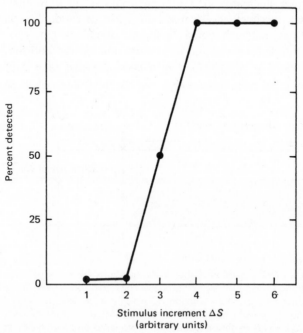

FIGURE 3.3 The rectilinear form of the psychometric function predicted by the neural quantum theory.

the expectations of the neural quantum theory. In this study, an observer listened to a continuous 1,000-Hz tone the intensity of which was increased by a fixed amount for 150 msec every 3 sec. The observer's task was to press a key upon hearing an increment in the loudness of the tone. The results, presented in Figure 3.4, show the rectilinear stepwise functions expected on the basis of the neural quantum theory.

Later, Stevens, Morgan, and Volkmann (1941) extended those results to pitch discrimination. In this second experiment, observers listened to a constant 1,000 Hz tone for a briefly presented, small increment in signal frequency and pressed a key whenever they heard an increment in pitch. As shown in Figure 3.5, the results of this study also seemed consistent with the step function predicted by the neural quantum hypothesis. Several investigations have also obtained rectilinear psychometric functions (DeCillis, 1944; Jerome, 1942; Larkin and Norman, 1964; Miller and Garner, 1944).

It is important to keep in mind that the neural quantum theory implies that the demonstration of quantal units in perception requires rigorous experimental controls. Among the recommended procedures necessary for observing quantal functions are (1) the use of well-motivated and highly trained observers, and (2) the use of brief incremental stimulus values which are added almost instantaneously to the standard.

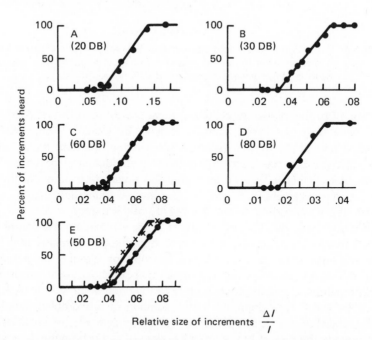

FIGURE 3.4   Neural quantum functions showing the percentage of increments heard as a function of the intensity of the increment added to a steady 1,000-Hz tone. (From Stevens and Volkmann, 1940)

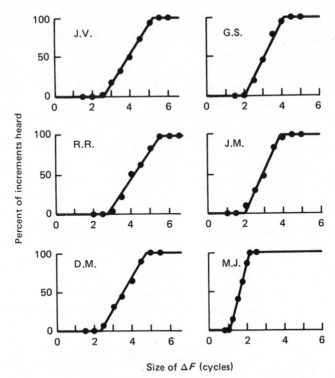

FIGURE 3.5 Neural quantum functions showing the percentage of pitch increments heard as a function of the size in the increment in frequency added to a steady 1,000-Hz tone. (From Stevens, Morgan, and Volkmann, 1941)

Not all of the investigations which have sought to uncover quantal functions have been successful. Careful reviews by Corso (1956, 1967) have identified several studies that failed to support the quantum theory. Furthermore, this position has been criticized on methodological grounds. For example, Blackwell (1953) has argued that the severe restrictions on the conditions of measurement imposed by the neural quantum theory make it difficult, if not impossible, to test the validity of the theory.

We now have two theoretical points of view regarding the nature of perceptual thresholds. One, the phi-gamma hypothesis, maintains that psychophysical performance is a continuous function of stimulus magnitude. The other, the neural quantum theory, argues that psychophysical performance is a discontinuous, stepwise process. How can we determine which of these positions is correct? One approach to the solution of this problem has been to employ statistical analysis to determine whether sigmoidal or rectilinear functions provide the best fit to the empirical data of a psychometric function. Figure 3.6 shows why this is not an easy task, since the differences in the curves fitted to the data on the basis of the phi-gamma and neural quantum theories

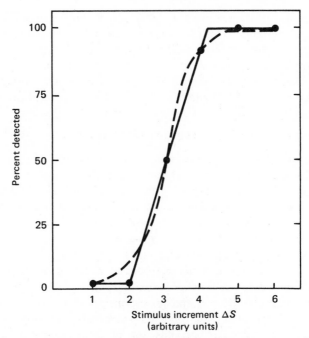

FIGURE 3.6   A psychometric function fit by curves based upon the phi-gamma hypothesis (dashed line) and the neural quantum theory (solid line).

are extremely small. Indeed, in an effort to defend the neural-quantum position, Stevens (1972) indicated that the data of some classical studies which could be described by the normal ogive could also be reanalyzed to fit a rectilinear function. But that implies, of course, that sigmoidal and step functions can often be made to fit the same experimental results!

At this time, the available evidence from curve-fitting experiments does not provide unequivocal support for one position over the other (Corso, 1956, 1967).As indicated by Corso (1963), by Norman (1973), and by Stevens (1972), this state of affairs may be due to the fact that available statistical procedures are not the most satisfactory means of testing the applicability of the phi-gamma and neural quantum theories to a set of psychophysical data.

An appeal to the neurophysiological mechanisms which may underlie psychophysical judgments also fails to provide a definitive answer to the phi-gamma–neural-quantum controversy. While it is true that neural processes follow the all-or-none law, this phenomenon is specific to impulses recorded from the axons of nerve cells. There is good evidence for the existence of graded impulses (often termed "generator potentials"), which are roughly proportional to the magnitude of the stimuli that elicit them, in the sensory nervous system. Such graded impulses may represent initial stages in the neural coding of physical stimuli (Uttal, 1973). Furthermore, most neurons in the central nervous system show "spontaneous" activity which occurs in the absence of any external stimulation (Granit, 1955). Evidently, the neural information which underlies perceptual responses is not conveyed simply in terms of the all-or-none law. Instead, the neural basis for psychophysical performance may consist of interactions between graded and ungraded impulses as well as the modulation of the spontaneous rate of nervous discharge.

Thresholds as Intervening Variables

The phi-gamma–neural-quantum controversy in regard to the nature of thresholds raises important questions about the fundamental nature of information processing in perception. After several decades of research, this issue remains essentially unresolved. Until such a resolution is reached, how shall we treat the nature of psychophysical discrimination? Typically, thresholds have been employed as *intervening* variables—i.e., theoretical constructs inserted between measured stimulus and response variables in an effort to account for the observed stimulus-response relations. Perhaps, for the time being, it would be best to adopt Corso's (1956) interesting suggestion that we consider thresholds from a strictly response-oriented point of view—that is, look upon them as nothing more than dependent variables or performance measures. Our task then becomes one of discovering the factors which influence these dependent variables.

Still another, more radical way to deal with the issues under discussion is to develop an approach to psychophysics which entirely avoids the threshold concept. The theory of signal detection (TSD) represents such an approach, and it is this important theory to which the rest of this chapter is devoted.

THE THEORY OF SIGNAL DETECTION

Two-State and Multi-State Positions

Signals in noise The theory of signal detection represents a radical innovation in thinking about the way in which information is processed in psychophysical experiments. As such, it constitutes *the* major theoretical development in psychophysics since Fechner's pioneering work of over a century ago.

Both of the models of psychophysical discrimination that we considered earlier, the phi-gamma and neural quantum positions, can be viewed as two-state theories of perceptual processing (Massaro, 1975). They imply that in any detection experiment, the perceptual system can signify only two possible states on a given trial—a detection state in which a stimulus is present and a nondetection state in which a stimulus is not present. The theory of signal detection, on the other hand, is a multi-state position. It assumes that every trial contains some degree of interference or "noise" which emanates from several possible sources, such as spontaneous firing in the nervous system, changes inherent in the environment or in the equipment used for generating stimuli, and factors deliberately introduced by the experimenter. Such noise always results in a greater-than-zero level of sensation, and the stimulus to be detected always occurs against a background of noise. Because sensory excitation is continually varying, the perceptual system can signify several different states, i.e., different values of sensory excitation when a stimulus is presented.

Consequently, TSD challenges the assumption of a perceptual threshold. It argues essentially that we cannot define the proper set of conditions for the measurement of such a "perceptual barrier." To put the argument more concretely, suppose we are interested in detecting an auditory signal. Clearly, the noise in the experimental room would place a limit on what an observer could detect at very low signal intensities. Even if we place the observer in an *anechoic chamber* where the walls are especially absorbent and the reduction of external noise is almost complete, we will not solve the problem, for a new source of noise will become apparent: the sound generated within the observer's body by heartbeats, by blood pulsing through vessels in the ears, and by the creaking of the muscles and joints. Similar effects occur in other sensory modalities as well. In short, if we insist on being really precise, we must recognize the fact that we cannot escape from the interfering presence of noise.

Because of this problem, TSD makes no systematic reference to the threshold concept. From the point of view of signal detection theory, the task of the observer in a detection situation is not to classify stimuli as above or below threshold; rather, it is to decide if the magnitude of sensation arising from a given experimental trial is sufficient to warrant a decision in favor of a positive (detection) or a negative (nondetection) response. Unlike the older positions, the emphasis of TSD is not upon a perceptual threshold but upon a *response threshold* anchored in the decision processes of the observer. The focusing of interest upon response thresholds and the view that noise is an inherent rather than an extraneous element of the psychophysical experiment constitute two of the crucial aspects of the approach adopted by TSD.

Sensing and decision making   Signal detection theory also maintains that an observer's report of the presence or absence of a stimulus is not dependent solely upon perceptual sensitivity; it is contingent upon nonperceptual factors as well. The latter include the observer's detection goals, expectations about the nature of the stimuli, and anticipated consequences of correct and incorrect responses. Taken together, these factors compose the observer's response criterion. This aspect of the detection problem is nicely described by Swets:

That probabilities and utilities influence outcomes in the important discriminations that people are called upon to make is perfectly clear—as when the clinician reads an X-ray, when the pilot emerges from a low ceiling, or when the Food and Drug administrator suspects that a product is harmful. Less clear, perhaps, is that these and similar biasing factors can play a large role in any discrimination problem, even those problems posed in the rarified atmosphere of the laboratory. A laboratory subject may have unrealistic notions about the prior probabilities of the alternatives presented to him, or about the sequential probabilities in random sequences of alternatives. One subject may not mind failing to notice a very small difference and feel foolish asserting a difference when there is none, while another subject may strive to detect the smallest possible difference and accept errors of commission as simply part of the game. (Swets, 1973, pp. 990–991.)

Perhaps the most important general feature of TSD is that it enables the independent assessment of the observer as a sensor and as a decision maker (Coombs, Dawes, and Tversky, 1970).

While this theory has had a profound influence on perceptual research, it is worth noting that it did not originate in a psychological laboratory. Signal detection theory has its roots in statistical decision theory and in electrical engineering through the efforts of communication scientists to develop sophisticated electronic sensing systems. The theory was initially adapted for use in regard to perceptual problems by Tanner and Swets (1954).

The Fundamental Detection Problem

Distributions of sensory effects   The theory of signal detection makes some important assumptions regarding the nature of the effects that are produced by signals and by noise. The theory assumes that the sensory effects produced by both signals and by noise vary randomly from moment to moment and that they follow a normal distribution with unit variance (standard deviation equal to 1). Adding a signal to the noise background shifts the average level of excitation upward in proportion to the magnitude of the signal, but it leaves the nature of the distribution of sensory effects unchanged. Thus, TSD maintains that adding a signal to the noise background merely adds an increment to the noise function. Accordingly, the theory postulates two distributions of sensory effects, both of which are normally distributed with equal variance—noise alone *(N)* and signal plus noise *(SN)*. These assumptions are portrayed graphically in Figure 3.7.

From the point of view of TSD, the fundamental detection problem is one in which an observation *(x)* is made during a fixed interval of time (trial), and the observer must decide if what was experienced during the observation interval was an instance drawn from the distribution of noise alone *(N)* or from the signal plus noise *(SN)* distribution. In other words, a sensory effect of some magnitude is produced on every trial, and the problem is one of deciding what produced it, noise or signal plus noise.

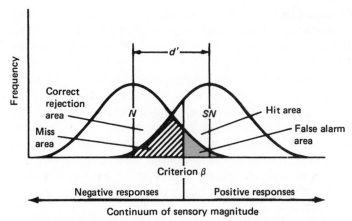

FIGURE 3.7   Hypothetical distributions of sensory events assumed by signal-detection theory. The magnitude of sensory excitations from weak to strong is arrayed from left to right along the horizontal axis, while the relative frequency of these excitations is represented along the vertical axis. The distribution of effects for noise alone (N) is shown in the left portion of the figure, that for signal plus noise (SN) in the right portion. Note that the presence of a signal shifts the SN distribution upward along the continuum of signal magnitude but leaves the nature of the distribution unchanged. The indices d' and β represent signal-detection parameters of sensitivity and response bias, respectively. See text for explanation.

The likelihood ratio   In order to arrive at such a decision, TSD assumes that the observer acts as a complex processor of information who proceeds along the following lines. On the basis of the level of excitation experienced during a given observation interval, the observer assesses the probability that observation *(x)* was an instance of noise and the probability that it was an instance of signal plus noise and then computes a ratio, known as the *likelihood ratio,* of these two conditional probabilities. This ratio expresses the odds that the observation *(x)* arose from *SN* relative to the odds that it arose from *N* alone. The theory also asserts that the observer establishes a *decision rule* such that the likelihood ratio based upon a given observation *(x)* must equal or exceed some cutoff value in order to report, "Yes, a signal was present." If the likelihood ratio falls below this value, the observer will report that a signal was not present. The cutoff value of the likelihood ratio is known as β (beta), and it represents the observer's response criterion.

Decision rules   Where should the observer place the response criterion in a given situation? Presumably, the criterion is established in accordance with the observer's detection goals and relevant situational factors. More specifically, the observer's decision on any trial can result in four possible outcomes: (1) a *hit,* a signal is reported when it was present; (2) a *false alarm,* a signal is reported when in fact it was not present; (3) a *correct rejection*, no signal is reported when no signal was presented; and (4) a *miss*, no signal is reported when in fact a signal was presented. These possibilities are outlined in Table 3.1.

The place along the sensory continuum at which the observer sets the response criterion will influence the relative frequency of these four outcomes. Reexamine Figure 3.7, in which one of many possible response criteria is indicated by the line labeled β. The figure illustrates that β represents a decision point along the sensory continuum and, consequently, along the continuum of likelihood ratios that is derived from sensory excitations. As shown in the figure, sensation values above (to the right of) the criterion will elicit positive responses whereas sensation values below (to the left of) the criterion will elicit negative responses.

Since the N and SN distributions overlap, some sensations could be produced either by N or by SN. Therefore, sensation magnitudes from the N distribution to the right of the criterion will elicit errors of commission or false alarms, and sensation magnitudes from the SN distribution which lie to the right of the criterion will elicit correct detections or hits. Similarly, sensation magnitudes from the N distribution which lie to the left of the criterion will result in correct rejections, while sensation magnitudes from the SN distribution which lie to the left of the criterion will elicit errors of omission or misses. If you study the figure carefully, it will become evident that as the observer becomes more cautious—that is, as the value of the criterion is shifted upward along the sensory continuum—less and less of the N and SN distributions will lie to the right of the decision point. Hence, decisions based upon increments in the criterion will result in a decrease in the probability of a false alarm at the expense of a decrease in the probability of a hit as well as an increase in the probabilities of both correct rejections and misses. Thus, a given criterion yields a particular balance among the four possible outcomes in the detection experiment.

According to TSD, the placement of the response criterion depends upon the willingness of the observer to tolerate errors in order to maximize correct responses. Consider the practical problem of a military radar operator in an early-warning system whose job it is to detect the presence of oncoming

TABLE 3.1   Contingency Table of Outcomes in a Signal Detection Experiment

Response	Stimulus Conditions	
	N	SN
Yes	$N(s)$	$SN(s)$
(s)	False Alarm	Hit
No	$N (n)$	$SN(n)$
(n)	Correct Rejection	Miss

enemy aircraft, and to alert the nation's defensive forces. A blip representing alien aircraft suddenly appears on the radar console. If it is peacetime, and an attack is considered unlikely, the operator might wait a bit to see if the blip continues. After all, sending defensive forces toward the enemy's air space if an attack is not really in progress may result in a dangerous international incident. In this case, the cost of a false alarm being great, the observer adopts a stringent response criterion and is reluctant to report a signal (enemy aircraft) as long as there is uncertainty about its interpretation. On the other hand, if war were already declared and an attack was considered to be imminent, the radar operator would be wise to sound the alert even at the slightest evidence of approaching enemy aircraft. In this case, the value of a hit far exceeds the cost of a false alarm, and thus the observer would adopt a lenient response criterion.

A similar state of affairs can occur in a laboratory setting. Suppose that an observer were told that the experimenter would sample equally between the N and the SN distributions and that a "payoff matrix" is arranged according to that in the left portion of Table 3.2.

According to this matrix, the observer would earn 10¢ for every hit and 1¢ for every correct rejection. There would be no penalties for errors (misses or false alarms). An observer instructed to maximize expected value would be wise to adopt a lenient criterion, for hits pay off substantially whereas correct rejections earn relatively little and errors have no cost at all. Consequently, the observer would be willing to accept making many false alarms in order to maximize the number of signals detected. By contrast, suppose that the payoff matrix were arranged as in the right portion of Table 3.2. In this matrix, the observer still earns 10¢ for every hit, but now correct rejections also pay off equally, and false alarms become quite costly: the observer is penalized 30¢ for each error of commission. Under these circumstances the observer would be wise to adopt a conservative criterion, which would reduce the chances of a hit but at the same time would increase the likelihood of a correct rejection and would also reduce the occurrence of the severe penalties for false alarms.

TABLE 3.2 Payoff Matrices Leading to Adoption of a Lenient and a Conservative Response Criterion

Lenient Criterion			Conservative Criterion		
Response	Stimulus Condition		Response	Stimulus Condition	
	N	SN		N	SN
Yes	N(s)	SN(s)	Yes	N(s)	SN(s)
(s)	0	+10¢	(s)	−30¢	+10¢
No	N(n)	SN(n)	No	N(n)	SN(n)
(n)	+1¢	0	(n)	+10¢	0

Performance Indices

Response criteria and perceptual sensitivity   The response criterion, β, represents one of the basic performance measures of TSD. It is a nonperceptual measure that reflects bias in responding. The *perceptual* index in TSD is termed d'. It specifies the sensitivity of a given observer and as such, reflects the observer's ability to discriminate signal from noise. The value d' is defined as the separation between the means of the N and SN distributions expressed in terms of their standard deviation, i.e.,

$$d' = \frac{M_{SN} - M_N}{\sigma_N}$$

This relation is portrayed graphically in Figure 3.7. The larger the value of d', the greater the separation of the N and SN distributions, the more detectable the signal, and/or the greater the sensory capability of the observer. A major assumption of TSD is that d' and β tap different aspects of performance, and are controlled by different factors. Indeed, the theory asserts that the value of d' is independent of the manner in which the observer sets the response criterion.

Computation of d' ***and*** β Let us take a concrete example to illustrate the computation of d' and β. Assume that an observer must detect a flash of light superimposed upon a constantly illuminated background. A warning signal heralds the start of each observation interval (trial), and the observer reports whether or not the flash of light appeared on the background. Two hundred trials are given, only half of which contain the light flash. The order of appearance of the trials which contain the flash (SN trials) and those which do not (N trials) is varied at random. The data of such an experiment would yield a 2×2 contingency table such as that illustrated in Table 3.1. The computation of d' and β uses only two values from such a table, the probability of hits $[P_{SN(s)}]$ and the probability of false alarms $[P_{N(s)}]$. These two are sufficient because the remaining two values are simply their complements. More specifically, the probability of a miss is equal to $1 - P_{SN(s)}$, and the probability of a correct rejection is equal to $1 - P_{N(s)}$.

Assume that the observer detects 85 of the 100 signals. The $P_{SN(s)}$ is equal to 85/100, or .85. Similarly, assume that the observer makes 5 false alarms. The $P_{N(s)}$ is equal to 5/100, or .05. In order to gain a high probability of hits such as .85, the observer's criterion must have been set well below (to the left of) the mean of the SN distribution. At the same time, the low probability of false alarms, only .05 in this case, suggests that the criterion must have been set well above (to the right of) the mean of the N distribution. The straightforward way to calculate d' and β from these probabilities is from a table of normal curve functions which gives the distance of the ob-

server's criterion from the means of the N and SN distributions in standard
deviation units or z-scores. Table 3.3 presents some representative z-scores
for different response probabilities.

On the basis of Table 3.3, $P_{SN(s)} = .85$ indicates that the criterion was located 1.04 standard deviation units below the mean of the SN distribution
(that is, $Z = -1.04$), and $P_{N(s)} = .05$ indicates that the criterion was located at
$+1.65$ standard deviation units above the mean of the N distribution. The
value of d' is given by the formula:

$$d' = Z_{p \ N(S)} - Z_{p \ SN(S)}$$

In this case, $d' = (1.65) - (-1.04)$, or 2.69

The measure β is determined as the ratio of the ordinate (height) of the
SN distribution to the ordinate of the N distribution at the point where the criterion was set. More specifically:

$$\beta = \frac{\text{ordinate } SN}{\text{ordinate } N}$$

Representative ordinate values for different response probabilities are presented in Table 3.3. In terms of the SN distribution, $P_{SN(s)} = .85$ has an associated ordinal value of .23. In terms of noise distribution, $P_{N(s)} = .05$ has an
associated ordinal value of .10. Therefore:

$$\beta = .23/.10 = 2.30$$

Computational procedures for d' and β have been illustrated in order to
show their basis in familiar statistical procedures. In actual practice, tables are
available which give d' and β for any set of hit and false-alarm probabilities

TABLE 3.3 Representative Z-Score Distances
and Ordinate Values of the
Normal Curve for Different
Response Probabilities

Response Probability	Z-Score	Ordinate Value
.05	+1.65	.10
.15	+1.04	.23
.25	+0.68	.32
.35	+0.38	.37
.45	+0.12	.40
.55	−0.12	.40
.65	−0.38	.37
.75	−0.68	.32
.85	−1.04	.23
.95	−1.65	.10

(Elliott, 1964; Grier, 1971; Hochhaus, 1972; Theodor, 1972). Values given in these tables will differ slightly from those in our illustrative example because of differences in the number of decimal places and the rounding procedures used in the computations.

Receiver operating characteristic curves   One of the fundamental ways of displaying data from a signal detection experiment is in terms of a "receiver operating characteristic" or "relative operating characteristic" curve (ROC curve), in which the proportion of false alarms is plotted against the proportion of hits. Such a curve is presented in Figure 3.8.

The ROC curve traces the relation between the proportions of hits and false alarms for a given degree of sensitivity (fixed level of d') as the observer's criterion is shifted in a stringent-to-lenient direction. The diagonal line in the figure represents a level of sensitivity in which the observer cannot distinguish signals from noise ($d' = 0$). It represents chance performance. As signal intensity is increased, or as observer sensitivity increases, the ROC curve forms an arc which is displaced further and further above the chance diagonal. There is, therefore, a family of ROC curves representative of different levels of d'. Movement in a left-to-right direction along *any* particular ROC curve reflects shifts toward a more lenient criterion. Because the ROC curve reflects criterion changes for a given degree of sensitivity, it is also termed an iso-sensitivity curve.

The ideal observer   An important concept in signal detection theory is that of an "ideal observer" or optimum detector which yields the best possible performance under specified conditions. This concept is important because it provides an absolute standard of reference against which human performance can be evaluated. In many cases, it is possible to state rather precisely the maximum possible value for d' given the known features of sig-

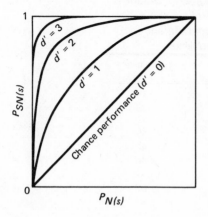

FIGURE 3.8   Receiver operating characteristic (ROC) curves for various levels of d'. Based on the assumption that the distributions of N and SN are normal and of equal variance. (After Green and Swets, 1966)

nal and noise and to compare this "ideal" performance with that actually obtained from a real observer. The ratio of the observed to the ideal d' is an index of the observer's absolute efficiency, which in TSD is symbolized as η.

As might be expected, the performance of the real observer often falls below that of the ideal observer in a given detection situation. In order to gain a further understanding of the nature of the detection process, it is instructive to try to isolate the reasons for the discrepancies that occur. Among the factors that may underlie such discrepancies are the presence of an unstable response criterion in the human observer's decision processes, noise in the perceptual system which masks the signal, and, perhaps most crucial, the human observer's uncertainty about the exact nature of the incoming signal (Swets, 1961).

Tests of the Model

The theory of signal detection represents an intricate mathematical model which describes the behavior of observers faced with the task of detecting weak signals. Before this theory could be accepted as an improvement on the older approaches to psychophysics, or even as a viable alternative to them, it was necessary to establish its validity. In this section, we will describe some of the many experimental attempts to do just that.

Variations of the response criterion   Perhaps the simplest and most direct test of TSD is to determine the effects of inducing the observer to alter the response criterion under conditions in which the physical magnitude of the signal remains constant. Since such a situation would manipulate nonsensory factors, one would expect that β would vary but that d' should be unaffected. In terms of ROC curves, changes in criterion should be reflected along a fixed iso-sensitivity function. An experiment by Tanner, Swets, and Green (1956) provided evidence to support this expectation. Observers were required to detect a tone burst in a background of noise. The level of noise and signal plus noise was kept constant. Changes in criterion were induced by varying the *a priori* probability of signal occurrence in separate blocks of 600 trials. The following values of signal probability were used and were known to the observer: .10, .30, .50, .70 and .90. A typical ROC curve for one observer is presented in Figure 3.9. The vertical dashed lines in the insert of the figure represent decision criteria corresponding to the data points.

It is evident in the figure that increasing the likelihood of a signal did induce the adoption of a more lenient criterion. Notice, however, that the data points fall along a single iso-sensitivity curve with $d' = .85$, confirming the crucial assumption in the theory of the independence of sensitivity and criterion.

In a second part of this experiment, the probability of a signal on any block of trials was kept constant at .50, and observers were induced to shift

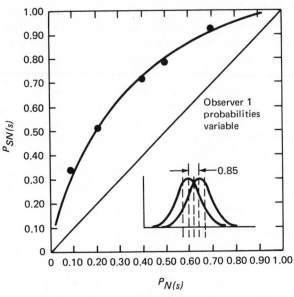

FIGURE 3.9   An ROC curve from an observer who was induced to vary the criterion by manipulating the a priori probability of a signal. The dashed lines of the insert
show the positions of the observer's criteria for each of the data points. The index d' is constant at .85. (From Green and Swets, 1974)

their criteria by systematically increasing the payoff for hits relative to that for
correct rejections. The results for this portion of the experiment for the same
observer as before are presented in Figure 3.10.

As can be seen in the insert, in which the dashed lines represent the decision criteria adopted by the observer, the experimental manipulations again
sulted in a marked change in the value of the criterion, but, as before, d'
remained stable at .85.

Support for TSD along similar lines comes from an experiment by Clark
(1966). This study made use of the fact that the temporal acuity of the eye is
limited and that a light which changes intensity very rapidly, for example, the
ordinary incandescent lamp which fluctuates in intensity 120 times per second, appears to have a steady rather than a flickering level of illumination.
The point at which a flickering visual stimulus just appears to be flickering
rather than steady is known as the critical flicker frequency (CFF). A great
deal of research has been conducted on the variables influencing CFF, such
as rate of fluctuation, target intensity, target area, and the light-dark ratio (see
Geldard, 1972; Kaufman, 1974; and Kelly, 1972, for recent discussions of this
problem).

The focus of Clark's experiment was upon the influence of facilitating and
inhibiting instructional sets on the point at which an intermittent light appeared steady. Under the facilitating instructions, observers were informed

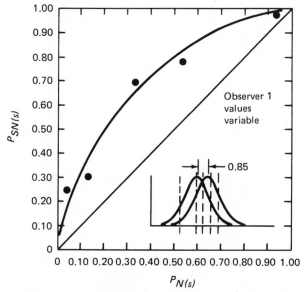

FIGURE 3.10   An ROC curve from the same observer as in Figure 3.9. In this case, changes in criteria were induced by varying the payoffs for hits and correct rejections. Each data point is the result of a different value for these decision outcomes. The dashed lines of the insert show the position of the observer's criterion for each data point. A priori signal probability was .50 under all conditions. The index d' is constant at .85. (From Green and Swets, 1974)

that "most people have very good vision . . . they see the light as flickering most of the time," while under inhibiting instructions they were told that "most people are careful about what they see . . . they do not report the light as flickering unless they are fairly certain." An analysis of the data by the method of constant stimuli suggested that the inhibiting instructions served to elevate the flicker threshold. However, a TSD analysis of the same data revealed that perceptual sensitivity remained unchanged under both instructional sets; the role of the inhibiting instructions was to induce a more stringent response criterion.

Variations in perceptual sensitivity   Signal detection theory offers the value d' as an alternate to the classical threshold measure as an index of perceptual sensitivity. If d' reflects the sensitivity of the observer, then it should increase with the clarity of the signal relative to the noise background. Figure 3.11 presents evidence for such a result from an experiment by Green, Birdsall, and Tanner (1957) on the detection of a pure tone embedded in a noise background.

In this investigation, both the energy level and the duration of the tone were varied systematically. As can be seen in the figure, the results for all four

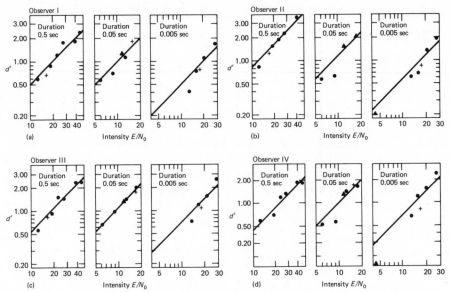

FIGURE 3.11   The detectability of an acoustic signal embedded in noise as a function of signal intensity and duration for four observers. Intensity values are expressed as
the ratio of signal energy to the noise spectrum—E/N_0. (From Green, Birdsall,
and Tanner, 1957)

observers in the experiment revealed that d' increased with increments in the
energy value of the stimulus and that it also increased with increments in the
duration of the signal within the range of .005 to .50 sec. Similar findings
have been reported for visual detection by Cohn, Thibos, and Kleinstein
(1974), for the detection of changes in stimulus duration by Creelman
(1964), for taste sensitivity by Engen (1971a), and for the detection of words
in noise by Green and Birdsall (1964). In addition, Cohn and Lasley (1974)
have shown in a visual-detection task that the value of d' decreases when the
specificity of the stimulus is degraded by making its spatial location uncertain.

As we have seen, one of the problems with the classical threshold measure has been that it depends upon the particular psychophysical procedure
that is used to collect the data. Thus, the results of psychophysical tests may
have very limited generality. By contrast, d' seems to remain relatively invariant over quite different experimental procedures. As described by Green
and Swets (1974), signal detection indices can be obtained from yes-no and
from forced-choice procedures as well as from techniques in which observers
rate their confidence in the decisions that a signal was present. Evidence is
accumulating to indicate that all of these procedures yield similar estimates for
d' for a given set of stimulus conditions (Green and Swets, 1974; Swets,
1961; Weintraub and Hake, 1962). Such a result implies, of course, that the

signal detection analysis may represent a substantial advance in psycho-physical technique.

Corrections for guessing We have pointed out earlier that classical threshold theories assume that on any trial the observer can report only the presence or absence of a signal. In terms of this approach, the threshold represents a lower limit on sensitivity, and the observer is not considered capable of making effective discriminations below a certain energy value. This "high threshold" position (Blackwell, 1953) argues that the threshold is rarely exceeded by noise alone. By contrast, TSD argues that the perceptual system can take several states on a given trial and that observers are indeed capable of ranking their observations and of giving a differential assessment of the likelihood of a signal on any given trial. These points of view lead to different implications with regard to the handling of false alarms in a psychophysical experiment.

For classical threshold theory, different rates of false alarms reflect varying degrees of bias in the observer's willingness to guess the presence of a signal. Thus, in order to obtain the "true" probability of a signal being above threshold, it is necessary to correct the psychometric function for guessing. The usual formula for this correction is:

$$\text{True Proportion of Correct Detections} = \frac{\text{Proportion of Hits} - \text{Proportion of False Alarms}}{1 - \text{Proportion of False Alarms}}$$

According to this approach, once the bias caused by guessing is removed, psychometric functions obtained under different false-alarm (guessing) rates should yield identical threshold values. The theory of signal detection, on the other hand, maintains that this should not be the case. Differences in false-alarm rates represent changes in β which cannot be removed simply by a correction for guessing.

This prediction from TSD was tested by Swets, Tanner, and Birdsall (1961) in an experiment which required observers to give a yes-no response, indicating their detection of a small spot of light briefly presented on a large, uniformly illuminated background. The proportion of correct detections for different values of signal intensity was determined for three different false-alarm rates, and the resulting psychometric functions are presented in Figure 3.12.

If we follow the customary procedure of taking a detection probability of .50 as the threshold, the data in Figure 3.12 reveal that the different false-alarm rates would lead to different estimates of the threshold value. These same psychometric functions corrected for guessing appear in Figure 3.13.

It is clearly evident in this figure that the prediction from TSD was borne

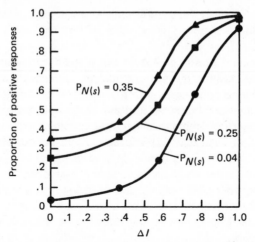

FIGURE 3.12   The relationship between the detection threshold for a spot of light presented on a uniformly illuminated background and false-alarm rate. (From Swets, Tanner, and Birdsall, 1961)

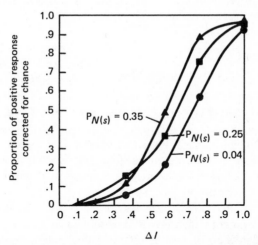

FIGURE 3.13   The relationship between the detection threshold and false-alarm rate with the three curves corrected for guessing. (From Swets, Tanner, and Birdsall, 1961)

out. The correction for guessing did not eliminate differences in the psycho-metric functions based upon different false-alarm rates. Even with the correction, the estimated 50 percent threshold values would vary inversely with the rate of false alarms.

The second-choice experiment   Further support for the signal-detection approach comes from another aspect of the work by Swets, Tanner, and

Birdsall (1961), known as the *second-choice experiment*. Once again observers were required to detect a small spot of light on an illuminated background. This time, however, four temporal intervals were defined on each trial, one of which contained the signal. The interesting feature of this experiment was that the observer was asked not only to indicate the interval most likely to have contained the signal, but to make a second choice as well.

How accurate should the second choice be? If the observer was incorrect on the first choice, the signal must have been below threshold, according to classical threshold theory. Hence, performance on the second choice should be no better than chance. From the viewpoint of TSD, however, the observer can differentially rate the likelihood that the signal appeared in any interval, and therefore the probability of a correct response on the second choice would be expected to exceed a chance value. Since the second choice in this study was made from the three remaining temporal intervals on each trial in which the first response was incorrect, the chance value for the second choice was .33. The results presented in Figure 3.14 reveal that the proportion of correct responses for the second choice did indeed exceed chance expectation, a result which cannot be accommodated by a rigid, high-threshold theory. This aspect of the work of Swets, Tanner, and Birdsall (1961) has been confirmed in additional experiments by Eijkman and Vendrik (1963) and by Kincaid and Hamilton (1959).

The Status of TSD

The theory of signal detection has passed some very rigorous experimental tests. While all aspects of this elaborate theory have not received unquali-

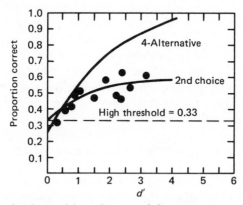

FIGURE 3.14 The results obtained from the second-choice experiment shown with the prediction from the theory of signal detection. The top curve is a theoretical function relating the proportion of correct first choices to d′; the lower curve is the theoretical relation of the proportion of correct second choices to d′. The data points represent the proportions of correct second choices obtained in the experiment. (From Tanner, Swets, and Birdsall, 1961)

fied support (Hohle, 1965; Parducci and Sandusky, 1970), enough favorable evidence has been accumulated so that it has gained general acceptance among investigators concerned with perceptual processes.

The principal advantage of TSD is that it permits the inherent detectability of the signal to be separated from attitudinal or motivational variables which influence the observer's criteria for judgment. Consequently, analysis along the lines of signal detection theory becomes useful when it is of interest to learn whether an experimental outcome is attributable to a change in the perceptual system, to variations in response bias, or, perhaps, to both.

The model in action   A recent study by Clark and Yang (1974) on acupunctural analgesia serves as a convenient illustration of this approach. One of the most startling developments in the management of pain during the early portion of this decade was the report by Chinese surgeons that acupuncture—the insertion of needles into specified areas of the body—can ameliorate surgical pain. Clark and Yang questioned whether the basis for this phenomenon was a reduction in pain sensitivity or a rise in the criterion for reporting pain. In order to answer this question, they presented high levels of painful radiant heat to both arms of a group of observers under conditions in which one arm was exposed to acupuncture and the other was not. The acupunctural procedure used by these investigators successfully produced functional analgesia: pain response in the acupunctured arm decreased when compared to the arm not treated with acupuncture. A TSD analysis of the data, however, revealed no differences in pain discriminability in the two arms of the observers. The sole effect of acupuncture was to cause the observers to set a higher pain criterion. Apparently, acupuncture was effective in controlling pain in this case because it operated on response bias and not on perceptual sensitivity. This, of course, does not lessen the utility of acupuncture; it might still be useful clinically, much as placebos can often be employed to reduce physical or psychological symptoms. But the TSD analysis does allow for a conclusion about the locus of the effect, which in turn should lead to a better understanding of how acupuncture actually works.

The theory of signal detection has been similarly applied to a wide variety of problems in perception; we will encounter some of these applications throughout the remainder of this book. Complete summaries of this work can be found in Green and Swets (1966, 1974); Pastore and Scheirer (1974), and Swets (1973).

The search for the threshold   What of the search for the threshold— does the advance of signal detection theory mean that it should be abandoned? Unfortunately, there is as yet no clear-cut answer to this question. The classical methods of psychophysics which have searched for thresholds have certainly provided important data on the exquisite sensitivity of perceptual functions. Furthermore, it is possible to generate versions of threshold theory, known as "low-threshold" theories, which specify a threshold that is exceeded a substantial portion of the time when only noise is present. Such low-threshold models can fit some of the same data used to support the TSD model (Luce, 1963a, 1963b; Atkinson, 1963; Swets, Tanner, and Birdsall, 1961). To complicate the matter still further, Stevens (1961a) has suggested that TSD may apply well only when observers must "dig" signals out of noise, but that the neural quantum theory may better apply when attempts to eliminate noise are successful. Of course, whether such attempts can ever really be successful remains to be seen.

The issue has perhaps been stated most cogently by Licklider (1959), who suggested that while the psychophysics of signal detection has, throughout most of its history, been a matter of determining thresholds, the threshold now has a competitor for its place as a basic concept. In this regard, it is interesting to note that Treisman and his co-workers (M. Treisman, 1964, 1973; Treisman and Leshowitz, 1969; Treisman and Watts, 1966) have developed ways of estimating d' from results obtained by the classical method of constant stimuli and of using the TSD model to explain the form of Weber's Law. Furthermore, Wright (1974) has developed a theoretical framework, based in part upon response bias, which attempts to bring together TSD, the phi-gamma hypothesis, and the neural quantum theory. The complexity of these investigations is beyond the scope of this chapter. They indicate, however, that the two major variants of classical threshold theory and the contemporary theory of signal detection may not be as far apart as they might seem. Indeed, it may eventually be possible to integrate these approaches under a single theoretical model.

4

The Quantification
of
Perceptual Magnitude
and
Stimulus Information

One of the most obvious properties of our everyday encounters with stimuli is that they vary over a considerable range of magnitudes. Sounds, for example, vary from faint to loud, lights from dim to bright, and so on. How can we measure this important aspect of perceptual experience, and how are such *psychological* measures related to *physical* measurements of the stimuli which yield variation in perceived magnitude? Contrary to what you might expect, the relation between these two sets of measures is far from simple. If, for example, the output of a sound or light source is doubled, the resulting increase in apparent loudness or brightness does not double, but, instead, seems considerably less than "twice as loud" or "twice as bright." On the other hand, if the strength of an electric current passed through the fingertip is doubled, the change in the perceived intensity of shock appears to be much greater than "twice as strong." Clearly, the perceptual system is not a simple, linear reflector of variations in the physical values of stimuli. Is there any mathematical equation which can adequately describe the relation between perceived and physical magnitude? The long and in part frustrating search for such an equation, often termed the *psychophysical law,* will provide the theme for the first section of the present chapter. In the second and briefer section, we examine some interesting techniques for quantifying the amount of information inherent in patterns and sequences of stimuli.

THE PSYCHOPHYSICAL LAW

Fechner's Law

Gustav Fechner (1860), whom we encountered in earlier chapters, made the initial empirical attempt to express the functional relationship between physical stimuli and their corresponding perceptual magnitudes, and thereby to link the inner world of perceived events with the outer world of stimulus energy. Fechner understood that in order to attack this problem experimentally it was first necessary to devise a means of scaling or measuring the subjective impressions of stimulus magnitude. Only then would it be possible to match these impressions to the known properties of the physical stimuli which elicit them.

The nature of measurement   Broadly speaking, measurement refers to the assignment of numbers to objects or events according to rules (Stevens, 1951b). In measuring physical variables, we often begin at an arbitrary starting point and mark off constant units of magnitude. Consider the establishment of a scale of weight. We could begin with any arbitrary value, find matching units with a pan balance, and go on to build successively equal units of weight against which we could compare or "measure" the heaviness of different objects. Fechner proceeded along similar lines in attempting to scale the subjective magnitude of stimuli.

Fechner acknowledged that a direct measure of subjective magnitude could be attained if people were able to judge that one stimulus was, say, twice or three times as intense as another, but he rejected the possibility of such judgments' being made in a meaningful fashion. Consequently, Fechner adopted an indirect approach, in which an index of perceptual magnitude was derived, as it were, "secondhand," through the measurement of some factor that could be accepted as reflecting the perceived magnitude of the stimulus. He reasoned that if this factor was composed of equal units, he might be able to count up these units (either literally or in principle) and in this way gauge the subjective impression produced by any stimulus over a whole range of physical values. All that was needed was a way of measuring the magnitude of one of these constituent units.

Fechner was aware of Weber's Law, which states that whereas the absolute value of a jnd increases as stimulus magnitude increases, the relative value of the jnd remains invariant. Or, as we noted in Chapter 2, a stimulus must be increased by a constant fraction of its value in order to be just noticeably different. Here, then, in the jnd was a suitable unit for measuring changes in perceived magnitude. Fechner argued that a subjective scale could be devised by adopting the absolute threshold as an arbitrary starting point and by using the jnd as an indirect but constant unit of measurement. In order to determine the apparent strength of a particular stimulus all that was necessary was to summate the number of jnd's that fell between that stimulus and the absolute threshold. Thus, if stimulus value x was 5 jnd's above the absolute threshold, its perceived magnitude was 5; if 50 jnd's separated stimulus value y and the absolute threshold, the perceived strength of that stimulus was 50.

Basic to any measurement scheme are the assumptions which underlie it. Fechner's scheme was founded on three crucial assumptions: (1) Weber's Law was true; (2) all jnd's are subjectively equal, and hence the difference between any pair of stimuli separated by one jnd will be the same regardless of the physical values of the stimuli; and (3) the perceived magnitude of a given stimulus is equal to the number of jnd units that precede it on the scale.

A logarithmic relation   Fechner carried out many careful experiments to establish the psychophysical law. Stepping off successive jnd's was a formidable task in these investigations, but Fechner was aided by mathematical equations which he developed to predict the subjective value of a given stimulus. Assuming that Weber's Law was true, he could write what he called the *Fundamentalformel,* or fundamental formula:

$$\Delta \psi = k \frac{\Delta M}{M}$$

where $\Delta\psi$ represents a perceived change in stimulus magnitude, M is the physical value of the stimulus, ΔM is the change in physical value necessary to make the stimulus just noticeably different, and k is a constant that depends upon the sense modality involved, the units of measurement used, and the choice of a zero point for apparent intensity. Fechner considered this formula as a differential equation, integrated it, and produced what he termed the *Massformel,* or measurement formula, which is now known as *Fechner's Law:*

$$\psi = k \log M$$

This equation states that perceived magnitude increases as the logarithm of the stimulus. An important characteristic of the logarithmic function is that larger and larger steps in physical magnitude are required for successively equal increments in the perceived magnitude of the stimulus. This aspect is shown in the left-hand portion of Figure 4.1.

Notice that the curve in the left portion of the figure is negatively accelerated — that is, successive steps in perceived magnitude require larger and larger increments in stimulus value.

A logarithmic relation between two variables also implies that as one increases geometrically the other increases arithmetically. In a geometric progression, each term except the first is derived from the preceding term by

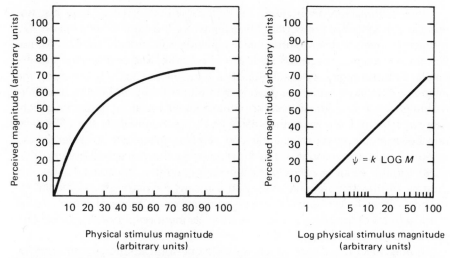

FIGURE 4.1   The psychophysical relation between physical stimulus magnitude and perceived magnitude proposed by Fechner.

multiplying by a constant number or ratio, e.g., 3, 6, 12, 24 = 3, 6 (or 3 × 2), 12 (or 6 × 2), 24 (or 12 × 2), while in an arithmetic progression, each term except the first is derived from the preceding term by the addition of a constant number, e.g., 3, 5, 7, 9 = 3, 5 (or 3 + 2), 7 (or 5 + 2), 9 (or 7 + 2). The logarithmic relation between a geometric and an arithmetic series can be illustrated by reference to the common logarithm of 10 and its multiples. Thus:

$$\text{Log } 10 = 1$$
$$\text{Log } 100 = 2$$
$$\text{Log } 1,000 = 3$$
$$\text{Log } 10,000 = 4$$
$$\text{Log } 100,000 = 5$$

Notice that the elements in the left side of the equations increase by a constant multiple (10) while those on the right side increase by a constant unit (1). Therefore, Fechner's logarithmic law can also be read as stating that perceived magnitude increases arithmetically as stimulus magnitude increases geometrically, or that equal differences in subjective magnitude correspond to equal ratios of physical magnitude.

Still another characteristic of a logarithmic function becomes evident when perceived magnitude in arithmetic units is plotted as a function of the log of the stimulus—curvature in the relation between these variables disappears and a straight line is obtained. This characteristic is illustrated in the right-hand portion of Figure 4.1.

Implications for perception   Fechner's method of cumulating just noticeable differences has important implications for the study of perception. On a practical level, scales of subjective magnitude can provide useful information for engineering specialties such as noise control and photometry. For example, acoustic engineers use the *decibel,* a logarithmic unit, in specifying the intensity of auditory stimuli, and workers in photography and optics use filters calibrated on a logarithmic scale to control variations in the intensity of light (Engen, 1971b). On a more theoretical level, psychophysicists study the relation between perceived magnitude and stimulus magnitude in order to develop a systematic account of the functioning of the perceptual system (Stevens, 1966b). More specifically, Fechner's logarithmic function held out the promise of providing psychologists with a means for making fundamental inferences about how observers process information in terms of the operating characteristics of the perceptual system, i.e., its input-output or "transduction" properties (Stevens, 1960, 1966b).

A *transducer* is a device which converts one form of energy into another. Microphones and photocells, which change acoustic and radiant energy into electrical energy, are examples of transducers. Luce (1972) has pointed out that measuring devices in general can be considered as transducers which transform one attribute into another. Thus, a spring balance transforms the force of weight into changes in the length of a spring, and a voltmeter translates electrical force into the spatial displacement of a needle. The sensory receptors of organisms, which form the initial stages of perceptual processing, can also be viewed as transducers for converting energy from the environment into neural form. If we consider the perceptual system as a measuring device, what can we say about its general transduction characteristic? Fechner's Law implies that this general characteristic is a logarithmic one. That is, the perceptual system translates physical magnitudes into psychological impressions on a logarithmic scale.

Fechner's proclamation of the logarithmic law provoked a great deal of controversy in the late nineteenth century. In summarizing these arguments, Marks (1974b) points out that some investigators challenged Fechner by maintaining that sensations are not amenable to quantitative investigation, and others attempted to establish alternative forms of the psychophysical law. One of the most important of these latter efforts was the proposal by Plateau (1872) that perceptual magnitude increased as a power function, not as a logarithmic function, of stimulus magnitude. That is, sensation magnitude is proportional to a power of the physical stimulus. The early attacks upon Fechner were not successful, however, and he was so convinced of the validity of his logarithmic function that he wrote:

The tower of Babel was never finished because the workers could not reach an understanding on how they should build it; my psychophysical edifice will stand because the workers will never agree on how to tear it down. (Fechner, 1877)

And he was right—up to a point. Fechner's form of the psychophysical law remained the generally accepted version until the midportion of the present century, at which time the work of S. S. Stevens (1961b) did much to effect its repeal.

Critique of Fechner's Law

Grounds for indictment   On the basis of data accumulated in the century since its formulation, Fechner's Law can be indicted on several grounds. First of all, it is based on the assumption that Weber's Law is true, and as we have seen (Chapter 2), Weber's Law generally does not hold for stimuli at the extreme ends of a sensory continuum. Thus, Fechner's summated jnd technique may introduce serious error into the form of the psychophysical relation between stimulus magnitude and subjective magnitude. In addition, Fechner's choice of the absolute threshold as an arbitrary starting point for a scale of psychological magnitude may not have been a judicious one, since, as we have seen in the previous chapter, the nature of the absolute threshold is in itself open to serious question. Finally, as Stevens (1957) has pointed out, Fechner's assumption that all jnd's are subjectively equal to each other, and therefore that each jnd contributes an equal increment to perceived magnitude, is contraindicated by empirical evidence.

In order to develop this last point, we need to consider a basic distinction that Stevens has drawn between two kinds of perceptual continua, *prothetic* and *metathetic* (Stevens, 1957; Stevens and Galanter, 1957). Prothetic continua are concerned with "how much" and represent dimensions on which discriminations involve an additive process on the physiological level. Examples of this type of continuum are loudness, brightness, heaviness, and duration. Metathetic continua are concerned with "what kind" or "where" and represent dimensions on which discriminations involve a substitutive process at the physiological level. Examples are pitch, azimuth, and apparent inclination. Stevens points out that while Fechner's assumption of the equality of jnd's may hold for metathetic dimensions, it definitely does not hold for prothetic dimensions.

Ratio scaling   Evidence for the lack of equality of jnd's along prothetic continua comes from studies using procedures in which perceptual magnitudes are measured by direct quantitative estimates on the part of observers rather than the indirect approach taken by Fechner. The developers of these "ratio-scaling" procedures assume that observers can do more than make crude judgments of similarity or simple equality matches. They operate on the conviction that people can validly assign numerical values to the magnitudes of their sensations. They further assume that if two stimuli are presented, an observer can assign a number to the ratio of the aroused perceptual magnitudes. For example, people can say with meaning that the perceived magni-

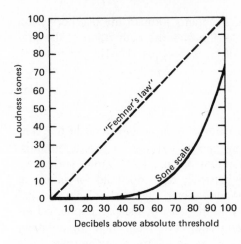

FIGURE 4.2 The sone scale of subjective loudness described by Stevens (1936). The solid line represents increments in judged loudness (sones) as a function of stimulus intensity in decibels. The dashed line represents the growth of loudness as predicted by Fechner's Law. (After Woodworth and Schlosberg, 1954)

tude of stimulus A is twice that of stimulus B, or that B's magnitude is one-half that of A's.

One of the principal ratio-scaling techniques is the "fractionation" method, in which observers are asked to set the physical value of a stimulus so that it appears to be half as intense as another stimulus. Stevens (1936) used this method to construct a subjective scale of loudness called the *sone scale*. He defined one sone as the loudness of a 1,000-Hz tone at 40 decibels above threshold. By working upward and downward in successive half-loudness steps from this reference point, he could construct the scale shown in Figure 4.2, in which apparent loudness in sones is plotted against stimulus intensity in decibels.

As mentioned before, a decibel is a logarithmic unit, which in terms of energy flow, is defined as

$$dB = 10 \log_{10} \frac{E_1}{E_0}$$

where E_1 is the energy value to be described in decibels and E_0 is a reference energy value, in this case stimulus energy at threshold.[1] Consequently, in plotting the sone scale in this way, psychological magnitude is represented in arithmetic units while physical magnitude is presented in logarithmic units. If, as Fechner's law maintains, perceived magnitude increases as the logarithm

[1] In this case, physical stimulus intensity is expressed as a relative measure, "decibels sensation level (dBSL)" — decibels above the observer's detection threshold. In acoustical work, it is also necessary to state the absolute physical intensity of a sound in terms of decibels sound pressure level (dBSPL). To accomplish this, an objective standard of 0.0002 dynes/cm² is usually taken as the reference value (E_0). While the decibel is most often associated with experiments in hearing, the general formula provides a convenient way of expressing the physical intensity of stimuli in other modalities as well.

of the stimulus, we should expect a linear function. Notice, however, that the result is far from linear: the curve in Figure 4.2 is concave upward.

This method of ratio scaling was used by Harper and Stevens (1948) to construct a scale of perceived weight, known as the *veg scale,* and more recently in a similar study by Engen (1971b). Engen's data are presented in Figure 4.3. Similarly, Hanes (1949a, 1949b) tried the halving method to produce a scale of apparent brightness of a patch of light known as the *bril scale,* which is presented in Figure 4.4.

In none of these cases does the form of the relation between perceived magnitude and physical magnitude conform to the expectations of Fechner's Law. It seems clear that with direct ratio scaling of the subjective magnitude of stimuli along prothetic continua, equal logarithmic steps are not psychologically equal. Instead, the observer behaves as if the subjective size of a perceived difference increases fairly regularly as the stimulus becomes more intense.

The Power Law

Magnitude methods In the historical development of theoretical ideas in science, it is one matter to provide logical criticism and empirical evidence to challenge an accepted position and another matter to displace it. The latter can only be accomplished by the formulation of an alternative position that is

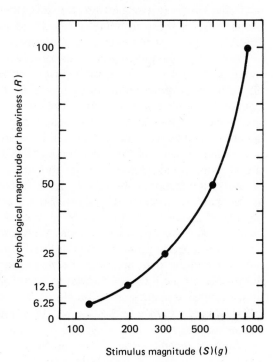

FIGURE 4.3 Subjective heaviness as a function of stimulus weight in grams. The data are plotted with psychological values in arithmetic coordinates and stimulus values in logarithmic coordinates. (From Engen, 1971b)

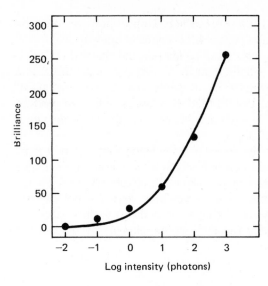

FIGURE 4.4 The bril scale of subjective brightness described by Hanes (1949). The data are plotted with psychological values (brils) in arithmetic coordinates and stimulus values in logarithmic coordinates. (From Hanes, 1949a)

bolstered by hard data. Stevens engaged in a program of research extending over four decades designed to do just that for the psychophysical law.

To begin with, Stevens developed direct-ratio-scaling techniques that are relatively simple to use and adaptable to many different experimental situations. One of these techniques, known as *magnitude estimation* (Stevens, 1956), requires that observers assign numbers directly to stimuli in proportion to their subjective magnitudes. The observer is presented with a standard stimulus called the *modulus* and is instructed to represent its subjective magnitude by a convenient number such as 100. The experimenter then presents in irregular order a series of stimuli above and below the standard and instructs the observer to assign to each stimulus a number proportional to its apparent magnitude. In other words, if the standard has a value of 100, what is the value of each of the other stimuli? If a stimulus appears to be twice as strong as the standard, the observer should say "200"; if it appears ten times as strong, the response should be "1,000"; if a stimulus seems half as strong as the standard, it should be called "50"; a quarter as strong, "25"; and so on. The observer is told to use any number that seems appropriate, whether fractions, decimals or whole numbers. With a series of usually six to ten stimuli, each is typically presented two or three times in a different order for each observer and the data are pooled across observers. The geometric mean or the median of the judgments given to each stimulus is taken as the measure of its central tendency and therefore as its perceived value (see Engen, 1971b; Marks, 1974b; and Stevens, 1956, for more detailed descriptions of this technique).

Another technique developed by Stevens, called *magnitude production,* is the logical inverse of magnitude estimation. Instead of presenting a series of stimuli and asking the observer to judge their apparent magnitudes, the experimenter names various magnitudes and asks the observer to adjust stimuli to proportionate subjective values. For example, in scaling the apparent length of lines the experimenter might present a standard length and call it "10." The observer is then instructed to form line segments with apparent lengths that are proportionate to numbers called out by the experimenter, e.g., 1, 2, 5, 10, 20, 30, 40, etc. Each number is called out two or three times in the course of the session in an irregular order. As in magnitude estimation, the geometric means or the medians of the settings obtained for each stimulus from individual observers and from a group of observers are taken as the measure of central tendency and therefore as the indices of perceived value. Though the results obtained by the method of magnitude production are not always identical to those obtained by magnitude estimation, the two methods yield very similar functions. Collectively, these techniques are referred to as "magnitude methods."

A power relation   Using the magnitude methods, Stevens found that psychological magnitude did not increase as a logarithmic function of stimulus magnitude, as Fechner had believed, but rather as a power function in accord with Plateau's (1872) prediction. That is, perceived magnitude is proportional to physical magnitude raised to some power, as represented in the formula:

$$\psi = kM^m$$

where ψ stands for perceived magnitude, M for physical stimulus value, m is the exponent, and k a constant determined by choice of units.

Some data based on magnitude estimations of electric shock through the fingers, line length, and the brightness of a luminous spot of light are presented in Figure 4.5.

It is evident in the figure that the perceived intensity of electric current through the fingers grows more and more rapidly as current increases (the

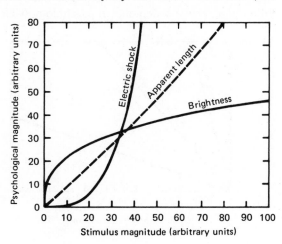

FIGURE 4.5 Magnitude estimates of the strength of electric shock, line length, and visual brightness as a function of stimulus intensity. The data are plotted in arithmetic coordinates. (From Stevens, 1962)

exponent in the power equation is greater than 1), whereas brightness grows less and less rapidly with increasing physical intensity (the exponent in the power equation is less than 1), and apparent length increases very nearly in direct proportion to physical length (the exponent in the power equation is almost 1). A convenient property of a power function is that when the data are replotted in log-log coordinates (logarithmic scales on both axes), curvature disappears, and the function becomes a straight line, as illustrated in Figure 4.6.

The exponent of a power function determines its curvature, and differences in curvature become differences in slope when the data are plotted in log-log coordinates. The high exponent for electric shock results in a steep slope, the low exponent for apparent brightness gives a relatively flat slope, and the nearly linear function for apparent length becomes a slope that is close to 45° in the log-log plot.

The psychophysical power equation described by Stevens has received a considerable amount of empirical support in relation to magnitude estimates of a very large number of prothetic dimensions. Examples of the wide range of dimensions for which power equations have been obtained are given in Table 4.1.

Stevens (1966b) has pointed out that power functions are obtained not only when observers are asked to judge a single attribute of a stimulus such as loudness, but also when different attributes of the same stimulus are judged in the same experiment. Thus, power functions have been observed for each attribute separately when observers were asked to judge the brightness, saturation (absence of gray), and duration of visual stimuli and the loudness, volume (space-filling quality), and density (compactness) of acoustic stimuli in different portions of the same experiment (Indow and Stevens, 1966; Stevens, 1966a; Stevens, Guirao, and Slawson, 1965). The consistency of the power function obtained in magnitude estimation experiments has led some writers to comment that this is one of the most firmly established quantitative statements in psychology (Cliff, 1973; Ekman and Sjöberg,

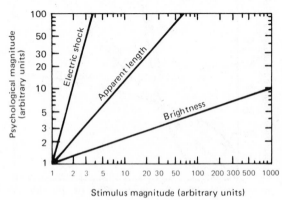

FIGURE 4.6 The data of Figure 4.5 replotted in log-log coordinates. The power function now plots as a straight line in which the exponent determines the slope. The exponents are electric shock through the fingers, 3.5; apparent length of lines, 1.1; brightness of a luminous spot, 0.33 (From Stevens, 1962)

TABLE 4.1   Representative Exponents of Power Functions Relating
Psychological Magnitude to Stimulus Magnitude on
Prothetic Continua (after Stevens, 1960)

Continuum	Exponent	Conditions
Loudness	0.6	Binaural
Loudness	0.55	Monaural
Brightness	0.33	5° target—dark-adapted eye
Brightness	0.5	Point source—dark-adapted eye
Lightness	1.2	Reflectance of gray papers
Smell	0.55	Coffee odor
Smell	0.6	Heptane
Taste	0.8	Saccharine
Taste	1.3	Sucrose
Taste	1.3	Salt
Temperature	1.0	Cold—on arm
Temperature	1.6	Warm—on arm
Vibration	0.95	60 c.p.s.—on finger
Vibration	0.6	250 c.p.s.—on finger
Duration	1.1	White noise stimulus
Repetition rate	1.0	Light, sound, touch, and shocks
Finger span	1.3	Thickness of wood blocks
Pressure on palm	1.1	Static force on skin
Heaviness	1.45	Lifted weights
Force of handgrip	1.7	Precision hand dynamometer
Vocal effort	1.1	Sound pressure of vocalization
Electric shock	3.5	60 c.p.s. through fingers

1965; Engen, 1971b; Marks, 1974b). The magnitude-judgment techniques have led to the development of what is called the "new psychophysics," in which perceived magnitude is measured directly rather than indirectly as in the classical approach taken by Fechner.

Implications of the power function   On the basis of the stability of his data, Stevens (1957, 1958, 1960, 1961b, 1962, 1968a, 1971, 1974, 1975) has proposed that the psychophysical law is best represented as a power relation rather than the logarithmic relation prescribed by Fechner. The power function implies that as stimulus magnitude increases geometrically, perceived magnitude also increases geometrically, so that equal stimulus ratios produce equal perceptual ratios. Stated another way, on sensory continua governed by a power law, a constant percentage change in stimulus magnitude produces a constant percentage change in perceptual magnitude.

The power law allows for great variation in psychological scales for various kinds of physical stimuli. As can be seen in Table 4.1, power functions differ markedly for different senses. In general, it appears that for sensory channels which are highly "buffered"—those, such as audition and vision, which encompass enormous ranges of energy—the exponents of the power equation are low, and psychological magnitude grows slowly with increments in physical magnitude. By contrast, for sensory channels in which the effective range is smaller — for example, temperature and pressure — the exponents are higher, and the effects of physical change are magnified. Stevens (1974) points out that in the case of exponents less than 1, the transduction properties of the sensory receptors reflect "compression," as, for example, when a billionfold change in sound energy becomes a thousandfold change in apparent loudness. He suggests that this might be nature's way of preventing the nervous system from being overloaded by the necessity of processing overwhelming changes in stimulus energy.

Stevens' power law leads to the same practical and theoretical implications as we noted for Fechner's Law. For example, the International Standards Organization has adopted a function of the form shown in Figure 4.7 as the relation between loudness and sound pressure to be used for engineering calculations (Stevens, 1962). With respect to the theoretical question of specifying the operating or transduction characteristics of the perceptual system, Stevens' law implies that physical magnitudes are translated into psychological impressions on a power scale, i.e., the subjective yardstick for stimulus magnitude is calibrated in terms of a power of the physical stimulus intensity (Stevens, 1960).

Support for the Power Law

Cross-modality matching Stevens was aware that the magnitude-estimation and magnitude-production techniques rely heavily upon the observer's having a moderately sophisticated understanding of the use of num-

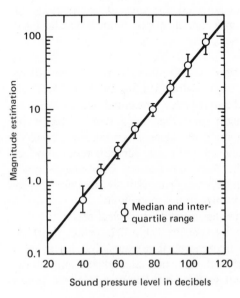

FIGURE 4.7 Loudness function for a 1,000-Hz tone of the form adopted by the International Standards Organization to be used for engineering calculations. The points are median magnitudes estimates obtained when the tone was presented twice at each of eight levels of intensity in irregular order to 26 listeners. (From Stevens, 1962)

bers. He argued that the validity of the power law would be enhanced if it were confirmed in a situation in which observers were not required to make any numerical estimations at all. A technique known as cross-modality matching provides a vehicle for such a test. In this technique observers are asked to match the perceived magnitude of a stimulus in one sensory modality with that of a stimulus in another modality, e.g., to equate the loudness of a sound to the brightness of a light. At first glance, such matches may seem arbitrary, but the comparison of perceived magnitudes across sensory channels is not something that people are totally unfamiliar with. As D'Amato describes it, "the rumble of a subway train is more akin to the brightness of midday than to the twilight of evening and there is more than poetic similarity between a whisper and a gentle breeze" (1970, p. 233). Stevens reasoned that cross-modality matches at various levels of stimulus intensity could be used to map out an "equal-sensation function," and the form of this function could then be compared with that predicted from magnitude scales for the two modalities involved in the match.

Specifically, mathematics tells us that if two sensory modalities are governed by power functions of the form $\psi_1 = kM^a$ and $\psi_2 = kM^b$ and the psychological values of ψ_1 and ψ_2 are equated by cross-modality matches at various intensity levels, then the resulting equal-sensation function will be linear in log-log coordinates, and its slope will be equal to the ratio of the exponents for ψ_1 and ψ_2. In other words, the equal-sensation function will itself be a power function whose exponent will equal the ratio of the exponents for the two modalities involved.

Stevens (1959) performed two complementary experiments in an effort to explore this possibility. In one study, the apparent loudness of a sound was adjusted to match the apparent intensity of 60-Hz mechanical vibration presented to the fingertips; in the other, apparent vibratory intensity was adjusted to match that of the sound. If you look again at Table 4.1, you will see that the exponent for the power function for loudness is 0.6 and that for 60-Hz mechanical vibration is 0.95. Therefore, when plotted in log-log coordinates the equal-sensation function for vibration and loudness should be linear with a slope equal to 0.6/0.95 or 0.63. The data from Stevens' experiments are presented in Figure 4.8. As predicted, the equal-sensation function was linear, with a slope of 0.60, a value remarkably close to the expected value of 0.63.

Since this early experiment, Stevens and his co-workers have conducted a large number of investigations on cross-modality matches. In many of these studies, cross-modal matches were secured by asking observers to emit squeezes on a hand dynamometer to equal the apparent intensity of a variety of test stimuli (Stevens, 1962). Equal-sensation functions obtained in this way are presented in Figure 4.9.

It is clear that a straight line in log-log coordinates provides a good fit for almost all of the data in Figure 4.9. Such cross-modality matches show that Stevens' ratio-scaling technique is internally consistent. In order to provide

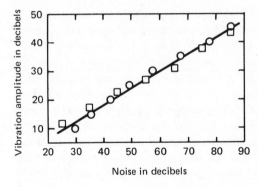

FIGURE 4.8 An equal-sensation function for vibration and loudness. Squares refer to the condition in which vibration was adjusted to match loudness; circles indicate the condition in which loudness was adjusted to match vibration. The slope of the linear function is 0.60. (From Stevens, 1959)

further evidence for such consistency, Stevens (1962) asked whether the exponents derived from the equal-sensation functions in Figure 4.9 for each of the nine sensory dimensions involved would agree with exponents for these dimensions calculated directly by magnitude estimation.

Stevens noted that the sensation of strain in the production of handgrip with the hand dynamometer grew as the 1.7 power of the physical force applied. Therefore, it was possible to derive the exponents of the power functions for each of the sensory dimensions in Figure 4.9 by multiplying the slopes of their equal-sensation functions by the factor 1.7. When this was done, the resulting values agreed quite closely with the exponents obtained

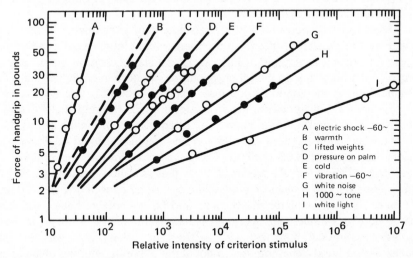

FIGURE 4.9 Equal-sensation functions obtained by matching force of handgrip to nine different criteria stimuli. Each point stands for the median force exerted by 10 or more observers to match the apparent intensity of the criterion stimulus. The relative position of a particular function along the horizontal axis (abscissa) is arbitrary. The dashed line shows a slope of 1.0 in these coordinates. (From Stevens, 1962)

independently by magnitude estimation. The largest discrepancy was only 0.07. Such close agreement over a wide range of dimensions provides formidable support for Stevens' approach.

In addition to these data, Stevens has provided families of matching functions based on matches involving brightness and various other continua (Stevens, 1967, 1968b, 1969a); other investigators have obtained loudness matches with taste (Moskowitz, 1971), temperature (J. C. Stevens and Marks, 1967; J. C. Stevens, Marks, and Gagge, 1969), and angular velocity (Brown, 1968). Ten additional equal-sensation functions based on matches of loudness to a variety of sensory dimensions are presented in Figure 4.10. While exceptions do occur (Mashour and Hosman, 1968), the great mass of evidence coming from the generation of equal-sensation functions seems to conform to predictions from the power law.

The physical correlate theory   As we have indicated, Stevens prefers to view the psychophysical power function as reflecting the basic operating or input-output characteristics of the perceptual system. The successful outcome of experiments on cross-modality matching permitted him to defend this point of view in the face of an alternate account proposed by Warren (1958, 1969, 1973). To explain the observation that equal stimulus ratios produce equal perceptual ratios, Warren offered a *physical correlate theory*, which maintains

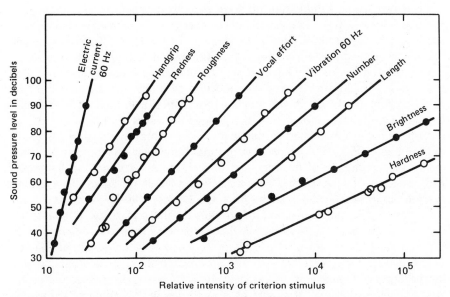

FIGURE 4.10   Examples of equal-sensation functions obtained by matches between loudness and perceptual values on 10 criteria stimuli. The straight lines through the data define power functions in log-log coordinates. The relative position of a particular function along the abscissa is arbitrary. (From Stevens, 1966b)

that the power function merely reflects how observers have learned to associate sensory impressions with some known aspect of the physical stimulus.

According to this point of view, observers learn through experience that a tone of constant intensity sounds softer at a distance than close up, and similarly that a light of constant intensity seems dimmer when viewed at a distance than at close range. Thus, loudness and brightness judgments are based on a learned relation between stimulation and distance from the stimulus source, and the procedures employed by Stevens reflect learned stimulus correlates, not the magnitude of internal experiences! The physical correlate theory leads to the expectation that direct judgments of stimulus magnitude such as half-loudness or half-brightness should be equivalent to doubling the distance of the stimulus source, i.e., a stimulus judged half as loud or half as bright as a standard should also be judged to be twice as far away. Indeed, Warren has provided empirical support for these expectations (Warren, 1973; Warren, Serson, and Pores, 1958; Warren and Warren, 1958), but Stevens (1960, 1975) has countered by appealing to the cross-modality matching experiments. He argued that it is difficult to conceive of how familiarity with the physical stimuli could account for the consistent results obtained with cross-modality matching over such a wide array of dimensions, and especially since many of these dimensions are relatively unfamiliar to the typical observer, at least as regards measures of stimulus intensity.

Reciprocity and individual differences   Still another line of support for the power law comes from experiments dealing with reciprocal relations between a stimulus attribute and its inverse. As D'Amato (1970) points out, if the perceived magnitude of a given stimulus, such as the loudness of a tone, is a power function of stimulus intensity, then the inverse of this attribute, that is, softness, should also be a power function of intensity with an exponent equal to that of the loudness function but opposite in sign. Stevens and Guirao (1962) have shown that the judged loudness and softness of an acoustic stimulus are related in this way. These same investigators (Stevens and Guirao, 1963, 1964) have demonstrated a similar relationship between magnitude judgments of the longness and shortness of lines, the largeness and smallness of squares, and the viscosity and fluidity of liquid. The former two functions are shown in Figures 4.11 and 4.12, respectively.

A last consideration in terms of support for the power law is related to the data of individual observers. We have pointed out in our description of the magnitude-estimation and magnitude-production techniques that the results of several observers are typically grouped together in determining the power function. However, if this function reflects some basic perceptual property, as Stevens believes, it should be able to describe the data of individual observers as well. A few investigations have reported that this is not the case (Luce and Mo, 1965; Pradhan and Hoffman, 1963), which implies that the

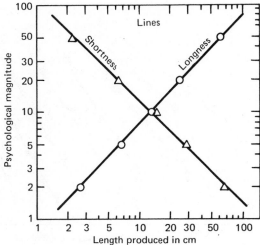

FIGURE 4.11 Reciprocity between the shortness and longness of lines. Data obtained by magnitude production. The slopes of the power functions are 1.0 for longness and −0.97 for shortness. (From Stevens and Guirao, 1963)

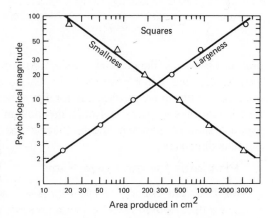

FIGURE 4.12 Reciprocity in magnitude productions of the largeness and smallness of squares. The slopes of the power functions are 0.62 for largeness and −0.72 for smallness. (From Stevens and Guirao, 1963)

power function may be artifactual—a result due to the averaging of data across observers. More generally, however, though individual differences are prevalent (Wanschura and Dawson, 1974; Zinnes, 1969), the bulk of evidence seems to favor the power law. Individual power functions have been obtained in many sensory modalities (Ekman and Åkesson, 1965; Ekman, Hosman, Lindman, Ljungberg, and Åkesson, 1968; Marks and Stevens, 1966; J. C. Stevens and Guirao, 1964; J. C. Stevens and Mack, 1959). An illustration of individual loudness functions based on magnitude estimation and production is presented in Figure 4.13.

In sum, it appears at this point that the power law has withstood some crucial tests. Its derivation is not subject to the conceptual pitfalls that afflict Fechner's Law, and it seems to describe data obtained for a vast array of

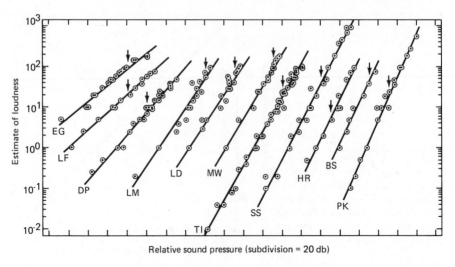

Relative sound pressure (subdivision = 20 db)

FIGURE 4.13   Individual loudness functions for 11 different observers. The data are based upon magnitude estimation and magnitude production responses. (From J. C. Stevens and Guirao, 1964)

prothetic stimulus dimensions on the basis of direct, magnitude-estimation techniques — data determined for individual observers as well as for groups of observers. Substantial verification for the power law has come from cross-modal matching experiments and, in addition, the expected reciprocity between a stimulus attribute and its inverse has been noted for a number of stimulus dimensions.

Problems for the Power Law

Method and theory   While impressive evidence exists for the power law, Stevens' assertion that this law represents the fundamental nature of the psychophysical relation must still be received with some caution. In previous chapters we have emphasized that the methods by which observations are made of perceptual events have an important bearing on the inferences that can be validly drawn about these events. In regard to the issue at hand, you may already have realized that the magnitude techniques which led to the development of the power law differ considerably from the indirect, summated jnd procedures used by Fechner to generate his version of the psychophysical law. A theoretical model is likely to be no better than the data which have shaped it, and the conditions of judgment must be considered before the results of one scaling technique can be accepted over those of another (Helson, 1964; Stevens, 1956, 1966b). Thus, the Fechner-Stevens controversy can be fought on methodological as well as conceptual grounds. To shed further light on this issue, it would be helpful to know if the psychophysical techniques employed in the development of one position are superior to those which led to the development of the other.

Category rating and magnitude scales   In addition to summated jnd scales, support for Fechner's logarithmic version of the psychophysical law can be gained from a more direct procedure known as the *category rating scale*. In this procedure, the observer is given a set of equally spaced categories designated by a finite set of numbers such as 1–7 or by a limited set of adjectives ranging, for example, from "very, very large" through "medium" to "very, very small." The observer is asked to place each of a series of stimuli, presented several times in a random order, into one of the available categories in such a way that the intervals between categories are subjectively equal. A scale relating perceived magnitude to physical magnitude is determined from the observer's judgments by calculating the mean category rating for each stimulus value (see D'Amato, 1970, and Guilford, 1954, for further descriptions of this technique). Scales determined in this way have shown that subjective magnitude is proportional to the logarithm of stimulus magnitude, as Fechner's Law demands (Engen, 1971b; Galanter, 1962; Snodgrass, 1975; Stevens and Galanter, 1957).

In an extensive series of experiments involving judgments of apparent area, brightness, duration, length, loudness, numerosity, and weight, Stevens and Galanter (1957) examined the relation between category rating scales and scales obtained by the magnitude methods. If both techniques provide equivalent measures of judged magnitude, then equal intervals on the category rating scale should correspond to equal intervals on the magnitude scale. Therefore, judgments obtained by the two procedures should be related to each other in a linear fashion in much the same way that measures of length obtained in inches and centimeters or measures of temperature expressed in Fahrenheit and centigrade are linearly related. Stevens and Galanter found, however, that on all of the prothetic dimensions they examined, category rating and magnitude judgments of the same stimuli were not linearly related. Figure 4.14 shows one of the many examples of this result. Moreover, nonlinearity between category rating and magnitude judgments has been confirmed in several additional investigations (Galanter and Messick, 1961; Stevens, 1966b, 1969b; Stevens and Guirao, 1963).

These seemingly equally plausible procedures for measuring perceived magnitudes have given discordant results. Which one is the more appropriate? A common explanation of the nonlinearity between category rating and magnitude judgments places the effect in a response-bias inherent in the category rating procedure. According to this account (Engen, 1971b), the observer's subjective categories are not, in fact, equally spaced. Instead, they are relatively narrow and exclusive for stimuli of small magnitudes but relatively wide and inclusive for stimuli of large magnitude. Consequently, when plotted

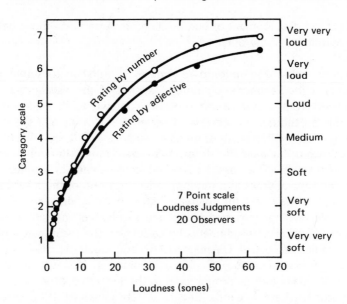

FIGURE 4.14   The non-linear relation between category rating and ratio judgments of loudness. (From Stevens and Galanter, 1957)

against a magnitude scale, the category rating scale is steeper at the low end
and flatter at the upper end. Because the magnitude methods are not subject
to such a bias, they would seem to be "purer" measures of perceptual magnitude.

Another criterion for deciding between the magnitude and category rating
procedures is the invariance of the results obtained by a given measure in the
face of contextual pressures. Ideally, a measure of perceived magnitude
should be related only to the stimulus dimension that is being scaled and not
to other extrinsic features of the experiment. Stevens and Galanter (1957) reported that the category rating scales which they obtained were influenced
dramatically by the spacing of stimuli along the range of values that were
studied, whereas the magnitude scales were relatively unaffected by this contextual factor. Thus, category rating values for particular stimuli were not as
closely tied to the stimuli themselves as were the values determined by the
magnitude procedure. In short, the category rating scale was more susceptible
to contextual perturbations. This result favors Stevens' approach to isolating
the "true" form of the psychophysical law.

Perceptual magnitude and perceptual dissimilarity   Stevens' power
law has gained support from results such as those just described. However,
additional investigations along these lines have exposed several complicating
factors which lead one to be somewhat skeptical as to whether Stevens' magnitude methods have entirely solved the riddle of the "true" form of the psy-

chophysical law. After an extensive review of studies using the category rating and magnitude methods, Marks (1974a) has suggested that these types of direct scaling procedures really tap *different* perceptual processes. He proposes that there are two basic underlying scales for any sensory attribute: Type I scales, which reflect perceptual magnitude, and Type II scales, which reflect perceptual dissimilarity. According to Marks, the former are most closely approximated by ratio scaling procedures of the sort used by Stevens and the latter by interval scaling procedures like category rating. Marks's suggestion can account for the results of an experiment conducted by Torgerson (1961) on brightness judgment in which observers produced power functions when instructed to judge ratios by means of a ratio scaling procedure and logarithmic functions when instructed to judge differences by means of a category rating procedure. If Marks's view is correct, then arguments in support of Stevens' approach on the basis of disparities between category rating and magnitude scales lose much of their potency.

Context effects and response bias   Furthermore, a large number of investigations have shown that the magnitude methods are not as impervious to contextual influences as the early study by Stevens and Galanter (1957) may have led us to believe. Much of this work has been summarized by Poulton (1968), who points out that (1) a small range of stimuli produces a steeper power function (larger exponent) than a large range of stimuli; (2) the slope of the power function is steeper as the stimuli involved approach the absolute threshold; and (3) the larger the size of the standard, or modulus, the steeper the slope of the power function. In addition, the size of the exponent is larger when the standard is present on every trial than when it is not (MacMillan, Moschetto, Bialostozky, and Engel, 1974), and, while magnitude production and magnitude estimation judgments both yield power functions, magnitude production results in larger exponents than does magnitude estimation (Stevens and Greenbaum, 1966). Magnitude estimates are also subject to at least two kinds of biases in responding. One of these is a tendency for observers to use numerical estimates which end in zero or 5—a bias which increases the coarseness of the grain of the data (Poulton, Simmonds, and Warren, 1968). The second is a tendency for stimulus magnitude to be biased in the direction of the value of the immediately preceding stimulus—a bias which results in underestimation of the exponent of the power function (Cross, 1973).

Still another line of disturbing evidence with respect to the magnitude methods comes from data on session-to-session correlations between the size of exponents for the same stimulus dimension. Such correlations are relatively high for short time spans but they tend to approach zero as the interval between two sessions increases (Teghtsoonian and Teghtsoonian, 1971). This suggests that the exponent may not reflect a persistent attribute of the observer's perceptual functioning. Data on between-session correlations in magnitude estimates of the area of circles, when the interval between two sessions spans an 11-week period, are presented in Figure 4.15.

Results such as these pose serious problems for the interpretation of data obtained by the magnitude procedures. These procedures are also subject to response bias and contextual effects, and therefore it is difficult to accept Stevens' version of the psychophysical law on the basis of the ultimate "purity" of the methodology that was used in its development. Even if the exponent of a power function does reflect the fundamental transduction properties of sensory receptors, as Stevens prefers to believe, it appears that the magnitude techniques do not provide an unbiased estimate of these properties. Indeed, Teghtsoonian (1971) has argued that there may be a *common* scale of sensory magnitudes for a wide variety of perceptual continua and that variations in power law exponents are a function of different dynamic ranges (the ratio of the greatest to the smallest stimulus intensity to which the observer is responsive) being mapped to this unitary subjective scale. Perhaps the best that can be said in the light of current knowledge is that the magnitude techniques represent a mixture of "how it seems" and "how I judge it," and the transduction properties revealed by these techniques are only part of the story (Poulton, 1968).

Neurophysiological ambiguity It has been argued that the ultimate validity of the logarithmic and power versions of the psychophysical law can be determined by appealing to neurophysiological evidence. According to this approach, if impulse rates in neural firing were found to be a logarithmic function of stimulus intensity, Fechner would be supported, while Stevens would be supported if the frequency of neural firing were found to be a power function of stimulus intensity. Although an appeal to neurophysiological data has some merit, it does not provide a satisfactory answer to the Fechner-Stevens controversy for two reasons. First, evidence for both logarithmic and power transformations has been found in nervous activity (Franzen, 1969; Hartline and Graham, 1932; Matthews, 1931; Stevens, 1970, 1971, 1974). Second, even if neurophysiological data did yield un-

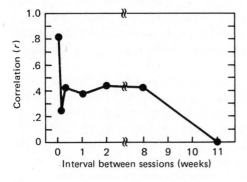

FIGURE 4.15 Product moment correlations (r) between individual power functions in magnitude estimates of the area of circles when the interval between two sessions varied over an 11-week span. Only the correlation for no delay differed significantly from zero. (From Teghtsoonian and Teghtsoonian, 1971)

equivocal support for one type of transformation at the receptor level, for example, a log function, the issue would still not be resolved, for it is possible that at still-higher levels in the nervous system information could be further transformed in terms of a power function (MacKay, 1963). Rosner and Goff (1967) have characterized the ambiguous relation between neurophysiological evidence and subjective scales of intensity by admonishing sensory physiologists "to beware of psychophysicists bearing gifts."

The Status of the Psychophysical Law

· It is disappointing to note that after more than a century of research, and the investment of large amounts of talent, ingenuity, and time, the "true" nature of the psychophysical law is still not resolved completely. Has all this effort been for naught? We think not. The study of perception has profited in terms of the technology generated for measuring subjective magnitude as well as in terms of the establishment of important regularities in performance. We have also learned a crucial lesson — even such an ostensibly simple problem as the perception of stimulus magnitude involves highly complex information processing. Stimuli are often judged as a conglomeration of elements rather than in terms of unitary properties (Hawkes, 1960; Ross and DiLollo, 1971), and the judgment of stimuli depends to a large extent upon the context in which they are presented and the way in which the human observer responds to them (Anderson, 1975).

In a summary statement regarding the status of the psychophysical law, Stevens (1971) has indicated that a matter of taste and opinion currently divides psychologists interested in this problem. Some, such as Stevens himself, prefer to hold that perceived magnitude follows simple laws and that under the proper conditions, the magnitude of sensations experienced by the typical observer grows as a power function of stimulus magnitude. For others, however, this view of a simple input-output function holds no compelling jurisdiction because of the complexities of the judgmental process. Until the many factors which contribute to such complexity can be isolated and fully explored, it is premature to speak of *the* psychophysical law. Our own sympathies lie with the second point of view.

At present, a number of attempts are being made to strike out in different directions. Some investigators are emphasizing the *relation between* stimuli rather than sensation magnitude as the basis of judgment (Krantz, 1972; Rule, Laye, and Curtis, 1974); others are developing networks of functional relations with respect to the integration of information in a compound stimulus (Anderson, 1970, 1975). Still other investigators are seeking ways to reconcile and synthesize the results of different experimental techniques (Baird, 1970a, 1970b; Baird, Kreindler, and Jones, 1971; Banks and Hill, 1974; Curtis, 1970; Green, 1962; Luce and Green, 1972; Montgomery and Eisler, 1974; Ward, 1972). Undoubtedly, these approaches are the wave of the future. They hold the promise of generating a broader approach to psychophysical measurement and, perhaps, of generating more general psychological laws, of which the psychophysical law may only be a special case.

INFORMATION THEORY

The Nature of Information

In our discussion of psychophysical problems up to this point, stimuli have been characterized in terms of physical units. We have spoken of the detectability and apparent magnitude of stimuli which vary in such units as centimeters, decibels, grams, nanometers, and photons. For some purposes, however, an understanding of perceptual processing requires that stimuli be characterized in still another way—along a dimension of *uncertainty* or *information value.*

Frequently, in our commerce with the perceptual world, our reactions to stimuli are determined not only by their physical properties, but also by the probabilities or likelihoods associated with their occurrence. That is, our responses depend not only on what occurs but also on the ensemble of events that might have taken place. Consider the case of recongizing the face of a friend whom you have not seen in a long while. You probably have shared the common experience that such a person is readily recognized if encountered in a familiar setting, where his or her presence is highly likely, but not as readily recognized if encountered unexpectedly in an unlikely situation. In the latter case, you might do a "double take" before approaching your friend, or else continue on your way convinced that the person you saw was a stranger.

In an earlier chapter, we pointed out that our perceptions of stimuli are often determined by the context in which they occur. The dimension of uncertainty is a critical aspect of the contextual framework which influences perceptual activities; one of the interesting developments in modern psychophysics has been the use of information theory to capture the uncertainty value of stimuli.

A communication model   Throughout the history of psychology, techniques have often been borrowed from other fields for use in solving psychological problems. We have encountered this in relation to signal detection theory, and it is also true with respect to information theory—an approach which was originally developed in the fields of communication and control engineering (Alluisi, 1970). The application of information theory to problems in engineering grew out of a series of seminal papers by Shannon and Weaver (1949) and Wiener (1948); it was introduced into psychology by Miller and Frick (1949).

One of the basic concepts of information theory is that of the flow of information through a general communications system. This conceptualization is diagrammed in Figure 4.16.

According to the information model, a specific message is selected from a source and coded into some form of signal by a device which prepares the message for transmission over a communication channel. Once transmitted, the signal is picked up by a receiver which decodes it into a form appropriate for delivery to its ultimate destination. In the process of transmission, undesirable changes may be introduced into the message. Such changes represent distortions of the signal which occur in the channel through the introduction of sources of error termed "noise." To make the model somewhat more concrete, we can view it with regard to the transmission of a television picture. For example, the source of information might be a scene in a World Series baseball game. This scene is coded by a TV camera into an electrical signal, transmitted as electromagnetic waves over an atmospheric channel, decoded by your home TV set into a picture for viewing by you, the destination. As you no doubt have experienced, the picture is sometimes subject to distortions by noise, resulting in an annoying loss of information.

The information model can also provide a conceptual tool for analyzing the flow of information within an individual perceiver. Such an analysis is diagrammed in Figure 4.17.

In this case, the selected message refers to a stimulus, the sensory receptors of the organism are the encoding devices, and the central nervous system is the communication channel. The message is decoded by cortical centers in the brain and the organism's response is the destination. The message is also subject to the degrading effects of "noise," stemming from events both within and outside the observer.

Whether our interest is in the flow of information with respect to an inanimate communication network or with respect to a human observer, we can ask some pertinent questions about the system involved: (1) What effect does varying the amount of information have on the performance of the sys-

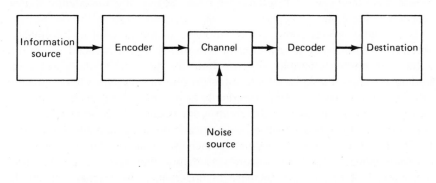

FIGURE 4.16 Schematic diagram of the flow of information through a general communications system. (After Shannon and Weaver, 1949)

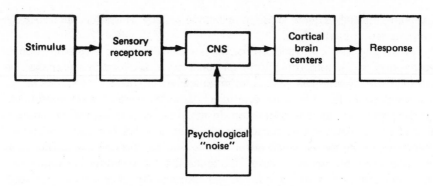

FIGURE 4.17   Schematic diagram of the flow of information within the perceiver.

tem? (2) What is the maximum amount of information *(channel capacity)* that the system can transmit? (3) What is the system's rate of transmission? (4) How does noise affect the efficiency of the system? Before we can answer such questions, we need a good definition of "information" and a means for measuring it.

The measurement of information   The technical meaning of the term "information" is not radically different from its meaning in everyday language. It is merely more precise and less general (Attneave, 1959; Fitts and Posner, 1967). Information is something we gain when an event tells us something that we did not already know. Suppose, for example, that you are looking for a book in your college library. You know that it is there, but you are uncertain where it is kept. If someone tells you that the book is in the library, the statement is not informative, since it does not add to your knowledge of the location of the book. If, on the other hand, you are told that the book is shelved in the Psychology Reading Room, the statement is informative, in that it adds to your knowledge of the location of the book. Thus, information is gained when it reduces to some degree the uncertainty that is present in a situation.

Uncertainty reflects some lack of knowledge; the amount of information gained is determined by the amount of uncertainty that is reduced. To return to the book-finding example, suppose that you proceed to the Psychology Reading Room. If the book of interest is on one of only two shelves present in the room, you will have little uncertainty as to which shelf it is on; if it is on one of four shelves present in the room, your uncertainty is greater; and if it is on one of eight possible shelves, your uncertainty is still greater. In general, the amount of uncertainty in a situation increases with the number of specifiable alternatives. If we can measure uncertainty, then we can also measure information in terms of the decrease in uncertainty. As Garner has put it, "these opposing concepts—uncertainty as a state of ignorance and information as the opposed reduction of uncertainty—are quantitatively the same thing" (1962, p. 30). An important point to notice in this definition of uncertainty and information is that no consideration is given to the context, purpose, or value of the information. Information theory is concerned only with the *amount* of information in the situation (Miller, 1953).

Technically, the measurement of uncertainty or information is based upon a binary counting system with respect to the number of alternatives in a situation. The unit of measurement is called the *bit* (a contraction for binary digit), and it represents the power to which the number 2 must be raised in order to arrive at the number of possible alternatives. Again, in our book-finding example, if there are only two shelves in the reading room, there are only two alternatives in locating the correct shelf. Consequently, there is only one bit of information (2^1) associated with the identification of the correct shelf in this case. If there were four shelves to choose from, there would be two bits of information (2^2), and if eight shelves, three bits of information (2^3), and so on. In general, the equation for measuring the amount of information is $A = 2^H$, where A is the number of equally likely alternatives from which a choice is made and H is the amount of uncertainty or information, expressed in bits. This is equivalent to saying that the number of bits equals the logarithm to the base 2 of the number of alternatives or, $H = \log_2 A$ (Attneave, 1959). It should be noted that this expression holds only when all alternatives are equally likely. A slightly more complex formula is needed when all alternatives are not equally likely (see Alluisi, 1970, and Attneave, 1959, for this more complex equation as well as for tables of $\log_2$ functions).

Armed with the conceptual model of information flow and the uncertainty metric, psychologists have been able to develop important functional relations with regard to the recognition, discrimination, and speed of processing of stimuli. In some cases, it has also been possible to pinpoint the phase in the information-processing sequence which is primarily responsible for the effects of stimulus uncertainty on perceptual performance.

Uncertainty and Recognition

The role of uncertainty   One of the most firmly established findings to come out of an information-theory analysis of perceptual performance is that the accuracy of recognition for a particular stimulus is inversely related to the number of alternative stimuli from which it can be drawn (Garner, 1962). A study by Miller, Heise, and Lichten (1951) on the recognition of words embedded in noise provides a nice demonstration of this effect. These investigators used test vocabularies of 2, 4, 8, 16, 32, or 256 familiar words, which correspond to uncertainty values of 1, 2, 3, 4, 5, and 8 bits, respectively. The words from each test vocabularly were read to listeners one at a time and the listeners indicated the word that they thought they heard by checking it off on an appropriate printed list. Test words were presented in a background of *white noise* produced by a sound source which emits all of the frequencies of the audible spectrum at equal energy values; such a background noise resembles hissing steam. Its intensity was varied from values in which the loudness of the noise exceeded that of the words — negative or low signal-to-noise (S/N) ratios — to those in which the loudness of the words exceeded that of the noise — positive or high S/N ratios. Figure 4.18 presents the percentages of correct recognitions for the various test vocabularies at several S/N ratios.

The figure shows that accuracy of recognition was influenced by both stimulus uncertainty and the noise background. The percentage of correct recognitions decreased as the size of the test vocabulary increased, and, in addition, the percentage of words correctly recognized increased as the S/N ratio increased. Furthermore, the effects of stimulus uncertainty and noise were interdependent. Look carefully at Figure 4.18, and you will see that the degrading effects of noise were considerably smaller when the test word was selected from only two alternatives (top curve) than when it was selected from 256 alternatives (bottom curve).

The findings of Miller, Heise, and Lichten were confirmed in a similar experiment by I. Miller (1957) in which listeners were required to recognize nonsense dissyllables (for example, MEEVOOM) presented in a noise background. The results of this study are shown in Figure 4.19.

From these two investigations we can see that the uncertainty context in which stimuli are presented has a strong influence upon recognition accuracy. Stimuli with high probability are recognized more accurately than those with low probability; furthermore, high stimulus probability can offset the disruptive effects of distortion on stimulus recognition. This latter point deserves more comment, since the relation between the uncertainty context and distortion is not as simple as our previous statements may make it appear. Whether or not high probability will have a beneficial influence in dealing

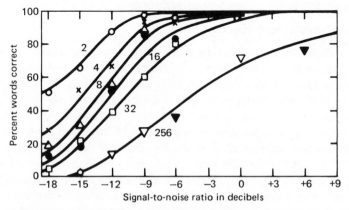

FIGURE 4.18   Recognition of English monosyllables heard in noise with test vocabularies of different sizes. (From Miller, Heise, and Lichten, 1951)

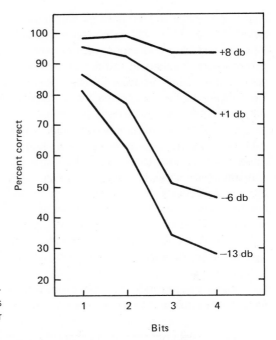

FIGURE 4.19 Recognition of non-sense dissyllables heard in noise as a function of uncertainty in bits per item. (From I. Miller, 1957)

with distortion of the stimulus often depends upon the perceptual goals of the perceiver. To take a practical example suggested by Fitts and Posner (1967), consider the case of reading a manuscript. If your interest lies in understanding the content of the manuscript, the contextual nature of the material may lead you to anticipate a particular word and thus to read it without difficulty even if it is misspelled (distorted). On the other hand, if your purpose is to proofread the manuscript, the same context con lead you to "see" the word as spelled correctly even if it is not (in case you have not already noticed, the word "can" in the preceding sentence has been misspelled).

Stimulus or response uncertainty   In the experiments just considered, the listeners were aware of the set of alternative possible stimuli prior to the presentation of the test words, and they knew that the size of the set of stimulus alternatives was always equal to the size of the set of response alternatives. Therefore, these experiments do not permit us to specify the locus of the uncertainty effect within the information-processing sequence. Does stimulus uncertainty affect encoding processes, or does uncertainty influence performance by affecting some later phase of the information-processing sequence such as the matching of appropriate responses to the already encoded stimulus input? One way of answering this question would be to perform an experiment in which stimulus uncertainty was manipulated independently of response uncertainty.

Just such an experiment has been reported by Pollack (1959). In this study, listeners were required to recognize familiar words from test vocabularies of 2, 4, 8, 16, 32, or 64 items presented in a noise background. Two types of response conditions were employed. In one, the number of alternative responses was equal to the number of stimulus alternatives, and thus response uncertainty equaled stimulus uncertainty. In the other, the listeners were aware of the size of the test vocabulary on each trial, but there were only two alternative responses to choose from regardless of the size of the test vocabulary. Thus, in this condition, response selection always required a 1-bit decision; hence, response uncertainty was not always equal to stimulus uncertainty. Pollack found that when stimulus uncertainty and response uncertainty were equal, recognition accuracy was inversely related to the size of the test vocabulary. By contrast, when response uncertainty always involved a 1-bit decision, the size of the test vocabulary had no effect on accuracy of recognition. Therefore, accuracy of recognition proved to be independent of the size of the set of *stimulus* alternatives but critically dependent upon the size of the set of *response* alternatives. These results are illustrated in Figure 4.20.

Pollack's study indicates that at least in some cases the locus of the effects of uncertainty on performance in a recognition task lies within the re-

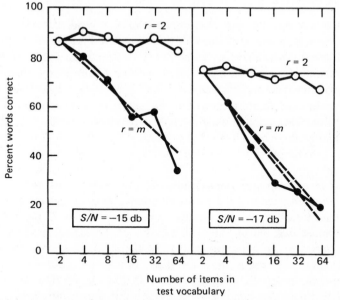

FIGURE 4.20 Recognition of familiar words heard in noise as a function of the size of the test vocabulary. Filled points represent results when the number of response alternatives equaled the number of stimulus alternatives. The open points represent results when only two response alternatives were provided. Data for two signal-to-noise ratios are plotted separately in each panel. (From Pollack, 1959)

sponse-selection phase and not within the stimulus-encoding phase of the information-processing sequence. In accounting for these results, Pollack offered the interesting suggestion that because its capacity to handle information is limited, the perceptual system may first place input information into some form of temporary storage for later selective processing; he then argued that uncertainty primarily influences the activities that go on after information is withdrawn from this temporary store.

Uncertainty and Discrimination

Absolute judgments In describing psychophysical tasks which require observers to discriminate among stimuli, it is often convenient to differentiate between *relative* and *absolute* judgments. A relative judgment is one in which the observers have the opportunity to compare two or more stimuli directly. They might be required to say that stimulus A is louder than stimulus B or that stimulus A is brighter than stimulus B, and so on. Relative judgments were involved in our previous discussions of difference thresholds and the measurement of perceptual magnitudes. In absolute-judgment tasks, there is no opportunity to make direct comparisons between stimuli. Instead, observers must identify a stimulus as belonging to a particular category without being able to compare it directly to any other stimulus. For example, they may state that a swatch of cloth is "red" when the cloth is presented by itself, or that a particular note on a piano is "middle C" when played by itself, or that a particular automobile is a "Chevrolet Impala" when seen alone on the highway. Such judgments are probably made by comparing the stimulus with some remembered standard, but the standard is not physically available for direct comparison. In the older literature in perception, the number of items that can be accurately discriminated on an absolute basis is referred to as the *span of apprehension.*

Channel capacity Information theory has been particularly useful in dealing with experiments on absolute judgment. In these experiments, the observer is considered as the now familiar communication channel and the question asked is, "What is the amount of information that the observer can transmit in an absolute-judgment task?" Or, more specifically, "What is the channel capacity of the perceiver with respect to the number of items that can be absolutely discriminated?" The situation can be described graphically as in Figure 4.21.

The left circle can be taken to represent the amount of input information, the right circle the amount of output information, and the overlap between the two the amount of transmitted information. The experimental problem, of course, is to vary the amount of input information and to measure the amount of information transmitted. If the observer's discriminatory ability is unlimited, output information will increase as a constant function of input. On

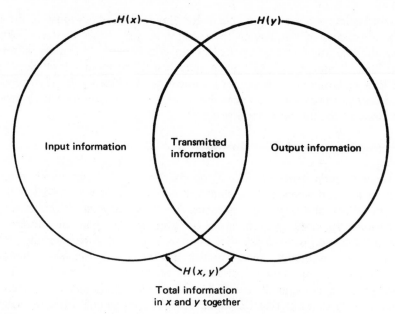

Total information
in *x* and *y* together

FIGURE 4.21   Schematic representation of several quantities of information that are involved in absolute judgments. (After Miller, 1953)

the other hand, if discriminatory ability is limited, as we increase the amount of input transmitted, information will at first increase but then level off at some asymptotic value. This asymptotic value provides a direct measure of channel capacity—the greatest amount of information that the observer can give us on the basis of an absolute judgment in a particular experimental situation (Miller, 1956). These ideas are illustrated in Figure 4.22.

Experiments on absolute judgments have focused upon our ability to discriminate between stimuli which lie along a single sensory dimension, such as brightness, loudness, pitch, duration, etc. In experiments of this sort, the investigator first familiarizes the observer with the stimuli that are to be used. For example, a set of five tones may be used that vary in 2-dB steps from 50 to 56 dB. Responses are typically assigned to the stimuli in the form of numbers arranged in ascending order, so that the softest tone would be called 1 and the loudest tone 6. Care must be taken to ensure that the stimuli employed would be easily differentiated in a test of comparative judgment and that they differ perceptually on only one attribute. After the observer has become thoroughly familiar with the stimuli and their assigned responses, the stimuli are presented several times in random order and the observer must identify each stimulus by responding with the appropriate number. Input information is varied by using different-sized sets of stimuli. For example, differ-

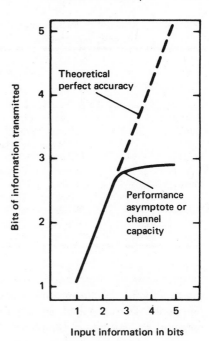

FIGURE 4.22 Schematic illustration of the amount of information transmitted in an absolute-judgment task.

ent observers may make judgments on sets varying from two to nine stimuli, or the same observers may be asked to make absolute judgments of each of these sets at different times.

Garner and Hake (1951) have devised a means of measuring the amount of information that an observer can transmit in such a situation. Essentially, this measure reflects the total number of items that the observer can discriminate without error. Thus, if the observer's responses indicate that two items were discriminated without error, one bit of information would be transmitted. If four items were discriminated without error, two bits of information would be transmitted, etc. To the extent that errors are introduced into the judgments, the amount of information transmitted is reduced. The mechanics of the calculations involved in this method are too complex to present here; students who wish to pursue this matter further should consult the paper by Garner and Hake or Alluisi (1970).

Using this kind of technique, researchers have determined the channel capacities for absolute judgments in several sensory modalities. The results of these investigations are strikingly similar, and they reveal a surprisingly small channel capacity for discriminating unidimensional stimuli. The results of representative experiments are summarized in Table 4.2.

In examining this table you will see that, in general, the maximum number of unidimensional stimuli that can be correctly discriminated in absolute

TABLE 4.2 Amount of Information in Absolute Judgments of Several
Stimulus Dimensions

Stimulus Dimension	Investigator	Channel Capacity in Bits	Approximate Number of Stimuli Discriminated
Brightness	Ericksen (1952)	1.7	3
Duration	Murphy (1966)	2.8	7
Hue	Chapanis and Halsey (1956)	3.6	12
Loudness	Garner (1953)	2.3	5
Odor intensity	Engen and Pfaffman (1959)	1.5	3
Pitch	Pollack (1953)	2.5	6
Position on a line	Hake and Garner (1951)	3.2	9
Saltiness	Beebe-Center, et.al. (1955)	1.9	4
Shock intensity	Hawkes and Warm (1960b)	1.7	3
Vibration intensity	Geldard (1961)	1.6	3

judgments varies from approximately 3 to 12. For any specific task studied, the exact value of the maximum channel capacity depends upon several experimental factors. Chief among these are the physical range of stimulus variation, the spacing of stimuli within this range, the number of stimulus and response categories, and the opportunity for the observer to obtain knowledge of results concerning judgment accuracy (Alluisi, 1957). Despite some differences, the general nature of these results has been so consistent that Miller (1956) described them as reflecting "the magical number seven plus or minus two." By this Miller meant that because of prior experience or the design of our nervous system, or both, our ability to distinguish accurately between unidimensional stimuli on an absolute-judgment basis is fixed at 7 ± 2, or around 5 to 9 items.

However, MacRae (1970) has pointed out that many of the early studies which led to Miller's "magic number seven" may be subject to a number of biases which somewhat distort the true functional relation between input and output information. He suggests that when these biases are corrected, the appropriate transmission curve does not reach a fixed asymptotic value, as was shown schematically in Figure 4.22. Instead, MacRae argues, the transmission curve has an initial increase followed by a decline: apparently people have limited but not fixed channel capacity when faced with this type of task. MacRae's proposal certainly merits further study. In any event, on the basis of the data currently available, it seems safe to say that human observers have a remarkably small capacity for making absolute judgments about stimuli which vary along a single dimension. In terms of information-processing characteristics, this small capacity contrasts sharply with what we have seen as the exquisite sensitivity of the perceptual system in detection tasks. It also stands in sharp relief with the finding that observers are able to distinguish between hundreds of hues and tones on the basis of comparative judgments (Chapanis, 1965; Fitts and Posner, 1967).

The factors which contribute to our limited capacity for absolute judgments are quite complex. Obviously, conditions which make the stimuli less different perceptually lead to problems of encoding or "getting the stimulus into the organism," which restrict the accuracy of absolute judgments (Clapp, 1972; Lockhead, 1966; Morgan and Alluisi, 1967; Spitz, 1973). In addition, events taking place farther along in the information-processing sequence have also been implicated. Several experiments have indicated that part of the problem rests with inexactness of memory in comparing a stimulus with previously stored data concerning its nature and the range of stimuli from which it comes (Clapp, 1973; Siegel and Siegel, 1972; Siegel, 1972; Ward and Lockhead, 1970). Moreover, evidence is accumulating to show that errors in judgment are also attributable to the activity of response-system processes involving the guessing strategies that observers employ when uncertain about the correct response (Ward and Lockhead, 1971).

Multidimensionality and recoding   The built-in limitation to information processing inherent in the concept of "the magic number seven" leads to an important practical question. If we are so limited, how is it possible for us to accomplish the many tasks of daily life which require us to distinguish on an absolute basis among a myriad of faces, voices, symbols, tunes, tastes, and spoken and written words? Clearly, there is a gap between the absolute judgments that people are called upon to make in "the real world" and in the "artificial world" of the laboratory.

One answer to this puzzle may lie in the fact that real-world stimuli are usually multidimensional; that is, they vary simultaneously along several dimensions. The letters of the alphabet, for example, differ in height and width, in the presence or absence of rounded features, and in the number and kinds of angles that they contain, as well as with respect to the sounds associated with them. Laboratory studies on absolute judgments with multidimensional stimuli have shown that performance with such stimuli is considerably better than with unidimensional items (Engen and Pfaffman, 1960; Ericksen and Hake, 1955; Klemmer and Frick, 1953; Hawkes, 1962; Lockhead, 1966). A particularly instructive experiment along these lines was performed by Pollack and Ficks (1954), who devised six different acoustic variables that could be independently manipulated: frequency, intensity, duration, on-time fraction, rate of interruption, and the spatial location of the signal. Under these multidimensional conditions, approximately 150 stimulus categories could be absolutely differentiated without error. In summarizing these findings, Miller (1956) has suggested that the general form of the relation between channel capacity in absolute judgments and the number of variable attributes of a stimulus may be something like that shown in Figure 4.23. This figure suggests that, in

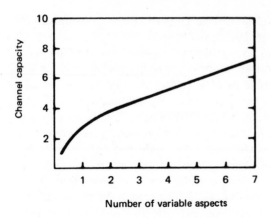

FIGURE 4.23 The general form of the relation between channel capacity (in bits) and the number of independently variable stimulus attributes. (After Miller, 1956)

general, when as many as seven dimensions are available on which to base a discrimination, channel capacity is a little more than 7 bits (a capacity of exactly 7 bits would allow for discriminating among 128 items without error).

In addition to basing their judgments on several stimulus dimensions, Miller (1956) has suggested that observers also stretch the informational limit in absolute judgments by reorganizing the stimuli in memory through a process known as *recoding*. In this process, individual items are grouped into larger psychological units called *chunks,* each of which contains several bits of information. While the memory system may be limited in its ability to process only 7 ± 2 chunks, each chunk contains a larger amount of information than the individual items alone.

In order to understand this approach, consider a task known as *memory span* in which a string of unrelated items, usually digits, is read to a subject, who must then repeat them back in the same order. The span for normal adults in this task is also approximately seven (Woodworth and Schlosberg, 1954), but it can be expanded considerably by reorganization. For example, the number sequence 19411861191717761812 containing 20 digits can be recalled easily if the digits are grouped into five units or chunks, such as 1941, 1861, 1917, 1776, 1812, or, if they are recoded into familiar dates in American history, i.e., "Pearl Harbor," "Civil War," "World War I," "Declaration of Independence," "War of 1812." In this way, large amounts of information can be combined into a few chunks to lessen the load on the memory system and thereby increase channel capacity in absolute judgments.

Support for this point of view comes from a large number of studies which reveal that organizational processes are useful in enhancing performance in a variety of perceptual and memory tasks (Vitz and Todd, 1969; Hilgard and Bower, 1975). A compelling demonstration of this effect has been described by Simon and Barenfeld (1969). They report that after only five seconds' sight of a chessboard, grandmasters can reproduce the positions of chess pieces without error if the positions are taken from actual game conditions. Weak players, on the other hand, make many errors. Apparently, the performance of the grandmasters stems from their ability to organize the pieces into meaningful constellations or chunks, as confirmed by the fact that when the chess pieces are randomly arrayed, the performance of the grand-masters falls to the level of the weak players.

Uncertainty and Speed of Responding

Reaction time   Picture an automobile driver speeding down an open road when, suddenly, an obstacle appears, blocking the entire road. The driver must apply the brakes in order to avoid collision, and a quick response is of the utmost importance. From your own experiences, you are aware that the driver will not react immediately; there will be some delay before the braking response that will bring the vehicle to a halt. The time between the occur-rence of a stimulus and the initiation of a response is known as *reaction time* (RT), and because of its obvious implications for adjustment to the environ-ment, the study of RT represents one of the oldest problems in psychology. It is also a problem which is easily adaptable to psychophysical investigation. ·

Since the pioneering experiments by Donders (1868), laboratory studies of RT can be classified into three basic paradigms: (1) type a, or simple RT, in which the subject must make a specific response to a single stimulus; (2) type b, choice or disjunctive RT, in which different responses are to be made to each of several possible signals; and (3) type c, in which several possible stimuli are presented, only one of which requires a response. For each para-digm we might ask, "Why is there a delay in responding and what happens during the RT interval?" Over the years, a vast amount of data has been gathered in answer to questions such as these, and there are many factors to be considered (see Teichner, 1954; Teichner and Krebs, 1972; Woodworth and Schlosberg, 1954). In this subsection, we will be concerned with only one such factor, stimulus uncertainty, and how information theory has con-tributed an understanding of the effects of uncertainty on reaction time, espe-cially in the case of choice RT tasks.

A finite amount of time is involved in all tasks which require us to take in information from the environment, process it, and execute an appropriate re-sponse. Broadly speaking, this overall RT can be considered to involve three component parts: first, the time required for a sense organ to be activated and for the resulting neural impulses to travel to the brain; second, the time necessary for central processes to identify the nature of the stimulus and initi-ate a response; and third, the time it takes to energize the muscular system in executing the response. Welford (1968) has pointed out that the central pro-cessing time involves, in part, the resolution of uncertainty from two sources. The subject often does not know exactly when the signal is coming and therefore when to respond and also does not know exactly what signal is coming and therefore what response to make.

Hick's law   One of the first experimental demonstrations of the effects of stimulus uncertainty on choice RT was provided by Merkel (1885). The stimuli were arabic and roman numerals varying in number from 1 to 10. The subject's fingers rested on ten keys; the subject reacted by releasing an appropriate key, depending on which numeral had been displayed. Merkel found that RT increased in proportion to the logarithm to the base 10 of the number of stimulus alternatives. This result reflected an interesting regularity in the nature of RT, but the general applicability of this regularity did not become fully apparent until the advent of information theory many years later.

Hick (1952) realized that the uncertainty produced by variations in the number of stimulus alternatives could be viewed in information-theory terms by expressing the number of alternatives in bits. Consequently, he repeated Merkel's experiment using one to ten lamps arrayed in an irregular circle. The subjects responded to the illumination of any one of the lamps by pressing the correct one of ten Morse Code keys. Hick found that RT increased as a linear function of the $\log_2$ of the number of stimulus alternatives and thus, in the language of information theory, RT was proportional to stimulus uncertainty. By and of itself, this was not a new discovery on Hick's part; it was merely a confirmation of Merkel's earlier finding, using a different scale for expressing the number of stimulus alternatives. However, by introducing the information metric into this problem, Hick made it possible to map a variety of ways of manipulating stimulus uncertainty onto a common scale. If it could be established that RT was proportional to stimulus uncertainty in several very different situations, then Hick's work would have laid the foundation for an important quantitative generalization about the speed of perceptual performance.

While there is some disagreement (for example, Kornblum, 1968), the general trend of the available data seems to indicate that choice RT is indeed proportional to stimulus information. Furthermore, within wide limits, it does not seem to matter if uncertainty is manipulated through variations in the number of stimulus alternatives or through variations in the probabilities of the stimuli or their sequential dependencies (Alluisi, 1970; Fitts, 1964; Garner, 1962; Smith, 1968; Teichner and Krebs, 1974; Welford, 1968). This relation is now referred to as *Hick's Law*. It states that the rate of processing of a signal is a linear increasing function of stimulus information, or that "the rate of gain of information is a constant." The general form of Hick's Law is illustrated in Figure 4.24.

Encoding and response selection   As in the case of recognition and discrimination, we might also inquire as to the phase of the information-processing sequence that might be responsible for the relation between uncertainty and the speed of choice reactions. Apparently, the answer lies in the central processing time required for both identifying the stimulus and for translating the stimulus information into appropriate responses. The evidence for the

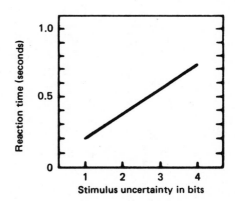

FIGURE 4.24 The general form of Hick's Law. Reaction time increases as a linear function of stimulus uncertainty. Absolute values of RT in this figure are arbitrary.

former is somewhat indirect and stems from results with type-c RT tasks. Welford (1968) has noted that the data on type-c reactions seem to indicate that even when no choice of response is required, RT increases with increases in the size of the set from which signals are drawn. This leads to the conclusion that in choice RT at least some of the time involved is taken up with identifying the stimulus.

The evidence with respect to coding stimuli into responses is more direct and stems from studies in which stimulus-response compatibility was varied. Compatibility refers to the directness or naturalness of association between stimulus-response pairings; it is most easily described through example. Consider an experiment by Alluisi, Strain, and Thurmond (1964), who asked subjects to make vocal responses at three levels of stimulus uncertainty to visually presented arabic numbers. The stimuli were paired with responses in such a way as to create ensembles of high, intermediate, and low stimulus-response compatibility. In the high-compatibility condition, the subjects responded to the appearance of a numeral by giving its usual name, i.e., "one" to the numeral 1, "two" to the numeral 2, and so forth. In the intermediate condition, the subjects responded by adding the constant 2 to each number name. Thus, they would respond "three" to the numeral 1, "four" to the numeral 2, etc. In the low-compatibility conditions, the names were paired with arabic numerals at random, i.e., a subject may have been instructed to respond to the numeral 1 by saying "five," to the numeral 2 by saying "eight," and so forth. The results of this study are shown in Figure 4.25.

The figure shows that the slope of the function relating RT to stimulus uncertainty was dependent upon the degree of compatibility in the stimulus-response pairings. The rate of rise in RT (steepness in slope) with increments in stimulus uncertainty declined as stimulus-response compatibility increased. In fact, at the high level of compatibility, there appears to be an almost negligible increase in RT with increments in uncertainty. Similar results have been reported in other experiments (Brainard, Irby, Fitts, and Alluisi, 1962; Leonard, 1959; Mowbray, 1960). Furthermore, it has also been found that when

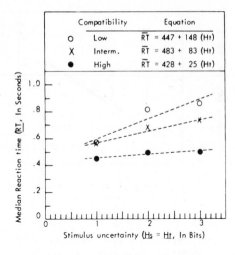

FIGURE 4.25   Reaction time as a function of stimulus uncertainty in bits at three levels of stimulus-response compatability. (From Alluisi, Strain, and Thurmond, 1964)

subjects are given sufficient practice with the stimulus-response ensembles, the rise in RT with uncertainty can be entirely eliminated or at least considerably reduced (Fitts and Seeger, 1953; Mowbray and Rhoades, 1959).

Thus, part of the relation between stimulus uncertainty and the speed of choice reactions must also involve the time required to match stimuli to responses. It is evident at this point that a complex sequence of information-processing activities is inherent in the factors which underlie Hick's Law. The development and testing of theoretical models which attempt to trace the course of these activities (for example, Broadbent, 1971; Smith, 1968; Teichner and Krebs, 1974; Welford, 1968) represents an exciting area of future investigation.

Information Theory in Perspective

Information theory represents a relatively recent innovation in the long history of psychophysics. At this point, it is appropriate to consider in a general way the extent to which this approach has enhanced our knowledge of perception.

On the basis of the material that we have presented, it is evident that information theory has provided a means by which we can capture more than just the physical properties of stimuli within our psychophysical nets. It enables us to quantify a more abstract property—uncertainty—and to relate this stimulus property to perceptual performance in a meaningful way. It is important to note, however, that information theory is not a substantive perceptual theory. Rather, it is a descriptive device, based on a very general type of mathematics, that permits us to integrate what may seem on the surface to be unrelated areas of investigation. For some psychologists (Alluisi, 1970; Garner, 1962), this may indeed be the primary contribution of information theory to research in perception.

While information theory basically provides a mode of description, it has also led to insights into the nature of the processes which mediate between stimuli and responses in perceptual experiments. These insights for the most part have been motivated by attempts to pinpoint the phase in the information-processing sequence which is primarily responsible for the effects of uncertainty on performance. Consequently, although essentially descriptive in nature, information theory may have borne considerable substantive fruit, having served as one of the major origins of the currently dominant information-processing approach to perceptual theory (Leeper, 1972).

5
Attention

The four preceding chapters have examined perception from a methodological point of view, with special emphasis on the problem of measurement. Having established this basic foundation to perceptual research, we can now proceed to examine issues of a more dynamic sort. In this chapter, we will consider the problem of attention or how people choose what to perceive. Specifically, we will examine two aspects of this broad concept: one is concerned with how people select information for processing over brief periods of time when they are being exposed to more information than they can handle; the other deals with people's efforts to sustain attention to infrequently occurring but important targets over extended time periods.

CONCEPTIONS OF ATTENTION

Attention and Perception

After reading this sentence, stop for a moment and consider the overall environment in which you are situated. In so doing, you may take notice of the hum of street noise outside your window or of the buzz of conversation in an adjoining room. You may also observe a shadow cast on your desk by your arm, or realize that your feet are cold. More generally, you may become aware of a rich variety of stimulation impinging upon you. If, as we hope, you were engrossed in reading this text, it is unlikely that you were cognizant of very much of this stimulation until we asked you to attend to it.

At practically every instant of our lives, the amount of stimulation available to us is incredibly large. We are showered with a plethora of sights, sounds, smells, and pressure and temperature sensations from stimuli in our external environment. At the same time, interoreceptors are monitoring the positions of our bodies and parts of our bodies, and feeding us information about various tissue needs and a host of other organismic functions. Any system, physical or biological, could easily become overloaded by this vast amount of information. Because of limits to the amount of information that it can effectively process, the perceptual system must be highly selective. This selective property of perception has long been designated by the term *attention* (Woodworth and Schlosberg, 1954).

The essence of the concept of attention is the focusing of awareness. Hernández-Peón (1966) has drawn the interesting analogy between attention and a beam of light in which illumination is brighter in the center, the focus of attention, than in the periphery, the fringe of attention. Those stimuli which occupy the focus of attention elicit a better-defined perceptual experience than those on the fringe. This analogy is illustrated schematically in Figure 5.1.

In terms of an information-processing approach to perception, the concept of attention implies an internal mechanism by which the organism controls the choice of stimuli which, in turn, will be allowed to influence its behavior (Kahneman, 1973). Such a mechanism can also be conceived of as one through which the organism trades off a gross loss of information for the opportunity to deal effectively with the small fraction of available information that is important to it at a given time (Boring, 1970; Egeth, 1967; Egeth and Bevan, 1973). Clearly, the choice of what to perceive is a fundamental step

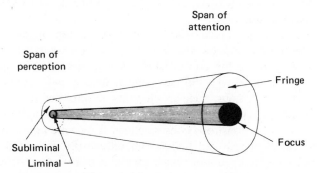

FIGURE 5.1   The span of attention and the span of perception. Stimuli located in the focus of attention are more clearly perceived than those in the fringe of attention. (From Hernández-Peón, 1966)

in perceptual experience, a step upon which all other experiences ultimately depend.

The Zeitgeist for Attention

A historical view   The concept of attention has had an uncertain history in psychology and has been the source of a theoretical dilemma. On the one hand, psychologists have often recognized the importance of the concept, but, on the other hand, they have had a difficult time placing it within major theoretical systems. During the early years of modern experimental psychology, interest in attentive phenomena as a basic aspect of perception was keen. Many laboratories were actively engaged in research on attention, and such people as James (1890), Pillsbury (1908), and Titchener (1908) wrote extensively about it. With the rise of radical behaviorism and Gestalt psychology a theoretical climate or Zeitgeist was established which, in effect, virtually eliminated this topic as a central factor in perceptual research for a considerable period of time. Both movements, for different reasons, regarded the concept of attention as unnecessary for an understanding of behavior. For the behaviorists, the key conceptual notion was the association of stimuli and responses. Attention was considered as a mentalistic concept which had no place in a scientific psychology. The Gestaltists, who had no quarrel with mentalistic concepts, nevertheless found attention to be an unnecessary concept. The Gestaltists relied on the notion of "field forces" within the nervous system to do the job which in other theories had been assigned to attention.

Modern developments   In recent years, the concept of attention has once again assumed a central role in psychological research in general and in perceptual investigations in particular. Several developments have led to a resurgence of interest in attention. One of these is the emergence of a new Zeitgeist, exemplified in the cognitive approach to behavior, which attributes to the organism a far greater degree of autonomy and spontaneity than the classical doctrines of behaviorism and Gestalt psychology were willing to acknowledge (Kahneman, 1973).

Another factor in the revitalization of interest in attention stems not from a change in theoretical outlook, but from the need for solutions to important practical problems. Since the end of World War II, specialists in applied psychology have been faced with the necessity of dealing with problems of human performance in settings, such as air traffic control centers, where operators must contend with very high rates of information flow and where human error can have disastrous consequences. It became important to know the extent to which people can handle stimultaneously presented signals, to determine how quickly they can switch attention from one task to another, and to assess how well they can maintain their attentiveness over time. In short, the study of attention became essential for an understanding of man-machine interactions in a world of advanced technology (Moray, 1969a).

Dimensions of attention   At present, the word "attention" is applicable to a wide range of activities and has a variety of different meanings to investigators whose main interest is in such fields as hearing, visual perception, speeded performance, etc. Moray (1969a) has distinguished among several subdivisions of attentive phenomena in addition to the *selective* aspect we have described. These include: concentration — the attempt to exclude stimuli which might interfere with the performance of a given task; search — a situation in which the observer hunts among a set of signals for some specified subset of signals; activation — readiness to deal with whatever stimuli appear; set — the preparation to respond in a certain way or to receive a particular type of stimulus; and vigilance, or sustained attention — the ability to maintain attention for prolonged periods of time. Moray has suggested that these subdivisions are not necessarily closely related to one another and that more than one theoretical model may be necessary to accommodate all of them. The present chapter will be concerned with just two of Moray's subdivisions, selective attention and vigilance. Other aspects of attention, such as set, will be taken up in later chapters.

SELECTIVE ATTENTION

Determinants of Attention

Granted that attention involves a selection process of some sort, a question which immediately comes to mind is: What factors make us notice one object rather than another when both are present at the same time? One means of answering this question is to examine the manner in which observers apportion the time they spend looking at objects around them. Of course, using such an index of attention might be questioned on grounds that a person could be looking at one object while actually attending to another. Nevertheless, an examination of spontaneous looking activity has frequently been used, with some success, as a vehicle for isolating the determinants of attention.

Physical characteristics   Spontaneous looking seems to be determined by two broad stimulus properties. One of these relates to the physical characteristics of stimuli, a property that was identified in some of the earliest work on attention. These early experiments made use of rather simple techniques in which observers were asked to look at a scene and describe which aspects stood out most clearly or else simply to examine a magazine for a while and then recall or recognize certain items. Later studies have examined looking activity more directly by recording eye fixations. Though the methods have differed, the results have been surprisingly consistent. In general, they have shown that *size, intensity,* and *motion* are important determinants of attention, with the advantage going to large, bright, and/or moving stimuli (Woodworth and Schlosberg, 1954). In a recent experiment, Lewis (1973) has introduced an innovation into this line of research by having observers record or recall items from 15-second motion pictures of natural scenes and animated cartoons. In both kinds of presentations, size and movement again proved to be crucial factors in "catching the observer's attention." Why these physical aspects of stimuli should be so successful in gaining attention is not entirely clear. Perhaps they represent a legacy from our biological past and reflect important attributes of salient elements in the environment such as animal predators.

Collative characteristics The second broad stimulus characteristic which attracts spontaneous attention has been designated by Berlyne (1960, 1966) as the *collative* properties of stimuli. These are properties which depend on comparison or collation of stimulus elements, and they are best described by such words as novelty, surprisingness, incongruity, and complexity. Visual patterns representing some of these collative properties are presented in Figures 5.2 and 5.3.

In a series of experiments, Berlyne and his co-workers devised a number of techniques to compare the ability of visual patterns to attract and sustain inspection when observers were given no special reason to attend to them. In some cases, observers were allowed access to a switch controlling stimulus presentations by which they could obtain as many brief glimpses of a pattern as they wished. In other cases, the amount of time spent looking at a pattern was measured, and in still others, eye-fixation recordings were used. These studies revealed that novel and incongruous objects are almost always selected or fixated in preference to others. The results with respect to complexity were somewhat less simple, since the function relating complexity to attention has the shape of an inverted U; that is, people seem to be attracted to patterns of intermediate complexity (Berlyne, 1966, 1970; Brown and Gregory, 1968). This issue and related topics will be addressed more fully in Chapter 11.

Kaufman and Richards (1969) have described an interesting technique for gauging spontaneous eye fixations. Their technique makes use of a phenomenon known as *Haidinger's brush.* Crystalline structures in the eye cast a shadow on the retina which is normally invisible. Using a slide projector and a polarizing filter, Kaufman and Richards devised a means of making Haidinger's brush visible as a "whirling propeller" by rotating the plane of polarization of blue light reflected off a screen containing a target figure. By asking the observer to mark the position of the "propeller" on the projected display, they could determine where the observer was looking. Research with this technique has demonstrated that in viewing visual forms, people attend predominantly to discontinuities, corners, contours, and the brighter sides of contours.

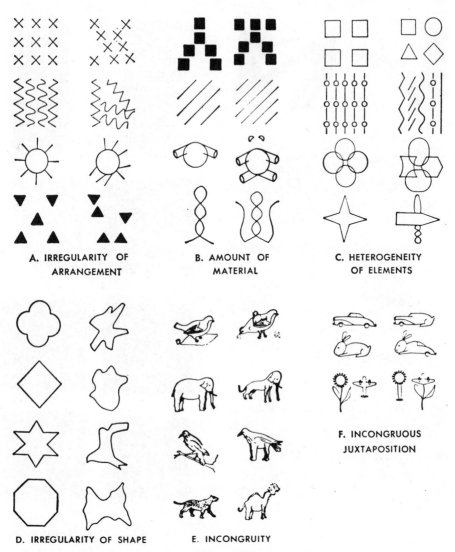

FIGURE 5.2 Visual patterns representing "complexity" and "incongruity" variables. (From Berlyne, 1966)

The orientation response Further insight into the determinants of attention might be gained by considering a characteristic pattern of skeletal and physiological changes which occur in the behavior of the organism shortly after stimuli are presented. This pattern is informally known as the "What is it?" response. More formally, it is termed the *orientation reflex* or the *orientation response* (Lynn, 1966; Sokolov, 1963). Some of the components of the

XA. NUMBER OF INDEPENDENT UNITS

XB. ASYMMETRY   **XC. RANDOM DISTRIBUTION**

FIGURE 5.3 Visual patterns representing "complexity" variables of a higher order than those of Figure 5.2. (From Berlyne, 1966)

orientation response are readily observed in animals, since they consist of gross skeletal adjustments. Dogs and cats, for example, may perk up their ears or point their heads toward a particular source of stimulation. Other aspects of the orientation response involve more subtle physiological manifestations, including enlargement of the pupils of the eyes, decreased electrical resistance of the skin (the GSR or galvanic skin response), and a transient breakdown of synchronized electrocortical activity as revealed in the electroencephalogram (EEG). A comprehensive listing of the bodily changes involved in the orientation response is given in Table 5.1.

The orientation response is frequently elicited by novel or intense stimuli, as well as by stimuli which have personal significance, such as one's own name or the announcement, "Fire!" As described by Kahneman (1973), the orientation response represents a disruption of ongoing activity by an attention-demanding stimulus, intense processing of that stimulus, and preparation for future stimuli and responses. The orientation response and responses associated with pain or fear (the "defense" response) share several physiological characteristics. However, the orientation response can be distinguished from the defense response by the state of the blood vessels in the head and limbs. The vessels dilate in the orientation response, whereas in the defense response, they exhibit vasoconstriction.

One of the important features of the orientation response is the fact that it habituates; that is, it diminishes with repeated presentation of a stimulus. This does not mean, however, that the organism ceases to process the stimulus. Quite the contrary. Sudden changes in the quantitative or qualitative characteristics of the stimulus will reinstate the orientation response (Mackworth, 1969), as will the omission of an expected stimulus in a recurrent sequence (Badia and Defran, 1970; Sokolov, 1969).

Some investigators (Lynn, 1966; Pribram, 1967; Sokolov, 1963) have interpreted such findings as indicating that the brain continually fabricates neuronal models of external events. Any event which does not adequately match the model of what is expected will trigger an orientation response. Conversely, the neural effects of events which match the model will be inhibited. Such an interpretation has some interesting implications for the conceptualization of perceptual processes in general and for the study of attention in particular. For one thing, it implies that the perceptual system actively attempts to reconstruct the external environment in an effort to cope with the massive volume of information it continually encounters. For another, the "match-mismatch" notion clearly identifies the unexpected as a, if not the, crucial determinant of attention.

TABLE 5.1 Bodily Changes Involved in the Orientation Response (after Beatty, 1975)

Local motor responses:	Orient animal toward stimulus. Ongoing activity inhibited.
General motor responses:	Increased electromyographic activity and muscle tone.
EEG:	Aroused pattern of cortical desynchrony.
Vascular changes:	Vasoconstriction in limbs. Vasodilation in head.
Heart rate:	Usually slows.
Electrodermal activity:	Galvanic skin response.
Respiration:	Breathing stops and then begins again with slow, deep breaths.
Pupil:	Pupillary dilation

Fluctuations of Attention

Eye movements and binocular rivalry   An interesting feature of selective attention is that the focus of attention continually shifts even when the stimulus field remains constant. Returning to our earlier analogy, it is as though the "attentional beam" is consistently probing the environment, illuminating one dark recess after another.

One way of observing fluctuations in attention is to examine the pattern whereby people spontaneously gaze at the parts of complex pictures. Eye-movement recordings of such behavior reveal that the fixation point wanders from area to area within the field of view, with a modal fixation duration of about 230 msec, or about four fixations per second (Woodworth and Schlosberg, 1954). An illustration of spontaneous eye-fixation patterns during the observation of a picture is presented in Figure 5.4.

The phenomenon of binocular rivalry has frequently been mentioned as one of the most spectacular demonstrations of fluctuations in attention (Helmholtz, 1866; James, 1890; Lack, 1974; Woodworth and Schlosberg, 1954). If radically different stimuli such as colors or figures are simultaneously presented to the corresponding areas of the two eyes, one of the stimuli tends to

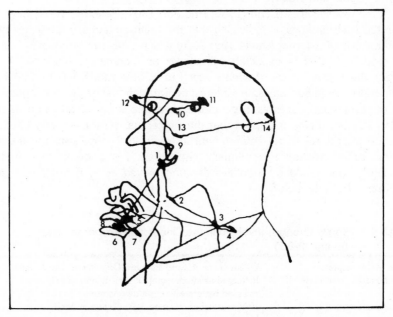

FIGURE 5.4   Illustration of spontaneous eye fixations made by a subject during a 20-second view of a drawing of an "old man." Numbers show the order of fixations on different portions of the drawing. The lines between the numbers represent rapid eye movements (saccades) from one fixation to another. (After Noton and Stark, 1971)

be seen and the other suppressed. As the double exposure continues, alternations in perception of the stimuli are experienced, so that what was previously invisible comes into view and what was visible disappears. Thus, cycles of dominance and suppression are established.

Several factors have been identified which control the rate of alternation and determine which of the competing stimuli will be the more dominant. An advantage accrues to a moving stimulus, as well as to the stimulus which is the more intense, or the more "interesting" (Woodworth and Schlosberg, 1954). Predominance can also be affected by the relative amount and clarity of contour in the stimuli (Crovitz and Lockhead, 1967; Levelt, 1968). In addition, predominance of one of the views can be established to some extent by voluntary effort (Lack, 1969; Meredith and Meredith, 1962).

The basis for rivalry   If binocular rivalry is to be attributed to some form of attentional oscillation, it is necessary to rule out the possibility that this phenomenon is controlled primarily by peripheral factors associated with the visual receptors. One possible candidate as a peripheral basis of rivalry is retinal adaptation or fatigue. However, since the contending stimuli are always physically present during both dominance and suppression, it is unlikely that these local retinal changes can explain the phenomenal changes characteristic of rivalry.

A somewhat less obvious peripheral factor that has been offered as the mediating mechanism for binocular rivalry involves differential changes in the thickness of the lens of each eye (Fry, 1936). According to this argument, rivalry is the result of differential accommodation and the consequent blurring of retinal images. Lack (1971) has provided a test of the accommodation hypothesis by using a drug which temporarily paralyzed the ciliary muscles of the eyes and rendered his subjects incapable of focusing properly. The stimuli in this study were presented in a *stereoscope*, a device which permits the differential exposure of stimuli to each eye (see Chapter 8). The stimuli consisted of a black ring with a vertical black bar in the center and a black ring within which a horizontal black bar was centered. Lack found that the ring-bar stimuli underwent rivalry even when accommodation was precluded by the paralyzing drug. These results indicate that differential accommodation does not play a significant role in controlling binocular rivalry.

Still another peripheral factor which might influence rivalry is eye movement. Our visual receptors are capable of exercising several different kinds of movements. Some of these are relatively extensive and are under conscious control. Examples are the sudden and "jerky" *saccadic* movements involving parallel changes in the position of both eyes when people shift their gaze from one point in space to another, and the slower and smoother pursuit movements which occur when people follow a moving target. In addition, smaller movements also take place which do not appear to be under conscious control. Even if you try as hard as you can, it is unlikely that you can keep your eyes completely still. During the steadiest effort at fixation, our eyes continually make extremely fine movements known collectively as *physiological nystagmus* (Alpern, 1971). Included in this category are slow drifts and rapid "flicks" called *microsaccades*. The latter tend to occur in a rather unpredictable manner. It is possible that the random adjustments in the position of the eyes inherent in microsaccades alter the effective strength of the rivalry stimuli and thereby trigger a cycle of dominance and suppression (Levelt, 1968). One way to check out the eye-movement hypothesis would be to fix or "stabilize" the visual images on the two retinas. And one method for creating stabilized retinal images is to use *afterimages* as rivalry stimuli. You probably have noticed that visual experience does not terminate abruptly upon termination of an intense stimulus. Rather, the visual sensation remains for a brief period of time, and under some conditions it may persist for several minutes. The retinal locus of the excitation which results in such afterimages remains fixed despite eye movements. Should afterimages yield binocular rivalry, the explanation of rivalry cannot lie in eye movements.

In an investigation based closely on the above logic, Blake, Fox, and McIntyre (1971) used the afterimage technique to study binocular rivalry. Rivalry targets were generated by means of a very-high-intensity electronic strobe-lamp flash, and afterimages were maintained by having the subjects gaze at an intermittently illuminated homogeneous field. Binocular rivalry was experienced even under these conditions. Other investigators have also demonstrated the occurrence of rivalry between afterimages (Lack, 1969; Wade, 1974).

In general, results of experiments designed to investigate potential peripheral contributions to binocular rivalry support the conclusion that rivalry is controlled not by peripheral factors but by some central mechanism such as fluctuations in attention.

Suppression and selectivity An interesting question which may be asked of the perceptual fluctuations which occur in rivalry concerns the extent to which suppression is selective. That is, does suppression selectively attenuate only certain classes of stimulus inputs, or is the suppression process nonselective in relation to physical properties of the suppressed stimuli? A series of studies by Fox and his co-workers has provided evidence to indicate that suppression is nonselective.

In order to attack this problem experimentally, Fox devised a means of measuring the relative sensitivity of the eye to a test probe that appeared during suppression or nonsuppression. In one study (Wales and Fox, 1970), rivalry targets were presented in a stereoscope, and the subjects pressed a switch to indicate when they had clear nonsuppression of the left- or right-eye target. Pressing the switch activated automatic electronic circuitry which delivered a test flash of light to either the suppressed or nonsuppressed eye on a given trial. The subjects were required to make a forced-choice judgment as to where the test flash appeared. The results of this study showed that the proportion of correct detections of the probe flash was greater in the nonsuppressed than in the suppressed eye; moreover, suppression resulted in an elevated detection threshold for the probe flash of about 0.56 log units. Using a similar technique, Fox and Check (1966, 1972) found that recognition thresholds are also elevated in the suppressed field when letters are used as test probes. In addition, these same investigators have reported that the detection of motion is attenuated during suppression (Fox and Check, 1968). Evidently, rivalry suppression represents an inhibitory state that attenuates all classes of inputs falling within the boundaries of the suppressed target. Thus, though the source of this kind of fluctuation in attention is central, it is also nonselective.

The switching time of attention   If we conceive of attention as a periodic phenomenon, it might be of interest to try to determine the time required to switch attention from one stimulus to another. This problem has been studied by several investigators in recent years, but the issue remains essentially unresolved. As yet, there does not appear to be enough evidence to warrant a firm statement regarding the exact time necessary to switch attention (Moray, 1969a). The wide range of estimates obtained from different experimental conditions is illustrated by the following investigations.

In an early study, Broadbent (1954) employed what is known as a *split-span* technique. Listeners were presented with pairs of digits, one number of each pair being delivered simultaneously to each ear. If the listeners were required to recall the digits in the order left-ear, right-ear, left-ear, right-ear (or vice versa), Broadbent found that they had great difficulty in doing so when the rate of presentation was faster than one pair every 1.5 sec. He concluded that an interval of about 1 or 2 sec is necessary for attention to shift from one input to another, at least under these conditions. Broadbent (1958) later revised his estimate of the switching time of attention downward to approximately 250 msec.

A much different approach has been taken by Kristofferson (1968), who makes the important assumption that attention can be directed at stimuli in only one sensory channel at a time. As a result, if one is attending to a given channel (for example, vision), the allocation of attention to input arriving in an unattended channel (for example, audition) will be delayed by the amount of time needed to switch attention between channels. A series of experiments based on this assumption (Kristofferson, 1967; Schmidt and Kristofferson, 1963) using pure tones and spots of light as stimuli has suggested that switching time is approximately 40–60 msec — a value considerably shorter than that suggested by Broadbent. Clearly, until the complex array of factors potentially inherent in the use of different experimental situations is more fully understood, an exact value for the time to switch attention will remain unavailable. Of course, it is also possible that no such unitary value exists. Instead, the time course of attention may encompass a spectrum of values that depends crucially upon the demands of the task imposed on the observer.

THEORIES OF SELECTIVE ATTENTION

Broadbent's Filter Theory

Information overload   Some of the most exciting work on attention has centered about attempts to develop theoretical models which describe the nature of the selection process. Perhaps the best-known of these is the *filter theory*, introduced by Broadbent in his influential book *Perception and Communication* (1958).

Theories of selective attention must address two basic problems. They have been phrased by Deutsch and Deutsch (1963) as follows. "The first is how different streams of information are kept distinct by the nervous system, and how a resultant babel is thereby avoided. The second is why only one of the messages (once it has been kept distinct and separate) is dealt with at any one time." Broadbent (1958) took the position that messages are kept distinct in part because they proceed along separate neurological pathways or channels. He assumed that the nervous system has a finite capacity for handling the deluge of information which arrives over different channels. To answer the question of how only one message comes to be handled at a time, Broadbent proposed that the brain contains a selective filter which chooses messages on the basis of physical characteristics toward which it is "tuned" and rejects others. The filter spares the limited-capacity system from being overloaded; complex forms of input are rejected on the basis of simple qualities, and a higher-level analysis of them need not occur. A flow diagram of the elements of Broadbent's proposal is presented in Figure 5.5.

According to the model, information enters the nervous system through a number of parallel channels. Since the total amount of information arriving within a given point in time usually exceeds the capacity of higher-level centers responsible for perceptual analysis (p system), a serious bottleneck in the flow of information would be expected. The bottleneck is reduced by the operation of a filter mechanism which has the ability to select information from one of the input lines and allow it direct access to the higher-level processing centers. Broadbent also proposed that there is a short-term memory store at the end of the sensory input lines. If two messages arrive simultaneously, one of them is immediately transmitted through the filter while the other is held briefly (on the order of seconds) in storage. During its time in storage, the representation of the message fades so that it is ultimately lost or at least seriously degraded when eventually gated through the filter. As is evident in Figure 5.5, the theory makes allowance for buttressing material in short-term storage through a feedback loop between the higher-level centers and the short-term store.

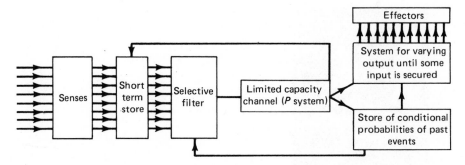

FIGURE 5.5 Information-flow diagram for Broadbent's filter theory. (From Broadbent, 1958)

In essence, the filter model views the selective nature of attention as resulting from restrictions in the capacity of the nervous system to process information. In addition, as Moray (1969a) has noted, the system is kept from being overloaded by an information-handling strategy in which parallel inputs are coded in a serial manner. An important feature of the filter theory is the notion that selection does not take place at random. Instead, Broadbent maintained that the filter biases its selections toward certain physical features of the stimuli. Preference is shown for novel or intense events, acoustic over visual signals, sounds of high frequency, and signals of biological importance to the organism.

Neurophysiological blocking   This unique and imaginative approach is supported by a broad array of empirical findings, both neurophysiological and behavioral. At the neurophysiological level, the notion of a filter that screens out certain classes of inputs fits nicely with the results of a pioneering series of experiments by Hernández-Peón (1966) and his co-workers which describe the blockage of incoming (afferent) impulses in sensory neurons when attention is distracted.

These experiments utilized electrophysiological recordings made in waking animals with electrodes permanently implanted in their brains. In one study, comparisons were made of activity triggered in peripheral auditory neurons of cats by click-stimuli both during relaxed wakefulness and also while the animals were gazing at a pair of mice in a jar. As shown in Figure 5.6, the magnitude of neural activity induced by the acoustic stimuli was considerably reduced when the mice were visible, and it returned to its usual level when the "distraction" was removed from view. Peripheral blocking of neural activity triggered by visual and tactual stimuli was also observed with feline subjects in additional experiments when fish odors and the sight of a rat in a jar were the distracting events.

Hernández-Peón and his associates have also reported some remarkable findings with respect to electrical potentials in the brains of human subjects

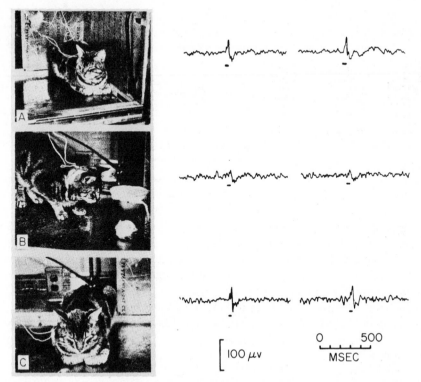

$$\begin{bmatrix} 100\ \mu v \end{bmatrix}$$

0   500
|_|_|_|_|
MSEC

FIGURE 5.6 Blocking effects of distraction upon click-evoked potentials in peripheral auditory neurons. Auditory-evoked potentials recorded during relaxed wakefulness (A) were reduced when the cat looked at a pair of mice in a jar (B) and then returned to their original level when the mice were removed (C). (From Hernández-Peón, Scherrer, and Jouvet, 1956)

evoked by flashes of light. They have indicated that the magnitude of these potentials was reduced during the performance of arithmetic calculations and that the degree of "blocking" was directly related to the difficulty of the problems involved. Other investigators (for example, García-Austt, Bogacz, and Vanzulli, 1964; Spong, Haider, and Lindsley, 1965) have also described attenuated electrocortical activity to stimuli in one sensory modality during distraction by events in another modality.

Experiments of this sort provide a dramatic illustration of the existence within the nervous system of a filter mechanism similar to the one proposed by Broadbent. The data must be considered with some caution, however. The work of Hernández-Peón's group on neural blocking in animals has been subjected to alternative interpretations which argue that these investigations may reflect methodological artifacts rather than true perceptual blocking (see Moray, 1969a; Schwartz, 1978). Furthermore, a discerning review of similar findings obtained from human subjects (Näätänen, 1975) argues that, in general, the results are neither entirely consistent nor conclusive.

Dichotic listening tasks   If we turn to more overt forms of behavior, it is possible to uncover several facts about attention which fall in line with a filtering principle. Much of this material comes from experiments involving *dichotic listening* situations, in which subjects are fed different messages simultaneously in each ear. The advantage of using these situations as a vehicle for studying selective processes in attention is that people cannot readily shut out acoustic signals in a simple, mechanical fashion. By contrast, unwanted visual signals can be ignored in most cases by the simple procedure of closing one's eyes. Thus, as Broadbent (1971) has noted, experiments in hearing are more likely to probe central processes in selection rather than peripheral, mechanical ones.

One form of dichotic listening task which has had extensive use in studies of selective attention is the *shadowing* procedure introduced by Cherry (1953). By means of a tape recorder, two different messages are played simultaneously, one in each ear. The listener is required to follow one message, by repeating it word by word, and to ignore the other. The task is illustrated in Figure 5.7. It represents a fairly close experimental analogue of the familiar "cocktail-party phenomenon" — that is, when you try to hear one conversation while participating in another, less interesting one.

Broadbent's filter model would imply that when engaged in a shadowing task, listeners should be unable to remember the content of the ignored message, since it would be screened from perceptual analysis by the action of the filter. The findings from Cherry's early investigations were consistent with this implication. His listeners could report almost nothing about what was directed to the nonshadowed ear. The language of the rejected message could change from French to German to English to Latin without being noticed. The listeners also failed to notice when the tape on which the rejected message was recorded was played backward. They were aware, however, of gross physical

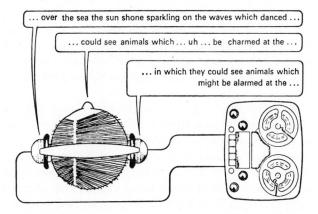

FIGURE 5.7   Illustration of the "shadowing" task used to study selective processes in attention. (From Moray, 1969b)

characteristics in the ignored message, such as changes from a male voice to a female voice or to a tone. This last finding is also consistent with Broadbent's view, since the filter is supposedly biased toward the frequency characteristics of the input signals.

Cherry's observations were later confirmed in an interesting study by Moray (1959) in which listeners were unable either to report or to recognize messages that were repeated 35 times in the unattended ear. Moray also found that instructions to stop shadowing were not heard when they were embedded in the rejected message, but that they were heard when part of the accepted message. A number of other experimenters have reported similar results in which the content of the nonattended message is degraded when listeners are engaged in a shadowing task (for example, Lewis, Honeck and Fishbein, 1975; Norman, 1969; Treisman, 1964b).

Additional evidence supporting the filter theory comes from a crucial experiment by Broadbent (1954) using the split-span method described earlier. In this study, subjects were presented with a string of three digits read serially into one ear, while at the same time a second string of three digits was read serially into the other. Presentation rate was approximately two digits per second. For example, the left ear might receive 6, 8, 2 and the right ear 9, 4, 5. Broadbent found that the listeners' reproduction of the digits was organized by ear of presentation rather than by the order in which they were heard. That is, the listeners would not recall the digits in the order 6, 9, 8, 4, 2, 5 or 9, 6, 4, 8, 5, 2. Instead, the series would be recalled as 6, 8, 2; 9, 4, 5 or 9, 4, 5; 6, 8, 2. Moreover, the first set recalled usually contained no errors, whereas errors were made in the second set recalled.

In terms of filter theory, these results would indicate that each ear served as a separate input channel with individual representations in short-term storage. At recall, the contents of one location in storage was passed by the filter, followed by the contents of the other. The short-term-storage feature of Broadbent's model gains further support from experiments by Norman (1969) and Glucksberg and Cowen (1970) using the shadowing procedure. These studies demonstrated that listeners can retain material in the rejected message if testing is conducted almost immediately after the information arrives in the nonattended ear, but not if testing is delayed for a few seconds.

Analysis for meaning The material that we have just examined fits nicely within Broadbent's filtering scheme. Nevertheless, shortly after is publication, data became available which indicated a need for some revision of this position. These studies focused upon the fate of rejected messages and revealed that in some cases the content of rejected information "leaks" through for perceptual analysis. Such results were crucial for the stance that Broadbent had adopted. They indicated that in addition to their *physical* properties, stimuli might be analyzed for *meaning* at a relatively early stage of processing. They also could be interpreted as indicating that a filtering concept is unnecessary: all information is processed at deeper levels of the nervous system than Broadbent had supposed.

A critical challenge to Broadbent's early conceptualization was provided by Gray and Wedderburn (1960) in a study which introduced a modification into the split-span technique. Instead of just presenting different sets of digits to each ear, they used material which represented different meaning classes. In one of their conditions, listeners were presented with three digits and a meaningful phrase intermingled in the two ears. For example, "6-mice-2" might be presented in the left ear and "eat-9-cheese" in the right ear. Such a procedure pits meaning class against input channel as a way for subjects to organize the material. Gray and Wedderburn found that their subjects were just as likely in their reproductions to group the words of the phrase together ("mice eat cheese") and keep the digits separate (6, 9, 2) as they were to group the items according to the ear in which they had been presented. These results do not necessarily demand that the filter concept be abandoned (Broadbent, 1971; Swets and Kristofferson, 1970). They can be taken to indicate, however, that simultaneous messages from two separate input lines are processed for linguistic content and that such content is a stimulus property which could be used for selection. Gray and Wedderburn's findings have been confirmed by Broadbent and Gregory (1964) and Yntema and Trask (1963). Furthermore, Bryden (1964) has reported that if two words presented simultaneously in the split-span procedure are common associates (for example, "fire" and "water"), the two may be reproduced together even though they come from different input channels.

The possibility that high-level perceptual analysis of unwanted signals may occur has been suggested by the results of shadowing experiments. Moray's (1959) study, which we cited earlier to support the filter concept, also provided one of the first demonstrations of the failure of the filter to screen out meaning. While it was true that the listeners in this study could remember little of the material in the nonshadowed message, certain meaningful elements did get through. The listeners were aware of their own names when they occurred in the nonshadowed ear, and they did notice some instructions in the nonattended message if such instructions were preceded by their own names. Related to these findings is an intriguing report by Oswald, Taylor, and Treisman (1960) involving records of electrocortical activity taken from sleeping subjects. These investigators found that during sleep, subjects tend to respond selectively to their own names relative to other more neutral names which were played to them.

Research with the shadowing task has provided several other lines of evidence to indicate that the message in the rejected ear is analyzed for meaning. Much of this evidence comes from clever experiments by Treisman. In one study (Treisman, 1960), messages were occasionally switched from ear to ear so that the message which had been in the shadowed ear was now in the ear to be ignored. Treisman found that when the message which the listeners were shadowing was highly redundant, they would follow it into the ear to be rejected before reverting back to the designated ear. This finding is incompatible with Broadbent's initial version of the characteristics of the filter. It implies that predictability of meaning may counteract instructions for channel selection and, therefore, that unwanted material is not necessarily rejected on the basis of simple physical characteristics in the early stages of processing.

A second important study by Treisman (1964b) also poses difficulties for Broadbent's argument that there is a substantial loss of information early in the processing pathways. Comparisons were made of the effects of verbal context on shadowing efficiency. The message to be shadowed was a passage from an English novel (Lord Jim), while the material to be rejected consisted of either a passage from the same novel or from a technical discussion of biochemistry. The listeners in this experiment had more difficulty in rejecting unwanted messages from the source with content similar to the target message (the same novel) than from the source with content quite dissimilar to that of the target message (the discussion of biochemistry). In another part of this investigation, Treisman examined the effects of presenting a French translation of the English target message to the rejected ear. Among those listeners who had little knowledge of French, only 2 percent of the subjects noticed the nature of the rejected information. By contrast, among listeners who were fluent in both languages, 55 percent of the subjects were aware of the nature of the rejected message. These results led to the conclusion that input information may receive very high levels of analysis even when it appears in a rejected channel.

The idea that rejected messages are analyzed as speech has been reinforced in a study by Lewis (1970) in which reaction times to shadow words were measured. He found that the reaction times to target words were increased (i.e., responses were relatively slow) if the word in the unattended ear was a synonym of the target word. When the unwanted word was an antonym, the time it took to shadow the target items decreased. Lewis' study clearly shows that the meaning of the word to be ignored was not "switched out," since both words would have to be recognized in order for effects such as those that he reported to occur.

Alternate Models of Selection

Filter attenuation theory   On the basis of findings such as those we have just considered, Treisman rejected the concept of a filter which screens out material solely in terms of physical properties. She proposed instead a modification of the filter theory which would render the notion of filtering in selective attention compatible with facts pointing to a more complete analysis of rejected information (Treisman, 1960, 1964a, 1969). The essence of this modification is that filtering is not an all-or-none affair. Treisman suggested that the filter does not cut off rejected messages entirely, but instead attenuates their strength. Thus, under some conditions, the weakened signals can still contact higher-level elements of the perceptual system. A flow diagram of Treisman's view of the process of selective attention is presented in Figure 5.8.

According to Treisman, selection is accomplished on the basis of a series of tests which are performed on incoming information in a hierarchical order. Incoming messages are first examined for crude physical properties such as pitch, intensity, spatial location, time of arrival, etc. The next stage of processing brings the action of the filter into play. On the basis of its "tuning" characteristics, the filter weakens the strength of signals coming from input lines that are to be rejected. For example, if a listener is instructed to attend to messages from one ear, those from the other ear are attenuated by the filter. In general, stimuli which do not possess the physical characteristics for which the filter is set are attenuated in strength.

After passing through the filter, both nonattenuated and attenuated messages go on to deeper levels of the nervous system where they activate high-level perceptual analyzers or "dictionary units." These units extract meaning from incoming stimuli, and complete selection is made on the basis of the responses of the perceptual analyzers. As conceived by Treisman, each analyzing unit has a threshold which must be exceeded by the input stimulus to which it is responsive in order for full awareness of the stimulus to occur. Un-

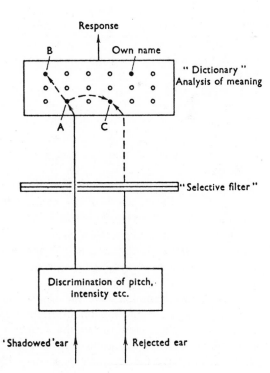

FIGURE 5.8 Information-flow diagram for Treisman's filter-attenuation theory. (From Treisman, 1960)

wanted signals, which have been weakened by the filter, will generally be unable to activate the higher-order perceptual units responsive to them and ordinarily will go unrecognized. On the other hand, wanted signals, which are not modified by the filter, will trigger their appropriate dictionary units and will thus be recognized.

In order to account for "leaks" of unwanted material into awareness, Treisman posited additional features of the perceptual analyzing units. She suggested that the thresholds of units which are responsive to highly significant stimuli are lower than those of other units. Thus, such stimuli will be fully perceived even if their strength is attenuated. Furthermore, Treisman asserted that transient modifications in thresholds may be brought about by instructional or contextual factors, and in this way highly probable events appearing in an unattended input line may be recognized even though attenuated by the filter. Treisman's modifications have enabled filter theory to handle successfully much of the material on selective attention that we have described, and these revisions have apparently been accepted by Broadbent (1971). Thus we may now speak of the Broadbent-Treisman filter attenuation model.

Response-selection positions   The same evidence which prompted Treisman to modify Broadbent's initial conceptualization of filter theory has led other psychologists to adopt a radically different stance with respect to the nature of selective attention. An alternate position was first formulated by Deutsch and Deutsch (1963), who maintained that *all* inputs are fully analyzed perceptually and that selection takes place only when the observer responds to stimuli.

Deutsch and Deutsch postulated the existence of central analyzing units similar to Treisman's which completely examine and recognize all incoming information. They suggested that the outputs of these central recognition structures have preset weightings of importance to the observer. At any point in time, the output of only that unit with the highest level of importance will be acted upon or remembered. On the other hand, if signals of more importance come along, they will be able to displace the previously most important signals. Thus, the most salient messages both capture attention and set the criterion of saliency that other signals must surpass in order to be heeded. Within this position, importance weightings were held to be dependent upon certain enduring predispositions of the observer. Additionally, transient changes in saliency could be brought about by contextual and instructional factors Moray (1969a).

The model formulated by the Deutsches argues that selective attention reflects a choice of information from memory and not perceptual filtering. Consequently, their view moves the selection mechanism farther back in the information-processing sequence. More recently, Norman (1968, 1976) and Keele (1973) have taken similar positions which, while differing in exact detail, also argue that all incoming signals receive a full analysis and that attention occurs at the level of activated memory and response organization.

The major distinctions in the theoretical positions that we have just outlined are nicely summarized in Figure 5.9 adopted from Kahneman (1973). Model A in the figure illustrates the filter approach, and Model B illustrates the activated memory-response selection point of view.

As Kahneman has pointed out, both positions assume that congestion occurs somewhere in the sequence of activities that take place in the processing of stimulus information. Filter theory holds that it occurs at or just prior to perceptual analysis and, therefore, that "attention controls perception" (Kahneman, 1973, p. 6). In contrast, the position adopted by the Deutsches, Norman, and Keele argues that the point of congestion takes place just before the selection of responses to fully analyzed stimuli and that such congestion prevents the execution of more than one response at a time. Consequently, the phenomenon of selective attention is postperceptual and reflects a choice by the organism of the most appropriate response for a given situation. Once again, we have the situation in which opposing points of view are arrayed against each other in an effort to solve a problem in perception. As you might expect, several attempts have been made to establish the validity of one over the other.

Tests of the Models

Support for filter theory   One of the first experimental attempts to determine if selective attention arises in perception or response organization was made by Treisman and Geffen (1967). They presented two messages simultaneously and required that listeners shadow the message appearing in one

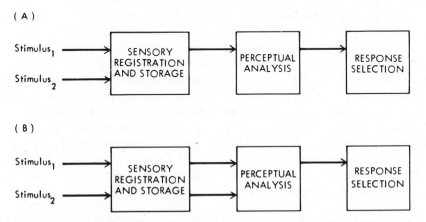

FIGURE 5.9   Outline of two general models of selective attention in which an information-processing bottleneck is considered to be located at different stages of analysis. (From Kahneman, 1973)

ear. In addition, the listeners were also required to execute a manual tapping response to critical target words which might occasionally appear in either ear. This procedure permitted different predictions to be generated from filter theory and the response-selection position.

According to filter theory, the shadowing requirement should preclude allocation of attention to messages arriving in the nondesignated ear, and consequently it should prevent the recognition of target items which occur in that ear. On the other hand, since perceptual recognition units should be primed for target items in either ear and since the tapping response was identical for target items in either ear, the response-selection position would imply that target items should be recognized regardless of ear of origin. The results of this study revealed that 87 percent of the target items were heard in the shadowed ear while only 8 percent of these items were heard in the nonshadowed ear. Accordingly, Treisman and Geffen concluded that the limit in selective attention was perceptual in nature and not due to response selection.

Although this experiment favors filter theory, it is subject to a potential methodological flaw. Deutsch and Deutsch (1967) have pointed out that the listeners had to make two responses to material in the shadowed ear—shadowing and tapping—but had to make only the tapping response to target words in the nonshadowed ear. This difference, they argued, could influence the "importance" attached to target items in the nonshadowed ear and thus bias the outcome in favor of filter theory. In response to such criticism, Treisman and Riley (1969) replicated the initial study with one important modification. Whenever the listeners heard a critical target item in either ear, they were immediately to stop shadowing. Therefore, the response differential to target items in each ear was eliminated. Once again, however, the results favored filter theory; the listeners detected 76 percent of the target items in the attended ear, but only 33 percent of the targets in the nonattended ear.

Further support for filter theory comes from an experiment by Moray and O'Brien (1967) in which subjects were asked to attend to streams of digits in one ear and to ignore digits presented simultaneously in the other. The subjects were also instructed to press a key whenever a letter appeared in the attended ear, and, although instructed to ignore material in the nonattended ear, they were asked to execute a key press if they happened to hear a letter in that ear as well. A signal-detection analysis of the data revealed that the subjects were perceptually more sensitive to letters in the attended ear (d' was higher), as filter theory might lead one to expect. However, contrary to implications from the response-selection view, the decision criterion (β) for target items did not vary between channels. Similar results have also been described by Broadbent and Gregory (1963).

Support for response selection While these studies bolster a filter-theory approach to selective attention, evidence is also available which falls in line with the response-selection point of view. This support comes from experiments which indicate that perceptual encoding does not require a limited-capacity mechanism — that subjects are capable of processing information from more than one channel at the same time. For example, Shaffer and Hardwick (1969) asked subjects to attend to simultaneous messages in each ear and to respond to critical target words which could appear in an unpredictable manner in either ear. The subjects were able to recognize 59–68 percent of the target messages under these conditions. The range of values for correct detections indicates that the task was difficult to perform, but this range is higher than the 50 percent which would be expected if listeners could only attend to one channel at a time.

An interesting experiment by Shiffrin, Pisoni, and Castaneda-Mendez (1974) also asked whether attention can be allocated simultaneously to stimuli from different sources. They arranged things so that in some conditions listeners had to pay attention to both ears at the same time, while in other conditions the listeners could devote attention entirely to one ear and then to the other in a sequential manner. The listeners were required to detect a speech-like target stimulus which appeared very briefly in one ear while a distracting foil was presented to the other. Simultaneous and sequential detections were essentially identical despite the need for sharing of attention between ears in the simultaneous condition. Such a result implies that processing of material from one source does not exclude processing material from another.

A potentially compelling result in favor of the response-selection position has been described by Corteen and Wood (1972). In this study, city names were first associated with electric shock and then embedded in material presented to the rejected ear in a shadowing situation. Although the shock-associated city names were not identified by the subjects and did not interfere with shadowing, they did elicit a large number of emotional responses as measured by changes in electrical skin conductance. The fact that the shock-associated stimuli produced emotional reactions without apparent awareness would seem to indicate that they were subjected to a rather sophisticated analysis, even though they were not chosen for selection in the shadowing response. This finding has been confirmed in studies by Corteen and Dunn (1974) and Von Wright, Anderson, and Stenman (1975). Unfortunately, a careful experiment conducted along similar lines by Wardlaw and Kroll (1976) could find no evidence for semantic processing of words without awareness. Apparently, the effect is difficult to obtain consistently and thus, while provocative, it should not be considered as definitive evidence in favor of a response-selection position.

The locus of selective attention   From what we have seen thus far, it seems clear that the debate over the locus of selective attention has not yet ended. It is tempting to conclude that more data are necessary before the issue can be resolved one way or the other. There is, however, another possible conclusion. It is conceivable that our cognitive capacities are more flexible than we have been willing to assume, and that both perceptual and response selection can take place under appropriate circumstances.

Indeed, studies by Greenwald (1972) and Moore and Massaro (1973) have suggested that the nature of the information-processing task facing the subject may determine whether limited perceptual capacity or response-organization effects will be found in selective-attention experiments. This same idea is offered by Kahneman (1973) and by Posner and Boies (1971), who argue that the limit on selective attention is not a structural one, reflecting congestion at some point of information processing. Instead, they argue, attention is limited by the mental resources demanded by a situation, and it is this limitation on the capacity to perform mental work which determines whether attention can be effectively allocated to different activities. A related but somewhat different view is proposed by Hochberg (1970), who attributes what is lost in selective attention to a failure of the person to encode and hence remember events which would overload the limited capacity of memory mechanisms. This new breed of attentional theory may very well prove of considerable value in directing research toward a more satisfactory solution to the mystery of selection attention.

SUSTAINED ATTENTION[1]

The Problem of Vigilance

Up to this point in our discussion, we have been concerned primarily with the ability of observers to focus awareness upon stimulus events. In this section we shift our own attention to a somewhat different issue. We are interested here in the ability of observers to maintain their focus of attention and remain alert to stimuli over prolonged periods of time, to engage in what is generally known as sustained attention or vigilance.

Practical implications   Earlier, we pointed out that current interest in attention is rooted, in part, in the difficulties encountered by technicians in handling practical information-processing tasks. This is especially true of vigilance. During World War II, British radar observers on antisubmarine patrol were often required to carry out their duties in a setting which included long-term monotonous waiting for uncertain stimulus events. Many hours were spent watching for an occasional blip of light on a radar screen which signified the presence of a hostile submarine. It seems safe to assume that these observers were highly motivated to detect those crucial signals. Nevertheless, despite a high level of accuracy early in their period of watchkeeping, a surprising change took place in their behavior as time wore on: they failed with increasing frequency to notice the critical blips displayed by their equipment.

Efforts to determine why this change occurred stimulated a substantial amount of research on the problem of sustained attention. This problem has

[1] This section is based on an earlier discussion of vigilance by J. S. Warm (1977).

obvious implications for military and industrial inspection tasks (Howell and Goldstein, 1971); it is also relevant to the medical setting, as for example when anesthesiologists monitor electronic equipment displaying a patient's life signs during prolonged surgery (Beatty, Ahern, and Katz, 1977). The importance of this problem extends even beyond these immediate practical concerns, for the capacity to maintain some level of alertness during the activities of the day represents one of the most fundamental elements of perceptual functioning (Jerison, 1977).

The decrement function   Controlled laboratory research on sustained attention is generally considered to date from the work of Norman Mackworth (1950), who devised a simulated radar display called the *clock test.* Subjects were asked to view the movements of a black pointer along the circumference of a blank-faced clock which contained no scale markings or reference points. The pointer moved 0.3 inch to a new position once every second. Occasionally, it executed a "double jump" of 0.6 inch, which was the critical signal for detection. The subjects were required to press a key whenever they spotted a movement of double length during a session which lasted continuously for two hours. In Mackworth's experiment, as in most of the vigilance experiments which have followed, the subjects were seated alone, their responses had no effect on occurrence of critical signals, and the signals to be detected occurred infrequently and aperiodically.

Using the clock test in this way, Mackworth was able to chart the course of the *decrement function,* or the progressive decline in performance over time. Some of his findings are illustrated in Figure 5.10.

Notice that the incidence of missed signals increased sharply from the first to the second half-hour of the session and then showed a more gradual decline for the remainder of the two-hour period. The decrement function is the most ubiquitous finding in vigilance experiments. Many studies, using a broad assortment of different displays, indicate that the decline in performance is complete from 20 to 35 minutes after the initiation of the vigil and that at least half of the final loss is completed within the first 15 minutes (Teichner, 1974). The most striking aspect of this finding is that it seems to result merely from the necessity of looking or listening for a relatively infrequent signal over a continuous period of time.

The body of data which has accumulated since Mackworth's seminal work has revealed that the factors which control the decrement function as well as the overall level of vigilance efficiency are quite complex. They encompass a wide spectrum of psychological processes and, evidently, need to be understood on a variety of levels involving sensory, cognitive, and psychophysiological considerations. As Broadbent (1971) has noted, the theoretical importance of the vigilance task is that it allows us to study in a controlled situation almost all of the factors that may be considered to influence attention. Simply stated, do observers fail to react in this task or react sluggishly be-

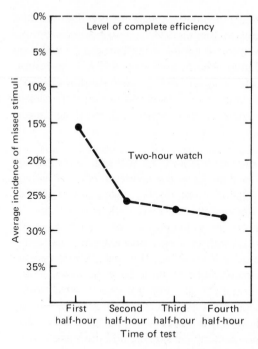

FIGURE 5.10 The decrement function in vigilance obtained in one of Mackworth's early experiments. (After Mackworth, 1950)

cause they are not looking or listening, because they are not expecting a signal, because they are too drowsy or otherwise physiologically unprepared to perform effectively, or because the cost of responding outweighs that of not responding?

The Psychophysics of Vigilance

Sensory factors As in the study of other perceptual phenomena, an important feature of research into the nature of sustained attention has been the precise determination of stimulus characteristics which influence performance. One important characteristic is the sensory modality in which stimuli are delivered to the observer. Performance efficiency in sustained-attention tasks involving auditory signals tends to be superior to that in tasks involving visuals signals; furthermore, several experiments have revealed rather low correlations between people's ability to sustain attention in different sensory channels (Baker, Ware, and Sipowitz, 1962; Buckner and McGrath, 1963; Colquhoun, 1975; Hatfield and Loeb, 1968; Jones and Kirk, 1970; Warm and Alluisi, 1971).

Such results are somewhat disturbing for our attempt to understand the nature of sustained attention, since they imply that vigilance performance may not reflect the properties of a single central process. Fortunately, evidence has begun to accumulate which affords a somewhat more optimistic view. This evidence indicates that auditory-visual correlations can be increased by closely equating the types of discriminations required in the two types of task; also pertinent are experiments showing that experience in one sensory modality can influence subsequent performance in another modality (Gunn and Loeb, 1967; Hatfield and Loeb, 1968; McFarland and Halcomb, 1970; Parasuraman and Davies, 1977; Tyler, Waag, and Halcomb, 1972). Thus, while specific sensory factors are of obvious importance in the maintenance of sustained attention, the notion remains viable that common factors are present in vigilance performance in different sensory channels.

Signal conspicuity   On the basis of our previous discussions of the detectability of stimuli under alerted conditions in psychophysical experiments, we would expect that the amplitude and duration of critical signals would be important factors in their detectability over prolonged periods. Indeed, such is the case. In general, performance efficiency increases as the signal-to-noise ratio of critical signals increases. This effect is nicely illustrated in a study by Loeb and Binford (1963) in which subjects listened for occasional increments in the loudness of recurrent pulses of auditory stimuli. Normal pulses had an intensity of 60 dB above the subject's absolute threshold, whereas the critical signals were pulses of 2.1, 3.6, or 5.1 dB above this level. As is shown in Figure 5.11, the number of missed signals was inversely related to the intensity of the critical stimuli. In addition, the figure also indicates that the decrement function, as indexed by a progressive increase in missed signals over time, was most pronounced at the lowest level of critical signal amplitude. Several other studies have demonstrated similar results (Adams, 1956; Tickner, Poulton, Copeman, and Simmonds, 1972; Wiener, 1964). Moreover, Hawkes and Loeb (1962) and Loeb and Schmidt (1963) have shown that response latency to correct detections decreases with increments in critical signal amplitude.

Vigilance performance is related in a similar manner to the duration of

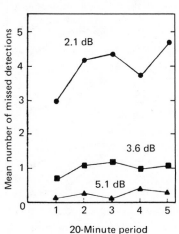

FIGURE 5.11   Effects of critical signal intensity on the detection of loudness increments in an auditory vigilance task. (After Loeb and Binford, 1963)

critical stimuli. Signals of brief duration are less likely to be detected than those which remain on the observer's display for longer periods of time (Adams, 1956; Baker, 1963b; Warm, Loeb, and Alluisi, 1970). An illustration of this effect is presented in Figure 5.12.

Event rate   In most vigilance experiments dynamic displays are employed in which critical signals are embedded within a matrix of regularly occurring neutral background events. In the clock test, for example, the small movements of the pointer constituted a set of neutral events in which the large "double jumps" occasionally appeared. Although the background events may be neutral in the sense that they require no overt response, they are by no means neutral in their influence upon the manner in which observers can maintain their attention to the task at hand. The frequency of neutral events, or the *background event rate*, turns out to be an important factor in determining performance efficiency.

Jerison and Pickett (1964) have provided a clear demonstration of the role of background event rate in vigilance tasks. In this experiment, subjects attended to the repetitive movements of a bar of light. An event was defined as a sequence of dual movements in which the bar moved a predetermined distance to the right, snapped back to its start position, again moved the same distance, and returned to its point of origin, where it remained for a while before the next dual movement or event took place. The critical signal for detection was an increment of 4 mm in the length of the second deflection within an event. Two event rates were used; a slow rate of 5 events/min and a faster rate of 30 events/min. Equal numbers of critical signals were presented at each event rate. The results of this study, shown in Figure 5.13, in-

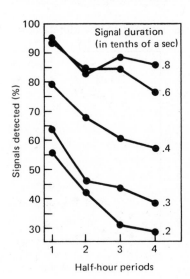

FIGURE 5.12   The percentage of signals detected during a vigilance task for several values of critical signal duration. (After Baker, 1963b)

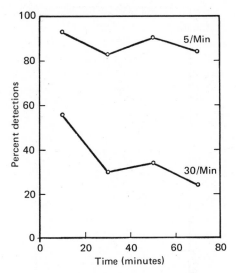

FIGURE 5.13 Effect of event rate on the detection of critical signals during an uninterrupted 80-minute vigil. Events to be judged as signal or nonsignal were repeated at the rate of 5 or 30 per minute. Critical signal frequency was constant at 15 signals per hour. (From Jerison and Pickett, 1964)

dicated that the percentage of signals correctly detected was considerably greater at the slow than at the fast event rate; moreover, the familiar decrement function occurred predominantly in the fast-event-rate condition. A substantial number of other investigations have confirmed the finding that the quality of sustained attention is inversely related to the rate of presentation of neutral events (Colquhoun, 1961; Guralnick, 1972; Johnston, Howell, and Goldstein, 1966; Krulewitz, Warm, and Wohl, 1975; Loeb and Binford, 1968; Taub and Osborne, 1968).

Not only does background event rate influence sustained attention in its own right, it also serves to modify the effects associated with other stimulus parameters. For example, Metzger, Warm, and Senter (1974) have shown that variations in event rate exert a strong influence on the effects of critical signal amplitude. Using a light-bar display similar to that described above, these investigators compared the effects of incremental excursions of 2 mm and 8 mm in the length of the second deflection within an event. Critical signals occurred within the context of a slow (6 events/min) and a fast (21 events/min) event rate. As is evident in Figure 5.14, the difference in detectability between the 2-mm and 8-mm signals was enhanced twofold within the context of the fast event rate. Thus, background event rate is a prepotent psychophysical factor in sustained attention, and we seem to reach the paradoxical conclusion that "the detectability of a signal is determined by what is going on at times when no signal is being presented" (Jerison and Pickett, 1964, p. 2).

Temporal and spatial uncertainty Factors such as the sensory modality of signals, their amplitude and duration, and the background event ma-

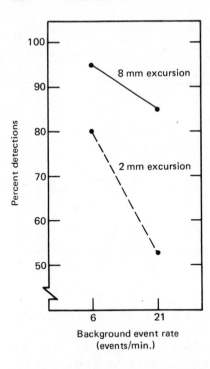

FIGURE 5.14 Percentage of correct detections as a function of background event rate for two levels of critical signal amplitude in a Jerison moving-light display. (From Metzger, Warm, and Senter, 1974)

trix in which they are embedded can be considered as first-order psychophysical factors in vigilance—factors in which some immediate physical property of the stimulus is manipulated. Second-order factors, those characteristics of the signal which must be derived by the observer on the basis of experience with the task, also play a vital role in the maintenance of sustained attention. These include the observer's uncertainty about both when (temporal) and where (spatial) the signal will appear.

One means of experimentally manipulating the observer's temporal uncertainty is through variations in the density or the number of critical signals. The more frequently such signals occur within a fixed time period, the less the observer's average uncertainty as to when they will occur. The effect of signal density can easily be seen by referring to Figure 5.15, which displays the results of several different experiments. Note that the percentage of signals detected increases as critical signal density increases over a broad range of values.

Variations in critical signal density also influence the speed with which critical signals are detected. Smith, Warm, and Alluisi (1966) employed an information-theory analysis to measure the density-determined temporal uncertainty in the appearance of critical signals. They studied monitoring efficiency over a density range of 6 to 96 signals/hour and found that the observer's response time could be represented as a linear increasing function of the temporal uncertainty due to density, as is indicated in Figure 5.16. This finding

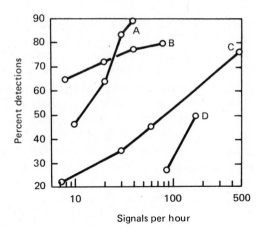

FIGURE 5.15 Percentage of signals detected as a function of log critical signal frequency in several vigilance experiments. (From Jerison and Pickett, 1963)

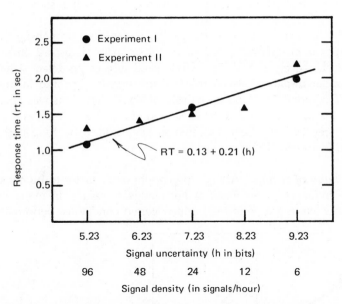

FIGURE 5.16 Response time to signal detections as a function of the temporal uncertainty due to signal density. Signal density values are given for reference. (From Smith, Warm, and Alluisi, 1966)

was later shown to hold equally well for visual and auditory signals (Warm and Alluisi, 1971). Apparently, Hick's Law, which, you may recall, states that response time is a linear increasing function of stimulus uncertainty, is applicable to vigilance tasks as well as to the choice–reaction-time tasks for which it was originally formulated.

Another means of manipulating the observer's temporal uncertainty is through variations in the intervals of time between critical signals. These intervals can be made to be highly irregular or quite regular and therefore easily predictable. For example, a regular series of intervals might be one in which critical signals appear once every minute, whereas an irregular series might be one in which critical signal appearances average one per minute, but range from 45 seconds to 5 minutes. For the most part, the more regular the inter-signal intervals, the greater the number of signal detections and the greater the speed of signal detections (Adams and Boulter, 1964; Baker, 1963a; Lisper and Törnros, 1974; McCormack, 1967; Warm, Epps, and Ferguson, 1974). It is of interest to note, however, that this source of temporal uncertainty appears to be closely tied to the background event matrix in which the critical signals are embedded. Moore and Gross (1973) have reported that under a fast event rate (30 events/min), the effects of signal regularity were maximal during the initial 30 minutes of a watchkeeping session, but under a slow event rate (5 events/min), effects of critical signal regularity were not apparent until the final 30 minutes of the session. This result is shown in Figure 5.17.

Spatial uncertainty has been studied by varying the probability that signals will appear in different positions in the monitored display. In a representative study, Nicely and Miller (1957) asked subjects to detect signals in a simulated radar display in which most of the signals appeared in only one quadrant. They found that the probability of signal detections was greatest in the part of the display in which the likelihood of signal appearances was highest. Similar results have been reported in later studies by Kulp and Alluisi (1967) and Milošević (1974).

Knowledge of results   A final "psychophysical" factor to be considered here is the influence of feedback or knowledge of results. In many psychophysical tasks which are performed under alerted conditions, performance ef-

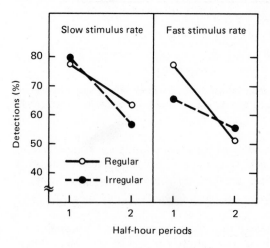

FIGURE 5.17 Percentage of correct detections as a function of time on watch for regularly and irregularly presented critical signals. Data for slow and fast background event rates are plotted separately in each panel. (From Moore and Gross, 1973)

ficiency can be substantially improved by giving the observers information as to how well they are doing (Gibson, 1969). Such improvement has also been demonstrated with respect to the maintenance of sustained attention. In his early work on the topic, Mackworth (1950) noted that provision of knowledge of results tended to increase the number of signals detected and to prevent the characteristic vigilance decrement. Several other experiments have also demonstrated that feedback enhances the frequency and the speed of signal detections in vigilance tasks (Adams and Humes, 1963; J. Mackworth, 1964; McCormack, 1967; Warm, Epps, and Ferguson, 1974; Warm, Hagner and Meyer, 1971; Warm, Riechmann, Grasha, and Seibel, 1973; Williges and North, 1972; Wiener, 1963, 1974).

While knowledge of results has been shown to be useful in maintaining sustained attention, the manner in which this is accomplished has given rise to an interesting debate. Specifically, is knowledge of results effective because it has cue properties which foster the subject's awareness of important task-relevant characteristics, or are the facilitative effects of feedback primarily motivational? When, as in most vigilance tasks, the required discriminations are simple, the latter alternative seems to be the most likely. The rationale for this statement stems from two rather surprising results.

The first of these relates to the use of false feedback—i.e., feedback which does not reflect the true nature of the subject's performance. Apparently, informing subjects that they missed a signal when in fact they did not, or giving them information about the speed of signal detections on a purely random basis, serves to improve overall performance efficiency (Loeb and Schmidt, 1963; J. Mackworth, 1964; Warm, Epps, and Ferguson, 1974). It seems unlikely that the observer can learn anything about crucial task characteristics under such conditions.

The second rather surprising result comes from a study by Warm, Kanfer, Kuwada, and Clark (1972), which compared the effects of accurate, experimenter-controlled feedback regarding response latencies with the effects of subject-controlled feedback taking the form of self-evaluations of the latency of their responses. The subjects in this study responded to the aperiodic disappearance of a visual signal during a one-hour session. Both feedback procedures enhanced performance compared with that of a control group receiving no evaluative information; in addition, groups of subjects operating under experimenter-controlled or subject-controlled feedback did not differ significantly from each other. These results occurred even though the subjects' self-provided information regarding detection latency was considerably less accurate than the veridical reports provided by the experimenter. Indeed, the accuracy of self-evaluations failed to exceed chance expectation! The outcome of this study is illustrated in Figure 5.18. Clearly, feedback is important, but since the feedback need not be accurate to be effective, it must play a motivational rather than an informational role.

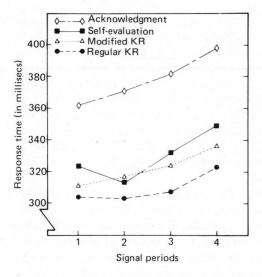

FIGURE 5.18 Response time to signal detections as a function of time on watch for different feedback conditions. Subjects in the Acknowledgment condition received no evaluative information. Those in the Modified KR and Regular KR conditions received feedback from the experimenter, while subjects in the Self-Evaluation condition provided the experimenter with evaluations of their own performance. (From Warm, Kanfer, Kuwada, and Clark, 1972)

Theories of Sustained Attention

Now that we have explored some of the psychophysical factors which influence sustained attention, we want to consider theoretical mechanisms which might be advanced to account for people's inability to detect signals over prolonged periods of time. Several different models have been proposed, and we do not have space in this brief section to describe them all. What we can do is to provide a sample of these models, with the aim of giving some indication of the scope of approaches adopted by psychologists in their attempt to solve the problem of vigilance. You will also see that these theoretical efforts have not yet been completely successful. More complete descriptions of the various theories of vigilance can be found in Broadbent (1971), Davies and Tune (1969), Loeb and Alluisi (1970, 1977), Stroh (1971), and Warm (1977).

Jerison and Pickett (1963) have suggested that the observer's behavior during a vigil can be analyzed into several task-relevant phases. Among these are: (1) storing background information, (2) observing and decision making, and (3) functioning of neural attention units. It is of interest to note that the various theories of sustained attention have approached the problem in terms of one or more of these phases.

Expectancy theory   It seems reasonable to argue that stored information about the signals to be detected and the conditions under which they appear can be of significant value in determining whether or not they will be detected. One model which emphasizes stored information is based on the *expectancy hypothesis* (Baker, 1963a; Deese, 1955). According to this position, observers in vigilance experiments act as temporal averaging instruments and form expectancies as to the approximate time course of critical signal appearances on the basis of samples of signal input. Readiness to detect a signal is assumed to be positively related to level of expectancy. In particular, the expectancy model maintains that the decrement function is brought about by a progressive deterioration in the observer's ability to predict accurately the time of appearance of critical signals. It also asserts that feedback improves the accuracy of the observer's expectations and helps reduce the typical performance decrement.

One prediction from this model is that vigilance efficiency would be enhanced by procedures that lower the observer's temporal uncertainty. As we have seen, this is indeed the case for increases in the density of critical signals and in their temporal regularity, both of which produce sizable improvements in signal detection. In addition, the expectancy hypothesis has received dramatic support from experiments which demonstrate that subjects who experience a high probability of signal appearances during a training phase of a vigilance session perform better in a subsequent test phase than those who initially experienced low signal probability during training (Colquhoun and Baddeley, 1964, 1967; McFarland and Halcomb, 1970).

In spite of these favorable findings, there are reasons to doubt that the expectancy hypothesis can provide a satisfactory account of all vigilance phenomena. For example, the complex relation between the effects of signal regularity and event rate described by Moore and Gross (1973) implies that more than just temporal averaging and extrapolation is going on; furthermore, as we noted earlier, the contribution of feedback seems not to be so much that of shoring up expectation as of enhancing motivation. Finally, the expectancy model leads to the prediction that the ability to estimate time accurately ought to be related to vigilance efficiency, but McGrath and O'Hanlon (1967) have reported that this is not the case.

For reasons such as these, Davies and Tune (1969) have suggested that while expectancy formation may play a part in sustained attention, its role is not one of overwhelming importance. They argue that observers will tend to utilize stored information about the temporal sequence of critical signals only if the task is difficult and other cues are not available. This line of reasoning is nicely supported in a recent study by Krulewitz and Warm (1977); their results revealed that the residual effects of experience with one level of critical signal probability during training on subsequent performance during testing may show up under the difficult conditions of a fast event rate but not under the easier conditions of a slow event rate.

The elicited observing rate hypothesis   An important feature of most vigilance tasks is the loose coupling between the observer and the stimulus display. Typically, subjects are free to make responses, involving movements of the head and eyes, that are incompatible with viewing the target to be detected, and evidence is accumulating to indicate that such responses do affect performance. For example, eyeblinks and the frequency and patterning of eye fixations have been shown to influence the detection of critical signals (Hatfield and Loeb, 1968; Mackworth, Kaplan, and Metlay, 1964; Schroeder and Holland, 1968). Recently, Warm, Wait, and Loeb (1976) have demonstrated that when positioning of the observer's head is restrained by a headrest, the detectability of low-amplitude critical signals is enhanced considerably and the degrading effects of high event rates are attenuated. These results might lead one to conclude that the relation between observing behavior and sustained attention is simple and straightforward. To the contrary, however, it is quite subtle, for failures to respond to critical signals occur even when the target is visually fixated (Baker, 1960; Mackworth, Kaplan, and Metlay, 1964), and the decrement function is not always related to systematic changes in overt observing activity (Baker, 1960; Broadbent, 1963b; Guralnick, 1973; Hockey, 1973). The complex relation between observing activity, decision processes, and vigilance is captured in a theory known as the *elicited observing rate hypothesis* (Jerison, 1970) as well as attempts to encompass vigilance within the framework of signal detection theory.

The elicited observing rate hypothesis assumes that during a vigilance task, the observer constantly makes sequential decisions about whether or not to emit observing responses toward the display to be monitored. Such responses are treated very broadly in the theory as "unitary attentive acts," which may involve some form of message selection by the central nervous system. The theory maintains that detection failures occur when the subject does not emit these observing responses or does so in an imperfect manner. It also proposes that the effort involved in observing has a definite energy cost and that decisions to observe or not to observe appropriately are based upon their utility, i.e., the overall cost of observing relative to the reward involved in detecting a critical signal. According to this view, the vigilance decrement is brought about by a deterioration in the frequency and quality of elicited observing activity over time. Such changes in observing behavior are due to progressive increments in the cost of observing produced by factors such as inhibition, fatigue, poor motivation, etc.

In addition to accounting for the decrement function, the elicited observing response model offers a means of explaining the effects of some of the major psychophysical factors which influence sustained attention. For example, it asserts that increasing event rate speeds up the pace with which the observer must look for target signals and thereby adds to the task demand. The resulting increase in the cost of observing leads to a decline in the subject's willingness to attend to the task, and, therefore, poorer detection efficiency. By the same token, factors which aid the observer in developing accurate expectations about the course of events in a vigilance task could be considered to enhance the utility of the observing responses. Hence, Jerison's model accounts for the beneficial effects involved in reducing the temporal and spatial uncertainty of signals; in that sense, it can encompass the expectancy hypothesis described previously.

Though the elicited observing rate hypothesis is an attractive one, definitive tests of its implications are difficult because the nature of the "internal" observing response is not specified precisely. We need a more detailed description of the character of the "unitary attentive acts" and of the factors which modify the utilities of observing. Jerison (1970) has clearly recognized these limitations and has suggested that the character of the observing response may be found in physiological indices such as variations in heart rate or evoked cortical potentials. These leads, however, remain to be developed more fully.

Signal detection theory   It is typical in vigilance experiments for the frequency of errors of commission, or false responses, to decline over time along with that of correct detections. This finding led Egan, Greenberg, and Schulman (1961) to propose that vigilance may be fruitfully analyzed from the viewpoint of signal detection theory. They suggested that the decrement function reflects a shift to a more conservative response criterion rather than a decline in alertness and perceptual sensitivity to signals. Their suggestion was supported in an experiment by Broadbent and Gregory (1963b), who found that the sensitivity index, d', remains stable during a vigil, whereas the response criterion, β, increases progressively over time. Several other investigators have described similar findings (Broadbent, 1971; Davies and Tune, 1969; Swets, 1973; Swets and Kristofferson, 1970).

This pattern of results is of potentially great importance. It implies that the locus of the decrement function can be pinpointed experimentally and that the decrement does not reflect a failure of perceptual sensitivity. Unfortunately, the picture is not really that clear. It has become evident that the vigilance decrement is not solely attributable to changes in decision processes and that in some types of vigilance tasks changes can be found in perceptual sensitivity to signals, as measured by a progressive decrement in the value of d'. Specifically, these are high-event-rate tasks requiring rapid comparison of successively presented stimuli for identity or nonidentity (Levine, Romashko, and Fleishman, 1973; Parasuraman and Davies, 1977; Swets, 1973). Why the decrement should reflect changes in alertness in this case but not in others remains unanswered.

Arousal theory   The theoretical positions just described are all essentially "cognitive." Attempts have also been made to seek a neurophysiological explanation of vigilance. One of these, known as the arousal or activation position, derives, in part, from Hebb's (1955) suggestion that sensory input has two general functions—to convey information about the environment and also to tone up the brain with a background of diffuse activity that aids in cortical transmission through increased alertness.

Hebb's suggestion stems from the fact that sensory signals from all parts of the body reach the cerebral cortex by two main routes. They travel directly along specified pathways to corresponding sensory cortical areas, and, in addition, they feed into a diverse neural network extending from the upper spinal cord to the thalamus known as the ascending reticular formation or the *reticular activating system* (RAS). A schematic diagram of the location of this system is presented in Figure 5.19. The RAS discharges a bombardment of impulses over a widespread area of the cerebral cortex to produce a general level of excitation and wakefulness. Deprived of the RAS, animals lapse into unconsciousness and coma (French, 1957; Malmo, 1959, 1975; Moruzzi and Magoun, 1949; Samuels, 1959). According to the arousal concept, a varied perceptual environment is necessary for optimal RAS functioning; when stimulus variability falls below a critical level, wakefulness is reduced. Thus, the activation hypothesis maintains that the monotonous aspects of sustained-attention tasks reduce the level of nonspecific activity necessary to maintain

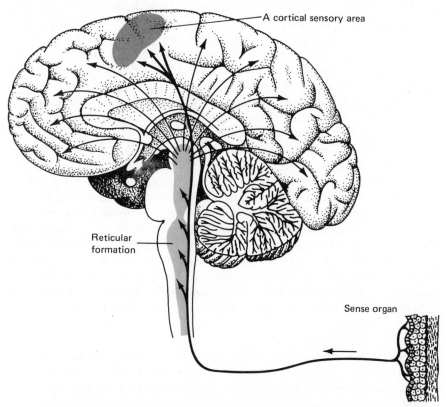

FIGURE 5.19 Schematic illustration of the reticular activating system (RAS). The reticular formation is the shaded area in this cross section of the brain. Impulses from a sense organ pass through the spinal cord to a sensory area in the cortex. These impulses also branch into the RAS, which provides the cortex with a diffuse bombardment of stimulation necessary for wakefulness. (From French, 1957)

continued alertness and thereby lead to a decline in the efficiency with which signals are detected.

A good deal of evidence is now available to link performance in vigilance tasks to neurophysiological indices of arousal. For example, decreases in the alpha activity of the electroencephalogram and in electrical skin conductance occur in sleep (Malmo, 1959). As illustrated in Figure 5.20, Davies and Krkovic (1965) have shown that a decrease in detection scores in a vigilance task is closely accompanied by decrements in these same indices of arousal.

Several other experiments have also shown that decrements in skin conductance parallel decrements in the frequency of signal detections (for example, Dardano, 1962; Milošević, 1975; Surwillo and Quilter, 1965) and that the deterioration of vigilance performance is accompanied by forms of electrocortical activity characteristic of lowered states of alertness (for example, Beatty, Greenberg, Deibler, and O'Hanlon, 1974; Gale, Haslum, and Lucas, 1972; Haider, Spong, and Lindsley, 1964; Parasuraman and Davies, 1975). Furthermore, the RAS is excited by the activity of biogenic stimulants such as epinephrine, and O'Hanlon (1965) has demonstrated that the epinephrine (adrenaline) level in the blood of observers is correlated with their detection performance in a vigilance task. This result is shown in Figure 5.21. Finally, the fact that vigilance performance can be improved by stimulant drugs and impaired by depressants fits nicely with an arousal position (Colquhoun and

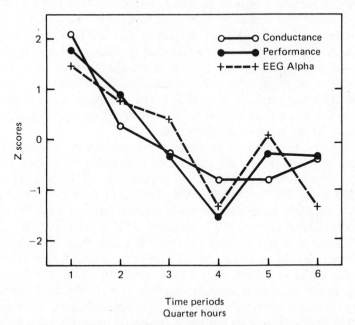

FIGURE 5.20 The relation between declining vigilance efficiency and physiological measures of alertness as indexed by skin conductance and EEG alpha activity. Data have been transformed to standard (Z) scores. (From Davies and Krkovic, 1965)

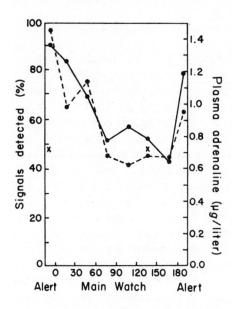

FIGURE 5.21 The percentage of signals detected (solid line) and plasma concentration of adrenaline (broken line) during alerted tests and time on watch (in minutes) during a vigilance session. (From O'Hanlon, 1965)

Edwards, 1975; Loeb, Hawkes, Evans, and Alluisi, 1965; J. Mackworth, 1965; Sharma and Moskowitz, 1974).

Although arousal seems to be clearly implicated as a factor in the vigilance decrement, the activation hypothesis is troubled by certain difficulties. The type and amount of external stimulation that will be related to measurable aspects of performance is not specified precisely, and the hypothesis is often ambiguous regarding the direction of change in performance to be expected with a given experimental manipulation (Broadbent, 1963a; Frankmann and Adams, 1962; Jerison, 1967). The validity of these points is evidenced by the fact that at a gross behavioral level tests of the arousal notion have generally produced equivocal results.

As might be expected on the basis of the activation position, added sensory input in the form of mild exercise or extraneous stimulation has been found to enhance vigilance efficiency (Davenport, 1974; Kirk and Hecht, 1963; McGrath, 1963; Randel, 1968; Tolin and Fisher, 1974; Zuercher, 1965). On the other hand, extraneous stimulation has also been found to degrade performance (Jones, 1971; McGrath, 1963). Moreover, the vigilance decrement has been noted under conditions in which there was a rich source of stimulation (Alluisi and Hall, 1963), and at least in one case (Broadbent, 1963a) the vigilance decrement was more profound under extremely stimulating circumstances than under less stimulating conditions. Such inconsistencies might be dealt with by arguing that detection efficiency is adversely affected both by too little or by too much arousal — that is, the relation between arousal and detection efficiency take the form of an inverted U-shaped function. Unfortunately, the point at which some experimental manipulation will fall on the curve cannot be specified until the experiment has been completed. Therefore, the arousal concept is not amenable to rigorous experimental test.

Habituation theory A somewhat different approach to the neurophysiology of vigilance has been suggested by Jane Mackworth (1968, 1969). She has proposed a theory anchored in the concept of habituation, which we encountered earlier in this chapter in our discussion of the determinants of selective attention. Habituation is defined as a waning of neural responsiveness due to repeated stimulation (Groves and Thompson, 1970). An active process of inhibition, it is differentiated from adaptation or fatigue by the phenomenon of dishabituation or the sudden reappearance of responsiveness following qualitative, quantitative, or temporal changes in the pattern of stimulation (Sharpless and Jasper, 1956). Generally, the degree of neural habituation in a given situation is directly related to the frequency of stimulus presentation.

Mackworth contends that the repetitive stimulation of the continuous background events of the vigilance task serves to habituate cortical responses to incoming stimuli. Thus, with the development of habituation, the observer's ability to discriminate critical signals is degraded, attending to the task becomes increasingly more difficult, and the observer's performance suffers a decline over time. With respect to event rate, the model maintains that habituation accumulates more rapidly at fast than at slow rates, resulting in poorer performance at fast event rates.

The habituation model is the most recent addition to the cast of vigilance theories. As in the case of the arousal hypothesis, the degree to which predictions from the model can be verified empirically is also questionable. On the positive side of the ledger, Siddle (1972) has indicated that subjects who show fast habituation of the galvanic skin response display a greater vigilance decrement than slow habituators. On the negative side, Lisper and Törnros (1974) have pointed out that the usual finding of a greater decrement with irregular as compared to regularly presented critical signals is embarrassing to the habituation model, since Mackworth maintains that the accumulation of inhibition is more rapid with regular than with irregular signals.

In a recent study, Krulewitz, Warm, and Wohl (1975) attempted to test predictions from the habituation model. They attacked the problem by shifting background event rates both in a slow-to-fast and in a fast-to-slow direction during a vigilance session. According to the habituation model, any change in stimulus conditions produces dishabituation, which should result in improved performance. Shifts in event rate represent a rather drastic change in such conditions. Therefore, the habituation model leads to the expectation that changes in event rate should enhance performance regardless of the direction of change. The results are displayed in Figure 5.22. Contrary to expectation, observers shifted in the slow-to-fast direction eventually performed more poorly than nonshifted controls. Moreover, while the performance of subjects shifted in the fast-to-slow direction tended to exceed that of the nonshifted controls, it did so only after the shifted group had experienced the new event rate for 20 minutes. This result does not coincide with the expected time-course of habituation and dishabituation, since habituated neural responses tend to dishabituate promptly after a change in stimulus conditions and then to rehabituate after repeated exposure to the habituating stimulus (Thompson and Spencer, 1966).

The Current Status of Vigilance Theories

It should be evident at this point that our understanding of the mechanisms involved in sustained attention is far from complete. A variety of theoretical models have been proposed to account for vigilance effects. Each has focused upon a somewhat different aspect of the problem, yet many can account for similar data. Further, it is difficult to establish a definitive test of one against the other, and they all invite important criticism.

Pribram (1969) has pointed out that the progress of research in a given

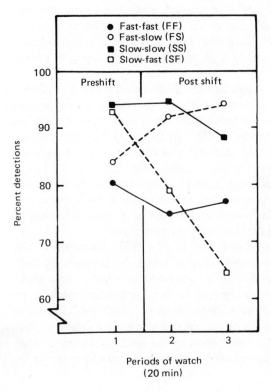

FIGURE 5.22 The effects of shifts in background event rate during a vigilance task on the detectability of critical signals. Data for preshift and postshift phases are plotted separately in each panel. The shift groups are indicated by open figures and dashed lines; nonshift control groups by filled figures and solid lines. (After Krulewitz, Warm, and Wohl, 1975)

area usually evolves through a series of stages: first, enthusiastic discovery; second, the accumulation of detailed information; third, a stage of deeper understanding and exploration; and fourth, an attempt at synthesis. It seems to us that research on sustained attention, and selective attention as well, is in the third stage. The task of theoretical synthesis remains to be accomplished.

6

The Stability
of
Perceptual Experience

PERCEPTUAL CONSTANCY

Stability and Change

In the first chapter of this book, we introduced the concepts of distal and proximal stimuli. You might recall that "distal" refers to an external object and the physical energy emanating from it, while "proximal" refers to this physical energy as it impinges on a sensory receptor. We pointed out that a key problem of perception is to understand how experience can be so nearly veridical given the considerable differences between the proximal and distal stimuli. As we noted, such differences lie along dimensions of size, spatial orientation, and form of energy. Now, we want to point out another dimension of difference which complicates the matter still further. The proximal stimulus is subject to substantial, continual change in our normal commerce with the environment. For example, the intensity of illumination received from a white tablecloth is diminished greatly when the tablecloth is seen in shadow relative to bright light; the retinal image of an automobile shrinks as the vehicle recedes from view; the retinal image of a dinner plate undergoes considerable alterations in shape and size as the perceiver moves in relation to it. Such gross variations in proximal stimulation might be expected to produce a kaleidoscopic perceptual world in which objects seem to change in brightness from moment to moment and appear to swell, shrink and warp with every movement. Yet, as you well know, this is normally not the case. Instead, our perceptual world remains remarkably stable in spite of the considerable insta- bility of proximal stimulation.

Such close matches between the object as it is perceived and the object as it "physically" is are called *perceptual constancies*. This ability to extract the inherent qualities of objects from continually changing proximal stimu- lation is one of the most impressive achievements of perception and one which has obvious significance for the biological survival of the perceiver. As Feldman and Weld (1939) have noted, it is based to a considerable extent upon the perceiver's ability to take into account the *circumstances* of stimu- lation and compensate accordingly. In this sense, the phenomenon of per- ceptual constancy, perhaps more than any other topic that we will consider, reflects the fact that perception does not depend only on isolated, local char- acteristics of stimulation. It illustrates, in very dramatic fashion, the point that perception is an active process of reconstruction and interpretation of stimulus information and is critically dependent on the total context in which particular stimuli are presented. In what follows, we will examine the phenomenon of perceptual constancy with regard to the dimensions of brightness and size.

LIGHTNESS CONSTANCY

The Perception of Brightness

A complex process   The amount of light reaching the eye may vary greatly from moment to moment. We easily become aware of general changes in overall illumination which occur when the sun ducks behind a cloud or when we move from a sunlit garden into a dimly illuminated room. Our ability to react differentially to the intensity or amount of light reaching the eye is a fundamental achievement of visual perception—one which ap- pears to be self-evident and immediate but, in reality, is accomplished in a complex manner.

We have considered some of this complexity in our earlier discussions of absolute and difference thresholds and in the material that we presented on psychophysical measurement. We showed, for example, that increments in perceived intensity do not grow as a simple linear function of stimulus in- tensity, as might be the case if we measured light intensity with a photometer. The subtlety of our reactions to changes in illumination is also revealed in the following demonstration described by Hurvich and Jameson (1966). Place a gray filter or sunglass in front of one of your eyes and look binocularly at this page. Now, cover the eye which has the filter in front of it and the page will appear to lighten. If, at this point, you uncover the eye with the filter, the page will appear to darken. Although the total amount of light that you re- ceived increased when the filtered eye was reopened, the added light resulted in a darkening rather than a lightening of the visual field! This effect, known as *Fechner's Paradox,* suggests that binocular impressions of brightness are keyed not to the total amount of excitation from the two eyes, but to some sort of averaging process.

Still another aspect of the subtle nature of our response to general changes in illumination can be appreciated when we consider the fact that our visual world is made up of an array of objects and surfaces varying in brightness and that the brightness of such objects tends to remain the same under very different conditions of illumination. This aspect of visual experience has been vividly described by Feldman and Weld:

In moonlight as well as in sunlight a white wall looks whitish; that is to say, the object appears the same under different illuminations. This fact becomes puzzling as soon as we realize that the amounts of light reflected into the eye differ enormously. How great this difference may be is brought home to us by the estimate that sunlight is 800,000 times as strong as full moonlight. If, instead of being more or less constant, the brightness of objects varied directly with the amount of light they reflect, we should find life very confusing. The white wall, for example, in moonlight would look black. Up to noon, when sunlight is most intense, all objects would grow whiter; and from noon on, they would gradually turn blacker. Similarly, the paper of this book would look white near the window but dark gray at the other end of the room. (Feldman and Weld, 1939, 425–426.)

Brightness and lightness   Thus, as we have already noted, the apparent brightness of objects is not entirely dependent upon the amount of light received from them. The tendency to maintain a constant apparent brightness under different amounts of illumination has traditionally been termed *brightness constancy.* Actually, this is a rather unfortunate term for it implies that the appearance of brightness may be more independent of the amount of light reaching the eye than is really the case. It is true that a piece of paper looks white and a lump of coal looks black in both direct sunlight and shadow. However, as Rock (1975) has pointed out, the paper in sunlight appears brighter but not *whiter* than it does in shadow, whereas the coal appears brighter but not *lighter.* For this reason, some investigators prefer the term "lightness" or "whiteness" constancy instead of the more traditional "brightness" constancy. This is an important point because the use of conflicting terminology has resulted in misunderstandings in the literature on the topic (Beck, 1974). In our discussion, we will adopt the current trend and use the term "lightness constancy" consistently from here onward.

Sources of illumination   Lightness constancy represents the maintenance of perceptual stability in the face of stimulus variability. Clearly, however, the effect must be related to *some* invariant physical property of the distal stimulus. To best convey what this property is we need first to consider the manner in which light reaches our eyes from surfaces in the environment.

Some objects, such as the sun, candles, electric lamps, cathode-ray tubes, and fireflies, emit radiant energy within the visible spectrum; they are called *luminous* objects. The great majority of objects, however, have no light-emitting capability, and are visible only because they reflect light which they receive from luminous sources. Consider Figure 6.1. The cat and the bedspread receive light from a lamp and transmit some of this light to the eye of an observer. In this way, they become visible. The incident light falling on objects such as the cat and the spread is called the *illuminance* and is specified in units known as *footcandles*. The flux of light proceeding to the eye of the observer from a reflecting surface is the *luminance* of the surface. This measure depends not only upon the amount of incident light but also upon the amount of the incident light that is reflected by the surface. If reflectance is defined as the ratio of reflected light to incident light, the luminance of a surface, often specified in units called *footlamberts,* is given by a simple equation, $L = IR$, where L refers to luminance, I to illuminance, and R to reflectance.

The critical fact for an understanding of lightness constancy is that the proportion of light reflected from a given surface remains constant under different levels of illumination. Thus, a good white reflects about 80 percent of the incident light and a good black about 3 percent. This holds true for objects viewed in brilliant sunlight or in the dim shadows of twilight. The constant index of reflection of a surface is known as its *albedo,* and it is this property of objects to which we may be responsive in maintaining lightness constancy. How this is accomplished is not completely understood as yet, even though the problem is an old one in research on perception. Several explanations have been offered, but before considering some of these, we need to describe how lightness constancy is measured in the laboratory.

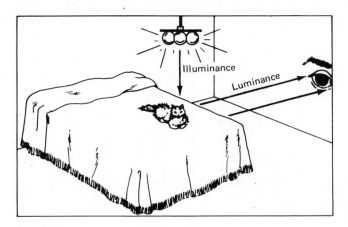

FIGURE 6.1   Illustration of the concepts of illuminance, the incident light falling on objects, and luminance, the light reflected from objects.

The Measurement of Lightness Constancy

The standard arrangement   Lightness constancy is often studied with the arrangement shown in Figure 6.2 and a device known as a color wheel. This consists of a disk composed of black and white sectors. The proportions of these sectors can be varied from zero to 360° by the experimenter or by the observer. When rotated at high speed, the surface of the disk takes on a uniform gray appearance, the shade of gray depending upon the relative amounts of black and white in the mixture. As shown in the figure, an observer views two color wheels, one standing in dim illumination and the other under a higher level of illumination. Typically, the disk in dim illumination is set at a given black-white mixture and designated as the standard. The observer's task is to vary the blend of black and white in the disk under high illumination so as to make its surface match the apparent gray of the standard.

If, in this situation, the match were made on the basis of the absolute amount of light reflected from each disk, the observer would adjust the amount of black in the comparison color wheel to be greater than that of the standard, thus compensating for the greater amount of light falling on the comparison. On the other hand, an observer exhibiting perfect lightness constancy would set the black-white mixture of the comparison stimulus to be identical with that of the standard. It is usually the case that the observer sets the proportion of black and white in the comparison stimulus to be similar but not identical to that of the standard. That is, lightness constancy is obtained, but it is less than perfect. In effect, it is a compromise between an albedo match and a match based upon the total amount of light coming from the object (stimulus match). Thouless (1931) has characterized such a result as "phenomenal regression to the real object." The technique that we have just described is only one of several procedures which have been used to study lightness constancy in the laboratory. Descriptions of these other proce-

FIGURE 6.2   Schematic illustration of the standard arrangement for studying lightness constancy.

dures can be found in Beck (1969), Cornsweet (1970), Forgus and Melamed (1976), Rock (1975), and Woodworth and Schlosberg (1954).

The Brunswik Ratio   Brunswik (1929) has provided a convenient way to specify the amount of constancy in studies of perceived lightness as well as in experiments on other forms of perceptual constancy. The general formula for the amount of constancy, known as the *Brunswik Ratio* is:

$$\text{Brunswik ratio} = \frac{(P-R)}{(C-R)}$$

where P is the judged property of an object, C refers to the objective or physical property of the object, and R is its sensory or proximal representation. The Brunswik Ratio expresses the difference between the judgment of a stimulus and its proximal representation relative to the difference between the objective nature of a stimulus and its proximal representation. If the ratio equals unity, constancy is perfect; a value of zero implies that the observer has made a stimulus match and constancy is nil. Values greater and less than unity indicate over and under constancy, respectively.

To illustrate the use of this measure, consider once again the example in Figure 6.2. Assume that the reflectance of the standard disk is set at 48 percent, and that the standard is placed under an illumination of 20 footcandles. The comparison disk is illuminated at a value of 80 footcandles, or four times the illumination of the standard. An observer who matched the apparent lightness of the disks on the basis of the absolute amount of light reflected by each stimulus would have to adjust the reflectance of the comparison disk to one-fourth that of the standard, or 12 percent (i.e., one-fourth of 48 percent). If lightness constancy were perfect, the observer would, of course, set the reflectance of the comparison disk at 48 percent. Suppose that the observer judges the two stimuli to be equal in lightness when the comparison disk has a reflectance of 45 percent. The Brunswik Ratio for this judgment would be $\frac{(45-12)}{(48-12)}$, or .92.[1] It is worth noting that while this ratio is the most commonly used index of constancy, other measures are available. A good description of these alternative measures has been provided by Hurvich and Jameson (1966).

[1] In using the Brunswik Ratio to index the amount of lightness constancy, students are often puzzled about the way in which the values for stimulus reflectance are obtained. When color wheels are used, reflectance is expressed as the angular degrees of white in the disk. Thus, in the illustrative example given above, if the reflectance of the standard were set at 48 percent, the white sector would have to be 48 percent of 360° or 172.8°. Similarly, the setting for a stimulus match of 12 percent reflectance would be 43.2° white and that for an equality judgment (45 percent reflectance) would be 162° white. Using these values we can compute the Brunswik Ratio as (162° − 43.2°/172.8° − 43.2°·, or .92, a value identical to that given above.

Film color and surface color   In studying lightness constancy, it is important to understand the distinction between film color and surface color. This distinction was introduced by Katz (1935), who pointed out that under some circumstances light appears to come from an undefined luminous expanse in the visual field, an expanse which does not seem to have material substance or a definite spatial location. Katz gave the name *film color* (or *aperture color*) to this type of experience. By contrast, the term *surface color* refers to the case in which the light we receive appears to be an integral part of the illuminated surface of some object. To make this distinction a bit clearer, consider the appearance of a white wall viewed from a few feet away. Ordinarily, it looks as though it were a continuous surface standing in a specific illumination. Its lightness seems to be an integral part of this surface. Now, if we view the wall through a pinhole in a dark card, the surface characteristic will no longer be evident. Instead, the patch of wall that we see will seem to be an incorporeal, self-luminous expanse. It has been well established that lightness constancy holds only for surface colors.

The breakdown of lightness constancy when the light that we receive takes on the characteristics of film color can easily be demonstrated in the laboratory. To do this, we can ask an observer to view two samples of gray through a *reduction screen* — an opaque screen with small apertures which permit the observer to see only the gray samples and not the area of the visual field which surrounds them. Figure 6.3 illustrates the use of a reduction screen in the standard arrangement for studying lightness constancy described earlier.

Under these conditions, the light reflected from the two samples assumes

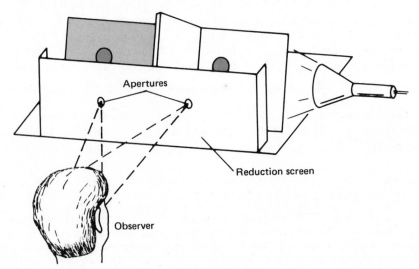

FIGURE 6.3   Schematic illustration of the use of a reduction screen in studying lightness constancy.

the characteristics of film color, and the observer departs from lightness constancy by making matches based upon the absolute amount of light in the two retinal images.

The Classical Theory of Lightness Constancy

Unconscious inference   One of the oldest accounts of lightness constancy was formulated by the German scientist Hermann von Helmholtz (1866), whose work has been influential in the fields of physics, physiology, and sensory mechanisms as well as in perception. Helmholtz was impressed by the contribution that past experience made to perception, and he developed a general theory of perception known as *Unbewuster Schluss* or "unconscious inference." Helmholtz argued that in perceiving, people make instantaneous, unconscious inferences about the nature of the distal stimulus that must be present in a given situation in order to produce the current pattern of proximal stimulation. These inferences, moreover, are presumably based upon prior experiences in similar situations.

As applied to the problem of lightness constancy, the notion of unconscious inference implies that we come to learn that an object's reflectance is relatively stable under different conditions of illumination; that we determine the amount of illuminance falling on the object at a given time; and that the illuminance is taken into account in assessing the amount of light reflected by the object. If, as we indicated before, luminance *(L)* is equal to illuminance *(I)* times reflectance *(R)*, Helmholtz suggested that observers can derive R from L by taking I into account, and that they implicitly solve the equation $R = L/I$. Thus, in terms of this position, a weakly illuminated piece of white paper is seen as white and a strongly illuminated piece of black paper is seen as black because the white paper is judged to reflect a greater proportion of the incident light falling upon it than does the black paper.

If you think carefully about Helmholtz's proposal, you might conclude initially that it is illogical if not impossible. In viewing a visual field, the only light entering the eye from an object is that reflected from the object itself. Incident illumination falling on the object is not registered directly. How, then, is it possible for us to become aware of illuminance and thus take it into account in our lightness judgments? One answer to this question is that we become aware of the general level of illumination indirectly on the basis of cues in the field of view.

Illumination cues   In natural scenes, there are numerous possible cues to the strength of illumination. One obvious possibility is through direct sight of the source of light. In addition, since more than one object is usually visible, impression of the amount of light falling on a particular object might be gained from the features of other objects such as highlights, flecks of sunlight under trees, or dust particles floating in a bright region of the field (Rock, 1975; Woodworth and Schlosberg, 1954). Another important cue to differences in illumination can come from realizing that an object stands in shadow; the existence of shadow itself is cued by the presence of a *penumbra,* the half-shadow or gradual transition from light to dark along the edges of a shadowed region. Realizing that an object is three-dimensional provides still another indication of shading and differential illumination. In this case, an observer might "decide" that the darker side of a gray box, for example, is so because it lies in shadow rather than because it is inherently a darker shade of gray (Hochberg, 1971a).

If we accept the possibility that illuminance can be registered indirectly, then Helmholtz's position can deal effectively with a number of interesting findings regarding lightness constancy. For one thing, it provides an explanation of the breakdown of constancy when stimuli are viewed through a reduction screen: under such conditions, cues to differential levels of illuminance are precluded. In a similar way, it also accounts for the results of the *ringed-shadow experiment* described by Hering (1907) many years ago. In this experiment, a shadow was cast on a white surface and the surface took on the appearance of a shaded white. When the penumbra of the shadow was outlined with a dark line, however, the surface no longer appeared shadowed, and the shaded portion appeared as a gray spot on the white surface. This effect is illustrated in Figure 6.4.

Helmholtz's explanation of lightness constancy also fits generally with the results of several other experiments which indicate that cues to illumination affect the perceived lightness of a surface. The best-known and most dramatic of these was provided by Gelb (1929). As shown in Figure 6.5, Gelb arranged things so that a wall and several objects stood in dim illumination pro-

FIGURE 6.4 Illustration of the ringed-shadow experiment. The ball on the left is shaded so that there is a gradual transition from light to dark. This transition zone, or penumbra, serves as a cue that the ball is illuminated in such a way as to be partially located in shadow. When the penumbra is removed by a dark line in the ball on the right, the appearance of a shadow is lost, and the ball no longer gives the impression of a surface with uniform brightness.

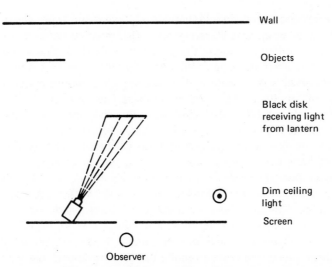

FIGURE 6.5   Gelb's concealed-illumination experiment. The light source at the left is not visible to the observer, and its illumination is limited to the black disk. The wall and other objects in the room are dimly illuminated by a ceiling lamp. (From Woodworth and Schlosberg, 1954)

vided by a ceiling lamp. A rotating black velvet disk in the foreground was illuminated by a concealed lantern in such a way that light from the lantern fell only on the disk, and no penumbra was visible either on the disk or on the background. Under these conditions, there was a complete breakdown of lightness constancy; the disk appeared white and standing in dim illumination rather than black and standing in high illumination. When, however, a piece of white paper was placed in front of the disk, constancy was restored. The paper now looked white and the disk black, most likely because the paper provided a clue to the added illumination falling on the disk. An important finding of the Gelb experiment was that the disk reverted to its former appearance when the white paper was removed. This aspect of Gelb's findings is not completely consistent with the notion that we come to learn that an object's reflectance is stable in different illuminations and then use this knowledge in taking illumination into account. Nevertheless, as Woodworth and Schlosberg (1954) have pointed out, it is possible that in this case observers need a concrete visible indicator of the additional illumination in order properly to correct their lightness judgments.

Using a similar procedure, Henneman (1935) substituted a white disk for a black one, and the white disk then appeared to be luminous. Such a result is also consistent with the notion that lightness constancy is coupled with judgments of illumination, since, under these conditions, the white disk would reflect more light than could be accounted for by the dim ceiling light which was the only visible source of illumination. In an analogous experiment, Kardos

(1934) determined what would happen if a shadow, produced by a concealed shadow caster, was placed upon a disk of white paper in such a way that the observer had no clue to the presence of shading. The white disk was seen as unshadowed and black. When the shadow caster was moved so as to reveal the presence of a shadow, the disk appeared as white with a shadow over it. In still another experiment along these lines, MacLeod (1932) placed a light-gray disk in a concealed shadow so that the disk looked black. When a visible shadow was cast on the background behind the disk so that the disk appeared to be in shadow, the disk took on a lighter-gray appearance.

The Helmholtzian point of view is also generally consistent with studies which have reported changes in the apparent lightness of an object when observers incorrectly infer the orientation of the object with respect to the direction of incident light and therefore inappropriately conclude that the target is not in shadow. For example, Hochberg and Beck (1954), using the arrangement shown in Figure 6.6, have reported that a fixed target under constant illumination is judged darker when made to appear perpendicular to the direction of illumination, and therefore not in shadow, than when it is perceived correctly to be parallel to the direction of illumination and therefore as standing in shadow.

Although the experiments just described coincide with expectations derived from the notion that lightness constancy depends upon unconscious illumination judgments, they cannot be considered as providing conclusive evidence in support of this position. In a thoughtful and extensive discussion of the problem, Hochberg (1971a) has pointed out that the most such experiments can do is show that stimulus conditions which accompany changes in illumination also result in changes in perceived lightness. They do not demonstrate unequivocally that the perception of lightness is based upon the observer's taking information about illumination into account. According to Hochberg, more conclusive evidence would come from investigations into the accuracy with which observers can make judgments of illumination under different conditions. Unfortunately, the evidence on this point does not favor the notion that lightness constancy depends upon unconscious judgments of illumination.

First of all, the available evidence suggests that good illumination judgments are difficult to come by and that they are not obtained consistently in different investigations (Beck, 1974; Katz, 1935). Second, a series of careful studies by Beck (1959, 1961) has shown that lightness constancy can be obtained from people who make extremely inaccurate judgments of incident illumination. These experiments investigated the judgment of the lightness and illumination of surface in a dark room. Four types of surfaces were used: speckled and striped surfaces, a stippled surface produced from shading materials, and a flannel cloth. Judgments of illuminance and lightness constancy were good for the speckled and striped surfaces. For the flannel surface, inaccurate judgments of illumination were accompanied by a complete absence

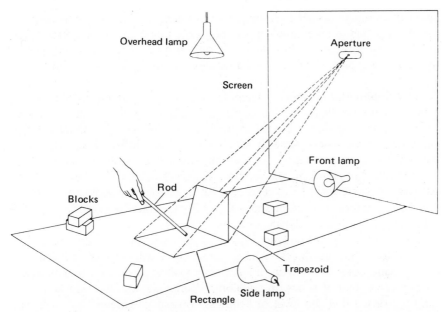

FIGURE 6.6 Illustration of the apparatus used by Hochberg and Beck (1954) to show that the perceived lightness of a surface is affected by the apparent spatial position of the surface. When viewed with one eye through the small aperture in the screen, the upright trapezoid is seen as a rectangle lying flat on the table. If viewed binocularly, through a larger opening in the screen, the trapezoid is correctly perceived as standing upright on the table. When the scene is illuminated from overhead, and the trapezoid appears upright and parallel to the direction of illumination, its surface appears to be shadowed. When seen as a flat rectangle at right angles to the perceived direction of illumination, the target is no longer seen as shadowed, but appears to have a darker surface color. (From Beck, 1975)

of constancy. However, for the stippled surface, inaccurate judgments of illuminance were accompanied by good lightness constancy. Beck (1965) has also provided further evidence against the Helmholtzian view in experiments on the role of the apparent spatial position of objects and shadow on perceived lightness. His studies show that changes in apparent illumination may not constitute a sufficient condition for changes in perceived lightness; hence, judgments of lightness and illumination may not be as closely coupled as Helmholtz believed.

The notion that lightness constancy depends upon a correction for illumination is really a difficult idea to pin down experimentally. While the discrepancies between judgments of illumination and lightness are inconsistent with this notion, they do not necessarily rule it out. As both Beck (1969) and Hochberg (1971a) have suggested, it could be argued that *conscious* judgments of illumination are not at all the same as the unconscious taking account of illumination that Helmholtz had in mind. In Hochberg's words, "the subject has had a lifetime of experience with trying to make correct judgments about reflectance, but he has rarely, if ever, had to concern himself with making explicit responses to illumination as such" (1971a, p. 406).

Developmental evidence   There is, however, still another source of evidence which casts doubt on the complete adequacy of the position taken by Helmholtz. This evidence comes from data on children and animals below man in the phylogenetic scale. If, as Helmholtz has suggested, lightness constancy is based, in part, upon our learning about the stability of object reflectance in different illumination, we might expect this form of constancy to be less well developed in young children than in older individuals and also less evident in creatures that do not have the ability to make the exquisite cognitive judgments that are characteristic of human beings.

Hochberg's (1971a) review of the available data indicates that age differences in the expected direction have been found with human subjects, but that in many cases the degree of lightness constancy exhibited by children is comparable to that of adults. In addition, experiments with fish, chickens, and monkeys reveal that the level of lightness constancy achieved by these animals closely approximates that of human observers (Burkamp, 1923; Köhler, 1917; Locke, 1935). Moreover, in the case of chickens, lightness constancy seems to be present soon after hatching, when the birds have had little, if any, opportunity for learning. Chickens have been shown to prefer pecking at light rather than dark grain. Gogel and Hess (1951) took advantage of this characteristic in an experiment in which chicks were raised in complete darkness until the time of testing. When given the opportunity to peck at light grain under dim illumination or dark grain under high illumination, the birds showed the usual light-grain preference. These results imply that a complex intellectual judgment may not be necessary in the mediation of lightness constancy and that, at least in one case, this perceptual achievement may be innate. Therefore, while Helmholtz's notion of unconscious inference may have some validity in explaining lightness constancy, it does not provide a complete account of the phenomenon, and therefore we are compelled to seek other more comprehensive explanations.

Contrast Theory of Lightness Constancy

Luminance relations   The major alternative to a "cognitive" explanation of lightness constancy relies entirely on reference to luminance relationships within the visual field. This approach ties lightness constancy to the familiar phenomenon of brightness contrast (see Figure 1.4 and accompanying text). Recall that brightness contrast refers to the observation that the apparent brightness of a target stimulus varies inversely with the brightness of the background on which it appears. Roughly stated, a contrast explanation of lightness constancy maintains that the perceived lightness of a test stimulus is strongly influenced by the apparent lightness of regions in the surrounding field. Thus, from this viewpoint, the apparent lightness of a test surface is not determined solely by the absolute level of its illumination or reflectance, but rather depends on the relation between its luminance and the luminance of surrounding surfaces (Freeman, 1967).

A classic experiment by Hess and Pretori (1894), using the apparatus shown in Figure 6.7, provided a clue to the way in which lightness constancy might be related to brightness contrast. In this study, test and comparison patches were entered upon surrounding fields. The luminance of the comparison patch was varied so that it did not match that of the test patch. The subject's task was to equate the perceived lightness of the comparison patch to that of the test patch by adjusting the luminance of the *field surrounding the comparison patch.* Within certain limits, Hess and Pretori found that a lightness match was made when the ratio of the luminance of the comparison patch to its surround equaled the ratio of the luminance of the test patch to its surround. Such an equation of apparent lightness occurred even though the absolute luminance values of the stimuli were not equal. Thus, as long as the luminance *ratios* were fixed, the apparent lightness of the comparison and test patches remained equal.

Several years later, Hans Wallach (1948, 1963) carried this line of investigation a step further in a series of clever experiments. In one study, he projected a disk of light on a screen in a dark room and surrounded the disk with an annulus, or ring, of light. The perceived lightness of the disk under these conditions could be shifted from light to dark simply by changing the luminance of the surrounding annulus from low to high levels. In another study, Wallach arranged things as shown in Figure 6.8. Two disks of light, each surrounded by a ring, were projected on a screen in an otherwise dark room. This study revealed that if the disk and ring in each pattern were illuminated with intensities in the same ratio, both disks appeared to be equal in lightness even when the absolute intensity of one pattern was reduced to a third or a quarter of that of the other. For example, the disk and ring on the left may have had luminance values of 180 and 360 footlamberts respectively

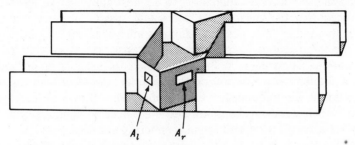

FIGURE 6.7 Schematic illustration of the apparatus used by Hess and Pretori (1894). The perceived lightness of the patches labeled A_l and A_r was manipulated by varying the luminance of their surrounds. (From Hurvich and Jameson, 1966)

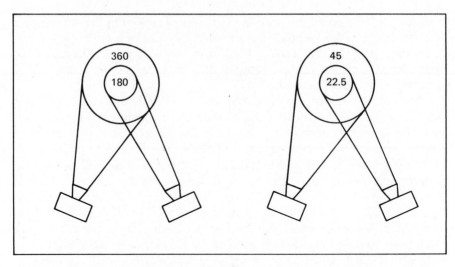

FIGURE 6.8   Illustration of Wallach's (1948) arrangement for demonstrating that lightness constancy is a function of luminous ratios. The intensities of the disks and rings are controlled by separate projectors. In the illustration, the values for the disk and ring on the left are 180 and 360 footlamberts, respectively, while those for the disk and ring on the left are 22.5 and 45 footlamberts, respectively. Thus, the ratio of light intensities between the disk and ring is the same (1:2) in both patterns, but the absolute intensities in the pattern on the left are greater than those on the right. In spite of variations in absolute intensity, the perceived lightness of the two disks is similar. (After Wallach, 1963)

(a luminance ratio of 1:2). Now, if the ring on the right had a luminance of 45 footlamberts, the disk in the right pattern appeared equal in lightness to that in the left when its luminance was approximately 22.5 footlamberts. Thus, in this case, a disk-ring luminance ratio of 1:2 resulted in an equality of perceived lightness between the disks even though the absolute luminance values of the two stimuli differed considerably.

These results led Wallach to propose a theory which is perhaps the most frequently cited of several variants of the contrast approach to lightness constancy. According to Wallach, the perceptual system abstracts information about relative rather than absolute stimulus intensities, and luminance ratios provide the stimulus invariants necessary for constancy. Thus, changes in the overall level of illumination in the visual field will produce a proportionate change in the luminance of any particular surface together with the regions that surround it. Consequently, the luminance ratio of one surface to others in the field of view remains constant, and the perceived lightness of an object seen against a background also remains generally constant.

Lateral inhibition   Now, one aim of contrast theories, such as Wallach's, is to get away from having to invoke cognitive processes in explaining lightness constancy. You might wonder, though, whether a system which "abstracts" information about relative stimulus intensities and which deals in luminance ratios must not, in effect, be calling on cognitive operations. It turns out, to the contrary, that a simple neural mechanism at the retinal level, called *lateral inhibition*, can accomplish that task. Thus, recent versions of the contrast theory have been supplemented by reference to a lateral inhibition mechanism (see Cornsweet, 1970).

A convincing demonstration of lateral inhibition at the retinal level was provided by Ratliff and Hartline (1959). Through the development of exceedingly precise techniques of dissection, they were able to record the electrical activity in a single neural cell in a living organism. These recordings were taken from the optic nerve of the horseshoe crab, *Limulus.* The *Limulus* eye, like that of many creatures of the insect world, such as the bee, for example, is structurally different from the mammalian eye. It is called a *compound eye* and, as illustrated in Figure 6.9, is composed of tightly packed segments called *ommatidia* (literally "little eyes"), each of which appears to function as a receptor unit. Nerve fibers arising from the ommatidia eventually form the optic nerve, which then proceeds to the optic lobe of the animal's brain.

The basic strategy adopted by Ratliff and Hartline was to record the electrical activity from a single fiber in the crab's optic nerve, and by probing the *Limulus* eye with a point of light, discover the ommatidium which activated that fiber. They found that as the point of light was moved so as to stimulate adjacent ommatidia, the electrical activity in the fiber under investigation was suppressed and that the amount of suppression, or lateral inhibition, was inversely related to the distance between the interacting ommatidia. An illustration of lateral inhibitory activity is presented in Figure 6.10.

This inhibitory effect of adjacent neurons upon one another, originally noted in the crab retina, has now been found in higher species, such as cats and monkeys, that have visual structures similar to the human eye. Furthermore, lateral inhibition is not limited to the visual modality; it occurs in other sensory systems as well (von Békésy, 1967). The discovery of lateral inhibition is one of the most important developments in the neurophysiology of perception. It indicates that stimulation can simultaneously elicit excitation and inhibition in the nervous system and that neural information processing is a joint product of excitation and inhibition.

The concept of lateral inhibition can be applied to a variety of perceptual phenomena. For example, it can be used to account for brightness contrast in general, and more specifically for the results of studies such as those reported by Leibowitz, Mote, and Thurlow (1953) and Stecher (1968), in which the perceived lightness of a target stimulus was found to be dependent upon the spatial proximity of other stimuli in the field of view.

To explain lightness constancy in terms of contrast and inhibition we might proceed as follows. Increments in the illumination falling both on the

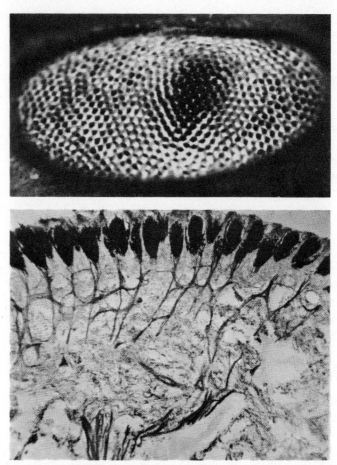

FIGURE 6.9 The lateral eye of the horseshoe crab, Limulus. Photograph at the top shows the corneal surface. The circular surfaces are the ommatidia. The lower section of the figure is a photomicrograph of a section of the compound eye of Limulus. The heavily pigmented parts of the ommatidia are at the top of the micrograph. Nerve fibers originating from each ommatidium join with those of other ommatidia to form the optic nerve. (From Ratliff, 1965)

target and its surround increase the excitation of neurons stimulated by the target, but this increase is compensated for by increments in lateral inhibition coming from the increased activity of neurons stimulated by the surround. Similarly, decrements in illumination falling on a target and its surround will decrease the excitation of neurons stimulated by the target but, at the same time, the decreased excitation is compensated by a lessening of inhibition produced by the activity of nervous elements stimulated by the surround. Therefore, in both cases, changes in excitation and inhibition essentially cancel each other, and the perceived lightness of the target remains relatively in-

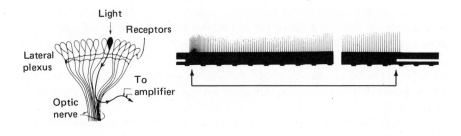

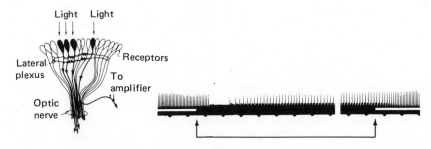

FIGURE 6.10 Oscillograms showing the rate of firing (vertical lines) in single optic-nerve fibers of Limulus. The top record illustrates the response of a single ommatidium to steady illumination. Duration of the visual signal is indicated by the brackets. Inhibition of the activity of a steadily illuminated ommatidium by the illumination of adjacent ommatidia is shown by a decrease in the rate of firing in the bottom record. Brackets indicate the illumination of neighboring ommatidia. Note the return to the earlier rate of activity when illumination of adjacent ommatidia is terminated. (After Ratliff, 1965)

variant with changes in illumination. In this way, lateral inhibition provides a vehicle by which luminance ratios may determine perceived lightness.

At this point in our discussion, it is of interest to consider an interpretation of lightness constancy offered by Cornsweet (1970), who makes the point that lightness constancy entails a *loss* rather than a gain of information by the visual system. What is lost is information about the absolute intensity of visual stimuli. But such a loss of information may nevertheless be adaptive. Recall from our earlier discussion of attention that the perceptual system is limited in the amount of information it can process. Hence, the rejection, at a peripheral level, of information which is less important for survival may preserve the ability of the system to process more vital information. And, as Cornsweet argues, it seems reasonable to assume that information about relative intensities is more crucial for human survival than is information concerning absolute intensity.

The adequacy of a contrast account An account of lightness constancy based on luminance relationships and inhibitory processes within the visual field would be attractive for several reasons. For example, if we make the assumption that contrast relations represent a lower order of perceptual processing than do "unconscious inferences," then a contrast approach might provide a convenient explanation for the lack of phylogenetic differentiation which seems to be characteristic of lightness constancy. In addition, a contrast approach can handle many of the same effects which fit within Helmholtz's point of view.

Consider the breakdown of constancy which occurs in experimental situations in which a reduction screen is used. As Rock (1975) has noted, the screen eliminates the surrounds which are usually visible around the standard and comparison stimuli and substitutes a different one—the screen itself. The intensity of light reflected by the screen is the same for both the standard and the comparison stimuli, and consequently both stimuli are now centered within a common surround. Therefore, a match based upon a luminance ratio would require the luminance of the two stimuli to be physically equal. In the typical lightness-constancy experiment, the illumination falling on the standard and the comparison surfaces is different, and the only way in which a luminance-ratio match could be achieved under these conditions with a reduction screen is to match on unequal reflectances. This, of course, is what happens when the reduction screen is employed.

A contrast approach can also be used in relation to the Gelb effect. The introduction of a piece of white paper in front of the black disk in the Gelb experiment may reveal the presence of a hidden light source, but it may also introduce an area of much higher luminance which could alter the luminance ratio of the disk to its surround. In other words, the white paper could be considered as providing a contrast-inducing field which could darken the appearance of the disk.

Support for this view comes from an experiment by Stewart (1959). Several studies of brightness contrast have shown that the influence of contrast-inducing fields on the apparent lightness of test areas depends upon the size of the inducing field and its position with respect to the test area (Freeman, 1967; Hurvich and Jameson, 1966). Stewart reported similar results in relation to the Gelb arrangement. Under these conditions, the black disk appeared darker when the white stimulus was made larger. For any-sized white stimulus, the darkening of the black disk was greatest when the white disk was placed closest to its center, and, in addition, the darkening effects produced by the white disk were not uniform over the surface of the black disk. Instead, they were greatest in the immediate vicinity of the white stimulus. Stewart's experiment indicates that the Gelb effect depends upon more than the observer's interpretation of the conditions of illumination. It also seems to be related to luminance interactions within the visual field. In a similar vein, it is possible to argue that results of several of the other studies reviewed earlier in this chapter on the effects of illumination cues in perceived lightness are based upon altered luminance relations within the field of view (Beck, 1971).

Like Helmholtz's notion of unconscious inference, a contrast interpretation may have some validity in explaining lightness constancy. However, it too does not provide a completely satisfactory account of this elusive
phenomenon. For one thing, the luminance ratio principle for lightness constancy seems to hold only for a limited range of ratio and luminance values.
These limitations were apparent in the early work of Hess and Pretori (1894)
and have been elegantly traced out in an experiment described by Jameson
and Hurvich (1961) and Hurvich and Jameson (1966). This study was designed to approximate a normal, everyday viewing situation wherein a variety
of surfaces of different reflectances (and thus different luminances) were subjected to gross changes in illumination. In order to do so, it made use of a
test pattern consisting of five areas of different luminances arrayed in the form
of a cross as shown in Figure 6.11. The area of greatest luminance at the
center of the cross is labeled 1, followed in decreasing order by those labeled
2 through 5, respectively. Such an arrangement permitted the investigators to
vary the overall illumination falling on the test pattern, while at the same time
keeping constant the luminance ratio of each test area to its neighbors and its
surround.

Since the luminance ratios remained constant, the ratio hypothesis would
predict that perceived lightness should remain invariant with changes in the
absolute illumination falling on the test field. Figure 6.12 shows what happened when the overall illumination increased in three steps over a range of
1.1 log units. It is evident in the figure that perceived lightness remained constant only in the case of area 4. For areas 1 through 3, apparent lightness increased with increments in illumination. In the case of test area 5, a paradoxical outcome was observed in which the perceived lightness of the test
patch decreased with increments in illumination. Several other investigations
have also revealed departures from constancy with changes in illumination

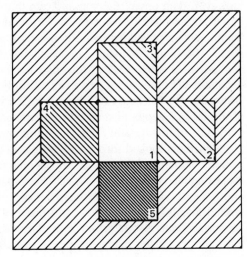

FIGURE 6.11 Outline of the test pattern used by Jameson and Hurvich
(1961). Striations of the pattern illustrate the luminance of different individual areas. The area labeled 1 had the
greatest luminance, followed by those
labeled 2 through 5. Numbers are for
reference only and did not appear on
the test pattern during the experiment.
(From Jameson and Hurvich, 1961)

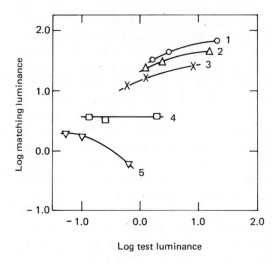

FIGURE 6.12 Perceived lightness of the five test areas in the experiment by Jameson and Hurvich (1961) at different levels of illumination. (From Hurvich and Jameson, 1966)

which depended upon the luminance ratios involved (Heinemann, 1955; Horeman, 1965; Leibowitz and Chinetti, 1957; Leibowitz, Myers, and Chinetti, 1955), as well as upon the relative areas of the target field and its surround (Hamison, 1974).

In addition to these results, other findings are available which also fail to support an interpretation of lightness constancy that is based strictly upon brightness contrast. As Rock (1975) has pointed out, if luminance ratios completely determine what is seen, then all that should matter is the contrast between the target surface and its surround. Thus, as long as the contrast ratio is unchanged, it should not make much difference if, for example, the target is perceived as lying at some distance in front of or behind the surround. However, data are available to indicate that the apparent spatial position of a target surface with respect to its surrounding field does exert a strong influence on perceived lightness. In a Gelb type of experiment, Gogel and Mershon (1969) and Mershon and Gogel (1970) have found that the effectiveness of a white disk in lowering the apparent lightness of a black disk decreases with increasing perceived depth between the two disks. A recent investigation by Gilchrist (1977) provides an even more striking demonstration of the role of depth-adjacency in determining perceived lightness. This study made use of the apparatus shown in the upper portion of Figure 6.13.

Observers looked through a pinhole in a screen through which they saw a dimly illuminated near wall. An opening in this wall permitted them also to see a brightly illuminated far wall. The target surface, a piece of white paper, and a piece of black paper were affixed to the near wall so that they extended into the opening. A second piece of white paper, identical to the target surface, was also attached to the far wall. Under some viewing conditions, the target could be made to appear to lie in the plane of the near wall. It

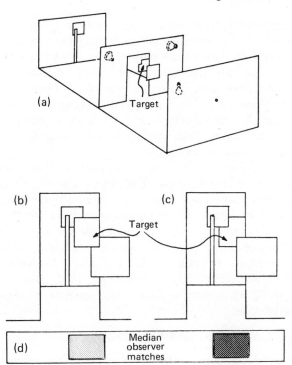

FIGURE 6.13   The arrangement used in Gilchrist's (1977) study of the role of depth-adjacency in perceived lightness. (a) presents a perspective view of the apparatus
showing hidden light bulbs. (b) and (c) indicate how the display appeared
when viewed through a pinhole. In (b), the target appears to be located in
the near plane, while in (c) it appears to be located in the far plane. (d)
shows the apparent lightness of the target when seen as lying in the near or
the far plane. (From Gilchrist, 1977)

could also be made to appear to be located on the distant wall by means of
two notches cut out of the corners of the target which coincided with the
edges of the near black paper and the far white paper. As illustrated in the
lower portion of the figure, altering the perceived location of the target in this
way greatly influenced its apparent lightness. The subjects judged the target
to be much lighter in the "near" than in the "far" condition. It is especially
noteworthy that this effect was obtained in the absence of any significant
change in the retinal pattern or the amount of illumination falling on the target or its background. These results are contrary to expectations to be derived from a contrast theory of lightness constancy, which emphasizes retinal
interactions and hence would predict no differences in the perceived lightness
of the target surface in Gilchrist's experiment. The results of this study, together with those reported by Gogel and Mershon, suggest that the perception of lightness involves more complex factors than just luminance ratios.

Another complicating factor for a simple contrast explanation of lightness constancy is revealed by experiments concerning the perception of transparency. Metelli (1974a, 1974b) has prepared demonstrations in which those portions of a gray stimulus that appear to be seen "through" a black figure are perceived as darker than those portions of an identical gray stimulus which appear to overlay the black figure. This experience is difficult to reconcile with an explanation based solely on contrast, since both gray stimuli are adjacent to black surrounds. Thus, organizational factors beyond black-white ratios contribute to perceived lightness.

The influence of organizational factors on perceived lightness is revealed in still another way in Figure 6.14. This figure illustrates a phenomenon known as *brightness assimilation.* Here, the gray stripes interspersed with black look darker than similar stripes interspersed with white. On the basis of brightness contrast, however, just the opposite effect would be expected. Finally, it should be noted that lightness judgments are highly susceptible to the influence of variations in instructional set and observational attitudes (Festinger, Coren, and Rivers, 1970; Henneman, 1935; Landauer and Rodger, 1964), a result which also suggests that higher-order cognitive factors may indeed be involved.

Contrast, Cognition, and Constancy

Given the variety of factors which influence lightness constancy, how are we to explain this phenomenon? Evidently, neither the cognitive approach adopted by Helmholtz nor a contrast approach can individually account for all of the data. Beck (1971) has suggested a possible integration of these two positions. According to Beck, the perception of lightness may involve two separate components: (1) neural signals resulting from the operation of sensory processes, such as contrast, which produce a pattern of excitation in accordance with peripheral luminance distributions; and (2) an integrative conceptual scheme into which these signals are incorporated. The sensory signals themselves do not specify a particular percept, but, instead, allow for alterna-

FIGURE 6.14   Brightness assimilation. The gray stripes interspersed with black appear darker than similar stripes interspersed with white.

tive percepts. Beck maintains that as a result of past experience, observers have stored multiple memories of the appearance of surfaces ranging from black to white under different illuminations. The perceived lightness of a given surface depends upon the matching of sensory signals to this stored information. You should keep in mind, of course, that Beck's "conceptual scheme" and other so-called cognitive factors are not incompatible with or antithetical to neurophysiology. Rather, the point is that a simple, retinal mechanism, such as lateral inhibition, does not seem adequate to account for all that is known about lightness constancy. Any complete neurophysiological explanation that is proposed must include more complex, central mechanisms to supplement what the simple retinal mechanisms are able to accomplish.

SIZE CONSTANCY

As an introduction to this next aspect of the general problem of perceptual constancy, try the following "experiment." Stand an object, such as a book, vertically on your desk and observe its size. Now, walk slowly away from the desk and continue to note the size of the object. You will probably find that as you move farther and farther away, the size of the object remains relatively unchanged; it does not appear to shrink with increasing distance. "So what?" you might say. "There is nothing remarkable about that!" But such a result is indeed a truly remarkable feature of your perceptual system, for as you move farther and farther away from the object, the image that it produces on your retina, its proximal or retinal image, will decrease markedly. The tendency for the perceived size of objects to remain relatively unchanged as their distance from you, and hence their proximal size, changes is known as *size constancy*.

Size constancy, as you well know if you have ever flown in an airplane, is not perfect. With great distances, constancy does break down, and perceived size does approach proximal rather than distal size. Thus, from a plane people do look like "ants" and houses resemble those on a Monopoly board. Furthermore, even at less extreme distances, perfect size constancy does not necessarily occur. There is usually a tendency for the object, when distant, to look somewhat smaller than when near. But this decrease in perceived size is trivial compared to what is happening to the size of the proximal image. In order to help you to appreciate this more fully, we need to describe how the proximal size of a stimulus is measured.

The Measurement of Proximal Size

Visual angle   The proximal size of a visual stimulus is conveniently measured, with the help of trigonometry, in terms of the angular size of the object at the observer's retina. This measure is commonly known as the *visual angle*. Figure 6.15 provides a schematic illustration of the visual angles, la-

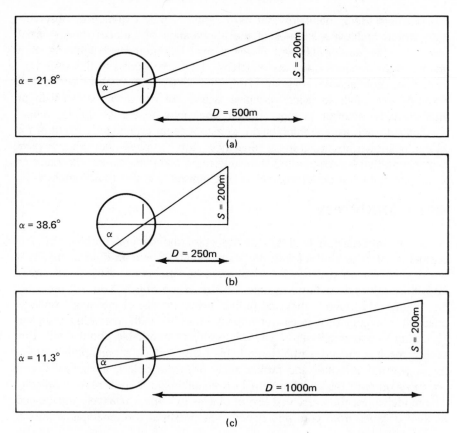

FIGURE 6.15   The visual angle (α) subtended on the retina by an object of constant size at different distances from an observer. In the illustration, the object is 200 meters high and is viewed from distances of 500 meters (a), 250 meters (b), and 1,000 meters (c).

beled α, subtended by an object of constant size *(S)* located at specified distances *(D)* from an observer.

Starting with (a) in the figure, let us assume that the observer is looking at a building which is 200 meters tall from a distance of 500 meters. The angular size (in this example, height) of the building, expressed in degrees of arc, is given by the formula:

$$\text{Tan } \alpha = \text{Size/Distance}$$

Thus, Tan α in (A) $= 200/500 = .40$, and $\alpha =$ Arctan of .40, or 21.8 degrees of arc.[2]

---

[2] The reader should note that this formula for the visual angle requires the construction of a right angle for computational purposes. For a more general expression, see Graham (1951).

Panel (b) of the figure illustrates the fate of the visual angle produced by the building if the observer's viewing distance is halved to 250 meters. As is evident in the figure, the visual angle grows larger. Using the formula given above, the visual angle in this case would be 38.6°, or almost twice as large as it was at a distance of 500 meters. Finally, panel (c) illustrates the change in visual angle which would occur if the observer's viewing distance were doubled to 1,000 meters. In this case, the angle would be reduced to 11.3°, a value approximately half of what it was at a viewing distance of 500 meters.

Retinal ambiguity   Since the visual angle subtended by an object on the retina is inversely proportional to the distance between the object and the observer, the proximal image of an object, by itself, is an inadequate cue to the object's size. That is, any number of objects could yield a retinal image of a given size if placed at the proper distance. Given this ambiguity, the challenge for psychologists is to find out how we are able to perceive the size of objects as we, or the objects we see, move about in our environment. Several relevant mechanisms have been identified which apparently operate at sensory as well as higher-order or "cognitive" levels.

Explanatory Factors

The reafference principle   From our discussion thus far, it should be clear that changes in retinal size can be produced both by movement of the external object and by movement of the perceiver. Thus, for example, the retinal image cast by an object will shrink if the object moves away from the observer or if the observer moves away from the object. Von Holst and Mittelstädt (1950) have applied the term *exafference* to changes in the retinal image produced by movement of an external object and *reafference* to changes produced by movement of the perceiver. Furthermore, in studies with dragonflies and fish they have demonstrated that organisms are capable of differentiating between exafferent and reafferent changes. The principle of reafference provides one possible mechanism for the maintenance of size constancy—a mechanism linked to the action of the eye itself. The applicability of the reafference principle to the problem of size constancy has been investigated by Leibowitz and his co-workers in a series of very careful experiments (Leibowitz, 1971).

When the fixation of our gaze shifts from a far to a near object, certain oculomotor adjustments occur which maintain the image in good focus on the retina. One type of adjustment, called *accommodation,* involves a change in the shape of the lens. As illustrated in Figure 6.16, the lens bulges more for near than it does for far objects. The accommodation of the lens—that is, its flattening or bulging—is controlled by the *ciliary* muscles. A second form of oculomotor adjustment involves convergent and divergent movements of the eyeballs controlled by the *rectus* and the *oblique* muscles outside the eye. *Convergence* occurs when fixation is directed at a close object, and the two

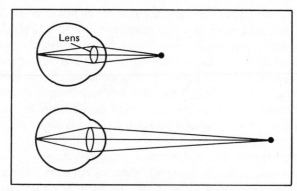

FIGURE 6.16   Schematic illustration of accommodation. Changes in the curvature of the lens
bring light rays reflected from objects at different distances into sharp focus on
the retina. The lens thickens to focus images of nearby objects and flattens to
focus on objects that are far away. These changes in the shape of the lens
are produced by the contraction and relaxation of the ciliary muscles which
are attached to the zonule fibers from which the lens is suspended (see Figure 2.5).

eyes rotate toward each other, as shown in Figure 6.17. *Divergence* is the opposite of that response, occurring when the eyes shift from fixation on a close
object to fixation on a far object.

As described by Leibowitz (1971), the reafference principle holds that the
initiation of movements for accommodation and convergence is coupled
with an expectation that this action will be accompanied by an alteration in
the size of the retinal image. Anticipating such a change, the organism corrects
for it and, in this way, maintains size constancy.

In order to assess the implications of the reafference principle, Leibowitz
and Moore (1966) asked subjects to view a white equilateral triangle in an
otherwise completely dark room. The triangle was placed at four viewing distances, namely 25, 50, 100, and 400 cm. At each distance, the triangle was
varied in physical size such that it always subtended a visual angle of 1°. Size
judgments were obtained by having the subjects adjust the size of a similar
triangle to that of the standard. A major feature of the experiment was a system of prisms and lenses which forced the observers to adjust their accommodation and convergence to distances which were closer to, or farther away
from, the actual test object in order to focus their gaze clearly. In this way,
the experimental arrangement permitted retinal size to remain fixed under all
conditions while allowing the hypothesized "expectations" of a change in retinal size to vary freely.

Such a situation leads to some interesting predictions on the basis of the
reafference principle. Normally, accommodation and convergence to a near
distance are accompanied by an enlarged retinal image. According to the
reafference notion, the appropriate correction to maintain size constancy

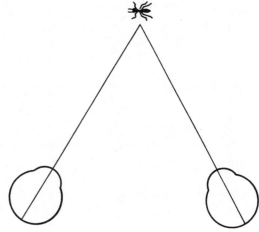

FIGURE 6.17 Convergence of the two eyes on a near object.

would be to diminish the size of the image. Under the conditions arranged by Leibowitz and Moore, however, oculomotor adjustments for near vision were not accompanied by a change in retinal size. Thus, if a "diminution correction" were to occur, as predicted from the reafference position, it would lead to a reduction of perceived size. A similar line of reasoning leads to the expectation of an increase in perceived size when the subjects were forced to make oculomotor adjustments for distances which were farther away than the actual test object.

Figure 6.18 presents the results of this experiment. Matched size is plotted as a function of "equivalent distance," or the distance to which the oculmotor adjustments induced by the system of prisms and lenses should correspond. In the figure, the diagonal lines represent the results to be expected if perceived size were proportional to equivalent distance, as the reafference principle would predict. By contrast, the horizontal lines reflect the results to be expected if oculomotor adjustments had no influence on perceived size, and judgments were made solely on the basis of retinal image size, which remained unchanged in all cases. It is evident that up to a viewing distance of 100 cm judged size corresponded quite well to predictions derived from the reafference principle. Beyond 100 cm, however, perceived size followed retinal size.

Leibowitz, Shiina, and Hennessy (1972) confirmed these findings in a second study. Additionally, through the use of laser-beam technology, they were able to measure the exact amount of accommodation in force without interfering with the accommodative process itself. In this way, they were able to verify independently that their system of prisms and lenses did in fact induce the required amounts of oculomotor change. The work of Leibowitz and his colleagues demonstrates in a rather elegant way that oculomotor adjustments do indeed play a role in size constancy. However, as they carefully

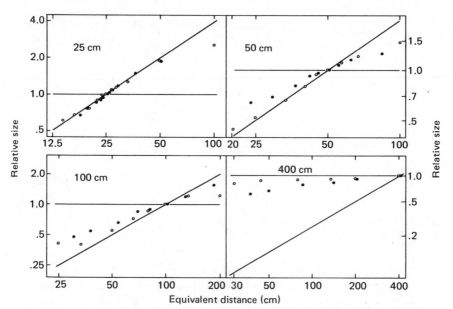

FIGURE 6.18 The role of reafference in size constancy. Matched size is plotted as a function of distances to which observers were forced to adjust their accommodation and convergence (equivalent distance) by a system of prisms and lenses. Each panel presents the results for a test object subtending 1 degree of visual angle at different physical distances from the observer. The diagonal line reflects the results to be expected if perceived size were proportional to equivalent distance (size constancy). The horizontal line represents the results to be expected if judgments were made solely in terms of retinal image size. (From Leibowitz, 1971)

point out, this role is only effective up to distances of about 100 cm, or 1 meter. Since size constancy obtains over viewing distances considerably greater than this, a complete account of size constancy compels us to search for additional mediating factors.

The invariance hypothesis   Another view which couples size to distance in a more general way dates back to Helmholtz (1866) and his notion of unconscious inference. In relation to size constancy, Helmholtz argued that observers learn through experience that an object's physical size remains invariant although its retinal size varies with distance. Thus, the perceptual system records the size of the retinal image and then modifies, or corrects, this record in light of available information about distance to arrive at judgments of object size. Since the retinal size subtended by an object is proportional to object size/distance, Helmholtz suggested that in perceiving object size, people implicitly solve the equation Object Size = Retinal Size × Distance.

More recently, this view of size constancy has been embodied in what is known as the size-distance invariance hypothesis (Epstein, Park, and Casey, 1961; Kilpatrick and Ittelson, 1953), which states that a particular retinal size specifies a unique or invariant relationship between perceived size and perceived distance. Thus, if the perceived value of one of these attributes accurately maps the corresponding physical value of an object— that is, if the perceived value is veridical—then the perceived value of the other attribute will also be veridical. According to the invariance hypothesis, accurate perception of an object's distance implies accurate perception of its size.

A straightforward demonstration of this type of linkage between size and distance was provided in a now-classic experiment by Holway and Boring (1941). In their experiment, a subject was seated in a chair at the intersection of two long corridors which formed a right angle. The stimuli to be judged— that is, the standard stimuli—were disks of light located in one of the corridors at various distances from the subject ranging from 10 to 120 feet. For each distance, a disk was selected which projected a retinal image of 1° of arc in diameter. To indicate their estimate of the size of a particular standard stimulus, the subjects made reference to a comparison disk located in the other chamber at a distance of 10 feet, in a direction of 90° removed from that of the standard. The experimenter continuously varied the size of the comparison disk until the subject indicated that a satisfactory match had been made. Four viewing conditions were employed: (1) binocular, (2) monocular, (3) monocular through an artificial pupil, and (4) monocular through a tunnel that virtually eliminated distance cues. The four conditions, in the order mentioned, were meant to provide the subjects with decreasing amounts of information about the distance of the objects for which size estimates were to be made.

The results of this study appear in Figure 6.19. The diagonal dotted line in this figure represents the results to be expected if perfect size constancy were obtained. Since the standard stimuli always cast a retinal image of 1°, their physical size necessarily increased with increased viewing distance. Consequently, accurate size judgments (size constancy) would reflect the increase in target size with increasing distance. The horizontal dotted line in the figure represents the results to be expected if size judgments were made solely on the basis of visual angle, which was the same in all conditions. It can be seen in the figure that under the binocular viewing conditions, which provided the richest supply of cues to distance, perceived size closely approximated physical size, and thus size constancy generally obtained. As demanded by the invariance hypothesis, the veridicality of size estimates decreased as distance cues were diminished. Under the most impoverished condition—viewing through the tunnel—estimates of size approached those implying sole dependence on the size of the retinal image. The results described by Holway and Boring have been confirmed in several other investigations which made use of different types of stimulus objects and techniques of impoverishing judgments of distance (Chalmers, 1952; Harvey and Leibowitz, 1967; Hastorf

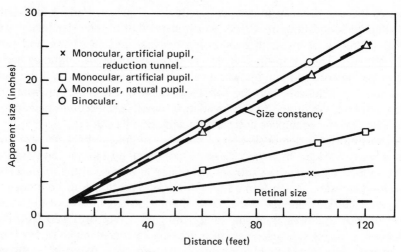

FIGURE 6.19   Perceived size as a function of distance for different viewing conditions in which depth cues were varied. (After Holway and Boring, 1941)

and Way, 1952; Lichten and Lurie, 1950; Rock and McDermott, 1964; Zeigler and Leibowitz, 1957).

Changes in perceived size under impoverished conditions for judging distance presumably represent strong support for the invariance hypothesis. However, there is a subtle problem which might seem to render the invariance hypothesis logically untenable. When cues to distance are eliminated, the perceived distance of a test object might be expected to tend toward zero. If the perceived size of the object is the product of retinal size times perceived distance and if apparent distance tends toward zero, then the perceived size of the object should not approach retinal size. Instead, a more radical effect should occur—the object should disappear. The reason is that the product of a value times zero is zero! (Epstein, Park, and Casey, 1961)

A solution to this problem for the invariance hypothesis comes from the fact that in the total absence of cues to distance two tendencies operate to provide people with some finite value of the perceived distance of stimuli (Gogel, 1973). (1) The *specific distance tendency* refers to the observation that objects appear at a near distance (approximately 4 to 8 feet) in the absence of cues to the actual distance of the object from the perceiver (Gogel, 1969). (2) The *equidistance tendency* refers to the observation that people generally perceive two or more objects as equidistant in depth when the effective cues to depth are absent or minimal; this tendency is strongest when there is little lateral separation between the objects (Gogel, 1956, 1965; Lodge and Wist, 1968). Thus, if a disk and a rectangle are placed at different distances from an observer, and there are no cues as to their distances from the observer, they will usually appear to be at the same distance. Furthermore, since the objects appear at the same distance, their perceived sizes will be proportional to their retinal sizes, a result which is in accord with the invariance hypothesis. For example, if the diameter of the disk equals the width of the rectangle and the rectangle is physically twice as far away as the disk, the perceived width of the rectangle will be half as large as the perceived diameter of the disk (Gogel, 1973).

The linkage between perceived size and perceived distance inherent in the invariance hypothesis may become evident in still another way if we consider the size not of objects themselves, but of their afterimages. If an afterimage is produced by a stimulus and is then projected onto a real surface so that it appears to be lying on that surface, the apparent size of the afterimage will increase as the perceived distance of the surface increases. This relation is known as *Emmert's Law.* Now, the area of the image on the retina has a fixed size. Therefore, if perceived size is a product of retinal size and perceived distance, it follows from the invariance hypothesis that increments in the perceived distance of the projection surface should be accompanied by increments in the perceived size of the afterimage. Though the relation between size perception and Emmert's Law is actually somewhat more complicated than is implied above (see Epstein, Park, and Casey, 1961; Furedy and Stanley, 1970; Gogel, 1965; and Weintraub and Gardner, 1970), this phenomenon may still be considered, at least in part, as supportive of the size-distance invariance hypothesis.

The invariance hypothesis is perhaps the most widely cited account of size constancy, and, as we have seen, there is supporting evidence for it. Nevertheless, it has also generated a considerable amount of controversy, and there are limits to its applicability. Problems for the invariance notion come from experiments which have adopted the strategy of requiring *both* size and distance judgments in the same situation. These studies have indicated that perceived size is not as strictly proportional to perceived distance as the invariance hypothesis demands.

For example, there are a number of investigations which have shown that apparent size tends to be overestimated with increasing distance. However, this effect is generally not accompanied by a tendency for apparent distance to increase more rapidly than perceived distance (Epstein, Park, and Casey, 1961). Such a tendency would be required if perceived size were strictly proportional to perceived distance. In addition, Gogel, Wist, and Harker (1963) have reported that perceived size is an increasing but not necessarily a linear function of perceived distance. Vogel and Teghtsoonian (1972) have shown that even when the product of retinal size and perceived distance remains constant, perceived size may still vary as a function of certain viewing conditions. Still another case of nonmatching judgments of size and distance has been reported in experiments by Epstein and Landauer (1969) and Landauer and Epstein (1969), which suggest that under some circumstances size and distance judgments may be made independently of one another.

These results, and others like them, add to the complexity of our understanding of the relation between size and distance. On the one hand, they force us to be skeptical about the ability of the invariance hypothesis to constitute a completely satisfactory account of the phenomenon of size constancy. On the other hand, there are reasons to argue that they do not necessarily overrule this hypothesis.

As in the case of judgments of lightness, size judgments are subject to variations in instructional set and modes of judgment. Several experiments have demonstrated that when size judgments are made under conditions which provide good cues to depth, subjects are capable of making accurate "proximal" or retinal matches as well as accurate "objective" or physical matches between a standard and a comparison stimulus. That is, subjects can bias their judgments toward size constancy or toward visual-angle projections depending on the instructions they receive (Carlson, 1962; Epstein, 1963a; Gilinsky, 1955; Jenkin and Hyman, 1959; Rock and McDermott, 1964). As Hochberg (1971b) has indicated, such results illustrate in a formal way your own informal experiences that railroad tracks do seem to converge on the horizon and that in some cases, far-off trees do seem smaller than near ones. It is possible, then, that different conditions of observation—the exact nature of which remains to be fully identified—may trigger judgmental attitudes which place different weightings on the relation between perceived size and perceived distance. Consequently, a less stringent statement of the invariance hypothesis may have validity, such as one recently provided by Gogel (1973). He suggests that for a given value of retinal size, perceived size will generally be an increasing function of perceived distance, but that this function will not necessarily be invariant under different conditions of observation.

The proportionality principle Perceived distance is not the only contextual factor which may provide a cue for size constancy. Rock and Ebenholtz (1959) have proposed that another possible cue for an object's perceived size is the ratio of the size of its retinal image to that of a neighboring object which can serve as a frame of reference. More specifically, consider a case in which an observer views a telephone pole which stands in front of a large building taller than the pole. The retinal image of the pole will be proportionate to the retinal image of the building. For convenience, let us assume a ratio of 1:3. Now, if the observer were to view the scene from a greater distance, the retinal images of both the pole and the building would shrink in absolute size, but the ratio of their relative sizes would remain constant. Such a ratio could conceivably serve as a stimulus invariant for the maintenance of size constancy. Rock and Ebenholtz point out that their hypothesis of a relational stimulus for apparent size is analogous to Wallach's (1948) explanation of lightness constancy, which, as we have seen, holds that perceived lightness of a surface is based upon the ratio of the luminance of the surface to that of its surround.

In order to test the relative size, or proportionality, hypothesis, Rock and

Ebenholtz asked observers to view two luminous stimuli in an otherwise dark room under conditions designed to eliminate cues to distance. The stimuli were rectangles in which a vertical line was embedded. As illustrated in Figure 6.20, one of the rectangles was smaller than the other, and the smaller one was designated as the standard. The subjects adjusted the height of the vertical line in the comparison rectangle until it matched that of the vertical line in the standard when the comparison rectangle was either two, three, five, or eight times as large as the standard.

If the proportionality hypothesis is valid, we should not expect the subjects in this experiment to perceive the vertical lines in the standard and comparison rectangles to be equal when they were physically identical in height. Instead, the lines should be perceived as equal when the ratios of their heights to the heights of the rectangles in which they were embedded were equal. The outcome of this experiment was generally consistent with this latter expectation, and we may therefore speak of a proportionality principle which appears to play a role in the judgment of size and in size constancy. However, inasmuch as the approximation to complete proportionality became progressively poorer as the disparity in the sizes of the standard and comparison rectangles increased, we must consider the contribution of the proportionality principle with some caution. Though it seems to be involved in size constancy, it does not completely determine this phenomenon.

A similar hypothesis concerning a relational stimulus for size has been advanced by Gibson (1966). He has suggested that one kind of information for detecting the size of an object in a terrestrial environment is the amount of surface texture that the object intercepts or covers. Large objects occlude more of the textural background of their immediate surroundings than do small objects. Furthermore, the retinal size of an object normally varies directly with the retinal size of the textural elements of the terrain so that even though an object's retinal size decreases with distance, the relative number of textural elements that it covers remains invariant. Gibson argues that this invariance may aid the observer in perceiving an object as generally unchanging in size while its proximal image varies. This effect has been termed the _textural scale-size-cue_ (Hochberg, 1971b). It is illustrated in Figure 6.21 under conditions in which an object is drawn so that its retinal size does not vary directly with that of the terrain texture as is usually the case. Both white squares are identical in size. However, square (a) occludes more of the textural elements than does square (b), and, in Gibson's view, this is why

FIGURE 6.20 Illustration of the configuration used to study the role of proportionality in size constancy. When cues to distance are eliminated, observers tend to judge the vertical lines in (a) and (b) as equal in height when the ratios of their heights to the rectangles in which they are embedded are equal. (From Rock and Ebenholtz, 1959)

(a)

(b)

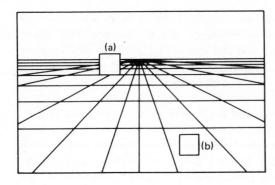

FIGURE 6.21 The textural scale-size-cue. An object of constant linear size appears larger when it occludes a greater amount of the surface texture of its surroundings.

square (a) appears to be larger than (b). While Gibson's suggestion clearly has merit, we should point out, as Kaufman (1974) has done, that our present knowledge of the effectiveness of the textural scale-size-cue is incomplete; the precise manner in which perceived size varies as a function of the amount of terrain texture hidden by an object remains to be investigated.

Known size Thus far, our discussion of the factors which mediate size constancy has focused upon forms of sensory information which provide cues to the size of an object. If the object is familiar to us, there is still another factor, involving information of a different sort, which may also be of use in maintaining the stability of perceived size—that is, stored knowledge of the nature of the object or similar objects. Many of the items that we encounter have a typical size, or at least a restricted range of sizes. A pen, for example, is usually about 5 to 7 inches long. It is rarely as long as a foot or as short as an inch. Thus, we probably "know" the sizes of many items in our immediate surroundings, and once an item has been identified we can give reasonably accurate judgments of its size even though its proximal image may vary from moment to moment.

An experimental demonstration that known or familiar size plays a part in size constancy has been provided by Bolles and Bailey (1956). They had subjects make two types of verbal estimates of the sizes of familiar things such as pencils, light fixtures, furniture, books, articles of clothing, automobiles. First, the subjects gave their estimates with eyes closed after the object had been identified for them. Afterward, they did so while looking at the object. The correlation between judged size and actual object size was .988 for nonvisual judgments and .994 for visual judgments. Moreover, the accuracy of nonvisual judgments was not enhanced appreciably by the addition of visual information. Once an item was identified, size constancy was almost perfect regardless of whether or not the object was actually seen.

The effect of known size on perceived size in visually rich environments has been confirmed in a number of other experiments (Brunswik, 1944;

Churchill, 1962; McKennel, 1960; Slack, 1956). Once again, however. we are faced with a limitation to our understanding of the degree to which a potential mediating factor is actually utilized. Studies by Schiffman and his colleagues (Fillenbaum, Schiffman, and Butcher, 1965; Schiffman, 1967) suggest that under ordinary viewing conditions, judgments of size are based primarily on the available visual information and that people resort to known size primarily when viewing conditions are poor. On the other hand, Gogel and Newton (1969) have presented evidence to show that under some conditions of impoverished viewing, perceived size is determined by both known size and retinal size.

Interaction of cues for constancy It should be evident from what we have been saying that no single mechanism in and of itself completely accounts for size constancy. Rather, this phenomenon is probably determined by several factors operating together, and the relative contributions made by these factors may vary under different circumstances. Thus, at close distances (1 meter or less), oculomotor adjustments and reafference seem to play an important role, whereas at distances beyond 1 meter, the "taking account" of cues to distance, the relative size context, and the observer's familiarity with the stimuli all become crucial.

A further indication of the complexity of size constancy is revealed if we examine it from a developmental point of view. As was true in the case of lightness constancy, size constancy has been observed in organisms below man in the phylogenetic scale (Heller, 1968; Shinkman, 1962; Walk, 1965). In addition, several investigations have revealed that children manifest size constancy (Gibson, 1969; and Wohlwill, 1960) and that it is observable even in infants as young as six to eight weeks of age (Bower, 1965, 1966). Unlike lightness constancy, however, size constancy shows a trend for improvement with age — a trend which is closely tied to viewing distance. Studies with children ranging from six to 12 years old have indicated that at short viewing distances, size constancy appears to be unrelated to age, but that with increasing distance, adults show a greater approximation to constancy than do children (Brislin and Leibowitz, 1970; Leibowitz, 1971; Leibowitz, Pollard, and Dickson, 1967; Zeigler and Leibowitz, 1957). Figure 6.22 illustrates this trend. Results such as these suggest that size constancy may represent a more intricate perceptual achievement than lightness constancy and that experience brings with it a sharpening of the perceiver's ability to make use of stored information and cues to size in the maintenance of a stable perceptual world.

SIZE ILLUSIONS

The Corridor Illusion

The various mechanisms for size constancy just described may provide an explanatory framework not only for veridical judgments of size but also for il-

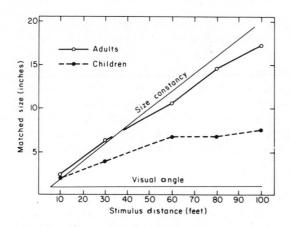

FIGURE 6.22 Age differences in size constancy. Matched size as a function of receiving distance for adults and children. (From Leibowitz, 1971)

lusions of size — conditions in which constancy fails and size is misperceived. Figure 6.21 is an example of such an illusion. A somewhat related example is the "corridor illusion" presented in Figure 6.23.

Although the two cylinders in this picture are identical in physical size, they vary in perceived size. The cylinders also appear to differ in spatial location. This illusion has been explained in terms of the size-distance relationship. Thus, if objects of the same physical size are perceived to be at different distances, the observer, taking apparent distance into account, perceives the object that appears to be farther away also as larger (Gregory, 1973; Rock and Kaufman, 1962; Richards and Miller, 1971). This illusion has also been accounted for in terms of the relative size context (Gibson, 1966), since the far cylinder intercepts more units of texture than the near one does. Several other illusions of size have been explained along similar lines. They will be considered further in our discussion of the geometrical illusions in Chapter 7. For now, we want to pay particular attention to a failure of size constancy which occurs in the natural setting of the evening sky.

The Moon Illusion

An ancient problem   At one time or another, you probably have noticed a rather striking change in the perceived size of the moon as you see it in different portions of the sky. Although the retinal image of the moon, regardless of its position, is about 0.5° (Boring, 1943; Kaufman and Rock, 1962; Restle, 1970), the moon seems much larger when it lies just over the horizon than when it is seen in elevation at the zenith. This effect is called the *moon illusion,* or, more generally, the *celestial illusion,* since it also occurs with respect to the sun. There is ample evidence to show that it is indeed perceptual in origin and not an artifact of physical conditions which distort the images of celestial bodies. Experiments have indicated that the apparent difference in the moon's size is not produced by factors such as the scattering of light by atmospheric conditions or disparities in the relative luminance of the

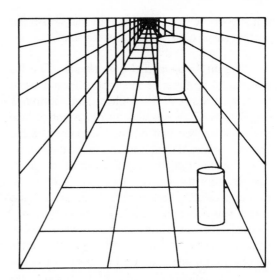

FIGURE 6.23   The corridor illusion.

moon in different sky locations, and, most important, the size difference does not show up in photographs taken of the moon in different positions (Boring, 1943; Kaufman and Rock, 1962; Solhkhah and Orbach, 1969). We are, therefore, concerned with a remarkable natural effect wherein retinal images of the moon which are of equal size give rise to radically different impressions of size when the moon appears in different parts of the sky.[3]

The moon illusion has been a puzzle since antiquity and was discussed repeatedly in ancient and medieval literature (Ross and Ross, 1976). One of the major accounts of this heavenly illusion is the *apparent distance theory,* often ascribed to Ptolemy, the Greek astronomer in the second century A.D. More recent evidence suggests, however, that credit for developing the apparent distance theory of the moon illusion belongs to Alhazen, an Arabian scientist of the 11th century, and to Roger Bacon of England in the 13th century (Ross and Ross, 1976). According to this view, the presence of intervening objects and terrain makes the horizon moon appear to be more distant than the zenith moon because filled space tends to produce a greater impression of depth than does unfilled space. Given equal retinal sizes, that object seems larger which seems farther away. Hence, the greater the appar-

[3] In this era of space exploration, many students wonder if there is also an "earth illusion" when our planet is seen from the moon. We consulted Dr. Neil Armstrong, the first astronaut to set foot on the moon. Unfortunately, Dr. Armstrong did not have the opportunity to look for this effect. Moonwalks took place only during "daylight" hours, and when the spacecraft passed from the dark side of the moon over the horizon, crew members were too much occupied with other tasks to note the apparent size of the earth. Dr. Armstrong did say that while traveling between earth and moon he observed no unexpected changes in the apparent size of either body. Perhaps the most striking effect for him was a marked shift from a two-dimensional to a three-dimensional body as the spacecraft neared the earth and the moon.

ent size of the horizon moon. In this sense, the moon illusion and the corridor illusion may reflect similar relationships.

The angle-of-regard hypothesis   The first systematic attempts at an experimental analysis of the moon illusion were made by Boring and his coworkers (Boring, 1943; Holway and Boring, 1940a, 1940b; Taylor and Boring, 1942). They rejected the apparent distance theory for the simple reason that when asked which moon appeared farther away, their observers unanimously reported that the moon in elevation looked more distant than the moon on the horizon. Such a report, of course, seems to invert the logic of the apparent-distance explanation. Boring and his associates were impressed by the possibility that postural changes involved in gazing at the zenith moon might somehow underlie the moon illusion. Specifically, an erect observer normally views the horizon moon with eyes straight ahead, whereas the eyes ordinarily are raised when looking at the zenith moon. Thus, the illusion may be due to the elevation of the observer's eyes.

To investigate this possibility, Boring and his colleagues conducted experiments using mirrors mounted on long beams which could make the moon appear at different positions in the sky. Observers were asked to match the size of the real moon with that of a disk of light projected on a nearby screen. By means of this technique, the apparent size of the moon could be charted at different sky locations, as shown in Figure 6.24. These investigations also revealed that the moon illusion could be eliminated if the observers tilted their heads so that they could look at the zenith moon with eyes level.

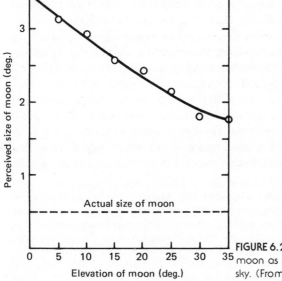

FIGURE 6.24   The perceived size of the moon as a function of its elevation in the sky. (From Boring, 1943)

Under some conditions, the illusion could even be reversed. If the observers lay supine on a flat table and hung their heads over the edge, the zenith moon seemed larger than the horizon moon. A similar result could also be obtained if the observers doubled over to view the moon from between their legs. In these cases, the horizon moon is viewed with eyes elevated and the zenith moon with eyes level. Such findings led Boring (1943) cautiously to advance the suggestion that, for some reason, eye elevation reduces the perceived size of the moon. His suggestion has come to be known as the *angle-of-regard hypothesis.* It has found support in a number of other investigations, which also indicate that perceived size of objects is influenced by eye elevation (Bilderback, Taylor, and Thor, 1964; Thor, Winters, and Hoats, 1969, 1970; Van Eyl, 1972; Wood, Zinkus, and Mountjoy, 1968).

Apparent distance revisited However, in what may by now be an all too familiar pattern of events, a series of important experiments by Kaufman and Rock (1962) and Rock and Kaufman (1962) challenged Boring's work and provided strong support for the apparent distance theory of the moon illusion. Kaufman and Rock pointed out that Boring's findings on the remoteness of the horizon and zenith moons were inconsistent with studies on the so-called half-arc-angle, which indicated that the horizon sky appears more distant than the sky at the zenith. They noted that when people are asked to point along a line which bisects the arc of the sky from the horizon to the zenith, they indicate a direction considerably less than 45° from the horizontal. Thus, the vault of the heavens appears to have the shape of a flattened soup bowl rather than a hemisphere, and the horizon seems farther away than the sky overhead. These ideas are illustrated in Figure 6.25. Kaufman and Rock argued that Boring's subjects made their distance estimates while experiencing the moon illusion, and consequently they might have judged the horizon moon as nearer because it seemed larger. If this were true, the distance information so obtained might not constitute a fair test of the apparent-distance notion. They also suggested that it may have been inappropriate for Boring to have asked observers to compare the size of the moon—an extremely distant object of virtually indeterminate size—with a disk of light of determinate size. Under such circumstances, the observers may have been trying to compare things that were actually incommensurate.

Accordingly Kaufman and Rock adopted a different approach to the study of the moon illusion, one in which two artificial moons seen against the sky could be compared with each other. They developed an optical device which permitted an observer to view an adjustable disk of light at optical infinity on the sky. With two such devices, one pointed at the horizon and one at the zenith, the sizes of the moons could be compared directly. Using this approach, Kaufman and Rock found that the moon illusion occurred regardless of whether observers viewed the zenith moon with eyes elevated or, by tilting

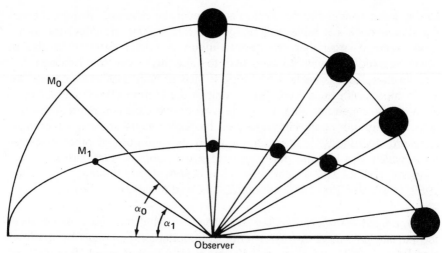

FIGURE 6.25   The apparent-distance theory of the moon illusion and the half-arc-angle measure. The circles in the top arc indicate the true distance and size of the moon as it ascends in the sky. At all points, the moon is equidistant from the observer and of constant size. The circles in the bottom arc illustrate the perceived distance of the moon at various positions in the sky and corresponding changes in its size. According to the apparent-distance theory, the moon appears farther away at the horizon than at the zenith. Points M_0 and M_1 represent the half-arc-angle measure. The midpoint of the actual arc connecting zenith to horizon is at M_0, and the actual half-arc-angle, α_0, is 45°. The midpoint of the perceived arc connecting zenith to horizon is at M_1, and the perceived half-arc-angle, α_1, is less than 45°. (After Kaufman and Rock, 1962)

their heads, with eyes level. Furthermore, when the sizes of the artificial moons were made unequal, the observers judged the larger one to be nearer no matter where it was seen in the sky. These investigators also asked their observers to judge the distances of the horizon and the zenith in a *moonless sky* and found that under these conditions, the horizon appeared to be more remote.

In a further effort to test the apparent distance theory, Kaufman and Rock instituted various conditions designed to alter the cues to distance provided by the terrain. Among other things, they found that the moon illusion disappeared when the observer's view of the terrain was obscured by a reduction screen and that the magnitude of the illusion was greater in scenes in which the physical distance from the viewing point to the horizon was largest. Additionally, through the use of prisms, they were able to create a situation in which the zenith moon appeared over a horizon at the end of an apparent terrain while the horizon was deprived of its terrain and seemed to be surrounded on all sides by sky. In this case, the zenith moon appeared to be larger than the horizon moon.

Kaufman and Rock's findings in support of the apparent distance theory of the moon illusion were reinforced by two other experiments which appeared at about the same time. King and Gruber (1962) reported the rather striking finding that the perceived size of an afterimage is greater if the afterimage is projected on the surface of the sky at the horizon than if projected at the zenith. On the basis of Emmert's Law, such a finding can be considered to support the belief that the horizon is perceived as more distant than the zenith. In addition, Gruber, King, and Link (1963) found that the moon illusion could be obtained in a laboratory setting with an artificial luminous ceiling, but only when cues to distance were available.

The relative size hypothesis   With the publication of these dramatic experiments, the apparent distance theory became the most prevalent explanation of the moon illusion. However, it has once again been questioned. Restle (1970) has argued that the apparent distance theory is an incomplete explanation of the moon illusion since it depends upon another as yet unexplained illusion—the remoteness of the zenith sky in relation to the horizon sky. Restle has proposed an alternative account that is not linked to apparent distance, but, instead, to the context of the visual field itself. His position is similar to the relative size hypothesis of Rock and Ebenholtz (1959). According to Restle, the moon seems small at the zenith because its immediate surroundings consist of the vast (90°), empty visual extent to the horizon. By contrast, the horizon moon appears larger because it is compared with a much smaller (1°) extent to the horizon. Thus, in Restle's view, the moon illusion represents a striking and naturally occurring example of the relativity of perceived size and how the same object may appear large in one context and small in another.

It should be evident by now that there may be no single answer to the ancient puzzle of the moon illusion. As in the case of veridical perceptions of size, it is probable that this illusion of size is multiply determined by the several factors that we have described and perhaps by others not yet thought of. Such a possibility was recognized by both Boring (1962) and by Wallach (1962) in their comments on the complexity of this effect. Indeed, we might consider the story of the efforts to understand the moon illusion as a microcosm of the larger problem of size constancy itself, and of the general problem of the various perceptual constancies.

THE STABILITY-INSTABILITY PARADOX

Homogeneous Stimulation

The main theme of the preceding discussion is that people perceive the world as relatively stable, and act effectively, despite ever changing, ambiguous proximal stimulation. Though we have concentrated on the dimensions of lightness and size, you should keep in mind that constancy is manifested in other stimulus attributes as well. For example, the perceived color or hue of a surface remains relatively the same in spite of variations in the color of the light falling on the surface (color constancy). Similarly, an object with a constant physical shape will have a stable perceived shape when viewed at different degrees of slant even though its retinal image takes on different configurations (shape constancy). Thus, a dinner plate will retain its circular appearance regardless of the angle from which it is seen. Similarly, a door will look rectangular even though, except when viewed head on, its visual image is trapezoidal. Moreover, an object moving at a constant speed across the field of view will not appear to change in speed when viewed at different distances even though the retinal distance that it covers will be less as its physical distance from the observer increases (motion constancy). It would become tedious to go into the mechanisms involved in these several forms of constancy. Needless to say, they are no less complex than those inherent in lightness and size constancy (see Epstein, 1977; Epstein and Park, 1963; Hochberg, 1971a, 1971b; Kaufman, 1974). In any event, it should be apparent that perceptual constancy is a truly remarkable achievement and that without constancy survival would be seriously jeopardized.

Given the adaptive significance of the perceptual stability that is normally maintained under conditions of stimulus flux and ambiguity, we might wonder what would happen if stimulus variability were physically eliminated. How would people react to situations in which sensory stimulation was essentially constant? If it were possible to create such conditions of ultrastability, shouldn't they be especially adaptive? Strangely enough, in the presence of a nonchanging environment, perceptual experience becomes grossly unstable. This effect has been observed in a number of experimental conditions.

Stopped images   We referred in the previous chapter to the fact that the eye is never absolutely stationary. Even the most careful attempts at steady fixation are accompanied by small, involuntary eye movements. This continual movement of the eyes implies a corresponding movement of the proximal stimulus over the retina. Each point in the proximal stimulus falls, in time, over several retinal receptors. Thus, the projection of a stationary target on a moving eye has the same effect as a moving image on a stationary eye. The influence that these "moving images" have on perception became amenable to empirical investigation in the early 1950s with the development of techniques to stop image movement. There are two general ways in which stopped images may be produced. The first, obviously, is to prevent the eyes from moving. However, a procedure for doing this would be likely to have undesirable side effects that would render it useless. Fortunately, there is a second possibility. It involves moving the stimulus in such a way as to compensate exactly for each eye movement. If, every time the eye were to move, the image were moved by the same amount and in the same direction, then a particular point on the stimulus would always fall on the same particular retinal point.

The actual technique for accomplishing this is simple in principle. Essentially, it involves making the location of the target dependent on the location of the eye. One way of doing so is to attach a small mirror to a contact lens covering one of the subject's eyes. The target stimulus is directed at the small mirror. Through a relatively simple optical system, the image on the retina is itself directed at a screen. It is the image on the screen that the subject sees. Now, as the subject's eye moves, the small mirror attached to the eye also moves; this in turn causes the stimulus image on the screen to move, and thus the image on the retina moves. The optical system is so arranged that the absolute extent of the eye movement is compensated for exactly by the movement of the retinal image. A schematic diagram of such a system is provided in Figure 6.26.

A vast amount of research has been conducted with image stabilization. Much of this work, along with alternate techniques for producing stopped images, has been described by Alpern (1971), Cornsweet (1970), Ditchburn

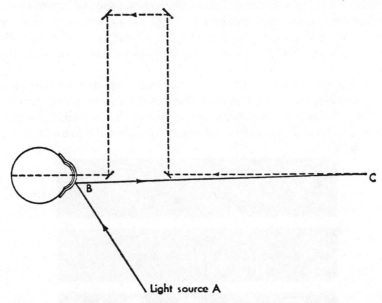

FIGURE 6.26 Schematic diagram of the apparatus for producing a stopped, or stabilized image on the retina. Light from the source at A is reflected from a tiny mirror, B, attached to a contact lens, onto the screen at C. The light from C reaches the subject's eye through the path indicated by the dotted lines. Whenever the eye moves through a given angle, the light at C moves through twice that angle. The length of the optical path from C to the eye is selected so as to compensate exactly for this difference in extent of angular movement. Thus, the image that reaches the retina remains fixed in location, or stopped on the retina, despite normal eye-movements. (After Riggs, Ratliff, Cornsweet and Cornsweet, 1953)

(1973), Heckenmueller (1965), and Pritchard (1961). What follows is a summary of some of the more dramatic effects that have been noted.

Within a few seconds of viewing a figure that is stabilized on the retina, people report that the perceived figure progressively disappears, leaving a homogeneous field. This field itself may darken, resulting in a complete loss of sensation. If the field being viewed contains colors, the colors will fade away, leaving an achromatic field of different lightness which, in turn, may also disappear after a while. Simple figures, such as fine black lines, vanish and, in some cases, never reappear. In others, the image, or fragments of it, will periodically appear and disappear.

An especially important finding with respect to stopped images is that the complexity of the image determines the extent of disappearance. More complex images—those which have a greater number of elements or images which have meaning—remain visible longer than simple ones. Moreover, complex images do not disintegrate in a haphazard way but, instead, tend to break up in organized units. For example, the profile of a face will remain in view longer than a curved line. When the profile fades, the top of the head or the front of the face may continue to be seen while the remainder vanishes. Similarly, if the stimulus is a monogram containing the letters H and B, one or the other letter or a fragment of it will be the unit seen. If an entire word such as "beer" is presented, partial fragmentation of the letters will result in other words being perceived. These types of effects are illustrated in Figure 6.27.

The disappearance of stopped images indicates that eye movements serve to maintain the perception of a stimulus. Exactly how eye movements perform this function is not entirely known, although reasonable guesses can be made. The most likely explanation is something like the following.

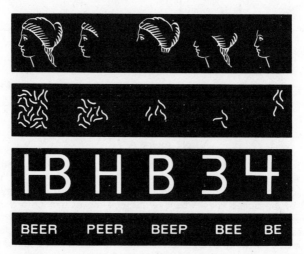

FIGURE 6.27   Illustration of the kinds of perceptual fragmentations that are experienced when observers view stopped images on the retina. (From Pritchard, 1961)

Electrophysiological studies (see Granit, 1955) have revealed that most of the retinal receptors fail to respond to steady light. The most vigorous response is to illumination change. The occurrence of activity in these receptors is thus dependent upon the occurrence of changes in illumination. One important source of change lies in the normal movements of the eye. With a stopped image, however, the light falls continuously on the same receptors. After their initial response to stimulation, these receptors stop firing; since very few, if any, new receptors are being stimulated, the target no longer has any effect on the activity of the system. The target might as well not be there; perceptually, the target disappears.

An explanation of the effects of stopped images based only on retinal adaptation is not entirely complete, however. There is also evidence to suggest that central nervous system components are involved in the disappearance of stabilized images. Suppose a stopped image, presented to one eye, has disappeared and is then presented to the other eye. It will disappear more rapidly in the second eye if it is projected on the same position of the retina in the second eye as it was in the first than if it is projected on noncorresponding retinal positions (Krauskopf and Riggs, 1959). Thus, some of the effects of a specific locus on the first eye must transfer, through the mediation of central mechanisms, to a corresponding locus on the second eye. Further evidence in support of the idea that central mechanisms are involved in stopped-image effects comes from the fact that the visibility of a stopped image in one eye is increased when the other eye receives external stimulation as compared to a condition in which stimulation of the other eye is occluded by an eyepatch (Cohen, 1961).

Luminous designs Effects which are similar to those found with stopped images have been described by McKinney (1963, 1964), using a different technique for impoverishing sensory input. He employed luminous drawings which were viewed under conditions of reduced illumination. In one of his experiments, subjects observed the designs presented in Figure 6.28. The stimuli were coated with luminous paint on purple construction paper and were viewed one at a time in a completely dark room. Within a short time, as little as three seconds in some cases, fragmentation of the figures began to occur, with parts disappearing and reappearing. As with stopped im-

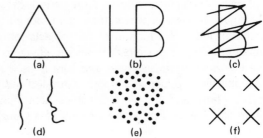

FIGURE 6.28 Designs used to study the fragmentation of luminous patterns viewed in a dark room. (From McKinney, 1963)

ages, complex figures remained intact longer than simple ones, and the disappearance occurred in perceptual units, not at random. Whole lines dropped away, and frequently meaningful figures resulted. For example, in (b), subjects reported seeing the letter H, then B, or the numbers 3 or 13. In (c), the letter B seemed to float out in front of the hatched lines, and in (f), subjects reported seeing four diagonal lines pointed in the same direction. Similar results with luminous figures observed in a dark room have also been described by other investigators (Hart, 1964; Schuck, Brock, and Becker, 1964).

The Ganzfeld Still another technique for restricting stimulus change is to place observers in a field of uniform brightness — that is, one containing no physical discontinuities. A visual environment of this sort is called a *homogeneous field* or a *Ganzfeld.* It sometimes is encountered in nature during high-altitude jet flights, when the visible field outside the aircraft contains no notable detail. This situation induces a phenomenon called *empty-field myopia,* in which pilots temporarily lose the ability to accommodate their eyes properly and become myopic or nearsighted (Matheny, 1961). It is a potentially dangerous condition, for it limits the pilot's ability to locate objects which might suddenly appear in the surrounding airspace.

Technically, it is difficult to create a perfect Ganzfeld in the laboratory, but close approximations to it have been constructed. The first laboratory Ganzfeld was produced by Metzger (1930), who placed subjects in front of a curved whitewashed wall which was homogeneously illuminated. Hochberg, Triebel, and Seaman (1951) achieved a fairly good Ganzfeld by placing halved Ping-Pong balls over the eyes of their subjects. A particularly effective Ganzfeld has been used in a series of experiments by Cohen (1957, 1958a, 1958b). It is composed of two intersecting spheres, A and B, each 1 meter in diameter. Each of the spheres is painted white on the inside, and so constructed that it acts as an integrator of all the light within it. That is, any light within a sphere becomes uniformly distributed over the entire inside surface through multiple reflection. Subjects looking with one eye into a small opening in sphere A see a uniformly illuminated field, provided that the illumination in sphere B is identical with that in A.

Some rather striking effects occur with the use of techniques such as these. When they first gaze into a Ganzfeld, viewers have the impression of looking into a diffuse mist or "sea of light" that appears to be at an indeterminate distance. After a short period, they become unable to tell where their gaze is fixed or where they have looked previously, and their ability to locate or judge the motion of test objects introduced into the field becomes impaired. One of the most impressive effects is the disappearance of color in the Ganzfeld. If, for example, red light is used to illuminate the field, subjects may initially experience a poorly saturated red fog. Very soon, the color begins to fade and the field becomes achromatic. Similar effects occur with other illuminants. Prolonged viewing of a Ganzfeld can result in a temporary cessation of vision or "blankout" in which observers become unable to recognize even familiar objects such as a circle or a star. A thorough account of research with the Ganzfeld can be found in a review by Avant (1965).

The Nature of the Paradox

Taken together with what we know of the perceptual constancies, the results of research on restricted visual environments that we have just mentioned suggest what we might call the "stability-instability paradox." On the one hand, we are capable of transcending a large amount of variability and ambiguity in proximal stimulation to arrive at a stable perceptual world. On the other hand, we seem to need stimulus change in order to maintain such stability. When confronted with situations featuring homogeneous stimulation, our perceptual world fragments. The fact that this occurs, and that it often does so in organized units, has important implications for the way in which perceptual experience is organized. This issue is taken up in the chapter to follow. In Chapter 11, we will address the general need which people seem to have for an optimal amount of stimulus change, an amount that is neither too little nor too much.

7

The Perception of Form

FIGURE FORMATION

Two-Dimensional Spatial Organization

The typical visual field consists of a variegated collection of dots, lines, brightenesses, colors, and other stimulus elements. Yet, as noted in the first chapter of this book, we usually do not experience these elements as a spatially unstructured and chaotic mosaic. Instead, our experiences are of meaningful objects which in some way "stand out from" or are segregated from their background. An interesting example of this point is provided in a drawing by the Dutch artist Maurits Escher reproduced in Figure 7.1. At first glance, the drawing may seem to consist of a random array of elements. After a bit of study, however, it becomes organized into figures representing either a group of fish on a dark background or a group of ducks in flight on a light background.

Visual figures appear whenever we look out into the real world. Whatever we look at, if there is something to be seen, we see it as figure or figures against some background. This fact points to an important aspect of our perceptual world: it is built, in part, upon figures which are sculptured out of a kaleidoscopic array of ambiguous stimulus elements and organized two-dimensionally on a plane surface. This accomplishment represents still another

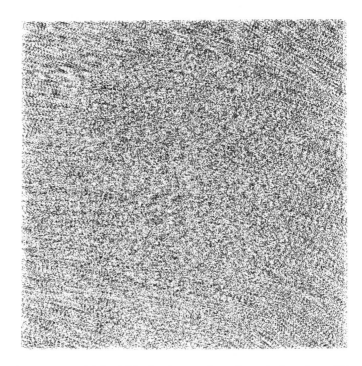

Plate 1.

A random-dot stereogram which yields the impression of a spiral surface. When viewed with a red filter over the right eye (Kodak Wratten gelatin filter No. 58) and a green filter over the left (Kodak Wratten gelatin filter No. 25), a spiral surface will appear to come forward off the page. (From Julesz, 1971, Copyright 1971 by Bell Telephone Laboratories, Inc. Reprinted by permission)

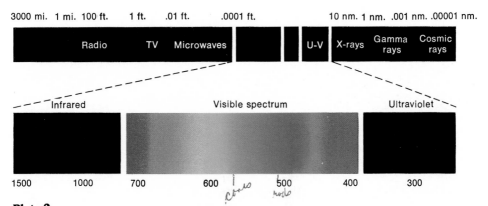

Plate 2.

The electromagnetic spectrum. The visible band of wavelengths is enlarged in the lower portion of the figure. This band extends from about 380 to 760 nanometers in wavelength. A nanometer is equivalent to a millionth of a millimeter. (From Bourne and Ekstrand, 1979)

Plate 3.
Protective coloration (camouflage). The coloration and contour of the mantid blends the insect's body into its surroundings. In this way, the mantid may remain concealed from potential predators. (From Ward's Natural Science Establishment, Inc.)

Plate 4.
A photograph of the village of St. Vincent, Italy, illustrating aerial perspective. The trees and houses in the foreground appear in sharp detail while the distant mountain peaks are hazy and have a bluish tint.

FIGURE 7.1   The segregation of objects from their background. In this drawing, it is possible to see a group of fish on a dark background or a group of ducks on a light background. (Based on a drawing, "Fish and Fowl," by M. Escher, 1971)

aspect of the way in which the perceptual system structures the world as we know it. In the present chapter, we shall take a broad view of the dynamics of form perception. Starting with processes which contribute to the formation of figures, we shall examine the factors involved in their organization, discrimination, and recognition.

The importance of contours   Perhaps the main, and most likely the indispensable, ingredient for the two-dimensional organization of the perceptual world is the presence of *contours* or borders. Contours are perceived when there is an abrupt change in the gradient of brightness or color between adjacent elements of the field of view. They represent an interface between a figure and its background (Zusne, 1970); indeed, figures have been defined as areas of the field which are set off from the remainder by visible contours (Hochberg, 1971a). This role of contour is illustrated in the drawing of a cat in Figure 7.2. The inner portion of the drawing has the same luminance as the page on which it appears. The drawing is set off from the page, however, by the abrupt change in brightness produced by the black lines which constitute its border. Similarly, in Figure 7.1, abrupt transitions between light and dark areas define the figures as "fish" and "fowl."

The importance of contour in the formation of figures is revealed when

FIGURE 7.2   A "sleeping cat." The black lines act as a border which sets off the figure from the surrounding area of the page. (From Attneave, 1954)

we interfere with the integrity of a figure's border. One means of doing this is to blur the border by projecting an image out of focus or by casting a shadow with relatively diffuse light. In an early study, Fry and Robertson (1935) reported that when targets with blurred borders are carefully fixated, they tend to disappear fairly quickly, apparently fusing with their background. Such results, of course, are reminiscent of our discussion in Chapter 6 of the perceptual fate of targets when inhomogeneity of stimulation is removed by presenting the stimuli in a Ganzfeld or under stopped-image conditions.

Still another way of interfering with the integrity of a figure's border is to embed the figure in a more complex design that incorporates its contours. An example of an "embedded figure" is given in Figure 7.3. The hexagon at the left is incorporated in both the parallelogram and the triangle; its own contours are now serving other functions and hence the simpler figure becomes harder to see or loses its identity entirely.

Camouflage   It is of interest to note that the phenomenon of embeddedness is not merely a clever laboratory demonstration; it is frequently encountered in the natural world in terms of protective camouflage. The coloration and striping of many animals enables them to blend with their background by avoiding sharp discontinuities of brightness and color. In this way, they remain concealed from potential prey or predators. The coloration of the mantid, for example, forms a pattern which does not coincide with the contour of the insect's body and thus aids in concealing its presence in foliage (see Plate 3). Along similar lines, military camouflage experts employ a variety of techniques to embed the contours of objects in the surrounding terrain or to make objects appear to be something that they are not (see Zusne, 1970, for a bibliographic survey of the military use of camouflage).

Neurophysiological Mechanisms

Retinal organization   One of the most exciting and important developments in our understanding of the perception of form has been the discovery of neural elements which are specialized for the detection of contours and for the coding of information regarding the features of patterns. In order to

FIGURE 7.3 An "embedded figure." The hexagon is concealed in the parallelogram and the triangle. (After Woodworth and Schlosberg, 1954)

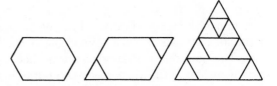

best describe some of these findings, it is necessary first to review some of the anatomical structures of the nerve-cell network in the retina. A highly simplified illustration of this network was presented in Figure 2.5. For the present purpose, a more elaborate illustration is provided in Figure 7.4.

The vertebrate retina contains three distinct neural layers. The first is the familiar layer of receptor cells—rods and cones—containing light-sensitive vi-

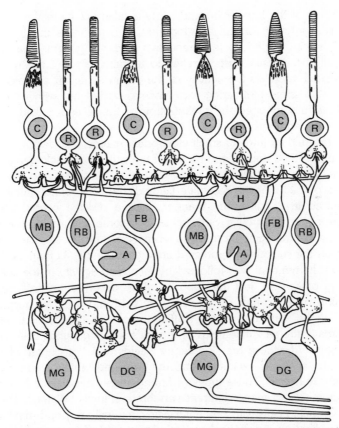

FIGURE 7.4 Schematic illustration of the interconnections in the nerve-cell network of the retina. A, amacrine; H, horizontal; C, cone; R, rod; MB, midget bipolar; RB, rod bipolar; FB, flat bipolar; MG, midget ganglion; DG, diffuse ganglion. (After Dowling and Boycott, 1966)

sual pigments. The second layer is made up of bipolar cells which receive inputs from the rods and cones. In addition, the second layer also contains horizontal cells, which make connections between the receptors and amacrine cells. The amacrine cells modify activity between the bipolars and the third layer (ganglion cells), which receives input from the bipolars. The axons of the ganglion cells form the optic nerve, which sends fibers to the brain. As Hubel (1963) has noted, the series of connections between layers does not represent a simple "bucket brigade" for impulses. Instead, the richness of the interconnections among retinal elements makes a variety of integrated mechanisms possible. You can gain some idea of the extent of the early processing and integration which takes place at the retinal level by noting that the optic nerve contains approximately 1 million myelinated fibers (Geldard, 1972), which transmit the information coming from approximately 130.5 million light-sensitive retinal cells!

One aspect of the integration and analysis taking place in the retina that is of particular interest for the development of contours is the behavior of ganglion cells with respect to their receptive fields. In general, the *receptive field* of a cell in the visual system refers to a limited area of the retina that, when stimulated, modifies the activity of the cell in either an excitatory or inhibitory way. In some pioneering experiments, carried out with cats, Kuffler (1953) successfully mapped the organization of the receptive fields of ganglion cells in the vertebrate retina.

Kuffler inserted exquisitely small electrodes (microelectrodes) into the retina of an anesthetized animal and recorded the activity of single ganglion cells when different areas of the retina were stimulated by a tiny, moving spot of light. He discovered that the receptive fields of the cat's retinal ganglion cells were organized in a concentric manner, with a disklike central area surrounded by a roughly circular outer zone. For some ganglia, a spot of light falling on the central region produced excitation ("on" response), whereas light falling on the surround suppressed activity in the cell as long as the light remained on. Its removal was followed by increased activity in the cell ("off" response). In other cells just the opposite effects occurred: an "off" response to illumination of the center of the receptive field and an "on" response to stimulation of the surround. Thus, Kuffler uncovered two distinct organizational patterns in the receptive fields of the cat's retinal ganglion cells. As illustrated in Figure 7.5, these are "on-center" fields and "off-center" fields. In the former, the center is excitatory and the surround inhibitory; in the latter just the opposite is true. These types of arrangements have since been found in the ganglion cells of many different vertebrate animals (Michael, 1969; Uttal, 1973). Ganglion cells with on-center fields generally respond maximally to small spots of light on a dark background; those with off-center fields respond most vigorously to small dark dots on an otherwise illuminated background (Rumelhart, 1977).

The center-surround arrangement has important implications for the reti-

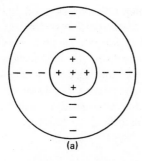
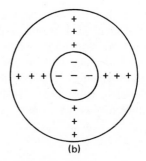

(a)   (b)

FIGURE 7.5 Schematic illustration of the receptive field organization of retinal ganglion cells described by Kuffler (1953). An "on-center" organization is presented in (a). Stimulation in the central region produces an excitation (+) response, whereas stimulation of the surrounding region inhibits the activity of the cell (−). The opposite type of organization, an "off-center" organization, is presented in (b).

nal processing of visual images. It suggests that ganglion cells act to compare the illumination of the center of their receptive fields with the illumination in the surround and thus are able to detect abrupt changes in illumination. This neural arrangement serves to accentuate edges and discontinuities in the optic array of light and enhances the ability of the visual system to extract contour information.

An example of how the center-surround arrangement may play a role in the detection of contours is presented in Figure 7.6. Most people viewing this design, called the *Hermann grid,* see "imaginary" contours in the form of dark spots at the intersections of the white stripes. Brown and Mueller (1965) have suggested the following explanation for the appearance of these spots. If

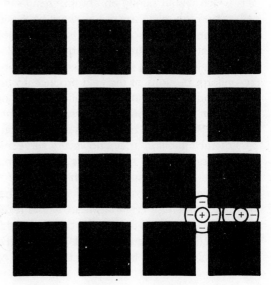

FIGURE 7.6 The Hermann grid. Dark spots appear at the intersections of the white stripes. Concentric circles at the lower right illustrate the mechanism proposed by Brown and Mueller to account for this effect. See text. (From Brown and Mueller, 1965)

we assume that the activation of an on-center unit signals a brightening in the field of view, such a unit would have a greater portion of its surrounding inhibitory zone illuminated when it is located at the intersection of the white stripes than a similar unit located some distance from the intersection. Thus, the center excitatory field of the unit at the intersection would be disproportionately subjected to inhibition and hence seem relatively dark. Following this suggestion, some investigators have attempted to use the Hermann grid to measure the size of visual receptive fields in humans (Jung and Spillman, 1970).

Lateral inhibition   In addition to the center-surround organization, there is still another mechanism by which the integrative action of the retinal network acts to aid in contour extraction. This mechanism is lateral inhibition, which we described in the previous chapter in regard to brightness contrast and lightness constancy. Recall that when a given cell in the visual system is stimulated, it may inhibit the activity of cells that are adjacent to it and that the amount of lateral suppression is inversely related to the distance between neighboring cells. A simple illustration of how such lateral interaction may help to augment the perception of sharp contours is sketched below with the help of Figure 7.7.

Suppose that the field of view consists of a black line on a white background that is otherwise strongly and uniformly illuminated. Stimulation from this field reaches ganglion cells A through E; the black line falls on cell C while the remainder of the field falls on cells A and B and D and E. Given the physical discontinuity in this pattern of stimulation, one might expect that it would be sufficient to elicit strong contrast in the activity of the network of cells which would signify an abrupt change in brightness. However, stimulus patterns on the retina are not as sharp as the illumination patterns which give rise to them. This is so because the eye is not a perfect optical device, and light is scattered within it. Consequently, cell C, upon which the black line falls, will also receive some diffuse stimulation. If we assume arbitrarily that the uniform portions of the field produce 15 units of excitation in cells A,B,D, and E, and that 9 units of excitation "leak" onto cell C, the activity rates of the cells in the network might resemble those shown in the left panel at the bottom of Figure 7.7 — excitation is present throughout the network.

Lateral inhibition may, however, serve as a built-in mechanism which dampens or clears up such "noise" on the retina. Let us assume, also arbitrarily, that when stimulated, each cell in the network exerts on its *immediately adjacent* neighbor a level of inhibition that is one-third of the excitation that it receives. Cell A, in this case, would receive 5 units of inhibition; cell B, 8 units (5 from A and 3 from C); cell C, 10 units (5 each from B and D); cell D, 8 units (3 from C and 5 from D); and cell D, 5 units. As a consequence of such lateral inhibitory interaction, the activity of cell C would be suppressed,

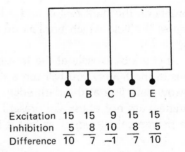

	A	B	C	D	E
Excitation	15	15	9	15	15
Inhibition	5	8	10	8	5
Difference	10	7	−1	7	10

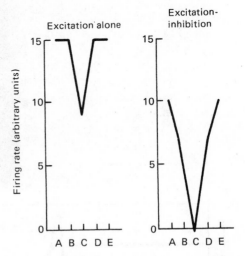

FIGURE 7.7 The role of lateral inhibition in aiding contour extraction. See text for explanation.

since the inhibition it receives (10 units) would exceed its excitation (9 units). Accordingly, as shown in the right panel of Figure 7.7, there would be a general decrease in the overall amount of activity, and more significantly a sharpening of the contrast between the activity of cell C and that of its neighbors. Thus, the neural coding of an abrupt change in stimulation, i.e., contour information, would be enhanced. While this illustration is highly simplified, it does depict the rudiments of how lateral inhibition can aid in the extraction of contours. More complex mathematical models of the role of lateral inhibition in this regard can be found in Ratliff (1965).

Evidence that the visual system acts in that way to extract and accentuate contours comes from work on an illusory phenomenon called *Mach bands* (or *Mach rings*) after the Austrian physicist-philosopher-psychologist Ernst Mach, who first discovered and investigated it. Mach bands refer to the perception of accentuated brightness and darkness in a visual field composed of a continuously changing distribution of intensity. More specifically, there is a band of increased apparent brightness in the bright region of the field which borders on the dark region and a band of increased darkness in the dark region of the field which borders on the bright region. An example is given in Figure 7.8.

If you look closely at the transition zone between the light and dark portions of the figure, you will see a narrow bright line at the bright edge and a narrow dark line at the dark edge. These bands of enhanced brightness and darkness are not physically present in the illustration; they are the product of the perceptual system. This fact is indicated by the solid line in the graph at

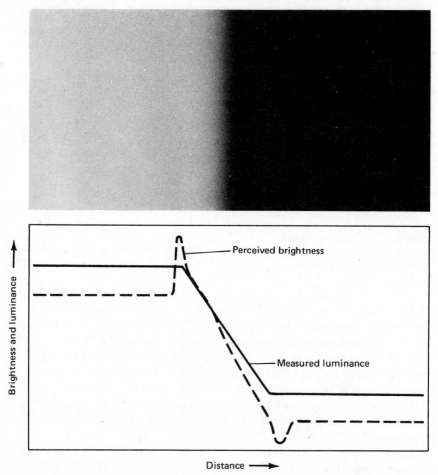

FIGURE 7.8 Mach bands. Examine the transition zone between the light and dark patches. Note a narrow line of increased brightness at the bright edge and a narrow line of increased darkness at the dark edge. The results of luminance measures across the surface of the figure and psychophysical measures of perceived brightness are shown in the accompanying graph. These curves reveal that the origin of the Mach bands is in the eye of the beholder; the bands are not physically present in the illustration (After Ratliff, 1972)

the bottom of Figure 7.8. It shows the results of measurements of the actual luminance in the figure. Note that there is a step-function of high luminance to a lower luminance to a still lower luminance. The dotted line illustrates the two sharp inflections in the perception of this pattern, one corresponding to the apparent bright band and the other to the apparent dark band.

Mach bands can also be seen in circular patterns, as shown in Figure 7.9. Within the circle you will note the presence of a dark ring that encloses the dark central circle. The ring seems even darker than the area it surrounds. Physically, however, there is no corresponding decrease in the region of the ring. The transition in intensity from the center to the circumference of the circle is continuous. The pattern in Figure 7.9 was actually obtained by photographing the pattern shown in Figure 7.10 while the pattern was rotating rapidly. Such a procedure yields a continuously changing intensity distribution.

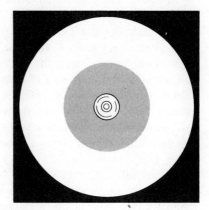

FIGURE 7.9   A Mach band in a circular pattern. Note the dark ring about halfway out from the center. The ring seems darker even than the circular area it encloses, despite the fact that the latter is physically darker than the portion of the surface where the ring appears.

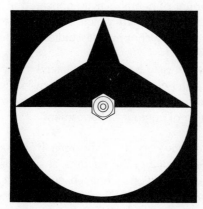

FIGURE 7.10   The stimulus which, when rapidly rotated, produced the Mach ring shown in Figure 7.9. Note that the ring in Figure 7.9 appears at the point of abrupt change in intensity.

Mach bands depend upon the spatial distribution of illumination. As described by Hurvich and Jameson (1966), they appear at those locations where the rate of change in luminance undergoes an increase or a decrease (mathematically, this phenomenon depends upon the second derivative, or the rate of change, in the slope of the spatial luminance distribution). The observation of Mach bands is not restricted to laboratory conditions; they can be experienced in several "real world" situations. For example, Ratliff (1965) has pointed out that you can see them at the edge of almost any shadow cast on a uniform surface by an object in sunlight. Bright bands appear at the transition zone from half-shadow to fully illuminated space, and dark bands are seen at the transition of full shadow to graded half-shadow. Indeed, as Ratliff has noted, artists and astronomers as well as psychologists have experienced Mach bands in the course of their work.

A careful study by Ratliff and Hartline (1959) using the eye of the horseshoe crab *Limulus* has provided compelling evidence that lateral inhibitory activity underlies the production of contours that is illustrated in the Mach band phenomenon. As a stimulus, they utilized a simple step pattern, similar to that in Figure 7.8, with the light area on the left and the dim on the right, and recorded the frequency of response in a single ommatidium. A mask with a tiny aperture was placed over the surface of the eye so that only one receptor unit could "see" the pattern, and the inhibitory influence of its neighbors was precluded. The pattern was moved in small steps across the eye and the activity of the single receptor cell was recorded at each step. As shown by the upper curve in Figure 7.11, the response of the ommatidium under these conditions faithfully followed the luminance pattern of the stimulus. When, however, the mask was removed, so that lateral interactions among the ommatidia could take place, a dramatically different result occurred. First, the overall amount of activity was lowered. Second, and most important, increases and decreases in the amount of neural activity appeared at the points of luminance transition in the stimulus pattern which correspond to the perception of bright and dark bands in psychophysical studies with human observers.

Still another phenomenon which may be based on lateral inhibitory activity in the visual system is the striking contour oscillation seen in Figure 7.12. Bridgeman (1971) has suggested that such oscillation results from overdriving a lateral inhibitory network capable of contour enhancement.

Feature detectors   The integrative action of the retinal network can be viewed as a preliminary means of analyzing the features of stimulus patterns. Neurophysiological research has, in addition, identified even more elaborate physiological analyzers which seem to be specialized for the detection of contours and other stimulus attributes. As Uttal (1973) has pointed out, these feature detectors emphasize the presence of complex processing in the periphery of the visual system.

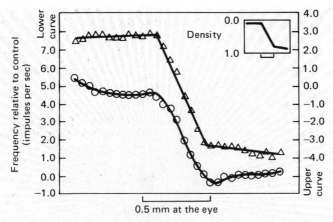

FIGURE 7.11 Mach bands and lateral inhibition. The discharge of impulses from a single ommatidium of the Limulus eye in response to a gradient of illumination (insert) moved across the retina. The upper curve (triangles) shows the form of this response relative to a control level when the eye was masked so that only the test receptor was illuminated. Note that the response of the ommatidium closely followed the luminance pattern of the stimulus. The lower curve (open circles) shows the response of the same receptor unit when the eye was unmasked and the receptor was then inhibited by the activity of adjacent ommatidia. (Data from Ratliff and Hartline, 1959; after Ratliff, 1965)

One of the first reports of such feature detectors was made by Lettvin, Maturana, McCulloch, and Pitts (1959) in a paper with the engaging title "What the Frog's Eye Tells the Frog's Brain." By means of electrodes inserted into the frog's optic nerve, these investigators observed the effects produced by spots of light, small dots, geometrical figures, and other stimuli which appeared within the animal's field of view. Lettvin and his colleagues were able to identify four different types of feature detectors in the frog's retina. One of these, called a sustained contrast detector, was responsive to a brightness disparity between two portions of the field of view. Another, termed a moving edge detector, responded only to moving edges, and a third, labeled a dimness detector, responded to any overall dimming of the field. The fourth type of detector, called a net convexity detector, responded to the presence of small moving spots. These types of detectors clearly have meaning for the frog's interaction with its environment. The first three could, for example, be involved in aiding the animal to notice looming predators, while the fourth could be termed a "bug detector" and be of use in locating insects, which are a staple of the frog's diet. These detectors also have meaning for an understanding of perception—they indicate how simple attributes of stimulus patterns can be extracted very early in visual processing.

Cellular units which analyze the properties of visual patterns can be found not only at the retinal level but throughout the visual system as well. This point has been demonstrated in a remarkable series of experiments by

FIGURE 7.12 A pattern that induces oscillating contours. (After MacKay, 1961)

Hubel and Wiesel (1959, 1962, 1963, 1968) conducted with cats and monkeys. In order to explore the neurophysiological activity which occurs in different regions of the neural pathways which lead from the eye to the brain, these investigators made use of an experimental arrangement like that shown in Figure 7.13. Anesthetized cats, for example, were positioned so that they faced a wide screen, and various stimuli consisting of edges, slits, and bars of

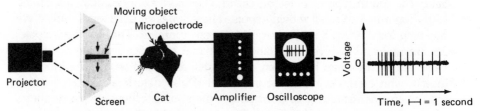

FIGURE 7.13 Experimental arrangement for studying the coding of form by single neurons in the visual system beyond the retina. See text for further explanation. (From Thompson, 1973)

light were projected onto the screen. Simultaneously, microelectrodes inserted into the brains of the animals recorded the activity triggered in single neurons by the stimuli flashed on the screen. In this way, Hubel and Wiesel successfully mapped receptive fields in a major relay station of the visual system, the lateral geniculate body of the thalamus, and in the visual projection areas of the cerebral cortex, the "striate region" of the optic lobe (see Figure 7.14 for a sketch of the neural pathway from the retina to the cortex).

Cells in the geniculate body were found to have many of the circumscribed "center-surround" receptive field characteristics that Kuffler described for retinal ganglion cells. Among other things, the geniculate cells seemed to have the function of enhancing responses to spatial differences in illumination that were initially encoded at the retinal level. Receptive fields in the cerebral cortex differed considerably from those present in the lower levels of the visual pathways. The concentric organization was no longer observed; instead, cortical receptive fields had side-to-side arrangements of excitatory and inhibitory areas separated by linear rather than circular boundaries. Some of these arrangements are illustrated in Figure 7.15.

One of the most stunning aspects of Hubel and Wiesel's work was the identification of four different classes of feature extractors which were anatomically arrayed in columns in the cortex and functionally organized in a multi-tiered manner. The most elementary of these was called a *simple cell.* Units of this sort responded to edges, bars, and slits of light which were oriented in a particular manner or moved in a particular direction with respect to the receptive field of the cell. Simple cortical cells were apparently stimulated by a large number of lateral geniculate cells whose "on" centers were arrayed along a straight line. Thus, a spot of light presented at any point along the line activated some of the geniculate cells, which, in turn, triggered a cortical cell. Another type of cortical cell was termed a *complex cell.* It responded to similar stimulus features as single cells, but its activity was less closely linked to the specific locus of the stimulus within its receptive field. Complex cells were apparently stimulated by simple cells. An illustration of the response of a complex cell is presented in Figure 7.16. At the highest level of this multi-tiered arrangement were *hypercomplex cells* which responded to edges, corners, and angles of particular sizes. These units could be divided into *lower-order hypercomplex cells,* which integrated information from complex cells, and *higher-order hypercomplex cells,* which received inputs from the lower-order units.

Thus, at the cortical level there appears to be a hierarchy of feature analyzers. Within each level, there are cells which respond maximally to particular properties of stimuli, and the activity of the cells at each level in the hierarchy integrates that of the cells in the next lower level (Uttal, 1973). Taken together with what we have learned of processing at the retinal and geniculate levels, it seems that the functional architecture of the visual system is

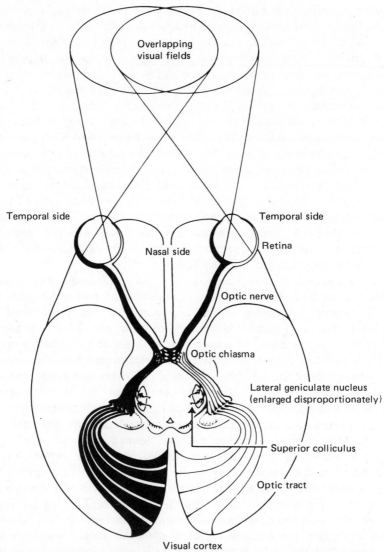

FIGURE 7.14 Schematic view of the underside of the human brain showing the major way stations in the neural pathways from the eye to the visual cortex. Fibers from retinal ganglion cells proceed to the optic chiasma. Here, those from the nasal halves of each eye cross to the opposite side of the brain and join with uncrossed fibers from the temporal half of the contralateral eye. In this way, both eyes are bilaterally represented in the higher visual centers. Beyond the chiasma, the majority of fibers continue on to a relay station in the thalamus, the lateral geniculate body. From this point, fibers proceed to the visual cortex. Some fibers leave the main optic tract and make synaptic connections in a midbrain center, the superior colliculus. This center is involved in controlling eye movements and the blink reflex to an object that appears suddenly in the visual field (From Bruce, 1977)

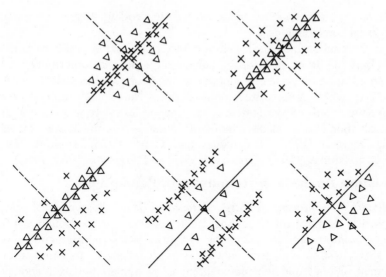

FIGURE 7.15 Some examples of cortical receptive fields. Triangles indicate areas giving inhibitory "off" responses; X's indicate areas giving excitatory "on" responses. (After Hubel and Wiesel, 1962)

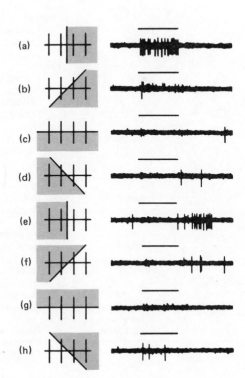

FIGURE 7.16 Response of a complex cell. The line above each record marks the presentation of a stimulus: (a), response to a vertical edge; (b–h), responses to various other orientations of the edge. (From Hubel and Wiesel, 1962)

geared for the extraction of contours and for coding abstract information about visual configurations.

The material on biological feature detectors presented in this section represents only the tip of an "iceberg" of neurophysiological information which has formed in recent years. A glimpse of the scope of this data is given in Table 7.1, which summarizes what Barlow, Narasimhan and Rosenfeld (1972) have called "trigger features" for a variety of neurons in several kinds of animals. For additional discussions of neural feature analyzers, you might consult Boynton (1970), Breitmeyer and Ganz (1976), Dodwell (1970), Lindsay and Norman (1977), Thomas (1970), and Weisstein (1969, 1973).

Feature Analysis in Human Form Perception

Identifying human feature detectors The discovery of neurophysiological feature analyzers has great potential for explaining the perception of contours and the formation of figures. We should remember, however, that these mechanisms have been identified in experiments with nonhuman animals and that generalizations to human behavior should be

TABLE 7.1   Trigger Features for a Variety of Neurons in Several Kinds of Animals

Anatomical Location	Trigger Feature
	Goldfish
Retina	Local redness or greenness
	Directed movement
	Frog
Retina	Convex edge
	Sustained edge
	Changing contrast
	Dimming
	Dark
Optic tectum	Newness
	Sameness
	Binocularity
	Pigeon
Retina	Directed movement
	Oriented edges
	Ground squirrel
Retina	Local brightening or dimming
	Local blueness of greenness
	Directed movement
Lateral geniculate body	Color coded units
Optic tectum	Directional units
	Oriented slits or bars
	Complex units

TABLE 7.1   Trigger Features for a Variety of Neurons in Several Kinds of Animals (continued)

Anatomical Location	Trigger Feature
	Rabbit
Retina	Local brightening or dimming
	Directed movement
	Fast or slow movement
	Edge detectors
	Oriented slits or bars
	Uniformity detectors
Lateral geniculate	Greater directional selectivity
Tectum	Habituating units
	Cat
Retina	Directed movement
	Uniformity detectors
Lateral geniculate	Local blueness or greenness
	Binocular, directional, and orientational units
Optic tectum	Directed movement
	Complex units
	Monkey
Retina	Local brightening or dimming
	Local redness, greenness, or blueness
Lateral geniculate	Various forms of color coding
Cortex	Similar to cat; some color coded
Inferotemporal cortex	Very complex; possible hand detector

Barlow, Narasimhan, and Rosenfeld, (1972).

made with caution. It would be comforting if, in addition to the presumption of phylogenetic continuity, we could find experimental evidence to support the belief that feature analyzing mechanisms are also at work in the human visual system. For obvious reasons, direct measures of single-cell activity are not readily available with human subjects. While there have been scattered efforts to chart the activity of single cells in the human visual cortex (for example, Marg, 1973), our knowledge of the operation of human pattern analyzers has been gained indirectly and is based, for the most part, upon inferences drawn from psychophysical experiments.

One source of such inferences is the work on stabilized images, luminous designs, and stimulation in the Ganzfeld described in the previous chapter. The finding that under these conditions patterns disintegrate in *organized units* has been taken by some psychologists as evidence that the human visual system contains elements which are sensitive to individual features of the stimulus field (Weisstein, 1969).

Still another means of drawing inferences about the operation of feature detectors is to make use of adaptation effects resulting from the prolonged viewing of a stimulus pattern. If feature detectors are involved in human perceptual functions, and observers are permitted to inspect a stimulus for a period of time, we might expect that specific feature detectors will fatigue. This should result in predictable differences in the perceptual response to subsequent stimulation.

Such a possibility was tested in an experiment by McCollough (1965), who had observers scan a grating containing vertical orange and black stripes which alternated every few seconds with a grating composed of horizontal blue and black stripes. After watching this alteration for two to four minutes, the observers were shown achromatic test gratings of vertical or horizontal white and black lines, as illustrated in Figure 7.17. The vertical test pattern appeared to be tinged with blue and the horizontal pattern with orange. A result of this sort suggests that the inspection period produced color adaptation of orientation-specific edge detectors in the visual system. McCollough's finding has been replicated and extended in several subsequent investigations (see Skowbo, Tinney, Gentry, and Morant, 1975) and is now generally known as the *color-contingent aftereffect* or, more simply, as the *McCollough effect.* An interesting demonstration of this effect which you can conduct yourself is described by Favreau and Corballis (1976).

The adaptation procedure has led to evidence for other types of feature detectors as well. For example, Riggs (1973) has described a curvature-contingent aftereffect which, as illustrated in Figure 7.18, suggests the presence of cortical cells for detecting the degree of curvature in a pattern. Similarly, Blakemore and Sutton (1969) have reported an aftereffect which implies the

FIGURE 7.17 Achromatic test pattern used to study color-contingent aftereffects. After inspecting vertical orange and black-striped and horizontal blue and black-striped gratings, the left half of the test grating appears to be tinged with blue and the right half with orange. (From McCollough, 1965)

Inspection   Test·

Red   Green   Achromatic

FIGURE 7.18 Samples of inspection and test patterns used to study curvature-contingent aftereffects. After gazing alternately at a red inspection pattern containing convex lines and a green pattern with concave lines, the corresponding lines on the achromatic test pattern are seen as greenish and pinkish, respectively. (After Riggs, 1973)

presence of spatial-frequency detecting neurons. These investigators found that if one looks at a wide-spaced grating pattern for about one minute and then scans a medium-spaced grating in the same orientation, the test grating will appear to be more narrowly spaced than it really is. Similarly, if the inspection grating is narrow, a medium-spaced test grating will appear more widely spaced than it really is. Presumably, the inspection grating selectively adapted low-frequency (wide-spacing) detectors in the former case and high-frequency (narrow-spacing) detectors in the latter. This effect is illustrated in Figure 7.19.

A related means for probing for the presence of human feature analyzers is to make use of a selective adaptation procedure in which the effects are noted of viewing contours in one orientation on the subsequent perception of contours with the same or different orientations. Underlying this procedure is the assumption that viewing contours in a given orientation will selectively adapt feature detectors "tuned" to that orientation, and thus the subsequent perception of contours having the same orientation will be degraded. This procedure has been termed a *forward masking* procedure; the test stimulus is designated as the "target" and the stimulus initially inspected is called the "mask."

A substantial number of experiments have demonstrated that prolonged viewing of a masking grating changes the perceptibility of a target grating that is identical or similar to the mask: discrimination thresholds to the target are elevated, the apparent contrast of the target is depressed, the accuracy with which the target can be identified is lowered, and the speed of identification is slowed. On the other hand, the perceptibility of target gratings which differ in orientation or size from the mask is unaffected (see Blakemore and Campbell, 1969; Gilinsky and Cohen, 1972; Pantle and Sekuler, 1968; Weisstein, 1969, 1973; Weisstein and Bisaha, 1972). Results such as these strongly imply the operation of feature detection mechanisms in the human visual system.

Contour formation: more than meets the eye From what has been said to this point, it would be tempting to conclude that the neural code for the two-dimensional spatial organization of the visual world has at least been partially determined. More specifically, we might say that contours are coded

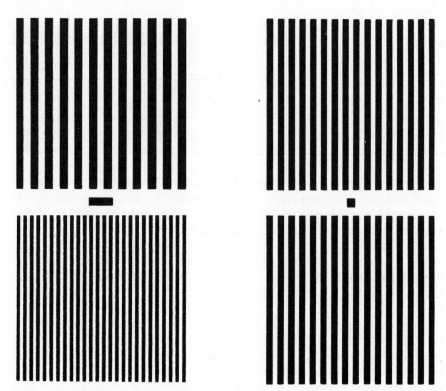

FIGURE 7.19   Inspection and test patterns used to demonstrate a spatial-frequency after-effect. The gratings on the right are identical. Place the illustration about 2 meters away from you and look at the pair of gratings on the left. Let your gaze wander back and forth along the horizontal fixation bar between the two gratings. After one minute, quickly shift your gaze to the fixation bar between the two gratings on the right. The grating above the fixation bar will now seem to have narrower stripes than the one below the bar. (After Blakemore and Sutton, 1969)

by the action of feature detectors functioning as elements in a system which performs a property-list analysis of stimuli. The wiring of such feature analyzers into neural networks enables us to perceive contours which are the primary ingredient for the two-dimensional organization of the visual scene.

A conclusion of this sort would certainly be attractive. Nevertheless, it would be premature given the present state of knowledge. For one thing, not all investigators are convinced that the results of psychophysical experiments such as those just described can be interpreted as reflecting the operation of feature analyzers. It has been argued, for example, that contingent after-effects, such as the McCollough effect, persist for periods of time that are too long to reflect the fatigue of physiological mechanisms. Instead, such after-effects may be based upon some form of associative learning (Jones and

Holding, 1975; Murch, 1972; Skowbo, Tinney, Gentry, and Morant, 1975). In addition, a relatively simple system of physiological analyzers does not adequately explain certain other perceptual experiences involving contour formation.

Uttal (1973) has pointed out that a crucial aspect of the view that contour development is dependent upon a simple feature analysis network is that the features to be detected must be present in the stimuli. However, experiments in which critical stimulus elements are missing suggest that in some cases contour formation may be determined more by contextual factors than by the presence or absence of specific features. In one such experiment, Uttal (1969) studied the recognition of alphabetic characters composed of the dot patterns shown in Figure 7.20. These patterns can be considered as forms with missing parts, for no continuous features are presented. Rather, the features are suggested by the statistical relation of the dots. The dot patterns of

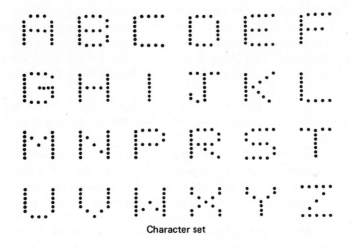

Character set

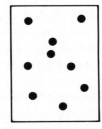 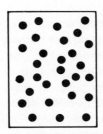 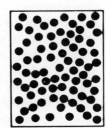

Visual noise backgrounds

FIGURE 7.20   Stimuli and backgrounds used to study the recognition of dotted letters in dynamic visual noise. The letters were placed within the limits of the visual noise field. (After Uttal, 1969)

letters were embedded in a field of "visual noise" which, as shown in Figure 7.20, consisted of a random array of dots. Presumably, presenting letters composed of periodic dots together with a random array of other similar dots should interfere with the suggestion of continuous features and result in reduced recognition of the letters. Indeed, the "noise" background lowered the recognizability of most letters to chance levels. However, a few—I, K, L and X—continued to be recognized with greater-than-chance accuracy. The fact that the contours of some alphabetic dot characters could be separated from noise under these conditions suggests that something more than a property-list analysis was involved in their perception.

In a related experiment, Uttal, Bunnell, and Corwin (1970) explored the effects of visual noise on the detectability of the orientation of dotted lines. In this case, observers were able to recognize the orientation of dotted test lines embedded in dotted visual noise beyond chance levels of accuracy. As the authors point out, the crucial aspect of this experiment was the requirement that the subjects select from several isolated point stimuli a particular set of stimuli which is aligned in some statistical manner along a common axis. Since the dots of the target line were no more interconnected with one another than they were with those of the noise, it is difficult to understand how a simple feature-extracting mechanism could operate to synthesize contour information in this situation.

Research with the forward-masking paradigm, which, as we have seen, has provided support for feature-specific detectors in contour formation, has also provided evidence to indicate that more complex mechanisms may be involved. Weisstein (1970) has reported that a masking grating will reduce the apparent brightness of a subsequent test grating even if the test grating is located within a portion of the mask that had been covered by a cubelike drawing (see Figure 7.21). Thus, adaptation effects occurred to a region of the mask that was not visible! Weisstein suggested that this result reflects the presence of neural mechanisms which convey the information "in back of." Such a mechanism, of course, implies the operation of higher-level symbolic functions which extend beyond neurophysiological feature mechanisms that have so far been identified.

As a final example of the complexities of contour formation, consider Figure 7.22. Most people report seeing a white triangle, a white square, and a white circle, respectively, in configurations (a), (b), and (c). The triangle, square, and circle appear to have sharp contours which surround a region of enhanced brightness. They also seem to have an opaque surface and to be superimposed upon the other elements of the scene. Figure 7.22(d) is just the reverse; you see a black triangle with distinct contours surrounding a region of enhanced blackness. The striking aspect of these illustrations is that you are perceiving figures set off by contours that are not physically present. Consequently, such contours are termed "subjective contours" (Coren, 1972; Kaniza, 1976; Lawson and Gulick, 1967) or "cognitive contours" (Gregory, 1972).

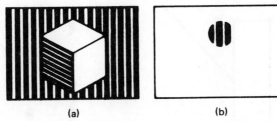

FIGURE 7.21   Inspection (a) and test (b) figures used to demonstrate that adaptation occurs not only to portions of a grating that are visible but also to those portions blocked from view. After studying the inspection figure, observers rated the relative brightness of the test figure, which was positioned to fall in the area of the field previously occupied by the top plane of the cube. The relative brightness of the test figure was reduced to some degree even though it appeared in the region of the inspection figure obscured by the cube. (After Weisstein, 1970)

Though subjective contours are not physically present, they are nonetheless real; they are perceptible and they can influence perceptual responses to other stimuli. For example, Figure 7.23(a) portrays the *Poggendorff illusion*, in which the slope of the oblique line seems to be distorted by the interruption of the "objective" rectangle. Figure 7.23(b) shows the same effect evoked by a "subjective" rectangle.

The phenomenon of contours which can be formed in the absence of physical brightness gradients is difficult to explain completely on the basis of

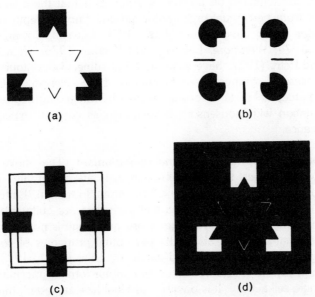

FIGURE 7.22   Subjective contours. Illustrated in (a) is a subjective white triangle; in (b), a subjective square; in (c), a subjective circle. In (d), a subjective triangle is shown with reversed brightness of that presented in (a). (From Coren, 1972)

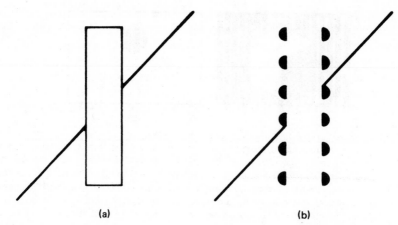

FIGURE 7.23 The Poggendorff illusion. In (a), it is generated by a physical contour, in (b), by a "subjective" contour. (After Gregory, 1972)

feature-specific physiological analyzers. While there is some evidence that lateral inhibitory or edge-detector effects may play a role in their formation (Coren and Theodor, 1977; Smith and Over, 1976), subjective contours imply that there is more than meets the eye in contour formation and that complex cognitive functions are involved. The exact nature of the higher-level functions which underlie the formation of subjective contours has stimulated considerable interest in recent years. One possibility suggested by Coren (1972) and substantiated by several experiments is that these subjective patterns result from perceptual organization around implicit depth cues (Coren and Theodor, 1975; Gregory and Harris, 1974; Lawson, Cowan, Gibbs, and Whitmore, 1974; Whitmore, Lawson, and Kozora, 1976). In a larger vein, Bradley and Petry (1977) have suggested that subjective contours may result from a process of synthesis (see Hochberg, 1968; Neisser, 1967) through which the perceptual system "builds" figures by integrating fragments of sensory information with nonsensory factors such as context, expectation, and past experience.

Contours, neurophysiology, and reductionism The above material is not intended to suggest that neurophysiological data are of little use in leading psychologists to an understanding of contour formation. Rather, our discussion is intended to stress the idea that such data are quite important, but, at the same time, current knowledge in psychobiology is not sufficient to account for all that is known about the perceptual properties of contours. We are voicing the same caution raised earlier by Uttal (1971, 1973) against a hasty attempt toward a total reduction of contour-forming mechanisms to aspects of single-cell activity. It is possible, as Uttal has suggested, that the physiological feature analyzers which have been identified to date are only parts of far more elaborate neurophysiological ensembles.

Along these lines, it now seems possible that the visual system may code contour information on the basis of a property-list analysis, but that the properties on the list are not direct aspects of stimulus features (Weisstein, 1973). It has long been known that in perceiving sound the auditory system performs a kind of Fourier analysis, in which complex sound vibrations are analyzed into simpler sine-wave components (Geldard, 1972; Yost and Nielsen, 1977). Recent evidence suggests that the visual system may be organized to perform a spectral decomposition, in which complex spatial patterns of brightness and darkness are separated into simpler functions. Contours may be coded in terms of this type of transformation (Blakemore and Campbell, 1969; Campbell and Robson, 1968; Cornsweet, 1970; Graham, 1977; Harmon and Julesz, 1973; Legge, 1976; Wenderoth and Beh, 1977). Indeed, spatial frequency analysis may prove to be the Rosetta stone for breaking the feature-detection code.

INHIBITING FIGURE FORMATION

Temporal Development of Figures

The problem   Under ordinary circumstances our percepts seem to be immediate and fully formed. However, we also know that the processes which intervene between stimulation and perception, though speedy, must take some time. How can we track the course of the temporal development ("microgenesis") of the perception of form? One procedure which has proved successful is to make use of a paradigm known as "backward masking."

The backward-masking paradigm   We used the phrase "forward masking" in an earlier section to refer to the case in which perception of a "target" stimulus was affected by prior presentation of a "masking" stimulus. In the backward-masking paradigm, it is the first stimulus which serves as the target and the second as the mask; again, perception of the target stimulus is degraded by presentation of the mask. This masking effect is especially intriguing since it seems to be working backward in time. For that reason, backward masking is of intrinsic interest to researchers in perception; in addition, it has been used as a device for studying the temporal development of perception. It provides a way of stopping perceptual processing or disrupting figure formation, thereby enabling one to determine how long it takes for a given percept to develop. We will look first at that use of the backward-masking paradigm and then turn to research on masking *per se*.

Figure formation: how much time?   If not instantaneously, how long does it take for a figure to form? In a series of experiments, Werner (1935) studied the backward masking of a black disk by a black masking ring which fit snugly around the disk. When, under proper circumstances, he repeated the sequence—disk-ring, disk-ring—he found that the disk could be made to disappear. What the observers saw was a black ring with an empty center —a doughnut. Werner argued that the disk disappeared because its developing contour had fused with the inner contour of the developing ring. With its contour lost in that fashion, the disk no longer existed as a figure.

It was important to Werner's argument that figure development proceeded from the center out. In his thinking, then, the disk was growing both temporally and spatially; it became obliterated as a figure when its *spreading boundary* met the inner edge of the ring just as the latter was beginning to evolve. For backward masking to occur, both the spatial and temporal relations between target and mask must be just right. In the case of the spatial relation, that meant close physical proximity—ideally, contiguity. But in the case of the temporal relation, optimal masking would occur when the target and mask onsets (referred to as *stimulus onset asynchrony,* or SOA) were separated in time rather than simultaneous. The separation also should not be too long; if so, disk formation would already have been completed when mask formation began, and the disk contour would no longer be vulnerable to disruption. Thus, it is to be expected that the curve relating extent of masking to SOA would be nonmonotonic, rising to a maximum and then falling to zero (an "inverted U-shaped function"). In Werner's experiments, and in many subsequent studies, an inverted U-shaped function has been obtained (panel [b] in Figure 7.24). The value of SOA that is optimal for masking typically

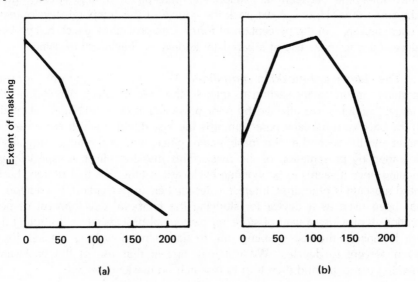

Stimulus onset asynchrony (msec)

FIGURE 7.24 Schematic illustration of two kinds of backward-masking functions. In (a), the extent of masking is greatest when target and mask come on at the same time. In (b), maximum masking occurs when the onset of the mask follows the onset of the target by 50 to 100 msec.

falls between 50 and 100 msec—that is, between $\frac{1}{20}$ and $\frac{1}{10}$ of a second. Masking declines to zero at about 200 msec. Clearly, then, in the case of simple figures, figure formation is complete in about 200 msec, though the developing figure is most vulnerable to disruption about 50 to 100 msec after its onset.

It turns out also (Kolers, 1962) that not all masking functions take the inverted U-shaped form. Under some circumstances extent of masking is greatest at a value of zero SOA (that is, target and mask come on at the same time), and declines as SOA increases (panel [a] in Figure 7.24). It has not been fully determined what conditions yield inverted U-shapes and what produce monotonic functions.

The evidence so far indicates that inverted U-shaped functions are most likely when target and mask are approximately equal in energy, when they are presented peripherally rather than to the central fovea, and when the subject's task involves some variant of target recognition (Breitmeyer and Ganz, 1976; Kahneman, 1968; Lefton, 1972; Weisstein, 1972). It is the inverted U-shaped functions which have proved the most interesting theoretically. Monotonic functions can be explained fairly simply by assuming that though separated in clock time, target and mask occupy the same "neural" time period. Thus, it has been argued, visual stimuli which occur within about 100 msec of one another are processed as though they were simultaneous. Given that assumption, it is possible to show that the backward-masking effect results from a summation of the luminances of the target and mask and a consequent reduction in the contrast between the target and its background (Eriksen and Lappin, 1964). Such an explanation, however, cannot be applied to masking results which follow the inverted U-shaped function, since the luminance summation, on which the explanation rests, should decrease with increasing SOA and thus too should contrast reduction and the resulting masking effect.

Theories of Backward Masking

Werner's account of masking, though clever and fruitful, was too vague and fanciful to be taken seriously, especially by those who insisted on a plausible underlying neurophysiological mechanism. In the past decade or two a host of alternative theories has been offered, among them the luminance summation-contrast reduction theory mentioned above. Most have taken as their main burden the generation of the troublesome inverted U-shaped function. All have been found wanting. Rather than review this history of frustration, we want to call your attention to the latest and most comprehensive of the masking theories—one proposed by Breitmeyer and Ganz (1976). A similar theory has also been developed by Weisstein, Ozog, and Szoc (1975).

Transient and sustained channels Breitmeyer and Ganz note the existence of two kinds of visual information-processing channels, *transient* and *sustained,* as revealed in neurophysiological investigations. Transient channels are triggered by sudden onset of a stimulus; they have a short latency and a fast conduction speed. They serve mainly to signal the occurrence of a visual stimulus. Sustained channels are slower to respond, in terms of both latency and conduction speed. They serve the function of extracting information about the spatial properties of a stimulus. Neurophysiological evidence also indicates that activity in transient channels can inhibit ongoing activity in the sustained channels.

With these two types of channel as the actors, the stage is set for an inverted U-shaped masking function. In effect, Breitmeyer and Ganz argue that backward masking occurs when the transient activity instigated by the masking stimulus overtakes and inhibits the sustained activity initiated by the target stimulus. With the process of extracting spatial (pattern) information about the target thus interrupted, the observer cannot accurately identify or recognize it. Moreover, the temporal properties of transient and sustained channels are such that an inverted U-shaped masking function is inevitable, with a peak around 50 msec, as illustrated in Figure 7.25.

One fundamental issue which Breitmeyer and Ganz also address has to do with the functional significance of backward masking. Ordinarily, we assume that over the course of evolution those structures and functions which have survived must, unless proved otherwise, have some adaptive value. Of what use is backward masking? Offhand, it would seem that masking must interfere with information processing and that being susceptible to masking is a liability rather than an asset. However, according to Breitmeyer and Ganz, what backward masking does is bias the organism in favor of new stimuli over old. It allows attention to be drawn to sudden, peripheral events, the sort that might signal, for example, predator or prey; in addition, masking clears the system, thereby making room for these new, potentially important events to be processed.

Target recovery   We have presented above only some of the highlights of the Breitmeyer and Ganz theory. Its virtues are many, but it does share one defect with the other masking theories. All set out to explain how backward masking might occur; that goal is achieved when the theory is so constructed that it does, indeed, predict masking under appropriate circumstances. The problem with all masking theories is that they overachieve their goal: they wipe out the target. That is a problem, rather than a virtue, only because of evidence that the masked target may not in fact be irretrievably erased. On the contrary, it has been shown that backward masking is not an irreversible process: a masked target, under special circumstances, can be recovered, at least to some extent. The following passage, excerpted from a talk given by one of your authors (Dember, 1976), tells the target-recovery story and offers what was intended as a light-hearted characterization of masking theories and of the implication for theory posed by the phenomenon of target recovery.

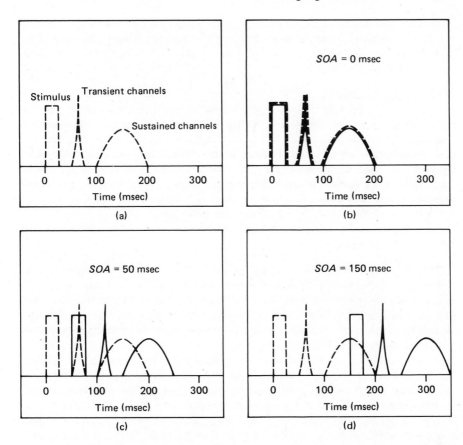

FIGURE 7.25 The generation of inverted U-shaped backward-masking functions according to the theory of Breitmeyer and Ganz (1976). The theory posits two types of neurophysiological responses to stimuli called transient-channel and sustained-channel responses. As shown in (a), the occurrence of a stimulus is signaled by a brief burst of transient-channel activity. This is followed by sustained channel activity which extracts pattern information from the stimulus. It is assumed that when they overlap in time, transient-channel responses inhibit those of the sustained channels.

In (b), a target stimulus (dotted lines) and a masking stimulus (solid lines) are presented simultaneously (SOA = 0). Since the transient response to the mask does not overlap the sustained response to the target, masking at this SOA is minimal. In (c), the SOA is increased to 50 msec, and the transient response to the mask now overlaps with the sustained response to the target. The sustained response would be inhibited, and masking would be maximal at this SOA. In (d), the SOA is increased still further to 150 msec. At this SOA, the sustained activity to the target is completed before the transient response to the mask is initiated; the target would be fully processed and masking would once again fall to a minimal level. (After Breitmeyer and Ganz, 1976)

I wondered whether it would be possible to restore the perception of a masked target by introducing a third stimulus into the standard target-mask paradigm. The third stimulus would have to be one that would effectively mask the original masking stimulus but have minimal direct effect on the original target. If such conditions could be met, would the target stimulus become *easier* to perceive than it is in the conventional masking paradigm?

Dean Purcell devoted a year of pilot testing to finding the parameters that we were seeking and a second year to doing two formal experiments to determine whether *target recovery,* as we came to call it, could be demonstrated. At about the point when he was writing up the research for his master's thesis, a similar study was reported by Daniel Robinson (1966). There were substantial methodological differences between the Purcell and the Robinson experiments, though both were designed to answer the same question. And both came up with the same positive answer.

The type of stimuli used by Purcell are shown in Figure [7.26.]

The target stimulus was one of two letters of the alphabet, D or O. Mask 1 was a black disc; mask 2 was a black ring.

The experimental design is outlined in Figure [7.27], which shows four conditions in which target recognition was measured: target alone; plus mask 1; target plus mask 1 plus mask 2; and a control condition in which the target and mask 2 were presented, to assess any direct effect of mask 2 on the target stimulus. In all four conditions the subject's task was to say what letter had been presented. A total of 100 trials was run in each condition, with 25 college-student volunteers, naive about the purpose of the experiment, serving as subjects.

The results of one of Purcell's two experiments are summarized in Figure [7.28.] The bars indicate mean percent correct target recognition. In this experiment the intervals between stimuli were such that mask 2, by itself, had relatively little effect on target recognition, as indicated in a comparison of conditions T and $T + M_2$. In Purcell's first experiment this was not the case, and a correction had to be built into the data analysis to partial out the direct effect of mask 2 on the target. Both experiments provided convincing evidence of target recovery (Dember and Purcell, 1967). The rele-

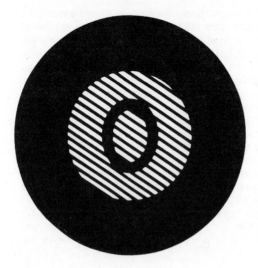

FIGURE 7.26 The spatial arrangement of the target letter, masking disk, and masking ring used in the target-recovery experiments. The disk (crosshatched in the figure) is Mask 1 and the ring is Mask 2. Both masks were solid black, as was the target letter (D or O)

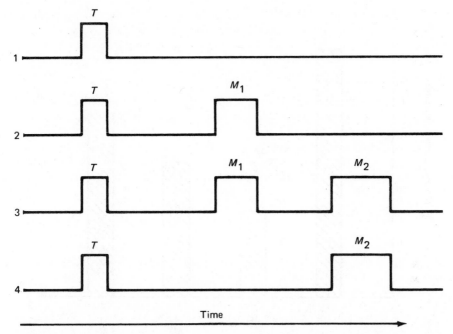

FIGURE 7.27   The four conditions of the Dember and Purcell (1967) target-recovery experiments. Vertical lines represent stimulus onset and termination. The target stimulus is designated by T, masking stimuli by M_1 and M_2.

vant comparison is that between conditions $T + M_1$ and $T + M_1 + M_2$; the difference in mean percentage of correct target recognition is significant and in a direction consistent with the notion of target recovery. However, comparison of conditions T and $T + M_1 + M_2$ indicates that the recovery of the target was not complete. . . .

What became clear to me only after the data were in was that target recovery has profound theoretical significance: it indicates that backward masking does not simply "erase" or in some other way irreversibly degrade the target stimulus. Some representation of the stimulus must remain after masking if the target subsequently can be recovered. Thus, target recovery eliminates a whole class of masking models, or at least suggests serious limits to their generality. . . .

In searching for an image to help communicate these ideas, I came up with the illustration in Figure [7.29]. You might think of this as the "fishy model" of backward masking. The work of such a model is completed when the big fish (the mask) has swallowed the little fish (the target).

Now, if adding a second mask to the standard paradigm simply iterated the process shown in Figure [7.29], then the outcome would be as depicted in the next figure [Fig. 7.30]. Obviously, such a model does not predict target recovery. If anything, the target should be even further engulfed by the addition of a second mask.

So much for conventional masking models; they don't seem to work in the recovery paradigm, possibly because they work too well in the standard situation. It may be a case of overkill. A better model would be one that didn't end up by wiping

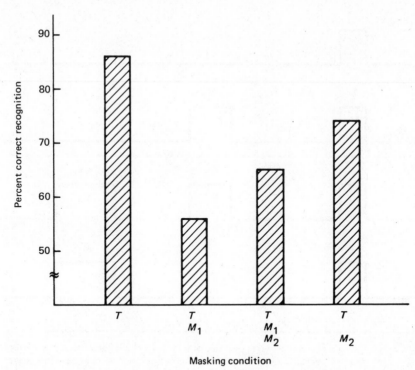

Masking condition

FIGURE 7.28   Mean percent target recognition (corrected for guessing) in each of the four conditions of one of the Dember and Purcell (1967) experiments. Target recovery is indicated by the difference between conditions $T + M_1$ and $T + M_1 + M_2$.

FIGURE 7.29   The "fishy model" of backward masking. See text for interpretation of this figure and Figures 7.30, 7.31, and 7.32. (All drawn by D. Kopriwa)

FIGURE 7.30   The "fishy model" extended to the target-recovery paradigm.

out the target, but rather by keeping it out of the perceptual stream. Of course, if it stayed out long enough, it would become a "dead fish," but for some brief period after being captured it could still be revived.

I know my metaphor isn't quite adequate, but maybe a better model could be built on the image depicted in the following two figures. In Figure [7.31] the big fish is shown capturing the little fish and holding it out of the water (that's masking); in Figure [7.32] (recovery), the biggest fish captures the bigger fish, who, in response, drops

FIGURE 7.31   A modified "fishy model" of masking.

FIGURE 7.32   The modified "fishy model" extended to target recovery.

the little fish back into the water, and the little fish continues on its way, perhaps with less than normal skill and vigor, you might say "floundering," up the stream to consciousness.

What seems to be needed is a better account of what happens in the standard backward-masking paradigm when, to use Breitmeyer and Ganz's concepts, the activities of the transient and sustained channels meet. Clearly, the inhibition imposed by transient on sustained channels involves some sort of temporary blockage rather than an immediate and permanent erasure. In addition, the question remains of whether the same concepts used to explain backward masking can by themselves simply be extended to handle target recovery.

PRINCIPLES OF ORGANIZATION

Figure and Ground

Basic characteristics   The formation of contours can be viewed as the initial phase in the dynamics of form perception or, as Rock (1973) has characterized it, contours provide the "building blocks" of form perception. In the sections to follow we move beyond the mechanics of this initial phase to consider more molar issues regarding the "structures" themselves. The first is the manner in which developed contours and the patterns to which they give rise are organized in two-dimensional space.

At the outset of this chapter, we stated that figures are always seen as standing out from or segregated from their background—some aspects of the field of view stand out in a distinctive way from the others. This statement re-

flects a fundamental principle of perceptual organization which was first articulated by the Danish psychologist Edgar Rubin (1915, 1921) in the concept
of figure and ground. That part of the field which appears as a sharply delineated unit is known as the *figure* while the remainder is termed the *ground.*
Figure-ground segregation is one of the most primitive aspects of perceptual
organization. It is present very early in life, and figural units are seen as separated from the ground even before they can be recognized as particular figures (see Chapter 12). In this latter sense, figure-ground segregation can be
considered in terms of what Neisser (1967) describes as a preattentive process—that is, an automatic global analysis which precedes the extraction or
the construction of figure detail.

The figure-ground aspect of two-dimensional spatial organization is often
illustrated by means of *reversible figures*—figures which are so structured that
they permit either of two possible figure-ground relations. You see either Figure A or Figure B. If Figure A is seen, then the part of the pattern that would
have been B becomes ground. Escher's "Fish and Fowl" painting portrayed
in Figure 7.1 is such a reversible figure. Other examples are presented in Figures 7.33 and 7.34.

Figure 7.33 can be seen as a radial array of dark arrows on a white background. It can also be seen as a white square with dark arrows superimposed
upon a dark square. In this case, some of the "arrow heads" now serve as
portions of the dark background. Similarly in Figure 7.34, one can view the
dark region as figure—two dancers—and the light region as ground, or the
light portion as figure—a face in three-quarter profile—and the dark as
ground. The cross in Figure 1.3 (Chapter 1) and Figures 9.2 and 9.3 (Chapter

FIGURE 7.33   A reversible figure in which it is possible to see a radial array of arrows on a
white background or a white square with dark arrows superimposed upon a
dark square. These organizations tend to alternate with continued inspection.

FIGURE 7.34 Reversible figure which, upon continued inspection, yields the alternate impressions of two dancers or a face in three-quarter profile. (Drawing by G. M. Rand)

9) are other examples of reversible figures (for some fascinating additional examples see Attneave, 1971).

If you examine these illustrations carefully, you will note that the phenomenal properties of the figure and the ground differ. These differences were described by Rubin, who pointed out that the figure has structure; further, a figure has "thing" quality, while the ground is relatively shapeless and unstructured. The figure also appears to lie in front of the ground, while the ground extends continuously behind the figure. Finally, the figure is more dominant than the ground; it is more likely to suggest meaning and to be remembered.

Figural persistence The memory element in figure-ground segregation leads to an interesting phenomenon called *figural persistence*, which was discovered by Rubin in his early work. Once an ambiguous field is structured by the perceiver into a particular figure-ground organization, that organization will tend to dominate on subsequent presentations of the field.

As reported by Woodworth and Schlosberg (1954), Rubin arranged things so that a series of 18 nonsense forms, such as those illustrated in Figure 7.35, could be projected on a screen. They appeared as irregular green areas surrounded by black. For half of the stimuli, Rubin instructed subjects to see the green area as figure and the black as ground, while the opposite instruction was given for the remaining stimuli. Approximately 30–45 minutes after an initial inspection period, the subjects were shown the stimuli again with no particular instructions as to which portions should be seen as figure. For each stimulus, they were simply to report whether the green or the black area now appeared as figure. Sixty-four percent of the ambiguous stimuli were seen in the same figure-ground organization as they were in the initial inspection period. In Woodworth and Schlosberg's words, "as the subject had divided the field the first time into figure and ground, so he was likely to do the second time even when remaining passive" (Woodworth and Schlosberg, 1954, p. 405). Although there has been some controversy over the validity of Rubin's finding (see Epstein, 1967), it seems to have been substantiated by later research (Cornwell, 1963; Engel, 1961; Epstein and DeShazo, 1961).

The generality of figure and ground   It is worth noting at this point that figure-ground segregation is not limited to visual phenomena; there are analogies in other sensory modalities. As applied to hearing, for example, the voice of someone with whom you are talking may be figural while other sounds in the room represent ground. With regard to music, melody represents figure while the chords and other accompaniments can be thought of as ground (Woodworth and Schlosberg, 1954). Similarly, an itch can be figure while other concomitant tactual sensations are ground, and the odor of skunk can be quite figural while the remaining fragrances of the forest are ground. Figure-

FIGURE 7.35   Illustration of the type of stimuli used by Rubin (1921) in studies of figural persistence. (After Woodworth and Schlosberg, 1954)

ground segregation, though typically considered with respect to vision, is a universal aspect of perceptual experience.

Gestalt Principles in Perceptual Grouping

The Law of Prägnanz   In discussing the nature of figure-ground organization, we have focused upon unitary relationships. In daily life, however, several figures may share a common ground, and figures tend to be seen to cluster together in groups. Are there any unifying principles which can tell us why some elements of the perceptual field form the figure while others become ground and why figural elements group together the way they do?

The experimental investigation of this question was initiated almost 65 years ago by a group of German psychologists led by Max Wertheimer and his chief collaborators, Kurt Koffka and Wolfgang Köhler. Their approach is known as Gestalt psychology (*Gestalt* is the German word for "form"), and, as we noted in Chapter 1, it emphasized the study of perception in terms of inherent organizational and configurational properties. The Gestalt psychologists argued that organization is intrinsic to the perceptual system, and they offered the Law of Prägnanz as the basic principle which governs the segregation of the field of view into separate forms. This principle states that "psychological organization will always be as 'good' as the prevailing conditions allow" (Koffka, 1935, p. 110). The definition of the term "good" is rather ambiguous, but, in general, it refers to the simplest, most stable figure possible. A "good" figure embodies such properties as regularity, symmetry, and simplicity. Perhaps the best example is a circle. In a very general way, figures are grouped together that "belong" together in the sense that making them figural and bringing them together achieves the simplest and therefore the "best" organization possible. In essence, the Law of Prägnanz holds that perception is organized through some sort of *minimum principle* by which the perceptual response that will occur in a given situation is the most economical response possible (Hochberg, 1971a). The Gestaltists generated a series of grouping principles supported by many compelling illustrations of the operation of the Law of Prägnanz. Some of these are considered below with the help of Figure 7.36.

Proximity   With all other factors constant, subgroups tend to be formed from parts which are spatially close to each other. An example of this principle is shown in Figure 7.36(a) and (b). In (a), spatial nearness leads to an organization of the squares into columns, while in (b) the squares are organized into rows by their spatial proximity. The principle of proximity is not limited to spatial factors; temporal contiguity can also lead to grouping. For example, in a series of irregularly occurring taps, those which appear close together in time will also tend to be grouped.

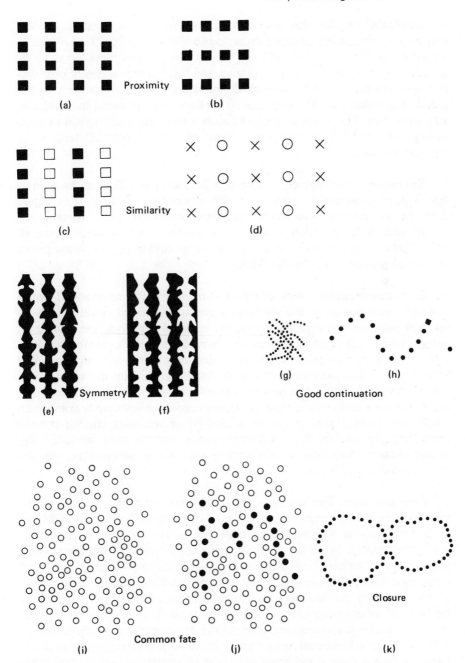

FIGURE 7.36 Gestalt principles of perceptual grouping. See text for explanation.

Similarity   Again, with other factors constant, the elements of a collection will be perceptually grouped according to their similarity. This principle is illustrated in Figure 7.36(c) and (d). In (c), the dark squares tend to be grouped together, as do the light squares, yielding the impression of organization into columns. In (d), perceptual organization occurs according to the shape of the elements. Organization by similarity also is found in other sensory modalities. For example, if you listen to a repetitive presentation of alternating high- and low-pitched tones, those of similar pitch will tend to be grouped into units.

Symmetry   Symmetrical regions of a field are more likely to be seen as figural than asymmetrical ones. Consider illustrations (e) and (f) in Figure 7.36. In (e), you can see either black symmetrical or white asymmetrical stripes, while in (f), the white stripes are symmetrical and the black asymmetrical. Most people see black stripes on a white ground in (e) and white stripes on a black ground in (f) (Koffka, 1935).

Good continuation   A collection of elements may be so arranged that as a viewer scans the array, the elements seem to be properly located with respect to each other just as the successive notes of a melody seem to fit together. When such "good continuation" prevails in spatially distributed visual elements, it is as though a pattern were generated by the smooth movement of a single element over each of the positions occupied by the separate figures that made up the actual pattern. Consider Figure 7.36(g) and (h). In (g), the dots form a uniform direction. A figure-ground arrangement is seen which makes the fewest interruptions in a straight or smoothly curving contour (Hochberg, 1971a). In (h), good continuation prevails over similarity; the square element "belongs" to the wave-shaped figure, whereas the circular element to the right is perceptually isolated.

Common fate   This principle relates to grouping based upon common movement or change among a collection of elements in the field. It is difficult to illustrate without elements that actually move. Nevertheless, consider Figure 7.36(i) and (j). In (i), you might imagine a collection of dots scattered at random over a surface. Now pick out a subset of those dots that would form a common figure if there was some basis for their perceptual organization, such as similarity. For example, as shown in Figure 7.36(j), you could make the letter M emerge simply by darkening some of the dots. We could obtain the same result—the emergence of the letter M—if these same dots, instead of being darkened, were all moved together. While in motion, the dots would form a coherent pattern by virtue of a type of similarity—that is, their common motion, or, to use the Gestalt phrase, their common fate.

Krech, Crutchfield, and Livson (1969) have made the interesting observation that common fate has an important role in choreography. When sev-

eral dancers are involved, the tendency to follow those who execute the
same movements transforms potential chaos into a complex procession of figural elements on a dynamic ground. Still another aspect of common fate is
worth noting. Recall our earlier discussion in Chapter 6 of the critical role
played by stimulus change in the maintenance of perceptual stability. Common fate is an additional example of the importance of change to perception.
In this case, the role of change is quite complex. Change serves to generate a
temporary correlation among the parts of an object, and to minimize any for-
tuitous correlations among elements of the object and those of its background. It is possible that something of this sort is operative also in the apparently simpler examples of the disappearance of stopped images, luminous
designs, and targets in a Ganzfeld.

Closure   A bounded region of the field tends to be seen as figural and
as a segregated unit more frequently than regions with incomplete contours.
Consider the pattern of dots shown in Figure 7.30(k). You are most likely to
see two closed regions, each self-contained or bounded. Note that you might
have seen a single line of dots arrayed perhaps as a figure-eight on its side.
The principle of good continuation might yield such an organization. In this
case, however, the factor of closure has entered in.

Modern developments   The perceptual grouping principles suggested by
the Gestaltists are convincing and provide a good start toward an understanding of perceptual segregation. There is, however, something still to be desired. The demonstrations used to illustrate the grouping principles represent
"evidence" only of a phenomenological sort, and they deal with relatively
simple cases. The job remains of working out the generality of the Gestalt
principles of grouping and the exact relations among them so that *a priori*
prediction can be made about how a particular pattern will be organized.

In the past few years a number of attempts have been made toward a
more objective and quantitative analysis of the grouping principles. These efforts have enabled us to learn more about the factors involved in perceptual
organization and the relations between them. For example, Rock and Brosgole (1964), using a stimulus array which could be tilted in depth, have
shown that the crucial factor in grouping by proximity is nearness in *perceived* space rather than simple retinal proximity. In addition, Hochberg and
his co-workers (Hochberg and Hardy, 1960; Hochberg and Silverstein, 1956)
have devised a technique to set the factors of proximity and similarity against
each other and thereby assess their relative strengths in different situations.

An important series of experiments by Beck has forced a reanalysis of the
factors involved in similarity grouping. In an initial study (Beck, 1966a), subjects were shown patterns such as the one illustrated in Figure 7.37 with instructions to divide the pattern into two regions along the boundary yielding

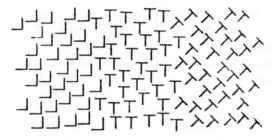

FIGURE 7.37 The role of line orientation in perceptual grouping. The backward Ls and upright Ts, figures in which line elements are in the same orientation, form a group distinct from the tilted Ts. This occurs even though the T figures have a physical configuration more similar to each other than to the L figures. (From Beck, 1966a)

the most natural demarcation. Beck found that figures having lines in the same orientation rather than figures having generally the same shape tended to be seen together. In Figure 7.37, the backward Ls and upright Ts tended to form a group distinct from the tilted Ts even though elements in the form of a T had greater physical similarity to one another than they did to elements in the shape of a backward L. In this study, line orientation took precedence over physical similarity in determining perceptual grouping.

#9

These results were corroborated in subsequent experiments (Beck, 1966b, 1967, 1972) in which threshold measures and ratings of clarity were used to index the effectiveness of perceptual segregation. In the light of his findings, Beck suggested that the processes in grouping are based upon spontaneous, pre-attentive responses to relatively simple properties such as brightness, size, and line direction. He also noted that the critical importance of line orientation is consistent with a suggestion by Gibson (1950) that the direction of a line is a primary element in the perception of a figure and with the work on cortical feature detectors for orientation such as that discussed earlier in this chapter.

Beck's finding that the orientation or slope of lines is a major factor in similarity grouping has been supported by Olson and Attneave (1970), using still a different experimental technique. These investigators explored the effectiveness of several variables in producing similarity grouping by measuring the time it took subjects to locate a disparate quadrant in a circular stimulus array. Examples of the arrays used in this study are shown in Figure 7.38.

Olson and Attneave found that arrays in which elements differed in terms of slope (line segments of one orientation opposed to others of a different orientation) yielded more "immediate" grouping times than arrays in which the same slopes were combined to form different angles. You can probably verify this for yourself by comparing the relative speed with which segregation seems to occur in Figures 7.38(a) (slope elements) and 7.38(b) (angle elements). As part of their extensive investigation, Olson and Attneave also discovered that grouping was dependent upon the orientation of the *entire* stimulus array; arrangements with horizontal and vertical elements gave better grouping than those with diagonal elements. Findings such as these led Olson

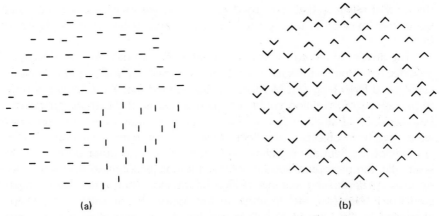

FIGURE 7.38   The role of slope and angle elements in perceptual grouping. Arrays in which the elements differ in terms of slope (a) segregate more readily than those (b) in which slopes are combined to form different angles. (From Olson and Attneave. 1970)

and Attneave to propose that grouping may depend upon the relation of elements to an internal reference system of x-y axes (that is, to an internal Cartesian frame of reference).

Most recently, Uttal (1975), using the paradigm described earlier in which dot figures must be recognized in visual noise, has provided some interesting evidence favoring the Law of Prägnanz in perceptual grouping. He performed a series of experiments designed to test a corollary of this law, namely, that "good" forms are seen better than poor ones. His research showed that regular and symmetrical dot patterns (for example, a dotted square) are segregated more accurately from dotted visual noise than less regular patterns (for example, a dotted parallelogram); moreover, the organization of a set of dotted lines into regular linear arrays enhances the accuracy of segregation over irregular arrangements.

PSYCHOPHYSICS OF FORM

The Metrics of Form

Information analysis   The principles of perceptual organization tell us how elements in a field are segregated into patterns. While these principles permit some insight into which elements bounded by a common contour will be seen as figural, they do not tell us *what* figures will be seen (Hochberg, 1971a), nor do they tell us what aspects of the resulting figures influence the discriminations that we make among them. For answers to questions such as these, it would be helpful if we could specify exactly the physical aspects of shapes that relate to their perceptibility. That is, we might learn more about the factors involved in form perception if we could build a psychophysics of form.

The advent of the concepts of information theory described in Chapter 4 provided an impetus for such an approach. In two seminal papers, Attneave (1954) and Hochberg and McAlister (1953) argued that the Gestalt principles of perceptual organization could be recast in terms of the more quantitative framework of information theory. They pointed out that the stimulation which we receive from objects in the field of view is often quite redundant. That is, portions of the field are repetitive and predictable from other portions. Consequently, the perceptual system obtains the most economical description of a stimulus by abstracting features of high information value—i.e., lines, angles, points of intersection, etc. In terms of this approach, the minimum principle expressed in the Law of Prägnanz can be viewed as stating that the perceptual system prefers those organizations which require a minimum number of physical components to specify them. "Good" forms are those that reduce uncertainty by having a high degree of redundancy.

Consider Figure 7.39. Most people see the pattern in 7.39(a) as two intersecting rectangles. It could be used as an illustration of "closure." However, from the information approach, seeing it as two rectangles can be conceived as permitting more succinct encoding—fewer numbers of line segments and angles are involved—than does perceiving it as five irregular shapes. Similarly, most people see Figure 7.39(b) as a simpler, two-dimensional object than Figure 7.39(c) (three-dimensional) because the former has fewer line segments, angles, and points of intersection than does the latter.

More recently, a related but somewhat different approach to the problem of figural goodness has been offered by Garner (1962, 1966). He, too, focuses upon the concept of redundancy or its inverse, uncertainty, and suggests that simple or "good" patterns are those which have few alternative modes of perceptual organization. More specifically, Garner proposes that the

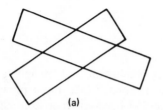  

(a)	(b)	(c)

FIGURE 7.39   The role of stimulus information in the encoding of form. (a) is perceived as two intersecting rectangles rather than as five irregular shapes because the former organization requires encoding fewer angles and lines than does the latter. (b) is seen as simpler (two-dimensional) than (c) (three-dimensional) because (b) has fewer angles, line segments, and points of intersection than does (c). (From Hochberg and McAlister, 1953)

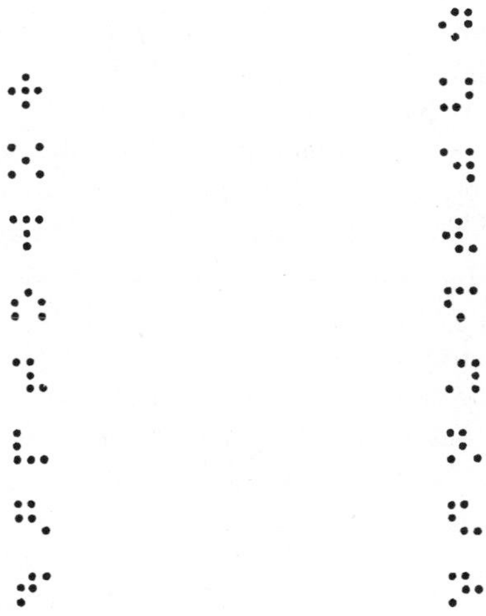

FIGURE 7.40 Samples of dot patterns used in testing the implications of an informational approach to figural goodness. (From Garner and Clement, 1963)

perceived goodness of a pattern is inversely related to the size of a subset of equivalent patterns from which an observer infers the pattern in question to have come. Briefly stated, good patterns come from small inferred subsets, and poor patterns come from large ones.

In order to put this idea to an experimental test, Garner and Clement (1963) prepared 90 dot patterns, like those illustrated in Figure 7.40, by placing dots in an imaginary 3 × 3 matrix. Two groups of subjects served in the study. One group provided ratings of goodness for all 90 patterns on a 7-point scale in which the definition of goodness was left essentially to the subjects' discretion. The other group of subjects provided data concerning the size of the inferred equivalence set for each pattern. The people in this group were instructed to arrange the patterns into eight sets on the basis of perceived similarity. The sets did not need to have equal numbers of patterns; indeed, the equivalence set index for a given pattern was the total number of stimuli placed in the set into which it was classified. Garner's hypotheses regarding pattern goodness would lead one to predict that patterns which received high ratings for goodness would come from small similarity sets. This is precisely what happened: good patterns were unique! The idea that good patterns are those with few alternative modes of organization has been substantiated by Garner in several additional experiments (Garner, 1970; Handel and Garner, 1966; Royer and Garner, 1966).

Synthetic forms The psychophysical analysis of form triggered by the information-theory approach is designed to provide explicit measures of the physical characteristics of shapes which relate to perceptual performance. Since forms may vary along many different dimensions, there are serious problems in specifying meaningful physical units and in generalizing the results from one experiment to another. In order to handle these problems, researchers developed the innovative solution of using what might be termed synthetic or algorithmic forms.

As described by Arnoult (1968), these are figures generated according to a set of formal construction rules, some of which are finite and some of which appeal to chance at certain decision points. Taken as a whole, the set of rules defines the population of all stimuli that could be constructed by these rules. Any particular set of stimuli selected for a given experiment constitutes a random sample from the population. The advantage offered by such synthetic forms is that they represent highly controlled stimulus materials. Moreover, the results obtained with one stimulus sample should be replicable, within the limits of sampling theory, to a different set of stimuli drawn from the same population. Several schemes for generating synthetic forms have been developed (see Alluisi, 1970; Dobson and Young, 1973; Snodgrass, 1971; Zusne, 1970). The most familiar of such forms are the "random polygons" devised by Attneave and Arnoult (1956), which are illustrated in Figure 7.41. These stimuli have been used extensively in experiments which probe the role of the geometry of forms in perceptual performance.

Structural elements Several structural elements have been identified which are related to the perceptual characteristics of forms. Among these characteristics are the dimensions of complexity and discriminability.

Whether forms are perceived as simple or complex objects seems to be related to the number of independent sides or turns that they contain (see Figure 11.5 for an illustration of random polygons with different levels of sidedness). In general, the judged complexity of a form increases with increments in the sidedness of the figures (Michels and Zusne, 1965; Zusne,

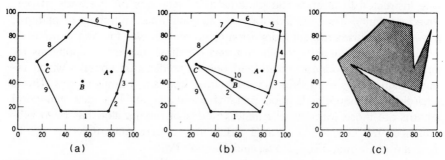

FIGURE 7.41 Successive stages in constructing a "random" polygon. Pairs of numbers between 1 and 100 are drawn from a table of random numbers. Each pair determines a coordinate that can be plotted on a 100 × 100 unit matrix. The outer points are joined to form a polygon (a). After assigning numbers to the sides of the polygon and letters to the inner points, a table of random numbers is used to determine the connections between the inner points and the sides (b). Joining the inner points to the sides (c) completes the figure. (From Attneave and Arnoult, 1956)

1970). An interesting aspect of the complexity-sidedness relation is that it appears to be independent of the sensory modality used for stimulus presentation. Brown and his co-workers (Brown and Brumaghim, 1968; Brumaghim and Brown, 1968; Owen and Brown, 1966) have found this relation to hold for visual random polygons and their tactual analogs constructed from sandpaper. The consistency of results for vision and touch is important; it indicates that the psychophysical relation between judgments of complexity and the sidedness of forms is a general perceptual characteristic. Since form is a multi-dimensional attribute, we might expect that, in addition to sidedness, other physical characteristics also contribute to judged complexity. This is indeed the case; among the other contributing factors are the symmetry and compactness of figures, the amount of variability in the sizes of their angles, and the ratio of perimeter squared to area (Arnoult, 1960; Attneave, 1957).

acct for 98% of variance

The parameter of sidedness, which, as we have seen, is a critical factor in the perceived complexity of forms, is also a factor in their discriminability. In this case, the psychophysical relation tends to be U-shaped—polygons of 8 to 12 sides seem to be more easily discriminated from each other than those of 4 or 16 sides. An experiment by Brown, Hitchcock, and Michels (1962) illustrates this point. Subjects were tested on a series of oddity problems in which they were required to detect the disparate member of a group of six random polygons. An example of a problem set and the results of the experiment are shown in Figure 7.42. As you can see, there was a nonmonotonic relation between discrimination time and the sidedness of the stimuli.

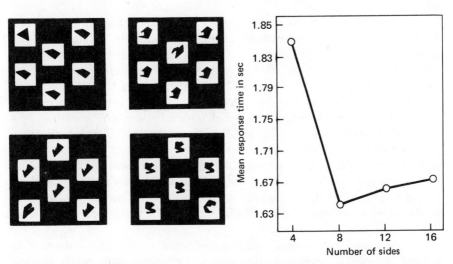

FIGURE 7.42   Samples of oddity problems used to study the effects of sidedness on the discrimination of random polygons. The accompanying graph shows that the time required to select the odd member of a group of patterns was a nonmonotonic function of the number of sides in the stimuli. (From Brown, Hitchcock, and Michels, 1962)

What might account for a relation such as this? One possibility is that there is both too little and too much information involved. More specifically, 4-sided polygons may have fewer degrees of freedom to vary from each other—i.e., they are less free to be unique, and are therefore less discriminable. On the other hand, figures with more than 8 to 12 sides may contain more information than can be optimally processed and therefore are also difficult to discriminate (Brown and Goldstein, 1967; Michels and Zusne, 1965). As was true for judged complexity, other higher-order physical dimensions are also related to people's ability to discriminate among shapes. These factors include the compactness, jaggedness, and elongation of the stimuli (Aiken and Brown, 1969; Brown and Andrews, 1968; Mavrides and Brown, 1969).

Spatial orientation   In addition to the structural elements just described, the psychophysical approach has identified other types of physical characteristics which are related to the way in which forms are perceived. One of the more interesting of these is the spatial orientation of the figures. Howard and Templeton (1966) have pointed out that at least two logically distinct questions might be asked about the influence of spatial orientation on people's ability to distinguish between patterns: (1) with no difference in orientation, what is the effect of the absolute orientation of the forms, and (2) how is discrimination influenced by differences in the relative orientation of the forms with respect to each other?

If the patterns to be discriminated have recognizable horizontal and vertical axes, their absolute orientation makes a considerable difference in our ability to discriminate between them. Visual patterns which are oriented about a vertical axis are more easily discriminated than those oriented about a horizontal axis (Howard and Templeton, 1966). The reasons for this effect have not been fully determined as yet. One possibility may lie in the activity of neurological feature detectors that are differentially sensitive to stimuli in a vertical orientation (see Appelle, 1972). Still another plausible interpretation of the superiority of vertical orientation comes from the fact that most natural visual objects such as trees and people, as well as constructed ones such as houses, are typically seen vertically and are often bilaterally symmetrical along the vertical axis. Perhaps through some process of perceptual learning, people develop general schema which vertically oriented objects "fit" better than other objects.

The relative or differential orientation of forms is also quite important. In general, differential orientation degrades the efficiency with which patterns may be discriminated (Hake, 1966; Howard and Templeton, 1966; Shinar and Owen, 1973; Warm, Clark, and Foulke, 1970). A particularly compelling example of this effect has been provided by Shepard and Metzler (1971). They measured the time required to determine whether pairs of perspective

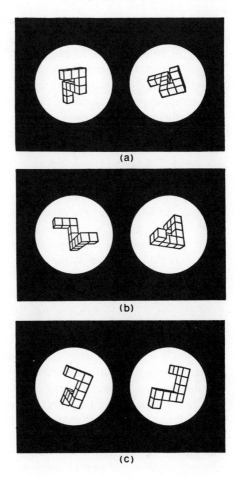

FIGURE 7.43 Examples of pairs of perspective line drawings used to study the influence of differential spatial orientation on the perception of form. (a) illustrates a pair of drawings that are physically identical but differ by an 80° rotation in the picture plane; (b) a physically identical pair, which differs by an 80° rotation in depth; (c) a nonidentical pair that cannot be brought into congruence by any rotation. (From Shepard and Metzler, 1971)

line drawings were of the same shape. Using figures such as those illustrated in Figure 7.43, Shepard and Metzler arranged things so that pairs of patterns could be differentially oriented with respect to each other in either a two-dimensional or a three-dimensional plane. For both conditions of differential orientation, discrimination time increased in a linear manner with the angular difference (degrees of differential orientation) between the two objects in the pair.

In accounting for how people go about determining the shape of differentially oriented objects, Shepard and Metzler suggested that observers may go through a process of first "mentally rotating" the objects into a common orientation and then assessing the fit or congruence of the stimuli. A similar proposal has been offered by Howard and Templeton (1966).

Support for a view of this sort comes from a study by Cooper (1975) in which subjects were asked whether test figures composed of random polygons were identical to previously learned standards. As might be expected from what has already been said, Cooper found that the time required to make this determination increased linearly with the angular departure of the test form from the normal orientation of the standard. She also found that this effect could be eliminated if the subjects were told in advance of each trial which of several standard forms would be tested on that trial and what the orientation of the upcoming test form would be. Under these conditions, however, the time needed by the subjects to *prepare* to view the test form increased linearly with the angular departure of the upcoming test items from the standard's learned orientation. Apparently, the subjects prepared for the upcoming test form by "mentally rotating" the remembered version of the form into the cued orientation. The greater the disorientation of the standard and the cued test item, the greater the time necessary to carry out this process.

In addition to the influence of absolute and differential spatial orientation on the discriminability of forms, there is still another aspect of spatial orientation that warrants examination. This is the relation between spatial orientation and the recognizability of forms. Consider Figure 7.44. Most likely it will seem to be an unfamiliar object, perhaps the profile of a bearded man. However, if you turn the book 90° in a counterclockwise direction, the drawing will take on a more familiar appearance—that of an outline map of the United States. This simple example makes an important point: the spatial orientation of a figure can determine its appearance and recognizability.

In order to understand this phenomenon more fully, it is necessary to specify the contextual framework within which the term "orientation" is being used. More specifically, if we rotate a figure, we will change the orientation of its image on the retina of an observer. At the same time, we will also alter its orientation with respect to the horizontal and vertical dimensions of the environment. Those portions of the figure which point upward or downward in relation to the axis of gravity, i.e., the sky and the ground, will also be modified. Which of these contextual frameworks, the retinal or the gravitational, is the main point of reference involved in the relation between spatial orientation and the appearance and recognizability of forms?

FIGURE 7.44 Spatial orientation and figure recognition. When viewed in a vertical orientation, the figure resembles the profile of a bearded man. If the page is rotated 90° counterclockwise, the figure takes on a different appearance, that of an outline map of the United States. (From Rock, 1973)

Rock and Heimer (1957) attacked this problem experimentally by separating the retinal and environmental frameworks. Subjects first reviewed a series of unfamiliar figures while seated in an upright position. Then they were required to recognize these figures when mixed with others in a test series. During this phase of the study, the subjects viewed the stimuli with their heads tilted 90° sideways resting on a table. The original figures were presented twice during the test phase, once upright with respect to the environment and once rotated 90° so that the top of the figure corresponded to the top of the observer's head—upright with respect to the retina. Recognition scores were better when the figures were upright with respect to the environment than when they were upright with respect to the retina. This study and several others conducted by Rock (1973, 1974) lead to the conclusion that the environmental framework takes precedence over the retinal in determining the effects of spatial orientation on the recognition of forms. Rock is careful to point out, however, that retinal image orientation is not an unimportant factor. Pictures of faces and printed and written words are difficult to recognize when viewed with a change in retinal orientation but no change in environmental orientation—i.e., when seen upright with the head tilted. In accounting for these findings, Rock has suggested that what is most important in regard to orientation is the assignment to a figure of the directions of top, bottom, left, and right. Ordinarily, these directions are assigned on the basis of the region of the figure that is at the top of the environment, and, when viewing with the head tilted, observers make corrections for the tilt. When, however, quite complex figures are involved, such as faces or words, the correction capacity of the perceptual system is overtaxed, and retinal orientation then becomes an important factor in recognition.

Problems for a Psychophysics of Form

Measurement and sampling   The psychophysical analysis of form has been of value in providing a way to determine certain aspects of the geometry of shapes which influence perceptual responses to them. We should note, however, that at this time our knowledge of the metrics of form is far from complete. Many problems remain to be unraveled. Two of the most critical concern the measurement and sampling of stimuli, particularly in relation to the use of synthetic forms.

For expository reasons our discussion has centered upon relatively simple physical dimensions. The choice of dimensions to examine is in reality a complex issue. With regard to random polygons, there appears to be a high correlation between various physical dimensions so that shapes selected for one dimension, say sidedness, tend to be selected at proportionate values on other dimensions, such as jaggedness. Thus, it is difficult to be sure which of the only partially independent dimensions actually accounts for performance variation (Brown and Owen, 1967).

The problem of sampling centers about the concept of *ecological validity* (Brunsv.ik, 1956). A stimulus is ecologically valid if it is representative of the domain of stimuli to which one wants to draw generalizations. As we have noted, synthetic forms have been used extensively in psychophysical studies on the perception of patterns. Because of the way in which they are constructed, a sample of synthetic forms is, most likely, representative of the population of synthetic forms from which it is drawn. But are synthetic forms themselves representative samples of the objects to which we most want to generalize—those in the natural world? This difficult question remains to be answered.

Associative factors   Although synthetic forms such as random polygons are ostensibly nonrepresentational or "nonsense forms," they are not necessarily devoid of meaning. This fact provides an added problem for a psychophysics of form. Vanderplas and Garvin (1959) have successfully scaled random polygons for meaning or association value, and a series of studies by Clark (1965, 1968) has demonstrated that random polygons of high association value are recognized more accurately than those of low association value. In addition, several other experiments have shown that verbalization facilitates recognition memory for form (see Ellis, 1972, 1973; Glanzer and Clark, 1964; Santa, 1975). Results such as these suggest that a psychophysics of form may need to incorporate the fact that more is involved in the perception of shapes than just their internal and external geometry.

Pattern Recognition and Memory

The Höffding step   The material presented in the previous section indicates that more than physical geometry is involved in the two-dimensional spatial organization of the perceptual world. The role of memory is clearly implicated, and considerable effort has been expended in recent years in studying the contact between perception and memory, especially in regard to the recognition of form. This issue goes by several names. For the Gestaltists, it is known as the *Höffding step* (Neisser, 1967), while for workers in artificial intelligence, who attempt to program computers to recognize and respond to different patterns, it is termed *character recognition* (see Uhr, 1966). The issue revolves about the manner in which the perceiver interrogates stored information in the process of recognizing a particular pattern. The literature on this topic, which brings two basic areas of experimental psychology together (perception and memory), is too extensive to review in detail here. Instead, we will concentrate on one key question. For further information, you might consult Corcoran (1971), Neisser (1967, 1976), Posner (1969), Reed (1973), Reynolds and Flagg (1977), and Rumelhart (1977).

Features and templates   A major question which arises in regard to pattern recognition and memory concerns the structure of the memory code against which incoming stimulation is compared. In the context of the present chapter, we might view this as the psychophysics of memory and form. One solution to the problem suggested by several investigators (E. Gibson, 1969; Selfridge, 1959; Sutherland, 1959) is the *distinctive features hypothesis,* which holds that a stimulus to be recognized is first analyzed in terms of its physical features. This pattern is then recognized by comparing some weighted combination of features with sets of attributes that characterize items stored in memory. In terms of this model, the presence of particular parts or particular features is decisive in determining the recognition response.

Evidence that some such process in involved in the recognition of patterns comes from a variety of sources. Chief among these are the data reviewed earlier indicating the presence of cells in the nervous system which are specialized for the extraction of specific stimulus features and the psychophysical data indicating that feature measures are related to the discrimination of form. Still another line of evidence for feature analysis in pattern recognition comes from studies of eye-movement recordings in the inspection of forms. These studies reveal that the pattern of eye fixations is systematically related to the physical structure of the stimuli (Gould and Dill, 1969) and that the frequency and the duration of fixations is greatest at places where changes of contour occur (Baker and Loeb, 1973; Mackworth and Morandi, 1967). Along these lines, Noton and Stark (1971) have suggested that patterns may be represented in memory by a series of sensory and motor traces which record a feature of the pattern and the eye movement required to reach the next feature.

The primary alternative to the distinctive feature hypothesis is a template-matching model. According to this view, patterns are coded in memory in terms of prototypes—abstractions that represent the basic elements or the central tendency of the stimuli. By way of example, we may note, as Klatzky (1975) has done, that the prototype of an airplane can be thought of as a long tube with two wings attached, all planes being some variant of this prototype. The template-matching model holds that a pattern is recognized by comparing its congruence with a particular stored prototype.

At first glance, such a model of pattern recognition might seem unreasonable. Stimuli of varying size or orientation or those with slight distortions might not fit their appropriate prototypes, and, thus, accuracy of recognition would be poor in many cases. However, the model can be adjusted to accommodate such problems if we also assume that a process of stimulus normalization (the institution of size or rotational transformations) occurs before prototype matching takes place. The process of "mental rotation" described above can be considered as an example of normalization.

Evidence in favor of a template-matching model is provided in a study by Franks and Bransford (1971). As illustrated in Figure 7.45, these investigators constructed prototypes consisting of structured arrays of geometric forms. They also constructed transformations of these prototypes by systematically

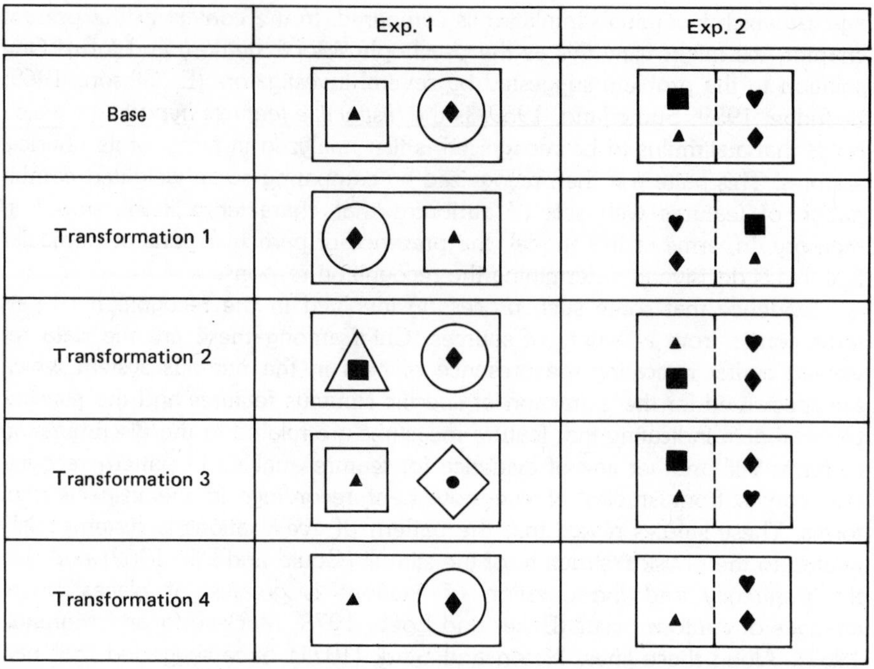

	Exp. 1	Exp. 2
Base		
Transformation 1		
Transformation 2		
Transformation 3		
Transformation 4		

FIGURE 7.45 Examples of bases (prototypes) and some transformations used to demonstrate template matching in pattern recognition. (After Franks and Bransford, 1971)

changing certain elements—for example reversing halves of the configurations, deleting elements, substituting elements, etc. Subjects were first shown only the transformations of the prototypes. Then they were given a recognition test consisting of the stimuli they had seen and others not previously seen, among which were the prototypes. The subjects were required to indicate whether each stimulus had been seen before and to rate the confidence of their judgments. The highest confidence ratings of being seen before were given to the prototypes even though these stimuli had *not* been shown during the first portion of the experiment. Similar results have been reported by Posner and Keele (1968); moreover, Evans and his co-workers have demonstrated that subjects can learn to discriminate synthetic forms derived from one prototype from those derived from another (Brown and Evans, 1969; Evans, 1967; Evans and Arnoult, 1967).

Research on the structure of the memory codes used in pattern recognition suggests that both feature-analysis and template-matching codes are involved. To strike a computer metaphor, the human observer is evidently multiply programmed. This result is not too surprising if we realize that forming a prototype involves the combination of a number of different features (Caldwell and Hall,1970). The problem, then, may not so much be one of deciding whether feature analysis or template matching is involved in pattern recognition as it is of determining the conditions under which observers will resort to one strategy or the other.

NONVERIDICAL PERCEPTION

Geometrical Illusions

The significance of illusions   Thus far, our discussion has focused upon the veridical or accurate perception of figures. There are cases, however, in which form perception is far from accurate. These cases, known collectively as the geometrical illusions, involve line drawings in which some attributes of the perceived stimuli (for example, size, shape, direction) differ considerably from their corresponding physical values. We have come across a few of these illusions previously in Figures 1.7 (Chapter 1) and 7.23.

Scientists have studied the geometrical illusions for more than a century. Some of this interest stems from the value of illusions as "curiosities." Like mountains to mountain climbers, illusions pose a challenge just because they are there. Still another motive has stimulated the study of illusions, one with a more serious aspect. This motive stems from the belief that in order to understand how form perception can be accurate, it is also necessary to account for why it can sometimes be inaccurate (Girgus and Coren, 1976). In other words, the study of illusions may provide special insights into the fundamentals of pattern perception.

Classification of illusions   In many areas of scientific endeavor, the development of classification systems or taxonomies has proved useful in the description and explanation of the phenomena under investigation. Examples of such systems are those for classifying families of plants and animals in biology and for classifying matter by atomic number in physics and chemistry. A taxonomic approach has also proven useful to research on geometrical illusions (Robinson, 1972). One of the most recent efforts along these lines has been described by Coren, Girgus, Erlichman, and Hakstian (1976). These investigators made use of a complex statistical technique known as factor analysis to examine the interrelationships among responses to 45 illusory configurations. The results of the analysis suggested two general types of geometrical illusions, those of extent and those of shape and direction. Figure 7.46 illustrates this general classification scheme.

The top row of the figure presents some illusions of extent. The familiar Müller-Lyer illusion is shown in (a). In this case, the shafts of the "arrows" are physically equal in length, but the one with the two "heads" looks shorter than the one with the two "tails." The Ponzo illusion, in which the upper horizontal line seems longer than the lower, is shown in (b). In (c), the hori-

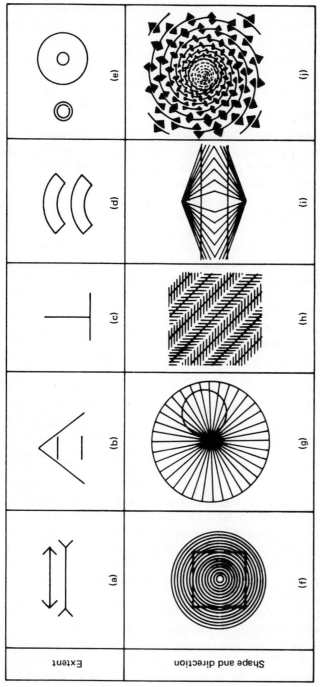

FIGURE 7.46 Some geometric illusions. Those that can be classified as illusions of extent are the Muller-Lyer (a), the Ponzo (b), the horizontal-vertical (c), the Jastrow (d), and the Delboef (e). Illusions of shape and direction are the Ehrnstein (f), the Orbison (g), the Zollner (h), the Wundt (i), and the twisted cord (j).

zontal-vertical illusion, the vertical line appears longer than the horizontal. The Jastrow illusion is illustrated in (d). In this case, the upper segment of the pattern seems smaller than the lower. Geometrically, the segments are congruent. Finally, (e) shows the Delboef illusion, in which the circle surrounded by the ring of small diameter seems larger than the circle surrounded by the ring of large diameter.

Illusions of shape and direction are presented in the bottom row of Figure 7.46. Distortions in the shape of a square and a circle appear in (f) (Ehrnstein illusion) and (g) (Orbison illusion), respectively. Distortions in the directions of parallel lines appear in (h) (Zöllner illusion) and (i) (Wundt illusion). The "twisted cord" illusion is shown in (j). Here, the concentric circles appear to form a spiral which turns inward. Figures 1.7 and 7.23 present illusions which also fit within the "shape and direction" category.

The illustrations shown in Figure 7.46 serve a dual purpose. They exemplify a reasonable taxonomic scheme for describing geometrical illusions, and, in addition, they help to make a point of primary significance for a general understanding of the perception of form. Embodied in these illustrations is the principle that knowledge of the physical characteristics of part of a stimulus is not sufficient information from which to predict how that part will be perceived. It is necessary to know the total pattern in which the part is embedded. This principle, of course, is consistent with our earlier discussion (Chapter 1) of the importance of context in determining perceptual responses.

Theories of Illusions

Although the geometrical illusions have been subjected to much systematic study, they remain difficult to explain. Several theoretical accounts have been offered, but none can successfully incorporate all of the known data.

In general, theories of illusions fall within three broad classes (Over, 1968). Some accounts focus upon errors which arise in sampling stimulus information. Others seek an explanation of illusions in terms of the "hardware" of the perceptual system, that is, at the neurophysiological level. Still others adopt a judgmental or cognitive approach to the problem. We shall not attempt a full description of all of these positions. Instead, we shall select a few from each of the three broad classes with the aim of illustrating the different approaches that have been taken and the problems which they face. More complete discussions of theories of illusions can be found in Hochberg (1971a), Over (1968), Rock (1975), and Zusne (1970).

Eye movement theory   One of the principal stimulus-sampling theories is based upon the role played by the eyes as they scan pattern configurations. This view holds that errors occur in the perception of illusory figures because surrounding contours modify the extent and direction of eye movements during the scanning of particular parts of the figures (Over, 1968). For example, the horizontal-vertical illusion could be accounted for by arguing that, with distance constant, vertical eye movements require more effort than horizontal movements and that the increased effort results in a greater impression of length. Similarly, in the case of the Müller-Lyer illusion, it could be argued that the outward-going lines of the "tails" induce scanning movements along the shaft which are of greater extent than those induced by the inward-going lines of the "heads" and that this difference leads to disparities in the perceived length of the shaft. Data are available to indicate that there is indeed a relationship between the magnitude of eye movements and the extent of the Müller-Lyer illusion (see Festinger, White, and Allyn, 1968). Unfortunately, this appealing theory is greatly embarrassed by the fact that geometric illusions can be obtained in the absence of such movements. Illusions occur even when exposure times are too brief for an eye movement to have taken place (Over, 1968; Schiffman and Thompson, 1974). They also can be obtained when the image of the stimulus is fixed on the retina by means of afterimage or stabilized-image techniques (Evans and Marsden, 1966; Pritchard, 1958).

Still another version of eye-movement theory—the efferent readiness hypothesis—asserts that eye movements themselves are not the crucial factor responsible for illusions. Instead, illusions are claimed to result from inappropriate instructions to the eye muscles to move in a particular manner which are induced by certain aspects of the stimulus configuration (Festinger, Burnham, Ono, and Bamber, 1967). The presence of illusions in the absence of eye movements poses no problem for this theory; illusions are perceived because there is readiness for particular eye movements: the movements themselves do not have to occur.

The efferent-readiness hypothesis can be put to an experimental test by taking advantage of the fact that prolonged inspection results in a decline in the magnitude of geometrical illusions (Coren and Girgus, 1972). According to the efferent-readiness view, this decline is due to the observer's discovery, in the course of scanning the stimulus, that the initial efferent commands are inappropriate and that recalibration of these commands is necessary. Accordingly, we might expect that illusion decrements should be more readily apparent when observers are permitted free eye movements than when scanning activity is restricted. Such a possibility has received empirical verification (Coren and Hoenig, 1972; Festinger, White, and Allyn, 1968). Even so, however, the efferent-readiness version of eye movement theory constitutes a rather incomplete account of illusions. We are left with the need to specify precisely how efferent readiness is related to particular stimulus properties and to explain why the hypothesized inappropriate motor commands occur in the first place.

A stimulus-sampling approach to illusions is also reflected in a proposal by Chiang (1968), who suggested that blur-inducing optical imperfections in the eye may play a role in geometrical illusions involving crossing lines.

This possibility has been supported by experiments which demonstrate that illusion magnitude can be reduced when care is taken to reduce retinal image blurring and that illusion magnitude can be amplified under conditions designed to increase image blurring (Coren, 1969; Ward and Coren, 1976 In addition, Pearce and Matin (1969), using the horizontal-vertical illusion, have reported that the magnitude of this illusion depends upon the area of the retina to which the stimulus configuration is presented. Evidently, the contribution of optical factors to the perception of illusions cannot be completely ruled out at present.

Neural inhibition   Ganz (1966) has proposed an account of geometric illusions which is anchored in the neurophysiology of contour formation. Ganz assumes that when two contours are adjacent to each other, lateral inhibitory processes within the retina modify the activity of the cells stimulated by the contours so as to shift the centers of the excitation distribution. As a result, the contours are phenomenally displaced away from each other. Other investigators have offered similar retinal-inhibitory explanations of illusions (Blakemore, Carpenter, and Georgeson, 1970; Burns and Pritchard, 1971; Robinson, 1968).

A neural-inhibition approach links many illusions of shape and direction to current thinking in the neurophysiology of contours. However, a view of this sort does not constitute a completely satisfactory account of such illusions. It places the locus of misperceptions in retinal interaction, but illusions of spatial displacement such as the Zöllner and Poggendorf figures persist even when different parts of the figures are presented to each eye to be combined by some central fusion mechanism (Julesz, 1971; Schiller and Wiener, 1962). Moreover, the Poggendorf illusion can be obtained even after deletion of the part of the oblique line which is ordinarily adjacent to the parallel inducing lines (Pressey and Wilson, 1974). Also, as we have seen in Figure 7.23, this illusion occurs when the inducing contours are "subjective contours."

Depth processing and misapplied constancy   As an example of a judgmental or cognitive approach to the explanation of illusions we might consider what has been termed the depth processing or misapplied constancy theory. It was introduced many years ago by Thiéry (1896) and has been popularized more recently by Day (1972) and Gregory (1968, 1973). This position states that illusions of size result when cues which generally permit the observer to maintain size constancy are utilized under conditions wherein retinal images are not actually varied in size. Thus, mechanisms which normally aid in the maintenance of perceptual stability lead to distortions in perception when applied inappropriately to illusory stimuli. More specifically, the misapplied-constancy view asserts that certain pictorial cues in illusory configurations trigger the impression of a separation in depth between parts of the figures which are physically the same size. If two portions of a configuration are equal in size but one seems to be farther away than the other, the part which seems more distant will also appear to be larger. We have encountered such a view in our general discussion of size constancy (Chapter 6) and have seen it applied to both the corridor illusion and the moon illusion.

The Ponzo illusion fits easily within this position. The cue to distance known as linear perspective (see Chapter 8) is provided by the converging lines. Thus, the upper horizontal seems farther away and hence larger than the lower horizontal. Gregory (1968, 1973) explains the Müller-Lyer illusion in a similar fashion. He argues that we experience an illusion with this config-uration because the shaft with the two "tails" appears as though it were the inside, *far* corner of a three-dimensional array while the shaft with the two "heads" is perceived as though it were the outside, *near* corner of a three-di-mensional array. Gregory's approach to explaining the Müller-Lyer illusion is illustrated in Figure 7.47.

Several interesting experiments provide some empirical support for the misapplied-constancy idea. For example, Leibowitz and his co-workers have studied the Ponzo illusion using real-world scenes, photographs and drawings in which potential cues to distance were varied in a systematic manner. They found the magnitude of the illusion to increase as the cues to a depth separa-tion between the two horizontal lines increased (Leibowitz, Brislin, Perlmutter, and Hennessy, 1969). The results of a developmental study of the Ponzo illusion by Leibowitz and Judisch (1967) are also consistent with the misapplied constancy theory. These investigators found that the magni-tude of the Ponzo illusion increases progressively with age in a manner which parallels the developmental trend for size constancy described in Chapter 6. While such a result does not necessarily imply causation, it does suggest that a size-distance correction mechanism is common to size constancy and the Ponzo illusion. In addition, with reference to the Müller-Lyer illusion, Gregory (1968) has reported that when coated with luminous paint and viewed in to-tal darkness the Müller-Lyer figures did indeed take on the appearance of corners. The shaft with the two "heads" resembled an outside near corner and was seen as smaller than the shaft with the two "tails," which looked like an inside far corner.

As in the case with other theories of illusions, there is also a body of evi-dence which runs counter to some implications of the misapplied-constancy view. Predictions derived from this position have not been substantiated in several experiments (Carlson, 1966; Dengler, 1972; Fisher, 1968; Holding, 1970; Kruger, 1972; Massaro and Anderson, 1970; Pressey, 1974; Stacey and Pike, 1968). The general acceptability of the theory is also weakened by the rather striking fact that many size illusions, including the Müller-Lyer, can be obtained in both blind and sighted individuals with tactual presentations

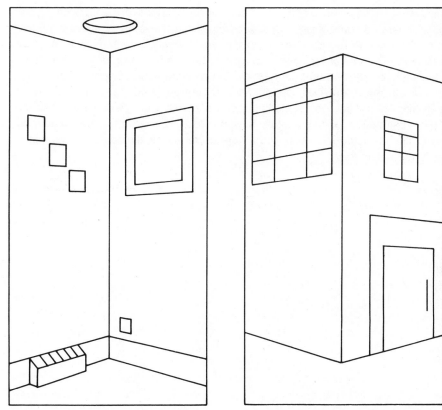

FIGURE 7.47   Gregory's (1968, 1973) concept of the Müller-Lyer illusion on the basis of the depth processing or misapplied constancy theory. This position suggests that the shaft with the two tails (left) appears as though it were the inside far corner of a physical structure, while the shaft with the two heads (right) resembles the outside near corner. Since the two shafts are of the same size, the part that appears more distant also appears larger.

which yield no impression of depth (Bean, 1938; Deregowski and Ellis, 1972; Eaglen and Kirkwood, 1970; Over, 1966, 1967; Patterson and Deffenbacher, 1972; Rudel and Teuber, 1963; Wong, Ho, and Ho, 1974). This suggests that more than pictorial cues to depth must be involved in the production of illusions.

Multiple determinants   Gregory (1968) has made the point that in thinking about the geometric illusions we should not consider them as reflecting flaws in the perceptual system. Instead, it might be better to view them as the product of imperfect solutions which are reached by the system when faced with the need to determine the nature of objects from ambiguous images. In our discussion of this phenomenon, we have seen that psychologists have generated some imaginative ideas regarding the sources of these imperfect solutions but that no single theory is entirely satisfactory. This state of affairs has led some investigators to reach the nonparsimonious but perhaps reasonable conclusion that geometric illusions stem from several different factors which may be of both peripheral and central origin. Any single factor is likely to account for only a limited portion of the data (Coren and Girgus, 1973). Estimation of the relative importance of the contributions made by these different factors to each of the various geometric illusions remains a task for future researchers.

8

Space, Time, and Motion

THREE-DIMENSIONAL SPATIAL ORGANIZATION

Depth and Distance

Perceptual organization Our discussion in the previous chapter focused upon ways in which perceptual experience is organized in two-dimensional space. Although the discussion was lengthy and complex, it described only a limited aspect of the spatial organization of the perceptual world. Perceptual experience is not just composed of figures organized two-dimensionally on a plane surface; it also contains a three-dimensional aspect. Objects have depth, and they are located phenomenally as well as physically at various distances from the observer.

Depth perception is one of the earliest topics to be studied by experimental psychologists. As a consequence of this early and continued interest, a great deal of information has been accumulated about the perception of depth and distance. We will consider the major aspects of this material in the first portion of the present chapter.

The retinal paradox Have you ever wondered how it is possible for you to see the world laid out in three-dimensional space? Most people probably simply take for granted their perception of depth and distance, as they do other perceptual abilities and experiences. To psychologists, however, and to others who specialize in understanding perception, our awareness of three-dimensional space represents both an impressive achievement and a challenging problem. The locus of the problem resides in the nature of retinal images. Such images are essentially flat; three-dimensionality is not inherent in them. Thus, retinal images, which constitute the proximal representation of the distal environment, provide information about the direction of objects, but they carry no direct information about the distance of objects from each other or from the observer. By the same token, a retinal image conveys no direct and unequivocal information about the solidity of objects.

This property of retinal images is illustrated in Figure 8.1, which shows how some points along a line of sight may be projected onto the retina. The fact that point A lies to the left of the observer and point B lies to the right of the observer is easily depicted in the retinal projection because their images (*a* and *b*) fall on different retinal locations (remember that retinal images are inverted). However, since all points lying along vector A or along B project to the same retinal loci (*a* or *b*), how can the observer determine that there is a difference in depth between points A_1, A_2, and A_3 or between points B_1, B_2, and B_3? How, then, is it possible for us to gain a three-dimensional view of the distal environment from two-dimensional proximal images?

Since information about depth is not immediately given in retinal images of objects, there must be other information in the optic array which permits us to "generate" an appreciation of depth and distance. The search for the particular characteristics of stimulus input—the cues—that result in the perception of depth and distance is a basic theme in the research on three-dimensional spatial organization.

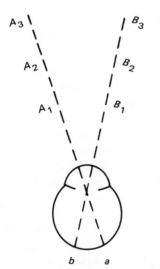

FIGURE 8.1 The retinal paradox for depth perception. Images from all objects lying along line A fall on a single retinal point, a. Those from all objects lying along line B fall on a single retinal point, b. Points a and b can indicate the direction of an object but not its distance from the eye. How, then, is it possible to determine that there are differences in depth among objects A_1, A_2, and A_3 or among objects B_1, B_2, and B_3? (After Woodworth and Schlosberg, 1954)

Several sources of input information about depth and distance have been identified. These sources can be classified and described in a number of ways. To this end, we will follow Kaufman's (1974) lead and consider them in terms of (1) *physiological cues,* which arise from properties of the optical apparatus itself, (2) *kinetic cues,* which come about from the relative movements of objects and observers, and (3) *pictorial cues,* attributes inherent in scenes which convey the impression of depth.

Physiological Cues

Accommodation and convergence   The optical apparatus of the visual system itself provides at least three potential sources of information regarding the distance of objects. Two of these sources come from the oculomotor adjustments that are made in order to maintain images in clear focus on the retina. These adjustments are termed accommodation and convergence; we encountered them earlier in our discussion of size constancy (Chapter 6). We now need to examine accommodation and convergence in a bit more detail.

When our eyes are fixated on a point in space, that point is sharply imaged on the retina. Other points, whether nearer or farther away than the point of fixation, will be blurred. When our gaze shifts from one point in space to another, the shape of the lens changes in order to maintain a sharp image of the object being fixated. The lens bulges to focus on near objects, and it flattens to focus on far objects. You will recall that this process is called *accommodation* and that it is controlled by ciliary muscles. Kinesthetic impulses emanating from the ciliary muscles represent a potential source of information regarding the distance of objects upon which the eye is focused. Since the ciliary muscles contract in order to thicken the lens, the greater the degree of contraction of these muscles, the nearer the object must be.

Closely related to accommodation is *convergence,* which refers to the process whereby the eyes pivot inward toward each other when fixating a near object. The function of convergence is to regulate the pattern of stimulation on each eye so as to avoid double images (diplopia) which arise by virtue of the fact that the two eyes view the world from different positions on the head. Ordinarily, we are not consciously aware of these double images, but they can be illustrated rather easily through a simple demonstration suggested by Woodworth (1938).

Hold a pencil vertically at a reading distance between your eyes and fixate upon a conspicuous and somewhat isolated object at the far end of the room. The pencil will be seen as double. Moreover, the double images of the pencil will be *crossed.* That is, the image in the right eye will be seen to the left of the distant object, and the image in the left eye will be seen to the right of the distant object. This effect can be observed by maintaining your fixation on the distant object and alternately covering each eye. Now, fixate on the pencil. In this case, the far object will be seen as double, and the double images of the far object will be *uncrossed.* That is, the image in the right eye will be seen to the right of the pencil and that of the left eye will be seen to the left of the pencil. Once again, you can observe this effect by alternately covering each eye; this time, however, maintain your fixation on the pencil. An explanation of crossed and uncrossed images is presented in Figure 8.2.

In order to yield a single image, the input from the two eyes must fall on *corresponding retinal points*. Points on the two retinas are said to correspond if they give rise to the same subjective impression of direction when stimulated. Such points are also geometrically related. As Graham (1965b) has indicated, corresponding points are those that would be coincident if one retina could be superimposed exactly on the other. This geometric correspondence is accompanied by an anatomical correspondence. That is, corresponding geometric points "report" to the same region of the cortex (Burian and von Noorden, 1974; Ogle, 1950, 1959).

When objects are viewed from a distance greater than 54 meters, the lines of sight are parallel, and the two images automatically fall on corresponding retinal points (Christman, 1971). If the gaze of the observer is shifted to a near object, however, the eyes must converge in order to place the images on corresponding retinal points. Since single vision for objects at different distances requires different degrees of convergence, kinesthetic feedback from the extraocular muscles, which control the movement of the eyeballs, might also provide a cue to the distance of the object being fixated.

The potential contribution of oculomotor adjustments to the perception of distance has been recognized for quite a while. As long ago as the early 18th century, the British philosopher Bishop Berkeley nominated accommodation and convergence as cues to distance. The empirical evidence

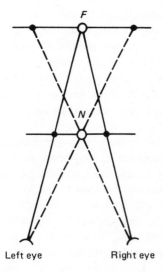

Left eye   Right eye

FIGURE 8.2 Crossed and uncrossed double images. When the eyes are converged upon a far point, F (illustrated by the solid lines), a near point, N (illustrated by the dotted lines) will give crossed images. That is, N will be seen by the right eye to be to the left of F and by the left eye to be to the right of F. When the eyes are converged upon a near point, a far point will give uncrossed images. In this case, F will be seen by the right eye to be to the right of N and by the left eye to be to the left of N. (After Woodworth, 1938)

on this issue, however, has been mixed. Both Ogle (1959) and Woodworth (1938), after thoroughly reviewing the reported research, concluded that accommodation was of little value as an aid to the perception of depth. A similar conclusion was reached by Künnapas (1968), who found that observers could not accurately judge the distance of circles coated with phosphorescent paint when viewed with one eye in a dark room. As for convergence, the early data were also unconvincing. All of the above experiments required observers to make direct judgments of distance.

Evidence has been accumulating to indicate that accommodation and convergence may indeed have some influence on distance perception. This evidence comes mainly from experiments which get at perceived distance indirectly, through the perception of size. We have come across a few of these studies before in our discussion of size constancy. For example, we noted that Leibowitz and his co-workers (Leibowitz, 1971; Leibowitz and Moore, 1966; Leibowitz, Shiina, and Hennessy, 1972) have shown that when the physical size of an object remains invariant, accommodating and converging the eyes for near vision results in a reduction in the perceived size of an object and that the opposite effect occurs with oculomotor adjustments for far vision. Similar kinds of results have also been reported in other experiments (Heinemann, Tulving, and Nachmias, 1959; Komoda and Ono, 1974; Wallach and Floor, 1971; Wallach and Norris, 1963). The changes in perceived size noted in these experiments suggest that observers do make use of distance information arising from oculomotor adjustments.

If we are to accept accommodation and convergence as meaningful sources of distance information, we must do so with at least three qualifications. First, on the basis of the data provided by Leibowitz and his colleagues and other factors (Graham, 1965b), these oculomotor cues are useful only for near space—that is, for distances of about 1 meter or less. Second, convergence seems to be of greater importance than accommodation. Ritter (1977) has described a complex "cue-dominance" experiment in which conditions were arranged so as to place accommodation and convergence in conflict: the values of the two oculomotor adjustments were set to correspond to contradictory values of observational distance. Under these conditions, direct judgments of depth were found to be based on the value of distance at which convergence was fixed. Accommodation, while simultaneously set at a different distance, showed no effect upon perceived distance. A study by Gogel and Sturm (1972), which also attempted to separate the contributions of accommodation and convergence, suggests a similar conclusion. Third, people vary considerably in their ability to make use of the convergence cue. Experiments involving direct judgments of distance by Gogel (1961) and Richards and Miller (1969) have indicated that some people can use this cue whereas others cannot. Indeed, in the latter investigation, convergence was of little use to approximately one third of the 25 subjects who were tested.

Binocular disparity Another "physiological" cue to distance—one which is generally acknowledged to be exceedingly potent—arises from the fact that we have two eyes—that is, binocular vision. This cue also involves a delicate and precisely controlled organization of the activity of the eyes. It provides information about the relative distance of parts of the same object, and is known variously as *binocular disparity, retinal disparity, stereopsis,* or *stereoacuity.*

Because the two eyes are separated from each other horizontally (the interpupillary distance is approximately 65 mm), each eye receives a slightly different view of the visual field: the two retinal images are somewhat disparate. You have already "seen" this fact in our demonstration of crossed and uncrossed images. It can also be illustrated with the help of Figure 8.3, which shows the basis of disparity in terms of geometric optics. A solid object, a cube, is pictured as located in the median plane of the head. Note that the right eye will observe somewhat more of the left surface of the cube and the left eye somewhat more of the right surface. The perceptual system integrates the disparate images from each eye to provide a three-dimensional percept. The nature of the percept depends upon the type of disparity. Crossed dis-

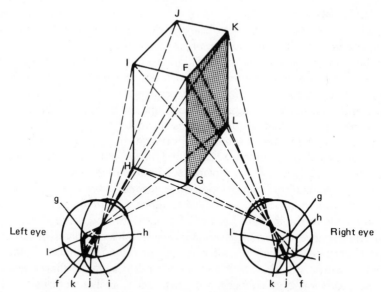

FIGURE 8.3 Geometric representation of binocular disparity. A solid object such as a cube placed in the median plane of the head produces slightly different or disparate images in the two eyes. The right eye observes somewhat more of the left surface of the cube and the left eye somewhat more of the right surface. The three-dimensional representations of the images in each eye serve to emphasize the differences in retinal projections. In actuality, these projections are flat. (From Burian and von Noorden, 1974)

parity (or a crossed image) results in seeing a nonfixated point as nearer than the fixation point, whereas uncrossed disparity results in localizing a non-fixated point as farther than the fixation point (Ogle, 1959).

Perceptual integration in depth occurs provided certain conditions are met. The images in each eye must be highly similar in brightness, size, and contour; otherwise, retinal rivalry (see Chapter 5) will occur. For singleness of vision, they must also fall within a limited area of corresponding retinal points. This latter condition is illustrated in Figure 8.4. When our eyes are converged on one point in space, a surface can be determined that will pass through the fixation point such that all spatial locations lying along the surface will stimulate corresponding retinal areas (Ogle, 1950, 1959). This surface is termed the *horopter*. It is formally defined as the locus of all points in space whose images fall on corresponding retinal areas for a given degree of convergence. Points lying along the horopter will give rise to single images. Those which lie off the horopter will stimulate disparate retinal areas, and, if the disparity is

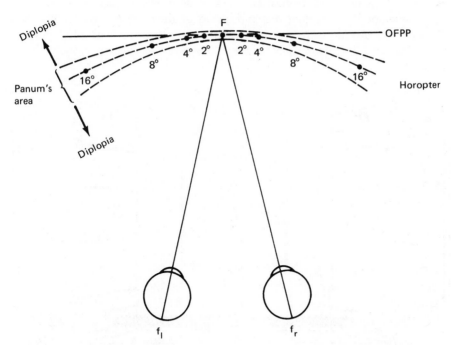

FIGURE 8.4   The horopter and Panum's area. The eyes are converged on point F; OFPP is the objective fronto-parallel plane. The horopter is an empirically determined surface passing through F such that all points lying along this surface stimulate corresponding retinal areas and are seen as single. The actual shape of the horopter depends upon target distance. Points lying off the horopter give rise to double vision except for those that fall in a narrow horizontal band known as Panum's area. (After Burian and von Noorden, 1974)

great enough, such points will produce diplopia. However, if the points lie within a narrow horizontal band about the horopter, the stimulation of horizontally disparate retinal areas will result in a single visual impression perceived in depth. The region about the horopter which yields single vision is known as *Panum's fusion area,* after the Danish physiologist who discovered it.

The initial demonstration that binocular disparity is a cue to depth was made by the British physicist Sir Charles Wheatstone (1838). From a knowledge of geometric optics, he prepared drawings of scenes as viewed by the right and the left eyes (stereograms). These drawings were presented in an optical device that he constructed known as a *stereoscope* (see Figure 8.5). Using it, with the aid of mirrors, he could control accommodation and convergence and also regulate the stimulation reaching the eyes. By manipulating the amount and kind of disparity, Wheatstone was able to simulate on a flat surface the conditions which prevail when the two eyes are viewing a solid object. Thus, by means of two-dimensional stereograms viewed in a stereoscope he was able to elicit a compelling impression of depth.

Since Wheatstone's stereoscope, several other stereoscopic devices have been developed for creating the impression of depth from two-dimensional stimuli. They use the technique of presenting the two eyes with photographs taken from slightly different perspectives. One of these devices, shown in Fig-

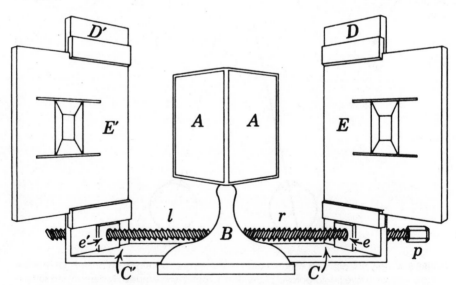

FIGURE 8.5 The Wheatstone stereoscope. Panels E'E house slightly different drawings of a common object. Images of the drawings are reflected into each eye as an observer faces the instrument by the mirrors, AA. The instrument can be calibrated for use by different observers by sliding E'E in the uprights D'D and by adjusting the distance between D'D and the mirrors by turning the screw, p.

FIGURE 8.6 A hand-held stereoscope. This instrument was a popular source of entertainment during the nineteenth century. (From Geldard, 1962)

ure 8.6, became a popular source of entertainment in the parlor rooms of the 19th century. A modern version of this device is the "Viewmaster," which you may have used as a child. If you have one of these in your possession, you can gain an impression of the value of disparity as a depth cue by performing the following "experiment." Point the "Viewmaster" directly at a light source so that both viewing fields are evenly illuminated, and look at a stimulus card with one field covered. After a short while, uncover the occluded field; the scene will appear to "jump out" at you in vivid depth.

Still another means of creating the impression of depth from separate two-dimensional pictures is the *anaglyph* technique. In this case, a picture is printed partly in red and partly in blue ink. A strong impression of depth appears when the picture is viewed with a red filter over one eye and a green filter over the other. This occurs because the filters induce different images in the two eyes (Kaufman, 1974). The eye covered by the red filter sees black in the green portion of the picture; the eye covered by the green filter sees black in the red portion. Plate 1 gives an example of this means of achieving stereopsis.

A major innovation in the study of stereopsis was introduced by Julesz (1964, 1971). Prior to his work, the stimulus patterns used in stereograms had been fine line drawings, geometric forms, or photographs of real-life scenes. It had been implicitly assumed that the stereoscopic effect requires recognizable objects or patterns. Julesz has shown, however, that stereopsis is possible with stereograms that consist of meaningless, unfamiliar, randomly determined patterns such as the ones given in Figure 8.7.

The Julesz stereograms were constructed in the following way. One stereogram was generated by a computer programmed to produce a random array of black and white elements of specified density. Another was copied from the first, except that in a block in the center, each element was displaced laterally by a prescribed amount. When viewed monocularly each of the stereograms appears to have the same random texture. When viewed in

FIGURE 8.7   Stereograms, composed of randomly arranged black and white elements. The elements in the central portion of one stereogram are laterally displaced to form the central portion of the other stereogram, thereby introducing binocular disparity. When the two fields are viewed stereoscopically, the central portion appears as a square that stands out in front of the background. (From Julesz, 1964)

a stereoscope or other equivalent device, however, the cluster of elements that is disparately displayed on the two retinas is seen in depth. The cluster appears either in front of or behind the rest of the pattern depending upon which stereogram is placed before which eye. In this manner, squares, spirals, and other forms are seen to come out from or recede into the background. In another study from Julesz's laboratory (Julesz and Spivack, 1967) random stereograms were generated using tiny breaks in horizontal or vertical lines which yielded a square standing out from a surface.

Other investigators have found that stereopsis can also be achieved by varying the brightness of disparate elements (Kaufman, 1964; Kaufman and Pitblado, 1965) as well as by selectively omitting certain elements of the array presented to each eye (Lawson and Gulick, 1967; Lawson and Mount, 1967; Lawson and Pandina, 1969). These findings are quite important. They indicate that binocular disparity is a dominant factor in the perception of depth. Evidently, it can be utilized when all familiarity cues are removed and oculomotor cues are held constant. Moreover, the correspondence of objects and patterns in the two retinal projections can be established without the viewer's actually recognizing the objects and patterns. According to Julesz (1964), this pattern matching is based on a process of finding connected clusters formed by adjacent points of similar brightness.

Just how good a cue to three-dimensional space is binocular disparity? While stereoacuity is affected by several factors, such as the luminance of objects, their lateral separation, retinal location, and observation distance (Graham, 1965b; Lit and Finn, 1976; Richards and Foley, 1974), disparity turns out to be a very powerful space cue. It operates over a considerable range of distances, a range of approximately 495 yards, or 445.5 meters (Graham, 1965b), and sensitivity to very small differences in disparity is exceptionally keen. As described by Hochberg (1971b), some observers can detect depth in retinal disparities of only 1/1800 of a degree, or about 2 sec of arc. A recent series of experiments by Ross (1976) gives further evidence of just how resourceful binocular perception can be. Ross has developed a computer system that extends Julesz's random-dot stereogram method. Points of light are presented on twin oscilloscopes that are optically separated so that one is visible to the left eye and the other to the right eye. The points of light are appropriately displaced in each oscilloscope to produce retinal disparity. When the display is viewed monocularly, the observer sees a swarm of dots moving across the display like "snow" on a television set. When viewed binocularly, the display is seen to contain objects in depth. Ross reports that some observers can see targets in depth when the optical system delivers points at the rate of 250,000 pairs per second and that they can tolerate a delay of 50 milliseconds between points. Evidently, the perceptual system can handle an incredibly high rate of binocular information, and binocular perception must incorporate a memory component capable of maintaining a record of the position of thousands of points for at least 50 milliseconds.

Our ability to perceive distance through disparate retinal images is a truly remarkable phenomenon. Although much is known of the psychophysics of this phenomenon, the manner in which stereoscopic information is coded in the brain has been a long-standing problem, and it still remains a mystery. Perhaps the most widely adopted explanation involves fusion theory. As summarized by Rock (1975), this view generally holds that the images of the two eyes fuse with each other in some way within the brain. Stimulation of corresponding retinal points results in fusion at one level within the neural network of the visual system. Stimulation of noncorresponding points results in fusion at some other level, and the greater the difference in the fusion levels within the neural network, the greater the impression of depth. The fusion model is intuitively appealing, but it is not completely satisfactory because it cannot handle several aspects of stereopsis. One of these is the fact that, within limits, depth may be perceived in a stereoscope even when the images are seen as double (Ogle, 1952, 1953, 1959). Several other models of stereopsis have been offered, some of which make use of exciting electrophysiological findings regarding disparity-detecting cells in the visual system (see Bishop, 1973). A good discussion of these models is available in Kaufman (1974), as well as in Bishop and Henry (1971), Dodwell (1970), Hochberg (1971b), and Julesz (1971).

Kinetic Cues

Motion parallax and motion perspective   It is important to keep in mind that perceiving people are moving people. Except under the most artificial circumstances, you are continually moving about, and your head rarely remains stationary for any length of time. As Gibson (1950a) has noted, if you are not walking or looking from a moving vehicle, even simple postural adjustments will produce some change in the position of your eyes in space. Such changes, of course, provide continuous shifts in the images on the retina, and these shifts serve to enrich your perception of distance.

When you move about on foot or in a vehicle, the projections of objects on the retina are alive with motion. In general, elements in the field of view that lie close to you appear to move at a greater velocity than those more distant. Furthermore, the direction of displacement is different. Objects nearer than the point of fixation appear to move in direction opposite to that of your own movement, whereas those beyond the point of fixation seem to move with you. This disparity in the apparent motion of objects at different distances, as the observer moves past them, is known as *motion parallax*. It is illustrated in Figure 8.8, which depicts the movement of terrain as seen by an observer from a train traveling toward the left. You can observe a similar effect when riding in an automobile. The next time you do so, notice how the posts of the guard rails along the highway seem to be moving much faster than and in the opposite direction from the trees off in the distance.

For another illustration, try the following. Hold up your two index fingers,

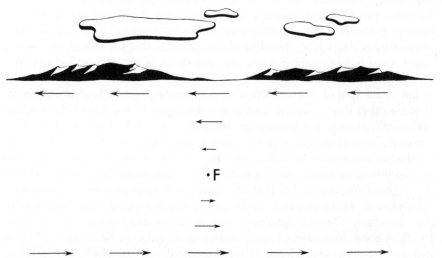

FIGURE 8.8   The optical flow in motion parallax. Assume that an observer moving toward the left fixates a point at F. Objects nearer than F will appear to move in a direction opposite to that of the movement of the observer; objects farther away than F will appear to move in the same direction as the observer. The length of the arrows signifies that the apparent velocity of the optical flow is directly related to the distance of objects from the fixation point. (From Gibson, 1950a)

one close to your face and the other at arm's length. First fixate on the near finger. Then, move your head laterally. Notice that the far finger seems to move in the same direction that your head is moving. Now, shift your fixation to the far finger, and again move your head laterally. This time, the near finger will seem to move in the direction opposite to your head movement. Formal experiments have confirmed these informal observations: motion parallax is, indeed, a useful source of information about relative distance (Gibson, Gibson, Smith, and Flock, 1959; Graham, Baker, Hecht, and Lloyd, 1948) and, in some instances, for the perception of absolute distance as well (Dees, 1966; Ferris, 1972).

Gibson (1950a, 1966) has made the interesting suggestion that motion parallax is part of a more general source of motion-produced distance information which he terms *motion perspective*. Gibson points out that when an observer is in motion, the retinal projections of objects undergo continuous transformations that are regular and lawful in character. Wherever the observer looks, the scene flows past in a continuous stream. The flow decreases at the top of the visual field and vanishes at the horizon. If we consider the terrain of the environment to be projected as a plane in front of the eye, the rate at which any element flows is inversely related to its physical distance from the observer. There is, in Gibson's terms, a gradient of velocity from a maximum at the bottom of the visual field — the ground over which we travel — to the horizon.

These ideas are illustrated in Figure 8.9, which shows the projected terrain ahead of the observer as seen from an airplane in level flight. In principle, the diagram would be similar for a person on foot or driving an automobile. The arrows in the figure represent the velocity and direction of flow of surface elements. As Gibson points out, in these circumstances the field ahead expands outward from a focus, and there is a gradient of decreasing velocities (shown by decreases in the length of the arrows) from the lower section of the scene to the horizon. There is also a gradient of changing directions from the mid-portion of the field to each side. On the other hand, the mountains and the clouds are at such great distances that the velocity of their deformations approaches zero. The gradients of continuous transformations of the entire retinal image arising from the motion of the perceiver is the motion perspective of which motion parallax is a part.

Kinetic depth effect The motion of objects can also provide cues to depth. Investigators have turned up some fascinating and subtle ways of creating the impression of depth with two-dimensional stimuli placed in motion. One of these lines of investigation has been pursued by Wallach and his associates (Wallach and O'Connell, 1953; Wallach, O'Connell, and Neisser, 1953) under the heading of the *kinetic depth effect*. These investigators conducted a series of experiments to test the hypothesis that the shadows cast by rotating objects of appropriate shape will be seen as three-dimensional. Their

FIGURE 8.9   Motion perspective. The optical flow in the visual field as an observer moves forward. The view is that as seen from an airplane in level flight. The direction of apparent movement in the terrain below is signified by the direction of the arrows; speed of apparent movement is indicated by the length of the arrows. From Gibson, 1950a)

experimental technique involved projecting the shadow of a rotating object onto a translucent screen. The shadow was cast by a point source of light located far from the object, which itself was placed behind, and very close to, the screen. The resulting shadow gave an undistorted, isometric projection of the object. The subjects viewed the shadow through the screen. Whenever the shadow-casting objects were of appropriate shape, the subjects reported seeing rotating, three-dimensional objects. That is, the shadows were described much as the objects themselves would be.

According to Wallach and his co-workers, objects of appropriate shape to yield a kinetic depth effect were those which cast shadows that underwent transformations of length and direction when rotated. Transformations of length or direction alone were not sufficient. This and related evidence indicates that the kinetic depth effect depends upon distortions in shape, though it is not any single distorted image which is responsible. Thus, if a rotating object were stopped at any one position, naive subjects viewing the resulting single shadow did not report depth. The depth effect comes, apparently, from the continuous sequence of distortions.

Complete rotation was not necessary to obtain the kinetic depth effect; partial rotation was quite effective. The use of solid objects was also not essential. Figures made up of wire bent into three dimensions worked quite as well. Indeed, the subjects not only perceived the shadows of such figures as three-dimensional, they often were able to reproduce the wire figures with remarkable accuracy just from seeing their rotating shadows.

These experiments reveal a very interesting cue to depth, a cue involving a temporal sequence of transformations in shape much like the motion perspective cue suggested by Gibson. Since the early work of Wallach and his colleagues, a number of investigators have generated other ways of producing the appearance of depth through motion. This research is nicely summarized in Braunstein (1962, 1976).

Pictorial Cues

Depth perception and Western painting The cues to depth that we have discussed so far have centered upon physiological properties of the visual system and changes in retinal images which arise when observers, or the objects that they look at, move about the environment. These cues can be considered to be "dynamic," and since they are tied to the activity of the observer, to be primary cues to depth. There are other indicants of a more "static" and secondary nature which can also be quite useful in conveying a three-dimensional impression. The discovery of most of these *pictorial cues* was made primarily by artists of the Renaissance in their efforts to portray depth on canvas. In this case, the role of psychologists has primarily been one of formalization and amplification rather than of initial discovery (Kaufman, 1974). What follows is a description of several of these pictorial cues.

Size Earlier in this book (Chapter 6), we spoke of the size-distance relationship when considering the problem of size constancy. At that time, we pointed out that knowledge of the distance of objects can serve as a cue to their size. The size-distance relationship can work the other way around as well; aspects of size can influence the perception of distance. Several pictorial cues to depth reflect this important fact.

Recall that as an object of fixed size moves away from an observer, there is a corresponding decrease in the image that the object casts on the retina (see Figure 6.6). Thus, the proximal size of a target is a potential source of information about its distance. Artists make use of this information to portray depth by drawing as smaller the one of two similar objects that is to appear the farther away.

The role of proximal size as an important determinant of apparent distance has been demonstrated in a number of laboratory investigations. These studies adopt the general technique of presenting two objects that are identical, except for the size of their retinal images, in an impoverished viewing situation from which all other distance cues are removed. Under these circumstances, the object which casts the retinal image having the larger visual angle appears nearer. An illustration of this effect can be found in the "balloon experiment" of Ittelson and Kilpatrick (1951). These investigators used two partly inflated balloons which were illuminated by a concealed source and viewed monocularly in a dark room. The relative size of the balloons was controlled by a bellows. When they were of equal size, the balloons appeared

to be glowing spheres at equal distances from the observer. When their relative size was continuously varied, the balloons appeared to move in a dramatic fashion back and forth through space. At any time, the balloon which
was larger seemed to be nearer than the smaller one. Similarly, Gogel (1968)
has reported that if two luminous rectangles of the same shape but different
retinal sizes are viewed in darkness, the relatively larger rectangle is perceived
as closer to the observer. Other studies showing the effects of proximal size
have been reported by Epstein and Franklin (1965), Gogel, Hartman, and
Harker (1957), Hochberg and Hochberg (1952), and Hochberg and
McAlister (1955).

The experiments just described represent the case in which *relative* retinal
size determines a perception of depth between objects. As Gogel (1964) has
noted, it is as if the observer assumes that the two objects are physically the
same size and therefore perceives the retinally smaller one as being more distant. There is still another aspect to size which also contributes to the perception of depth—the *familiar* or *assumed* size of an object.

One of the earliest descriptions of the role of familiar size on apparent
distance was provided by Ittelson (1951). In order to study this problem, he
employed what is known as a "thereness-thatness" apparatus in which a test
object with a familiar (or assumed) size is presented in a visually impoverished field. Its perceived distance is measured by comparing its spatial location with that of a comparison object seen in a field that is rich with cues to
distance. In one part of Ittelson's experiment, subjects judged the distance of
three playing cards: a normal-size card, a card that was twice normal size,
and one that was half-sized. All stimuli were presented in the thereness-thatness apparatus at a constant distance of 7.5 feet. On the average, the normal-sized card was judged to be 7.46 feet away, the double-sized card to be
about half that distance (4.61 feet), and the half-sized card to be approximately twice as far away as the normal-sized card (14.99 feet). Evidently,
given the "known" size of a normal playing card, the double-sized card appeared to be "too large" and was seen as close by, whereas the half-sized
card seemed "too small" and therefore farther away. These results supported
the hypothesis that perceived distance is related to the familiar size of objects.
A similar study by Hastorf (1950) led to the same conclusion.

The experiments by Ittelson and Hastorf triggered a considerable debate
regarding the contribution of familiar size to the perception of distance (see
Epstein, 1967; Gogel, 1964; Gogel, Hartman, and Harker, 1957). In part, the
debate hinged upon the use of the thereness-thatness apparatus in the early
experiments. Since this apparatus involves an apparent distance judgment between a test and a comparison object, the observers' responses may not reflect the influence of familiar size at all, but instead may be based upon the
relative sizes of the objects being compared.

One way to avoid this criticism is to show that perceived distance depends upon familiar size when distance judgments are obtained without using

comparison objects. This approach was taken by Epstein (1965) in a study in which observers made distance judgments by signaling when an amount of rope pulled through their hands equaled the perceived distance of targets seen under reduced-cue conditions. The targets were photographs of coins which would normally be expected to vary in familiar size. In this case, however, their actual retinal sizes were the same. The stimuli consisted of a photograph of a normal-sized quarter, a dime photographically enlarged to the size of a quarter, and a half-dollar reduced to the size of a quarter. The apparent distance of these stimuli varied as a function of familiar size; the dime, which was larger than its usual size, seemed closest, followed in order by the normal-sized quarter and by the half-dollar, which was smaller than its usual size.

Still another means of showing the influence of familiar size on perceived distance is to use a paradigm in which familiar size and relative size are placed in opposition. Such an approach was taken by Ono (1969). In one portion of his experiment, subjects judged the distance of circles presented under reduced-cue conditions. As expected, Ono's subjects judged a large circle to be nearer than a smaller one when both were physically the same distance away. In another portion of the study, "familiar object" connotations were added to the abstract circles, and this addition greatly modified the results. The photograph of a normal-sized golf ball was placed on the smaller circle, while that of a baseball, which was smaller than that of a full-sized baseball but larger than a golf ball, was placed on the larger circle. Under those conditions, the circle containing the baseball should appear closer if relative size alone is operative, but farther away on the basis of familiar size. Ono found that the larger object was still judged nearer. However, the apparent distance between it and the smaller object was considerably reduced when compared to the condition where plain circles were the stimuli. In this case, familiar size acted to minimize the effect of relative size. Indeed, a variety of experiments (for example, Baird, 1963; Coltheart, 1971; Epstein, 1963b; Epstein and Baratz, 1964; Gogel, 1976; Gogel and Mertens, 1968; Newman, 1972; Park and Michaelson, 1974) demonstrate that both relative size and familiar size are pictorial cues which can determine the perceived distance of objects.

Linear perspective   As one looks along a flat and continuous expanse of terrain, such as a road, parallel lines appear to converge as they recede into the distance. This phenomenon is termed *linear perspective,* and it is one of the most important pictorial cues to depth. A familiar illustration of linear perspective is shown in Figure 8.10. Note that the railroad tracks, which are distally parallel, appear to meet as they become more distant from the observer. Moreover, the ties between the tracks appear to become shorter and shorter and, indeed, the perceived length of a tie at any point is equivalent to the distance between the tracks at that point.

FIGURE 8.10   An illustration of linear perspective. The railroad tracks, which are distally parallel, converge in the picture as they would on the retina in accordance with the relation between proximal size and distal distance. (Photo by Leventhal)

Linear perspective is a further example of the important relationship between size and distance. Recall once more that the projected size of objects on the retina decreases with increasing distance from the observer. Thus, if two objects, such as the rails in Figure 8.10, are parallel and extend toward the horizon, the visual angle which describes the separation between any two points on the rails will grow smaller with increments in the distance of the points from the eye, and the rails will eventually meet at a "vanishing point" — the horizon. The same principle explains the decreasing size of the ties. Linear perspective is based upon the geometric concept of a flat plane. You might wonder why this principle works as well as it does, since the surface of the earth is, of course, curved and not flat. The answer, as Kaufman (1974) has noted, is that the radius of curvature is so large in comparison to our own size that, for perceptual purposes, the surface of the earth is seen as a flat plane.

Texture gradients   A variable of special interest in studies of depth perception is the texture gradient provided by the stimulus field. Imagine yourself looking up the wall of a tall brick building. As your gaze moves up the wall, the retinal size of the bricks becomes smaller, and the number of bricks per unit of retinal area becomes greater. Think of the bricks as the elements composing the texture of the wall's surface. The *texture density* of the surface is defined as the number of proximal elements per unit area. In this sense, then, there is a gradient of texture density along the surface of the wall, with the densest texture at the top of the building.

The same kind of texture gradient is created as you stand on a pebbly beach and look along it into the distance, or as you look down a cobblestone path. Most natural surfaces, in fact, are characterized by gradients of texture density. The correlation between texture density and distance provides the basis for another pictorial distance cue. An illustration of this type of distance-relevant information is given in Figures 8.11 and 8.12.

Credit for pointing up the importance of texture gradients as a cue to distance belongs to the psychologist James J. Gibson (1950a, 1966). In one of his experiments on this problem, Gibson (1950b) investigated the influence of texture-density gradients on the perceived slant of a surface. Perceived slant,

FIGURE 8.11   Illustrations of texture gradients. In the picture on the left, note how the bricks grow smaller and more densely packed from bottom to top, providing a cue to distance. The distance effect is enhanced by the presence of linear perspective. Perspective is absent in the picture on the right, leaving the texture gradient as the only distance cue. (Photos by Leventhal)

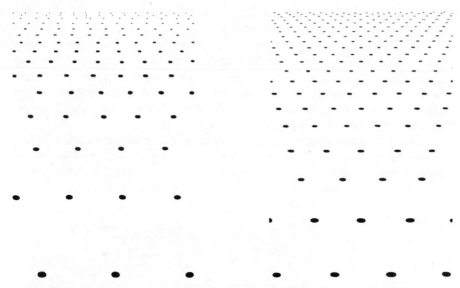

FIGURE 8.12   Spot distributions which create a strong perceived depth effect. (After Gibson, 1950a)

of course, is a special case of perceived distance. Thus, an unslanted surface is perpendicular to the line of regard; its top and bottom are equidistant from the observer. When the surface is slanted, its top and bottom are no longer equidistant from the observer; as the top recedes, the bottom moves closer. For example, as you stand at one end of a room, looking straight ahead, both the floor and the ceiling are slanted with respect to your line of regard — the ceiling slants down and the floor slants up. According to Gibson, the perception of the degree of slant of a surface is, in the absence of other cues, dependent upon the rate of change of the texture density which the surface projects on the retina. This hypothesis derives from the geometric relation between size and distance that we have previously discussed — the farther away from the observer an array of elements is, the smaller their interelement distance will be on the retina, or the greater their density.

To test this hypothesis Gibson carefully constructed a situation that allowed texture density to vary while eliminating other distance cues. The experimental stimuli were photographic slides of real surfaces slanted at the desired angles. The slides were projected on an unslanted screen, and it was these projections which the subjects viewed.

Two kinds of surfaces were photographed, at each of the four angles — 10°, 22°, 30°, and 45°. One surface contained elements of constant size arranged in a regular pattern, such as the surface of a brick wall would provide. The other surface contained elements of irregular size, arranged in haphazard order. It was expected that the irregular surface would yield less stable judgments of slant than the regular surface. The subjects indicated the perceived slant of each stimulus by adjusting the slant of a board provided for that purpose. In relative terms, the estimates of perceived slant agreed well with the "actual" slant of the stimuli. As expected, the regular pattern resulted in more accurate and more reliable judgments than did the irregular pattern.

These results support the validity of gradients of texture density as distance cues. Further experiments have substantiated Gibson's general results (Beck and Gibson, 1955; Epstein, Bontranger, and Park, 1962; Flock, 1964; Kraft and Winnick, 1967; Newman, 1970; Vickers, 1971) and have also added some complexity to the original hypothesis. For example, slants tend to be underestimated when texture is the only cue available (Clark, Smith, and Rabe, 1956a, 1956b), and certain combinations of element size and interelement separation are necessary for slant estimation; maximum utilization of texture as a cue to distance occurs at intermediate levels of density (Gruber and Clark, 1956). Moreover, the saliency of texture gradients as a cue to distance depends upon viewing conditions. Subjects place less weight on texture gradients when using binocular vision than when they are restricted to monocular viewing (Newman, 1972b).

Relative height Another pictorial cue to perceived depth which seems to be related to texture gradients is the relative height of objects. Other things being equal, the higher of two objects in a visual field will tend to appear the more distant. The linkage between this cue and texture gradients was suggested by Epstein (1966), who pointed out that compared to objects that are low in the field, those which are higher up are usually adjacent to denser portions of the optical gradient of texture and hence associated with the perceptually more distant portions of the ground surface. Therefore, the higher object appears to be farther away.

In order to test this idea, Epstein had subjects make judgments of the apparent distance between pairs of dots presented one above the other in a frontal parallel plane. The dots were separated vertically by either 3.5, 5.5, or 7.5 inches and were presented against three types of backgrounds: a null background, consisting of a black surface, an outline background without surface texture, and a background with texture gradients (see Figure 8.13). The dots and the outline and textured backgrounds were coated with fluorescent paint and made visible in a completely dark laboratory by the light of an ultraviolet tube. Vertical separation of the dots produced no differences in the perceived distance between them when the dots were viewed against the null background. When viewed against the outline or textured backgrounds, however, the top dot was judged as farther away than the bottom one. With the outline background, this difference in perceived depth increased by about 3 inches over the range of vertical separations; with the textured background, the difference in the apparent depth between the dots increased by about 10 inches over the same range of vertical separations.

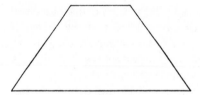

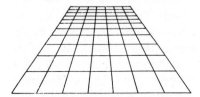

FIGURE 8.13 Outline and textured backgrounds used by Epstein to test the optical adjacency explanation of the relation between relative height and perceived distance. (From Epstein, 1966)

These results provide strong support for Epstein's optical adjacency explanation of the effects of relative height on perceived depth. They led him to conclude that the relative height cue might best be thought of as relative height *in the field* rather than vertical separation *per se,* considered in isolation in empty space.

Aerial perspective   Should the air between the observer and an object (say a building) not be clear—an increasingly chronic condition in most urban regions—the light which is reflected from the object will undergo a wide variety of transformations, such as scattering and filtering, that changes its original character. Under these conditions objects at a considerable distance appear to have a bluish tint, and their detail as less distinct than those nearby. The farther away the object, the greater the effect, which is called *aerial perspective.* It is illustrated in Plate 4, a photograph of the village of St. Vincent nestled in the foothills of the Italian Alps. Notice how the trees and houses in the foreground appear in sharp detail, while the distant mountain peaks are blurred and hazy.

Aerial perspective is used to advantage by artists to convey the impression of great distance. It is of interest to note, as Dember and Jenkins (1970) have done, that "if a person has come to expect the aerial perspective effect to prevail, its absence can lead to a considerable error in judging the distance of objects. For this reason, in the relatively clear air of mountainous regions, the peaks seem much closer than they are and, as a result, people are often misled into thinking that a distant mountain is only an hour's walk away, when in fact it is several days away."

Proximal brightness   Brightness is another attribute of stimuli that is correlated with their distance, and hence brightness can also serve as a pictorial distance cue. Other things being equal, if the position of the observer and a source of light remain constant, the brighter of two otherwise identical objects will seem nearer. This effect is based upon an important relation in the physics of light known as the *inverse square law*, which states that illumination intensity at any point is inversely proportional to the square of its distance from the source of light. Thus, as the distance of an object from a source of light increases, the illumination falling on the object decreases (Kaufman, 1974).

Shading and shadow Still another pictorial depth cue arising from illumination conditions is *shading* and *shadow*. Objects are normally illuminated in such a way that the distribution of light on their surface is nonuniform. The nonuniformity is a consequence of their three-dimensionality. The resulting pattern of light and shadow can serve as a cue to the relative distance between objects or to the distance between objects and surfaces. It can give the impression of a textured relief to a surface as well. In the hands of a skilled artist (see Arnheim, 1974), shading and shadow can produce a compelling impression of depth in a two-dimensional picture. This effect is illustrated in a sketch of a three-dimensional rectangle in Figure 8.14. When drawn with shading and shadow the rectangle appears to rise vertically off the page. Notice how much flatter this sketch seems to be when shading and shadow are eliminated.

The role of shading and shadow in giving a textured appearance to objects is illustrated in Figure 8.15. The object shown is a piece of natural glass called Tektite. Notice that the surface of the object appears to be pockmarked by small craters. If we alter the direction of the shadows by turning the page upside down, the craters turn into bumps or mounds.

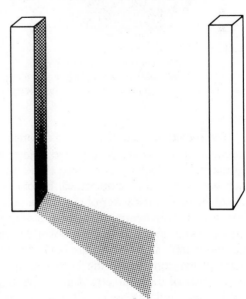

FIGURE 8.14 The role of shading and shadow in producing the impression of depth. Notice how much flatter the rectangle appears when shading and shadow are absent.

FIGURE 8.15 The role of shading and shadow in giving a textured appearance to objects. The surfaces of pieces of natural glass called Tektite appear to be pock-marked by small craters. If the figure is turned upside down, the craters become bumps or mounds. (From King, 1976)

Interposition   The final cue to distance that we shall consider is based on the fact that relative distance of two objects may be represented on the retina by the partial blocking of one by the other. If two objects overlap laterally, then part of the farther object will be blocked from view by the nearer. The retinal image of the nearer object is interposed over that of the farther object. One example of interposition as a distance cue with geometrical figures is represented in Figure 8.16. A real-world illustration of this cue is presented in the photograph shown in Figure 8.17. Notice how the trees in the foreground intercept the contours of the house, as also does the lamp post. Moreover, the contour of the garage roof intercepts that of the remainder of the building. Dember and Jenkins (1970) have noted that interposition can be manip-

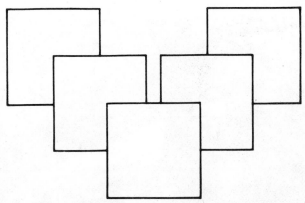

FIGURE 8.16   Interposition. The squares appear to fan out behind each other. Each square intercepts the contour of the one behind it.

ulated not only to yield a veridical impression of depth, but also to reverse apparent distance relations. Thus, it is possible to make the closer of two objects seem farther, as in Figure 8.18.

Distance cues and perceptual dynamics   The several cues to distance described in the preceeding sections reveal how we are able to solve the retinal paradox and gain a three-dimensional view of the distal environment from two-dimensional proximal images. No doubt, you have noticed that some of these cues, namely, convergence and binocular disparity, involve a complex coordination of the two eyes; the remaining cues can be effective when only one eye is used. You should bear in mind that for experimental reasons the cues to distance are often studied individually. In nature, however, they are rarely separated. Instead, they occur together in complex combinations. As an example, consider Figure 8.19, a flat picture which gives a strong impression of depth. How many of the pictorial cues which we have mentioned can you find operating in this scene?

It is clear that we make use of a wide variety of cues, no one of which is itself "three-dimensional," in order to achieve an awareness of depth, highlighting once again the active, constructive nature of perception. The view of perception as a dynamic process is, of course, a recurrent theme throughout this book.

TIME: THE FOURTH DIMENSION

The Temporal Framework of Events

The ubiquity of time   In addition to its spatial framework, the perceptual world is organized in terms of an ever-present matrix of time. Perceptual events have a beginning and an end; they occur simultaneously, or

FIGURE 8.17 A real-world scene featuring interposition as a cue to distance.

successively, or partially overlap; they endure for different durations. Consider how your everyday activities are partitioned in time. You rise, eat, work, play, and sleep at specified temporal intervals, and it is likely that you frequently consult your watch to "time" some aspect of an event in which you are engaged. As Ornstein (1969) has put it, time constitutes a basic thread in the fabric of existence.

The importance of time in human experience was recognized early in the development of experimental psychology (Boring, 1942), and the literature on this topic is extensive (see Doob, 1971; Eisler, 1976; Fraisse, 1963; Hicks, Miller, and Kinsbourne, 1976; Underwood, 1966; and Wallace and Rabin, 1960, for comprehensive summaries). We will describe some of this information in the sections to follow.

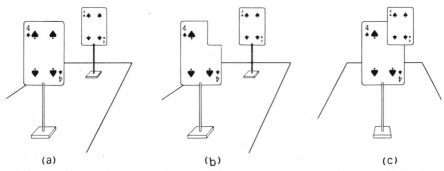

(a)   (b)   (c)

FIGURE 8.18   How interposition can override both size and familiarity cues in the perception of distance. The playing cards and their stands are viewed monocularly and are the only objects illuminated. In panel (a), the two cards seem to be about equal in size, and the right-hand card is seen as the farther away. The same is true of the arrangement in panel (b), where a piece of the left-hand card has been cut out. In (c), however, with the right-hand card "filling" the opening, and with its stand obscured, the right-hand card appears nearer, though much smaller, than the left-hand card. (From Dember and Jenkins, 1970)

FIGURE 8.19   A mountain road in Colorado. How many pictorial cues to distance can you detect in this scene? (Photo by G.M. Rand)

The interaction between space and time   Before doing so, however, we want to examine the nature of the relationship between the spatial and temporal frameworks within which perceptual experience may be ordered. Just as space and time are tied together in the physical world, they are also closely related in the world of perception. One way to illustrate this linkage is to consider experiments which explore the effects of variations in the temporal interval between stimulus events on the perception of their spatial separation. Such an experiment was performed by Helson and King (1931). They arranged things so that three equidistant points, A, B and C, could be stimulated on the forearms of subjects. When the interval of time between the stimulation of points A and B exceeded that between B and C, the subjects reported that the spatial separation between A and B seemed to be greater than that between B and C. This result, termed the *tau effect,* also occurs when the stimuli are flashes of light separated in visual space (Abbe, 1937; Bill and Teft, 1969). Furthermore, its converse, the *kappa effect,* has been demonstrated experimentally—the perceived temporal interlude between two successive visual or cutaneous stimuli varies directly with their spatial separations (Abbe, 1936; Adkins, 1972; Cohen, Hansel, and Sylvester, 1953, 1955; Price-Williams, 1954; Suto, 1952). The tau and kappa effects are compelling demonstrations of the relativity of, and interaction between, space and time in perceptual experience.

Psychophysical Factors in Perceived Duration

The elusive nature of time   While it is true that there are parallels in the perception of space and time, it is also true that the perception of time differs in important ways from the perception of space as well as from the perception of other stimulus attributes such as brightness, loudness, form, and size. In the case of time, there is an absence of specific cues which provide an invariant basis for judgment. Moreover, perceptual responses to other attributes can often be made while the relevant stimuli are physically present, but perceptual responses to the durative aspect of events cannot be made until after the events have run their course. The ephemeral nature of the experience of time is captured in this 14th-century Hebrew meditation:

> And remember that the companionship of Time is but of
> short duration. It flies more quickly than the shades
> of evening. We are like a child that grasps in his
> hand a sunbeam. He opens his hand soon again, but, to
> his amazement, finds it empty and the brightness gone.
>
> —Yedaya Penini

In a careful examination of the nature of temporal experience, Woodrow (1951) has pointed out that the perception of duration is not an immediate property of stimuli, but rather an indirect property—one that is apprehended on the basis of cues which become progressively altered with the lapse of physical time. If we accept Woodrow's analysis, then we might expect that the experience of time will fluctuate considerably with variations in the conditions under which judgments of duration are to be made. This is indeed the case: as a result, it is often difficult to come up with principles of time perception that have broad generality of application.

Stimulus characteristics   Any discussion of the psychophysics of time needs to consider the stimulus characteristics which influence perceived duration. Among the most important of these are the stimulus patterns used to demark intervals, the energy value and sensory modality of the signals involved, and the complexity of the stimuli.

Psychophysical studies of temporal perception typically make use of two types of stimulus patterns. One of these is called a *filled interval,* since it is marked off by a signal, such as a flash of light or a tone, which lasts continuously for a period of time. The other is termed an *unfilled* or *empty* interval. It consists of a period of time between two brief bounding signals, for example, pulses of light, or sound. Though the same amount of clock time can obviously be delineated by each type of stimulus pattern, the response to these patterns turns out not to be the same. Filled intervals are perceived to be longer than unfilled intervals of equal physical duration (Buffardi, 1971; Craig, 1973; Goldstone and Goldfarb, 1963; Thomas and Brown, 1974). This effect is termed the *filled-duration illusion,* and it is reminiscent of the filled-space illusion described in Chapter 6.

Several explanations have been offered for the filled-duration illusion. One of the more interesting is Craig's (1973) suggestion that in heralding the start of an unfilled interval, the representation of the initial bounding stimulus lasts beyond the signal's offset. This "leakage" into the interval causes the beginning of the gap between the two bounding signals to be perceptually delayed, and hence the unfilled interval seems shorter than a filled interval of equal duration. Some support for this delay hypothesis comes from studies showing that the perception of the duration of a signal grows over time and that it is not completed at the moment the stimulus is physically terminated. For example, Massaro and Idson (1976), using a backward-masking paradigm, have demonstrated that the apparent duration of an acoustic stimulus is influenced by a masking stimulus which comes on after the target stimulus has gone off.

Along these lines, it is of interest to note that the perceived duration of a burst of white noise is not shortened when the burst is sandwiched between two brief tones (Craig, 1973). Such an arrangement, however, presents a similar stimulus pattern for the judgment of a filled interval as is present in the construction of an unfilled interval — that is, a period of time set off by two bounding markers. In this case, it could be argued that the noise burst interrupts the perseveration of the initial bounding signal and, in this way, avoids the shortening effect that occurs when two bounding signals surround an unfilled gap.

The results with respect to the effects of stimulus energy on perceived duration are complex. On the other hand, several experimenters have reported that judgments of the absolute duration of a signal are directly related to the signal's intensity (Lifshitz, 1933; Needham, 1935; Oléron, 1952; Treisman, 1963; Zelkind and Uléhla, 1968). On the other hand, when asked to judge the relative durations of two successive stimuli, subjects seem to ignore energy differences in the stimuli. As long as the signals are easily detectable, disparities in their intensities are not incorporated into judgments of their relative durations (Abel, 1972; Allan and Kristofferson, 1974; Carbotte and Kristofferson, 1973; Creelman, 1964; Nilsson, 1969; Rafales, 1976). The question of why information about intensity should be incorporated into judgments of absolute duration but not into discriminations of relative duration remains unanswered at present. This state of affairs does, however, serve to highlight an important point—judgments of absolute and relative duration may very well involve different psychological processes with respect to the coding of time.

Sensory differences represent still another complicating factor in the psychophysics of time. Behar and Bevan (1960, 1961) explored the effects of the sensory modality used for stimulus presentation by means of a category-scaling procedure. Subjects judged the durations of acoustic (white noise) and visual (white light) signals ranging from 1 to 5 seconds. As shown in Figure 8.20, they found that the apparent duration of filled intervals of light was less

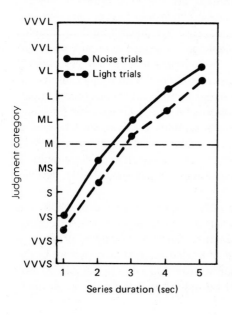

FIGURE 8.20 The perceived duration of auditory and visual intervals. L = long; S = short; V = very; M = medium (After Behar and Bevan, 1961)

than that of filled intervals of sound. This sensory difference has been confirmed in a series of experiments by Goldstone and his co-workers (Goldstone, 1968; Goldstone, Boardman, and Lhamon, 1959; Goldstone and Goldfarb, 1964, 1966). In addition, the durations of visual intervals also appear to be shorter than those marked off by cutaneous stimulation (Hawkes, Bailey, and Warm, 1961). Results such as these indicate that input modality is a relevant factor in the perception of time. They also raise some important questions for theories of time perception, to be discussed more fully in a later section, which generally ignore peripheral encoding factors and assume that duration judgments are the product of central processing mechanisms. Fortunately for our understanding of the processes of time perception, there is evidence to indicate that temporal experiences in different sensory modalities may share central processing units. For example, correlations computed between people's judgments of auditory and visual durations are quite high (Eijkman and Vendrik, 1965; Loeb, Behar, and Warm, 1966); furthermore, skill in making precise temporal judgments acquired through training in one modality readily transfers to another (Warm, Stutz, and Vassolo, 1975).

Variations in stimulus complexity play an important role in perceived duration. In general, the apparent duration of a stimulus event tends to vary directly with the complexity of the stimuli used to demark it. This effect has been demonstrated in several ways.

For example, Frankenhaeuser (1959) secured judgments of a broad range of intervals filled with the beating of a metronome. When the metronome was run at a fast rate (92 beats/min.), elapsed time seemed longer than when it was run at a slow rate (42 beats/min.). The finding that judged duration expands with increments in the number of discrete events presented during an interval has been replicated in several other experiments using a variety of techniques to vary the number and kinds of discrete events presented (Adams, 1977; Buffardi, 1971; Jones and MacLean, 1966; Mulhern, Warm, and Clark, 1974; Schiffman and Bobko, 1974, 1977; Thomas and Brown, 1974; Vroon, 1970). In addition, increases in amount of information in a stimulus, as indexed by the number of angles of a random polygon (Ornstein, 1969) or the numerosity of a dot pattern (Mo, 1975), have been found to be positively related to increases in the perceived duration of the stimulus.

Task characteristics   In addition to assessing the effects of the physical characteristics of stimuli on their perceived duration, psychologists have also been concerned with the way in which subjects keep track of time in different experimental tasks. In your own experience, you have probably noted that boring tasks, such as listening to a dull lecture, seem interminable, while interesting tasks end all too quickly. William James (1890) was one of the first to give formal expression to this experience when he stated that intervals filled with diversified and interesting activity seem shorter than those made up of monotonous tasks. A great deal of research has accumulated in the past quarter of a century to verify this statement (see Doob, 1971; Fraisse, 1963; Loehlin, 1959). In addition, data are available to indicate that perceived duration varies inversely with the muscular effort expended in a task (Warm, Smith, and Caldwell, 1967) and that it expands when elements of danger (Langer, Wapner, and Werner, 1961) or painful stimulation (Falk and Bindra, 1954) are introduced into the situation.

A pervasive finding with regard to task factors and temporal experience is a decrease in perceived duration when judgments of intervals are made while subjects are performing a concurrent nontemporal task. For example, the requirement to perform mental arithmetic shortens the duration of intervals (Burnside, 1971; Gulliksen, 1927). A recent study by Hicks, Miller, Gaes, and Bierman (1977) varied the amount of concurrent information processing in a quantitatively graded manner. Subjects were required to judge the time spent sorting playing cards under conditions that differed in processing demand, as indexed by response uncertainty: (1) sorting the cards into a single stack, (2) sorting into two stacks on the basis of color, (3) sorting into four stacks on the basis of color and suit. In terms of information theory, these conditions contained 0, 1, or 2 bits of response uncertainty, respectively. The experiment also featured a control group in which subjects judged time in the absence of a concurrent task. As shown in Figure 8.21, judged duration was longest in the control condition and declined progressively as the concurrent task became intellectually more demanding. Hicks and his co-workers account for such effects by arguing that the perception of time requires processing or attentional capacity and that distraction from attending to time by the need to process the ancillary task decreases the experience of duration.

Still another means of varying the nature of concurrent tasks has been used in experiments which have examined the effects of stimulus familiarity on perceived duration. In an initial set of experiments (Warm, Greenberg, and Dube, 1964; Warm, and McCray, 1969) subjects were asked to judge the durations of familiar words (for example, "Market," "Poetry," "Savings") and unfamiliar words (for example, "Benign," "Elegies," "Mundane") that were flashed on a screen. All of the stimuli were presented for one second. The subjects were told that a word would be shown for a brief period of time and that when it disappeared, they were to write down the word that was exposed and indicate their estimate of the exposure duration on a scale ranging from .09 to 9.99 sec. Under these conditions, familiar words were consistently judged to have been presented for a longer duration than the unfamiliar words. Such results can also be explained by appealing to differential attention to time. Specifically, it is likely that the familiar stimuli will be recognized more rapidly than the unfamiliar items (see Chapter 9), and thus during the exposure interval the subjects will have more time to attend to duration when presented with familiar than with unfamiliar words.

The "stimulus familiarity" effect has been confirmed in a study by

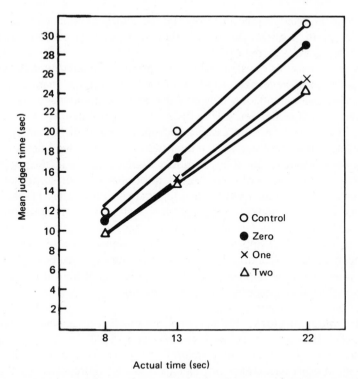

FIGURE 8.21   Perceived duration of card sorting and response uncertainty in bits. Zero bits of uncertainty: sort into a single stack; one bit: sort into two stacks on the basis of color; two bits: sort into four stacks on the basis of color and suit. In the control condition, time was judged in the absence of a concurrent card-sorting task. (From Hicks, Miller, Gaes, and Bierman, 1977)

Devane (1974), but it has not been replicated in several other experiments (Avant and Lyman, 1975; Thomas and Weaver, 1975; White, 1973). Recently, Miller (1977) has shown that this effect depends, in part, upon the requirement actively to process some aspect of the stimuli other than their duration *per se*. Using letter strings which differed in their approximation to English words (for example, ZTMGHKL as compared to THATERE), he found that the perceived duration of the letter strings increased with their approximation to words if the subjects were required to report both the duration of the stimuli and the letters in the strings. However, no differences in apparent duration were noted if the subjects were only required to attend to the elapsed time of the stimulus presentations.

Theories of Temporal Perception

Absolute and relative duration   It should be clear that a substantial body of information is available with regard to the perception of time. We have examined some theoretical explanations for specific temporal phenomena such as the filled-duration illusion and the effects of concurrent task activity. At this point, we want to ask whether there are any comprehensive accounts of temporal experience.

The answer to this question is both yes and no. Several quantitatively sophisticated models have been proposed to account for the manner in which people make discriminations between the relative durations of two stimuli (see Allan and Kristofferson, 1974; Eisler, 1975; Kristofferson, 1977). These models, however, do not necessarily address the issue of time-in-passing or the absolute duration of events. General theories of perceived absolute duration are also available, but they do not necessarily speak to the problem of differential discrimination of time. This state of affairs is not surprising, since, as we have seen, absolute and relative judgments of time may involve somewhat different psychological processes. Inasmuch as our previous discussion has focused primarily on the phenomenon of absolute duration, we shall consider here two general approaches to absolute impressions of interval duration: one, a physiological approach based upon internal metabolic factors, the other a more cognitive approach based upon the registration and retention of stimulus events which occur within a given interval.

The biological clock   Physiological approaches to explaining temporal experience can be characterized as adopting a "time base metaphor" (Ornstein, 1969). They take the position that the flow of subjective time is related to an internal pacemaker or "biological clock" represented by the functioning of some body mechanism that acts in a periodic or "pulse-dispensing" manner. The biological clock serves as a time base for judgments of duration. The greater the rate of physiological activity, the faster the output of the internal pacemaker and hence the swifter the flow of subjective time.

This point of view was introduced by Hoagland (1933), who suggested that psychological time is directly related to the velocity of chemical processes within the body. Similar proposals have been made by Lecomte Du Nouy (1937) and Piéron (1952). These ideas have been incorporated into a more recent "information-processing" model of the time-keeping mechanisms by Treisman (1963). The Treisman model features an arousal center which governs the output of a pacemaker. The latter is considered to produce a regular series of pulses which serve as a biological standard against which the duration of events is compared.

Evidence in support of the concept of a "biological clock" comes from some interesting experiments concerning the effects of variations in body temperature on perceived duration. The first of these was reported by François (1927), who required subjects to tap a key at the rate of three taps per second for a 10-second interval. He found that the rate of tapping, and thus the flow of subjective time, increased when the subjects' body temperatures were elevated through the use of a diathermy procedure. These findings were replicated by Hoagland (1933) under conditions of artificial temperature elevation as well as in the case of an individual (his wife) with a fever produced by influenza. More recent studies, using artificial techniques to elevate body temperature, have reported similar results (Fox, Bradbury, Hampton, and Legg, 1967; Kleber, Lhamon, and Goldstone, 1963). Furthermore, Pfaff (1968) has shown that the passage of subjective time is correlated with normal daily variations in body temperature. The perceived duration of intervals is less in the morning, when body temperature is at its lowest ebb, and increases in the afternoon, when diurnal variations in temperature typically reach their highest levels. The notion that subjective time is related to a temperature-sensitive internal clock is also supported by the finding that the perceived duration of intervals is shortened when body temperature is lowered while subjects are immersed in cold water (Baddeley, 1966).

Additional evidence for the support of a "biological clock" comes from experiments which demonstrate that apparent duration is expanded by stimulant drugs and shortened by depressants (Adam, Castro, and Clark, 1974; Adam, Rosner, Hosick, and Clark, 1971; Frankenhaeuser, 1959; Goldstone, Boardman, and Lhamon, 1958; Hawkes, Joy, and Evans, 1962) and that temporal experience is related to measures of electrocortical rhythms (Anliker, 1963; Holubář, 1969).

We should note that support for a physiological time-keeping mechanism has not been uniformly consistent. Bell and his co-workers (Bell, 1965; Bell and Provins, 1963) and Lockhart (1967) could find no systematic relation between body temperature and temporal judgments; other investigators have been unable to establish a link between temporal experience and electrocortical activity (Adam, Rosner, Hosick, and Clark, 1971; Jasper and Shagass, 1941). On the whole, however, the available evidence seems to confirm the notion of a biological clock which mediates temporal experience.

Memory and cognition   As an alternate to the "time base metaphor," we might view the experience of duration as a cognitive process in which the "mental content" of an interval determines the perception of duration. Such an approach has been suggested by Fraisse (1963). He maintains that any factor which influences the degree of stimulus change observed during a temporal interval has the effect of expanding or reducing its apparent duration. Within this framework, attention to the passage of time becomes a special case of the awareness of the number and quality of events occurring during a given period. According to Fraisse, the greater the unity of stimulus elements which occur during an interval, the smaller the number of perceived changes and hence the shorter the apparent duration of the interval.

A similar approach has been taken by Ornstein (1969). It is characterized by what he terms the "storage size metaphor." According to Ornstein, the experience of duration is constructed from the amount of information registered in consciousness and stored in memory during the passage of an interval of time. Increments in the number or complexity of stimulus events increase the size of storage, and as storage size increases, perceived duration also expands.

Cognitive theories such as those proposed by Fraisse and Ornstein can be applied to a number of temporal phenomena, for example, the filled-interval illusion, the effects of stimulus intensity and complexity, and the role of concurrent task activity. Ornstein also maintains that the storage-size hypothesis can incorporate the effects noted with regard to variations in body temperature and the administration of pharmacological agents; that is, conditions which from one point of view act to speed up the "biological clock" increase the subject's sensitivity to and awareness of the stimulus array and thus result in placing more information in storage. Consequently, Ornstein suggests that the search for neurophysiological correlates of temporal experience should concentrate on the mechanisms which underlie the registration, coding, and storage of information.

The cognitive formulations of Fraisse and Ornstein are imaginative and certainly have the advantage of broad generality. We need to point out, however, that the mere registration and retention of events may not be the sole factor in determining perceived duration. Hicks, Miller, and Kinsbourne (1976) have made the important observation that care must be taken to differentiate between prospective and retrospective judgments of time. The former refers to the case in which subjects know in advance that temporal judgments will be required before an interval of time is presented. The latter represents the case in which temporal judgments are made without this foreknowledge. Similar variations in the information content of intervals do not result in similar effects with both types of judgments. For example, using the card-sorting task described earlier, Hicks, Miller, and Kinsbourne (1976) found that perceived duration decreased with increments in response uncertainty under prospective judgment conditions, but that the same sorting task had no effect on retrospective judgments of duration.

As so frequently happens, we have two alternative theoretical views to explain an aspect of perception, in this case, the experience of time. At present, a definitive conclusion about which view is the more reasonable is not dictated by the evidence. Indeed, as Adam (1971) has noted, the question remains open as to whether temporal experience is mediated by one or by several mechanisms.

MOTION: ACTIVITY IN SPACE AND TIME

The Problem of Motion Perception

Dynamics in space and time The final topic to be addressed in this chapter is the perception of motion. Thus far our discussion has characterized the structure of the perceptual world in terms of a framework of space and time. It is important to note that the denizens of this world do not lead a static existence within the "walls" of that framework. Instead, perceivers and the objects that they perceive are often mobile; this mobility lends a dynamic quality to perceptual experience. In physics, the concepts of space, time, and motion are closely related. For example, the velocity (V) of motion is given by the equation $V = d/t$, where d and t are the spatial and temporal extents traversed by a body in motion. As you will see, this linkage is evident in the perception of motion as well.

Proximal stimulus ambiguity At first glance, the perception of motion would not seem to pose much of a problem for psychological analysis. Given the simplicity of the equation for physical velocity, it might be expected that perceived motion will also be determined merely by the displacement in space and time of a stimulus passing continuously over the mosaic of the retina. But quite to the contrary, the perception of motion poses a highly complex problem for psychologists, and retinal displacement is only a small part of the story.

The crux of the problem lies in the fact that physical displacement and perceived movement are far from perfectly correlated. For example, hold up the index finger of your right hand and move it across your field of view in a right-to-left direction. In this case, the image of the finger will pass across the retina of your eye, and it will, of course, be seen as moving. Now, hold up the same finger and sweep your gaze across it in a left-to-right direction. In this case, your finger will appear to remain stationary, even though its image will cross the retina in the same manner as before! For another example, recall that our eyes are never still; they continuously execute small movements known collectively as physiological nystagmus (see Chapter 5). Consequently, the images of objects are always in motion on the retina; yet we do not ordinarily perceive the world as "swimming" before us. If, however, you induce artificial motion to the eyes by gently rotating your eyeballs with your fingers, the visual world will appear to move.

As Spigel (1965) has noted, the lack of correspondence between physical displacement and perceived movement also becomes evident if we consider the hands of a clock, or the moon in a cloudless sky, or shadows cast by an object in sunlight. Over a prolonged period of time, these stimuli will appear to have been displaced in space, but we typically do not see them moving. What seems to be needed for the perception of motion is a perceptible rate of change in the position of a stimulus with respect to some other stimulus, for example, a figure with respect to its ground. But even that is not a necessary condition for the perception of motion. The reason why it is not is captured in the distinction between two classes of motion perception: *real motion,* in which stimuli undergo objective and continuous spatial displacement and *apparent motion,* in which motion is attributed to stimuli which are physically stationary or in which continuous motion is seen when successive and discrete retinal loci are stimulated.

The moral of all of this is clear: as in the case of many other perceptual phenomena, the proximal stimulus is highly ambiguous with respect to motion. An understanding of the perception of motion requires that we go beyond the proximal stimulus itself. In what follows, we will first examine some of the factors which influence the perception of real motion and then turn our attention to some examples of apparent motion.

Real Motion

Motion thresholds   There are several interesting questions that can be asked about the perception of real motion. One of these, is "how fast must an object be moving in order for its movement to be detectable?" Such a question requires a complex answer, for several factors are involved.

In the first place, psychophysical studies which seek to provide data with respect to this issue distinguish between two types of motion thresholds: the *velocity threshold,* or the minimum speed per unit time which can be detected, and the *displacement threshold,* the minimum distance over which movement can be detected. In the second place, the perceptibility of motion depends upon more than the physical velocity of the target.

One of the critical stimulus parameters for motion detection is the retinal locus of the target. Though it is true that sudden movements in the peripheral field of view are effective in capturing attention, it is also true that thresholds for the detection of motion are considerably higher for targets presented to the periphery of the eye than for those in foveal vision (Graham, 1965a). A study by Leibowitz, Johnson, and Isabelle (1972) illustrates this effect and also isolates one of the factors responsible for it. These investigators point out that peripheral visual fields are subject to large refractory errors which degrade the quality of retinal images. Therefore, higher motion thresholds for peripheral targets may be due, at least in part, to poor image quality. To test this possibility, Leibowitz and his co-workers used special lenses to "tailor" the correction of peripheral refractive error in the eyes of three subjects. The results of their experiment are shown in Figure 8.22.

It is evident in the figure that without the corrective lenses peripheral motion thresholds were considerably higher than those obtained with foveal stimuli (0° retinal eccentricity). Indeed, at 80° in the periphery, the threshold is almost 10 times greater than it is at the fovea. Moreover, the figure shows considerable variability among the three subjects in the absence of the corrective lenses. With correction, the figure indicates that peripheral motion thresholds were reduced almost 50 percent and that individual differences were practically eliminated. Additional evidence implicating poor image quality as a factor in elevated motion thresholds in peripheral vision has been provided by Johnson and Leibowitz (1974).

Besides retinal location, motion thresholds are also dependent upon the luminance and duration of the stimuli and upon the presence of reference

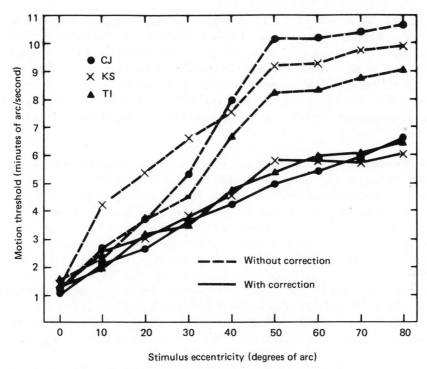

FIGURE 8.22 Motion thresholds as a function of the retinal locus of the stimulus. Data are for three observers (CJ, KS, and TI) with and without correction for peripheral refractive errors. (From Leibowitz, Johnson, and Isabelle, 1972)

points in the field of view. In general, increasing either the luminance or the duration of the target lowers the threshold for motion (Brown and Conklin, 1954; Harvey and Michon, 1974; Henderson, 1971; Leibowitz, 1955b). Under some conditions, Bloch's Law, $I \times T = k$ (see Chapter 2), holds for the detection of motion (Brown, 1955), and a similar reciprocity exists between velocity and time, $V \times T = k$ (Cohen and Bonnet, 1972). The presence of reference points can also modify detection efficiency to a considerable degree. Graham (1965a) has reviewed several early experiments which indicate that motion thresholds for a target seen in the absence of stationary reference points may be approximately 10 times larger than thresholds obtained when reference points are clearly visible. Later studies have confirmed the importance of reference points and demonstrated that their utility depends upon target duration: for the introduction of reference points to have a substantial effect on motion thresholds, target exposure should exceed four seconds (Harvey and Michon, 1974; Leibowitz, 1955a; Mates, 1969).

Knowledge about the nature of motion thresholds has important practical implications. For example, you may have read or heard about safety reports indicating that night driving is more hazardous than driving in daylight. If accurate perception of the motion of objects, such as other vehicles, is necessary for "highway survival," some of the reasons for the danger of driving at night should be evident. The lower levels of illumination at night will elevate motion thresholds directly and also indirectly by rendering reference points less visible. Moreover, the problem will be compounded by high speed, which reduces the amount of time you have to assess the motion of other vehicles.

Motion and context   The perception of motion is dependent not only upon the stimulus factors just described but is also conditioned by the structure and general properties of the visual field in which a target stimulus appears. The effects of context on the perception of motion are revealed in an experiment by Brown (1931) involving what is known as the *motion transposition effect*. In this study, observers were asked to equate apparent velocity in two displays containing black squares moving in a downward direction within a rectangular framework (see Figure 8.23). The linear dimensions of the framework and squares of one display were twice as large as those of the other. Brown found that in order for the squares to be equated in apparent velocity, those in the larger frame needed to move at twice the physical speed of those in the smaller frame. Thus, the perceived velocity of a target

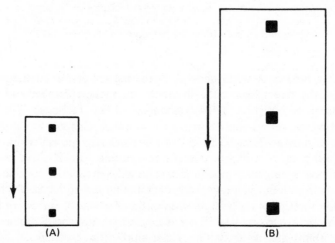

(A)   (B)

FIGURE 8.23   The type of displays used by Brown (1931) to study the motion-transposition effect. Observers equated the apparent velocities of black squares moving in a downward direction within two rectangular frameworks. The linear dimensions of the framework and squares in (B) were twice as large as those in (A). In order to be equated in apparent velocity, the squares in (B) needed to move at twice the physical speed of those in (A).

tends to be inversely proportional to the size of the framework surrounding it. If the size of the field containing a moving target is increased (transposed), the physical speed of the target must be increased proportionately in order for the target's apparent velocity to remain the same.

Context effects in apparent motion are also evident in a phenomenon known as *induced movement*. In this case, context not only determines perceived velocity, it also determines what appears to move. You have probably experienced this effect when looking at the moon in a partly cloudy sky. The moon seems to "race" behind the clouds when, in reality, the moon is moving at an imperceptible rate: it is the clouds, of course, which are drifting rapidly in front of the moon. Laboratory studies have demonstrated that this contextual determinant of perceived movement is related to several factors. In general, motion induction is produced in a smaller, enclosed object by a larger object which encloses it even though it is the larger object which is actually in motion (Duncker, 1938). Past experience is important in the induction effect; objects which we expect to move, people or vehicles for example, are more susceptible to motion induction than neutral objects (Hochberg, 1971b). In addition, the induction effect decreases with increases in the apparent depth sepating the test and induction objects (Gogel and Koslow, 1971, 1972; Gogel and Tietz, 1976).

Motion and the size-distance relation   In our discussion of perceived size and distance we made frequent mention of the size-distance relation – the fact that the retinal size of an object decreases with increases in object distance. This relation also has important implications for the perception of motion.

Consider Figure 8.24. It shows that the same geometrical principles which account for decreases in the retinal size of an object with increasing observer-object distance also dictate that the retinal distance traversed by an object in motion grows smaller as the observer-object distance increases. This geometrical relation would lead us to suspect that the perceived velocity of nearby objects would be more rapid than that of objects farther away. To some extent, such is the case. While driving, for example, vehicles located at great distances from us do seem to be moving at a "snail's pace" compared to vehicles in the more immediate vicinity; similarly, airplanes flying high in the sky appear to travel more slowly than those nearer to the ground. Nevertheless, the perceptual system does exhibit a remarkable amount of motion constancy (Wallach, 1939), and an important ingredient in this achievement is the availability of spatial cues to distance.

The role of distance cues in motion constancy was demonstrated by Rock, Hill, and Fineman (1968) through an experiment in which observers compared the speeds of two luminous circles moving in a downward direction in an otherwise dark room. A standard circle was located at a near dis-

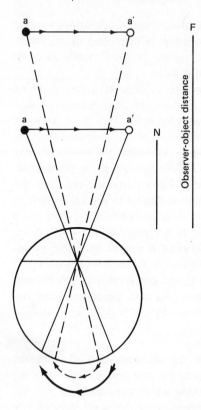

Observer-object distance

FIGURE 8.24 Retinal velocity and observer-object distance. The image of an
object moving across the field of view
from a to a' in time t will cover a greater
distance on the retina when the object is
located at a near point in space, N (solid
lines), than when it is located at a farther
viewing distance, F (broken lines). Since
movement time is the same in both cases
and since retinal velocity is equal to retinal
distance/t, the retinal velocity of the object
will be faster at the near viewing distance.
(After Day, 1969)

tance from the observer, and a comparison circle was positioned at a distance
four times farther away than that of the standard. When distance cues in the
form of accommodation and convergence were available, the observers demonstrated a high degree of constancy in setting the speed of the comparison
circle to equal that of the nearby standard. When distance cues were obliterated by requiring the observers to view the stimuli monocularly through a
small aperture, constancy was lost and velocity was judged on the basis of visual angle. In this case, the physical velocity of the comparison circle had to
be four times faster than that of the nearby standard in order to appear equal
to that of the standard.

Day (1969) has noted that the linkage between an object's retinal velocity, retinal size, and its distance from an observer leads to an interesting prediction, derived from the size-distance invariance hypothesis. The prediction
involves a reciprocity in the relation between motion and distance, namely,
that distance cues aid in the perception of motion and that changes in velocity can serve as a cue to distance. If we assume that increments in velocity
can indicate a decrease in observer-object distance, then, if the retinal size of
an object remains constant, increases in its velocity should result in a shrink-

age in its apparent size. More specifically, recall that the size-distance invariance hypothesis states that apparent size is equal to the product of retinal size and perceived distance (see Chapter 6). A decrease in perceived distance produced by an increase in a target's velocity will lower the product of retinal size and perceived distance and thereby result in a reduction in the apparent size of the target.

Such an effect does indeed occur. Ansbacher (1944) asked subjects to judge the size of a lighted arc positioned on the edge of a disk while the disk was rotated in a dark room. As the velocity of rotation increased, the apparent length of the arc of light decreased. This change in apparent size with change in velocity is now known as the *Ansbacher effect*. It has been substantiated in other experiments (Marshall and Stanley, 1964; Stanley, 1970), and it represents a striking demonstration of the relativity of space, time, and motion in visual perception.

The Ansbacher effect has a real-world exemplification in the game of baseball. A ball thrown by a very fast pitcher seems much smaller than usual; frustrated batters refer to it as an "aspirin tablet" or a "pill." Of course, understanding why a fastball seems small in no way guarantees that you will be able to hit it!

Mechanisms for the perception of motion   An important part of the study of motion perception has been the search for underlying mechanisms. From what we have presented so far of perceived motion, you might expect that the search would not be an easy one, and you would be right. Current knowledge indicates that the perception of motion is probably mediated by the combined action of several mechanisms.

As in the case of the perception of form, research into the mechanisms of motion perception has profited from neurophysiological investigations. These studies have isolated cells at the retinal and cortical levels of the nervous system which are specialized for detecting the presence of a moving stimulus, its direction of movement, and its velocity (for example, Barlow and Hill, 1963; Barlow, Hill, and Levick, 1964; Baumgartner, Brown, and Schultz, 1964; Bridgeman, 1972; Finkelstein and Grüsser, 1965; Hubel and Wiesel, 1962; Lettvin, Maturana, McCulloch, and Pitts; 1959; Teyler, Shaw, and Thompson, 1972). The discovery of these neurophysiological "feature analyzers" implies that motion is signaled by the operation of detector systems triggered, in part, by the sequential firing of receptors as a moving target passes over the retina. Such a system has been described by Gregory (1973) as an *image/retina system*.

In addition to providing an account of veridical motion, the image/retina system also offers a convenient way to explain some illusions of motion. One of these is a class of illusions known as *motion aftereffects* — changes in the perceived motion of a stimulus after prolonged viewing. One aftereffect, which can be experienced outside the laboratory, is called the *waterfall illu-*

sion. If you gaze at a waterfall for a while and then look at the surrounding terrain, trees and other stationary objects will seem to float upward—that is, in a direction opposite that of the falling water. A similar effect which can be produced in the laboratory is the *spiral aftereffect*. If you watch a rotating spiral such as that in Figure 8.25 for a minute or two, and the spiral appears to expand during rotation, it will appear to contract when the rotation is stopped.

Sekuler and Ganz (1963) have argued that aftereffects of seen motion may be attributable to the fact that prolonged viewing of movement in one direction fatigues the motion-detection cells tuned to that direction. Upon subsequent viewing of a stationary image, the fatigued cells would emit less activity than usual, and apparent movement in the opposite direction would result. It follows from this argument that prolonged inspection of a stimulus moving in one direction should selectively elevate the threshold for the subsequent detection of movement in that direction, and this is precisely what occurs. Sekuler and Ganz measured thresholds for the detection of stripes moving in one direction, say from right to left; they found that subsequent thresholds for detecting the motion of stripes in that direction were elevated in comparison to thresholds for stripes moving in the opposite, nonadapted,

FIGURE 8.25 Stimulus for producing the spiral aftereffect. When rotated, the spiral will appear to expand or contract depending upon the direction of rotation. If it is seen to expand when rotating, it will appear to contract when rotation is stopped, and vice versa.

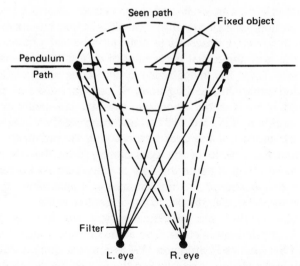

Pendulum
Path

Seen path

Fixed object

Filter

L. eye   R. eye

FIGURE 8.26   The Pulfrich effect. When a pendulum placed in motion in a straight path normal to the line of sight is viewed binocularly with a dark filter over one eye,
it does not appear to swing in a straight line. Instead, it seems to move in an
eliptical orbit toward and away from the viewer. The pendulum will appear
to move in a clockwise direction when the filter covers the left eye and in a
counterclockwise direction when the filter covers the right eye. (From Harker,
1967)

direction. Other studies have reported similar results (Mayhew; 1973; Pantle
and Sekuler, 1969).

Still another motion illusion which might fit within the bounds of the im-
age/retina system is a curious distortion in the path of seen movement called
the *Pulfrich effect.* As shown in Figure 8.26, this effect occurs when an object
such as a pendulum is placed in motion in a straight path normal to the line
of sight and is viewed binocularly with a dark filter over one eye. Under these
conditions, an oscillating object does not appear to swing in a straight line,
but rather seems to move through an elliptical path toward and away from
the viewer. Although there is some disagreement among investigators (see
Harker, 1967), the most common explanation of the Pulfrich effect is based
upon an increase in the time of response of receptors in the filtered
eye (Bartley, 1969; Brauner and Lit, 1976; Gregory, 1973). Specifically,
since the dark filter reduces the light reaching the filtered eye, there is a delay
in the time of arrival of signals from that eye at higher levels in the visual system. Consequently, the position of the oscillating object coded by the filtered
eye lags behind that of the unfiltered eye, and this disparity is interpreted as
reflecting the movement of an object in an elliptical path.

While the neurophysiological evidence for an image/retina system is abundant, such a system by itself cannot account for all of the known aspects of perceived motion. One of the chief difficulties is that the system makes no provision for the ability of observers to distinguish between motion on the retina brought about by the actual movement of objects and by the movement of the eye itself. Thus, the image/retina system does not provide an answer to the question posed in the beginning of our discussion of motion as to why the world remains stable when our eyes are constantly in motion. To handle that problem, Gregory (1973) has suggested an *eye/head system* which takes the motion of the eyes into account. According to Gregory, information about the activity of the eyes coming from the eye/head system is compared to information about the flow of images across the retina signaled by the image/retina system. During normal eye movements, these sources of information interact to give stability to the perceptual world.

The manner in which the perceptual system monitors eye position has been a topic of considerable debate. The argument has centered upon the *inflow* theory of Sir Charles Sherrington (1918) and the *outflow* theory of Herman von Helmholtz (1866). According to the former, proprioceptive information fed back to the brain from stretch receptors in the extraocular muscles signals the position of the eyes. By contrast, Helmholtz maintained that our knowledge of eye position is based on command signals sent from the brain to the extraocular muscles. The evidence favors Helmholtz. For example, in a dramatic experiment, Brindley and Merton (1960) covered the eye of an observer, anesthetized its surface and surrounding tissues, and moved the eye mechanically. Under these conditions, inflow information was available to the observers, but they were unable to tell that their eyes were being moved. Further support for the outflow theory has come from studies which demonstrate that when the eye is moved artificially, it is a target in space rather than the eye which appears to move. When the eye is restrained during an attempted eye movement, a target is perceived to move in the direction of the aborted movement. And when the normal correspondence between inflow and outflow information is disrupted experimentally, the localization of the subjective straight-ahead depends upon outflow information (see Skavenski, Haddad, and Steinman, 1972).

In addition to the contributions of the image/retina and eye/head systems, James Gibson (1966, 1968) has made the important observation that motion information is inherent in the different kinds of transformations in the retinal projections produced by an object in motion and by the motion of the observer. He points out that as an object moves through space, it produces *kinetic optical occlusion*. That is, it progressively covers and uncovers the physical texture of the surfaces that lie behind it. In Gibson's terms, there is a "wiping out" of background texture at the leading border of the moving target, an "unwiping" at its trailing border, and a "shearing" of the background texture at the lateral borders of the moving figure. Such "rupturing" of the continuity of background texture is invariably associated with an object in motion. In contrast, when objects are stationary and the observer is moving, a transformation of the entire optic array results, which, as we described in connection with depth perception, is known as *motion perspective*. In this case, the whole optic array springs into motion (see Figure 8.9). The phenomena of kinetic optical occlusion and motion perspective provide potent cues to differentiate object and observer-object motion.

The importance for motion perception of projective relations in the optical flow on the retina has also been suggested by Johansson (1973, 1975), who notes that in decoding the total optical flow, the perceptual system tends to extract components of projective invariances. As an example, he points to a complex pattern of motions that occur in everyday life—the *biological motions* generated by people as they move about in space.

We can tell rather quickly whether someone is running, walking, or dancing. Johansson maintains that different types of human actions are built up from pendulum-like motions which are highly specific for different forms of locomotion. These specific patterns of movement yield projective invariances that are abstracted by the perceptual system. In order to test this idea, Johansson attached flashlight bulbs to the shoulders, elbows, wrists, hips, knees, and ankles of an actor and made a motion picture in a darkened room while the actor was stationary or moving about. Naive observers who viewed the film perceived only a meaningless collection of points of light when the actor sat motionless in a chair. A striking effect occurred, however, when the actor rose and started to move. The observers immediately perceived that the lights were attached to an otherwise invisible human being. They could differentiate between walking and jogging movements and could also report anomalies in gait, as when the actor feigned a limp. Such results provide a compelling demonstration of the role of projective relations in the optic array as cues to the perception of motion.

The contribution of projective relations in the optical flow to motion perception can also be observed in terms of a phenomenon known as *looming*—spatial and temporal transformations that signal an impending collision with some object in the environment (Schiff, 1965; Schiffman, 1976). If an object hurtles toward us so that a collision is imminent, it is accompanied by a rapidly expanding retinal image that suddenly "fills" the visual field. The fact that such temporal and spatial transformations in the optic array serve to specify a collision is revealed in experiments which make use of shadow-casting devices to project the silhouette of an object onto a screen. Human infants and a variety of animals react with avoidance responses when such "looming" configurations are presented (see Shiffman, 1976).

On the basis of the available evidence it seems clear that there are multiple mechanisms for motion perception. It is another remarkable achievement of the visual system that the information processed by these several mechanisms is integrated in such a way as to produce a smooth, unified, and typically veridical perceptual experience.

Apparent Movement

Throughout this book we have described several kinds of illusions. Apparent movement is still another form of illusory experience. In this case, we are concerned with illusions of motion — instances of perceived movement which are not the products of real physical motion. Several forms of apparent motion have been identified. We shall consider only four of them: stroboscopic motion, the autokinetic effect, sensory saltation and phantom movement. The first two have been known for many years; the last two are more recent discoveries.

Stroboscopic movement The most familiar and the most thoroughly investigated form of apparent movement is known as *stroboscopic movement*. It is also termed *beta movement* and is sometimes referred to as the *phi phenomenon*. Reduced to its simplest elements, this effect can be generated by two lights separated in space. Light A comes on and goes off, followed by light B. If the conditions are just right, observers will not see the successive onset and offset of two spatially separated stimuli. Instead, a single object will be seen moving smoothly back and forth from one spatial position to another.

The appearance of optimum stroboscopic movement depends upon several stimulus parameters. These include the luminance of the stimuli, the distance between them, and the time between them. The relationships between these parameters have been worked out by Korte (1915), who established several rules for determining optimum apparent movement now known as *Korte's Laws*. They have been summarized by Boring (1942) and by Graham (1965a). In part, they state that (1) if the time interval between the stimuli is constant, the optimal distance for apparent movement varies directly with stimulus intensity; (2) if the distance between the stimuli is constant, the optimum value of stimulus intensity needed to produce apparent movement varies inversely with the time interval between the lights; and (3) if the intensity is held constant, the optimum value for the distance between the stimuli varies directly with the time interval between them. Korte's Laws have been revised and extended in subsequent experiments (Kahneman and Wolman, 1970; Kolers, 1964; Neff, 1936; Neuhaus, 1930; Sgro, 1963), and several other stimulus determinants of optimal movement have been described (for example, Attneave and Block, 1973; Beck, Elsner, and Silverstein, 1977; Bell and Lappin, 1973; Pantle and Picciano, 1976.

Stroboscopic movement forms the basis of many devices designed to "catch" our attention such as the "moving lights" seen at railroad crossings, in advertising displays, and on theater marquees. The best examples of the practical application of stroboscopic movement are motion pictures and television. Both of these devices present a series of stationary pictures containing small variations in the positions of objects or parts of objects. When shown at the proper rate, the succession of discrete pictures yields a compelling impression of smooth and continuous motion that is often indistinguishable from real physical movement.

There is one anomalous effect in motion pictures which is puzzling to many people—seeing the wheels of a vehicle move backward while the vehicle itself moves forward. Since the motion picture is itself illusory, this effect, known as the *wagon wheel effect,* might seem to be an "illusion within an illusion." Christman (1971) points out, however, that such is not the case, and he offers an explanation along the following lines. Christman notes that movie cameras take 24 pictures per second. If the wheel being photographed turns at 23 revolutions per second, each successive frame of film will capture it slightly before a full revolution has been completed. Therefore, when the film is projected, the wheel is seen to be turning in reverse at the rate of one complete revolution per second. If the wheel turns at precisely 24 revolutions per second, it is seen as stationary, and if it revolves 25 times per second, it is seen as turning in the same direction as the vehicle to which it is attached at the rate of one revolution per second.

It is worth noting that stroboscopic movement can be seen by many different kinds of animals, and indeed it seems to be an innate perceptual characteristic. Strong evidence for its innateness comes from an ingenious experiment by Rock, Tauber, and Heller (1965), which made use of the *optokinetic reflex,* the tendency for animals to orient toward a rotating striped pattern with turning movements of the eyes, head, or total body. This reflex is often studied by placing subjects within a rotating cylinder containing vertical black and white stripes. Rock and his co-workers found that the optokinetic reflex could be elicited in newborn guppies and newly hatched praying mantids when these animals were placed in a stationary cylinder and the striped patterns were flashed stroboscopically in such a way as to simulate true rotation. Using a similar arrangement, Tauber and Koffler (1966) were able to elicit the optokinetic reflex in newborn human infants as well.

The autokinetic effect When an observer fixates upon a stationary point of light in darkness, the light, after a time, seems to move to and fro in a rather aimless manner. The apparent dance of the wandering light is known as the *autokinetic effect.* It is an illusion of motion that has intrigued scientists since 1799 when the astronomer von Humbolt noticed that the stars seemed to drift about when he looked at them through his telescope (Howard and Templeton, 1966). Airplane pilots are familiar with this phenomenon, since it presents a hazard in night flight. As Geldard (1975) has pointed out, a pilot holding steady fixation on the wing light of a nearby plane while flying in formation may see the autokinetic drift and interpret it as a change in flight path. Upon attempting to follow or to take evasive action, the pilot is likely to move on a collision course with another aircraft or to go into a dangerous spin.

The autokinetic effect is due, at least in part, to fluctuations in the retinal location of the target image produced by peripheral eye movements. The contribution of eye movements to this phenomenon was illustrated in a careful study by Matin and MacKinnon (1964). These investigators used a stabilized image technique to eliminate horizontal eye movements and compared autokinesis viewed under these conditions with that viewed normally. As is evident in Figure 8.27, the elimination of horizontal eye movements dramatically reduced the overall number of autokinetic responses given by the two subjects who participated in the study. Moreover, the reductions in autokinesis occurred primarily in the horizontal direction—the direction in which the retinal images were stabilized. Additional support for the role of eye movements in autokinesis comes from experiments by Lehman (1965) and Pola and Matin (1977) indicating that eye movements are correlated with the onset and direction of autokinetic activity.

In addition to peripheral factors, autokinesis has been related to more central processes. Gregory and Zangwill (1963) have noted that fixating a stimulus with the eyes held in one direction affects the direction of subsequent autokinetic movement. For example, if the eyes are held over toward

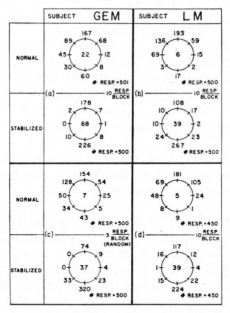

FIGURE 8.27 Eye movements and the autokinetic effect. The frequencies of autokinetic movements in a given direction under normal viewing conditions compared to those obtained when horizontal eye movements were eliminated by means of a stopped-image technique. Numbers along the circumference of a circle indicate the frequency of autokinetic motion seen in a given direction during an observation period of a little over one minute. The number in the center of each circle gives the frequency of failure to report movement in any direction. (After Matin and Mackinnon, 1964)

the nasal and temporal portions of the visual field for several seconds and then returned to their central position, a dim light seen in the dark will move either in the direction in which the eyes were held or the opposite direction, but in no other plane. This led Gregory (1973) to suggest that in maintaining fixation on a target, the eye muscles fatigue and autokinetic movements result from corrective outflow commands issued by the brain to compensate for the effects of fatigue. In this sense, the autokinetic effect is due to a loss of calibration in the visual system. The target remains fixed in a constant retinal position in the presence of outflow signals to move the eyes: the result is apparent movement of the target.

While the eye movement and outflow explanations of the autokinetic effect have merit, we must note that they do not provide a complete account of this phenomenon. Autokinesis is dependent upon several stimulus factors, such as the shape and size of the target and the nature of surrounding patterns and is also highly susceptible to suggestion (see Levy, 1972). These complex results do not fit easily within a simple eye movement or outflow explanation. The autokinetic effect has been studied extensively and much is known about it. However, a complete understanding of this puzzling phenomenon remains to be developed.

Sensory saltation   "Saltation" is an action word that expresses jumping or leaping. Recently, Geldard and Sherrick (1972) have described a curious phenomenon of apparent motion characterized by such a saltatory effect. Their initial experiment made use of cutaneous stimulation in which three vibrators were placed about 4 inches apart on the forearm, as shown in Figure 8.28. If the three vibrators were put into operation sequentially, each in turn

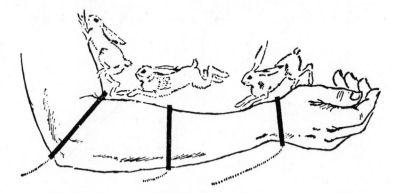

FIGURE 8.28 The cutaneous rabbit. Sequential bursts of stimulation from three vibrators spaced about four inches apart on the forearm produce a feeling of a slow sweeping movement punctuated by taps—much like a "rabbit" hopping up the arm. Reprinted with the permission of the author and publisher from Geldard, F.A., Sensory saltation: Melastability in the perceptual world. Hillsdale, N.J.: Lawrence Erlbaum Associates, 1975.

delivering five rapid pulses, the observers did not, as we might expect from the arrangement of the vibrators, report three well-spaced bursts of vibration. Instead, they reported feeling a slow, sweeping movement punctuated by the taps. Geldard and Sherrick described the experience as that of a tiny "rabbit" hopping up the arm. In later experiments (Geldard, 1975), these investigators were able to show that the saltation effect occurs in vision as well as in touch. If small lamps, L_1 and L_2 were arrayed about 5° apart in the periphery of the eye and flashed sequentially with an interflash interval of about 100 msec, the saltatory effect was clearly perceived, and jumps of about one quarter of the $L_1 - L_2$ distance were reported by several observers. As shown in Figure 8.29, this effect was noted with combinations of flashes in a variety of retinal locations as long as the stimuli were presented in peripheral vision.

At first glance, you might think that sensory saltation is simply an instance of stroboscopic movement in vision and touch. As Geldard (1975) points out, however, this is not the case. Stroboscopic movement is a continuous affair, whereas the essence of the saltation effect is its discontinuity and discreteness.

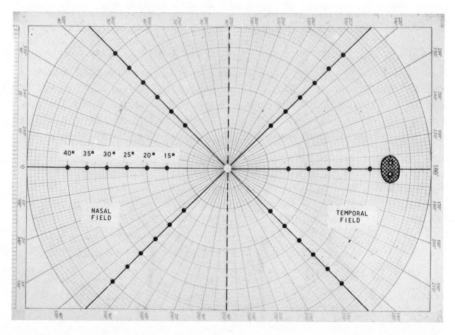

FIGURE 8.29   Map of the retinal fields used to study the saltation effect in vision. Dots indicate the locations of the flashing spots of light. All major radii except the vertical were tested. An illustration of the configuration of the light spots and their common surround is presented at the 40° position in the temporal field. Reprinted with the permission of the author and publisher from Geldard, F.A., Sensory saltation: Metastability in the perceptual world. Hillsdale, N.J.: Lawrence Erlbaum Associates, 1975.

We might add that stroboscopic motion is easy to see in foveal vision, but the "rabbit" only appears in peripheral vision. It is still too early to tell what factors underlie the saltation effect; it presents a challenging problem for future research. Many of the directions for this research are laid out in Geldard's (1975) fascinating little book.

Phantom movement   An important characteristic of the perceptual system is that regions of blindness often go unobserved; the system tends to complete a percept across a gap _(scotoma)_ in the visual field. Perhaps the best example of this characteristic is the optic disk or blind spot—the portion of the retina where the optic nerve exits (see Figure 2.5). The optic disk is a natural scotoma in the retinal mosaic which normally goes unnoticed. In a recent study, Tynan and Sekuler (1975) discovered a new form of completion effect involving apparent movement.

In their study, segments of vertical stripes were made to drift across the face of an oscilloscope above and below a homogeneous region formed by black construction paper. As the vertical stripes moved physically across the face of the oscilloscope, observers reported seeing a dim "phantom" grating drift across the black gap in phase with the actual moving pattern flanking the gap. The phantom appeared when the actual grating was set in motion; it disappeared when the real grating stopped moving, and its spatial frequency covaried with that of the inducing grating.

The phantom movement described by Tynan and Sekuler appears to be central in origin. When the top section of the inducing grating was presented to the right eye of an observer and the bottom section to the left eye, the phantoms did not appear in either eye if the display was viewed monocularly. They did show up, however, when the display was seen by both eyes. Although phantom movement seems reminiscent of induced movement, the two phenomena are quite different. In the case of induced motion, a moving contour surrounds a physically stationary contour, and the apparent motion induced in the stationary contour is in a direction opposite to that of the inducing contour. In phantom motion, apparent motion is attributed to a contour that is not physically present, and the phantom shares all of the characteristics of the motion of the inducing contour, including its directionality.

As Tynan and Sekuler have noted, the moving phantoms illustrate that the perceptual system abhors a gap. The observation of phantom movement has been confirmed by Weisstein, Maguire, and Berbaum (1977), who have also shown that phantom movement is associated with a _phantom movement aftereffect._ Immediately after viewing phantom movement, subjects were presented with stationary stripes in the previously empty region, where the phantom stripes had appeared; the stationary stripes seemed to move in the opposite direction. This is an important finding; it indicates that motion aftereffects are not restricted to the areas of the visual field where actual visual movement had occurred.

Real and apparent movement   We have examined several dramatic illusions of motion. At this point, it is appropriate to ask if real and illusory movement are mediated by the same processes. This question has most frequently been posed with respect to stroboscopic motion. Several investigators have reported that when the rates of apparent displacement are equal, observers are usually unable to distinguish between real and stroboscopic movement (Dimmick and Scahill, 1925; Gibson, 1954; Kennedy, 1936). Such a result would imply that both types of motion experience are mediated by common mechanisms. Indeed, this was the point of view adopted by Max Wertheimer (1912) in his early studies of apparent movement from which Gestalt psychology was initiated. Wertheimer believed that both types of perceived motion depended upon the spreading of cortical excitation from one region of the brain to another. More recently, Frisby (1972) has suggested that stroboscopic motion might be based on the action of motion detectors in the visual system. Just as these cells fire when an object moves across their receptive fields, they might also fire when light first falls upon one region of the receptive field, then on another.

On the other hand, there are reasons to believe that real and apparent motion reflect different perceptual mechanisms. Kolers (1964) has provided an especially cogent discussion of this issue. He points out that conditions which produce these experiences differ in several ways. For one thing, apparent movement tends to be slower than real movement. The speed of an object in real movement has to be made less than the calculated speed of an object in illusory movement in order for their rates of apparent displacement to appear equal. Moreover, real motion produces a blur at high speed, while a blurry appearance occurs in the case of stroboscopic motion under the opposite conditions—that is, when the rate of flashing between two lights is slower than that required for optimum movement.

Kolers (1963, 1964) has described an interesting experiment which permitted him to make a direct comparison of the perceptual consequences of real and apparent movement. Subjects were required to detect the presence of a stationary thin line of light which appeared in the path of a larger moving line. The latter could be a line in actual motion or one in illusory motion. When the moving line was actually in motion, it interfered with the detectability of the stationary line as the two came close together. In contrast, when the moving line was in illusory motion, it interfered with the detectability of the stationary line only when it had passed well beyond it and neared the terminus of the motion path. These results led Kolers to conclude that the mechanisms underlying real and apparent motion must be quite different.

Two other experiments lead to the same conclusion. One of them indicates that under some conditions for generating stroboscopic movement, apparent movement begins at speeds when an object in real movement starts to blur (Kaufman, Cryulnick, Kaplowitz, Melnick, and Stof, 1971). The other demonstrates that retinal displacement is not a necessary condition for the perception of apparent movement. In this case, two flashing lights were seen in apparent movement when their images fell on the identical retinal area (Rock and Ebenholtz, 1962).

If we conclude that real and apparent movement are mediated by different mechanisms, we might wonder why many animals are so constructed as to be innately susceptible to illusory motion. What biological purpose does it serve? Rock (1975) has made the intriguing suggestion that stroboscopic motion might reflect a system that takes over when the speed of a moving object exceeds the capabilities of the real-motion detection systems. He points out that the perception of an object moving at extremely rapid speed is essentially stroboscopic; it is based on stationary stimulation from its terminal positions. In this case, the stroboscopic mechanisms might then mediate the perception of rapid, real movement.

9

Cognitive Influences on Perception

In the present chapter, we examine in detail a body of research which deals with purported effects on perception of a class of variables called "cognitive"; in Chapter 10, we do the same for possible motivational and emotional ("affective") influences on perception. Our main concern in both chapters is more empirical than theoretical: What, if any, cognitive or affective influences on perception can be convincingly demonstrated? In seeking an answer to that question, we will turn in large part to a research strategy which calls for measuring people's thresholds for identifying target stimuli. As you will see, there are flaws in such an approach: it often is difficult to determine whether the obtained effects are truly perceptual. However, the research cited in both chapters goes beyond the use of threshold measurement. That is, in addition to asking whether people's cognitive and motivational status can affect how well they perceive, or fail to perceive, certain target stimuli, we also examine the closely related issue of possible contributions that cognition and affect make to people's judgments about qualitative and quantitative aspects of stimuli. For example, in considering motivational influences on perception, we might ask not only whether hungry people detect food-related objects more readily than they do neutral stimuli, but also whether they perceive food-related objects as, say, larger, or closer, or brighter than neutral stimuli. While

many of the latter kinds of experiments are also open to alternative interpretations, they provide in general a more convincing case than do the seemingly more "objective" studies employing classical psychophysical procedures.

TARGET IDENTIFICATION

Set

A variety of cognitive variables can be distinguished on the basis of the
kinds of operations that are used to manipulate them. Such concepts as *set,
attitude, expectancy, meaning, instructions, hypotheses, tuning,* etc. have all
been used in this regard.

The one conept which seems to include most of the others and which, at
the same time, is relatively neutral theoretically is that of *set.* We shall use the
word "set" to refer in a general way to all of the cognitive variables that are
of interest in this chapter. The specific operations for manipulating set in a
given experiment will be described in conjunction with the general description
of that experiment.

The active observer   Though the various details of the set-perception
relation will become evident as you read further in the chapter, it may be
helpful at this point to state the general principle emerging from this material.
Briefly, stimulation does not fall on a passive receiver. The individual, on the
contrary, is "prepared," implicitly or explicitly, for certain kinds of input; the
input is actively dealt with on the basis of this preparation. The fate of any input is at least partly dependent on the nature of the preparation.

A very crude analogy might be made, in this regard, between the individual and a computing machine. The machine is fed information, and in turn
yields information—the latter being some kind of transformation of the
former. But note that what comes out of the machine is dependent not only
on what goes in—that is, the data—but also on the machine's *program.* The
program is a set of instructions which are fed into the machine, telling it, in
effect, how to deal with the input. Such instructions might be, very simply,
"Find the sum of the squares of these numbers." The machine's instructions,
or program, obviously determine the treatment applied to the incoming information, and thus also determine the machine's output.

In an analogous fashion, the fate of the stimulation inpinging on an individual is determined by the individual's preparation, or set. The relation between set and perception is, of course, much more complex and much more
subtle than the relation between a machine's program and its output. Living
organisms are much more complex than computing machines. Nevertheless,
something like a machine's program seems to be operating in the individual,
as we shall presently see.

Explicit and implicit instructions   We alluded earlier to the point that set may be provided *explicitly* or *implicitly.* Instructions may be given the individual which directly and overtly are meant to manipulate set. Instructions may also be given in a less direct and obvious, more covert, fashion. Experiments on set can be categorized into two types on the basis of the degree of explicitness of the set-inducing operation.

Explicit Instructions

Perceptual tuning   A classic in this category is the very simple, but very instructive, experiment by Chapman (1932). The stimulus materials consisted of a group of cards on which were printed several capital letters. The cards varied in three ways: (1) number of letters, from four to eight; (2) identity of letters; and (3) spatial arrangement of letters. The cards were presented tachistoscopically, under conditions of illumination and expsosure duration that yielded less-than-perfect recognition on any of the three attributes.

Set was manipulated through instructing the subject to report on one of the three characteristics of a card on each exposure — that is, how many letters were on the card, or what letters they were, or how they were spatially arranged. The instructions about which of the three attributes to report on were given either *before* the exposure or *after* it.

When the instructions were provided before the exposure, the subject presumably was specifically set, or *tuned,* for the appropriate attribute. Instructions given after the presentation of the stimulus could not influence the subject's set.

As expected from the perceptual tuning hypothesis, there were fewer errors under the *before* condition than under the *after* condition. This was unequivocally true for the letter-naming and spatial-arrangement tasks, and somewhat less so for the counting task. The counting task was also the easiest of the three tasks.

Unfortunately for the perceptual tuning hypothesis, an experiment by Lawrence and Coles (1954) casts some doubt on the original interpretation of Chapman's results. In essence, Lawrence and Coles argue that Chapman's set-inducing instructions had their effect not directly on the perceptual process itself, but rather on the memory trace of the stimulus, which is tapped at the time the subject responds.

To test their interpretation, Lawrence and Coles designed an experiment involving variation in the time when instructions were given and variation in the nature of the instructions. The instructions consisted of four alternative responses which the subjects were to use in identifying a series of tachistoscopically exposed pictures. One of the four alternatives correctly identified the picture. The subjects in one group, the *before* condition, were given the alternatives prior to the exposure of each picture. The alternatives varied from picture to picture, minimizing any carryover of implicit instructions from one trial to the next. This was particularly important for the subjects in the *after* condition, who received their instructions subsequent to the exposure of each picture. A third group of controls received no alternatives, either before or after the stimulus exposure.

On half of the trials, the alternatives were quite similar to one another, and on half they were quite distinct from one another. For example, two similar alternatives might be: (2) a man in a gray flannel suit, and (b) a boy in a baseball uniform; a distinct alternative to replace (b) above might be: a red barn. The use of similar and distinct sets of alternatives was suggested by the following, rather complex, line of reasoning.

Suppose that there are really two ways in which instructions can influence accuracy of response. One way is by tuning the perceptual process, and the other is by tuning the memory trace. Assume further that the memory trace is generally a less informative basis of identification than the immediate perceptual material, of which the memory trace is a rather poor replica. Now, when subjects are faced with a relatively easy task, as for example when they are provided with distinct alternatives, then it should make little difference whether the alternatives are given before or after the stimulus exposure. Presumably, according to Lawrence and Coles, the memory trace would be sufficiently informative so that even after-instructions should facilitate recognition.

However, when the task is quite difficult, as when the alternatives are very similar to each other, then instructions given prior to the stimulus should facilitate recognition through perceptual tuning, whereas instructions given after the stimulus should be relatively ineffective. By the time instructions are provided, the memory trace should be too impoverished to benefit from them.

To summarize the argument, when the task is easy, tuning of the memory trace should be about as effective as tuning of the perceptual process; when the task is difficult, perceptual tuning should be more effective than tuning of the memory trace. This kind of reasoning led Lawrence and Coles to the following explicit prediction: The time when the alternatives are provided and the nature of the alternatives should interact to influence accuracy of response. Accuracy should not vary with time of instructions when the alternatives are distinct; however, when the alternatives are similar, performance in the *before* condition should be superior to that in the *after* condition.

Note that the prediction is based on the assumption that perceptual tuning does occur. If perceptual tuning is not operative, the instructions can influence only the memory trace. In that case, it should not matter when the instructions were given, provided, of course, that they were not unduly delayed. Since Lawrence and Coles were skeptical of the perceptual tuning hypothesis, it was their expectation that the predicted interaction between time and kind of alternatives would not in fact be found.

The results supported this expectation. First of all, subjects given the al-

ternatives either before or after the stimulus did better than the control subjects, even when the data were corrected for chance guessing. Second, the
distinct-alternatives condition yielded higher accuracy scores than did the sim-
ilar-alternatives condition. Finally, and most crucial, there was no difference
between *before* and *after* conditions, and no interaction between time and
type of alternative.

The facilitative effect of instructions in this experiment is thus apparently
on the memory trace, not on the perceptual process itself. Of course, this
conclusion is based on the failure to obtain a statistically significant interaction. Such indirect evidence is not as convincing as evidence would be
which allowed rejection of the null hypothesis. In addition, the prediction of
an interaction effect was suggested only by a rather loose, though appealing,
argument, containing some unproved assumptions. Finally, as pointed out by
Egeth (1967), one can ask whether verbal instructions can reasonably be expected to have much impact on perceptual tuning for complex *pictorial* stimuli. If not, then a more promising procedure for setting the subject might be
to use pictorial rather than verbal representations of the types of stimuli to be
presented on the subsequent test trial. Thus, when the test stimulus is to be a
house, for example, the subject might be shown a picture of a house, along
with pictures of incorrect alternatives. Employing this type of procedure,
Egeth and Smith (1967) report striking confirmation of the perceptual tuning
hypothesis. We seem to have come full circle. But even discounting their
data, there remains the argument by Lawrence and Coles that *before* instructions derive their advantage from the opportunity to operate on the memory
trace more quickly than instructions given after the stimulus. The latter meet
the memory trace after some delay; they operate on a somewhat faded trace,
whereas instructions given before the stimulus get to the memory trace while
it is at its freshest. That the memory trace can indeed fade so rapidly is clearly
supported in the work reported below.

Visual information storage   The issue raised by Lawrence and Coles
has been reopened, in somewhat modified form, by a host of researchers interested in pursuing the analogy of human beings as living computers. With
computers as models, these researchers attempt to specify the manner in
which people process incoming information. A typical theoretical strategy is to
postulate different stages through which information passes; in the course of
this passage the original input may undergo various kinds of transformations,
including partial or total "erasure" as well as temporary and sometimes permanent "storage."

In a now classic experiment, Sperling (1960) attempted to find out some
of the properties of the early stages in the processing of visually presented information. His main question, in effect, was: How much information can be
initially received by the visual system? Suppose the units of information to be

employed are symbols, such as numbers and letters. How might one go about determining how many such items a person can "see" in a very brief presentation? One way to do this would be to present large arrays of symbols and ask subjects to report what they saw on each of several trials. With suitable corrections for guessing and response bias, we could then assess the number of items correctly identified, and perhaps take as our best estimate the average performance of a large number of normal subjects. Using a procedure like this, Sperling found an average value of about 4.5 symbols over a range of exposure durations from 5 to 500 msec.

The notion, however, of a rapidly fading memory trace, as raised by Lawrence and Coles, suggested a major flaw in the above procedure: by the time subjects have reported the first few items they saw, some of the others may already have been forgotten. That is, subjects may very well be able to see more symbols than they can accurately report. Sperling devised a technique that in large part gets around that problem — the *partial-report technique*. The stimulus items (letters and numbers) are arranged as three rows of four symbols each. On any trial the subject is to report only one row; which row to report is indicated to the subject by an auditory signal that comes on immediately following the 50-msec-long presentation of the visual array. Thus, if the auditory signal is a high-pitched tone, the top row is called for, if medium-pitched, the middle row, if low-pitched, the bottom row. In this way, the amount of information immediately available to the subject following stimulus presentation is sampled; the average performance level over a large number of trials can be used to estimate how many items would have been correctly identified if a complete report had been possible and asked for.

In the experiment just described, the average value found by Sperling was about 76 percent correct (that is, about three correct out of the four items in a row). The inference is then made that the subjects had actually been able to see about 9.1 symbols (76 percent of 12). In another study, using a larger array of stimulus items (18) and a somewhat different procedure, Averbach and Sperling (1961) were able to conclude that as many as 17 items were available to subjects immediately after visual presentation.

How rapidly is this visual information lost? In the experiment using a 12-item array (Sperling, 1960), if the auditory signal was delayed by as little as 1 second, performance level fell from 76 percent to 36 percent correct (9.1 items to 4.3). In the Averbach and Sperling study, performance fell abruptly to 25 percent correct after a signal delay of only ½ second if the field containing the stimulus items was followed by a brightly illuminated post-exposure field. When the post-exposure field was dark, performance fell gradually to 25 percent correct after a delay of 5 seconds, and delays beyond 5 seconds had little if any further effect. That the nature of the post-exposure field can markedly affect performance adds weight to Sperling's suggestion that the stimulus items persist as visual images (*icons*) for a brief period following the termination of the physical stimulus field itself.

Sperling's research has been followed up by many other investigators, who in the past decade have uncovered a great deal of detail about the way information is processed by the visual (and auditory) system and about the intricate relations between perception and memory. It would take us well beyond the scope of this book to go further in that detail. A very thorough review of this work is available, however (Neisser, 1967, 1976), and several of the original articles reporting specific experiments have been reprinted in a volume edited by Haber (1969).

Figural uncertainty   Uncertainty of figure identity characterizes many stimuli that people encounter in their daily lives. This uncertainty often arises when not all the cues necessary for exact specification of a figure are available. For example, imagine sitting in a parked car on a rainy day waiting for a friend to come out of a building across the street. Looking through a wet windshield, perhaps with your view partly obstructed by passing cars, you may have difficulty telling which of the several people emerging from the building is your friend. You might even mistakenly perceive a stranger as the person you are expecting. Such instances of misidentification of, or failure to identify, a target stimulus are indeed far from rare; they occur whenever conditions allow only an impoverished or degraded version of the target stimulus.

A well-known laboratory analogue of degraded stimuli is illustrated in Figure 9.1, showing one of the "Street figures" (Street, 1931). If you look long enough, you will probably abruptly see a familiar figure in what initially appears as a meaningless pattern of black and white patches. Once having seen the figure, you will have little trouble seeing it again. Another way to facilitate perception of Street figures is to provide the viewer with an appropriate set. In the case of Figure 9.1, for example, it might help to be told that it is a scene one might see at a race track.

Another way of introducing uncertainty into figure identity is to construct stimuli with ambiguous figure-ground relations. Recall that such stimuli can be seen in more than one way. As illustrated in Figure 9.2, you can see the figure as a vase, but it is also possible to perceive two profiles facing each other. When one figure is dominant, the other forms part of the background.

Stimuli which are so constructed are highly subject to the influence of set. For example, it sometimes happens that a particular figure-ground relation will not emerge until its possibility is mentioned. At that point the figure seems to leap out of its background, and from then on it is difficult not to see it.

Figure 9.3 illustrates such an ambiguous figure. Obviously, it is the picture of a young woman. Most of you will see it as a young woman on first presentation. The picture, however, can also be seen as that of an ugly old woman. Once that set has been established, you will probably see both figures alternately. This ambiguous figure, incidentally, is usually referred to as

FIGURE 9.1 One of the Street figures. What do you see?

"my wife and my mother-in-law," and was brought to the attention of psychologists by Boring (1930).

The influence of two kinds of set-inducing instructions on Boring's figure and on an ambiguous pirate-rabbit figure was experimentally investigated by Leeper (1935). Three groups of subjects took part. The first, a control group, was simply shown the ambiguous figures and asked to describe them. One experimental group heard a verbal description of either of the two alternative figure-ground organizations before being shown the ambiguous figures. For

FIGURE 9.2 A classical illustration of figure-ground reversal. It is possible to see either the light region as figure, a vase, and the dark as ground; or the dark portion as figure, two profiles, and the light as ground. The two possible organizations tend to alternate with continued inspection.

FIGURE 9.3 "My wife and my mother-in-law," an illustration of an ambiguous figure used for investigating the influence of set on perception. (From Boring, 1930)

half of the group, the old woman and the rabbit were described; for half, the young woman and the pirate. The second experimental group received its instructions perceptually, by means of prior exposure to a nonambiguous young woman or old woman, and a nonambiguous pirate or rabbit.

The young woman and the pirate tended to predominate in the descriptions of the control group, with 65 percent of the subjects seeing the young woman only, and 75 percent seeing the pirate only. The experimental group which received prior verbal descriptions differed from the control group only on the pirate-rabbit picture. The group which had the set-inducing perceptual experience differed from the control group, in the expected direction, on both pictures.

Since the two pictures were responded to somewhat differently by the control group, no special meaning can be attributed to the differences in results yielded by the two pictures in the experimental groups. For our purposes, the finding of importance is the influence of the set-inducing operations on figure-ground organization. It should be mentioned that Leeper himself makes a great deal of the difference in effectiveness between the verbal and the perceptual "instructions." The experiment, however, was not sufficiently well designed to allow for such fine intergroup comparisons.

Multiple and misleading set   Explicit instructions about what to expect in an impending stimulus presentation do seem to have a strong effect on performance. Whether that effect can be a purely perceptual one is still open to question, although the question can be dismissed if "perception" is allowed to include events occurring shortly after the stimulus has terminated.

Holding that issue in abeyance, we can now ask what happens to performance if preparatory instructions are ambiguous or misleading. In the one case ambiguity is introduced by providing the subject with more than one set; in the other, the subject is instructed to expect a stimulus with particular properties, but is actually presented with a somewhat different target stimulus.

A direct comparison between single- and mulitple-set conditions has been made by Postman and Bruner (1949). Pairs of words were presented tachistoscopically; the words were arranged so that they crossed with a 45° angle between them. Recognition thresholds were measured by an ascending method of limits, with exposure duration the dependent variable.

Subjects were run under two kinds of instructions. In the single-set condition, subjects were told that one word of each pair would be the name of a color, and the other would not be; the task was to identify the color word. In the dual-set condition, subjects were told that one word would be either a color name or a food name; the other word of each pair would be neither.

It was found that the recognition thresholds under the single-set condition #34 were slightly lower than those under the dual-set condition. The mean recognition threshold for color-name words under single-set instructions was about 0.19 second; under dual-set instructions it was about 0.23 second.

Some suggestive auxilliary findings were also reported. The first meaningful guess—that is, any word whatever—was made at a lower exposure duration in the single-set condition than in the dual-set condition. The first meaningful guesses were more frequently incongruent with the set instructions in the dual-set than in the single-set condition, an incongruent guess being one that did not fit the category specified in the instructions. Finally, there were more blanks—that is, failures to respond at all—in the dual-set condition. Multiple set, in short, does seem to have a disruptive effect on the recognition process.

Of course, single set may also disrupt perception if the set is misleading. And misleading sets need not always be imposed or suggested from outside. For example, under difficult viewing conditions people may generate incorrect hypotheses about what they are looking at; these self-administered misleading sets may impede accurate recognition when the same target stimulus is subsequently presented more clearly. A convincing experimental demonstration of this type of effect has been provided by Bruner and Potter (1964). Their subjects' task was to identify stimuli projected on a screen; the task was made difficult by projecting the stimulus out of focus. Each time the subject failed to identify a stimulus, the focus would be improved until eventually a correct response was made. Some stimuli were initially encountered very badly out of focus and some less so. The former, it turned out, had higher identification thresholds than the latter. Bruner and Potter argue that the subjects' own incorrect hypotheses on the "hard" trials interfere with performance on later easy trials.

That misleading set can interfere with the recognition of a complex target may not be entirely surprising. Perhaps more dramatic is the occurrence of similar effects in situations simply requiring target detection. Thus, subjects who are prepared for one kind of stimulus, but presented with another, are less likely to detect the stimulus than they would otherwise be. An experiment nicely illustrating this point has been done with auditory stimuli (Karoly and Isaacson, 1956).

In this experiment, detection thresholds were measured by the temporal forced-choice technique. The target, a tone of a given frequency, would appear in one of four time intervals, and the subject's task was to indicate the interval in which the tone occurred. Randomly interspersed among normal trials would be trials in which the target was a tone of a different frequency. Even though that tone was the only target on a trial, and the subject's task remained simple detection, the detection of the unexpected tone was markedly impaired. The probability of detecting the set-incongruent tone was much lower than in control experiments in which the tone's detectability was measured under standard conditions. In this experiment, then, a set for one target stimulus interfered with the detection of a somewhat different stimulus.

In a variant of the Karoly and Isaacson procedure, subjects are informed that either of two tones will be presented on each trial. The task is simply to detect the occurrence of the target (not to identify which of the two tones was actually presented). This type of dual-set turns out also to impair detection, as compared with the case when only one target tone is expected. Furthermore, as the two target stimuli are increasingly far apart in tonal frequency, the loss in their detectability becomes greater (for example, Creelman, 1960). It is as though subjects can attend to only one restricted band of tonal frequencies at a time; if they are anticipating a target within one frequency band, but happen to be presented with a tone outside that band, then the likelihood of their detecting the unexpected tone decreases markedly.

Results quite similar to these have been reported by Kristofferson (1967) in experiments requiring attention to stimuli in two sensory modalities, vision and hearing. In this research (mentioned in Chapter 5 in connection with the attempt to determine how long it takes to switch attention between sensory channels), the subjects' task is to respond as quickly as possible when a signal occurs. In a dual-set condition, the subjects are instructed that the reaction-time signal will be either a light or a tone; whichever one occurs, they are to make the same response. Reaction times in this condition turn out to be considerably slower than when subjects know that the signal will consistently be either the tone or the light. Again, it seems that subjects can attend to only one modality at a time; if they are listening for a tone, their response to a light will be delayed, and vice versa.

Implicit Instructions

Interelement contingencies Contained within the results of the Postman and Bruner (1949) and similar experiments (for example, Freeman and Engler, 1955) is the finding that familiar or frequently used words have lower thresholds than unfamiliar or infrequently used words. For example, the color name *brown* would have a lower recognition threshold than *azure*. The differential thresholds of words varying in familiarity, or frequency of usage, have been the subject of an extensive series of experiments. It is possible to interpret frequency and familiarity as set-inducing operations in which the set is implicit rather than explicit. The remainder of this section is devoted to a discussion of implicit set, with familiarity and frequency of usage two of the set-inducing variables to be considered.

Various operations have been employed for manipulating set implicitly. All of these seem to have one property in common. That is, they all utilize probability relations that have been built into the subject before the experiment. The subject's past learning experience is such that certain patterns of stimulus elements are more likely to occur than others. Given some information about part of a particulr stimulus pattern, the total pattern is reconstructed — that is, the stimulus is identified, correctly or incorrectly — under the influence of the previously established probability relations.

Some concrete examples will help to clarify this point. Suppose that subjects are shown tachistoscopically the word "quiz." The information has been explicitly provided that the stimulus is an English word. If the subjects recognize the first letter as *q*, they will "expect" the second letter to be *u*, because in English an initial *q* is always followed by *u*. The subjects may not verbalize this relation, but, presumably, the high probability of a *q* followed by *u* will aid the recognition of *u*, given recognition of *q*.

Similarly, the probability is also very high that the third letter will be a vowel. Again, the subjects may not be aware of these probability relations while trying to recognize the word, but if probability relations operate as set inducers, they should facilitate recognition.

Consider another example. The words "quiz" and "quit" are much more likely to occur in the experience of most subjects than the word "quip." "Quiz" and "quit" are more frequently used than "quip," they are probably more familiar than "quip," and they are likely to be more meaningful. Given recognition of the first three letters, subjects should recognize the entire word more readily if it is "quiz" or "quit" than if it is "quip."

In the first two examples above, probability relations between pairs of letters within a word constituted the set-inducing operation. In the third example, relative probability of occurrence of the complete words served as the set-inducing operation.

Other kinds of probability relations have also been experienced by most subjects. For example, most people have learned that clubs and spades are black and that hearts and diamonds are red. The form and the color of the four playing-card categories have been tied together through past learning. In an experiment by Bruner and Postman (1949) which will be described later in this section, this relation was utilized as a means of inducing misleading, or stimulus-incongruent, sets.

The probability that one particular element of a pattern will occur when another is present—that is, the probability of B given A—may be perfect or less than perfect. In the playing-card example, the probability of red color, given diamond form, is 1.00 or very close to it in the experience of most people. The same is true of *u* given *q*. The probability of *z* given *qui* is higher than the probability of *p* given *qui*, but obviously neither probability is perfect.

In summary, then, implicit set-inducing operations can be thought of as based on learned probability relations associated with total stimulus patterns or relations between elements of a pattern. In this respect, implicit and explicit instructions do not differ qualitatively. Telling a subject that the stimulus to be presented is a "color name" is merely one easy and reliable way to establish a very high probability relation. That is, the subject is being told that the probability is perfect that the word will be in the category of color names.

Now, knowing that the word is in the category of color names helps to delimit the size of the population from which the particular word is drawn. It is no longer one of the huge population of English words; it is one of the much smaller subgroup of English color-name words. A decreased population from which the particular exposure word is drawn means an increased probability of occurrence associated with that particular word.

The population of color names is still large, so that the probability of a particular color name remains relatively small. Nevertheless, this kind of information, as we have seen, may increase the likelihood of recognition.

Word frequency   Perhaps the most extensively investigated operation for manipulating set implicitly is *word frequency*. Natural languages contain words that are used, in speaking or in writing, with differential frequency. Some words are hardly ever used; some are overworked. It is theoretically possible to associate with each word a measure representing its relative frequency of occurrence. Practically, this is a forbiddingly difficult job. Nevertheless, some attempt at measuring frequency of usage has been made. One such procedure involved counting the number of times each word was used in a set of popular magazines over a period of several years. The results of this study are available in a book by Thorndike and Lorge (1944).

From the Thorndike and Lorge book one can select words from different frequency levels. Of course, it should be remembered that the measures are strictly pertinent only to the sample of magazines employed and to the population of readers of those magazines. In particular, the Thorndike and Lorge measures may not accurately reflect frequency of spoken usage. Thus, obscene and vulgar expressions, used with great frequency in the spoken language, will be extremely rare in the counts from magazines published 30 to 40 years ago.

On several grounds, then, the frequency of usage measures which are available are far from perfect, and yet they probably reflect in a rough but adequate manner the kind of information desired. At any rate, such measures have been used experimentally and have yielded generally satisfactory results. The high-frequency words have different behavioral effects than the low-frequency words. In particular, recognition thresholds are inversely related to frequency of usage. This result has been obtained in an impressively large number of investigations, both with visual and with auditory presentation. Not all of these experiments need be described here; a few of the classic studies should suffice to illustrate the general methodology employed and the general outcome.

One of the first of these studies was reported by Howes and Solomon (1951). The recognition thresholds of words varying in frequency were measured by an ascending method of limits, with exposure duration manipulated. In the first of two experiments, 60 words were used, and 20 subjects participated. The frequency measure of each word was assigned on the basis of the Thorndike and Lorge values and also on the basis of another count, taken from a different sample of printed material—the *Literary Digest*, popular books of fiction, etc. A third measure, the average of the first two, was also computed. Three recognition-threshold measures were obtained for each word by taking the mean, the median, and the mean of the ten lowest-duration-threshold values of each word over the 20 subjects.

Product-moment correlation coefficients were computed for each of the three threshold measures and the logarithm of each of the frequency measures. The lowest correlation obtained was -0.68, and the highest was -0.75.

The list of 60 words used in the first experiment had been constructed for another purpose and contained some characteristics that might have influenced the results. To rule out this possibility, a second experiment was run with a new list of 15 words and with an attempt at random selection. This list contained the words "country," "promise," and "example" at the high-frequency end, and "titular," "figment," and "machete" at the low end. Recognition thresholds were obtained as in the first experiment, and correlations were computed using the three measures of frequency and the three threshold measures. Again, high negative correlations were found for all pairs of measures.

Since the Howes and Solomon study, many other experiments have revealed very similar results. A common feature of these experiments is their reliance on word counts for the assessment of frequency of usage. An interesting departure from this practice was employed by Solomon and Postman (1952), who attempted to manipulate frequency experimentally. This was accomplished in the following way. Subjects were given a deck of cards with a nonsense word printed on each. The nonsense words were composed of seven letters and were pronounceable, but had no meaning in English. Examples of these words are "nansoma," "lokanta," "zabulon." The subjects were instructed to read each word and pronounce it aloud.

Twenty-four words were distributed among 100 cards. Fourteen words appeared once; two appeared twice; two appeared five times; two appeared ten times; and two appeared 25 times. In this way, "frequency of usage" was varied exactly, instead of being crudely estimated.

Following a second task, irrelevant to the experiment, the subjects were given a recognition task, with thresholds measured in the usual way. A total of 30 words were used in this part of the experiment. Ten were real English words, 10 were nonsense words never before encountered by the subjects, and 10 were taken from the original list of 24, with all 8 of the multiply presented words and 2 of the 14 singly presented words being used.

As expected, recognition thresholds varied inversely with frequency of usage. The largest threshold difference occurred between the words experienced once and those that were completely novel. There was also a sizable drop in threshold between the single- and double-presentation words. Between the values of 2 and 25, the threshold decreased linearly.

The general conclusion, that frequency of usage and recognition threshold are inversely related, is clearly supported in the two experiments described above, and in several others as well (Pierce, 1963). Note, however, that these experiments give no indication of how the frequency variable operates. Is it frequency of *experience* — that is, number of times a word has been encountered in the past — or frequency of *usage* — that is, number of times the subject has actually uttered the word? It is difficult, though theoretically possible, to separate these two aspects of the frequency variable, and it may be that an answer to this question will be long in coming.

Another, more crucial question can also be raised in the interpretation of the frequency-threshold relation. Does frequency have its effect on the input side (on d', in the terminology of signal detection theory), or is the effect mediated simply by characteristics of the individual's response tendencies (i.e., on β)? Fuller discussion of this question will be deferred until the effects of some other frequencylike variables have been described.

Familiarity and meaningfulness   The attempt to pin down the exact manner in which frequency of usage influences recognition thresholds has led to the investigation of two other variables, *familiarity* and *meaningfulness*. *Frequency* relates to past events, from which a present state may be inferred. More direct measures of present state are available, however. Thus, a more frequently used word may be more familiar or more meaningful than a less frequently used word. It may be through these attributes that the relation with recognition thresholds is mediated. The first step suggested by this idea is to determine the familiarity and meaningfulness of words directly and to relate these measures to recognition thresholds. This step was taken in an experiment by Kristofferson (1957).

The meaningfulness and familiarity of a set of words were assessed by techniques developed by Noble (1953). Familiarity was measured by a rating-scale method. Meaningfulness was measured by a method utilizing the number of associations given to each word. Both measures were found to predict recognition thresholds, with rank-order correlations around −0.60. These results are about as good as those obtained with frequency of usage as the independent variable. Frequency is, of course, not eliminated from consideration as a relevant variable because of these results, but the possible mediating role of familiarity and meaningfulness is certainly substantiated.

Perceptual sensitivity or response bias?   Now that we have seen the kinds of variables that influence recognition thresholds, we should consider the question, raised earlier, of whether these experiments really have anything to do with effects of set on perception.

All of the word-recognition experiments can be interpreted in terms of *response biases.* Frequency, familiarity, and meaningfulness may operate not on the input itself, but on the output. They may influence the subject's responses independently of any influence on perception. For example, suppose that a subject is told to guess what word the experimenter has just randomly selected from the dictionary. The subject, who is never shown the word, begins emitting guesses, and in so doing is more likely to utter familiar words than unfamiliar words. Now, if the experimenter's word is a familiar one, the subject will eventually hit on it, by chance, sooner than if it were an unfamiliar word. The subject would appear to be better able to guess familiar words than unfamiliar ones. Of course, the difference would really be the result of the subject's biased distribution of guesses.

If the example above does not make the point, consider a more extreme case. Suppose that the experimenter has two dictionaries, one English and the other French, and draws one word from each. The subject, however, is merely told that the words were taken from a dictionary, and assumes that just one, an English dictionary, was involved. The subject emits English words and continues to do so until hitting on the correct word. It could only be the English word.

An experiment to test the response-bias interpretation has been done by Goldiamond and Hawkins (1958). A technique like that of the Solomon and Postman experiment was used to produce, experimentally, differential frequency of usage in a set of nonsense syllables. Then the subjects were put through a mock threshold-measurement procedure, in which they were told that the nonsense words would appear subliminally. No words, however, were actually presented. But when the data were treated as though there had been real stimulus words, the inverse relation between frequency and recognition threshold was obtained.

In short, the effects of such variables as frequency, familiarity, etc. may have nothing to do with perceptual sensitivity. They may, instead, impose biases on response probability.

A detailed analysis by Broadbent (1967) reveals that "response bias" is itself not an unambiguous term. He favors an interpretation that is consistent with a signal-detection-theory approach, where the biasing influence is on the subject's criterion. If such bias does indeed account for all of the effects of "cognitive" variables on word recognition, then the data of such experiments clearly have no bearing on perception *per se*. Then why have we spent so much time on experiments that may not involve perception at all? There are two reasons. First, these experiments are extremely instructive in demonstrating the necessity for care in the design and interpretation of research on perception. One must be very cautious in categorizing an effect as perceptual when it may be something else altogether.

The word-recognition experiments are important for a second reason. They may, after all, really be what we first described them as: experiments that show the effects of set-inducing variables on perception. In this regard, recall our discussion in Chapter 1 of Neisser's (1954) seeing vs. saying study.

Words and Objects as Context Providers

The experiments discussed in the preceding section involve the recognition of whole words. There has also developed an interesting line of research in which the target stimulus is a single letter. The essence of this body of research is the finding that embedding a target letter in a word enhances the letter's recognizability.

The initial experiment in this line was conducted by Reicher (1968); a subsequent elaborate follow-up by Wheeler (1970) verified the original finding, while ruling out several possible artifactual bases for the results. This enhanced recognition of letters when they are constituent elements of words has become known as the *Reicher-Wheeler* or the *word-superiority effect*. Analogous results involving lines and angles as elements of pictorial representations of objects have also been obtained; not surprisingly, this type of result has become known as the *object-superiority effect*.

Word-superiority effect The word-superiority effect actually appeared as an unanticipated finding in Reicher's experiment, which was addressed primarily at the issue of whether the letters composing a word are processed all at the same time (*parallel processing*) or one at a time (*serial processing*). That issue, in various forms, has been of central concern in the field of cognitive psychology. For our purpose, we can bypass the theoretical arguments and focus on Reicher's methodology.

A schematic diagram of the stimuli and the procedure is given in Figure 9.4. Note first that there were three ways of presenting target letters: (1) singly; (2) as elements in meaningful four-letter words; (3) as elements in four-letter nonwords, or "quadrigrams." The duration of the stimulus display varied; termination of the stimulus display was followed by a field consisting of randomly placed dots—a "masking field"—which was introduced as a means of insuring that no further cognitive processing of the target stimulus would occur following its physical termination. To minimize possible response biases,

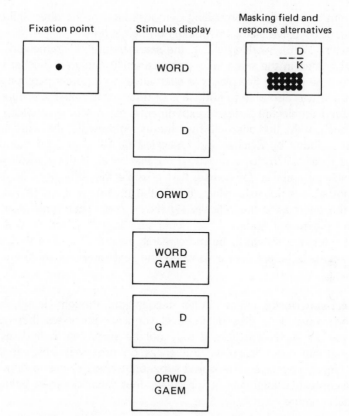

Fixation point   Stimulus display

Masking field and
response alternatives

FIGURE 9.4 Examples of tachistoscopic displays used by Reicher (1968). The stimulus display always consisted of either one or two stimuli of the same type, words, letters, or quadrigrams. (From Reicher, 1968)

the subjects were given on each trial two alternative letters from which to select their response. In one condition, the response alternatives were provided both before the target stimulus was presented and after termination of the masking field; in a second condition, the response alternatives were provided only afterward. The former condition was instituted in order to keep to a minimum possible differential memory requirements imposed by the different experimental conditions (that is, display duration and number of letters in the stimulus array). Again, the exact rationale for these procedures need not concern us; they follow from the type of model Reicher was working with and the questions he was trying to answer.

The data of interest here, as mentioned earlier, show that a letter is easier to recognize when part of a four-letter word than when part of a nonword or when presented alone. If alternative interpretations, such as response bias, differential memory requirements, and so on, can be ruled out, this result would seem to provide a compelling demonstration of the direct influence of an important cognitive factor (meaning?) on perception.

Wheeler (1970), working within the same theoretical framework as Reicher, and indeed in the same laboratory, carefully analyzed Reicher's procedure and came up with five plausible alternatives to a purely perceptual interpretation. He was also able to find ways of testing these alternate hypotheses; there ensued an elegant series of experiments, the outcome of which was to rule out each of the five alternate hypotheses. Apparently, the word-superiority effect, as found by Reicher and replicated by Wheeler (and many others since: see Estes, 1975, for a review of the literature), is not a trivial result of methodological artifacts. Of course, it is possible that Wheeler's list of alternate hypotheses is not exhaustive, but in the meantime it seems reasonable to treat the effect as a theoretically significant one. That conclusion is supported by the recent finding of a "letter-superiority" effect, in which fragments of letters are shown to be more readily recognized when they are presented as parts of letters than as isolated line segments (Schendel and Shaw, 1976).

Object-superiority effect Letter recognition, though clearly involving perception, most likely taps higher-level cognitive processes than just perception *per se*. In that respect, it may not be surprising to find, as in the word-superiority effect, cognitive influences on processes which themselves may be largely cognitive. The object-superiority effect seems to demonstrate cognitive-contextual influence on processes that seem closer to being purely perceptual in nature.

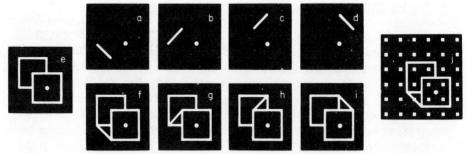

FIGURE 9.5   Briefly flashed stimuli used in two experiments. The subject's task on each trial was always to indicate which one of the four line segments a-d (differing in orientation and location relative to the continuously visible fixation point) was present. The target line was always accompanied by context lines, such as the squares in e, producing compound patterns such as f-i. Each stimulus flash was followed immediately by a 100-msec dotted masking stimulus, shown in j superimposed on a stimulus pattern. (From Weisstein and Harris, 1974)

In the object-superiority experiments (for example, Weisstein and Harris, 1974), lines are the analogues of letters, and line drawings of solid objects are the counterparts of words. An example of the stimuli used is given in Figure 9.5. The subject's task is an objective one—e.g., to select from four alternatives the line having the same orientation as the target line. The results show that a target line embedded in the drawing of a three-dimensional object is easier to detect than when that same line is presented as part of a collection of other lines which do not yield the perception of a solid object (an analogue of Reicher's and Wheeler's letter strings, or quadrigrams).

As in the case of the word-superiority effect, the object-superiority effect is impressive as a demonstration of how a meaningful configuration provides a context which enhances the recognition of an elementary constituent. This certainly has the ring of the Gestalt principle that "the whole is greater than the sum of its parts"—that, indeed, parts gain their status from the wholes which they compose. What is still missing is a simple, convincing account of how this might happen—i.e., how, exactly, wholes come to provide superior contexts for their parts.

SET AND THE PERCEPTION OF COLOR

Language and Color Coding

We have seen that where verbal reports are used as indicators of perceptual processes, there is the danger of the experimenter's equating the process with the report. Incorrect inferences may be drawn about perception from such a naive interpretation of verbal responses. For example, it has been reported that in a languge called Iakuti there is a single word for green and blue (Seroshevskii, 1896). Speakers of this language would respond with the same word to stimuli from the green and the blue portions of the spectrum. This, of course, does not prove that they are incapable of any discrimination between the two stimuli. Such a conclusion would obviously be unjustified without other kinds of data.

Even a careful use of verbal responses does not, however, eliminate the possibility of a linguistic effect on empirical data and hence on the conclusions drawn from these data. Verbal responses may inject artifacts into experimental data. This is one way in which it might be said that language influences perception.

The Whorf hypothesis There is also another, more subtle influence which language may have on the perceptual processes themselves rather than on the verbal indicators of perception. It has been hypothesized, most convincingly by the linguist Whorf (1950), that language may directly influence perception. Thus, speakers of Iakuti may *see* green and blue as more similar than do English-speaking subjects, and, if so, nonlinguistic responses should reveal this difference between the two kinds of people.

For another example of Whorf's hypothesis, consider Eskimos, who have in their vocabulary a separate word for each of three kinds of snow. Many speakers of English have only one word, "snow," for all three varieties, though they may invent phrases—for example "good skiing snow"—with which to represent its various properties. The easy accessibility of simple and separate names for the different kinds of snow may facilitate the Eskimos' recognition of and perhaps discrimination between them. Though others may be capable of the same behavior, they are, as a result of the set-inducing properties of their language, less likely to make the Eskimos' spontaneous responses to snow. Language, thus, may implicitly influence set, and hence partly shape people's immediate perception of their environment. To the extent that set, broadly defined, can influence perception, language may reasonably be expected to exert the same influence. From this point of view, Whorf's hypothesis becomes a special case of the more general postulation of a relation between set and perception.

Though Whorf's hypothesis has excited interest and controversy among linguists, anthropologists, philosophers, and psychologists, it has, so far, generated very little experimental research. One study, however, by Brown and Lenneberg (1954), nicely illustrates the way in which very general and somewhat vague hypotheses, of the Whorfian variety, can be put to empirical test.

The Brown and Lenneberg experiment   Whorf's hypothesis refers to two aspects of language—its structure, or grammar and syntax; and its lexical content, or vocabulary. It is with respect to content that the Brown and Lenneberg experiment is oriented. In particular, their experiment is concerned with the relation between the *codability* of colors, for English-speaking subjects, and the subjects' ability to recognize the colors. The specific operations for measuring these two variables, codability and recognizability, are described below.

A set of 24 stimuli was selected from the 240 colors of highest saturation, or purity, in the Munsell series. Eight of these were chosen on the basis of choices made by five judges, who were asked to pick out the best red, orange, yellow, green, blue, purple, pink, and brown. The remaining 16 stimuli were chosen by the experimenters from the rest of the color series.

Each of the 24 experimental subjects was shown the 24 stimuli as a group and was then asked to name each of the colors as it was presented individually; the naming was to be done both quickly and accurately. Five measures of the codability of each color were drived from the subjects' responses: (1) the average length of the naming response in syllables; (2) the average length in words; (3) the average reaction time; (4) intersubject agreement; and (5) intrasubject reliability.

Intercorrelations among these five measures were high, ranging from .355 to .864. A factor analysis was performed on the set of intercorrelations, and a single factor, "codability," emerged. The measure with the highest loading on this factor was the amount of intersubject agreement; it was this measure that was used in the second phase of the experiment.

The meaning of the first two measures may be somewhat obscure. The length of the response is relevant to codability on the basis of another linguistic hypothesis. According to Zipf (1935), frequency of usage and word length are inversely related. A short word is, therefore, one that is probably used frequently, and is hence easily accessible as a coding response for a particular color.

The purpose of the second phase of the experiment was to obtain measures of the recognizability of the 24 color stimuli. For this purpose, a larger group of colors, 120, was taken from the Munsell series; this list included the 24 stimuli of the first phase. The 120 colors were mounted together on a large card, with hue systematically varied along the vertical dimension and brightness along the horizontal.

A new group of subjects was then run through a recogition task. The subject was shown, simultaneously, 4 of the critical 24 colors. The 4 were then removed, and the subject had to point, on the large card containing the 120 stimuli, to the colors just seen. For each of the 24 colors a recognition score was obtained from the number of correct identifications made.

Thus, two measures were available for each of the 24 stimuli—its codability as measured by intersubject agreement, and its recognizability. These two variables were found to have a rank-order correlation of about .42, in confirmation of the hypothesis.

When a measure of the discriminability of the stimuli was obtained, it was found to correlate with recognizability, but not with codability. With discriminability held constant by statistical manipulation, the correlation between codability and recognizability increased, somewhat, to about .44. Codability and recognizability were significantly related, independently of stimulus discriminability.

Correlation, of course, does not imply causation. It may be that certain colors are difficult to name, or to "code," because they are not easily recognized. Or it may be that recognition, as hypothesized, is facilitated by easy codability. This ambiguity in interpretation might be cleared up by a study in which stimulus coding was experimentally manipulated, in contrast to the correlational approach used by Brown and Lenneberg.

At any rate, the Brown and Lenneberg study does provide some confirmation, even though indirect, of one prediction derived from the general Whorf hypothesis. Obviously, there is still a great deal more to be learned about the relation between language and perception. See, in this regard, the work of Rosch (1977), cited in Chapter 12.

Color Judgments

Incongruous playing cards   We have referred previously to misleading or incongruent sets arising implicitly from the individual's past experience. Bruner and Postman (1949) took advantage of their subjects' past experience to produce a set of incongruous playing cards. One crucial feature of their study involves the kinds of errors made by some of the subjects. These results, as we shall see, strongly indicate a truly perceptual effect. As you well know, clubs and spades are black; diamonds and hearts are red. Bruner and Postman created their incongruous stimuli by mixing suit and color, as for example by painting spades red. Recognition thresholds for these incongruous stimuli were higher than for normal playing cards, a finding that has been replicated by Lasko and Lindauer (1968).

By now, the response-bias interpretation should be obvious. Even with their eyes closed, subjects would be more likely to "recognize" normal cards than incongruous ones, simply because they are very unlikely to utter such incongruous combinations of words as "black four of hearts."

That this is not the only effect, however, is suggested by one of the kinds of errors that subjects made in their descriptions of what they saw in the Bruner and Postman study. Two frequent kinds of errors were noted by the experimenters; one was called *dominance* reactions, the other *compromise* reactions. In the first, the subject tends to assimilate either the suit to the color or the color to the suit. For example, if the subject called a black four of hearts either a red four of hearts or a black four of spades (or clubs), this would be classified as a dominance reaction.

Dominance reactions may simply represent response biases. Compromise reactions, however, cannot be explained in this way. Such responses involve a color which is neither red nor black, but somewhere between the two. Thus, a red spade might be called "brown," or "purple," or "rusty black," or "black with red edges." Compromise reactions of this sort sometimes occurred with normal cards, but much more frequently with the trick cards. The occurrence of compromise reactions, which have a very low *a priori* probability, indicates that the elevated thresholds of the trick cards were more than simply another example of artifacts introduced through response biases. The observation by Bruner and Postman (1949) of compromise reactions was an unexpected bonus of their experiment. It also suggests that cognitive influences on perception can be most clearly studied where the subject's task requires some sort of explicit judgment about an attribute of the target stimulus rather than about its identity. Experiments of this sort have been conducted, capitalizing on the fact that many classes of objects have associated with them rather limited values on certain attributes, particularly the attribute of color. Clubs and spades, as we have said, are black; hearts and diamonds, red. Lemons are generally yellow; limes, green; plums, purple. Elephants are gray; panthers, black; frogs, green.

Though the relation between class of object and color is rarely perfect (for example, apples are usually red, but may be green or yellow), there is often a high probability that a given object will have a given color. This relation is strong enough, in many instances, to justify the assumption that the classification of an object carries with it implicit set-inducing consequences.

The influence of such implicitly induced sets on attributive judgments has been studied in several experiments. Does an implicit color set, for example, have an effect on the perceived color of the set-inducing object? Will a stimulus which the individual identifies as a lemon appear more yellow than a meaningless stimulus? This type of question has been investigated in experiments by Duncker (1939), Bruner, Postman, and Rodrigues (1951), and Harper (1953). A review of these three experiments should suffice to illustrate the ways in which the question has been attacked and the methodological problems that have arisen.

Duncker's donkey   Out of the same green material, Duncker fashioned two targets, one in the shape of a donkey, the other in the shape of a leaf. Each of these figures was placed on a white background and presented in a field illuminated by red light. The combination of red light and green object was such that stimuli without a characteristic natural color should look gray. Set, however, might be expected to make the leaf look somewhat green by facilitating color constancy; the donkey, ordinarily gray, should be seen as gray, or at least as less green than the leaf.

The procedure for testing this hypothesis was as follows. The subject was shown one of the targets, and then looked at a disk, illuminated by white light, whose color could be varied. The subject attempted to match the disk to the target by instructing the experimenter how to modify the color of the disk. When a satisfactory match had been made with one target, it was replaced by the other. Several matches were made on each target by each of several subjects. Note that the inspection of the target and the color mixer was successive, not simultaneous.

In general, more green was required to match the disk to the leaf than to the donkey. This result was not obtained with every subject, but neither were there any reversals. Though the extent of the difference was small, it was in the direction specified by the hypothesis.

The Bruner, Postman, and Rodrigues experiment   Apparently, one of the essential features of an experiment such as Duncker's is the ambiguity of the color of the target. In his experiment Duncker achieved ambiguity by illuminating the green targets and their surrounding field with red light. Bruner, Postman, and Rodrigues used a different technique to accomplish the same end. Their experiment made use of various set-inducing figures, such as a lobster claw, a lemon, and a banana, as well as control figures similar in form to the experimental figures. Ambiguous color was created in the targets through simultaneous color contrast. The stimuli were actually gray, but they were presented on a blue-green background. The complement of the background, "brownish orange," was faintly induced in the stimulus figures. Each of the figures was verbally labeled by the experimenter.

The subject's task was to match the color of each figure with a color mixer, just as in Duncker's experiment. It was found that under conditions of successive observation of target and color mixer, the set-inducing figures required more color (for example, red in the case of the lobster claw and yellow for the banana) than did the control forms. The "red" and "yellow" experimental figures differed markedly from each other. This occurred despite many of the subjects' protests that all of their matches were the same. Again, set is claimed to have influenced perceived color.

Harper's modification   As with many of the dramatic experiments in this field, a question can be raised about the exact nature of the effect. Is it perception itself that has been influenced, or is the effect really on some other system? This question has been raised in connection with the two experiments described above. Perhaps the subjects were setting the color mixer to match not the perceived value of the stimulus, but rather some idea of what the color of the stimulus ought to be. The results that were obtained could certainly have been found in the absence of the stimulus.

For example, suppose that the subjects were asked to set the color mixer so that it looked like "the color of an apple," or like "the color of a circle." In all probability, more red would be used in the former case than in the latter. Even with the stimuli present and the instructions directed at how the stimuli looked, not how they ought to look, there is the danger of the subjects' responding cognitively rather than purely perceptually. This is especially likely to happen when the match is made with successive instead of simultaneous presentations.

Harper tried to get around this problem by modifying the matching procedure. In his experiment the set-inducing stimuli were an apple, a heart, and a lobster, all typically red objects. The control stimuli were an oval, a triangle, and a Y. All figures were cut out of orange paper. Rather than have the subjects match a color mixer to the target stimuli, with the two spatially separated, Harper superimposed the stimuli on the color mixer. The target served as figure, with the mixer as ground. The subjects' task was to report, as the color mixer was varied from red to orange, when the figure disappeared. Presumably, this procedure gets much closer to a pure perceptual effect than the usual matching procedure.

Using this modification, Harper still obtained the hypothesized effect of set. The set-inducing stimuli required more red in the background before they disappeared than the control stimuli did. The results support the hypothesis in a much more convincing fashion than those of the previous experiments.

There is one feature of Harper's procedure, however, which still leaves some ambiguity in the interpretation of the locus of the effect. That is, each of the set-inducing stimuli was not only labeled; it was also described by the experimenter as "reddish." The control stimuli were described as "yellowish-orange." Again, it may be that the subjects, in making their judgments, were to some extent complying with the experimenter's suggestions. Were the additional verbal instructions necessary, or would the less explicit set induced by the stimulus categories alone have been sufficient to yield the effect? This question can easily be investigated and a little more ambiguity perhaps eliminated.

10

Motivational Influences on Perception

The burden of the preceding chapter was to examine the proposition that we see, in part, what we *expect* to see. Does the same apply to motivational variables? Do we see what we *want* to see (and fail to see what we want not to see)? Motivational influences on perception (as well as on other processes, such as thinking, dreaming, memory, and so on) are postulated in psychoanalytic theory, as formulated by Sigmund Freud and his followers, and have by now become an accepted part of general psychological lore.

Having already seen how hard it is to validate experimentally the proposition relating cognitive and perceptual variables, you might anticipate a similar difficulty in demonstrating, with convincing empirical evidence, the motivation-perception relation. In this chapter, we look at some of the experimental attempts to obtain such evidence. As in the preceding chapter, the research cited is of two broad sorts: one where the task involves target identification or recognition, the other where the subjects make judgments about some aspect of a stimulus that is well above threshold. Throughout, the effort is to determine whether perceptual functioning can be influenced by motivational variables, where "motivational" is broadly defined to include: (1) the primary physiological drives, such as hunger, thirst, and pain; (2) the so-called acquired, or social drives, such as need for achievement; and (3) the psychoanalytically defined impulses, conflicts, and defenses.

TARGET IDENTIFICATION

Perceptual Vigilance

We have discussed in the preceding chapter how set might operate to affect perceptual selection. The problem here is the same. Do people who are hungry see more food-related stimuli, or see them sooner or more clearly, than people who are not hungry? Are socially insecure individuals hypersensitive to subtle rejecting aspects of the behavior of other people? What is the perceptual fate of stimuli with anxiety-arousing properties?

There was a time when one could review the relevant experimental literature and come up with some tentative answers to such questions. However, just in the past two decades research on this general topic has been voluminous, and unfortunately the literature is replete with contradictory findings, alternative interpretations of data, and reports of complex interactions among stimulus, situational, task, and subject variables. It simply is not possible to do justice to this vast amount of material in the present chapter. We, too, must be selective. For comprehensive reviews of various aspects of this literature, you are invited to examine the following references: Brown (1961), Dixon (1971), Erdelyi (1974), Eriksen (1960), Minard (1965), Natsoulas (1965), and Saugstad (1966). What we will do here is to concentrate on the pioneering experiments that have been done in this area and the kinds of problems that have arisen in their interpretation. We will also consider some of the follow-up research aimed at resolving those problems. As you might by now imagine, the problems arise mainly from the difficulty in segregating perceptual effects from other potential influences on the responses that are used as perceptual indicators.

Achievement motivation and the identification of achievement-related words   An experiment by McClelland and Liberman (1949) nicely illustrates a very common approach to the issue. A set of 30 words was chosen such that 10 were related to the "achievement motive," while the other 20 were either neutral or had implications for other motives. Of the 10 achievement-related words, 3 connoted failure (for example, "unable"), 3 connoted goal-seeking (for example, "strive"), and 4 connoted gratification (for example, "perfect").

Each of the 30 words was presented tachistoscopically at increasing durations until the subject correctly identified the word. In this way an *identification threshold* was obtained for each word. To control for individual differences in general perceptual sensitivity, the thresholds for the achievement-related words were expressed as functions of the neutral-word thresholds.

The subjects for whom the threshold measures were available could also be categorized, by their scores on a projective test, into those relatively high in achievement motivation and those relatively low. It was found that the highly motivated subjects had lower thresholds for the 7 words connoting goal-seeking or attainment than did those low in achievement motivation. The two groups did not differ, however, in their thresholds for the 3 "failure" words. In general, for all subjects, the words with failure connotation had higher thresholds than any other category of words. This latter result might, of course, be specific to the particular words themselves; 3 is a rather small sample to represent all "failure" words.

For our purpose, the important point here is the difference between the two types of subject in their identification of the other 7 achievement-related words. Apparently, subjects highly motivated for achievement are more sensitive to words connoting satisfaction of that motive than are subjects presumably less achievement-motivated. Further elaboration of this conclusion will continue after a discussion of some closely related studies.

Identification thresholds of value- or need-related words The McClelland and Liberman experiment actually followed, chronologically and methodologically, a somewhat more complex study by Postman, Bruner, and McGinnies (1948), who were also interested in the role of needs and values in perceptual selectivity. Their categorization of subjects was made on the basis of the Allport-Vernon scale of values. According to their responses to a questionnaire, subjects may be assigned relative scores in each of six "value areas"—theoretical, aesthetic, economic, social, political, religious. These are broad areas in which people may or may not seek gratification of certain of their motives.

It was hypothesized that people who valued one area highly would be more sensitive to words related to that area than to words in an area they valued less highly. As above, this hypothesis was generally confirmed. For example, a subject high in economic interest and low in religious interest would tend to have lower identification thresholds for words related to the economic area (for example, "income") than for those related to religion (for example, "sacred").

Results very similar to these were reported by Vanderplas and Blake (1949), who repeated the experiment above as closely as possible, except that the words were presented aurally rather than visually.

It should be noted that in both experiments not every subject shows the group result. Indeed, for some subjects, the relationship between value-area rank and identification threshold is reversed. But enough subjects do conform to the general trend to make the group data meaningful. This was true in the Vanderplas and Blake study, for example, for 17 of the 22 subjects.

In the work described above, motivation was inferred either from projective tests, as in the McClelland and Liberman experiment, or from personality inventories, as in the Postman, Bruner, and McGinnies experiment. Subjects were categorized on the basis of their scores on these tests; these categories were used to form the different motivational conditions (for example, high and low need for achievement). Such a procedure for manipulating the values of the independent variable (often referred to as a "natural groups de-sign"; see Underwood and Shaughnessy, 1975) does not fulfill the usual statistical requirement that subjects be randomly assigned to the different conditions. The subjects, in a sense, assign themselves. There is the danger, with such a procedure, of introducing biases into the composition of the groups; these biases may impose properties on the data which are erroneously attributed to the independent variable.

The best way to get around this problem is to use experimental manipulations to create the different conditions. Subjects are assigned at random to the conditions; after this assignment the experimental manipulations are performed.

An experiment by Wispé and Drambarean (1953) conforms to this latter approach. A group of 60 subjects was randomly divided into three experimental groups. One group went without food and water for 24 hours, the second group for 10 hours, and the third was a nondeprived control group. In this way three levels of motivation were experimentally created. The subjects were then put through a procedure in which identification thresholds were measured for 24 words. Of the 24, 12 were neutral with respect to hunger and thirst, and 12 were motive-relevant. The words could also be categorized into "common" and "uncommon." Thresholds were measured in the typical manner of increasing presentation duration until the subject correctly identified the word.

The finding of major interest here is that the deprived subjects had lower thresholds for need-related words than the nondeprived subjects. Their thresholds for the neutral words did not differ from those of the control group. This result held for both the common and the uncommon words, though the latter, as expected, had higher thresholds than the former. The 10- and 24-hour deprivation groups, incidentally, did not differ from each other.

Though the results of such experiments as have been described so far demonstrate a relationship between motivation and identification thresholds, their interpretation is not unambiguous. Thus, it has been argued that people high in one value area will be more familiar with words related to that area than they will with words associated with a low-value area. Since word familiarity is believed to influence thresholds, this factor in itself might be sufficient to account for the apparent effect of motivation. Of course, this argument is not applicable to the Wispé and Drambarean study, where the different levels of motivation were experimentally induced.

Another variation on this general theme, and one that might apply as well to the Wispé and Drambarean study as to the others, is the argument that motivation can influence thresholds by way of the subjects' verbal response probabilities. That is, motivation may not influence the perceptual process itself, but only the behavior from which characteristics of the perceptual process are inferred. For example, people who are highly concerned about achievement are likely to utter more achievement-related words than persons who are less motivated for achievement, and especially so in an ambiguous and indeed somewhat achievement-oriented experimental setting. They would therefore also be more likely to utter the correct words by chance. This argument should be a familiar one by now.

One way to test the response-probability suggestion is to examine the prerecognition guesses made by the subjects in the different motivational conditions. In the McClelland and Liberman study the high- and low-achievement motivated groups did not differ with respect to the number of achievement-related prerecognition guesses. On the other hand, the difference does appear in the Wispé and Drambarean experiment. The deprived groups did utter more need-related prerecognition guesses than the nondeprived group. This result tends to verify the response-probability argument, though there is still some room for ambiguity. If the deprived subjects were busy guessing need-related words, they should have somewhat higher thresholds for the neutral words than the nondeprived subjects. This did not happen. The neutral-word thresholds remained constant over the three experimental groups.

In summary, several experiments have demonstrated a relationship between motivation and stimulus thresholds. Some of these results are subject to alternative interpretations. Thus, all but the Wispé and Drambarean experiment are open to the argument that it is differential familiarity with motive-related words that mediates the relationship. The Wispé and Drambarean study is to some extent open to the argument that it is differential prerecognition response probability that mediates the relationship.

That neither familiarity nor response probability can entirely account for the relationship between motivation and perceptual selection is the contention of Atkinson and Walker (1956), whose experiment was specifically designed to obviate both interpretations.

Affiliation need and selection of affiliation-related pictures   To get around the problems of interpretation mentioned above, Atkinson and Walker used nonverbal stimuli and a very simple perceptual task. Subjects were shown, tachistoscopically, a set of four pictures, arranged in the pattern top, bottom, left, and right. One of the four pictures was of a face or several faces. The other three pictures were of common objects (for example, a typewriter). The subject was asked to indicate which picture—top, bottom, left, or right—seemed to stand out the most, or seemed the clearest. The experiment was so designed that one of four "people-pictures" was present on each trial, with the location of the picture systematically varied so as to occupy each position an equal number of times. The illumination and exposure duration were such that the contents of the pictures were *never* identified by the subjects.

Measures of the relative strength of the subjects' affiliation need were obtained via a projective test in much the same way as the achievement-need measures previously referred to. It was predicted, and found, that those subjects with a high affiliation need selected, as "clearest," more people-pictures than those low in that need.

Here the interpretation based on verbal response probabilities is obviously inapplicable. It also seems unlikely that the high-need subjects were more familiar with pictures of human faces than the low-need subjects.

Indeed, since the subjects could not identify the pictures, it is baffling to conceive of just how the relation between motivation and subthreshold perceptual selection is mediated. It seems unsatisfactory merely to assert that motivation influences perceptual selection, especially since the subjects were unaware of what they were selecting. And yet there has accumulated an impressive amount of evidence supporting the notion of "perception without awareness." We digress a bit from the main problem to consider this topic in more detail. Incidentally, we shall return throughout this section to the problem of perception without awareness as we introduce material that clarifies the issue.

The problem of a mediating mechanism   In the studies presented above the subjects in general were more responsive to need-related or value-related stimuli than to neutral stimuli. This responsiveness shows up in the form of decreased thresholds or in the form of increased selection of the relevant stimuli as those that stand out the most, even though, in the latter case, all stimuli were well below the identification threshold. This phenomenon, often referred to as *perceptual vigilance,* fits the conception of the motivation-perception relationship as an adaptive one. It is obviously useful to the organism to be sensitized to stimuli that are potential need satisfiers. But the adaptiveness of a relationship does not explain its mode of operation. It is this problem—the problem of *mechanism*—which has proved troublesome to those who are not satisfied merely to accept the demonstration of the relationship. And, parenthetically, it is this problem which has led many either to ignore or to deny the relationship itself.

Though it has taken several forms, the problem of mechanism essentially is this: For the relationship to occur, subjects must somehow first classify a stimulus as being either need-relevant or irrelevant; having made the initial classification, why should they then "throw away" some of the information on which the classification was based? For example, if achievement-motivated subjects have somewhere along the line been able to classify the word "friendship" as unimportant, why should they then be unable to report what the word was? Or, stated somewhat differently, how can a person classify a stimulus as need-relevant without knowing what the word is?

A similar problem arises out of experiments in which it has been found that so-called traumatic stimuli (for example, obscene words) have higher thresholds than neutral stimuli. This phenomenon has been labeled *perceptual defense.* The usual interpretation of this type of result is that by avoiding awareness of traumatic stimuli, people protect themselves from anxiety. Presumably the process is the same as that postulated in psychoanalytic theory, where unacceptable or anxiety-provoking impulses are, through the various defense mechanisms, kept out of consciousness.

The problem of mechanism here is perhaps even clearer than that posed by the perceptual vigilance experiments. In order to defend against anxiety-producing stimuli, you must first be able to classify them; to classify them, you must identify them. And yet, to be emotionally useful, the identification and classification must take place outside of awareness. How can you perform these required operations and still be unable to report what the traumatic stimulus was? We have not finished with this problem but in order to make the issue more concrete we shall describe some experiments representative of this latter type.

Perceptual Defense

The phrase "perceptual defense" was coined by Postman, Bruner, and McGinnies (1948) to refer to the relatively high thresholds of their low-value words. That is, not only were the high-value words more quickly identified than neutral words, but words related to low-value areas were less easily identified than the neutral words.

As we indicated previously, this particular relationship between value and threshold could be mediated by a nonmotivational variable such as familiarity. In this case the neutral words would fall between the high- and low-value words in familiarity, and concepts of sensitization or defense would be superfluous. Or, alternatively, as Eriksen (1954) has pointed out, the relation could be accounted for entirely by the perceptual vigilance concept, with the individual decreasingly sensitive to words of decreasing personal importance. At any rate, a single concept seems sufficient to handle these results. The perceptual-defense concept has been useful, however, in other contexts; its status, then, does not depend on the somewhat ambiguous experiments of the Postman, Bruner, and McGinnies variety. Blum (1954), for example, used both concepts, vigilance and defense, in designing and interpreting the provocative study described below.

Blum and Blacky   Blum's experiment derives from psychoanalytic ideas of the sort mentioned above, according to which potential anxiety-provoking stimuli are defended against. Blum's closer reading of the theory, however, led him to a more interesting hypothesis than that of a simple perceptual defense. Without discussing the problem of mechanism, Blum argued that traumatic stimuli would have either of two fates, low or high thresholds, depending on their proximity to conscious awareness. At low levels of awareness, the individual would be sensitized to threatening impulses and impulse-related stimuli; but if the stimuli were close to awareness, defense would occur. Thus, both perceptual vigilance and defense are predicted, depending on the level of awareness.

The stimuli for Blum's experiment were taken from the Blacky pictures, a set of cartoons about a family of dogs; the set of pictures was developed by Blum as a means of measuring various types of psychosexual conflict.

The experiment was conducted in three parts. The general procedure in the first part of the experiment was similar to that used by Atkinson and Walker (who, in fact, had borrowed the technique from Blum). The subject was shown four pictures at a time at an exposure duration below any possibility of picture recognition; the duration used was 0.03 second. The subject's task was to say which one of the four pictures, the top, bottom, left, or right one, stood out the most. A total of 54 trials was given in this part.

This procedure was followed before the subject had had any acquaintance with the stimuli, and was intended to provide a base line, or control series, with which to compare the next set of responses. Prior to the next repetition of the task, the subject was shown two of the four pictures; one was described in terms designed to elicit anxiety, the other in neutral terms. The traumatic picture for male subjects was used as the neutral picture for females, and vice versa. Along with the anxiety-provoking description, the subject was also asked to look at each picture and think about personal experiences similar to those depicted. Another 54 trials then followed. It was expected that in this second part of the experiment the subjects would be sensitive to the traumatic stimulus and select it more frequently than it had been selected in the control series. This was found to hold for 11 of the 14 subjects, a result significantly different from chance.

In the next part of the experiment the exposure duration was changed to 0.20 second, and the subject was asked to locate a particular picture on each trial; on half the trials the subject had to find the neutral picture, on half, the traumatic one. It was predicted that now the anxiety-provoking picture would be less easily located than the neutral picture. The exposure duration was long enough to permit some awareness of the contents of the picture, and hence perceptual defense was expected. This is what happened for 12 of the 14 subjects.

If we accept these results and Blum's interpretation of them, we seem forced to postulate both processes, perceptual vigilance and defense. Blum's interpretation, however, is not entirely unquestionable. The tasks used in the "vigilance" and "defense" parts of the experiment were not identical. In the first and second parts the subject was asked to select the picture which "stood out the most." In the third part the task was to locate a particular picture. Though it is not unreasonable to consider these two tasks as psychologically equivalent, they are not necessarily so. In particular, there is some ambiguity about the interpretation of the "vigilance" task. Suppose that four pictures are presented; three look about the same, but the fourth is different in some respect. This fourth picture is probably the one you would select as the one that stood out the most. You would choose that picture even if what made it different from the others was its fuzziness, or unclarity. That is, the traumatic picture might have been selected not because it was the clearest, but just for the opposite reason. What Blum interprets as vigilance may actually have been defense. It would be instructive, in this regard, to repeat Blum's experiment with one group of subjects being asked, "Which picture seems the fuzziest?"

You may wonder why Blum did not use the same task in all parts of the experiment. For example, why not, at the 0.03-second exposure duration, ask the subject to locate a particular picture? There were two reasons why this was not done. First, this procedure would eliminate the possibility of the baseline series, since that part depended on the subject's not having experienced the stimuli. More important, the task was meant not to be ego-involving; ego involvement would call into play the defense mechanisms and thereby rule out perceptual vigilance. The recognition task was considered by Blum to be just such an ego-involving task; it would have been as inappropriate to the vigilance part as it was appropriate to the defense part.

For the same reasons Blum preferred not to use the vigilance task in the defense series. He wanted ego-involvement in that part as a means of assuring the operation of the defense mechanisms.

Some replications of Blum's experiment   It turns out, however, that use of the perceptual vigilance task at the longer stimulus duration yields the same pattern of results as did Blum's recognition task (Mattson and Natsoulas, 1962). That is, when asked to pick out the location with the clearest picture, subjects selected with greater-than-chance frequency the traumatic picture at the brief exposure duration (.03 second), but significantly avoided picking that picture at the .20-second exposure duration. These results obviate a possible criticism stemming from the fact that different tasks were used for the vigilance and defense parts of Blum's experiment. In addition, Mattson and Natsoulas designed their study in such a way as to control for a possible order effect inherent in Blum's experiment, in which the defense task always followed the vigilance task. In the Mattson and Natsoulas experiment both orders of stimulus exposure were used (.03 followed by .20 and .20 followed by .03), and no effect of order appeared in the results.

In a host of other experiments, using increasingly complex designs, attempts have been made to tease out effects that can be considered "truly perceptual." Some of these seem successfully to have demonstrated such effects (for example, Bootzin and Natsoulas, 1965; Minard, 1965). For the sake of further argument let us assume that under some, as yet unspecified, experimental circumstances it is possible to show motivational effects on stimulus recognition or stimulus selection.

This still does not leave us with a very satisfactory mechanism to explain the operation of perceptual vigilance, defense, or both. Blum's notion of different levels of awareness, however, suggests a possible lead for specualtion. Can an individual react to a stimulus at a "low" level but not at a "higher" one?

There are experiments that seem to require just such an interpretation. Following a discussion of these experiments, we shall return to a more detailed consideration of the problem of mechanism.

Autonomic Discrimination without Awareness

McGinnies' experiment   It was an experiment by McGinnies in 1949 which actually set off much of the later work in the area we have been discussing. In brief, McGinnies presented his subjects with a set of words, some of which were neutral in affect and some "taboo" and presumably anxiety-arousing. Identification thresholds were measured by increasing the exposure duration of a word until it was correctly read by the subject. At the same time that these thresholds were being measured, a recording of the subjects' galvanic skin response (GSR) was also taken.

Two major results emerged. First, the taboo words had higher thresholds than the neutral words—presumably a demonstration of perceptual defense. Second, and more pertinent to our immediate interest, during the pre-identification trials, subjects gave higher GSRs to the taboo words than to the neutral words. That is, on those trials on which subjects could not correctly identify the words, they still gave a differential GSR to the two kinds of words. This result has been interpreted as evidence of *autonomic discrimination without awareness*. Somehow, enough information is transmitted to the autonomic nervous system to yield a differential GSR to the two classes of words, but insufficient information reaches the brain centers responsible for correct verbal classification.

Alternative explanations   As is the case with many of the experiments in this controversial area, alternative explanations are possible and have been vigorously offered by McGinnies' critics. Perhaps the simplest suggestion is given by Howes and Solomon (1950), who argue that the subjects' higher thresholds for the taboo words resulted from their reluctance to utter these words without more confidence in their guesses than they required for neutral words. If this were so, it would account not only for the elevated thresholds, but also for the differential GSR during the "pre-identification" period.

Another suggestion offered by Howes and Solomon is that the taboo words have a lower frequency of occurrence in the written language than do the neutral words; this difference could explain the threshold difference, but it would leave intact the discrimination-without-awareness aspect of the results.

Experiments have been performed to investigate some of these criticisms. For example, Cowen and Beier (1954) investigated the effects of both response withholding and differential frequency. Subjects were read a list of words and were told that some of the words would be the stimuli in a later recognition threshold test. Half of the words were of the taboo variety, and half were neutral. The subjects heard the taboo words spoken by the experimenter; they expected some of these words to appear in the recognition test; finally, they were encouraged, in preparation for the recognition test, to do as well as possible and especially not to withhold any guesses.

Despite these deliberate attempts to eliminate response withholding, the taboo words had higher recognition thresholds than the neutral words. Moreover, statistical analysis of the data revealed no correlation between recognition threshold and the conventional measure of frequency of word usage. It seems, therefore, that neither of the two factors suggested by Howes and Solomon can account for the higher thresholds of the taboo words in the Cowen and Beier experiment. By implication, their interpretation of the McGinnies results is probably also inadequate.

Lazarus and McCleary   The Cowen and Beier experiment provides one type of support for the perceptual defense hypothesis. It is not, however, directly relevant to the issue of discrimination without awareness. An experiment by Lazarus and McCleary (1951) bears directly on this problem.

To get around the criticisms aimed at McGinnies' study, Lazarus and McCleary experimentally created traumatic and neutral stimuli. Five nonsense syllables were paired with shock during a training period, while five others were presented but not paired with shock. After a sufficient number of trials the shock-paired stimuli became threatening to the subjects, but there was no threat involved in their being uttered by the subjects. Thus, the problem of response withholding was circumvented in this experiment. At the same time there was no problem of differential familiarity, since the two classes of nonsense syllables were equally unfamiliar.

Following the training period, recognition thresholds were measured in the usual way, and the GSR was also recorded. On those trials when the subject's guess was incorrect, there was a higher GSR to the shock-paired than to the neutral syllables. These data constitute strong support for the notion of autonomic discrimination without awareness.

The Problem of a Mediating Mechanism Resumed

We should stop at this point to remind you of the original problem. Starting with the general question about the influence of motivation on perception, we were led to consider experiments purporting to demonstrate "perceptual vigilance" and "perceptual defense." Both phenomena, granted the validity of the results on which they are established, require a mechanism whereby stimuli can be classified into a few broad categories—for example, need-relevant versus neutral—but beyond this crude classification cannot be otherwise identified. Though such a mechanism at first seems totally implausible, there is some evidence to support at least the assumption that stimuli can be differentially responded to outside of the subject's awareness.

Thus, it seems possible that the information reaching the level of awareness can be screened at lower levels. Though the postulation of such a screening mechanism invites all sorts of dangers in theory construction — for example, postulating, in effect, a little censor inside the head to do the screening — we do not see that it is necessary to fall into these easy traps.

Levels of classification   Much of the confusion in this area results from considering perception a unitary and immediate process. Some of the confusion could be dispelled by postulating different levels of classification, with all but the very lowest level subject to motivational influences. Thus, at the lowest level the individual is equally sensitive to all stimuli that are psychophysically equivalent. Enough information is extracted at this level to classify a stimulus as relevant or irrelevant, and as threatening or rewarding. At this point, the motivational influence can be exerted. Attention is directed more toward the relevant than the irrelevant, so that different amounts of further information are obtained from the two types of stimuli.

Either at this level or at succeeding levels, the motivational influence may again be felt. The classification of a stimulus as relevant and threatening, for example, leads to an increase in emotional response. This emotional response, of which the GSR is a component, may itself help to block or disrupt those finer, high-level classifications necessary for correct identification or recognition of the stimulus. Evidence in support of this idea has been reported by Walters, Banks, and Ryder (1959).

A conception of the perceptual process as one which operates in stages is not in itself very difficult to accept. (See Erdelyi, 1974, for elaboration of this notion). Nor is the idea unacceptable that events which influence behavior can occur without the individual's awareness. Indeed, that seems to be more the rule than the exception (Nisbett and Wilson, 1977). What may be difficult to grasp is the idea that some of the complex psychological functions, especially those that involve language and meaning, can take place at "low" levels but not at "high." How can the meaning and emotional connotations of a word be responded to when the word itself cannot be identified? It is this question that seems to constitute the main source of resistance to any theory postulating levels of classification. Levels by themselves are fine. But levels that act in reverse order seem at best paradoxical and at worst nonsensical.

Responses to subliminal stimuli   Is there any evidence outside of the perceptual vigilance and defense experiments which bears on this issue? In particular, can it be shown that behavior is influenced by the connotations of stimuli which the individual cannot identify and perhaps not even detect? There is, indeed, some evidence that people can respond to input of which they are unaware.

The prototype of such experiments can be found in a clinical investigation by Alfred Binet (1896). Binet reported on some patients with hysterical anesthesias. One woman, for example, had no tactual sensitivity on her neck. Nevertheless, when Binet pressed a medallion against the skin of her neck and asked her to draw whatever images came to mind, her drawings bore a remarkable resemblance to the figure on the medallion.

By modern standards, Binet's methodology is, of course, quite crude. But analogous effects, obtained through carefully controlled experiments, seem to support the notion of behavioral impact of *subliminal stimulation*.

An experiment by Bach and Klein (1957) provides an illustration of this kind of evidence. Subjects (all females) were asked to describe a line drawing of a face, which was projected on a screen before them. Unknown to the subjects, the word "happy" was superimposed on the face on half the trials and the word "angry" on the other half of the trials. The words were presented in such a way that the subjects were never aware of their presence. An effect of the words could, however, be detected in the subjects' descriptions of the faces. With the word "happy" present, the descriptions tended to include such adjectives as "happy," "smiling," "open," "soft," and other words and phrases generally connoting pleasant affect. When "angry" was present, the descriptions tended to include words such as "angry," "mad," "stern," "hard," etc. Through a complex scoring system, each subject was classified in terms of her conforming to the predicted effect. Of the 22 subjects, 16 responded according to the prediction, 5 went opposite to prediction, and 1 was neutral. The effect of the subthreshold stimuli was small, but significant.

In a similar and even more subtle experiment, Fox (1959) obtained similar results. Here the subliminal stimuli were two sets of lines that, when supraliminally superimposed on a supraliminal face, gave the face a "happy" or an "angry" appearance, as shown in Figure 10.1. During the experiment, of course, these lines were presented at an intensity that was, for each subject individually, below the detection threshold.

The 48 male subjects in this experiment performed three tasks: (1) They selected ten adjectives from a checklist to describe the faces; (2) they described the faces in their own words; (3) they reported any images that occurred after looking at the faces. Analysis of the data revealed the presence of a subliminal effect under the latter two conditions, with the extent of the effect increasing from description to imagery. These results have been replicated in a subsequent study by Allison (1963).

There are enough well-designed experiments of the above sort (see, for example, Fiss, 1966; Klein, Spence, Holt, and Gourevitch, 1958; Shevrin and Fritzler, 1968; Shevrin and Luborsky, 1958; Spence, 1961) to warrant the conclusion that stimuli of which persons are unaware can influence some aspects of their behavior. Typically, in these experiments, it is the meaning, and

FIGURE 10.1   Left to right, the neutral, "happy," and "angry" faces used in the experiment by Fox (1959).

often the emotional significance, of the subliminal stimuli to which the subjects respond.

How meaning is learned   We keep returning to the same question: How can the meaning of a stimulus be responded to when the stimulus has not even been seen? Meaning is learned; and this learning must depend on the higher brain centers. Suppose that the meaning of a stimulus is considered as consisting of a complex set of responses that occur, after learning, when the stimulus is presented. These "meaning responses" depend, presumably, on the activation of those brain centers that mediated the original learning. Now, it seems reasonable that the whole set of meaning responses should occur when the higher centers are activated by the presentation of a stimulus. Among this set of responses, let us consider two general categories: (1) identifying responses and (2) affective responses. Each category of responses has been attached, through learning, to the stimulus. Thus, when a particular stimulus is presented, the individual should simultaneously identify it and be affectively aroused by it.

In the context of the line of reasoning above, subliminal effects on behavior, autonomic discrimination without awareness, and perceptual vigilance and defense are all impossible. If we accept these phenomena, we obviously must change our way of thinking about the acquisition of meaning and its activation.

There is room in the account above for several changes. What follows is meant to suggest a way of thinking about the acquisition and activation of meaning responses that will encompass the otherwise mysterious phenomena discussed so far in this chapter.

Suppose that the two categories of meaning responses, the identifying and the affective responses, are not learned in identical fashions. In particular, suppose it is true that in the early stages of learning both require the mediation of the same higher centers. But once learning has progressed, the affective responses "move down" in the nervous system; they can be aroused through the activation of lower centers. On the other hand, the identification responses remain dependent on the original higher centers for their activation. In this way the two categories of responses become independent of each other. More exactly, the affective responses can be aroused by stimulation that is not sufficiently informative to arouse the appropriate identification responses; when the stimulation can arouse the identification responses, it will probably also arouse the affective responses.

The analysis above implies that arousal of the lower centers requires less stimulus information than does arousal of the higher centers. A mere fragment of a total stimulus pattern is all that is necessary to set off the diffusely reacting lower centers, while much more of the total stimulus pattern must be present before the higher centers will "allow" an identifying response. The higher centers are thus harder to activate (have a higher criterion), and are thus also subject to less error.

How can a fragment of a stimulus pattern activate the lower centers? This is a problem only if the idea is retained that the total stimulus pattern is always present when the meaning responses are acquired. But this need not be the case.

Not every angry face is obviously and completely angry. A slight tightening of the lips at one time, a contraction of the pupils at another; at one time a momentary furrowing of the brow, a barely noticeable tensing of the neck muscles; each or all of these may be present, but hardly noticed, at times when an affective response, appropriate to an agner-provoking situation, is aroused.

For example, the infant may have done something which, in the past, has elicited open anger from the parent. "Anticipating" anger again, the infant responds emotionally. The parent appears, notices the misdemeanor, tries not to be angry, but reacts nevertheless with a slight frown. This facial configuration of the parent, present during the infant's emotional response, becomes attached to it, to some extent, through the learning process.

Such learning goes on continually during children's early years. At the same time that subtle cues are being attached to emotional responses, they are also learning to be "precise" in their perceptions. They are learning to see things as they "really" are, and to call things by their "right" names. They may even be learning to respond *verbally* to some stimuli in a way that is inconsistent with their affective responses. ("Don't be silly, darling," Mother might say with a slight frown, "I'm not the least bit angry at you.") While the affective system is learning to respond to one set of cues, the identification system is learning a different set of meanings. Children are especially learning not to "confuse" what they feel with what they see. In the process, they are learning to ignore subtle, fragmentary, fleeting, and therefore unreliable stimuli.

Imagine such people, now college sophomores, serving as subjects in an experiment. They are shown a face and asked to describe it. On part of the face there are lines, just below threshold, which connote anger, or pleasure. All their past history has led the subjects not to notice these lines. But their past history has also been such that these lines (which are really there in the stimulus, though subthreshold) arouse a vague, subtle change in mood.

It is this slight nudge which the stimulus gives to the total affective reaction that makes dysphoric responses predominate with the angry face, and euphoric responses with the happy face. The change in behavior is small; the emotional effect of the subliminal lines must compete with other sources of arousal. But if the subjects are relaxed, passive, accepting of the situation, and not trying hard to be accurate, the lines push them far enough one way and then the other so that their verbalizations are appropriately more happy than angry, more angry than happy. This emotional effect of the lines is strong enough—often enough within a subject, and over enough subjects—so that a behavioral effect can be detected by a sensitive, well-trained psychologist.

The above is fanciful, incomplete in detail, and undocumented by data. And yet, what it suggests seems no less theoretically plausible than the model of perception which insists that stimuli be identified before they can be affect-arousing.

This is, perhaps, already more speculation than the topic deserves. One further idea will close the issue. Suppose that instead of naive college sophomores one used as subjects, in an experiment like Fox's, the sensitive, well-trained psychologists mentioned above. Let these be people who can adopt the nondefensive attitude necessary to the subjects in such an experiment. Once they have responded, however, they can look critically at their own behavior. By reacting to the mood expressed in their own verbalizations, let them decide which "subliminal" stimulus had just been presented.

Now, let this decision be taken as a judgment, as though in response to the recognition question "Which of the two stimuli were you just presented with?" Under these peculiar conditions of measurement, the subjects' recognition thresholds ought to be as low as those implied in their descriptions of the pictures. That is, there should be no "subliminal" effect. Their judgments should be as sensitive to the stimuli as their descriptions are.

The point of this hypothetical experiment is this: "Subliminal" effects are demonstrated by showing a discrepancy between two forms of behavior, one usually a simple judgment and the other a more complex, less restricted response. The discrepancy is there because people have learned to react emotionally to subtle, fragmentary cues, but to ignore these same cues in making rational, precise judgments about external stimuli. Very simply, the threshold measurements derived from such judgments can be thought of as spuriously high. Looked at in this way, the phenomena described so far in this chapter become less mysterious, but no less interesting.

SELECTION AND JUDGMENT

Ambiguous Figures

We have been discussing experiments in which the influence of motivation on perceptual selection has been studied at the threshold or subthreshold level. Here we take up a set of experiments concerned with the effect of motivation on the perception of ambiguous figures—that is, figures which are so constructed that they may be seen, with respect to the figure-ground relation, in either of two ways.

The Schafer and Murphy experiment   The first of these studies was reported in 1943 by Schafer and Murphy. Basically, the procedure consisted of a training session followed by a testing session. In each of 100 training trials the subject was shown, for about ⅓ second, one of the four "profiles" illustrated in Figure 10.2. Note that profiles (a) and (b) fit together, as do (c) and (d). The name associated with each profile was announced by the experimenter before each trial, and subjects were instructed to learn the name that went with each face. Along with this, they were also told that whenever they saw two of these faces, they would be rewarded with either 2 or 4 cents, and whenever they saw the other two faces they would lose 2 or 4 cents.

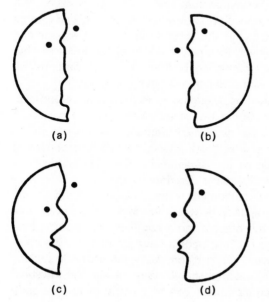

(a)   (b)

(c)   (d)

FIGURE 10.2 The training stimuli used in the Schafer and Murphy experiment. One of the two profiles of each pair was rewarded following its presentation, the other punished. (After Schafer and Murphy (1943)

The reward-punishment schedule was so arranged that the subjects actually ended up about 15 cents ahead by the end of the training session.

Lest any profile ever be seen in its oppostie aspect [e.g., lest (a) be seen as (b)] during training, the subjects were provided with unambiguous copies of the four possible faces. An attempt was also made to control for differences in the various reward-punishment pairs among the five subjects. Finally, a guessing procedure was instituted such that the subjects were led to believe that they could to some extent control the rewards and punishments. This was included as one means of maintaining interest in the experiment.

In the testing session, the subjects were shown the stimuli illustrated in Figure 10.3. Stimulus (A) is composed of training stimuli (a) and (b); stimulus (B) of (c) and (d). The test stimuli could be seen in either of two ways, with either of the two training profiles as figure and the other as ground. It was hypothesized that the effect of the training would be to make the rewarded profile dominant; when shown the test stimulus, the subjects would see it as one of the rewarded faces and call it by the name associated during training with that face.

In some preliminary work it was found that the reward-punishment effect was masked by a stronger factor—a "direction set." Subjects tended to see all the profiles pointing in the same direction. To overcome this, it was found helpful to follow each test trial with a face unambiguously pointing in the direction opposite that implied in the subject's previous response. With this procedure, the hypothesized result was obtained. On the first 16 test trials the number of rewarded profiles reported significantly exceeded the number of punished profiles. This result, incidentally, tended to disappear after about the 16th test trial, as might be expected from the principle of extinction. That is, learned behavior should fail to occur after a series of nonrewarded trials.

Three points are worth emphasizing about this study. The first is the small sample size: there were only five subjects. The second is the ease with which the presumed effect of reward could be masked by a direction set. Of course,

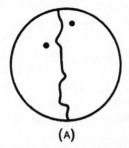   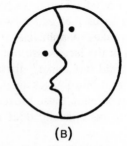

(A)   (B)

FIGURE 10.3   The test stimuli in the Schafer and Murphy experiment. The figure on the left is the composite of profiles a and b; the figure on the right is the composite of c and d. (After Schafer and Murphy, 1943)

the tenuousness of the reward effect may simply have been a function of the triviality of the reward.

The third point is the most important. As with all investigations of perception, it was necessary to utilize, in the collection of data, an indicator response. In many of these studies it is not clear whether the experimental manipulations have affected the percept directly or whether the effect has been on the indicator response itself. Thus, in the Schafer and Murphy experiment, it may be that the reward during training was merely strengthening the subjects' tendency to utter a particular name, and that their percepts were unaffected. It should be possible, however, in designing such experiments, to establish the control groups necessary to separate out these two sources of behavior, or to utilize indicator responses that would eliminate this ambiguity.

In summary, the Schafer and Murphy experiment gave results that were at best suggestive of the hypothesized effect of reward and punishment on perceptual selection. If nothing else, though, the experiment did serve to stimulate further work on the motivation-perception problem. Some of this we report below.

Further experiments of the Schafer and Murphy type   Since the Schafer and Murphy experiment, despite its weaknesses, had begun to assume considerable importance in the thinking of many perceptual theorists, an attempt at replication was made by Rock and Fleck (1950). The Schafer and Murphy procedure was followed as closely as possible, with a few variations (one of these, as we shall see later, turned out to be critical). The results of this replication, however, in no way confirmed the original conclusion. The rewarded faces were not seen, in the test series, more frequently than the punished faces.

Along with this discrepancy in results, two other behavioral differences should be noted. First, the Rock and Fleck subjects apparently did not learn to identify the training faces nearly so well as did the Schafer and Murphy subjects. Second, in a follow-up interview, the Rock and Fleck subjects indicated either indifference to or disdain of the rewards and punishments; many could not tell which faces had been rewarded and which punished.

It seems to us that either of these facts, aside from any methodological differences, makes meaningless a comparison of the main results of the two experiments. If the faces were not sufficiently learned, and if the rewards and punishments did not "take," then it is pointless to expect a confirmation of the Schafer and Murphy results. Of course, it is legitimate to inquire into the difficulty of replicating these procedural aspects of the Schafer and Murphy experiment, but this difficulty does not constitute a refutation of their original conclusion.

The task of investigating the differences between the two studies was undertaken by Jackson (1954). Two experiments were performed. In the first, the Schafer and Murphy procedure was followed, with a few minor changes and an increase in the amount of the rewards and punishments to 15 cents. Under these conditions Jackson obtained the Schafer and Murphy effect.

In the second experiment essentially the same procedure was used, except that the method of stimulus presentation was changed to conform to that used by Rock and Fleck. This is the feature that we referred to previously as the critical source of difference between the two experiments.

In the Schafer and Murphy experiment the stimuli were presented in a tachistoscope, such that the diameter of the figures was about 2–3 inches, at a distance of about 18 inches from the subject. Further, the pre-exposure field was illuminated, and the faces were imposed on this already lighted area. In the Rock and Fleck experiment, a projection tachistoscope was used. The stimuli were presented at a distance of about 54 inches, with a diameter of about 12 inches, and there was no pre-exposure field. Thus, the Rock and Fleck stimuli were relatively large; there was a marked contrast in illumination from pre-exposure to exposure; and fixation was difficult.

Now, with a presentation method similar to that used by Rock and Fleck, Jackson, in his second experiment, obtained results much like those of Rock and Fleck. The subjects made many more errors in recognizing the faces than they did in the first experiment; they tended to assume direction sets; and though they did report more rewarded than punished faces, the difference was not significant on the first 16 test trials.

The Schafer and Murphy phenomenon has received additional verification since the Jackson replication. In an experiment by Snyder and Snyder (1956) the subjects listened to each of two voices speaking in a meaningful set of sentences. While the subjects were hearing one of the voices, they were rewarded with nickels; when they listened to the other voice, some nickels were taken away from them. Following this training period, the subjects listened to a recording on which the two voices were superimposed, each reading a different passage. The subjects were asked to reproduce as much as possible of what they had heard of this mixed recording. Note the analogy between this situation and the usual visual task in the Schafer and Murphy situation. The subjects were presented with stimulation that could be perceived in alternative ways: they could attend to one voice or the other, but not to both simultaneously. The data indicated a significant tendency for subjects to report more material from the rewarded voice than from the punished voice.

In another experiment very similar in content to the original Schafer and Murphy study, Sommer (1957) found that reward produced the expected effect, but punishment did not. The effect of punishment was in the direction of stimulus avoidance, but even with more than 100 subjects the results were not significant.

The Sommer experiment involved a procedure in which rewarded or punished profiles were pitted against neutral profiles. In a separate experiment, with different subjects, reward was pitted directly against punishment.

The rewarded profile was selected over the punished profile in a ratio of about 2:1. This is about the same ratio with which the rewarded face was selected over the neutral face in the previous experiment. Thus, it appears that in the coin experiments, when reward and punishment are used concurrently, it is reward which is primarily responsible for the outcome.

The effects of punishment in the form of electric shock were investigated in an experiment by Ayllon and Sommer (1956). Here, the profiles consisted of a groove through which the subjects ran their index finger. One groove was embedded in a visual context such that it was perceived as the left profile of "Rufus." The same groove in another visual context was perceived as the right profile of "Clem." The subjects were told to run their index finger through the groove so that they might later be able to identify the profiles while blindfolded. The presentation of one of the profiles (for example, Clem) was followed by a shock on five trials, which were interspersed among non-shock presentations of Clem, Rufus, and an unambiguous, set-breaking groove of "Horace."

Following this training period, a series of 14 presentations was given with the subjects blindfolded. Their task was to identify the profile. Of course, as in all of these experiments, the test groove could be perceived, realistically, as identical with either of the two training profiles.

The subjects were classified, in terms of their own subjective reports and in terms of the experimenter's rating of their reactions to the shock, into two groups, those who found the shock only "slightly unpleasant" and those who found it "moderately or very unpleasant." The "slightly unpleasant" subjects tended to avoid the shocked profile, but the "very unpleasant" subjects significantly selected the shocked over the nonshocked profile. Ayllon and Sommer consider these results analogous to the defense and vigilance phenomena discussed earlier in this chapter.

In summary, there seems to be sufficient data to conclude that reward associated with a simple figure increases the probability that that figure will be selected in preference to an equally noticeable neutral figure. The effects of punishment in such a situation are less clear. There is some indication that very mild punishment (for example, taking away coins) has no effect; that somewhat stronger punishment (for example, mild shock) produces avoidance; and that even stronger punishment yields selection of the figure associated with punishment. It is conceivable that very severe punishment will again yield stimulus avoidance. In any event, the main question remains open to debate: Is the effect directly perceptual or does it merely reflect response bias?

Solley and Sommer   An experiment by Solley and Sommer (1957) to some extent answers that nagging question and also serves as a bridge between the experiments discussed above and those to follow. The subjects in this study were young children. A variation of the Schafer and Murphy technique was employed, and the children showed the usual effect. Presented with an ambiguous figure, they responded with the name of the alternative that had been associated with reward.

Along with this conventional measure, Solley and Sommer also obtained judgments from the children concerning attributes of the stimuli. In general, the children tended to call the rewarded profile closer, brighter, and happier than the nonrewarded profile.

Unfortunately, the judgmental task (e.g., "Which face is brighter?") was so designed that these latter results may be spurious. That is, the children may simply have been responding with the name of the rewarded face to every question, or at least to every ambiguous question. The questions were so phrased that if the rewarded face were indiscriminately used by the children, it would appear to fall on the more favorable end of the attribute. The way to eliminate this ambiguity is simply to reverse the polarity of the questions for half of the subjects. For example, half of the subjects should be asked, "Which face is darker?"

Whether or not the Solley and Sommer interpretation of their data can be accepted, their experiment serves to illustrate a type of motivation-perception relationship that has been the subject of a great deal of research—and controversy. This is the relationship between motivation and attributive judgments.

Attributive Judgments

The Schafer and Murphy type of experiment is concerned with the effects of motivational variables on figural dominance. A related problem, anticipated above, involves the effect of motivational variables on the perceived value of stimuli on certain attributes. This line of research was initiated by Bruner and Goodman in 1947. In their classic experiment they investigated the hypothesis that the perceived size of a valued object would be greater than that of a neutral object of equal physical size. Thus, motivation is expected to influence not only *what* stimuli are selected for attention, but is also hypothesized to affect the *manner* in which these stimuli are perceived. When the attributes on which this effect is supposed to take place are so primary as, for example, size, this becomes a very radical hypothesis. As with all extreme proposals, this one too has its avid supporters and bitter critics. Again, it is data that will ultimately decide the issue.

The Bruner and Goodman experiment To test their hypothesis, Bruner and Goodman had 10-year-old children judge the size of various coins. One group of 10 children was taken from a lower-class settlement house; a second group was composed of 10 children from a wealthy progressive school. It was assumed that the lower-class children differed from the others in their need for money. For them the coins should have more value and hence, according to the hypothesis, seem larger than for the wealthier children. Along with these two groups there was a control group of 10 children who judged the size of cardboard disks equal in size to the various coins.

The size judgments were made in the following manner. Each child was seated before an apparatus on the face of which was a ground-glass screen and a knob. Projected onto the screen was an almost circular patch of light; the diameter of the light patch could be varied by manipulating the knob. Each child was first asked to set the knob so that the size of the patch of light equaled that of a penny, a nickel, a dime, a quarter, and a half-dollar. These judgments were made without any coins present.

In the next phase of the experiment the same judgments were made, only this time with the child holding the appropriate coin in one hand, about 6 inches to the side of the light patch. Children in the control group also performed this task, but instead of coins, they held the cardboard disks in one hand and matched the light patch to them.

The results of the judgments made with the coins present can be summarized as follows. First, the experimental subjects overestimated the size of the coins, as compared with the control subjects. Second, the poor children overestimated the size of the coins even more than the wealthy children did. Third, except for the half-dollar, the amount of overestimation tended to increase as the monetary value of the coin increased. All of the results are in accord with the Bruner and Goodman hypothesis.

The results with the coins absent were less striking. The poor children did overestimate, but less than they did with the coins present. The wealthy children overestimated only the quarter and half-dollar.

Attempts at replication   Attempts at replicating the Bruner and Goodman results have not been uniformly successful. Carter and Schooler (1949), for example, followed the original design rather closely, but failed to obtain a significant difference between the judgments of rich and poor children when the judgments were made with the coins present. When, however, the judgments were made with the coins absent, the two groups did differ. The judgments of the poor children were larger than those of the rich children. It was only with respect to the quarter and half-dollar, though, that a substantial amount of overestimation occurred. Note that in the Bruner and Goodman experiment, the judgments with coins absent showed less of an effect than those with the coins present.

Very often, when the results of an experiment fail to be verified, it is possible to find major differences in procedure that might account for the differences in results. In the present case it is difficult to discover in the Carter and Schooler procedure any such important differences. If these were the only experiments of this type, we should be at something of an impasse. There are further experiments, however, that do yield results in support of the Bruner and Goodman hypothesis.

The most ingenious of the coin experiments is one reported by Ashley,

Harper, and Runyon (1951). It was their argument that the poor and wealthy children in the Bruner and Goodman study must certainly have differed in important ways other than mere need for money. For example, the two groups might have differed in their familiarity with the coins, especially the ones of higher denomination. Given such differences, it would be rash to attribute the differences in their judgments solely to the need variable.

Ashley, Harper, and Runyon therefore attempted to manipulate need experimentally while holding all other variables constant. To do this, they used the same individual in a "poor," a "rich," and a neutral condition. To establish the appropriate "need" state, the experimenters would hypnotize their subjects and then read them "descriptions" of their past life. The descriptions would involve a history of either poverty or wealth. From each subject judgments were obtained under poor, rich, and neutral conditions. Judgments were made both with the coins present and with the coins absent. In general, the subjects overestimated the size of the coins when in the "poor" state, and underestimated the size of the coins when in the "rich" state.

In a supplementary phase of the experiment the subjects judged the size of a metal slug, under hypnotically induced rich and poor states. Judgments were made with the slug given each of four names—lead, silver, white gold, and platinum. The results showed that as the value of the metal increased, the estimated size increased, with the "poor" judgments consistently larger than the "rich."

Though the mechanisms underlying hypnotic suggestion are far from understood, there is little reason to discount the Ashley, Harper, and Runyon experiments on that ground. At the same time, there is enough uncertainty about hypnosis to make tentative any conclusions from this one study.

Another very clever method of testing the Bruner and Goodman hypothesis was used by Lambert, Solomon, and Watson (1949). As in the previous study, their purpose was to manipulate the value variable experimentally rather than using specially selected groups of subjects.

The subjects in this experiment were 54 children, 3 to 5 years old. Of these, 37 served in the experimental group and 17 were controls. The experimental manipulation was designed to attach value to a previously neutral poker chip. This was accomplished in the following manner. The experimental subjects were shown how to turn a crank in order to get a poker chip; this chip could then be inserted into a slot in return for a piece of candy. The control subjects also learned to turn the crank, but they received the candy directly, without the mediation of the poker chip. This procedure was carried out for ten days.

Size judgments of the poker chips were made, using the Bruner and Goodman apparatus, both before and after the value-inducing procedure. On the 11th day of the experiment, the value of the poker chip was "extinguished": it no longer yielded candy from the slot machine. For the control subjects, turning the crank also no longer produced candy. A size judgment was made following this extinction period. On the next day there was a relearning session followed by another size judgment.

The results indicated that the experimental manipulations did have an effect on the size judgments. For the experimental group, the size judgments increased significantly following the value-inducing procedure; after extinction the judgments returned to the pre-experimental level; following relearning, the judgments again increased. The judgments of the control subjects remained relatively stable.

In comparing the judgments of the two groups immediately after training, one might argue that the difference is one in familiarity and not induced value. The experimental subjects had had more experience with the poker chips. The drop to the pretraining level following extinction, however, provides evidence contrary to the familiarity argument.

In summary, the Bruner and Goodman hypothesis has received verification in both the Ashley, Harper, and Runyon and the Lambert, Solomon, and Watson experiments. The specifics of the original Bruner and Goodman results are perhaps not replicable. However, their general hypothesis of a relation between object value and perceived size seems to have been adequately demonstrated. There remains, though, the possibility that the relation is itself mediated by a learned association between size and value. An interpretation of this sort has been offered by Tajfel (1957), along with some supporting experimental evidence (1959).

11

Novelty and Complexity: Determinants of Preference and Affect

BACKGROUND

Efficient processing of information about their internal and external environments is of paramount importance to organisms in the struggle for survival. What we have treated so far of perceptual selection might be thought of as its utilitarian aspect: How does the perceptual system receive, select, and organize the information upon which adaptive behavior depends? Granted the importance of that question, we must be careful not to neglect an obvious but easily slighted aspect of perceptual functioning—one that we might call "nonutilitarian" in the sense that it bears no simple, immediate relation to the task of survival. But, as we shall see, if we ask, "Survival for what end?" then this aspect will turn out to be blatantly utilitarian and far from trivial.

Perception: Means or End?

In this chapter we shall review the wide variety of evidence which bears on the motivational and emotional properties of perception. Here, we view perception not as only a means to the end of adaptation, but also as *an end in its own right*. This review will carry us through such diverse topics as the exploratory behavior of a rat in a maze; curiosity in monkeys, chimpanzees, human infants, and adults; the perceptual determinants of surprise and fear;

and the emotional and cognitive effects of both extremely monotonous and excessively stimulating environments.

To impose some structure on this heterogeneous collection of material, we have organized the chapter around the conceptual relation between behavior broadly classified as "exploratory" and behavior instigated by the so-called "primary" or "physiological" drives, such as hunger and thirst. In the course of examining that relation, we will offer a particular theoretical model of exploratory behavior and cite some of the anecdotal and experimental evidence that bears on the model.

Curiosity and Primary Drives: Some Similarities

Casual observations of animals and human beings reveal the prevalence of behavior that seems appropriately labeled "exploratory." For those theorists who feel obligated to identify an underlying motive for each distinctive behavior pattern (as "hunger" is specified as the motive on which eating and related behaviors are based), exploratory behavior is typically associated with a motive variously labeled "curiosity," "stimulus-seeking," and so on.

Theoretical issues aside, it is clear that individuals do interact with a vast array of stimuli that appear to be unrelated to their immediate physiological needs and drives. Indeed, such interactions are likely to be most evident when the individual is not preoccupied with strong drives. At the same time, exploratory behavior does share some of the important characteristics of drive-instigated behaviors such as eating and drinking. Three of these characteristics are suggested below. Each, in turn, is then made the central topic of a separate section of this chapter.

Preference   First, it is quite evident that a hungry individual ordinarily will spend a great deal of time and energy seeking and ingesting food to the virtual exclusion of other potential behavior. A "curious" person or animal will similarly devote a considerable share of its behavior to making and maintaining contact with "interesting" stimuli. Of course, hungry people will literally consume the food which they encounter, whereas curious people merely inspect or manipulate the interesting stimuli which they have found. But what is clearly common to the two situations is the disproportionate amount of *attention* devoted to, or *preference* shown for, the motive-relevant object (technically, the *incentive* or *goal object*).

Reward   Second, it is well known that objects which reduce the intensity of a physiological drive such as hunger can serve as very potent rewards or reinforcers; their application following a response will increase the strength of the tendency to make that response on subsequent occasions. Whether all learning follows this principle (the "law of effect") is an unsettled issue. That drive-reducing objects are effective reinforcers is not, however, controversial.

And so one might ask of the "interesting stimuli" that are the incentives for exploratory behavior whether they also can function as reinforcers. For example, if one can train hungry rats always to turn left in a T-maze by reinforcing left turns with food, can one accomplish the same thing by providing an appropriate goal object following each left-turning response of a curiosity-motivated animal?

Emotional consequences   Third, severe deprivation of drive-reducing objects is quite likely to have serious emotional consequences. People whose important drives and motives are unsatisfied or otherwise blocked from expression are far from emotionally tranquil; they may be, to various degrees, uncomfortable, angry, furious, apprehensive, fearful, anxious, terrified, depressed, suicidal, and so on. Are there comparable consequences of preventing a person from having commerce with appropriate curiosity incentives?

ATTENTION AND PREFERENCE

We have already asked in Chapter 5, and to some extent answered the question, what it is that enables certain stimuli to attract attention. It is quite clear that stimulus *change* is an important determinant of perceptual preference. We will take up the concept of stimulus change, and its implications for an understanding of attention and exploration, following a brief discussion of a simple behavior pattern exhibited by rats and many other species, called *spontaneous alternation*.

Spontaneous Alternation

Suppose that a rat is placed in the starting alley of a T-maze and is allowed to enter one of the goal arms of the maze. The rat is then removed from the goal arm and is replaced in the starting alley for a second trial. The chances are very high that for this second choice the animal will enter the goal arm that had previously been rejected. The animal will rarely enter the same arm twice in succession. This switching from one alternative to the other is what is referred to as *spontaneous alternation*. What is the relevance of spontaneous-alternation behavior to a book on perception? The answer to this question will become clear as we trace the development of theories about alternation behavior.

Reactive inhibition   Until recently, the most widely held view was that alternation behavior could be completely explained via the concept of *reactive inhibition,* or I_r in the symbolic language of Hull's learning theory (1943). Reactive inhibition is a concept, borrowed from Pavlov, originally invoked to account for experimental extinction. When a learned response is no longer followed by reward, it eventually stops being performed: it undergoes experimental extinction. The extinction is explained as resulting from the buildup of a quantity of inhibition each time a response is made. The inhibition decreases the likelihood that the response will be repeated.

As long as the response is not rewarded, the strength of learning does not increase; each response that is made, however, adds to the amount of inhibition. Finally, when there is more inhibition than excitation present, the response ceases to be performed. In short, the occurrence of a response decreases the probability of its recurrence.

It is not difficult to see how the reactive-inhibition concept might be applied to the explanation of alternation behavior. A rat turns right in a T-maze. Right-turning inhibition is built up, but without reward there is no corresponding addition to habit strength. The right-turning inhibition is sufficient to tip the scales in favor of a subsequent left turn at the choice point.

Stimulus satiation   The I_r account of alternation stood until it was challenged by some simple but decisive experiments by Montgomery (1952) and Glanzer (1953). Both experimenters hypothesized that the rat's alternation was a manifestation not of response inhibition, but rather of some kind of perceptual inhibition. The rat was alternating stimuli, not responses. To test this hypothesis, Montgomery and Glanzer independently devised the following kind of experiment.

A cross-maze was employed instead of a simple T-maze. On any trial, however, the cross was used as a T—the top half of the cross on one trial and the bottom half on the other. Thus, if the rat approached the choice point from the south, for example, on the first trial, it would have to ap-

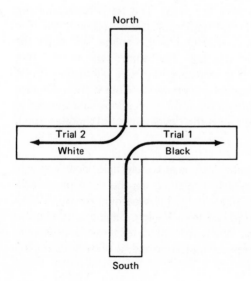

FIGURE 11.1 Schematic diagram of the stimulus versus response alternation test. If the rat is started from the south on the first trial, it is started from the north on the second. When one starting alley is used, the other is blocked by a gate, as represented by the dotted lines. The arrows indicate the behavior on two successive trials. On the first, the animal turned right, and thereby went into the black arm. On the second trial, the animal also turned right, thereby entering the white arm. Turning responses were repeated, but maze arms were alternated.

proach from the north on the second trial. The experimental arrangement is diagrammed in Figure 11.1.

Now, consider the following situation. Let the west goal arm be white and the east arm black. A rat approaches the choice point on the first trial from the south and enters the east, or black, goal arm. To do this, it makes a right-turning response. The rat is then removed from the goal arm and placed in the north starting alley, with the south alley, of course, blocked off. To alternate turning response, the rat must go left on this trial, since it had turned right previously. But a left turn will take it into the east, or black arm. Alternating turning responses in this situation means repeating goal arms. To alternate arms, the rat must repeat its previous turning response.

If Montgomery and Glanzer were correct in hypothesizing that rats alternate stimuli and not responses in the conventional T-maze situation, then this same behavior should also occur in the cross-maze experiment. The rats should alternate goal arms, even if to do so means repeating turning responses. And that is just what happened in both the Glanzer and the Montgomery studies. Similar results have since been obtained in other experiments (for example, Walker, Dember, Earl, and Karoly, 1955).

According to Glanzer's formulation, whenever an individual is exposed to a stimulus, a certain amount of *satiation* is built up for that stimulus, rendering the individual less responsive to that stimulus and to similar ones as well. Glanzer's satiation concept is analogous to Hull's reactive inhibition, except that the "inhibition" is associated with a stimulus, not with a response.

There have been several lines of development in research on alternation. The most recent concerns the exact identity of the stimuli which serve as cues for the alternation response. It is now well established that visual stimuli play a negligible role as alternation cues for rats. Two other classes of cues seem to be of much greater significance. These are (1) the odor trail which the rat leaves on the floor of the maze and (2) the rat's orientation in space, with the latter the more important of the two (Douglas, 1966). Indeed, there may be no simple generalization that will cover all species; thus, for gerbils, odor trail may be more potent than spatial orientation (Dember and Kleinman, 1973). Furthermore, the animal's sex may also be relevant (Brill, 1967). In any event, at a time when less was known about alternation, and the issues were relatively simple, it seemed worthwhile to follow up Glanzer's hypothesis that mere exposure to a stimulus (implicitly, a visual stimulus) is adequate to build up some satiation for it. One line of research was directed at testing that hypothesis.

Response to Change

Kivy, Earl, and Walker   As a very simple test of Glanzer's hypothesis, Kivy, Earl, and Walker (1956) conducted the following experiment. Rats were placed in the starting alley of a T-maze and were allowed to wander into the choice-point region. They were prevented from entering the goal arms, however, by means of glass partitions. The two goal arms were of the same brightness — for example, black. The arms could be seen by the animals, but not entered.

Exposure to the blackness of the goal arms should have decreased the rat's subsequent responsiveness to black arms. In particular, given a choice, following exposure of the sort described, between a black and a white arm, the rats should prefer the white. The results of the experiment confirmed that hypothesis.

Dember's experiment   An interpretation of the results somewhat different from the one offered by Kivy, Earl, and Walker led Dember (1956) to perform an experiment that was essentially the same as the one outlined above, except that the goal arms were equal in brightness on the choice trial and different during the exposure period. The modification in procedure was introduced as a way of allowing a test of Dember's interpretation of the Kivy, Earl, and Walker study. The animals in the latter experiment, so the argument ran, chose to enter the arm with the nonexposed brightness value because it was a *changed* arm, while the other remained unchanged. Thus, if both arms were black on the exposure trial, and then the animal was given a choice between a black arm and a white one, it entered the latter not because it was "satiated" for blackness, but because it was attracted by the change in brightness.

The response-to-change interpretation predicts the same behavior as the satiation hypothesis. With the modified procedure, however, it is possible to differentiate between the two interpretations. In the Dember experiment the animal is given a choice between two arms equal in brightness. From the satiation point of view, the rat should exhibit no preference for either arm, since it is equally satiated for both. The response-to-change position, on the other hand, would expect the rat to show a preference for one of the arms — that is, the one that had been changed in brightness from the exposure trial. For example, if on the exposure trial the left arm had been black, and the right arm white, and on the choice trial both arms were black, then the rat should enter the right arm. The experiment was conducted, and the response-to-change prediction was verified: 17 of 20 rats entered the changed arm. This result has subsequently been replicated by others (for example, Fowler, 1958; O'Connell, 1964; Walk, 1960; Woods and Jennings, 1959 — all with rats as subjects — and Hughes, 1965, with ferrets).

Though visual cues are unimportant for alternation behavior (either entirely so, according to Douglas, 1966, or relatively so, as suggested by Eisenberger, Myers, Sanders, and Shanab, 1970), they clearly operate in the response-to-change situation. This discrepancy poses a problem for the interpretation of alternation as a special case of a response-to-change tendency. It may thus turn out, as O'Connell (1964) has argued, that response to change and spontaneous alternation do not share a common psychological mechanism. Be that as it may, the phenomenon of response to change itself seems very well established, and it is nicely illustrative of the attention-attracting potency of an abrupt change in stimulation.

Novelty   The experimental operation of changing a stimulus object on one or more of its attributes has often been labeled one that produces *novelty*. It is frequently implied by those who use the term that novelty is a property of stimuli, independent of the perceiving individual. Such an assumption is obviously misleading. Novelty-producing operations can be performed without regard for their impact on the experimental subject, but without the subject the operations have no psychological meaning. Novelty must be thought of in terms of an interaction between stimulus and perceiver. In particular, it is instructive to think of novelty as involving a *discrepancy* between the individual's expectancy about and present perception of a stimulus. The usefulness of this way of thinking will become more apparent when we discuss later in the chapter the relation between novelty and another important concept, *stimulus complexity*.

Novelty and exploration   We have seen how rats are attracted by novel stimuli. Novelty produces not only an initial approach response, as in the T-maze studies, but it also keeps the animal investigating, or exploring, the novel stimulus object. That is, given a choice among otherwise equivalent objects, animals will spend their time examining novel objects in preference to thoroughly familiar ones. This function of novelty is nicely illustrated in experiments by Berlyne (1955) and Thompson and Solomon (1954) with rats, and by Welker (1956) with chimpanzees.

As part of a much larger series, Berlyne performed the following experiment. Three groups of rats were established, labeled F, N, and O. Group F, the familiarity group, was exposed for a period of 10 minutes on each of four successive days to a small wooden cube. The exposure took place in an otherwise empty box. On the fourth day, the animals in group F were placed in a new box following exposure to the cube, which itself was also placed in an alcove in the new box. The number of times each animal approached the alcove was recorded.

Group N, the novelty group, was tested in the same manner as group F, but the animals in group N had had no prior exposure to the cube. For these rats the cube was completely novel; for the group-F rats, the cube was familiar as an object, although located, on the test trial, in a new context.

Group O had had no experience with the cube before testing, and during the test trial the cube was not present in the alcove. The animals' approach responses to the empty alcove were recorded.

As expected, the animals in group N showed the greatest number of approach responses; group F was second; and group O third. The novelty of the cube attracted the group-N rats to the alcove. For the F rats, the cube was less novel, and the alcove therefore less attractive. The empty alcove was even less enticing to the rats of group O.

The influence of novelty on exploration and investigation is illustrated in an analogous way by Thompson and Solomon. In their experiment two groups of rats were used. All rats were exposed for 10 minutes to a pattern of vertical stripes. Following a 2-minute rest period, half the animals were again allowed access to the striped pattern, while half were presented with a novel pattern, a triangle. The experimenters recorded the amount of time the rats "sniffed at" the patterns, "looked at" them, and spent inside the box containing the patterns. It was found that the group tested with the triangle—the novel stimulus—was more responsive on all three measures than the group tested with the familiar striped pattern.

Some phylogenetic generality is added to the obvious conclusion drawn from the experiments on rats by the work of Welker with chimpanzees. For purposes of illustration we have again selected only one part of an extensive series of studies by Welker on play and exploration in the chimpanzee.

Over a period of many days Welker's chimpanzees were tested on a variety of stimulus objects. On a given day, the animals would be presented with a pair of objects and allowed to play with them for 6 minutes. The same pair of objects would be presented over several consecutive days, and then a new pair would be introduced. Our interest at this point is in three of Welker's findings.

First, there was a decline in amount of responsiveness, defined in terms of both manipulation and observation, within each day from the 1st to the 6th minute. This result is similar to that generally found in the exploratory behavior of rats.

Second, the chimpanzees' responsiveness to a given pair of objects increased from the end of one day's session to the beginning of the next. Some of the within-day decrement in responsiveness was temporary.

Third, when a new pair of objects was substituted for an old pair, the animals' responsiveness was greatly increased. Thus, there was some relatively permanent decrement in responsiveness associated with a pair of familiar stimuli.

On the basis of the experiments described here and others like them, the conclusion seems inevitable that novelty is an important determinant of initial attraction to a stimulus and continued responsiveness to it. The very same principle seems to hold for human subjects as well as animals.

Influence of novelty on human behavior   We need not go into the laboratory to be convinced of the influence of novelty on human behavior. The world of advertising, fashion, and entertainment is filled with examples. Of course, there are variables other than novelty that determine the attention-arousing and attention-maintaining value of a stimulus. These variables are often more powerful than novelty. A familiar but "good" style in clothing, for example, is likely to prevail over a novel but "poor" one. Nevertheless, with these other variables held constant, novelty certainly seems to be an important determinant of attention and interest in human beings.

Given the overwhelming anecdotal evidence available to us, it seems redundant to investigate novelty experimentally. And yet, experimentation can provide information otherwise unavailable. It is one thing to be convinced of the importance of novelty; it is another to know precisely how novelty operates, to know just what influence novelty does have, and to know exactly how novelty interacts with other variables. These details can be obtained only through carefully controlled and designed experimentation. Our own experience can suggest where to look and what to look for, but it cannot supply the precision necessary for the construction and testing of theoretical systems. Fortunately, a great deal of such research with human subjects has been done. Some illustrations of this kind of research are given below.

Attention to change   Berlyne (1951) performed some of the early studies on the effect of stimulus change on attention. The basic procedure involved presenting adult subjects, in a "familiarization phase," with one, two, or three identical stimuli. Following the familiarization phase, a novel stimulus was introduced, novelty being produced by a change in shape, color, or both. The subjects' task, throughout the entire experiment, was to respond to one of the stimuli currently presented by depressing one of three keys.

For example, in one experiment the subjects would be shown, in the familiarization phase, one, two, or three white circles, and were simply to press the key indicating which stimulus they had attended to. This phase, consisting of 48 such trials, was followed by two further phases of 48 trials each, during which a white square might be presented along with one or two of the original white circles. In another experiment the novel stimulus might be a red circle. Suitable control groups were run in which the stimuli of the familiarization phase were the same as those used in the second and third phases of the experimental conditions.

It was expected that the experimental subjects would, in the test phases, attend more to the novel stimuli than to the familiar ones. This result was also expected to be more prominent in the second than in the third phase. The results very clearly bore out these expectations. The behavior of the control subjects allowed the conclusion that it was *change* that was responsible for the results.

In a later experiment employing a somewhat modified procedure, Berlyne (1957a) obtained the same general result. When asked to respond to the stimulus they "noticed first," the subjects tended to select the novel member of a pair. The effect of novelty was absent in this experiment if, during the familiarization phase, the subjects were not required to perform the key-pressing response, but merely observed the stimuli, or if a 24-hour interval separated the familiarization from the test phase.

If it has not already become evident, you should note the very close similarity in procedure and results between the Berlyne experiments and the experiments on response to change in rats previously described. Concepts, methods, and results in this area of psychological investigation are remarkably generalizable across species. Moreover, the studies reported below, using human infants as subjects, add ontogenetic generality. This unusual state of affairs seems a strong argument that the processes being studied are indeed basic ones.

Response to novelty by human infants   Recent investigations of visual performance by human infants typically follow a general procedure developed by Fantz (for example, see Fantz, Ordy, and Udelf, 1962). In effect, an infant, lying supine in a crib, is presented with a pair of visual stimuli, as shown in Figure 11.2. If the direction of the infant's visual fixation is significantly biased toward one stimulus over the other, with stimulus position

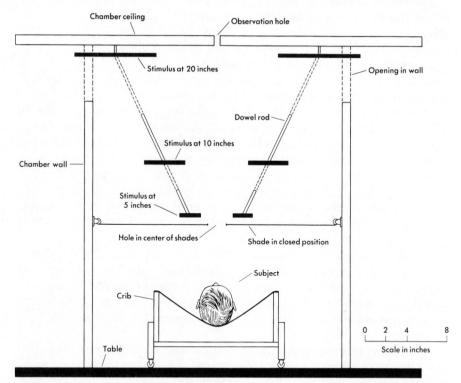

FIGURE 11.2   Schematic cross section through the middle of the testing chamber, with the stimulus objects used at the three test distances superimposed on the same drawing. The drawing is to scale except for the 1/4-inch observation hole. (After Fantz, Ordy, and Udelf, 1962)

controlled for, then it is a safe inference that the infant is able to discriminate between them.

This procedure has uncovered a remarkable degree of discrimination ability in very young infants: the infant's visual world is not the "blooming, buzzing confusion" posited by William James (1890). Moreover, infants exhibit reliable preferences for certain stimuli (to be described more fully later in this chapter) that appear to be based, at least in part, on stimulus complexity.

Directly pertinent to the present topic is the frequent finding that "looking time" tends to decline with continued, or repeated, exposure to a given stimulus. That this "habituation" of the looking response is stimulus-specific, rather than the result of a general decrease in responsiveness to all stimuli, is illustrated in a study by Saayman, Ames, and Moffett (1964), who used 3-month-old infants as subjects. Their experimental procedure was composed of three phases. (1) In a "prefamiliarization phase," pairs of stimuli were presented for two 30-second periods; stimulus positions were switched between periods, to control for possible position biases. Looking times for each member of a stimulus pair were recorded, allowing the experimenters to identify a set of preferred and a set of nonpreferred stimuli. (2) In a "familiarization phase," the infants were allowed to look for 4½ minutes at a single stimulus, either a preferred or a nonpreferred one. (3) Then, in a "postfamiliarization" phase, two 30-second preference tests were again administered, pitting a familiarized stimulus with one that differed from it either in color, in shape, or in both color and shape. If, for example, the familiarization stimulus was a red circle, it might be paired in the third phase with either a red cross, a black circle, or a black cross.

The results showed that looking time declined for all stimuli during the course of the 4½-minute familiarization phase—the typical habituation effect. Moreover, comparison of the results in the postfamiliarization phase with those of the first phase revealed an increase in looking time for the novel stimulus, provided that the familiarized stimulus had initially been preferred and that the novel stimulus differed from its mate in both color and shape.

Some discrepant results   There is a line of research, beginning with experiments by Zajonc and his colleagues (for example, Zajonc, 1968), which casts serious doubt on any monolithic view of the effects of novelty. This research demonstrates that under some circumstances it is the highly familiar stimulus, rather than the relatively unfamiliar one, that people prefer. For example, when asked to rate their liking for photographs of men's faces, people assign the higher ratings to faces to which they have been more frequently exposed.

Research addressed at accounting for these surprising results has uncovered some factors which limit their generality (for example, Stang, 1973; Zajonc, Swap, Harrison, and Roberts, 1971). Nevertheless, the basic data remain to be reconciled with what seem to be exactly opposite findings—in essence, that the overly familiar is boring and the novel is interesting.

One possible way out of this dilemma is to note that what the novelty literature emphasizes is not so much that novel stimuli are affectively pleasing as that they are attention-arousing. You may, for example, find yourself almost compelled to look at a grotesquely deformed person, but it is unlikely that you would give such a "stimulus" a high rating on a scale of "liking."

A second way of understanding the apparent preference for familiar items requires considering the factor of their complexity, a variable to be discussed more fully in the following section. That is, it may be that for relatively complex, multifaceted stimuli, repeated exposure enhances their attractiveness by allowing them to become better organized or understood by the subjects; only after some optimal level of familiarity has been achieved will additional exposure begin to make such stimuli seem less pleasant. In this regard, think what happens to a new piece of music. When it is first introduced, it may not be particularly appealing. But after you have heard it played several times (spread out over many days or weeks), you become very fond of it. However, after that point it will begin to lose its appeal if you hear it too often (see Heyduk, 1974).

It may also be that people (and animals) need access to some very familiar stimuli if they are to be able to handle the flood of stimulation continually impinging on them: they may need the comic strips in order to cope with the disasters and surprises on the news pages. In short, people may need access to both familiar and novel stimuli; in particular, novelty (and complexity) may appeal only in the context of a familiar, stable, comfortable environment. This seems to be the case, anecdotally, for people, and it has been convincingly demonstrated in experiments on animals; see, for example, the discussion of fear of novelty (*neophobia*) in rodents by Barnett (1963).

Stimulus Complexity

Two stimuli may be equally familiar, or novel, but one may still be more attractive than the other. Of the possible variables, besides novelty, one in particular has been identified as a major determinant of attention and exploration in both animals and people. This variable has been labeled *stimulus complexity.*

The exact definition of complexity has been the subject of controversy among psychologists, although agreement on an intuitive level is not lacking. Attempts at providing formal definitions have made use of the concepts of information theory (Glanzer, 1958), of conflict theory (Berlyne, 1957b), and even of Coombs's scaling theory (Dember and Earl, 1957). All of these definitions seem to share the general psychological assumption that the more complex stimulus is the one the individual can *do more with:* it affords more potential opportunities for responding than does the less complex stimulus.

This idea will become clearer as we examine some of the experimental operations that have been used in research in this area. Having looked at some of the experiments utilizing the complexity variable, we shall return to a theoretical discussion, and in particular show how complexity and novelty are related.

Preference for complexity by rats   One of the early sets of experiments that showed the influence of stimulus complexity on the behavior of rats was performed by Krechevsky. In one experiment (1937a) a Dashiell maze—an apparatus that has many correct paths to the goal—was employed. In such a maze an animal can exhibit behavior ranging from the stereotyped choice of the same path on successive trials to the very flexible selection of different paths on successive trials. Krechevsky found that normal rats tended to be more flexible than rats with cortical lesions.

In a second experiment (1937b) animals could arrive at the goal box via either of two routes. One route was simple and direct; the other was varied and took longer to traverse. Again, normal rats preferred to reach the goal over the path that offered variety, while the brain-damaged rats tended to select the simple, short path.

The brain-damaged rats could be enticed into a preference for the variable path if it were made shorter than the simple path. Under these conditions, the normal rats showed an even greater preference than before for the variable path (1937c).

We have identified the variable path as more *complex* than the stereotyped or direct path on the assumption that it provides the rat with more to see and more to do. In the experiments by Krechevsky, normal rats showed a decided preference for the more complex path. Analogous results have been obtained in a study by Havelka (1956). In this study rats were allowed to obtain food reinforcement in either of two ways: (1) They could take an unobstructed route to the goal, or (2) they could choose a route which contained a problem, and access to the goal required the rat first to solve the problem. Somewhat surprisingly, rats preferred the problem-containing alternative to the unobstructed one. In a similar vein, rats have been shown to prefer to press a bar to obtain food rather than simply to obtain it "free" from a cup—at least if not too many bar presses per food pellet are required (Carder and Berkowitz, 1970).

Further evidence of rats' preference for complex stimulation is provided in a study by Dember, Earl, and Paradise (1957). In this study the complexity variable was confined to a visual manipulation. The study also contains evidence on the way in which preference for the more complex stimulus develops with experience.

Two experiments were performed, similar in basic design but different in certain other respects. The general procedure involved allowing rats free access to two contiguous circular pathways, joined together so as to form a figure-eight. Translucent ceilings and floors kept out extraneous visual stimuli, but enabled the animals' wandering in the maze to be traced and recorded by the experimenter, who was sitting beneath the maze.

In the first experiment, each rat was allowed a period of about 45 minutes in the maze on each of two successive days. The two pathways were made different in visual complexity by lining their walls with different patterns. The walls of one path were lined with black and white stripes oriented in a vertical direction; the other path was decorated with similar stripes oriented horizontally. In terms of the total amount of black and white, the two paths were identical. It was assumed, however, that the path with the vertically striped walls was visually more complex than the other; it contained more discontinuities in illumination per rat length than did the horizontally striped path.

A complete record was kept of each rat's location in the maze during the entire period of the experiment. To facilitate data analysis, each day's record was divided into successive 2-minute periods. It was then determined, for each period, in which path the rat had spent the greater amount of time. A "vertical" and "horizontal" score could then be assigned to each rat, the score representing the number of 2-minute periods during which a preference was shown for one or the other path.

On the first day, 9 of 17 subjects showed a significant preference, and two showed an almost significant preference for the more complex path. Two subjects showed a significant preference and one an almost significant preference for the less complex path. The remaining three subjects failed to show a preference for either path which approached significance.

Of particular interest is the fact that of the 13 rats that could be classified, without regard to significance, as having an initial vertical preference, only one shifted to a preference for the horizontal on the second day. On the other hand, all four of the rats with initial horizontal preferences shifted to a vertical preference on the second day. This result is in conformity with the prediction: *"Any change in preference will be from the less to the more complex path."* (Dember, Earl, and Paradise, 1957, p. 514.) We shall have more to say about the theoretical basis of this prediction later in the chapter.

In the second experiment, 16 new animals were run for 60 minutes per day on five consecutive days. One path was lined with horizontal stripes, as before, and the other path was either homogeneously white or black. Here it was assumed that the path lined with horizontal stripes was the more complex.

On the first day, eight of the sixteen rats preferred the more complex path; all eight maintained their preference over the succeeding four days. Of the eight rats that initially preferred the less complex path, four shifted to the more complex on the second day, and the remaining four shifted on the third day. No subject regressed to a preference for the less complex path, again in accord with the prediction quoted above.

Complexity and attention in the chimpanzee We have already referred to an experiment by Welker (1956) in connection with the influence of novelty on play and exploration. In that same experiment the effect of stimulus complexity was also studied. Many of the pairs of stimuli offered to the chimpanzees could be ordered on relative complexity. Using time spent examining each object of a pair as a measure of preference, Welker reports that significant preferences were exhibited and that these "preferences were predominantly to the more movable, larger, brighter, more heterogeneous, and changing (auditory, visual) stimulus configurations" (p. 88). At least three of the characteristics Welker mentions—movable, heterogeneous, and changing—seem to fit our conception of complexity as a variable related to the opportunity which an object affords for responding.

Complexity and attention in human infants and adults Two experiments by Berlyne add further support to the idea that stimulus complexity is an important determinant of attention. In one study (1958b) the subjects were human infants, from 3 to 9 months of age. The procedure very simply involved placing two stimuli before the infant and noticing which one was looked at first. The stimuli consisted of four sets of three cards each. Within a set, six pairs of stimuli could be formed, making 24 pairs in all over the four sets. Each subject was tested twice on each of the 24 pairs, with stimulus position varied between replications.

For two of the sets, the stimuli could be ordered, intuitively, with respect to relative complexity. In each of these sets, the most complex stimulus was preferred to each of the other two. Initial fixation was the measure of preference. An illustration of one of the sets of stimuli is given in Figure 11.3 from which it should be possible to see how an *a priori* ordering on complexity can reasonably be made.

Though Berlyne's results seem consistent with expectation, the experiment itself might have been more informative if something beyond initial fixation had been observed. For example, it would have been possible to mea-

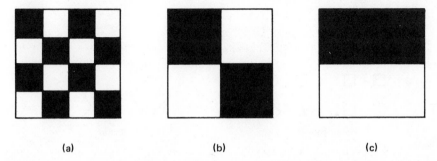

    (a)   (b)   (c)

FIGURE 11.3   A set of stimuli varying in complexity, with (a) the most complex and (c) the least. (After Berlyne, 1958b)

sure how long each stimulus was fixated over a period of minutes, analogous to Welker's measure, and perhaps how soon the subjects lost interest in each pair of stimuli.

The second experiment on complexity (Berlyne, 1958a, 1966), in which subjects were human adults, has already been mentioned in Chapter 5. The procedure was similar to that of the previous complexity experiments in that the subject was presented with pairs of stimuli and visual fixation was noted. Here, however, both initial fixation and total fixation over a 10-second period were measured. The subjects, incidentally, were told that the experiment was on "number-estimation ability."

The stimuli were grouped into six categories, with four pairs of stimuli in each of five categories and two pairs in the sixth. Each category was meant to represent a different aspect of complexity. For each pair within a category, it was possible to order the two stimuli on complexity. The six categories were labeled: irregularity of arrangement, amount of material, heterogeneity of elements, irregularity of shape, incongruity, and incongruous juxtaposition (see Figure 5.2). One pair from each of the first four categories is shown in Figure 11.4. Incongruity was exemplified by such figures as an elephant's massive head on a very fragile body, incongruous juxtaposition by a rabbit's head forming the front part of an automobile. From the illustration it should be apparent how the ordering between stimuli was made and how these categories are appropriate to the general conception of complexity expressed in this chapter.

The results of the experiment were as clear-cut as could be desired. Initial fixation failed to be related to the complexity variable, mainly because of a strong tendency on the part of the subjects to fixate first to the left, as in reading. However, the measure of total time spent looking at each figure was

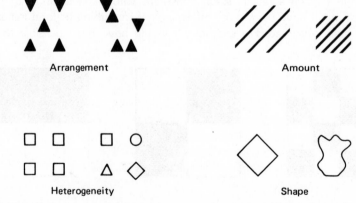

FIGURE 11.4 Four pairs of stimuli varying in complexity; the right-hand member of each pair is the more complex. (After Berlyne, 1958a)

consistently greater for the more complex member of each pair. This was true for each of the six categories, with the heterogeneity category showing perhaps the most pronounced effect.

Though a preference for the more complex stimulus is revealed in his data, Berlyne is careful to point out that the "more complex" stimuli were not extremely complex. Stimuli that were "too complex" might not be preferred. This is a point to which we shall return shortly.

Novelty and complexity   Novelty and complexity are variables that influence attention and exploration. The operations for manipulating these two variables are different. In the case of novelty, the operation involves exposing the individual to a stimulus and then presenting the stimulus again with a modification on one or more attributes. Psychologically, this kind of operation entails creating an expectancy and then failing to confirm it.

In the case of complexity, the operational procedure is single-stage; there is no explicit pre-exposure period. Stimuli varying in complexity are selected by the experimenter on certain *a priori* grounds and are presented to the subject. The *a priori* grounds are difficult to summarize in physical terms, though Berlyne's experiments provide excellent illustrations of what is involved. The psychological basis of complexity seems clearly to lie in the fact that some stimuli potentially convey more information than others. As we have stated earlier, the individual can do more with some stimuli than with others.

Despite superficial differences at the operational level, it is apparent that novelty and complexity are not different psychologically. Novelty is based on temporal change; complexity, at least in some instances, is based on spatial heterogeneity. But spatial heterogeneity can be thought of as a special case of temporal change, induced as a complex stimulus is scanned.

In other instances, complexity is based on incongruity. Here, too, the equivalence between complexity and novelty is evident. Incongruity, after all, involves a discrepancy between present perception and expectancy derived from past experience. The pre-exposure which is employed to create discrepancy in the case of novelty operations is not necessary in the case of complexity. Implicit expectations which the individual brings to the situation are substituted for explicit set-inducing operations.

In short, novelty and complexity can be thought of as psychologically equivalent variables. Both have as their basis a discrepancy between expectancy and present stimulation. The expectancy may arise from the individual's experience outside the laboratory, or it may derive from recent experience with different parts of the experimental stimuli themselves.

If we grant that novelty and complexity are different operations for activating equivalent psychological processes, and that they produce equivalent behavioral effects (see Stang, 1977, for further details), we see that any stimulus might have both novelty and complexity as sources of attractiveness. In general, sheer novelty should be less durable in effectiveness than complexity. Even complex stimuli, however, should lose their attractive power once they have been thoroughly investigated. The most interesting painting, for example, cannot be viewed interminably. The finest symphony, if repeated often enough, becomes banal and commonplace. The best book cannot bear continual rereading.

Of course, it is the essence of a lasting artistic creation that it contain fresh surprises upon each new presentation. For this to occur, however, it is necessary that the perceiver be capable of discovering these previously hidden facets of the work. The attractiveness of an object is a function both of its own complexity and of the ability of the individual to appreciate its complexity. In brief, the *effective complexity* of a stimulus cannot be evaluated independently of the "complexity" of the responding individual.

The Dember-Earl Theory

The ideal level of complexity Suppose that the members of a set of stimuli can be discriminated from one another on the basis of their complexity. Suppose further that the individual is free to respond to any of these stimuli. It seems intuitively obvious that some of the stimuli will be responded to in preference to others. That is, some of the stimuli may be too simple to arouse more than brief interest; others may be too complex to deal with in any satisfactory manner. Some stimuli, however, will be just complex enough to be attractive. It is with these stimuli that the individual will spend the most time. Each individual can be thought of as having a preferred complexity level, or an *ideal* complexity level. The ideal complexity level is characteristic of the individual at a given moment in time and with respect to specific stimulus attributes.

Across individuals, the ideal will vary. What is too simple for an adult may be just right for a child. What is too complex for the novice may be ideal for the sophisticate.

How do individuals come to have different ideals? The answer seems to be: through experience. With hereditary capacities held constant, two individuals will have different ideals as a function of differential contact with the appropriate stimuli. It is through experience with certain kinds of stimuli that an individual's ideal can change and, in particular, increase. What are these crucial stimuli?

Pacers According to a theory proposed by Dember and Earl (1957), the stimuli that serve the function of increasing the ideal are those that are slightly more complex than the individual's momentary ideal. These stimuli are called *pacers*. In effect, through contact with a pacer, an individual's ideal, on a given attribute, is moved toward the value of the pacer—that is, it is moved up in complexity value. As long as there are suitable pacers available, the individual's ideal complexity level will continue to increase up to whatever limit is imposed by hereditary endowment.

Note that complexity changes occur on specific attributes. An individual may be moving up on one attribute while remaining stationary on another.

The theory sketched above led to the previously described experiment by Dember, Earl, and Paradise (1957). It should now be apparent why, in that experiment, the prediction was made that shifts in preference, if they occurred, would be in the direction from simple to complex.

Tests of the Dember-Earl theory   Subsequent to the publication of the Dember and Earl model several experiments have been reported, some explicitly for the purpose of testing its validity and generality, others relevant, but conducted within somewhat different theoretical frameworks. Theory aside, the general outcome of this substantial body of research is a strong confirmation of the importance of the complexity variable for animal and human behavior.

In an elaborate experiment (Musselman, 1963), rats were tested in a maze with five choice compartments. The general procedure was composed of two phases. First, a rat would be put in the apparatus with the walls of all five choice compartments decorated the same. The walls were lined with either a homogeneous (black or white), a black-and-white-striped, or a black-and-white-checkerboard pattern. Following 12 minutes of exposure to a given pattern, the animal would be removed, the two outermost compartments would be blocked, and the walls of two of the three remaining compartments would be redecorated so that the animal was faced with a choice among a homogeneous, a striped, and a checkerboard pattern. In the second phase of the procedure, then, the rats would be allowed to enter one of the three compartments. Of interest was the relation between the stimulus pattern present during the exposure phase and the pattern selected by the animal on the choice trial.

Two important assumptions must be mentioned before a summary of the results can meaningfully be presented. First, the experimenter assumed that the three patterns—homogeneous, striped, and checkerboard—are ordered, as listed, from low to high complexity; a similar assumption was made, you will recall, by Dember, Earl, and Paradise. Second, it was assumed that the 12-minute exposure to a given pattern was an adequate procedure for assuring that the subjects were psychologically at the corresponding level of complexity on the test trial.

Given the above assumptions, and the conception of choice behavior already alluded to in our description of the Dember and Earl model, Musselman was able quite successfully to predict the rats' behavior. Consider, for example, animals exposed to the checkerboard pattern; among those that do not choose the checkerboard in phase two, more should prefer the striped than the homogeneous stimulus, and that is how the results turned out. Similar predictions were made (based on an analysis too elaborate to present here) and verified for other combinations of adaptation and test stimuli.

The major weakness in Musselman's research is his reliance on his own rather than his subjects' assessment of the complexity values of the stimuli. This problem has been tackled in an experiment that employed cats as subjects. Thomas (1969) developed a method for obtaining relevant complexity measures from each of his subjects through a scaling procedure. He was able to make and test predictions about stimulus selection for each cat individually. The pattern of results fit remarkably well the predictions based on the Dember and Earl model.

Returning to research on human subjects that bears on the model, we can note a class of experiments requiring *preference judgments* rather than direct measures of differential commerce with stimuli. A few illustrative studies are described below.

One line of research (Munsinger and Kessen, 1964) employed "nonsense" figures. Figure complexity was manipulated by constructing the borders of the figures with varying numbers of "turns," a turn being a point where the border of the figure changes direction. Twelve complexity levels were used, ranging from 3 to 40 turns in approximately logarithmic steps. Some examples are given in Figure 11.5.

The figures were projected in pairs, and the subjects (high school or college students) were asked simply to indicate which of the two figures in each pair they "liked better." These choices were obtained for all pairs and the results transformed to yield a preference score for the stimuli at each of the 12 complexity levels. In general, figures with an intermediate number of turns (8–13) were the most preferred. However, exceptions did occur at both extremes of the complexity range—that is, for both the three- and four-turn stimuli and the figures in the 25–40-turn range, all of which had excessively high preference scores. Additional data collected to determine possible bases for these departures from prediction suggest that the three- and four-turn figures were being evaluated on a dimension other than complexity, perhaps because they were the only figures for which subjects had a readily available verbal label ("triangle," "quadrilateral"). Furthermore, though the stimuli were intended to be nonsense figures, subjects' spontaneous comments indicated that parts of the highly complex figures "looked like things." A formal experiment was conducted to assess the possible contribution of this factor to the preference judgments. Pairs of figures (over the range of 5–40 turns) were presented and the subjects' task was to choose the one that was the "more meaningful." It turned out that judged meaningfulness was highest for the most complex figures, again suggesting that the preference scores of those figures reflected something else besides complexity *per se*.

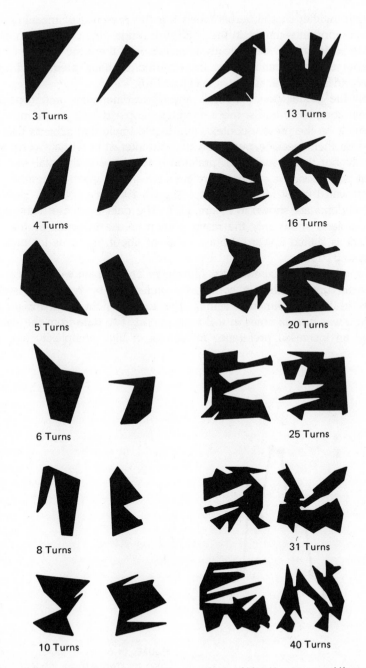

FIGURE 11.5 Examples of stimuli varying in complexity. (After Munsinger and Kessen, 1964)

Where neither special verbal labels nor the presence of meaningful sub-parts are important—that is, in the 5–23-turn range—the contribution of complexity to preference is most clearly revealed. And there the relation between complexity and preference takes the inverted U-shape predicted from the Dember and Earl model, as shown in Figure 11.6.

Now the model, you will recall, attends to differences among people in their own complexity levels: more complex people should prefer more complex stimuli. In the present context, that would imply that subjects who were selected for their special experience with, and interest in, visual figures should show a higher than usual peak preference for the experimental stimuli. To test that prediction, the standard preference task was given to a group of art students, with the full range of complexity (3–40 turns) covered. Results for the art students are shown in Figure 11.7. The data for these highly sophisticated subjects show only the rising portion of the inverted U; their peak preference is shifted upward, from a value of about ten turns for unselected subjects to 31 turns.

In another set of experiments, Munsinger and Kessen were able to demonstrate an upward shift in complexity preference by repeatedly exposing subjects to the experimental stimuli. For example, the standard judgment procedure was run six times in a 2-hour period. The data from the sixth trial revealed an increased preference for stimuli of high complexity and a de-

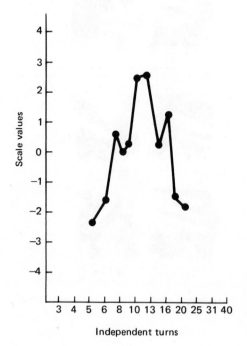

FIGURE 11.6 Scale scores of preference for asymmetrical random shapes varying in number of independent turns from 5 to 23. (From Munsinger and Kessen, 1964)

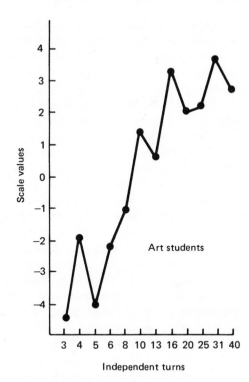

Scale values

Art students

FIGURE 11.7 Scale scores of preference of art students for asymmetrical random shapes varying in number of independent turns from 3 to 40. (From Munsinger and Kessen, 1964)

Independent turns

crease for low-complexity figures, though the peak preference itself remained at the typical 10-turn value.

In their main features, then, the Munsinger and Kessen experiments yielded data remarkably consistent with predictions that follow from the Dember and Earl model. Similar results have been reported by Vitz (1966a, 1966b), using visual figures in one case and auditory patterns in another, and by Dorfman and McKenna (1966), again with visual figures. Confirmation of the model and further extension of its generality have also been provided in the results of an experiment by Kammann (1966), who used poems as stimuli and an innovative approach to the problem of measuring both subject and stimulus complexity.

Kammann employed a procedure known as the Cloze technique (Taylor, 1953). In essence, this technique involves presenting to subjects passages of written material (in Kammann's research, poems) from which every nth word has been deleted. The subjects are asked to fill in the blanks—that is, to complete the passages by replacing the missing words. For example, suppose you were asked to fill in the blanks contained in the following very familiar lines: "Jack and Jill __ up the hill __ fetch a pail __ water." This would be an easy task, because the line is so familiar and the style so simple. The task would be much more difficult if the lines were taken from the work of an obscure poet who used highly unconventional poetic forms.

Kammann argued that the difficulty of the Cloze task reflects the overall complexity level of a passage; similarly, a person's ability to perform the task reflects that person's own complexity level for such material. Thus, looking at the data from the point of view of the subjects' performance, we find that the greater the number of correct responses made by a given subject to the set of incomplete poems, the more complex is that subject.

To examine the relation between poem complexity, individual complexity, and preference, it is then only necessary to obtain a preference measure from each subject for each of the intact poems. Kammann obtained ratings of the "goodness" of the poems, as well as less direct indicants of preference, from the same college-student subjects who performed the Cloze task. In general, the group data showed the inverted U-shaped relation between poem complexity and preference expected from the Dember-Earl model. Furthermore, the complexity level of the most preferred poems was highly correlated with individuals' complexity measures.

The Cloze technique has subsequently been used with prose passages, and results similar to Kammann's have been obtained (Evans, 1970). That is, subjects rated passages of intermediate complexity as most pleasing and most preferred. In addition, the Cloze measure itself was validated against subjective ratings on a "simplicity-complexity" scale.

The experiments cited so far, and many others, both confirm the predicted relation between complexity and preference and also attest to its generality over a wide range of stimulus materials and types of subjects. It should also be noted that the shape of the relation between complexity and "preference" depends on the nature of the measure of preference employed. For example, "looking time" tends to increase monotonically with increasing stimulus complexity (for example, Nunnally and Lemond, 1973), whereas "pleasingness" judgments tend to follow the inverted U-shaped function (for example, Aitken, 1974; Murray, 1975). Nevertheless, the potency of complexity as an influence on preference has been more than amply demonstrated.

THE REWARD VALUE OF COMPLEXITY

Task and Species Generality

Of the various types of learning situations, *instrumental learning* is characterized by the acquisition of a response pattern that is instrumental in providing the learner with "reward." The kinds of reward ordinarily employed in experiments on instrumental learning are those that help to reduce a primary drive, or "tissue need." Typical rewards are food, water, and shock reduction. Secondary, or acquired, rewards have also been used in the study of instrumental learning; these are rewards with value derived from their previous association with primary rewards.

It has become increasingly clear that primary and secondary rewards are not the only commodities that can facilitate instrumental learning. In particular, it has been shown in a variety of species, and with a variety of techniques, that instrumental learning can be acquired with nothing more than exposure to "stimulus complexity" as the rewarding condition. The kinds of stimulus situations we have already seen influencing attention and exploration can also serve as rewarding operations for instrumental learning.

Bar-pressing for stimulus change   We have noted that rats will attend to a change in the environment. Even more interesting is evidence that rats will perform responses to *produce* such changes. It has been shown, for example, that rats will learn to press a bar if the response is followed by a change in illumination (for example, Kish, 1955). The bar-pressing behavior observed in these experiments is of the same form as that observed in experiments utilizing conventional rewards. Similar results have been obtained with monkeys (Moon and Lodahl, 1956). They, too, will learn to press a bar when the only reward is either the onset or the cessation of illumination.

Running for stimulus change   Along with bar-pressing, running down a straight alley is a favorite response for observation by contemporary experimenters in the area of learning. An increase in running speed over rewarded trials is taken as evidence of learning. Though here, too, the rewards conventionally employed are primary-drive reducers, it has been found that stimulus novelty can also do the job. Thus, Mote and Finger (1942) obtained some evidence of increased running speed over trials where the only reward was apparently provided by the experimenter's interchanging goal boxes between trials. The effect in this experiment was not very striking, however, probably because of the intrinsic simplicity of the goal boxes. As we have indicated, sheer novelty is not likely to serve as a very durable reward, particularly when it is produced by the repeated interchange of the same two stimuli.

Simple maze performance and exploratory rewards   The simple Y- or T-maze has also been widely popular as a device for studying learning in animals. Learning is usually indicated by the animal's consistent selection of one of the alternatives, the one designated by the experimenter as correct. Again, primary-drive reduction has been the usual rewarding operation in such experiments. And again, rats have been shown to learn in these situations for clearly "exploratory" rewards. Three experiments are especially pertinent in this connection.

Montgomery (1954) reported an experiment in which rats would find, at the end of one arm of a T-maze, a complex stimulus situation and, at the end of the other arm, a simple stimulus situation. The complex stimulus was a large Dashiell maze which the rats could investigate. The simple stimulus was a small empty goal box. Learning was exhibited by the rats both through their increasing selection of the arm leading to the Dashiell maze and by their increased speed in running to the goal.

In a subsequent experiment, the animals had to learn a black-white discrimination in order to select the arm with the complex maze appended (Montgomery and Segall, 1955). That is, the reward — opportunity to investigate the Dashiell maze — was associated with the brightness of the goal arm rather than its location, as in the previous study. Despite the increased difficulty of this problem, these rats also showed evidence of learning. Their selection of the correct arm increased over trials.

Complexity in the Montgomery experiments may have been nothing more than "spaciousness." The Dashiell maze may simply have afforded the rats greater freedom of movement than the small goal box at the end of the incorrect arm. If true, this interpretation would leave the results of the experiments still of interest, but of limited generality. An experiment by Berlyne and Slater (1957), however, has shown very similar results, with spaciousness held constant between the two goal stimuli. One alternative provided a richer perceptual situation than the other, but the two were otherwise equivalent, particularly with respect to opportunity for locomotion.

It seems clear that stimulus complexity can serve as a reward for simple maze-learning in rats. The same result has also been obtained with kittens as subjects, and either manipulation or exploration the only rewards (Miles, 1958).

Learning in the shuttle-box   An apparatus for studying escape and avoidance behavior in animals, called the *Miller-Mowrer shuttle-box,* has yielded further evidence of learning based on exploratory reward. The box is composed of two compartments that may be separated by a barrier or a door. The animal is shocked in one compartment and must learn to escape or avoid the shock by moving into the other, safe compartment. To do this, it may be necessary simply to cross over from one to the other, to leap over a barrier, or perhaps to press a bar that opens the door between compartments. With such an apparatus Miller (1948) and others have extensively studied the acquired drive of fear.

An attempt by Myers and Miller (1954), using the shuttle-box, to demonstrate an acquired drive based on hunger was not successful. The data, however, indicated that learning had taken place in the rats. The learning was based, so it seemed, on an exploratory reward.

A new experiment was designed to test this hypothesis. It was found that naive animals, satiated for food and water, would learn to press the bar that opened the door and allowed them access to the other compartment. Various controls made it clear that the effective reward in this situation was the novelty of the unoccupied compartment.

Discrimination learning in monkeys   The rewarding power of stimulus complexity has been demonstrated in monkeys with both visual and auditory goal objects. The animals, for example, learned a color-discrimination problem whose solution caused a peephole to be opened, allowing the monkeys a brief look at various visual stimuli. Such stimuli as a moving electric train were used, or simply the adjoining experimental room with its attendant activity (Butler, 1953). The monkeys' performance was remarkably persistent; they would keep at such a task for several hours without apparent satiation (Butler and Harlow, 1954). In a similar experiment, monkeys were trained to press one of two levers, this time for a chance to hear brief selections from a recording of noises in a monkey colony (Butler, 1957).

The persistence of the monkeys' behavior in these experiments makes it unlikely that the visual and auditory rewards were effective because of any secondary reward value they might have had. If that were the case, the reward value would be expected to decrease, through extinction, over trials.

Non-nutritive sucking in human infants   The sucking response is high in the human infant's behavioral hierarchy, and it will occur even in the absence of nutritive consequences. It has been demonstrated (Siqueland and DeLucia, 1969) that the rate of such non-nutritive sucking can be increased by reinforcing sucking with visual stimulation. Furthermore, having once been established, high sucking rates can subsequently be reduced by imposing an extinction procedure—that is, by omitting the visual reinforcement.

Two studies were reported by Siqueland and DeLucia. In one, the subjects were 4 months old, an age when sucking is prepotent. A nipple was placed in the subject's mouth; the nipple was so constructed that it could be used to record the amount of pressure exerted by the infant each time it sucked. The experimenters established as a criterion for reinforcement a pressure amplitude higher than that typically emitted by infants of this age. Then, whenever a sucking response occurred that was of sufficiently high amplitude, a slide projector was activated and a picture appeared on a screen in view of the infant; the faster the rate at which the infant emitted such high-amplitude sucking responses, the brighter the picture became. The pictures serving as reinforcers were of geometric forms, cartoon drawings, and human faces, all in color. Eight pictures were used with a new picture being presented every 30 seconds to preclude loss of reinforcement value through habituation. This reinforcement procedure proved highly effective, and suitable control conditions allowed the conclusion that the change in sucking rate so effected was indeed a manifestation of instrumental learning.

In a second study, the subjects were 12 months old. By that age non-nutritive sucking is low in the behavioral hierarchy; in fact, for many 12-month-olds the nipple proved aversive. Nevertheless, using the same reinforcement procedure as in the first study, the experimenters were again able to modify the rate of high-amplitude sucking in ways that closely parallel those found with conventional reinforcers.

Stimulus Complexity and Primary Drives

It is evident that stimulus complexity can serve as a rewarding operation in the establishment of instrumental learning. In this respect complexity functions in a manner similar to that of the so-called primary rewards. For this reason, it seems sensible to hypothesize that the two types of operation have a common psychological basis.

Add one more drive to the list?   In accord with such a hypothesis, some experimenters have attempted to fit the two into a single category by considering complexity as merely another primary reward. More exactly, an exploratory drive is postulated, and complexity is treated as the reward appropriate to that drive, just as food is the reward associated with the hunger drive.

An effort at integration   There is another, and more interesting, way to integrate the two types of rewarding operation within a single system. That is, it is possible to locate the conventional primary drives and rewards in the framework of a theory that holds stimulus complexity and exploratory behavior to be central concepts. One virtue of this approach is that it may provide a satisfactory psychological explanation of the obvious power of the primary drives and rewards. The alternative approach has never successfully dealt with the question of how the primary rewards function. Their effectiveness has largely been taken for granted.

From the present point of view, the primary rewards can be thought of as having at least two aspects. In the first place, being stimuli, they have complexity values. An "interesting" meal is no different, in this respect, from an interesting concert. And the tastiest dish, served at every meal, will soon lose its appeal.

Second, primary rewards decrease or eliminate the stimulation arising from the primary drives. Hunger, thirst, and electric shock have characteristic perceptual concomitants. Consider hunger pangs, for example. They are, phenomenally, intense, persistent, structurally simple, and consistent in quality from one occasion to the next. In short, they are terribly boring as stimuli, and terribly familiar. But being intense, they cannot be ignored. You can drop a dull novel, turn off the television set, leave the theater, buy a new record; there is only one way to get rid of hunger pangs, and that is by finding food and ingesting it. Once that is done, you can return to your quest for ideal stimulation.

EMOTIONAL EFFECTS OF NONOPTIMAL STIMULATION

Inadequate Stimulation

Given free choice, an individual will attend most to stimuli with near-ideal complexity values. Occasionally, attention may revert to very simple stimuli, but not for long. What happens when simple stimuli are imposed on a person? The consequences of forced attention to simple stimuli are striking and unequivocal: intellectual disruption, severe emotional disturbance, and even hallucinations.

Anecdotal evidence from a variety of sources has long pointed to these effects. Such evidence can be found in the reports of prisoners in solitary confinement; in the reports of Arctic explorers; and, more recently, in the experiences of radar operators, forced to stare continuously at an unchanging screen, and of truck drivers on long night trips over straight highways through barren country.

Sensory-deprivation experiments This interesting anecdotal evidence has received experimental support in some research originated in Canada by Hebb and his colleagues and followed up in a host of other laboratories. The original experiment was reported by Bexton, Heron, and Scott (1954).

College students were recruited as subjects and paid $20 a day to serve in the experiment. The amount of money they could earn in this way was substantially larger than they normally could have earned outside the laboratory. The subjects, therefore, were highly motivated to remain in the experiment.

At first glance, their task seemed not only unforbidding, but even pleasant. They simply had to lie in a bed, in a small isolated cubicle, with their eyes covered by translucent goggles, their hands in gloves and encased in cardboard cuffs. Their bodily needs were to be taken care of, and they could leave the experiment whenever they requested. Many subjects saw their participation as a lucrative means of catching up on some much needed rest, and of doing some leisurely thinking. It promised to be a pleasant holiday.

It turned out quite otherwise. The subjects did sleep in the beginning of the experiment, but sleep was soon replaced by the disturbances mentioned above. As described by the experimenters:

Later they slept less, became bored, and appeared eager for stimulation. They would sing, whistle, talk to themselves, tap the cuffs together, or explore the cubicle with them. This bordeom seemed to be partly due to deterioration in the capacity to think systematically and productively. . . . The subjects also became very restless, displaying constant random movement, and they described the restlessness as unpleasant. Hence it was difficult to keep subjects for more than two or three days. . . . (Bexton, Heron, and Scott, 1954, p. 71).

The subjects' intellectual deterioration was assessed by a variety of simple tasks, such as arithmetic problems, anagrams, and block-design problems. On all of these tests the experimental subjects were inferior to controls.

Even more dramatic than this intellectual impairment was the unexpected but widespread occurrence of hallucinations that were mainly visual in content, and ranged from very simple geometric patterns through single objects (for example, "a row of little yellow men with black caps on and their mouths open") to complex, dreamlike scenes (for example, "prehistoric animals walking about in a jungle").

The experimenters report that the subjects were initially amused and entertained by their hallucinations. This suggests that the hallucinations may have served to replace the missing and much desired perceptual variety normally provided by the environment. For some, however, the hallucinations became unpleasant, and may have been responsible for part of the general emotional disturbance expressed by most of the subjects.

For practical reasons, the sensory deprivation provided by the conditions of the Bexton, Heron, and Scott studies was only relatively thorough. More rapid and intense effects have been obtained in experiments where control over the environment was more complete. Lilly (1956) for example, reported vivid and very disturbing hallucinations very soon after total immersion in a pool of water. Under these conditions, stimulus variability was reduced to a minimum (see also Shurley, 1960).

The original sensory-deprivation studies stimulated a great deal of subsequent research, much of it devoted to teasing out the specific variables that are operative—for example, whether the concomitant social isolation is an important factor in subjects' responses to the situation, whether the reported hallucinations are suggested to the subjects by the experimenter or would occur anyway, whether there are systematic differences in the way different people react to the deprivation situation, and so on (see, for example, Corso, 1967; Solomon and Mendelson, 1962; Zubek, 1969). Closer to the central issue of this chapter are experiments in which isolated subjects are allowed to perform an operant response to obtain doses of visual stimulation of various degrees of complexity (e.g., Jones, Wilkinson, and Braden, 1961). Without going into the details of these experiments, it is sufficient to note that sensory deprivation is a manipulation with considerable emotional impact. In that respect, deprivation of adequate sensory input parallels deprivation of commodities, such as food, conventionally considered to be incentives for primary, or physiological, drives.

Marasmus and autism   The results of the sensory-deprivation experiments very convincingly support the idea that perceptual variety is basic to the motivational and emotional states of the individual. People, so it appears, are strongly motivated to seek out stimulation of ideal complexity; when forced by circumstances to attend to stimuli that do not provide enough complexity, they become bored, restless, and miserable.

This point of view may provide some insight into a phenomenon observed by Spitz (1945) in certain institutionalized infants. For a variety of reasons, some institutions for orphaned and foster children made a practice of raising infants under conditions that, in some respects, resembled those of a sensory-deprivation experiment. The infants were isolated from each other, their cribs enclosed by white sheets, and contact with adults was minimal. They had no toys to play with, no mobiles to look at, not even any interesting wallpaper to study.

Many such infants developed what has been called *marasmus*. They became apathetic, emotionally unresponsive, listless; their physical and intellectual development was subnormal, and indeed a large number of them simply seemed to give up and die.

Now, the interpretation offered by Spitz for this severe emotional and physical disturbance is based on psychoanalytic concepts. The infants, according to this interpretation, were deprived of love, and it was to this type of deprivation that they reacted.

Though such an interpretation may prove valid, it seems reasonable, from the present point of view, to suppose that at least some of the disturbance arose from sheer sensory deprivation. Two days of monotony were enough to drive many of the Bexton, Heron, and Scott subjects out of the experiment. Six months of rather extensive stimulus deprivation might be expected to have an even more severe effect on the delicate emotional and physical development of the human infant. Indeed, it may well be that for the infant, a loving mother is in large part a rich supply of perceptual input. Such a hypothesis has been seriously entertained (see, for example, Casler, 1961) both for the type of children studied by Spitz and others (for example, Bowlby, 1951; Provence and Lipton, 1962) and for children with a similar type of psychopathology, *early infantile autism*. Autistic children are variously described, but certain diagnostic signs are fairly commonly employed, chief among them being the child's aloofness from and lack of responsiveness to human relationships, failure to use language as a means of communication, highly stereotyped behavior and a compulsive effort at maintaining an external environment that is unchanging and ordered in simple, repetitive patterns. The etiology of this affliction is still unknown (more than three decades since it was described by Kanner in 1943); however, one formulation argues that the autistic child lacks in its early environment the "varying, novel, patterned stimulation" that adequate mothers normally provide (Ward, 1970, p. 361).

The notion that adequate mothering means adequate sensory stimulation is partly supported in the well-known research of Harlow and his associates, who have studied the developmental consequences of raising infant monkeys with different types of surrogate mothers (for example, Harlow, 1958; Harlow and Suomi, 1970). For example, it turns out that it is more important for an infant's emotional well-being that its surrogate mother provide "contact comfort," through a soft "skin," than that she be a source of milk. However, even the best inanimate mothers are not enough to assure normal social and sexual development. For these, infant monkeys need access, if only sporadically and briefly, to living members of their own species (Harlow, 1962). Even so, one could argue that what distinguishes living from inanimate monkeys is the living monkeys' ability to provide a much more complex and responsive environment with which to interact. In any event, it is clear that a severely restricted early environment is likely to have later pathological consequences, in the emotional sphere, whether for the developing monkey or for the human being.

Excessive Complexity

We have seen how forced exposure to stimuli that are not sufficiently complex for the individual can lead to emotional and intellectual disruption. Stimuli can also be too complex for an individual. Ordinarily, as with simple stimuli, such stimuli would be avoided in favor of those with near-ideal complexity. The emotional impact of such stimuli, however, can be studied in situations where individuals do not have complete control over the stimuli with which they make contact—that is, in experimental situations. Effects of too much complexity seem to vary from mild surprise and disruption to discomfort, anger, and fear.

Surprise and disruption It has already been demonstrated how novel stimuli lead to attention and exploration. At the same time, novelty may have slightly disruptive consequences, with *surprise* as the phenomenal concomitant and slight disorganization of ongoing activity as the behavioral manifestation. Desai (1939), for example, found that stimuli which clashed with expectation tended to increase reaction time and to interfere with the smooth operation of motor performance.

An even more severe disruption of fluent performance and a greater emotional effect are illustrated in experiments with a special kind of technique for creating discrepancy between perception and expectancy. These are experiments utilizing what is called *delayed speech feedback*.

Whenever you talk, you are also ordinarily aware of your own voice: your speech returns as auditory feedback. The feedback, through experience, is strongly associated with speech movements. That is, there is a powerful implicit set established such that certain speech movements are expected to be followed, almost immediately, by certain auditory patterns. Interference with these feedback patterns is one way of producing set-perception discrepancy.

A particularly effective form of manipulation is to delay the onset of the feedback; this can be done rather easily with modern tape-recording and electronic instruments. The effects of delayed feedback are very dramatic. Behaviorally, most subjects exhibit a marked slowing down of speech, the maximal effect occurring with a delay of about 0.18 seconds. Most subjects also show more severe forms of speech disturbance under conditions of delayed feedback, such as "blocking of speech, facial contortions, the prolongation and slurring of sounds, and repetitions of sounds and syllables" (Black, 1951, p. 58). Their speech resembles that of the worst stutterer. In addition, subjects report considerable surprise and frustration (Lee, 1950).

Rage and fear   Under circumstances somewhat difficult to specify, too much complexity, particularly as it arises from set-perception discrepancy, can lead to reactions of rage and fear. For example, the first performance, in 1913, of Stravinsky's *Rite of Spring* is said to have incited a near-riot among the outraged audience because of its wildly novel style. Innovations in automobile or dress styles often lead to much more emotional reaction than they deserve. That it is novelty, and nothing intrinsic to the style itself, which causes the disturbance is evidenced by the ultimate acceptance, at least emotionally, of the initially rejected innovations.

Some fascinating experimental observations in this area have been made by Hebb. In his work with chimpanzees, Hebb discovered that he could elicit profound emotional reactions by presenting seemingly innocuous stimuli. To quote from Hebb:

> I discovered accidentally that some of the chimpanzees of the Yerkes colony might have a paroxysm of terror at being shown a model of a human or chimpanzee head detached from the body; young infants showed no fear, increasing excitement was evident in the older (half-grown) animals and those adults that were not frankly terrified were still considerably excited.[2]

These observations were followed up by Hebb, using such objects as "an isolated eye and eyebrow, a cast of a chimpanzee's face, a skull, a cured chimpanzee hide, an anesthetized chimpanzee." Reactions to these objects included general excitement, fear, avoidance, aggression, and sometimes "apparent friendliness" (p. 243).

Hebb points out that, to similar stimuli, human beings exhibit behavior very similar to that of the chimpanzees. The best monsters of horror movies, for example, are those that are similar to familiar creatures, but deformed or grotesque in certain features. To be really effective, emotion-arousing stimuli must elicit conventional expectancies and then fail to confirm them in unexpected ways. (Hebb, 1949, p. 243).

12

Perceptual Development

The many perceptual phenomena we have discussed so far are assumed to be typical of the adult human being. Certainly the data from which perceptual principles have been induced were taken largely from the standard subject pool of psychological research, that is, college students, graduate students and sometimes the researchers themselves serving as their own subjects. Now, there are no logical grounds on which to expect that the results of research on adult subjects will not generalize to immature individuals; however, there are many precedents, both within and outside of psychology, for anticipating that what is true of the adult may not hold, in all respects, for the child. For example, we take for granted the intellectual differences between adult and child, both in terms of content and style; the adult knows more, has greater intellectual "power," and even thinks differently. Similar differences pervade other areas of psychological functioning, as for example are revealed in a comparison of the emotional and motivational repertoires of children and adults.

BACKGROUND

We refer in general to those changes which are presumed to occur as the newborn grows into an adult as *developmental*. The term "development" in

418

this context is theoretically neutral. It does not "take sides" on the ancient philosophical issue of whether those psychological changes which accompany aging are the product of what happens to the individual as time goes by or whether they simply reflect the unfolding of genetically determined, "built-in," or, to use the modern jargon, "programmed" modifications in structure and function. Development, then, may imply changes attributable either to experience and consequent *learning,* or to those which are identified as the result of *maturation*—or indeed to both.

The Nature-Nurture Controversy

Is there any basis in fact for reference to "perceptual development"? If so, is it possible to segregate the potential contributions of learning and maturation to whatever instances of perceptual development might be uncovered? It is the burden of the present chapter to consider these two questions. You might already suspect that the answer to the first question is yes, if only because we have devoted a separate chapter to the topic of perceptual development. The second question is the harder and the more interesting one to grapple with. Indeed, it may be that any attempt to isolate maturational from experiential factors in any psychological domain will prove futile. Be that as it may, the concern with that question has motivated a great deal of fascinating research which might otherwise not have been done. Before examining the research efforts and their products, we might first look in somewhat greater detail at the historical antecedents of the main question, which conventionally is referred to as the *nature-nurture* or the *nativism-empiricism issue.*

Empiricism   The position known as empiricism, in its most radical form, would assert that all mental contents are derived from experience. Empiricism, as a philosophical tradition, is primarily identified with a line of British thinkers, including such well-known figures as Thomas Hobbes, John Locke, Bishop Berkeley, and David Hume, and spanning the 17th and 18th centuries.

Locke expresses the essence of empiricism in his "Essay on the Human Understanding," a volume devoted to the general problem of *epistemology,* or how one can have valid knowledge of the external world. We can know nothing, Locke argues in the following passage, without the intervention of experience; there are no innate mental elements, or "ideas" in Locke's terminology; the mind is initially a *tabula rasa,* a blank tablet on which experience makes its imprint:

Let us then suppose the mind to be, as we say, white paper, void of all characters, without any ideas; how comes it to be furnished? Whence comes it by that vast store which the busy and boundless fancy of men has painted on it with an almost endless variety? Whence has it all the material of reason and knowledge? To this, I answer, in one word, from experience; in that all our knowledge is founded, and from that it ultimately derives itself. (Locke, 1690, Book II, Ch. 1, paragraph 2).

Locke goes on to say that there are two sources of experience, one sensations and the other the operations which the mind performs on these sensations. Reference to this latter source of experience — the mind watching itself work — perhaps takes Locke out of the category of pure empiricists, since the mental operations he alludes to (e.g., comparison of two sensations) must be "built-in." Nevertheless, these operations would have no opportunity to be observed if they were not fed by sensory inputs, so that ultimately it is experience aroused by external objects which predominates in mental development.

Now, in the ordinary course of living, sensations do not arise in a random, helter-skelter fashion. Rather, they tend to come in clusters or in ordered sequences. Thus, the presentation of an apple to the sense organs gives rise to a complex of sensations, e.g., redness, smoothness, roundness, in the visual modality, along with, perhaps, typical odors, tastes, tactual sensations, and even sounds if the apple is not only seen but also held in the hand, bitten into and chewed. By virtue of their simultaneous occurrence these many sensations tend to become organized into a total percept through a process of *association*. As a result of the association of these sensations the percept, apple, takes on a close correspondence with the real object, apple. In this way, complex percepts come to mirror faithfully the objects in which they originated.

A similar association takes place in the case of sequences of sensory elements which occur with some regularity. Thus, events which in the physical world are highly interdependent generate their mental counterpart, through the simple process of association, in the person who has experienced them.

It is association, then, which imposes order on what would otherwise be perceptual and intellectual chaos if experience alone were the only determinant of mental development. Empiricism and associationism thus are both necessary characteristics of the Lockean position: experience is the source of mental elements, and association puts them together in patterns that reflect the way their physical counterparts are organized.

Nativism   The empiricist-associationist philosophy was developed in opposition to a strong nativist tradition, expressed by such philosophers as Plato and in Locke's own time and later by Descartes, Leibnitz, and Kant. In general, the nativists argued that certain categories of knowledge were built into the human intellect and did not depend for their existence or development on the vagaries of individual experience. For example, Plato argued that education consisted not in implanting knowledge, but rather in drawing out, through skillful questioning, what was already latent in the intellect. The other nativistic philosophers agreed with Plato that certain ideas were intrinsic to mental functioning, such as the axioms of geometry, basic spatial and temporal concepts, and so on. But just as Locke was unable to hold to a purely empiricist position, a strictly nativistic philosophy has also proved untenable. Thus, empiricism and nativism are not polar opposites, but rather should be thought of as labels for systems in which one or the other source of knowledge predominates.

Whatever its merits as a legitimate philosophical issue, the nativism-empiricism controversy has had considerable impact on psychological theory and research. The research, at least, can be evaluated on its own merits, leaving aside the philosophical-theoretical motivation behind it. In this chapter, then, the primary emphasis is on the data which are available that relate to perceptual development, as well as on the methodological approaches which have been developed to study the topic. Where it seems appropriate, the pertinence of the data to the nature-nurture issue will be pointed out.

Some Methodological Considerations

Longitudinal and cross-sectional designs If the research question is posed in terms of whether some perceptual phenomenon shows developmental trends, then the research strategy is quite straightforward, in principle if not in practice. One simply examines the phenomenon in subjects who are otherwise comparable, but who vary in age. Two ways of making age-related comparisons are conventionally employed in developmental studies of all sorts. First, the same subjects can be studied at frequent intervals as they get older; this is the *longitudinal* approach. It has the advantage of allowing subjects to serve as their own controls, and hence problems of adequately matching subjects on variables other than age can be bypassed. The primary disadvantage of the longitudinal method is that repeated measurements on the same persons may introduce changes in them that ordinarily would not have occurred. This problem is especially salient in the case of intelligence measurement, but it is potentially present even in such innocuous-appearing contexts as those involving the measurement of basic perceptual processes. It is a psychological fact of life that in observing people we often change them.

An alternative to the longitudinal method, and one that gets around the problem just mentioned, is the *cross-sectional* method. Here, groups of subjects are sampled at each of several ages, and a given subject appears in only one group. A further asset of the cross-sectional method is that there is not the danger of losing subjects that characterizes the longitudinal method. A person who has served as a subject in a cross-sectional study is of no further interest to the researcher. But in a longitudinal study, the identity of each subject must be preserved from one age point to the next. It should also be apparent that a longitudinal study must take as long to complete as the age range it covers. If a wide age range is desired, the only convenient way to gather the data—while the researcher still retains interest in the problem—is via cross-sectional investigations. One major liability of cross-sectional investigations is that the subjects in the several groups differ not only in chronological age, but also with respect to the particular years in which they were born and raised. Thus, what may appear to be age-related differences may in fact reflect differences in the "social climate" prevailing during the subjects' development.

Experimental manipulations It is a fair generalization to assert that most developmental research in psychology has relied on cross-sectional designs. There are some exceptions, however; for example, a study by Witkin, Goodenough, and Karp (1967) used a combination of the two approaches.

If the researcher wishes to go beyond the demonstrations of a developmental trend, and attempts to segregate innate from learned components of a perceptual phenomenon, then other methodological problems must be faced. In particular, it becomes necessary to regulate certain aspects of the developing individual's experience so that the impact of the experimental variable can be assessed. For example, it may be pertinent to control the amount of experience a young infant has with color, or with two- or three-dimensional visual patterns. The several barriers to accomplishing such control, both practical and ethical, should immediately be apparent.

As for the practical problems imposed by an attempt to establish quantitative variation in amount of visual experience in different subgroups of experimental subjects, one solution has been to establish only a few gross categories and sometimes just the two endpoints, *normal* experience for one group and *no* experience for another. A variation on this procedure has been to contrast a normal-experience group with one that is offered an *enriched* environment. In some research the three conditions are employed—impoverished, normal, and enriched experience. We will describe below some experiments representative of these approaches.

Ethical issues But what about ethical problems? Is it legitimate to tamper with the normal experience of a developing human being, especially when the consequences are unknown? Indeed, if they were known, there would be no need to do the research. There are two ways of circumventing the ethical issue. One is to use animals as subjects, and much of the research requiring manipulation of the subjects' early environment has followed this route. The other is to take advantage of "nature's experiments," i.e., instances which mimic conditions that an experimenter might want to establish, but which have occurred for reasons outside the experimenter's control.

For example, certain people might have been reared in unusual environments, for medical, socioeconomic, or cultural reasons, or perhaps because of parental idiosyncrasies. If one could assess their perceptual functioning and compare it with control subjects, then inferences might be drawn about any relation between early experience and perceptual development. One of the most fruitful of the studies to be discussed below—von Senden's investigation of visual perception in persons born blind who had vision restored through surgical techniques—is of this sort. Another to be mentioned is a cross-cultural comparison of visual illusions by Segall, Campbell, and Herskovits (1966), who were able to study people in certain African tribes reared under unusual visual conditions—conditions that might be expected to affect particular illusory phenomena if those phenomena are, at least in part, the product of learning.

Indicator response   Finally, with regard to issues of methodology, is the problem of the *indicator response*. If, for example, one is to study perception in young infants, by what means can one find out about how the child perceives certain stimuli? Clearly, verbalization, both by the experimenter (who might need in some way to "instruct" the subject) and by the subject, is precluded. The same, of course, holds for animals. In what follows, you might be alert to the several ways in which this major methodological problem has been faced.

VISUAL PERCEPTION IN THE HUMAN INFANT

One can investigate the perceptual system of the human neonate without any special interest in the nature-nurture issue. However, it seems a fair assumption that very little, if any, learning can have occurred prenatally, at least in the case of vision; if so, then neonatal performance must closely reflect the innate component of perceptual organization. Thus, what studies there are of neonatal perception easily lend themselves to interpretation in terms of that issue. How much significance one wants to attribute to the data from such research does depend, though, on how much time one is willing to let lapse between birth and the first measurement of perceptual performance. How old can a neonate be (in minutes, hours, days?) before it has had too much experience to be considered perceptually naive? Depending on the answer to that question, the research mentioned immediately below will be more or less relevant to the nature-nurture issue. Fortunately, the human infant is sufficiently fascinating so that whatever we find out about it is intrinsically of interest, regardless of its bearing on any particular theoretical controversy.

Pattern Discrimination and Visual Acuity

Discrimination learning   As suggested earlier, a major barrier to the study of perceptual processes in infants is posed by the lack of an easy medium of communication between subject and experimenter. This same problem characterizes attempts to work with animals. In the case of animals, a standard solution to the problem of communication has been to employ some sort of simple, learned response on the part of the animal; the experimenter's "instructions" take the form of providing or withholding rewards, depending on the animal's response. For example, suppose the issue is whether rats can discriminate a circle from a square. How might one go about finding this out?

One procedure might be to employ a *jumping stand,* as depicted in Figure 12.1. The rat, after considerable taming and pretraining, is placed on a small perch and encouraged to jump through one of the two available "windows" located several inches from the perch. After jumping through a window, it lands on a platform behind the window and is given the opportunity to eat a small amount of some highly preferred food. Once the animal is freely jumping, the open windows are gradually occluded, until eventually the rat must jump into and knock over the window covers in order to land on the platform and get the food. After this response has been acquired, the window covers, previously equivalent, are visually differentiated. On one a black circle is located, and on the other a black square. Furthermore, one of these is designated by the experimenter as "correct" and the other as "incorrect." If the rat jumps at the window cover containing the correct form, say the circle, the cover falls over as usual, and the rat gets to the food; however, whenever it jumps at the cover containing the incorrect form—in this example the square—the cover fails to fall over. The rat does not get the food on that trial; moreover, it may receive a painful bump on the nose. Clearly, if the rat is going to continue jumping, it is to its advantage to attend to the two forms (which are switched randomly from one window to the other by the experimenter) and learn to jump to the correct one.

Now, exactly how animals come to make the appropriate response in a discrimination-learning situation is an unsettled theoretical question, but fortu-

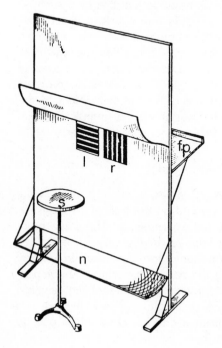

FIGURE 12.1 A jumping stand, used to test rats' discrimination abilities. The animal is induced to jump from the stand, s, at one of the covered windows, l and r. If it chooses the correct pattern, the window cover falls over, and it gains access to food on the food platform, f.p. An incorrect choice results in a bumped nose and a fall into the net, n. (From Lashley, 1930)

nately one that is not relevant to the present discussion. What is relevant is that the rat's consistent performance of the correct response implies that the two forms have been discriminated; without the discrimination, the correct response could not be performed.

We have described the discrimination-learning paradigm in sufficient detail so that its potential applicability to the problem of assessing the perceptual capacities of the human neonate should be apparent. It may also be evident, however, that there are practical impediments to its use. For one, the technique requires that the organism be capable of acquiring the response which serves as the indicator of discrimination. Even if there were some readily established response of this sort, its use in the discrimination-learning situation would require the imposition of a schedule of rewards and nonrewards (or perhaps "punishments") that might not be in the infant's best interest. For a variety of reasons of this sort, discrimination-learning techniques, as well as others taken from the repertoire of the learning laboratory, such as Pavlovian conditioning, have not been as useful as they might seem on superficial examination. Fortunately, in recent years alternative procedures have been developed which have already proved fruitful. Instead of relying on learned, or perhaps more appropriately, "trained" responses, these techniques take advantage of naturally occurring tendencies to respond differentially to stimuli which vary along dimensions of interest to the researcher, such as form and color.

Natural preferences   One of the psychologists who has pioneered in the development of this kind of perceptual indicator is Robert Fantz; his approach, as you will recall, was described in Chapter 11, in connection with research on infants' reactions to novelty.

In essence, the Fantz technique consists in displaying pairs of visual stimuli and noting the amount of time the infant spends fixating each member of a pair. If a reliable preference is exhibited, then the inference is made that the infant has indeed discriminated between the two stimuli. Reliability of preference can be assessed in various ways, as for example by determining whether the proportion of a group of subjects who devote the majority of "looking time" to a given member of a stimulus pair is significantly greater than would be likely to occur by chance. An analogous analysis can be performed on the behavior of a single subject if the data are properly obtained.

What is of prime concern here is the successful use of the Fantz technique with very young children. In the case of neonates and somewhat older infants, an apparatus like the one shown in Figure 11.2 is employed. The infant lies comfortably on its back and views the stimuli which are located at the top of the apparatus; the experimenter observes, or perhaps photographs, the infant's eyes to determine where it is looking.

The results of one of Fantz's early experiments are given in Figure 12.2, along with examples of the kinds of visual stimuli which can be discriminated.

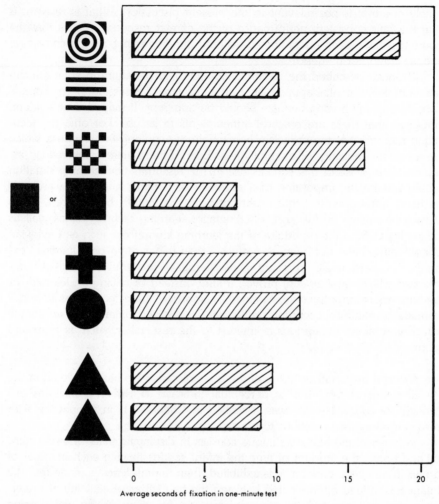

Average seconds of fixation in one-minute test

FIGURE 12.2 Various pairs of visual patterns used to assess infants' ability to discriminate forms. The results show a preference (greater duration of fixation) for the more complex patterns. (From Fantz, 1961)

Evidence of discrimination based on form is available, via the Fantz technique, for neonates as young as 10 hours (Fantz, 1963). While there may have been some opportunity for perceptual learning to have taken place even in that brief time period since birth, it would seem from such evidence that a considerable degree of perceptual organization is already present at birth in the human being.

Visual acuity The preference technique has been used to investigate other aspects of visual discrimination in infants. Fantz, for example, studied acuity in that way, based on the following rationale. In general, stimuli containing internal contours tend to be preferred over homogeneous stimuli. A striped rectangle, for example, would elicit longer looking times than a uniformly gray rectangle. Now, a physically striped stimulus will appear uniform if the stripes are sufficiently narrow to exceed the limits of the observer's acuity. Thus, if an infant is faced with two stimuli, one striped and the other homogeneous, any preference for the former will disappear at that point where the infant's acuity is no longer adequate to distinguish between the two stimuli. In this way, preference can be translated into an indicator of acuity.

Fantz's research, based upon the above logic, revealed a considerably greater degree of visual acuity in infants than many had previously suspected. While the data show that acuity does increase with age, they also indicate acuity to be quite respectable in very young infants—that is, 20/200 at about 2 months of age and 20/100 at 4 months (Fantz and Ordy, 1959; Fantz, Ordy, and Udelf, 1962).

Color

Some classical studies of color preference   Differentiation among visual stimuli according to hue is an important property of adult human visual functioning. Elaborate methods have been developed for the purpose of investigating color discrimination in adults. Unfortunately, these methods are not readily transferable to young children, and a variety of special techniques has been developed to determine simply whether color discrimination is present or absent in the very young.

The most successful of the several methods is one which, like the Fantz procedure, enlisted the infant's natural preferences for certain stimuli over others. Indeed, this method, as employed by Staples (1932), antedated Fantz's somewhat more sophisticated version by more than two decades.

One major methodological problem in research on hue discrimination arises from the fact that lights of different wavelength vary not only in hue but also in apparent brightness. Thus, a green light appears brighter than a blue one of equal physical intensity. Should an infant prefer one colored stimulus over another, or one colored stimulus over an achromatic stimulus, the preference may indicate a response to brightness differences rather than to hue differences.

Now, enough is known about the relation between wavelength and brightness (expressed as the *luminosity* or *visibility function;* see Figure 2.6) for adults that it is possible, at least in principle, to equate the apparent brightness of two chromatic stimuli, or one chromatic and one achromatic stimulus, by adjusting their relative intensities. That procedure was followed in Staples' experiments. However, there is no luminosity function available for infants, and so the equation procedure must rely on the adult luminosity function. To do so, of course, requires assuming that the adult luminosity function is essentially the same as that for infants.

As a supplementary control for possible contamination of her data by brightness differences, Staples tried varying the intensity of some of the stimuli along with variation in wavelength. It was her conclusion that brightness differences of the magnitude in question have little if any effect on preference. This conclusion is supported by the results of some experiments by Chase (1937), who found that infants would visually track a moving spot of light if the spot differed in hue from its background, but not if it differed only in brightness.

If one accepts Staples' precautions as adequate, then her main results support the assertion that young children — in her study as young as 2 months — differentiated each of the four hues, red, yellow, green, and blue, from gray. In a group of older children, from about 6 months to 2 years old, the child's reaching toward one of the stimuli with its hands was used as the indicator response instead of visual fixation. Again, colored stimuli were preferred to gray, with the degree of preference increasing with age.

Of course, even if the gray had been preferred to colored stimuli, the conclusion concerning discrimination would remain the same. It is interesting, however, that color is an effective attention-getter. In this regard, Staples' data indicate that yellow and red are more preferred than blue and green, especially for the younger children. A further refinement of those relations is made possible by the results of still another study, again with children from about 6 months to 2 years in age, in which the various colors were paired with each other, rather than pitted individually against gray. The rank order of preferability, induced from the children's reaching responses, is red, yellow, blue, green. Changes in that ordering are noted among older children and adults in a subsequent investigation, so that, for example, elementary-school children yield the order blue, red, green, yellow.

It has been argued by Bornstein (1975) that infants' preference for colors is mediated by the amplitude of neural excitation, or perhaps by the rate of neural firing, stimulated by varying wavelengths. Bornstein, citing DeValois, Abramov, and Jacobs (1966), points out, in support of this hypothesis, that within the lateral geniculate nucleus of the thalamus the firing rates of single neural cells are maximal when stimulation is provided by lights in the blue, green, yellow, and red regions of the spectrum. Individual cells, of course, respond maximally only to one of these colors. As noted above, and as indicated by the results of highly sophisticated research by Bornstein and colleagues (for example, Bornstein, Kessen, and Weiskopf, 1976), color preference in infants is also strongest in those regions. These and related data imply that color preferences, as well as the way colors are categorized, are largely determined by built-in differential neural sensitivity to different wavelengths of light, rather than by cultural and/or linguistic factors, as suggested by the Whorf hypothesis (see Chapter 9).

Through careful theoretical analysis, examination of existing cross-cultural data, and collection of new data, Rosch (1977) has convincingly shown an impressive degree of uniformity in color perception across a wide variety of different cultures. She distinguishes between "focal" and "nonfocal" colors. The former are colors chosen by people when asked to select from a large array of color chips those colors which best represent "basic" color terms in the language of a given culture. Basic color terms, in turn, are defined according to a set of linguistic criteria. For example, a basic, by contrast with a secondary, term has only one unit of meaning ("blue" as compared with "navy blue") and refers only to colors and not also to objects ("yellow" as compared with "lemon"). First, it turns out that no language investigated contained more than 11 basic color terms, of which 8 refer to chromatic experience and 3 to brightness. Second, there is considerable uniformity in the color chips which people choose when asked to select representatives of these eight basic chromatic color terms. It is these colors which Rosch referred to as "focal." Finally, the focal colors turn out to be the same across diverse cultures (for example, Berlin and Kay, 1969). The cultural-linguistic differences which anthropologists and others have noted do indeed still occur, but not with regard to focal colors. The differences have to do with where people in different cultures locate boundaries between colors. Thus, the cross-cultural evidence, when gathered and interpreted properly, supports the conclusion from developmental studies that basic color experience derives from a built-in, essentially fixed neural coding system.

SUSCEPTIBILITY TO VISUAL ILLUSIONS

Types of Illusions

So far, the fixation-preference technique exploited by Fantz and others for investigating perception in infants has been successfully applied only to a limited number of phenomena. Developmental studies of other aspects of human perception have relied on conventional methods, and hence also have been restricted to older children. Nevertheless, these experiments have turned out to be quite fruitful, by virtue of the considerable changes in perception which continue to occur well beyond infancy. The topic of developmental susceptibility to visual illusions is a good case in point.

Some examples   There seem to be two classes of illusions, from the developmental point of view. One class is characterized by a decrease in the illusory effect with increasing age (though there may be a reversal in this trend with very old subjects), while in the other class the illusory effect increases with age (see Wohlwill, 1960). Instances of the first type are such classical illusions as the Poggendorff (for example, Leibowitz and Gwozdecki, 1967) as illustrated in Figure 7.23 in Chapter 7. An example of the second class is the size-weight illusion, wherein the apparent weight of an object is influenced by its perceived bulk. Thus, of two boxes, equal in weight, the larger will seem the lighter. Another example of the second type is the *Usnadze illusion*, as depicted in Figure 12.3. As noted in the legend of the figure, the illusory effect is dependent on the integration of visual elements which are presented successively.

Possible bases   One way of understanding the difference between the two classes of illusions is to consider the first class (where the effect declines with age) to be the product of the young child's inability to segregate elements from each other; the illusion occurs because of the failure on the part of the immature organism to prevent the interaction among elements that yields illusory effects. On the other hand, the second class of illusion is dependent for its occurrence upon an integrative act on the part of the organism. In the case of the Usnadze illusion, the two items, in order to interact, must be "put together" by the observer; otherwise, their temporal separation negates any tendency for them to influence each other. Similarly, the size-weight illusion is dependent upon the presence of expectancies that large objects typically are heavier than small ones; these expectancies, in turn, are built on the kinds of experience of which the older person has had more than the younger.

A basis for illusions of the second class is not hard to imagine. The fascinating issue relates to the developmental processes which underlie the relationship typified by the illusions of the first class. Why does the older person segregate elements to a greater extent than the young child? We will return to that question after describing in some detail one particular phenomenon of the class-one variety which has been studied extensively by Witkin and his collaborators and which has generated a great deal of interest among those concerned not only with perception, but with the broad topic of personality development (Witkin, Dyk, Faterson, Goodenough, and Karp, 1962).

Field-Dependence and Independence

Measurement and generality   The term "field-dependence" was coined by Witkin to characterize a group of adult subjects who performed in an extreme fashion on a simple perceptual task. Subjects were placed in a dark room and saw nothing but a luminous, square frame within which was a luminous rod, as shown in Figure 12.4. The subjects' task was to align the rod with the vertical—for example, to make it parallel to the flagpole outside the lab building. On some trials, the rod would be set by the experimenter to the

FIGURE 12.3   The Usnadze illusion. The two small circles are presented alternately with the large circle. The latter makes the small circle it encloses seem even smaller. Susceptibility to this illusion increases with age.

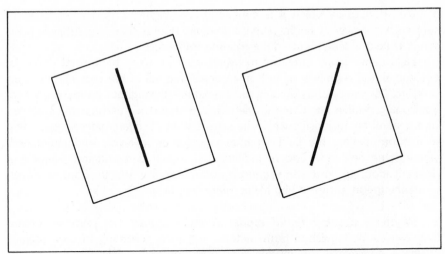

FIGURE 12.4   Schematic drawing of the kinds of stimulus situations facing subjects in the rod-and-frame test. The task is to set the rod to the true vertical. Field-independent people are those who can do so despite the misleading context provided by the tilted frame.

left of the true vertical, on others to the right, with the extent of deviation also varied from trial to trial. Following verbal instructions from the subject, the experimenter would then rotate the rod until it appeared to the subject to be properly aligned. Furthermore, the frame in which the rod was embedded could also be rotated, so that it was sometimes tilted and sometimes straight.

For some subjects, the orientation of the frame had little effect on their judgments of the rod's verticality. Other subjects, however, made gross errors in aligning the rod when the frame was tilted. Rather than set the rod vertical, they seemed to be making it parallel to the sides of the frame (or perpendicular to the frame's top and bottom). A large middle group of subjects seemed to be only partly influenced by the orientation of the frame. Thinking of the frame as composing the background or visual "field" for the rod, Witkin designated those subjects whose judgments were heavily influenced by the orientation of the frame as "field-dependent," while those whose judgments were highly accurate in spite of the misleading context provided by the tilted frame were called "field-independent." Subsequent research showed children to be, in general, more field-dependent than older subjects.

The designation of certain people as field-dependent or field-independent was found to have considerable generality. For example, field-dependence as measured by the rod-and-frame test is highly correlated with performance on the *embedded-figures test,* which also requires that a visual element be segregated from its context. In the embedded-figures test, the subject is shown a simple geometric form and then is asked to pick out that form from a more complex pattern in which it is contained (see Figure 7.3). Field-dependent subjects are slower at finding such embedded figures than are subjects measured as field-independent on the rod-and-frame test.

Field-dependence turns out to be reflected in many behavioral domains, perceptual and cognitive, as well as in areas that fall in the province of "personality." By virtue of its ubiquitous appearance throughout the person's total functioning, Witkin has come to view field-dependence as one manifestation of a general characteristic, which he calls degree of *differentiation*. According to this formulation, the field-dependent person is relatively undifferentiated, whereas the field-independent individual is highly differentiated. Degree of differentiation, in turn, is a concept borrowed by Witkin from a developmental theory proposed by Heinz Werner (1948).

Werner's developmental model   Werner argues that primitive organisms can be distinguished from mature organisms according to their relative positions on several dimensions. For these purposes, Werner classifies as "primitive" those species which are low on the phylogenetic scale, and those persons who are young, mentally ill, or from cultures which have not reached the "advanced" state of highly civilized societies. Among the dimensions on which primitive and mature organisms differ is one which Werner calls the *syncretic-discrete dimension*. On the discrete end of that dimension (where the mature organism falls), psychological items are kept separate which can be segregated and which "ought" to be segregated for the sake of optimal functioning. Thus, mature persons can, and typically do, separate the contents of the several sensory systems; they do not confuse visual and auditory stimulation, for example. Similarly, objects can be viewed according to their perceptual properties, unaffected by the kinds of motor impulses they might elicit, or the kinds of emotional responses they arouse.

By contrast, the primitive organism often fails to treat separate items discretely; these items, instead, interact in a syncretic manner. Thus, auditory stimuli may arouse visual images (*synesthesia*), or at least affect the quality of visual sensations. Further, stimuli are perceived not entirely in accord with their objective properties, but also in terms of the actions they elicit. Emotion permeates perception and cognition, so that colors, for example, are responded to primarily as warm or cold, arousing or relaxing, rather than in terms of their purely visual qualities. Objects are endowed with *physiognomic* value; that is, they are responded to as though they were faces, so that, for example, the letter A might be seen as "cruel" or "threatening" rather than simply as three lines intersecting to form a particular geometric relationship.

Syncretism, then, permeates the functioning of the young child; thus, exaggerated susceptibility to geometric illusions is seen as one instance of that general characteristic. With maturation, behavior moves in the direction of increased discreteness, and hence those illusory effects which reflect a failure to segregate parts become less and less extreme. The developmental trend noted by Witkin toward decreased field-dependence clearly fits this conceptualization.

Unfortunately, Werner has not provided an account of the specific mechanisms which might mediate the shift from syncretic to discrete functioning. In part, the answer may lie in some as yet unspecified maturational processes inherent in the nervous system. But several lines of evidence suggest that learning plays an important role in this developmental trend just as it does in others. For example, females are typically more field-dependent than are males. This difference might have purely biological roots, but it is simpler to consider it the outcome of the different behavioral styles imposed on the two sexes by cultural pressures: in Western culture at least, men traditionally have been expected to be more analytic in their thinking, and generally more active and assertive; women, by contrast, have been reared to be relatively passive, to let themselves be molded by external influences, to be more responsive to the emotional connotations of events and less tied to their objective properties. In Werner's terms, Western culture seems to have directed women to be somewhat more syncretic than men—and it shows in their perceptual style. Other evidence, supportive of a "learning" interpretation of the developmental tendency toward increased discreteness of psychological functioning, as revealed in field-dependence and related measures, can be found in Witkin's publications (see Witkin, Lewis, et al., 1954; Witkin, Dyk, et al., 1962).

Now, to say that learning carries a large proportion of the developmental trend discussed above is still not to say *how* this is accomplished. While some attempts have been made to deal with this important theoretical problem (see, for example, Epstein, 1967; Hebb, 1949; Piaget, 1969; Solley and Murphy, 1960), it remains far from solved.

MANIPULATIONS OF EARLY EXPERIENCE

Stimulus Deprivation

In none of the studies of perceptual development cited so far was an attempt made to *manipulate* the conditions prevailing during the developmental period. In this section we will consider some of the research conducted according to the conventional experimental design whereby a particular manipulation is imposed on one group of subjects, and their performance is compared with that of an unmanipulated control group. As noted earlier, to do such research on human beings poses serious ethical and practical problems, so that much of this kind of work has had to be done on animals.

Nevertheless, we can begin with reference to some observations on the perceptual effects of depriving human beings, from birth, of normal pattern vision; these "subjects" became available for observation by virtue of their having been born with cataracts of the lens which were subsequently removed surgically. The cataracts prevented patterned illumination from reaching the retina, although exposure to variation in quantity of illumination was not precluded.

Clinical studies: the von Senden report   Reports of the effects of this kind of "manipulation" were collected by a German psychologist, von Senden, and published in 1932. This monograph was made available in English translation in 1960. The information summarized by von Senden was virtually neglected by psychologists until Donald O. Hebb (1949) incorporated it into his theory of perception contained in the book *The Organization of Behavior*. The material we present here is taken from Hebb's account of the von Senden data. You should keep in mind that this information was not obtained as part of a carefully designed experimental plan. The evidence it provides is therefore only fragmentary and suggestive. For example, we are given no data on visual thresholds, nor on acuity or luminosity functions, and little on color discrimination. In general, the bulk of the evidence concerns form perception, and it is this which we now examine.

In describing the visual ability of the von Senden patients, Hebb distinguishes between two processes, *unity* and *identity*. By *unity* Hebb refers to the mere detection of the existence of a figure, in the sense that the figure stands out from its background. The patient is able to say, "There is an object." *Identity,* as Hebb uses the concept, requires more. Not only must a figure be segregated from its background; it must be recognized as a member of a class of figures. The patient must be able to say, at the least, "This figure is different from that figure." At a higher level of identification, the patient might say, "That is (like) the object I was shown yesterday," or, finally, "That is a triangle."

The distinction between unity and identity very nicely describes the basic difference between the visually naive and the visually sophisticated. Von Senden's patients at first were capable of the perception of unity, but required a long and difficult period of training before figural identity approximated that of normal subjects. To quote from Hebb:

Investigators (of vision following operation for congenital cataract) are unanimous in reporting that the perception of a square, circle, or triangle, or of a sphere or cube, is very poor. To see one of these as a whole object, with distinctive characteristics immediately evident, is not possible for a long period. The most intelligent and best-motivated patient has to seek corners painstakingly even to distinguish a triangle from a circle. The newly seeing patient can frequently find a difference between two such figures shown together, ... but the differences are not remembered. There is for weeks practically zero capacity to learn names for such figures, even when tactual recognition is prompt and complete. (D. O. Hebb, 1949, p. 28).

Even after the patient has learned to identify an object, identification is often completely disrupted if some slight (to a normal subject) change in context is introduced. Thus, a patient may learn to identify a lump of sugar in the examiner's hand, but fail to recognize it when it is suspended from a string. In such examples the learning has not *generalized*.

You might expect that learning to identify geometric forms or simple inanimate objects would not be very important to these patients, and thus would proceed slowly. On the other hand, you might expect that learning to identify the faces of friends, relatives, doctors, etc. would be relatively rapid. And yet Hebb cites the case of one patient who was described as exceptionally intelligent, but could identify only four or five faces as long as 2 years after operation.

It is unlikely, then, that the slow acquisition of the ability to identify objects or figures by way of their visual characteristics results from a lack of motivation. Further, since these patients were capable of making such identifications through sense modalities other than vision (for example, touch), their visual retardation is not merely symptomatic of a general perceptual deficiency. Finally, it seems clear that they were not suffering from permanent structural defects, other than loss of their lenses, in the visual receptor system. For they did, eventually, acquire many of the visual abilities lacking in the period following operation. This indicates that the potential for such behavior existed from the beginning in the visual apparatus.

The presumed difficulty of early learning   The evidence collected by von Senden strongly suggests that at least some aspects of visual pattern perception are acquired through learning. For von Senden's patients this acquisition was slow and inefficient. In interpreting these data, Hebb takes the position that the same learning is equally difficult for normally developing human infants. While this inference is quite plausible, we must remember that there is no good direct evidence for it. Indeed, Hebb's interpretation of the von Senden data has been the subject of some criticism. It has been pointed out that the poor postoperative vision of von Senden's patients was not solely a matter of inexperience. To quote in part from one of Hebb's critics:

there are certain post-operative inhibitions which every patient must overcome before he can be said to have had his vision restored. ... These inhibitory effects work against good vision immediately on removal of the bandages: dazzle, narrowing of the visual field, and eye-muscle cramp. (Wertheimer, 1951, p. 134.)

To some extent the early inefficiency of von Senden's patients must be attributed to these inhibitory influences. Unfortunately we have no information as to how long these distracting effects remain important. If, for example, the "dazzle" effect is nothing more than the result of exposing a thoroughly dark-adapted eye to intense light, then we might expect it to be of short-term duration. At any rate, such factors must be kept in mind in our own evaluation of Hebb's inference that perceptual learning in infancy is slow and difficult.

The possibility of critical periods   Another type of evidence may also be pertinent to this issue. In the case of certain sensory-motor habits in lower species there seem to be "critical periods" of development during which practice is most efficient, whereas practice following this period is relatively ineffective. The development of the pecking response in chickens provides a classical example.

The normally raised chicken is quite skillful in obtaining food from the ground by pecking at it. The behavior has almost the appearance of a reflex, but research has revealed that a period of practice is required before the response reaches full efficiency. Further research has shown that unless this practice occurs within about the first 14 days after hatching, the chicks are permanently retarded in their pecking ability (Padilla, 1935).

Now, if you were to observe the crude, bumbling pecking attempts of a "deprived" chicken, you might be tempted to conclude that this same inefficiency characterized the acquisition of the pecking response in baby chicks. Of course, it is a big phylogenetic step from chicken to man. But at least there is some precedent for considering the possibility that the same learning, so difficult for von Senden's mature patients, may proceed more quickly and easily in infancy.

There is a similar, more familiar illustration of critical periods associated with the development of a strong attachment by recently hatched fowl, such as ducks, to their mothers. This phenomenon, popularized by the ethologist Konrad Lorenz (1937), is known as *imprinting,* and it may apply to a wide variety of species, perhaps, in some form, even including human beings (Sluckin, 1965). The essence of imprinting, as investigated in fowl, is that the young bird develops a strong tendency to follow, and apparently be comforted by, whatever happens to be the first salient object it encounters. Typically, that object is the mother, but inanimate objects with the right set of attributes (for example, movement, color, sound) can also serve (Hess, 1973).

Lorenz considers imprinting to be based on a process different from ordinary associative learning for several reasons. Pertinent to our present discussion is the argument that unlike Pavlovian and operant conditioning, imprinting can occur only during a brief, critical period shortly after hatching or birth. If the proper stimulation is not applied during this critical period, then subsequent stimulation will be ineffective. Now, there is some controversy about Lorenz's assertion of the special nature of imprinting, and there is some question about the absolute nature of the so-called critical period for imprinting (see, for example, Moltz, 1960). Nevertheless, the evidence is quite clear that there is a brief period in the young animal's life during which conditions are optimal for imprinting. Such data, again, suggest the possibility of critical or quasi-critical periods in perceptual development.

We return now to other sensory-deprivation studies in which animal subjects, from pigeon to chimpanzee, were used. Such experiments were specifically designed to test hypotheses about perceptual learning and thus provide us with data, if not as dramatic as von Senden's, then certainly more precise. As well as covering a wide range of species, these studies also involve deprivation in sense modalities other than vision.

Visual deprivation in the chimpanzee   In conjunction with the evidence from von Senden's report, Hebb cites an experiment by Riesen (1949) on the effects of visual deprivation in the chimpanzee. The Riesen study was an attempt to reproduce experimentally the conditions under which von Senden's human subjects developed. Of course Riesen could not use human subjects. Instead he used an animal that is phylogenetically close to man, the chimpanzee.

A simple way to deprive an organism of visual experience is to prevent exposure to light. In this manner — raising a chimpanzee in complete darkness — Riesen hoped to accomplish what the cataracts of von Senden's patients had done. "Turning on the lights" would be analogous to surgical removal of the cataracts. However, Riesen's technique did more than was desired, and thereby made his results ambiguous. In short, it was found, upon careful examination, that there was actual physical degeneration in the retinal structures of the light-deprived chimpanzee. The poor visual performance of the chimpanzee after deprivation could not be attributed solely to lack of perceptual learning.

You may wonder why von Senden's data are not subject to the same criticism as Riesen's. In the first place, there was no ophthalmological evidence of retinal degeneration in von Senden's cases. Second, since their visual ability did develop with experience, it is unlikely that any permanent structural defect was present. Finally, the two deprivation procedures, cataracts and raising in complete darkness, are quite different and should not be expected to have the same structural results. The effect of the cataracts was to eliminate *pattern* vision; the cataracts did not eliminate all light stimulation of the retina. That seems to be the crucial difference. Apparently, normal development of the retinal mechanism requires some light stimulation.

Thus, the use of the results of Riesen's experiment as evidence favorable to the perceptual-learning hypothesis has become questionable. However, subsequent research by Riesen, in which structural defects did not confound interpretation, yields results very similar to those on which Hebb originally relied. It is this latter research we now describe.

Cognizant of the possibility of retinal degeneration, Riesen (1950) repeated his original experiment, but this time with three subjects. One chimpanzee, Debi, was raised in complete darkness for 7 months. The second, Kora, was also raised in darkness except for 1½ hours each day when she was exposed to diffuse illumination. In this way the retina was stimulated, but no *pattern* experience was given. The third chimpanzee, Lad, was allowed 1½ hours each day of normal visual stimulation.

As in the previous experiment the totally deprived chimpanzee, Debi, showed ophthalmological signs of structural defect. Neither of the other animals, however, showed any such evidence. The conditions imposed on Kora are therefore most like those of the cataract patients.

Behaviorally, Lad did not differ from normally raised chimps. Apparently, 1½ hours per day of exposure to pattern stimulation is sufficient, over a 7-month period, for normal pattern vision to develop. Both Debi and Kora, on the other hand, were markedly retarded, even in simple oculomotor tasks. To quote from Riesen:

> Kora did not develop the blink response to a moving object until six days after her removal from darkness, and Debi not until 15 days. It took Kora 13 days and Debi 30 days to acquire the ability to pursue a moving person with the eyes, and they did this by a series of refixations instead of following smoothly as normal animals of comparable age do; it took Kora 20 days and Debi 16 days to pursue visually a moving feeding bottle; Kora 13 days and Debi 30 days to fixate the image of a stationary person. (Riesen, 1950, p. 18.)

In another test Riesen paired the presentation of a large black-and-yellow-striped disk with mild electric shock. Normally-raised chimps showed an avoidance response to the disk after one or two of these pairings. It took Kora 13 and Debi 15 days, two trials a day, to show a consistent avoidance response.

The evidence Riesen reports fits well with the von Senden data. Though it provides little new information about specific effects of deprivation, the Riesen study does utilize a better-controlled deprivation procedure than that imposed by cataracts. Also, unlike the von Senden patients, Riesen's chimpanzees had the use of their lenses in the test sessions. And for those with a comparative approach to psychological problems, Riesen's data add some phylogenetic generality to the von Senden results.

Tactual deprivation in the chimpanzee   In an attempt to generalize the findings of previous research on visual deprivation to other sense modalities, Nissen, Chow, and Semmes (1951) restricted the tactual experience of a chimpanzee, Rob. From 4 weeks of age until 31 months Rob was deprived of normal tactual stimulation of the hands, forearms, feet, and legs. Beginning at the age of 15 weeks, his limbs, from elbow to fingertips and knee to toes, were encased in cardboard tubes. Prior to this, the limbs had been covered with bandages. Since movement was also partially restricted, deprivation was not confined to tactual experience. It is only the results of the latter, however, that we shall present here. Movement deprivation had effects comparable to the tactual effects.

After 31 months of confinement, Rob was freed of his cardboard tubes and given a tactual discrimination task. In brief, Rob had to indicate by appropriate head movement which one of his hands had just been stimulated. If his right-hand index finger was squeezed by the experimenter, he would be rewarded for turning his head to the right. If his left-hand finger was stimulated, he was to turn to the left. No other cues were provided; the solution of this simple learning problem depended on tactual discrimination of a very gross sort. Rob simply had to be able to tell his right hand from his left.

Despite the apparent simplicity of the task, Rob never showed much evidence of having learned, even after as many as 2,000 trials. A nondeprived control chimpanzee reached a level of almost perfect responding after one-tenth the number of trials given Rob. That Rob was not otherwise retarded was indicated by his normal performance on a series of visual discrimination tasks.

Nissen, Chow, and Semmes are cautious in generalizing from results obtained on only one experimental and one control animal. They tentatively conclude, however, that experience does play an important part in the development of tactual sensitivity, just as it does in the visual mode.

Visual deprivation in rats and birds   So far we have discussed experiments employing primates as subjects. Studies of visual deprivation in rats and birds have also yielded results consistent with a perceptual-learning hypothesis.

Hebb (1937) reports one experiment in which rats were raised in darkness and subsequently compared with normal controls on visual pattern-discrimination problems. Though the deprived rats were at first markedly inferior to the controls, it did not take them long to catch up. Their performance approached that of the normally-raised rats after only about 60 minutes of experience with visual pattern stimulation. Hebb argues that perceptual learning in lower species should be expected to proceed much more rapidly than in the primates.

In a similar experiment, Siegel (1953) deprived ringdoves of visual pattern experience by covering their heads with translucent plastic hoods. With this method, the birds were stimulated by diffuse light in much the same manner as the chimpanzee Kora in the Riesen study had been. The birds were hooded on the third day after hatching, before their eyes had opened. Between the ages of 8 and 12 weeks the birds were given training in jumping, while still hooded, from a perch to a platform. This was to be the response in the testing situation. After 20 days and 400 trials of this training, a window was cut in the hood over one eye, thus allowing monocular vision.

The birds were then tested for form discrimination, with a circle and a triangle the stimuli to be discriminated. Their performance on this task was significantly inferior to that of normally-raised controls. The experimental doves required an average of about 127 trials to reach the criterion of nine correct jumps out of ten, while the control doves required an average of about 78 trials. In a test for visual acuity, no difference was found between the deprived and the control birds. Siegel presents several arguments that his results can best be explained in terms of perceptual learning.

Depth perception   One of the earliest experimental investigations of the perceptual learning hypothesis was made by Lashley and Russell in 1934. The subjects were rats that had been raised in the dark. Three days after they had been removed from the light-deprivation condition, the rats were tested for accuracy of distance judgment. The animals were placed on a stand and induced to jump to a platform located at various distances from the stand. It was found that the force with which the rats jumped was graded according to the particular stand-platform distance, indicating that the rats were capable of accurate distance perception. The further inference, that distance perception is "unlearned," does not, however, necessarily follow. The 3-day period in the light, prior to testing, may have been sufficient for distance-perception learning to have taken place.

A later series of experiments utilizing an apparatus called the *visual cliff* (Figure 12.5) tests the perceptual learning hypothesis in a more suitable man-

FIGURE 12.5   The visual cliff, used for investigating depth perception in the young. Subjects with well-developed depth perception avoid the steeper—appearing side. (From Gibson and Walk, 1960)

ner. In one of the first studies in this series (Walk, Gibson, and Tighe, 1957), rats were raised in the dark for 90 days and were tested for distance perception within 20 minutes of their removal from the dark. The testing situation was very cleverly designed to yield a sufficient amount of useful data in a minimum of time, and therefore with minimal contamination of the test itself on the behavior being studied. The testing apparatus consisted of a narrow platform; on either side of the platform, and 3 inches below it, were two glass plates. Sandwiched between the two thicknesses of one plate was a rectangle of wallpaper. The same wallpaper pattern was placed several feet below the other glass plate. Optically, the first plate looked much closer to the platform than the other plate. It was assumed that if rats were to leave the platform, they would prefer to descend onto the glass plate that appeared to be the closer. Demonstration of such a preference would imply an ability to make a distance discrimination.

The rats raised in the dark showed this preference, and to the same extent as that of a normally raised control group. About 82 percent of the dark-raised rats and 85 percent of the normally raised rats descended on the optically "near" side. These data offer strong evidence that distance perception in rats does not depend on learning.

Similar experiments have been done with a variety of species, including chicks, kittens, goats, and even human infants, not always, however, incorporating visual deprivation into the procedure. The general conclusion emerging from this sizable body of research is that whatever process mediates preference for the optically shallow side is present as soon as the species tested is able to reveal its preference through locomotor activity (see Hinde, 1970, p. 474).

As far as the question of the role of learning in this kind of discrimination is concerned, the most convincing data come from those studies which employed animals capable of locomotion immediately after birth, or hatching. Indeed, for this purpose chickens are the ideal subjects, since they can be tested on the visual cliff very shortly after hatching. In several experiments using newly hatched chicks, the typical preference for the shallow surface was exhibited (Shinkman, 1963; Tallarico, 1961; Walk and Gibson, 1961).

The evidence seems clear that visually naive chicks discriminate between the two visual patterns provided by the shallow and deep sides of the cliff; however, the implications of this evidence for the more general question of the development of depth perception remain unsettled. First, the results may apply solely to chickens and not to other species. Second, there is some reason to suspect that the chicks' preference for the shallow surface may be mediated by a process that is only incidentally related to depth perception.

The results of several studies (for example, Palen, 1965; Schiffman and Walk, 1963; Walk and Gibson, 1961) point to the conclusion that with one exception none of the possible cues to depth (for example, binocular disparity, sharpness of visual image, size of pattern elements) is indispensable.

The one exception is motion parallax—i.e., the relative rate at which pattern elements move over the retina as the chicken scans the two sides of the cliff. It is the nearer elements, of course, which travel the faster over the retinal surface. The suggestion has been made (Simner, 1967) that rate of element movement may not serve for the young chick as a cue to depth, but rather may be a stimulus which directly elicits approach or withdrawal tendencies. Simner argues that the chick is highly responsive to visual flicker and that the chick's eye is so constructed that a flickering effect is established on the retina through scanning of patterned stimuli of the sort used on the visual cliff. In short, the chick's alighting on the shallow side may simply reflect a preference for the flicker rate induced by that side relative to the rate associated with the deep side. Simner presents some experimental evidence in support of his hypothesis; chicks can be made to reduce their typical preference for the shallow side by properly manipulating the size of the pattern elements on the two sides.

That cats do not exhibit normal behavior on the visual cliff without appropriate prior experience is clearly demonstrated in an experiment by Held and Hein (1963). That experiment, in addition, provides insight into what characterizes "appropriate" experience for the developing cat. In particular, visual experience alone is not sufficient. What the cat needs is the opportunity to integrate visual experience and locomotor activity. This was demonstrated in the following manner:

Newborn kittens were raised by their mothers in the dark for several weeks. Then, some of the kittens, between 8 and 12 weeks of age, were allowed to walk around in a visually patterned environment. Each locomoting kitten was paired with another kitten that got a "free ride" through the same environment, confined in a little gondola which the moving kitten propelled (Figure 12.6). Thus, the two kittens had essentially the same visual experience, but one was deprived of the events normally associated with moving (motor activity, kinesthetic feedback, tactual stimulation, etc.).

The kittens were tested for a visually-guided paw-placing reflex and for depth perception on the visual cliff. Those kittens given the chance to move actively through the visually patterned environment showed the normal preference for the "shallow" side of the visual cliff, whereas the kittens allowed only passive observation of the visual environment still appeared insensitive to the difference between the deep and shallow sides. When the latter animals were given an additional 48 hours of opportunity to move actively in a lighted environment, they then exhibited normal behavior on the visual cliff and other evidence, from simple tests of visual-motor reflexes, of normal visual ability.

Sensitivity to specific stimulus features   The deprivation procedures employed in the experiments described to this point have been relatively gross. Other experiments have addressed the issue of whether depriving de-

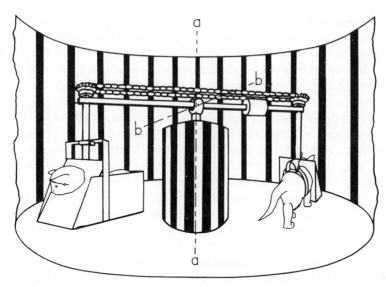

FIGURE 12.6 Sketch of the apparatus for equating motion and consequent visual stimulation for an actively moving and a passively moving kitten. (From Held and Hein, 1963)

veloping animals of exposure to specific features of stimuli will create later perceptual deficits. Some of these experiments have employed electrophysiological recordings from brain cells to assess the neurophysiological effects of the deprivation procedures along with behavioral indicators, whereas others have relied solely on behavioral indicators. Both types of research have yielded dramatic results.

Illustrative of this type of research is the work of Blakemore and Cooper (1970). In one of their experiments, kittens were reared between the ages of about 3 to 13 weeks in a visual environment which restricted their experience either to vertical or to horizontal stripes. When restored to a normal environment, the kittens showed behavioral evidence of being insensitive to objects oriented in the direction characterizing the type of deprivation they had undergone. Thus, it was noticed that animals deprived of exposure to vertical stripes tended to bump into objects such as chair legs, as though they could not see them. But those same kittens had no trouble with horizontally oriented objects, such as the seats of chairs, or table tops. Analogous observations were made of the behavior of those kittens that had been deprived of exposure to horizontal stripes. The kittens' perceptual deficits seemed to be confined quite narrowly to the specific feature of the visual environment (verticality or horizontalness) in which their early experience had been lacking.

Electrophysiological recordings from cells in the cats' visual cortex supported this conclusion. If you recall an earlier discussion (Chapter 7), there are specific neural cells in the brain which are maximally sensitive to specific features of visual stimuli (e.g., edge detectors, movement detectors, orientation detectors). Such feature detectors were evident in the visual cortex of the deprived kittens with the exception of detectors tuned to the feature that had been missing in their early experience. Apparently, if the cat's visual cortex is to develop the kind of organization that makes it selectively responsive to specific features of visual stimulation, the developing brain must be "nourished" by stimulation containing those specific features.

Subsequent behavioral research has demonstrated that the kind of perceptual deficit described above is relative rather than absolute. Thus, Muir and Mitchell (1973) raised two kittens from the age of 3 weeks to 5 months and one from 3 weeks to 5 weeks in an environment which restricted their experience either to vertical or to horizontal gratings. When not in those special environments, the kittens were kept in the dark. They were then treated normally from about the age of 6 months, and were tested for visual acuity 3 to 6 months after that. Compared with two cats that had been reared normally from birth the deprived cats showed markedly decreased acuity when tested for their ability to discriminate between a grating and a gray field. The deficit, however, was evident only for gratings oriented in one direction — that is, the direction, vertical or horizontal, which had been absent from the stimulation they received early in their development. Muir and Mitchell are careful to point out that the cats were not *blind* to vertically or horizontally oriented stimuli; rather, they were markedly insensitive to one or the other of those dimensions. In either case, of course, the evidence indicates that normal visual sensitivity to such basic features as verticality and horizontalness is the end product of a developmental process which has an important experiential component.

The behavioral evidence of a relative deficit in acuity rather than an absolute blindness is consistent with further neurophysiological data provided and interpreted by Grobstein and Chow (1975). Putting together results of their own neurophysiological research on rabbits with experiments by others on cats, such as those mentioned above, and some work on monkeys, Grobstein and Chow conclude that deprivation of experience with specific visual features reduces the frequency with which cortical neurons can be identified that are tuned to those features. Some such neurons are present before the young animal has had any visual experience at all, indicating that experience is not necessary for their development. However, in normally-reared animals an increase is noted in the frequency with which such neurons can be found by electrophysiological recording techniques (the recording of the electrical activity of single neural cells by implanted microelectrodes) as the animal matures. That increase is delayed in deprived animals but not irreversibly prevented.

A more severe deficit seems to result from depriving kittens of normal binocular stimulation. In normally-reared adult cats, electrophysiological recording from single cells in the visual cortex reveals the presence of a large number of neurons which appear to be involved in the process of binocular depth perception. Such cells give their maximum electrical response when both eyes are stimulated and when the stimulation is restricted to very delimited areas on each retina, as would ordinarily be the case when the animal was looking at a single object in space. Just as some neurons are especially sensitive to specific features such as orientation, movement, and direction, these cortical neurons are specialized for the feature of "binocularity."

Results of experiments (for example, Hubel and Wiesel, 1965; Schlaer, 1971) employing various methods for preventing normal binocular stimulation in developing cats indicate that adult animals so deprived lack the normal complement of "binocularity" neurons. In reviewing these and related behavioral studies, Grobstein and Chow (1975, p. 355) conclude that "they establish a fairly strong case that, during normal development, it is left to individual experience to establish exactly which pairs of retinal regions activate single cortical neurons."

There is an interesting finding, somewhat tangential to the line of research described above, but perhaps relevant and certainly worth noting. *Adult* cats were confined for 1 hour a day, over a period of 2 weeks, in an environment containing only vertical stripes, and in darkness for the rest of the time. Within 12 hours of the final exposure to the vertically striped environment, the cats, with no intervening visual stimulation, were tested neurophysiologically for responsiveness to variously oriented stripes. The results indicated a marked decline, relative to normal control animals, in the number of neural cells in the visual cortex that responded to vertically oriented stimuli. Responsiveness to horizontally oriented stimuli were unaffected (Cruetzfeldt and Heggelund, 1975). Thus, a manipulation which has one effect in developing cats seemingly has the opposite effect in mature cats. The authors remark on the similarity of their results with cats to those obtained when human subjects are exposed to gratings — that is, a subsequent decline in sensitivity to test gratings which are oriented in the same manner as the exposure gratings. Why adults show such adaptation effects of exposure to specific features of stimulation such as orientation while developing organisms show the opposite effect (or, at least, decreased sensitivity to nonexposed features) is as yet an unanswered question.

The overall conclusion from clinical and experimental investigations of the effects of perceptual deprivation during the early phases of development is that such deprivation does indeed result in perceptual deficits and abnormalities in underlying neurophysiological functioning. Specific details probably vary greatly over different species, different types and times of deprivation, and different perceptual functions. A similar conclusion seems warranted on the basis of experiments designed to assess the consequences of providing enriched environments to developing organisms. Some of those experiments are discussed in the following section.

Stimulus Enrichment

In essence, enrichment procedures involve exposing subjects to a greater quantity and/or variety of stimulation during infancy than is typically encountered. In some experiments, the procedure may be restricted to the addition of a few specific stimulus patterns to the normal environment.

Free-environment experiments   Hebb (1949) reports in *The Organization of Behavior* an informal experiment that illustrates the essential features of the enrichment method. One group of rats was moved at an early age from the laboratory to Dr. Hebb's home. There they become the pets of the Hebb children. They had "toys" to play with and a great deal of varied territory to explore. In short, their environment was much more varied perceptually than the rather dull and limited cage world of their laboratory siblings, the normal control group.

After several weeks of this plush life the experimental rats were returned to the laboratory for an intelligence test. Their performance on this test (a series of specially designed maze problems) was consistently superior to that of the control group. Furthermore, the difference between the scores of the two groups increased upon successive retests, indicating that the initial advantage of the experimental rats was not attributable only to their being more accustomed to handling than the controls. Hebb argues that their early, special experience made the experimental animals more intelligent than they would have been had they remained in their cages. This increase in intelligence, according to Hebb, is a manifestation of their greater perceptual ability, developed simply through contact with a varied and complex environment.

Several experiments of the same sort, but with more rigorous control of conditions, have since been performed. Hymovitch (1952) reports a series of studies examining Hebb's hypothesis. In one experiment rats were raised in four types of environments. Group 1 lived in a "free environment," a large box containing runways, blind alleys, and objects that could be visually explored and manipulated. Group 2 lived in small mesh cages that restricted the rats' activity somewhat but afforded a rich visual environment. The mesh cages were moved each day to a different location in the laboratory, with six of these locations inside the free-environment box. Group 3 lived in small stovepipes, which allowed little movement and presented a very limited visual world. The animals in Group 4 were raised in enclosed activity wheels; visually, they were as restricted as the rats of Group 3, but they were not deprived of motor activity.

After a little over 6 weeks of living under these conditions, the rats were tested, over a period of 3 weeks, in the intelligence-testing apparatus used by Hebb, the "closed-field" test. It was found that groups 1 and 2 were superior to groups 3 and 4, while neither 1 and 2 nor 3 and 4 differed from each other. Groups 1 and 2 averaged about 138 errors; groups 3 and 4 about 234 errors.

It appears that the crucial aspect of the extra experience given Groups 1 and 2 was exposure to varied *visual* stimulation. Their increased opportunity for motor activity and object manipulation did not seem to benefit the rats in Group 1. Similarly, the Group-4 animals, raised in activity wheels were not superior to the stovepipe subjects of Group 3.

There is nothing in Hebb's theory that would lead to a general expectation that extra *visual* experience should far outweigh the effects of enriched experience in the other sensory systems. It seems most likely, then, that the lack of difference between Groups 1 and 2 is attributable to specific features of the closed-field test itself. Good performance on the test is perhaps a function of both intelligence and well-developed distance vision. Some data bearing on this point are provided in an experiment by Forgus, which we shall discuss presently.

It is, of course, not possible to say whether the superior performance of Groups 1 and 2 was the result of their extra experience or was simply a reflection of the poor performance of the two restricted groups. No normally-raised control group was used in the experiment just described. However, such a group was used in another study by Hymovitch, discussed below. The average score of these normally-reared rats, about 222 errors, falls between the scores of the enriched and the deprived groups, indicating that both special procedures were effective.

In a second experiment Hymovitch showed that early free-environment experience is more effective than the same experience later in life. For this study four groups of rats were used. Group 1 had free-environment stimulation for about 6 weeks, starting at 1 month of age. During this period the Group-2 rats were living in stovepipe cages. There followed a 10-day period in which both groups were kept in normal cages, and then Group 1 was put in the stovepipes and Group 2 was given 6 weeks of the free-environment treatment. The subjects in Group 3 had both early and late free-environment exposure, while those in Group 4 spent the entire period in normal cages.

These animals were also tested in the closed-field maze. The results of the test were as follows: Group 1 made an average of about 161 errors; Group 2,249; Group 3,153; Group 4,222. Group 1 made significantly fewer errors than Group 2. This is consistent with the hypothesis that early experience is more effective than the same experience later in life. Group 3 was not significantly better than Group 1, again indicating the relative unimportance of late experience. The same inference can be drawn from the failure of Group 2 to perform better than Group 4.

What is learned in a free environment?   As we have anticipated above, an experiment by Forgus (1954) gets at the question of what specifically is learned as a result of exposure to a free environment. Forgus used three groups of rats. Group 1 was raised in a free environment very similar to that used by Hymovitch. These animals could traverse as well as see their complex environment. Group-2 rats could only see the environment; they lived in a glass house located in the middle of a free environment. The subjects in Group 3 were raised in small cages affording a minimum of visual or manipulative variety. This treatment lasted for a total of 60 days, beginning at day 24 after birth.

Following a week in normal living cages, during which a food-deprivation schedule was established, a series of three behavioral tests was begun. The first was a test of activity, emotionality, and variability. In brief, the rats in Groups 1 and 2 did not differ on these measures, but both groups differed significantly from Group 3, with the free-environment animals more active, more variable, and less emotional than the restricted subjects.

The second test involved a visual form-discrimination problem. Here, Group 2 performed significantly better than Group 1, and both excelled Group 3. In a subsequent test of generalization the difference between the two free-environment groups disappeared, but both were still superior to the restricted group.

The third test required a spatial solution rather than a visual form solution. On this test, Groups 1 and 2 did not differ; again Group 3 was significantly inferior to the other two groups.

Of special interest to us at this point is the superior performance of Group 2 in the form-discrimination problem. Focus argues that the Group-1 rats were in effect temporarily at a disadvantage on this problem because of their greater number of nonform hypotheses. That is, they came to the problem with a much richer set of "perceptual responses" than did the animals in Group 2. The irrelevant responses in this set, being prepotent for rats in general over form hypotheses, would at first tend to interfere with a solution of the problem. The Group-2 rats, on the other hand, had fewer nonform hypotheses because of the previous restriction on their motor activity.

This type of argument places a slightly different emphasis on the interpretation of what is being learned in the enrichment studies and what is *not learned* in the deprivation experiments. We shall take up this point again following a discussion of some experiments in which the extra experience is limited to a few specific stimulus patterns, and later discrimination testing is conducted with these or similar stimuli. Some experiments by E. Gibson and others nicely illustrate the general procedure.

In one such study, Gibson and Walk (1956) raised rats from birth under two conditions. In the experimental condition the walls of the animals' living cages contained four metal plaques, two triangles and two circles. The walls of the control rats' cages were plain white. After about 3 months of this treatment, the animals were given a learning task in which the triangle and the circle had to be discriminated. The experimental group performed consistently better than the controls, reaching about 90 percent correct choices while the controls were still operating at a chance level.

Similar results were obtained in a second study (Walk, Gibson, Pick, and Tighe, 1958). Here, only one stimulus pattern was present in the experimental rats' cages. In the subsequent testing period, half the experimental subjects had to approach the pattern, while for the other half the pattern was the avoidance stimulus. The two experimental groups did not differ from each other in performance, but both groups were superior to comparable controls.

In a third experiment (Gibson, Walk, Pick, and Tighe, 1958), the exposure was to an equilateral triangle and a circle, and the discrimination test involved an isosceles triangle and an ellipse. The experimental subjects again were superior to control rats, indicating that whatever learning had taken place during exposure was not specific to the stimulus patterns used. This result could perhaps be anticipated on the basis of the free-environment studies, where learning seemed to have been of a very general type. Of course, any final interpretation of this particular experiment would depend on the demonstration that equilateral and isosceles triangles, and circle and ellipse, are in fact discriminable for rats. It would be most revealing to test "exposed" animals with stimuli markedly different from the original exposure stimuli. In this way it might be possible to determine whether the perceptual learning was of the general, free-environment type, or whether it was specific to the exposure patterns. One such test has been conducted by Gibson, Walk, Pick, and Tighe (1958), with results favorable to the specificity interpretation.

Both Hymovitch, using general enrichment, and Forgus (1956), using exposure to specific stimuli, found early experience to have a greater effect on perception than later experience. On the basis of these and similar results, we might infer that perceptual learning in infants proceeds more quickly than the same learning in equally naive adults. This is not to say that infants in general learn more quickly than adults in general. On the contrary, as Hebb cogently argues, learning in adults is much more efficient than infant learning for the reason that it makes use of early learning—which itself has little to build on. But note that Hebb is referring to *sophisticated* adults, those who have already undergone the arduous process of early learning. What we do suggest is that *naive adults are inferior learners compared with naive infants*. It is this idea which makes us reluctant to accept Hebb's conclusion that early learning must always be as slow as it was for von Senden's adult subjects.

One possible explanation of the greater efficacy of early experience is based on the concept of "critical periods" in perceptual learning, as mentioned in our earlier discussion of stimulus-deprivation experiments. A related, but less extreme, explanation is expressed in the familiar adage, "You can't teach an old dog new tricks." Why not? Because the "old tricks" interfere. In learning terminology, there is *proactive inhibition*. Earlier learned responses are incompatible with, and hence interfere with, the acquisition of the new responses.

In the same way it may be that individuals raised without visual experience have learned to adjust to the world through the mediation of other sense modalities. The *use* of smell, hearing, touch, etc. in solving the problems of cage life constitute the "old tricks" of, for example, the visually deprived pigeon. Suddenly its hood is removed, and it must now learn a new trick—for example, to avoid punishment by solving a visual problem. It is possible that the slow learning exhibited in such a situation is simply a manifestation of the bird's trying out its old tricks first. It may be perfectly capable of discriminating a circle from a triangle, but nothing in its past experience would lead it to "expect" that such percepts have any relevance. This idea gains support from the results of the experiment by Forgus (1954) in which the efficacy of a particular type of free-environment exposure was shown to depend on the nature of the learning task.

Stated in extreme form, the issue is this: Does visual deprivation retard visual discrimination learning by preventing the development of visual *ability* or by decreasing the *probability* of an individual's using a visually related response? One way to get at this question might be to expose the deprived individual to problems requiring brightness discrimination. This procedure would at least increase the probability of trying a *visual* solution to *later* pattern-soluble problems. It might thereby indirectly increase the chances of using a visual pattern solution.

The argument above is developed in the context of the deprivation procedure. It might at first seem inapplicable to studies using early exposure to figures. The geometric forms decorating the walls of the living cages are obviously not relevant to any experimenter-imposed problems. It is possible, though, that these figures are used by the rats in "games" or problems of their own making. Certainly the forms must be attended to in some manner by the rats if their presence in the cages is to benefit the animals' later performance This latter point is developed by Gibson, Walk, and Tighe (1959), who found that only three-dimensional exposure figures have a facilitating effect on later discrimination learning.

A more powerful criticism of the probability argument, and one we are not entirely prepared to dismiss, would point to the original von Senden data. Here, through the use of language, the experimenter very effectively can direct the subject's attention to the relevant modality, vision, and to specific visual attributes. There is no need for the period of trial-and-error hypothesis testing which we suggest may be taking place in the animal studies. At a gross level—that is, *the use of vision*—the probability argument seems inappropriate if applied to the von Senden data. Of course, this does not necessarily make the argument equally inappropriate to the animal studies.

Moreover, it may be that at a more specific level—that is, the level of squares and triangles—something analogous to a probability argument is valid. Just because instructions say to use form and ignore color and brightness does not imply that the individual will be able to do so. Color, for example, may be innately so dominant as to render the experimenter's instructions ineffective, even in the best-motivated subject. To expect verbal instructions to "take" completely under such circumstances would be as unrealistic as to expect complete compliance in children who, on Christmas Eve, are told to stop thinking about their presents and go to sleep. Thus, the deprived individual may be able to "see" a triangle but, because of strong interfering responses, be unable to make use of this percept in the special way required by the experimenter.

We are suggesting, in short, that early experience may not affect perceptual capacity *per se,* but rather the likelihood of perceptual systems being used in the normal fashion. A related argument is made by Fuller (1967), who has extensively studied the behavioral development of dogs. He interprets the profound effects on dogs of impoverished early experience as being largely the result of the dog's inability to cope with the excessive stimulation which a "normal" environment presents to a stimulus-deprived animal. In essence, Fuller's point is that the dog's early experience establishes an adaptation level against which current stimulation is assessed. When current stimulation exceeds the adaptation level, a powerful emotional reaction ensues, which in turn interferes with such delicate processes as discrimination, learning, and problem solving.

Should our interpretation or Fuller's, or indeed both, prove valid, it may still be the case that there is a direct perceptual effect of early experience. The point here is that for such an effect to be clearly revealed, it is necessary to control for the general cognitive and emotional effects of manipulations intended to have purely perceptual consequences.

While the neurochemical mechanisms underlying learning are not yet known in detail, there is evidence of such effects on the brain of variation in early experience (for example, Rosenzweig, Bennett, and Diamond, 1972). Thus, rats reared in sensorially enriched environments develop heavier than normal portions of the brain. Furthermore, biochemical analysis of brain tissue reveals differences in such substances as cholinesterase in brain loci that are consistent with the notion that enriched experience leaves a physiological residue. In short, the brains of enriched animals are better developed than those of normal or deprived subjects. Such results, together with the electrophysiological data reported in the previous section, support the hypothesis that early experience does have a direct effect on perceptual development; however, the possibility has not been ruled out of an emotional, or "arousal," basis for differences in brain biochemistry (Walsh and Cummins, 1975).

Practical implications   It is not often that basic research in psychology is avidly greeted by people whose concerns are mainly practical. This may be just as well, since psychological research is so often equivocal, and its procedures and results so difficult to replicate. The environmental-enrichment studies, despite their flaws and ambiguities, were nevertheless seized on, during a period of rising social consciousness in the United States (the 1960s), as both a rationale and a model for attempts to enhance the general intellectual development of "culturally deprived" infants and children. The argument, in essence, was that by virtue of cultural style and economic disadvantage, many children were denied the early stimulation necessary for their optimal development. The solution, obviously, was to encourage parents to provide such stimulation. or to compensate for parental inaction by institutionally-sponsored programs of perceptual and cognitive enrichment. That, in essence, was the scientific basis for such ambitious efforts as Head Start, and a host of related programs and procedures. Although it is extremely difficult to assess accurately the effectiveness of social programs, there is reason to believe that some success, in some instances, may be achievable by interventions of this sort. For example. White and Held (1966) report acceleration in the development of normal infants' (1½ to 3½ months of age) visual-motor behavior through enriching the amount and quality of the visual and visual-motor stimulation available to the infants in their cribs. Other interventions involving extra handling, verbalization, access to toys, and specific perceptual-motor training have also been tried (see, for example, Hess and Bear, 1968). Though promising, such procedures are still very much in the initial stages of development, and solid experimental evidence of their effectiveness is still in short supply.

SOME PERCEPTUAL PHENOMENA IN ADULTS DEMANDING A LEARNING EXPLANATION

The developmental studies reviewed so far, of both the descriptive and manipulative types, strongly suggest some role for learning in the formation of adult perceptual experience. That, of course, is the position taken by empiricists on the basis of their analysis of adult perception *per se*. A host of perceptual phenomena seem to demand an explanation which incorporates the concept of learning even though direct experimental evidence may be lacking for the specific manner in which the presumed learning has taken place.

Several such phenomena are amenable to convincing demonstration. However, while often very dramatic, these demonstrations offer only circumstantial evidence that learning does indeed influence the course of perceptual development.

The Ames Demonstrations

The so-called Ames demonstrations were developed by Adelbert Ames, Jr. and his co-workers in conjunction with their *transactional theory of perception*. The transactional theory is based on the observation that any stimulus pattern that impinges on the retina could have come from an "infinity" of objects. Despite the infinity of possible perceptions that might arise from a given retinal distribution, the actual perception is usually quite restricted. The transactional theory attempts to account for this restriction in perception by referring to the learning that takes place during the life of the individual. This

FIGURE 12.7   Schematic drawing of a rotating trapezoidal window. When in motion, the window seems to oscillate rather than to rotate. (From Ames, 1951)

learning occurs as a result of people's actively dealing with their environment. Somehow, through their "transactions" with the environment, people's perceptions become limited, and usually in a way that corresponds closely with the world or real objects.

The Ames demonstrations were designed to illustrate the role of learning in perception. They do this, in general, by showing how, under specially constructed stimulus conditions, the correspondence between perception and reality can be made to break down. The "assumptions" that people have developed in the course of their transactions lead them astray in these special circumstances. People do not see things veridically, but rather in ways that are compatible with their assumptions. The demonstrations are most dramatic when one set of assumptions must be violated in order to preserve another.

The rotating window   The rotating trapezoidal window, as depicted in Figure 12.7, is one of the best-known of this latter type of demonstration. To be fully appreciated, the demonstration should be seen in action. As the next best thing, we quote from two of Ames's collaborators, Ittleson and Kilpatrick:

By means of a piece of apparatus called the "rotating trapezoidal window" it has been possible to extend the investigation to complex perceptual situations involving movement. This device consists of a trapezoidal surface with panes cut in it and shadows painted on it to give the appearance of a window. It is mounted on a rod connected to a motor so that it rotates at a slow constant speed in an upright position about its own axis. When an observer views the rotating surface with one eye from about 10 feet or more or with both eyes from about 25 feet or more, he sees not a rotating trapezoid but an oscillating rectangle. Its speed of movement and its shape appear to vary markedly as it turns. If a small cube is attached by a short rod to the upper part of the short side of the trapezoid, it seems to become detached, sail freely around the front of the trapezoid and attach itself again as the apparatus rotates.[2]

Though the apparent oscillation of the window is contrary to reality, it is not disturbing, at least until the observer gets a closer look at the apparatus. But the behavior of the cube is bizarre. Even more bewildering to the observer is the strange behavior of a rod that is inserted through the window. In the course of the apparent oscillation of the window, the rod undergoes a variety of "impossible" distortions. Part of the time it seems to be rotating in a direction opposite to that of the window itself. At one point the rod begins to bend, and then suddenly it snaps back straight. Some even see the rod as passing through the solid mullions of the window.

A detailed explanation of this demonstration in terms of geometric optics is possible, but it is too complex to present here. The important point is that what is seen as an oscillating rectangular window, with all its bizarre accompaniments, could just as well be seen as a rotating trapezoid. That it is not, the transactionalists attribute to learning. The cues of the situation are so constructed that the object is seen as a *window*. If it is seen as a window, it must, because of all our past experience, be seen as a rectangular window. If it is seen as a rectangular window, then it must be seen as oscillating.

The distorted room   This same point is demonstrated by the "distorted room," illustrated in Figure 12.8. To quote again from Ittelson and Kilpatrick:

the floor of the room slopes up to the right of the observer, the rear wall recedes from right to left and the windows are of different sizes and trapezoidal in shape. When an observer looks at this room with one eye from a certain point, the room appears completely normal, as if the floor were level, the rear wall at right angles to the line of sight and the windows rectangular and of the same size. (From W. H. Ittelson and F. P. Kilpatrick, "Experiments in perception." *Scientific American, 1951, 185, No. 2, p. 55. Reprinted by permission of Scientific American*).

Since the room is seen as normal, the two faces in Figure 12.8 seem equidistant from the observer; hence the two are seen as grossly different in size.

Notice that in both examples, the rotating trapezoid and the distorted room, normality of one aspect of the environment is attained at the expense of abnormality in other aspects. Why not see the two faces as approximately equal in size, and the room for what it is—that is, distorted? Though the transactionalists are vague on this point, the answer presumably lies in the learning experience of the individual. Rooms are always "normal," whereas people do differ in size. Windows are almost always rectangular, but things that look stiff—for example, toy rubber daggers—do sometimes bend.

FIGURE 12.8 The perceptual effects of a distorted room. The person on the right seems to have a much larger head than the one on the left. (From Ittelson and Kilpatrick, 1951)

Cross-cultural studies How would the rotating trapezoid be seen by people who have had no experience with rectangular windows, or with rectangular forms in general? According to the transactionalist approach, the effect of the demonstration depends on the individual's identifying the object as a window, and hence as rectangular. A person who has had no experience with windows would not make this identification, and hence should be less subject to the effect.

This hypothesis was tested in a study by Allport and Pettigrew (1957). Their subjects were members of a Zulu group which very well fulfills the conditions described above. This particular group lives in a "spherical" culture. Their huts are round, rather than rectangular, and are usually arranged in circles. The huts have no windows. Their cooking implements are round, and their fields follow the contour of the land, rather than being laid out in rectangular plots. Their language has no word for "square" or "rectangle," but there are words for "round" and "circle." Such people seem ideal subjects to test with the trapezoidal window.

The basic experiment was run under four viewing conditions: (1) monocular viewing at 20 feet; (2) binocular at 20 feet; (3) monocular at 10 feet; (4) binocular at 10 feet. The first condition is optimal for getting the effect of an oscillating rectangle; the fourth condition is least likely to elicit the effect, since it provides many cues to the true movement.

Along with the subjects from the group described above, appropriate control groups were run. The hypothesized difference was obtained most strongly in the fourth condition above—that is, under binocular viewing at 10 feet. This is the condition under which it is most difficult to see the oscillation. Here the experimental subjects, as expected, reported oscillation much less frequently than the control subjects. As it became easier to get the effect, the difference between experimental and control subjects decreased, until under the condition of monocular viewing at 20 feet the groups did not differ. Almost all subjects reported the oscillation. Subsequent replication with other subjects verified these original findings.

The results of these experiments give partial support to the transactional point of view. When it is difficult to see the oscillation, the "inexperienced" subjects rarely report it. However, under optimal conditions, even the inexperienced subjects report oscillation. Experience with rectangular windows and with rectangular objects in general is not essential to the effect, but strongly contributes to it.

Of course, the "inexperience" of the Zulu subjects was probably not complete. Their world is not entirely spherical: people walk at right angles to the earth, trees grow perpendicularly, outstretched arms make right angles with the body. The Zulu subjects, then, were only relatively deprived of the appropriate experience. It is the strong effect of this relative deprivation which is perhaps most striking about the Allport and Pettigrew results.

A more ambitious anthropological investigation of perceptual differences was conducted by Segall, Campbell, and Herskovits (1966), who examined a wide range of perceptual phenomena, especially illusions, in a variety of cultures. Their results pointed convincingly to perceptual differences that could reasonably be attributed to differences in the environments characteristic of the various cultures. For example, the environments of the Western cultures could be described as "carpentered"; these environments are replete with right-angled visual patterns, mainly of human construction. Other groups, like the Zulus mentioned above, live in environments which are essentially "non-carpentered." That profound environmental difference shows up in differences in the way the various groups respond to visual illusions. For example, subjects from Western cultures are more susceptible to the Müller-Lyer illusion (see Figure 7.46) than are non-Western people, who have been reared in relatively noncarpentered environments. This particular finding makes sense if it is assumed that the Müller-Lyer illusion is based on subjects' interpreting the lines making up the illusory patterns as part of a three-dimensional figure. As an aside, you might note that, contrary to Werner's conception, which was mentioned earlier, it is the "primitive" people in this instance who show the lesser susceptibility to the illusory effect. Perhaps the Müller-

Lyer is a class-2 illusion, dependent on the person's transforming a two-dimensional array with meager depth cues into a three-dimensional figure.

Similar cross-cultural differences have been reported for visual acuity. Whereas "typical" subjects show maximal acuity for stimuli aligned either along the horizontal or vertical meridians, rather than obliquely, Cree Indians show no meridional differences (Annis and Frost, 1973). Their uniform acuity is attributed to the nature of the visual environment in which they live—the east coast of James Bay in Canada, a rural environment not dominated by rectilinear human constructions. In fact, the tepees in which they dwell provide stimulation by oblique contours, a type of stimulation relatively lacking in urban communities.

What Role Does Learning Play?

The Ames demonstrations, as we have indicated, seem most plausibly accounted for by reference to the observer's past experience. This, obviously, is another way of saying that the kinds of perceptual phenomena involved in these demonstrations are influenced by learning. But just where in the process does the learning play its part?

The rotating trapezoid is seen as an oscillating rectangle, partly because it is seen as a window: windows are rectangular. Seeing the ambiguous object as a window clearly involves the mediation of learning. The same is true of the "assumption" that windows are rectangular. Whether learning is involved in, or, more strongly, necessary to, any other part of the process is not so clear. For example, if the object really were an oscillating rectangle, and it were seen as such, would it be necessary to invoke learning to explain the perception? The Ames demonstrations do not answer such questions, though the transactional theory, by implication, does. According to Ittleson and Kilpatrick:

All these experiments, and many more that have been made, suggest strongly that perception is never a sure thing, never an absolute revelation of "what is." Rather, what we see is a prediction—our own personal construction designed to give us the best possible bet for carrying out our purposes in action. We make these bets on the basis of our past experience. (Ittelson and Kilpatrick, 1951, p. 55.)

A great deal more experimental evidence is necessary before such a position can claim verification. In the meantime, it is fairly certain that learning does play a role at several points in the development of perceptual processes. The full extent of this role is yet to be determined.

References

Abbe, M. The spatial effect upon the perception of time. *Japanese Journal of Psychology*, 1936, *3*, 1–52.

Abbe, M. The temporal effect upon the perception of space. *Japanese Journal of Experimental Psychology*, 1937, *4*, 83–93.

Abel, S. Duration discrimination of noise and tone bursts. *Journal of the Acoustical Society of America*, 1972, *51*, 1219–1223.

Adam, N. Mechanisms of time perception: T.-I.-T. *Journal of Life Sciences*, 1971, *1*, 41–52.

Adam, N., Castro, A. D., arid Clark, D. L. Production estimation and reproduction of time intervals during inhalation of a general anesthetic in man. *Journal of Experimental Psychology*, 1974, *102*, 609–614.

Adam, N., Rosner, B. S., Hosick, E. C., and Clark, D. L. Effect of anesthetic drugs on time production and alpha rhythm. *Perception & Psychophysics*, 1971, *10*, 133–136.

Adams, J. A. Vigilance in the detection of low-intensity visual stimuli. *Journal of Experimental Psychology*, 1956, *52*, 204–208.

Adams, J. A., and Boulter, L. R. Spatial and temporal uncertainty as determinants of vigilance performance. *Journal of Experimental Psychology*, 1964, *67*, 127–131.

Adams, J. A., and Humes, J. M. Monitoring of complex visual displays: IV. Training for vigilance. *Human Factors*, 1963, *5*, 147–153.

Adams, R. D. Intervening stimulus effects on category judgments of duration. *Perception & Psychophysics*, 1977, *21*, 527–534.

Adkins, C. J. Verbal estimations of time at four spatial distances. *Perceptual and Motor Skills*, 1972, *35*, 411–418.

Aiken, L. S., and Brown, D. R. Visual form perception: Congruence among spatial configurations. *Perception & Psychophysics*, 1969, *5*, 155–160.

Aitken, P. P. Judgments of pleasingness and interestingness as functions of visual complexity. *Journal of Experimental Psychology*, 1974, *103*, 240–244.

Allan, L. G., and Kristofferson, A. B. Psychophysical theories of duration discrimination. *Perception & Psychophysics*, 1974, *16*, 26–34.

Allison, J. Cognitive structure and receptivity to low intensity stimulation. *Journal of Abnormal and Social Psychology*, 1963, *67*, 132–138.

Allport, F. H. *Theories of perception and the concept of structure*. New York: Wiley, 1955.

Allport, G. W., and Pettigrew, T. F. Cultural influence on the perception of movement: The trapezoidal illusion among Zulus. *Journal of Abnormal and Social Psychology*, 1957, *55*, 104–113.

Alluisi, E. A. Conditions affecting the amount of information in absolute judgments. *Psychological Review*, 1957, *64*, 97–103.

Alluisi, E. A. Information and uncertainty: The metrics of communications. In K. B. DeGreene (Ed.), *Systems psychology*. New York: McGraw-Hill, 1970.

Alluisi, E. A., and Hall, T. J. Declines in auditory vigilance during periods of high multiple-task activity. *Perceptual and Motor Skills*, 1963, *16*, 739–740.

Alluisi, E. A., Strain G. S., and Thurmond, J. B. Stimulus-response compatibility and the rate of gain of information. *Psychonomic Science*, 1964, *1*, 111–112.

Alpern, M. Effector mechanisms in vision. In J. W. Kling and L. A. Riggs (Eds.), *Woodworth & Schlosberg's experimental psychology*, 3d ed. New York: Holt, Rinehart and Winston, 1971.

Ames, A., Jr. Visual perception and the rotating trapezoidal window. *Psychological Monographs*, 1951, *65*, Whole No. 324.

Anderson, N. H. Functional measurement and psychophysical judgment. *Psychological Review*, 1970, *77*, 153–170.

Anderson, N. H. On the role of context effects in psychophysical judgment. *Psychological Review*, 1975, *82*, 462–482.

Anliker, J. Variations in alpha voltage of the electroencephalogram and time perception. *Science*, 1963, *140*, 1307–1309.

Annis, R. C., and Frost, B. Human visual ecology and orientation anisotropies in acuity. *Science*, 1973, *182*, 729–731.

Anokhin, P. K. A new conception of the physiological architecture of conditioned reflex. In J. F. Delafresnaye (Ed.), *Brain mechanisms and learning*. Oxford: Blackwell Scientific Publications, 1961.

Ansbacher, H. C. Distortion in the perception of real movement. *Journal of Experimental Psychology*, 1944, *34*, 1–23.

Appelle, S. Perception and discrimination as a function of stimulus orientation: The "oblique effect" in man and animals. *Psychological Bulletin*, 1972, *78*, 266–278.

Arand, D. Metacontrast with internal contours in target and mask. Unpublished masters thesis, University of Cincinnati, 1974.

Arand, D., and Dember, W. N. Metacontrast with internal contours in target and mask. *Bulletin of the Psychonomic Society*, 1976, *7*, 370–372.

Arnheim, R. *Art and visual perception*, rev. ed. Berkeley: University of California Press, 1974.

Arnoult, M. D. Prediction of perceptual responses from structural characteristics of the stimulus. *Perceptual and Motor Skills*, 1960, *11*, 261–268.

Arnoult, M. D. Psychophysical models for pattern perception. U.S. Army Human Engineering Laboratories, Aberdeen Proving Ground, Maryland, Technical Memorandum 17–68, 1968, 63–68.

Ashley, W., Harper, R., and Runyon, D. The perceived size of coins in normal and hypnotically induced economic states. *American Journal of Psychology*, 1951, *64*, 564–572.

Atkinson, J. W., and Walker, E. L. The affiliation motive and perceptual sensitivity to faces. *Journal of Abnormal and Social Psychology*, 1956, *53*, 38–41.

Atkinson, R. C. A variable sensitivity theory of signal detection. *Psychological Review*, 1963, *70*, 91–106.

Attneave, F. Some informational aspects of visual perception. *Psychological Review*, 1954, *61*, 183–193.

Attneave, F. Physical determinants of the judged complexity of shapes. *Journal of Experimental Psychology*, 1957, *53*, 221–227.

Attneave, F. *Applications of information theory to psychology.* New York: Holt, Rinehart and Winston, 1959.

Attneave, F. Perception and related areas. In S. Koch (Ed.), *Psychology: A study of a science,* Vol. 4. New York: McGraw-Hill, 1962.

Attneave, F. Multistability in perception. *Scientific American,* 1971, *225,* 63–71.

Attneave, F., and Arnoult, M. D. The quantitative study of shape and pattern perception. *Psychological Bulletin,* 1956, *53,* 452–471.

Attneave, F., and Block, G. Apparent movement in tridimensional space. *Perception & Psychophysics,* 1973, *13,* 301–307.

Avant, L. L. Vision in the Ganzfeld. *Psychological Bulletin,* 1965, *64,* 246–258.

Avant, L. L., and Lyman, P. J. Stimulus familiarity modifies perceived duration in prerecognition visual processing. *Journal of Experimental Psychology: Human Perception and Performance,* 1975, *1,* 205–213.

Averbach, E., and Sperling, G. Short term storage of information in vision. In C. Cherry (Ed.), *Information theory.* London: Butterworth, 1961, 196–211.

Ayllon, T., and Sommer, R. Autism, emphasis, and figure-ground perception. *Journal of Psychology,* 1956, *41,* 163–176.

Bach, S., and Klein, G. S. The effects of prolonged subliminal exposure of words. *American Psychologist,* 1957, *12,* 397–398.

Baddeley, A. D. Time estimation at reduced body temperature. *American Journal of Psychology,* 1966, *79,* 475–479.

Badia, P., and Defran, R. H. Orienting responses and GSR conditioning: A dilemma. *Psychological Review,* 1970, *77,* 171–181.

Baird, J. C. Retinal and assumed size cues as determinants of size and distance perception. *Journal of Experimental Psychology,* 1963, *66,* 155–162.

Baird, J. C. A cognitive theory of psychophysics: II. Fechner's law and Stevens' law. *Scandinavian Journal of Psychology,* 1970, *11,* 89–102. (a)

Baird, J. C. A cognitive theory of psychophysics, information transmission, partitioning and Weber's law. *Scandinavian Journal of Psychology,* 1970, *11,* 35–46. (b)

Baird, J. C., Kreindler, M., and Jones, K. Generation of multiple ratio scales with a fixed stimulus attribute. *Perception & Psychophysics,* 1971, *9,* 399–403.

Baker, C. H. Observing behavior in a vigilance task. *Science,* 1960, *132,* 674–675.

Baker, C. H. Further toward a theory of vigilance. In D. N. Buckner and J. J. McGrath (Eds.), *Vigilance: A symposium.* New York: McGraw-Hill, 1963. (a)

Baker, C. H. Signal duration as a factor in vigilance tasks. *Science,* 1963, *141,* 1196–1197. (b)

Baker, M. A., and Loeb, M. Implications of measurement of eye fixations for a psychophysics of form perception. *Perception & Psychophysics,* 1973, *13,* 185–192.

Baker, R. A., Ware, J. R., and Sipowicz, R. R. Vigilance: A comparison in auditory, visual, and combined audio-visual tasks. *Canadian Journal of Psychology,* 1962, *16,* 192–198.

Banks, W. P., and Hill, D. K. The apparent magnitude of number scaled by random production. *Journal of Experimental Psychology,* 1974, *102,* 353–376.

Barlow, H. B., and Hill, R. M. Selective sensitivity to direction of movement in ganglion cells of the rabbit retina. *Science,* 1963, *139,* 412–414.

Barlow, H. B., Hill, R. M., and Levick, W. R. Retinal ganglion cells responding selectively to direction and speed of image motion in the rabbit. *Journal of Physiology,* 1964, *173,* 377–407.

Barlow, H. B., Narasimhan, R., and Rosenfeld, A. Visual pattern analysis in machines and animals. *Science,* 1972, *177,* 567–575.

Barnett, S. A. *The rat.* Chicago: Aldine, 1963.

Bartlett, N. R. Thresholds as dependent on some energy relations and characteristics of the subject. In C. H. Graham (Ed.), *Vision and visual perception.* New York: Wiley, 1965.

Bartley, S. H. *Principles of perception,* 2d ed. New York: Harper & Row, 1969.

Baumgartner, G., Brown, J. L., and Schultz, A. Visual motion detection in the cat. *Science,* 1964, *146,* 1070–1071.

Bean, C. H. The blind have "optical illusions." *Journal of Experimental Psychology,* 1938, *22,* 283–289.

Beatty, J. *Introduction to physiological psychology: Information processing in the nervous system.* Monterey, Calif.: Brooks/Cole, 1975.

Beatty, J., Ahern, S. K., and Katz, R. Sleep deprivation and the vigilance of anesthesiologists during simulated surgery. In R. R. Mackie (Ed.), *Vigilance: Theory, operational performance and physiological correlates.* New York: Plenum, 1977.

Beatty, J., Greenberg, A., Deibler, W. P., and O'Hanlon, J. F. Operant control of occipital theta rhythm affects performance in a radar monitoring task. *Science,* 1974, *183,* 871–873.

Beck, J. Stimulus correlates for the judged illumination of a surface. *Journal of Experimental Psychology,* 1959, *58,* 267–274.

Beck, J. Judgments of surface illumination and lightness. *Journal of Experimental Psychology,* 1961, *61,* 368–375.

Beck. J. Apparent spatial position and the perception of lightness. *Journal of Experimental Psychology,* 1965, *69,* 170–179.

Beck, J. Effect of orientation and of shape similarity on perceptual grouping. *Perception & Psychophysics,* 1966, *1,* 300–302. (a)

Beck, J. Perceptual grouping produced by changes in orientation and shape. *Science,* 1966, *154,* 538–540. (b)

Beck, J. Perceptual grouping produced by line figures. *Perception & Psychophysics,* 1967, *2,* 491–495.

Beck, J. Surface color perception. In G. S. Reynolds (Ed.), *Experimental Psychology,* Vol. II. Glenview, Ill.: Scott, Foresman, 1969.

Beck, J. Surface lightness and cues for illumination. *American Journal of Psychology,* 1971, *84,* 1–11.

Beck, J. Similarity grouping and peripheral discriminability under uncertainty. *American Journal of Psychology,* 1972, *85,* 1–19.

Beck, J. Dimensions of an achromatic surface color. In R. B. MacLeod and H. L. Pick (Eds.), *Perception: Essays in honor of James J. Gibson.* Ithaca, N.Y.: Cornell University Press, 1974.

Beck, J. The perception of surface color. *Scientific American,* 1975, *233,* 62–75.

Beck, J., Elsner, A., and Silverstein, C. Position uncertainty and the perception of apparent movement. *Perception & Psychophysics,* 1977, *21,* 33–38.

Beck, J., and Gibson, J. J. The relation of apparent shape to apparent slant in the perception of objects. *Journal of Experimental Psychology,* 1955, *50,* 125–133.

Beebe-Center, J. G., Rogers, M. S., and O'Connell, D. N. Transmission of information about sucrose and saline solutions through the sense of taste. *Journal of Psychology,* 1955, *39,* 157–160.

Behar, I., and Bevan, W. Analysis of the prime psychophysical judgment. *Perceptual and Motor Skills,* 1960, *10,* 82.

Behar, I., and Bevan, W. The perceived duration of auditory and visual intervals: Cross-modal comparison and interaction. *American Journal of Psychology,* 1961, *74,* 17–26.

Békésy, G. von. *Experiments in hearing.* New York: McGraw-Hill, 1960.

Békésy, G. von. *Sensory inhibition.* Princeton, N.J.: Princeton University Press, 1967.

Bell, C. R. Time estimation and increases in body temperature. *Journal of Experimental Psychology,* 1965, *70,* 232–234.

Bell, C. R., and Provins, K. A. Relation between physiological responses to environmental heat and time judgments. *Journal of Experimental Psychology,* 1963, *66,* 572–579.

Bell, H. H., and Lappin, J. S. Sufficient conditions for the discrimination of motion. *Perception & Psychophysics,* 1973, *14,* 45–50.

Berlin, B., and Kay, P. *Basic color terms: Their universality and evolution.* Berkeley: University of California Press, 1969.

Berlyne, D. E. Attention to change. *British Journal of Psychology,* 1951, *42,* 269–278.

Berlyne, D. E. The arousal and satiation of perceptual curiosity in the rat. *Journal of Comparative and Physiological Psychology,* 1955, *48,* 238–246.

Berlyne, D. E. Attention to change, conditioned inhibition (slr) and stimulus satiation. *British Journal of Psychology,* 1957, *48,* 138–140. (a)

Berlyne, D. E. Uncertainty and conflict: A point of contact between information-theory and behavior-theory concepts. *Psychological Review,* 1957, *64,* 329–339. (b)

Berlyne, D. E. The influence of complexity and change in visual figures on orienting responses. *Journal of Experimental Psychology,* 1958, *55,* 289–296. (a)

Berlyne, D. E. The influence of albedo and complexity of stimuli on visual fixation in the human infant. *British Journal of Psychology,* 1958, *49,* 315–318. (b)

Berlyne, D. E., *Conflict, arousal and curiosity.* New York: McGraw-Hill, 1960.

Berlyne, D. E. Curiosity and exploration. *Science,* 1966, *153,* 25–33.

Berlyne, D. E. Attention as a problem in behavior theory. In D. I. Mostofsky (Ed.), *Attention: Contemporary theory and analysis.* New York: Academic Press, 1970.

Berlyne, D. E., and Slater, J. Perceptual curiosity, exploratory behavior, and maze learning. *Journal of Comparative and Physiological Psychology,* 1957, *50,* 228–232.

Bexton, W. H., Heron, W., and Scott, T. H. Effects of decreased variation in the sensory environment. *Canadian Journal of Psychology,* 1954, *8,* 70–76.

Biederman, I. Perceiving real-world scenes. *Science,* 1972, *177,* 77–80.

Bilderback, L. G., Taylor, R. E., and Thor, D. H. Distance perception in darkness. *Science,* 1964, *145,* 294–295.

Bill, J. C., and Teft, L. W. Space-time relations: Effects of time on perceived visual extent. *Journal of Experimental Psychology,* 1969, *81,* 196–199.

Binet, A. *Alterations of personality.* New York: D. Appleton & Co., 1896.

Bishop, P. O. Neurophysiology of binocular single vision and stereopsis. In R. Jung (Ed.), *Handbook of sensory physiology: Vol. VII/3. Central processing of visual information, Part A.* New York: Springer-Verlag, 1973.

Bishop, P. O., and Henry, G. H. Spatial vision. In P. H. Mussen and M. R. Rosenzweig (Eds.), *Annual review of psychology,* Palo Alto, Calif.: Annual Reviews, Inc., 1972.

Black, J. W. The effect of delayed side-tone upon vocal rate and intensity. *Journal of Speech and Hearing Disorders,* 1951, *16,* 56–60.

Blackwell, H. R. *Psychophysical thresholds: Experimental studies of methods of measurement.* Bulletin of the Engineering Research Institute, University of Michigan, No. 36, 1953.

Blake, R. R., Fox, R., and McIntyre, C. Stochastic properties of stabilized-image binocular rivalry alternations. *Journal of Experimental Psychology,* 1971, *88,* 327–332.

Blakemore, C., and Campbell, F. W. On the existence of neurons in the human visual system selectively sensitive to the orientation and size of retinal images. *Journal of Physiology,* 1969, *203,* 237–260.

Blakemore, C., Carpenter, R. H. S., and Georgeson, M. A. Lateral inhibition between orientation detectors in the human visual system. *Nature,* 1970, *228,* 37–39.

Blakemore, C., and Cooper, G. F. Development of the brain depends on visual environment. *Nature,* 1970, *228,* 447–478.

Blakemore, C., and Sutton, P. Size adaptation: A new aftereffect. *Science,* 1969, *166,* 245–247.

Blum, G. S. An experimental reunion of psychoanalytic theory with perceptual vigilance and defense. *Journal of Abnormal and Social Psychology,* 1954, *49,* 94–98.

Bolles, R. C., and Bailey, D. E. Importance of object recognition in size constancy. *Journal of Experimental Psychology,* 1956, *51,* 222–225.

Bootzin, R. R., and Natsoulas, T. Evidence for perceptual defense uncontaminated by response bias. *Journal of Personality and Social Psychology,* 1965, *1,* 461–468.

Boring, E. G. A new ambiguous figure. *American Journal of Psychology,* 1930, *42,* 444–445.

Boring, E. G. *Sensation and perception in the history of experimental psychology.* New York: Appleton, 1942.

Boring, E. G. The moon illusion. *American Journal of Physics,* 1943, *11,* 55–60.

Boring, E. G. *A history of experimental psychology,* 2d ed. New York: Appleton, 1950.

Boring, E. G. On the moon illusion (letters to the editor). *Science,* 1962, *137,* 902–906.

Boring, E. G. Attention: Research and beliefs concerning the conception in scientific psychology before 1930. In D. I. Mostofsky (Ed.), *Attention: Contemporary theory and analysis.* New York: Academic Press, 1970.

Boring, E. G., Langfeld, H. S., and Weld, H. P. *Introduction to psychology.* New York: Wiley, 1939.

Bornstein, M. H. Qualities of color vision in infancy. *Journal of Experimental Child Psychology,* 1975, *19,* 401–419.

Bornstein, M. H., Kessen, W., and Weiskopf, S. Color vision and hue categorization in young human infants. *Journal of Experimental Psychology: Human Perception and Performance,* 1976, *2,* 115–129.

Bourne, L. E., and Ekstrand, B. R. *Psychology: Its principles and meanings:* 2d ed. New York: Holt, Rinehart and Winston, 1979.

Bower, T. G. R. Stimulus variables determining space perception in infants. *Science,* 1965, *149,* 88–89.

Bower, T. G. R. The visual world of infants. *Scientific American,* 1966, *215,* 80–92.

Bowlby, J. *Maternal care and mental health.* World Health Organization, 1951.

Boynton, R. M. Retinal contrast mechanisms. In F. A. Young and D. B. Lindsley

(Eds.), *Early experience and visual information processing in perceptual and reading disorders*. Washington, D.C.: National Academy of Sciences, 1970.

Brackman, J., and Collier, G. The dependence of probability of response on size of step interval in the method of limits. *Journal of Experimental Psychology*, 1958, *5*, 423–428.

Bradley, D. R., and Petry, H. M. Organizational determinants of subjective contour: The subjective Necker cube. *American Journal of Psychology*, 1977, *90*, 253–262.

Brainard, R. W., Irby, T. S., Fitts, P. M., and Alluisi, E. A. Some variables influencing the rate of gain of information. *Journal of Experimental Psychology*, 1962, *63*, 105–110.

Brauner, J. D., and Lit, A. The Pulfrich effect, simple reaction time, and intensity discrimination. *American Journal of Psychology*, 1976, *89*, 105–114.

Braunstein, M. L. The perception of depth through motion. *Psychological Bulletin*, 1962, *59*, 422–433.

Braunstein, M. L. *Depth perception through motion*. New York: Academic Press, 1976.

Breitmeyer, B. G., and Ganz, L. Implications of sustained and transient channels for theories of visual pattern masking, saccadic suppression, and information processing. *Psychological Review*, 1976, *83*, 1–36.

Bridgeman, B. Metacontrast and lateral inhibition. *Psychological Review*, 1971, *78*, 528–539.

Bridgeman, B. Visual receptive fields sensitive to absolute and relative motion during tracking. *Science*, 1972, *178*, 1106–1108.

Brill, M. Parameters of odor-trail avoidance in the spontaneous alternation of the rat. Unpublished doctoral dissertation, University of Cincinnati, 1967.

Brindley, G. S., and Merton, P. A. The absence of position sense in the human eye. *Journal of Physiology*. 1960, *153*, 127–130.

Brislin, R. W., and Leibowitz, H. W. The effect of separation between test and comparison objects on size constancy at various age-levels. *American Journal of Psychology*, 1970, *83*, 372–376.

Broadbent, D. E. The role of auditory localization and attention in memory span. *Journal of Experimental Psychology*, 1954, *47*, 191–196.

Broadbent, D. E. *Perception and communication*. Oxford: Pergamon, 1958.

Broadbent, D. E. Possibilities and difficulties in the concept of arousal. In D. N. Buckner and J. J. McGrath (Eds.), *Vigilance: A symposium*. New York: McGraw-Hill, 1963. (a)

Broadbent, D. E. Some recent studies from the applied psychology research unit. In D. N. Buckner and J. J. McGrath (Eds.), *Vigilance: A symposium*. New York: McGraw-Hill, 1963. (b)

Broadbent, D. E. Information processing in the nervous system. *Science*, 1965, *150*, 457–462.

Broadbent, D. E. Word-frequency effect and response bias. *Psychological Review*, 1967, *74*, 1–15.

Broadbent, D. E. *Decision and stress*. New York: Academic Press, 1971.

Broadbent, D. E., and Gregory, M. Division of attention and the decision theory of signal detection. *Proceedings of the Royal Society*, London 1963, *158*, 222–231. (a)

Broadbent, D. E., and Gregory, M. Vigilance considered as a statistical decision. *British Journal of Psychology*, 1963, *54*, 309–323. (b)

Broadbent, D. E., and Gregory M. Stimulus set and response set: The alternation of attention. *Quarterly Journal of Experimental Psychology,* 1964, *16,* 309–317.

Brown, B. R., and Evans, S. H. Perceptual learning in pattern discrimination tasks with two and three schema categories. *Psychonomic Science,* 1969, *15,* 101–103.

Brown, D. R., and Andrews, M. H. Visual form discrimination: Multidimensional analyses. *Perception & Psychophysics,* 1968, *3,* 401-406.

Brown, D. R., and Brumaghim, S. H. Perceptual equivalence, pattern perception, and multidimensional methods. *Perception & Psychophysics,* 1968, *4,* 253–256.

Brown, D. R., and Goldstein, J. A. Stimulus correlates of the discrimination behavior of children. *Psychonomic Science,* 1967, *9,* 177–178.

Brown, D. R., Hitchcock, L. Jr., and Michels, K. M. Quantitative studies in form perception: An evaluation of the role of selected stimulus parameters in the visual discrimination performance of human subjects. *Perceptual and Motor Skills,* 1962, *14,* 519–529.

Brown, D. R., and Owen, D. H. The metrics of visual form: Methodological dyspepsia. *Psychological Bulletin,* 1967, *68,* 243–259.

Brown, J. F. The visual perception of velocity. *Psychologische Forschung,* 1931, *14,* 199–232. Reprinted in I. M. Spigel (Ed.), *Readings in the study of visually perceived movement.* New York: Harper & Row, 1965.

Brown, J. H. Cross-modal estimation of angular velocity. *Perception & Psychophysics,* 1968, *3,* 115–117.

Brown, J. L., and Mueller, C. G. Brightness discrimination and brightness contrast. In C. H. Graham (Ed.), *Vision and visual perception.* New York: Wiley, 1965.

Brown, J. S. *The motivation of behavior.* New York: McGraw-Hill, 1961.

Brown, L. T., and Gregory, L. P. Attentional response of humans and squirrel monkeys to visual patterns: Final studies and resumé. *Perceptual and Motor Skills,* 1968, *27,* 787–814.

Brown, R. H. Velocity discrimination and the intensity-time relation. *Journal of the Optical Society of America,* 1955, *45,* 189–192.

Brown, R. H., and Conklin, J. E. The lower threshold of visible movement as a function of exposure time. *American Journal of Psychology,* 1954, *67,* 104–110.

Brown, R. W., and Lenneberg, E. H. A study in language and cognition. *Journal of Abnormal and Social Psychology,* 1954, *49,* 454–462.

Bruce, R. L. *Fundamentals of physiological psychology.* New York: Holt, Rinehart and Winston, 1977.

Brumaghim, S. H., and Brown, D. R. Perceptual equivalence between visual and tactual pattern perception: An anchoring study. *Perception & Psychophysics,* 1968, *4,* 175–179.

Bruner, J. S., and Goodman, C. C. Value and need as organizing factors in perception. *Journal of Abnormal and Social Psychology,* 1947, *42,* 33–44.

Bruner, J. S., and Postman, L. On the perception of incongruity: A paradigm. *Journal of Personality,* 1949, *18,* 206–223.

Bruner, J. S., Postman, L., and Rodrigues, J. Expectation and the perception of color. *American Journal of Psychology,* 1951, *64,* 216–227.

Bruner, J. S., and Potter, M. C. Interference in visual recognition. *Science,* 1964, *144,* 424–425.

Brunswik, E. Zur Entwicklung der Albedowahrnehmung. *Zeitschrift für Psychologie,* 1929, *109,* 40–115.

Brunswik, E. Distal focusing of perception. Size constancy in a representative sample of situations. *Psychological Monographs,* 1944, *56,* Whole No. 254.

Brunswik, E. *Perception and the representative design of psychological experiments.* Berkeley: University of California Press, 1956.

Bryden, M. P. The manipulation of strategies of report in dichotic listening. *Canadian Journal of Psychology,* 1964, *18,* 126–138.

Buckner, D. N., and McGrath, J. J. A comparison of performances on single and dual sensory mode vigilance tasks. In D. N. Buckner and J. J. McGrath (Eds.), *Vigilance: A symposium.* New York: McGraw-Hill, 1963.

Buffardi, L. Factors affecting the filled-duration illusion in the auditory, tactual, and visual modalities. *Perception & Psychophysics,* 1971, *10,* 292–294.

Burian, H. M., and von Noorden, G. K. *Binocular vision and ocular motility.* St. Louis: Mosby, 1974.

Burkamp, W. Versuche über das Farbenwiedererkennen der Fische. *Zeitschrift für Sinnesphysik,* 1923, *55,* 133–170

Burns, B. D., and Pritchard, R. Geometrical illusions and the response of neurons in the cat's visual cortex to angle patterns. *Journal of Physiology,* 1971, *213,* 599–616.

Burnside, W. Judgment of short time intervals while performing mathematical tasks. *Perception & Psychophysics,* 1971, *9,* 404–406.

Butler, R. A. Discrimination learning by rhesus monkeys to auditory incentives. *Journal of Comparative and Physiological Psychology,* 1953, *46,* 95–98.

Butler, R. A. Discrimination learning by rhesus monkeys to auditory incentives. *Journal of Comparative and Physiological Psychology,* 1957, *50,* 239–241.

Butler, R. A., and Harlow, H. F. Persistence of visual exploration in monkeys. *Journal of Comparative and Physiological Psychology,* 1954, *47,* 258–263.

Caldwell, E. C., and Hall, V. C. Distinctive-features versus prototype learning reexamined. *Journal of Experimental Psychology,* 1970, *83,* 7–12.

Campbell, F. W., and Robson, J. G. Application of Fourier analysis to the visibility of gratings. *Journal of Physiology,* 1968, *197,* 551–556.

Carbotte, R. M., and Kristofferson, A. B. On energy dependent cues in duration discrimination. *Perception & Psychophysics,* 1973, *14,* 501–505.

Carder, B., and Berkowitz, K. Rats' preference for earned in comparison with free food. *Science,* 1970, *167,* 1273–1274.

Carlson, J. H. Effect of instructions and perspective-drawing ability on perceptual constancies and geometrical illusions. *Journal of Experimental Psychology,* 1966, *72,* 874–879.

Carlson, V. R. Size-constancy judgments and perceptual compromise. *Journal of Experimental Psychology,* 1962, *63,* 68–73.

Carter, L. F., and Schooler, K. Value, need, and other factors in perception. *Psychological Review,* 1949, *56,* 200–207.

Casler, L. Maternal deprivation: A critical review of the literature. *Monographs of the Society for Research in Child Development,* 1961, *26,* No. 2.

Chalmers, E. L. Monocular and binocular cues in the perception of size and distance. *American Journal of Psychology,* 1952, *65,* 415–423.

Chapanis, A. How we see: A summary of basic principles. In *Human factors in undersea warfare.* Washington, D.C.: National Research Council, 1949.

Chapanis, A. Color names for color space. *American Scientist,* 1965, *53,* 327–346.

Chapanis, A., and Halsey, R. M. Absolute judgments of spectrum colors. *Journal of Psychology,* 1956, *42,* 99–103.

Chapman, D. W. Relative effects of determinate and indeterminate *Aufgaben. American Journal of Psychology,* 1932, *44,* 163–174.

Chase, W. P. Color vision in infants. *Journal of Experimental Psychology,* 1937, *20,* 203–222.

Cherry, E. C. Some experiments on the recognition of speech with one and with two ears. *Journal of the Acoustical Society of America,* 1953, *25,* 975–979.

Chiang, C. A new theory to explain geometrical illusions produced by crossing lines. *Perception & Psychophysics,* 1968, *3* 174–176.

Christman, R. J. *Sensory experience.* Scranton, Pa.: Intext, 1971.

Churchill, A. V. Supplementary report: Effect of mode of response on judgment of familiar size. *Journal of Experimental Psychology,* 1962, *64,* 198–199.

Clapp, D. F. Information processing in mental retardation: The effects of sensory modality on the absolute judgment of stimulus duration. Unpublished masters thesis, University of Cincinnati, 1972.

Clapp, D. F. Information processing in normals and mental retardates: The effects of organizational and memory factors in absolute judgments of spatial position. Unpublished doctoral dissertation, University of Cincinnati, 1973.

Clark, H. J. Recognition memory for random shapes as a function of complexity, association value, and delay. *Journal of Experimental Psychology,* 1965, *69,* 590–595.

Clark, H. J. Random shape recognition at brief exposure durations. *Psychonomic Science,* 1968, *12,* 245–246.

Clark, J. L., Warm, J. S., and Schumsky, D. A. General and specific factors in the intersensory transfer of form. *Journal of Experimental Psychology,* 1972, *95,* 184–188.

Clark, W. C. The psych in psychophysics: A sensory-decision theory analysis of the effect of instructions on flicker sensitivity and response bias. *Psychological Bulletin,* 1966, *65,* 358–367.

Clark, W. C., Smith, A. H., and Rabe, A. Retinal gradients of outline distortion and binocular disparity as stimuli for slant. *Canadian Journal of Psychology,* 1956, *10,* 77–81. (a)

Clark, W. C., Smith, A. H., and Rabe, A. The interaction of surface texture, outline gradient, and ground in the perception of slant. *Canadian Journal of Psychology,* 1956, *10,* 1–8. (b)

Clark, W. C., and Yang, J. C. Acupunctural analgesia: Evaluation by signal detection theory. *Science,* 1974, *184,* 1096–1098.

Cliff, N. Scaling. In P. H. Mussen and M. R. Rosenzweig (Eds.), *Annual review of psychology.* Palo Alto, Calif.: Annual Reviews, Inc., 1973.

Cohen, H. B. The effect of contralateral visual stimulation on visibility with stabilized retinal images. *Canadian Journal of Psychology,* 1961, *15,* 212–219.

Cohen, J., Hansel, C. E. M., and Sylvester, J. D. A new phenomenon in time judgment. *Nature,* 1953, *172,* 901–903.

Cohen, J., Hansel, C. E. M., and Sylvester, J. D. Interdependence in judgments of space, time and movement. *Acta Psychologica,* 1955, *11,* 360–372.

Cohen, R. L., and Bonnet, C. Movement detection thresholds and stimulus duration. *Perception & Psychophysics,* 1972, *12,* 269–272.

Cohen, W. Spatial and textural characteristics of the *Ganzfeld. American Journal of Psychology,* 1957, *70,* 403–410.

Cohen, W. Color perception in the chromatic *Ganzfeld*. *American Journal of Psychology*, 1958, *71*, 390–394. (a)

Cohen, W. Apparent movement of simple figures in the *Ganzfeld*. *Perceptual and Motor Skills*, 1958, *8*, 32. (b)

Cohn, T. E., and Lasley, D. J. Detectability of a luminance increment: Effect of spatial uncertainty. *Journal of the Optical Society of America*, 1974, *64*, 1715–1719.

Cohn, T. E., Thibos, L. N., and Kleinstein, R. N. Detectability of a luminance increment. *Journal of the Optical Society of America*, 1974, *64*, 1321–1327.

Colquhoun, W. P. The effect of "unwanted" signals on performance in a vigilance task. *Ergonomics*, 1961, *4*, 42–51.

Colquhoun, W. P. Evaluation of auditory, visual, and dual-mode displays for prolonged sonar monitoring in repeated sessions. *Human Factors*, 1975, *17*, 425–437.

Colquhoun, W. P., and Baddeley, A. D. Role of pretest expectancy in vigilance decrement. *Journal of Experimental Psychology*, 1964, *68*, 156–160.

Colquhoun, W. P., and Baddeley, A. D. Influence of signal probability during pretraining on vigilance decrement. *Journal of Experimental Psychology*, 1967, *73*, 153–155.

Colquhoun, W. P., and Edwards, R. S. Interaction of noise with alcohol on a task of sustained attention. *Ergonomics*, 1975, *18*, 81–87.

Coltheart, M. The effect of verbal size information upon visual judgments of absolute distance. *Perception & Psychophysics*, 1971, *9*, 222–223.

Conant, J. B. *On understanding science*. New Haven: Yale University Press, 1947.

Coombs, C. H., Dawes, R. M., and Tversky, A. *Mathematical psychology: An elementary introduction*. Englewood Cliffs, N.J.: Prentice-Hall, 1970.

Cooper, L. A. Mental rotation of random two-dimensional shapes. *Cognitive Psychology*, 1975, *7*, 20–43.

Corcoran, D. W. J. *Pattern recognition*. Baltimore: Penguin, 1971.

Coren, S. The influence of optical aberrations on the magnitude of the Poggendorff illusion. *Perception & Psychophysics*, 1969, *6*, 185–186.

Coren, S. Subjective contours and apparent depth. *Psychological Review*, 1972, *79*, 359–367.

Coren, S., and Girgus, J. S. Illusion decrement in intersecting line figures. *Psychonomic Science*, 1972, *26*, 108–110.

Coren, S., and Girgus, J. S. Visual spatial illusions: Many explanations. *Science*, 1973, *179*, 503–504.

Coren, S., Girgus, J. S., Erlichman, H., and Hakstian, A. R. An empirical taxonomy of visual illusions. *Perception & Psychophysics*, 1976, *20*, 129–137.

Coren, S., and Hoenig, P. Eye movements and decrement in the Oppel–Kundt illusion. *Perception & Psychophysics*, 1972, *12*, 224–225.

Coren, S., and Theodor, L. H. Subjective contour: The inadequacy of brightness contrast as an explanation. *Bulletin of the Psychonomic Society*, 1975, *6*, 87–89.

Coren, S., and Theodor, L. H. Neural interactions and subjective contours. *Perception*, 1977, *6*, 107–111.

Cornsweet, T. N. The staircase-method in psychophysics. *American Journal of Psychology*, 1962, *75*, 485–491.

Cornsweet, T. N. *Visual perception*. New York: Academic Press, 1970.

Cornwell, H. G. Prior experience as a determinant of figure–ground organization. *Journal of Experimental Psychology*, 1963, *65*, 156–162.

Corso, J. F. The neural quantum theory of sensory discrimination. *Psychological Bulletin,* 1956, *53,* 371–393.

Corso, J. F. A theoretico-historical review of the threshold concept. *Psychological Bulletin,* 1963, *60,* 356–370.

Corso, J. F. *The experimental psychology of sensory behavior.* New York: Holt, Rinehart and Winston, 1967.

Corteen, R. S., and Dunn, D. Shock-associated words in a nonattended message: A test for momentary awareness. *Journal of Experimental Psychology,* 1974, *102,* 1143–1144.

Corteen, R. S., and Wood, B. Autonomic responses to shock-associated words in an unattended channel. *Journal of Experimental Psychology,* 1972, *94,* 308–313.

Cowen, E. L., and Beier, E. G. Threat-expectancy, word frequencies, and perceptual prerecognition hypotheses. *Journal of Abnormal and Social Psychology,* 1954, *49,* 178–182.

Craig, J. C. A constant error in the perception of brief temporal intervals. *Perception & Psychophysics,* 1973, *13,* 99–104.

Creelman, C. D. Detection of signals of uncertain frequency. *Journal of the Acoustical Society of America,* 1960, *32,* 805–810.

Creelman, C. D. Human discrimination of auditory duration. In J. A. Swets (Ed.), *Signal detection and recognition by human observers: Contemporary readings.* New York: Wiley, 1964.

Crovitz, H. F., and Lockhead, G. R. Possible monocular predictors of binocular rivalry contours. *Perception & Psychophysics,* 1967, *2,* 83–85.

Cross, D. V. Sequential dependencies and regression in psychophysical judgments. *Perception & Psychophysics,* 1973, *14,* 547–552.

Cruetzfelt, O. D., and Heggelund, P. Neural plasticity in visual cortex of adult cats after exposure to visual patterns. *Science,* 1975, *188,* 1025–1027.

Curtis, D. W. Magnitude estimations and category judgments of brightness and brightness intervals: A two-stage process. *Journal of Experimental Psychology,* 1970, *83,* 201–208.

D'Amato, M. R. *Experimental psychology: Methodology, psychophysics and learning.* New York: McGraw-Hill, 1970.

Dardano, J. F. Relationships of intermittent noise, intersignal interval and skin conductance to vigilance behavior. *Journal of Applied Psychology,* 1962, *46,* 106–114.

Davenport, W. G. Arousal theory and vigilance: Schedules for background stimulation. *Journal of General Psychology,* 1974, *91,* 51–59.

Davies, D. R., and Krkovic, J. Skin-conductance, alpha-activity and vigilance. *American Journal of Psychology,* 1965, *78,* 304–306.

Davies, D. R., and Tune, G. S. *Human vigilance performance.* New York: American Elsevier, 1969.

Day, R. H. *Human perception.* New York: Wiley, 1969.

Day, R. H. Visual spatial illusions: A general explanation. *Science,* 1972, *175,* 1335–1340.

DeCillis, O. E. Absolute thresholds for the perception of tactual movement. *Archives of Psychology,* 1944, *294,* 1–52.

Dees, J. W. Accuracy of absolute visual distance and size estimation in space as a function of stereopsis and motion parallax. *Journal of Experimental Psychology,* 1966, *72,* 466–476.

Deese, J. Some problems in the theory of vigilance. *Psychological Review*, 1955, *62*, 359–368.

Dember, W. N. Response by the rat to environmental change. *Journal of Comparative and Physiological Psychology*, 1956, *49*, 93–95.

Dember, W. N. Looking backward. Presidential address, Midwestern Psychological Association, Chicago, Ill., 1976.

Dember, W. N., and Earl, R. W. Analysis of exploratory, manipulatory, and curiosity behaviors. *Psychological Review*, 1957, *64*, 91–96.

Dember, W. N., Earl, R. W., and Paradise, N. Response by rats to differential stimulus complexity. *Journal of Comparative and Physiological Psychology*, 1957, *50*, 514–518.

Dember, W. N., and Jenkins, J. J. *General psychology: Modeling behavior and experience*. Englewood Cliffs, N.J.: Prentice-Hall, 1970.

Dember, W. N., and Kleinman, R. Cues for spontaneous alternation by gerbils. *Animal Learning & Behavior*, 1973, *1*, 287–289.

Dember, W. N., and Purcell, D. G. Recovery of masked visual targets by inhibition of the masking stimulus. *Science*, 1967, *157*, 1335–1336.

Dengler, M. A test of constancy scaling theory in a modified Mueller–Lyer illusion. *Perception & Psychophysics*, 1972, *12*, 339–341.

Deregowski, J., and Ellis, H. D. Effect of stimulus orientation upon haptic perception of the horizontal–vertical illusion. *Journal of Experimental Psychology*, 1972, *95*, 14–19.

Desai, M. M. Surprise. *British Journal of Psychology, Monograph Supplements*, 1939, No. 22.

Detwiler, S. R. Some biological aspects of vision. *Sigma Xi Quarterly*, 1941, *29*, 112–129.

Deutsch, J. A., and Deutsch, D. Attention: Some theoretical considerations. *Psychological Review*, 1963, *70*, 80–90.

Deutsch, J. A., and Deutsch, D. Comments on "Selective attention: Perception or response?" *Quarterly Journal of Experimental Psychology*, 1967, *19*, 362–363.

DeValois, R. L., Abramov, I., and Jacobs, G. H. Analysis of response patterns of LGN cells. *Journal of the Optical Society of America*, 1966, *56*, 966–977.

Devane, J. R. Word characteristics and judged duration for two response sequences. *Perceptual and Motor Skills*, 1974, *38*, 525–526.

Dimmick, F. L., and Scahill, H. G. Visual perception of movement. *American Journal of Psychology*, 1925, *36*, 412–417.

Ditchburn, R. W. *Eye-movements and visual perception*. Oxford: Clarendon Press, 1973.

Dixon, N. F. *Subliminal perception: The nature of a controversy*. London: McGraw-Hill, 1971.

Dixon, W. J., and Massey, F. J., Jr. *Introduction to statistical analysis*, 2d ed. New York: McGraw-Hill, 1957.

Dobson, R., and Young, F. W. On the perception of a class of bilaterally symmetric forms. *Perception & Psychophysics*, 1973, *13*, 431–438.

Dodwell, P. C. *Visual pattern recognition*. New York: Holt, Rinehart and Winston, 1970.

Donders, F. E. Die Schnelligkeit Psychischer Processe. *Archiv Anatomie und Physiologie*, 1868, 657–681.

Doob, L. W. *Patterning of time.* New Haven: Yale University Press, 1971.

Dorfman, D. D., and McKenna, H. Pattern preference as a function of pattern uncertainty. *Canadian Journal of Psychology,* 1966, *62,* 171–183.

Douglas, R. J. Cues for spontaneous alternation. *Journal of Comparative and Physiological Psychology,* 1966, *62,* 171–183.

Dowling, J. E., and Boycott, B. B. Organization of the primate retina: Electron microscopy. *Proceedings of the Royal Society, London,* 1966, *166B,* 80–111.

Duncker, K. Induced motion. In W. D. Ellis (Ed.), *A source book of Gestalt psychology.* New York: Harcourt, Brace, 1938.

Duncker, K. The influence of past experience upon perceptual properties. *American Journal of Psychology,* 1939, *52,* 255–265.

Eaglen, J., and Kirkwood, B. The effect of instructions on judgment of the Müller-Lyer illusion with normal and haptically mediated visual inspection. *Perception & Psychophysics,* 1970, *8,* 35–36.

Egan, J. P., Greenberg, G. Z., and Schulman, A. I. Operating characteristics, signal detectability, and the method of free response. *Journal of the Acoustical Society of America,* 1961, *33,* 993–1007.

Egeth, H. Selective attention. *Psychological Bulletin,* 1967, *67,* 41–57.

Egeth, H., and Bevan, W. Attention. In B. B. Wolman (Ed.), *Handbook of general psychology.* Englewood Cliffs, N.J.: Prentice-Hall, 1973.

Egeth, H., and Smith, E. E. Perceptual selectivity in a visual recognition task. *Journal of Experimental Psychology,* 1967, *74,* 543–549.

Eijkman, E., and Vendrik, A. J. H. Detection theory applied to the absolute sensitivity of sensory systems. *Biophysics Journal,* 1963, *3,* 65–77.

Eijkman, E., and Vendrik, A. J. H. Can a sensory system be specified by its internal noise? *Journal of the Acoustical Society of America,* 1965, *37,* 1102–1109.

Eisenberger, R., Myers, A. K., Sanders, R., and Shanab, M. Stimulus control of spontaneous alternation in the rat. *Journal of Comparative and Physiological Psychology,* 1970, *70,* 136–140.

Eisler, H. Subjective duration and psychophysics. *Psychological Review,* 1975, *82,* 429–450.

Eisler, H. Experiments on subjective duration, 1868–1975: A collection of power function exponents. *Psychological Bulletin,* 1976, *83,* 1154–1171.

Ekman, G., and Åkesson, C. Saltiness, sweetness, and preference. *Scandinavian Journal of Psychology,* 1965, *6,* 241–253.

Ekman, G., Hosman, B., Lindman, R., Ljungberg, L., and Åkesson, C. Interindividual differences in scaling performance. *Perceptual and Motor Skills,* 1968, *26,* 815–823.

Ekman, G., and Sjöberg, L. Scaling. In P. R. Farnsworth (Ed.), *Annual review of psychology.* Palo Alto, Calif.: Annual Reviews, Inc., 1965.

Elliott, P. B. Tables of d'. In J. A. Swets (Ed.), *Signal detection and recognition by human observers: Contemporary readings.* New York: Wiley, 1964.

Ellis, H. C. Verbal processes in the encoding of pattern information: An approach to language, perception and memory. In M. E. Meyer (Ed.), *Third Western symposium on learning: Cognitive learning.* Bellingham: Western Washington State College, 1972.

Ellis, H. C. Stimulus encoding processes in human learning and memory. In G. H. Bower (Ed.), *The psychology of learning and motivation,* Vol. 7. New York: Academic Press, 1973.

Engel, E. Binocular methods in psychological research. In F. P. Kilpatrick (Ed.), *Explorations in transactional psychology.* New York: New York University Press, 1961.

Engen, T. Psychophysics I. Discrimination and detection. In J. W. Kling and L. A. Riggs (Eds.), *Woodworth & Schlosberg's experimental psychology,* 3d ed. New York: Holt, Rinehart and Winston, 1971. (a)

Engen, T. Psychophysics II. Scaling methods. In J. W. Kling and L. A. Riggs (Eds.), *Woodworth & Schlosberg's experimental psychology,* 3d ed. New York: Holt, Rinehart and Winston, 1971. (b)

Engen, T., and Pfaffmann, C. Absolute judgments of odor intensity. *Journal of Experimental Psychology,* 1959, *58,* 23-26.

Engen, T., and Pfaffmann, C. Absolute judgments of odor quality. *Journal of Experimental Psychology,* 1960, *59,* 214-219.

Epstein, W. Attitudes of judgment and the size-distance invariance hypothesis. *Journal of Experimental Psychology,* 1963, *66,* 78-83. (a)

Epstein, W. The influence of assumed size on apparent distance. *American Journal of Psychology,* 1963, *76,* 257-265. (b)

Epstein, W. Nonrelational judgments of size and distance. *American Journal of Psychology,* 1965, *78,* 120-123.

Epstein, W. Perceived depth as a function of relative height under three background conditions. *Journal of Experimental Psychology,* 1966, *72,* 335-338.

Epstein, W. *Varieties of perceptual learning.* New York: McGraw-Hill, 1967.

Epstein, W., Ed. *Stability and constancy in visual perception.* New York: Wiley, 1977.

Epstein, W., and Baratz, S. S. Relative size in isolation as a stimulus for relative perceived distance. *Journal of Experimental Psychology,* 1964, *67,* 507-513.

Epstein, W., Bontranger, H., and Park, J. The induction of nonveridical slant and the perception of shape. *Journal of Experimental Psychology,* 1962, *63,* 472-479.

Epstein, W., and DeShazo, D. Recency as a function of perceptual oscillation. *American Journal of Psychology,* 1961, *74,* 215-223.

Epstein, W., and Franklin, S. Some conditions of the effect of relative size on perceived relative distance. *American Journal of Psychology,* 1965, *78,* 466-470.

Epstein, W., and Landauer, A. A. Size and distance judgments under reduced conditions of viewing. *Perception & Psychophysics,* 1969, *6,* 269-272.

Epstein, W., and Park, J. Shape constancy: Functional relationships and theoretical formulations. *Psychological Bulletin,* 1963, *60,* 265-288.

Epstein, W., Park, J., and Casey, A. The current status of the size-distance hypothesis. *Psychological Bulletin,* 1961, *58,* 491-514.

Erdelyi, M. H. A new look at the new look: Perceptual defense and vigilance. *Psychological Review,* 1974, *81,* 1-25.

Eriksen, C. W. Location of objects on a visual display as a function of the number of dimensions on which the objects differ. *Journal of Experimental Psychology,* 1952, *44,* 56-60.

Eriksen, C. W. The case for perceptual defense. *Psychological Review,* 1954, *61,* 175-182.

Eriksen, C. W. Discrimination and learning without awareness: A methodological survey and evaluation. *Psychological Review,* 1960, *67,* 279-300.

Eriksen, C. W., and Hake, H. W. Multidimensional stimulus differences and accuracy of discrimination. *Journal of Experimental Psychology,* 1955, *50,* 153-160.

Eriksen, C. W., and Lappin, J. S. Luminance summation-contrast reduction as a basis for certain forward and backward masking effects. *Psychonomic Science,* 1964, *1,* 313–314.

Escher, M. C. *The graphic work of M. C. Escher.* New York: Ballantine Books, 1971.

Estes, W. K. The locus of inferential and perceptual processes in letter identification. *Journal of Experimental Psychology: General,* 1975, *104,* 122–145.

Evans, C. R., and Marsden, R. P. A study of the effect of perfect retinal stabilization on some well-known visual illusions, using the after-image as a method of compensating for eye movement. *British Journal of Physiological Optics,* 1966, *23,* 242–248.

Evans, D. R. Conceptual complexity, arousal, and epistemic behavior. *Canadian Journal of Psychology,* 1970, *24,* 249–260.

Evans, S. H. A brief statement of schema theory. *Psychonomic Science,* 1967, *8,* 87–88.

Evans, S. H., and Arnoult, M. D. Schematic concept formation: Demonstration in a free sorting task. *Psychonomic Science,* 1967, *9,* 221–222.

Falk, J. L., and Bindra, D. Judgment of time as a function of serial position and stress. *Journal of Experimental Psychology,* 1954, *47,* 279–284.

Fantz, R. L. The origin of form perception. *Scientific American,* 1961, *204,* 66–72.

Fantz, R. L. Pattern vision in new-born infants. *Science,* 1963, *140,* 296–297.

Fantz, R. L., and Ordy, J. M. A visual acuity test for infants under six months of age. *Psychological Record,* 1959, *9,* 159–164.

Fantz, R. L., Ordy, J. M., and Udelf, M. S. Maturation of pattern vision in infants during the first six months. *Journal of Comparative and Physiological Psychology,* 1962, *55,* 907–917.

Favreau, O. E., and Corballis, M. C. Negative aftereffects in visual perception. *Scientific American,* 1976, *235,* 42–48.

Fechner, G. T. *Elemente der psychophysik.* Leipzig: Breitkopf & Härtel, 1860. English translation of Vol. 1 by H. E. Adler (D. H. Howes, and E. G. Boring, Eds.). New York: Holt, Rinehart and Winston, 1966.

Fechner, G. T. *In sachen der psychophysik.* Leipzig: 1877.

Feldman, S., and Weld, H. P. Perception. In E. G. Boring, H. S. Langfeld, and H. P. Weld, *Introduction to psychology.* New York: Wiley, 1939.

Ferris, S. H. Motion parallax and absolute distance. *Journal of Experimental Psychology,* 1972, *95,* 258–263.

Festinger, L., Burnham, C. A., Ono, H., and Bamber, D. Efference and the conscious experience of perception. *Journal of Experimental Psychology, Monograph Supplement,* 1967, *74,* 4, Whole No. 637.

Festinger, L., Coren, S., and Rivers, G. The effect of attention on brightness contrast and assimilation. *American Journal of Psychology,* 1970, *83,* 189–207.

Festinger, L., White, C. W., and Allyn, M. R. Eye movements and decrement in the Müller–Lyer illusion. *Perception & Psychophysics,* 1968, *3,* 376–382.

Fillenbaum, S., Schiffman, H. R., and Butcher, J. Perception of off-size versions of a familiar object under conditions of rich information. *Journal of Experimental Psychology,* 1965, *69,* 298–303.

Finkelstein, D., and Grüsser, O. J. Frog retina: Detection of movement. *Science,* 1965, *150,* 1050–1051.

Fisher, G. H. An experimental and theoretical appraisal of the inappropriate size-depth theories of illusions. *British Journal of Psychology,* 1968, *59,* 373–383.

Fiss, H. The effects of experimentally induced changes in alertness on response to subliminal stimulation. *Journal of Personality,* 1966, *34,* 577–595.

Fitts, P. M. Perceptual-motor skill learning. In A. W. Melton (Ed.), *Categories of human learning.* New York: Academic Press, 1964.

Fitts, P. M., and Posner, M. I. *Human performance.* Belmont, Calif.: Brooks/Cole, 1967.

Fitts, P. M., and Seeger, C. M. S–R compatibility: Spatial characteristics of stimulus and response codes. *Journal of Experimental Psychology,* 1953, *46,* 199–210.

Flock, H. R. Three theoretical views of slant perception. *Psychological Bulletin,* 1964, *62,* 110–121.

Forgus, R. H. The effect of early perceptual learning on the behavioral organization of adult rats. *Journal of Comparative and Physiological Psychology,* 1954, *47,* 331–336.

Forgus, R. H. Advantage of early over late perceptual experience in improving form discrimination. *Canadian Journal of Psychology,* 1956, *10,* 147–155.

Forgus, R. H., and Melamed, L. E. *Perception,* 2d ed. New York: McGraw-Hill, 1976.

Fowler, H. Response to environmental change: A positive replication. *Psychological Reports,* 1958, *4,* 506.

Fox, C. Modification of perceptual and associative response by subthreshold stimuli. Unpublished doctoral dissertation, Yale University, 1959.

Fox, R. H., Bradbury, P. A., Hampton, I. F. G., and Legg, C. F. Time judgment and body temperature. *Journal of Experimental Psychology,* 1967, *75,* 88–96.

Fox, R., and Check, R. Forced-choice form recognition during binocular rivalry. *Psychonomic Science,* 1966, *6,* 471–472.

Fox, R., and Check, R. Detection of motion during binocular rivalry suppression. *Journal of Experimental Psychology,* 1968, *78,* 388–395.

Fox, R., and Check, R. Independence between binocular rivalry suppression duration and magnitude of suppression. *Journal of Experimental Psychology,* 1972, *93,* 283–289.

Fraisse, P. *The psychology of time.* New York: Harper & Row, 1963.

François, M. Contribution à l'étude du sens du temps: La temperature interne comme facteur de variation de l'appréciation subjective des durées. *Année Psychologique,* 1927, *28,* 186–204.

Frankenhaeuser, M. *Estimation of time: An experimental study.* Stockholm: Almqvist & Wiksell, 1959.

Frankmann, J. P., and Adams, J. A. Theories of vigilance. *Psychological Bulletin,* 1962, *59,* 257–272.

Franks, J. J., and Bransford, J. D. Abstraction of visual patterns. *Journal of Experimental Psychology,* 1971, *90,* 65–74.

Franzen, O. On spatial summation in the tactual sense. A psychophysical and neurophysiological study. *Scandinavian Journal of Psychology,* 1969, *10,* 193–208.

Freeman, J. T., and Engler, J. Perceptual recognition thresholds as a function of multiple and single set and frequency of usage of the stimulus material. *Perceptual and Motor Skills,* 1955, *5,* 149–154.

Freeman, R. B., Jr. Contrast interpretation of brightness constancy. *Psychological Bulletin,* 1967, *67,* 165–187.

Freides, D. Human information processing and sensory modality: Cross-modal functions, information complexity, memory, and deficit. *Psychological Bulletin,* 1974, *81,* 284–310.

French, J. D. The reticular formation. *Scientific American,* 1957, *196,* 54–60.

Frisby, J. P. Real and apparent movement — same or different mechanisms? *Vision Research,* 1972, *12,* 1051–1056.

Fry, G. A. The relation of accommodation to the suppression of vision in one eye. *American Journal of Opthalmology,* 1936, *19,* 135–138.

Fry, G. A., and Robertson, V. M. The physiological basis of the periodic merging of area into background. *American Journal of Psychology,* 1935, *47,* 644–655.

Fuller, J. L. Experiential deprivation and later behavior. *Science,* 1967, *158,* 1645–1652.

Furedy, J. J., and Stanley, G. The apparent size of "projected" afterimages under conditions where size-constancy holds. *Perception & Psychophysics,* 1970, *7,* 165–167.

Galanter, E. Contemporary psychophysics. In R. Brown, E. Galanter, E. Hess, and G. Mandler, *New directions in psychology.* New York: Holt, Rinehart and Winston, 1962.

Galanter, E., and Messick, S. The relation between category and magnitude scales of loudness. *Psychological Review,* 1961, *68,* 363–372.

Gale, A., Haslum, M., and Lucas, B. Arousal value of the stimulus and EEG abundance in an auditory vigilance task. *British Journal of Psychology,* 1972, *63,* 515–522.

García-Austt, E., Bogacz, J., and Vanzulli, A. Effects of attention and inattention upon evoked visual response. *Electroencephalography and Clinical Neurophysiology,* 1964, *17,* 136–143.

Garner, W. R. An informational analysis of absolute judgments of loudness. *Journal of Experimental Psychology,* 1953, *46,* 373–380.

Garner, W. R. *Uncertainty and structure as psychological concepts.* New York: Wiley, 1962.

Garner, W. R. To perceive is to know. *American Psychologist,* 1966, *21,* 11–19.

Garner, W. R. Good patterns have few alternatives. *American Scientist,* 1970, *58,* 34–42.

Garner, W. R., and Clement, D. E. Goodness of pattern and pattern uncertainty. *Journal of Verbal Learning and Verbal Behavior,* 1963, *2,* 446–452.

Garner, W. R., and Hake, H. W. The amount of information in absolute judgments. *Psychological Review,* 1951, *58,* 446–459.

Garner, W. R., Hake, H. W., and Eriksen, C. W. Operationism and the concept of perception. *Psychological Review,* 1956, *63,* 149–159.

Ganz, L. Mechanism of the figural aftereffects. *Psychological Review,* 1966, *73,* 128–150.

Gelb, A. Die "Farbenkonstanz" der Sehdinge. *Handbuch der Normalen und Pathologischen Physiologie,* 1929, *12,* 594–678.

Geldard, F. A. Cutaneous channels of communication. In W. A. Rosenblith (Ed.), *Sensory communication.* Cambridge, Mass.: M.I.T. Press, 1961.

Geldard, F. A. *Fundamentals of psychology.* New York: Wiley, 1962.

Geldard, F. A. *The human senses,* 2d ed. New York: Wiley, 1972.

Geldard, F. A. *Sensory saltation.* Hillsdale, N.J.: Lawrence Erlbaum Associates, 1975.

Geldard, F. A., and Sherrick, C. E. The cutaneous "rabbit": A perceptual illusion. *Science,* 1972, *178,* 178–179.

Gibson, E. J. *Principles of perceptual learning and development.* New York: Appleton, 1969.

Gibson, E. J., Gibson, J. J., Smith, O. W., and Flock, H. Motion parallax as a determinant of perceived depth. *Journal of Experimental Psychology,* 1959, *58,* 40–51.

Gibson, E. J., and Walk, R. D. The effect of prolonged exposure to visually presented patterns on learning to discriminate them. *Journal of Comparative and Physiological Psychology,* 1956, *49,* 239–242.

Gibson, E. J., and Walk, R. D. The visual cliff. *Scientific American,* 1960, *202,* 64–71.

Gibson, E. J., Walk, R. D., Pick, H. L., Jr., and Tighe, T. J. The effect of prolonged exposure to visual patterns on learning to discriminate similar and different patterns. *Journal of Comparative and Physiological Psychology,* 1958, *51,* 584–587.

Gibson, E. J., Walk, R. D., and Tighe, T. J. Enhancement and deprivation of visual stimulation during rearing as factors in visual discrimination learning. *Journal of Comparative and Physiological Psychology,* 1959, *52,* 74–81.

Gibson, J. J. *The perception of the visual world.* Boston: Houghton Mifflin, 1950. (a)

Gibson, J. J. The perception of visual surfaces. *American Journal of Psychology,* 1950, *63,* 367–384. (b)

Gibson, J. J. The visual perception of objective motion and subjective movement. *Psychological Review,* 1954, *61,* 304–314.

Gibson, J. J. *The senses considered as perceptual systems.* Boston: Houghton Mifflin, 1966.

Gibson, J. J. What gives rise to the perception of motion? *Psychological Review,* 1968, *75,* 335–346.

Gilchrist, A. L. Perceived lightness depends on perceived spatial arrangement. *Science,* 1977, *195,* 185–187.

Gilinsky, A. S. The effect of attitude upon the perception of size. *American Journal of Psychology,* 1955, *68,* 173–192.

Gilinsky, A. S., and Cohen, H. H. Reaction time to change in visual orientation. *Perception & Psychophysics,* 1972, *11,* 129–134.

Girgus, J. S., and Coren, S. Seeing is deceiving. In H. H. Siegel and H. P. Zeigler (Eds.), *Psychological research: The inside story.* New York: Harper & Row, 1976.

Glanzer, M. The role of stimulus satiation in spontaneous alternation. *Journal of Experimental Psychology,* 1953, *45,* 387–393.

Glanzer, M. Curiosity, exploratory drive, and stimulus satiation. *Psychological Bulletin,* 1958, *55,* 302–315.

Glanzer, M., and Clark, W. H. The verbal-loop hypothesis: Conventional figures. *American Journal of Psychology,* 1964, *77,* 621–626.

Glucksberg, S., and Cowen, G. N., Jr. Memory for nonattended auditory material. *Cognitive Psychology,* 1970, *1,* 149–156.

Gogel, W. C. The tendency to see objects as equidistant and its inverse relation to lateral separation. *Psychological Monographs,* 1956, *70,* Whole No. 411.

Gogel, W. C. Convergence as a cue to absolute distance. *Journal of Psychology,* 1961, *52,* 287–301.

Gogel, W. C. Size cue to visually perceived distance. *Psychological Bulletin,* 1964, *62,* 217–235.

Gogel, W. C. Equidistance tendency and its consequences. *Psychological Bulletin,* 1965, *64,* 153–163.

Gogel, W. C. The measurement of perceived size and distance. In W. D. Neff (Ed.), *Contributions to sensory physiology.* New York: Academic Press, 1968.

Gogel, W. C. The sensing of retinal size. *Vision Research,* 1969, *9,* 3–24.

Gogel, W. C. The organization of perceived space, I. Perceptual interactions. *Psychologische Forschung,* 1973, *36,* 195–221.

Gogel, W. C. An indirect method of measuring perceived distance from familiar size. *Perception & Psychophysics,* 1976, *20,* 419–429.

Gogel, W. C., Hartman, B. O., and Harker, G. S. The retinal size of a familiar object as a determiner of apparent distance. *Psychological Monographs,* 1957, *71,* 13, Whole No. 442.

Gogel, W. C., and Hess, E. H. A study of color constancy in the newly hatched chick by means of an innate color preference. *American Journal of Psychology,* 1951, *6,* 282.

Gogel, W. C., and Koslow, M. The effect of perceived distance on induced movement. *Perception & Psychophysics,* 1971, *10,* 142–146.

Gogel, W. C., and Koslow, M. The adjacency principle and induced movement. *Perception & Psychophysics,* 1972, *11,* 309–314.

Gogel, W. C., and Mershon, D. H. Depth adjacency and simultaneous contrast. *Perception & Psychophysics,* 1969, *5,* 13–17.

Gogel, W. C., and Mertens, H. W. Perceived depth between familiar objects. *Journal of Experimental Psychology,* 1968, *77,* 206–211.

Gogel, W. C., and Newton, R. E. Perception of off-sized objects. *Perception & Psychophysics,* 1969, *5,* 7–9.

Gogel, W. C., and Sturm, R. D. A comparison of accommodative and fusional convergence as cues to distance. *Perception & Psychophysics,* 1972, *11,* 166–168.

Gogel, W. C., and Tietz, J. D. Adjacency and attention as determiners of perceived motion. *Vision Research,* 1976, *16,* 839–845.

Gogel, W. C., Wist, E. R., and Harker, G. S. A test of the invariance of the ratio of perceived size to perceived distance. *American Journal of Psychology,* 1963, *76,* 537–553.

Goldiamond, I., and Hawkins, W. F. Vexierversuch: The log relationship between word-frequency and recognition obtained in the absence of stimulus words. *Journal of Experimental Psychology,* 1958, *56,* 457–463.

Goldstone, S. Production and reproduction of duration: Intersensory comparisons. *Perceptual and Motor Skills,* 1968, *26,* 755–760.

Goldstone, S., Boardman, W. K., and Lhamon, W. T. Effect of quinal barbitone, dextroamphetamine, and placebo on apparent time. *British Journal of Psychology,* 1958, *49,* 324–328.

Goldstone, S., Boardman, W. K., and Lhamon, W. T. Intersensory comparisons of temporal judgments. *Journal of Experimental Psychology,* 1959, *57,* 243–248.

Goldstone, S., and Goldfarb, J. L. Judgment of filled and unfilled durations: Intersensory factors. *Perceptual and Motor Skills,* 1963, *17,* 763–774.

Goldstone, S., and Goldfarb, J. L. Direct comparison of auditory and visual durations. *Journal of Experimental Psychology,* 1964, *67,* 483–485.

Goldstone, S., and Goldfarb, J. L. The perception of time by children. In A. H. Kidd and J. L. Rivoire (Eds.), *Perceptual development in children.* New York: International Universities Press, 1966.

Gould, J. D., and Dill, A. B. Eye-movement parameters and pattern discrimination. *Perception & Psychophysics,* 1969, *6,* 311–320.

Graham, C. H. Visual perception. In S. S. Stevens (Ed.), *Handbook of experimental psychology.* New York: Wiley, 1951.

Graham, C. H. Perception of movement. In C. H. Graham (Ed.), *Vision and visual perception.* New York: Wiley, 1965. (a)

Graham, C. H. Visual space perception. In C. H. Graham (Ed.), *Vision and visual perception.* New York: Wiley, 1965. (b)

Graham, C. H., Baker, K. E., Hecht, M., and Lloyd, V. V. Factors in influencing thresholds for monocular movement parallax. *Journal of Experimental Psychology,* 1948, *38,* 205–223.

Graham, N. Visual detection of aperiodic spatial stimuli by probability summation among narrowband channels. *Vision Research,* 1977, *17,* 637–652.

Granit, R. *Receptors and sensory perception.* New Haven: Yale University Press, 1955.

Gray, J. A., and Wedderburn, A. A. Grouping strategies with simultaneous stimuli. *Quarterly Journal of Experimental Psychology,* 1960, *12,* 180–185.

Green, D. M., and Birdsall, T. G. The effect of vocabulary size on articulation score. In J. A. Swets (Ed.), *Signal detection and recognition by human observers: Contemporary readings.* New York: Wiley, 1964.

Green, D. M., Birdsall, T. G., and Tanner, W. P., Jr. Signal detection as a function of signal intensity and duration. *Journal of the Acoustical Society of America,* 1957, *29,* 523–531.

Green, D. M., and Swets, J. A. *Signal detection theory and psychophysics.* New York: Wiley, 1966.

Green, D. M., and Swets, J. A. *Signal detection theory and psychophysics* (reprint with corrections). Huntington, N.Y.: Krieger, 1974.

Green, E. E. Correspondence between Stevens' terminal brightness function and the discriminability law. *Science,* 1962, *138,* 1274–1275.

Greenwald, A. G. Evidence of both perceptual filtering and response suppression for rejected messages in selective attention. *Journal of Experimental Psychology,* 1972, *94,* 58–67.

Gregory, R. L. Visual illusions. *Scientific American,* 1968, *219,* 66–76.

Gregory, R. L. Cognitive contours. *Nature,* 1972, *238,* 51–52.

Gregory, R. L. *Eye and brain,* 2d ed. New York: McGraw-Hill, 1973.

Gregory, R. L., and Harris, J. P. Illusory contours and stereo depth. *Perception & Psychophysics,* 1974, *15,* 411–416.

Gregory, R. L., and Zangwill, O. L. The origin of the autokinetic effect. *Quarterly Journal of Experimental Psychology,* 1963, *15,* 252–261.

Grier, J. B. Nonparametric indexes for sensitivity and bias: Computing formulas. *Psychological Bulletin,* 1971, *75,* 424–429.

Grobstein, P., and Chow, K. L. Receptive field development and individual experience. *Science,* 1975, *190,* 352–358.

Groves, P. M., and Thompson, R. F. Habituation: A dual process theory. *Psychological Review,* 1970, *77,* 419–450.

Gruber, H. E., and Clark, W. C. Perception of slanted surfaces. *Perceptual and Motor Skills,* 1956, *6,* 97–106.

Gruber, H. E., King, W. L., and Link, S. Moon illusion: An event in imaginary space. *Science,* 1963, *139,* 750–751.

Guilford, J. P. *Psychometric methods,* 2d ed. New York: McGraw-Hill, 1954.

Gulliksen, H. The influence of occupation upon the perception of time. *Journal of Experimental Psychology,* 1927, *10,* 52–59.

Gunn, W. J., and Loeb, M. Correlation of performance in detecting visual and auditory signals. *American Journal of Psychology,* 1967, *80,* 236–242.

Guralnick, M. J. Observing responses and decision processes in vigilance. *Journal of Experimental Psychology,* 1972, *93,* 239–244.

Guralnick, M. J. Effects of event rate and signal difficulty on observing responses and detection measures in vigilance. *Journal of Experimental Psychology,* 1973, *99,* 261–265.

Haber, R. N., Ed. *Information-processing approaches to visual perception.* New York: Holt, Rinehart and Winston, 1969.

Haider, M., Spong, P., and Lindsley, D. B. Attention, vigilance, and cortical evoked-potentials in humans. *Science,* 1964, *144,* 180–182.

Hake, H. W. Form discrimination and the invariance of form. In L. Uhr (Ed.), *Pattern recognition.* New York: Wiley, 1966.

Hake, H. W., and Garner, W. R. The effect of presenting various numbers of discrete steps on scale reading accuracy. *Journal of Experimental Psychology,* 1951, *42,* 358–366.

Hamison, B. R. The response criterion, the stimulus configuration and the relationship between brightness contrast and brightness constancy. *Perception & Psychophysics,* 1974, *16,* 347–354.

Handel, S., and Garner, W. R. The structure of visual pattern associates and pattern goodness. *Perception & Psychophysics,* 1966, *1,* 33–38.

Hanes, R. M. A scale of subjective brightness. *Journal of Experimental Psychology,* 1949, *39,* 438–452. (a)

Hanes, R. M. The construction of subjective brightness scales from fractionation data: A validation. *Journal of Experimental Psychology,* 1949, *39,* 719–728. (b)

Harker, G. S. A saccadic suppression explanation of the Pulfrich phenomenom. *Perception & Psychophysics,* 1967, *2,* 423–426.

Harlow, H. F. The nature of love. *American Psychologist,* 1958, *13,* 673–685.

Harlow, H. F. The heterosexual affectional system in monkeys. *American Psychologist,* 1962, *17,* 1–9.

Harlow, H. F., and Suomi, S. J. Nature of love—simplified. *American Psychologist,* 1970, *25,* 161–168.

Harmon, L. D., and Julesz, B. Masking in visual recognition: Effects of two-dimensional filtered noise. *Science,* 1973, *180,* 1194–1197.

Harper, R. S. The perceptual modification of colored figures. *American Journal of Psychology,* 1953, *66,* 86–89.

Harper, R. S., and Stevens, S. S. A psychological scale of weight and a formula for its derivation. *American Journal of Psychology,* 1948, *61,* 343–351.

Hart, J. T. Luminous figures: Influence of point of fixation on their disappearance. *Science,* 1964, *143,* 1193–1194.

Hartline, H. K., and Graham, C. H. Nerve impulses from single receptors in the eye. *Journal of Cellular Comparative Physiology,* 1932, *1,* 277–295.

Harvey, L. O. Jr., and Leibowitz, H. W. Effects of exposure duration, cue reduction and temporary monocularity on size matching at short distances. *Journal of the Optical Society of America,* 1967, *57,* 249–253.

Harvey, L. O. Jr., and Michon, J. A. Detectability of relative motion as a function of exposure duration, angular separation and background. *Journal of Experimental Psychology,* 1974, *103,* 317–325.

Hastorf, A. H. The influence of suggestion on the relationship between stimulus size and perceived distance. *Journal of Psychology,* 1950, *29,* 195–217.

Hastorf, A. H., and Way, K. S. Apparent size with and without distance cues. *Journal of General Psychology,* 1952, *47,* 181–188.

Hatfield, J. L., and Loeb, M. Sense mode coupling in a vigilance task. *Perception & Psychophysics,* 1968, *4,* 29–36.

Havelka, J. Problem-seeking behavior in rats. *Canadian Journal of Psychology,* 1956, *10,* 91–97.

Hawkes, G. R. An evaluation of the magnitude estimation technique. *Journal of Psychology,* 1960, *50,* 303–313.

Hawkes, G. R. Predictability of multidimensional absolute identifications from information transmitted with unidimensional stimuli. *Journal of Psychology,* 1962, *54,* 309–316.

Hawkes, G. R., Bailey, R. W., and Warm, J. S. Method and modality in judgments of brief stimulus duration. *Journal of Auditory Research,* 1961, *1,* 133–144.

Hawkes, G. R., Joy, R. J. T., and Evans, W. O. Autonomic effects on estimates of time: Evidence for a physiological correlate of temporal experience. *Journal of Psychology,* 1962, *53,* 183–191.

Hawkes, G. R., and Loeb, M. Vigilance for cutaneous and auditory stimuli as a function of intersignal interval and signal strength. *Journal of Psychology,* 1962, *53,* 211–218.

Hawkes, G. R., and Warm, J. S. The sensory range of electrical stimulation of the skin. *American Journal of Psychology,* 1960, *73,* 485–487. (a)

Hawkes, G. R., and Warm, J. S. Maximum I_t for absolute identification of cutaneous electrical intensity level. *Journal of Psychology,* 1960, *49,* 279–288. (b)

Hebb, D. O. The innate organization of visual activity: I. Perception of figures by rats reared in total darkness. *Journal of Genetic Psychology,* 1937, *51,* 101–126.

Hebb, D. O. *The organization of behavior.* New York: Wiley, 1949.

Hebb, D. O. Drives and the C.N.S. (conceptual nervous system). *Psychological Review,* 1955, *62,* 243–254.

Hebb, D. O. *Textbook of psychology,* 3d ed. Philadelphia: Saunders, 1972.

Hecht, S., and Shlaer, S. An adoptometer for measuring human dark adaptation. *Journal of the Optical Society of America,* 1938, *28,* 269–275.

Hecht, S., Shlaer, S., and Pirenne, M. H. Energy, quanta, and vision. *Journal of General Physiology,* 1942, *25,* 819–840.

Heckenmueller, E. G. Stabilization of the retinal image: A review of method, effects and theory. *Psychological Bulletin,* 1965, *63,* 157–169.

Heinemann, E. G. Simultaneous brightness induction as a function of inducing- and test-field luminance. *Journal of Experimental Psychology,* 1955, *50,* 89–96.

Heinemann, E. G., Tulving, E., and Nachmias, J. The effect of oculomotor adjustments on apparent size. *American Journal of Psychology,* 1959, *72,* 32–45.

Held, R., and Hein, A. Movement-produced stimulation in the development of visually guided behavior. *Journal of Comparative and Physiological Psychology,* 1963, *56,* 872–876.

Heller, D. P. Absence of size constancy in visually deprived rats. *Journal of Comparative and Physiological Psychology,* 1968, *65,* 336–339.

Helmholtz, H. von. *Treatise on physiological optics,* Vol. III. Originally published 1866, translated from the 3d German ed., J. P. C. Southall, Ed. New York: Dover, 1962.

Helson, H. *Adaptation-level theory.* New York: Harper & Row, 1964.

Helson, H., and King, S. M. The tau-effect: An example of psychological relativity. *Journal of Experimental Psychology,* 1931, *14,* 202–218.

Henderson, D. C. The relationships among time, distance, and intensity as determinants of motion discrimination. *Perception & Psychophysics,* 1971, *10,* 313–320.

Henneman, R. H. A photometric study of the perception of object color. *Archives of Psychology,* 1935, No. 179, 5–89.

Hering, E. *Outlines of a theory of the light sense.* Translated by L. M. Hurvich and D. Jameson. Cambridge, Mass.: Harvard University Press, 1964 (originally published 1907).

Hernández-Peón, R. Physiological mechanisms in attention. In R. W. Russell (Ed.), *Frontiers in physiological psychology.* New York: Academic Press, 1966.

Hernández-Peón, R., Scherrer, H., and Jouvet, M. Modification of electric activity in cochlear nucleus during "attention" in unanesthetized cats. *Science,* 1956, *123,* 331–332.

Herrick, R. M. Psychophysical methodology: Comparison of thresholds of the method of limits and of the method of constant stimuli. *Perceptual and Motor Skills,* 1967, *24,* 915–922.

Herrick, R. M. Psychophysical methodology: VI. Random method of limits. *Perception & Psychophysics,* 1973, *13,* 548–554.

Hess, C., and Pretori, H. Messende Untersuchungen über die Gesetzmässigkeit des simultanen Helligkeits-Contrastes. *Archiv für Opthalmologie,* 1894, *40,* 1–24. As described in L. M. Hurvich and D. Jameson, *The perception of brightness and darkness.* Boston: Allyn & Bacon, 1966.

Hess, E. H. *Imprinting.* New York: Von Nostrand, 1973.

Hess, R. D., and Bear, R. M. *Early education.* Chicago: Aldine, 1968.

Heyduk, R. G. Rated preference for musical compositions as it relates to complexity and exposure frequency. *Perception & Psychophysics,* 1974, *17,* 84–90.

Hick, W. E. On the rate of gain of information. *Quarterly Journal of Experimental Psychology,* 1952, *4,* 11–26.

Hicks, R. E., Miller, G. W., Gaes, G., and Bierman, K. Concurrent processing demands and the experience of time-in-passing. *American Journal of Psychology,* 1977, *90,* 431–446.

Hicks, R. E., Miller, G. W., and Kinsbourne, M. Prospective and retrospective judgments of time as a function of amount of information processed. *American Journal of Psychology,* 1976, *89,* 719–730.

Hilgard, E. R., and Bower, G. H. *Theories of learning,* 4th ed. Englewood Cliffs, N.J.: Prentice-Hall, 1975.

Hinde, R. A. *Animal behavior,* 2d ed. New York: McGraw-Hill, 1970.

Hoagland, H. The physiological control of judgments of duration: Evidence for a chemical clock. *Journal of General Psychology,* 1933, *9,* 267–287.

Hochberg, C. B., and Hochberg, J. E. Familiar size and the perception of depth. *Journal of Psychology,* 1952, *34,* 107–114.

Hochberg, J. E. Perception: Toward the recovery of a definition. *Psychological Review,* 1956, *63,* 400–405.

Hochberg, J. E. In the mind's eye. In R. N. Haber (Ed.), *Contemporary theory and research in visual perception.* New York: Holt, Rinehart and Winston, 1968.

Hochberg, J. E. Attention, organization, and consciousness. In D. I. Mostofsky (Ed.), *Attention: Contemporary theory and analysis.* New York: Appleton, 1970.

Hochberg, J. E. Perception: I. Color and shape. In J. W. Kling and L. A. Riggs (Eds.), *Woodworth & Schlosberg's experimental psychology,* 3d ed. New York: Holt, Rinehart and Winston, 1971. (a)

Hochberg, J. E. Perception: II. Space and movement. In J. W. Kling and L. A. Riggs (Eds.), *Woodworth & Schlosberg's experimental psychology,* 3d ed. New York: Holt, Rinehart and Winston, 1971. (b)

Hochberg, J. E., and Beck, J. Apparent spatial arrangement and perceived brightness. *Journal of Experimental Psychology,* 1954, *47,* 263–266.

Hochberg, J. E., and Hardy, D. Brightness and proximity factors in grouping. *Perceptual and Motor Skills,* 1960, *10,* 22.

Hochberg, J. E., and McAlister, E. A quantitative approach to figural "goodness." *Journal of Experimental Psychology,* 1953, *46,* 361–364.

Hochberg, J. E., and McAlister, E. Relative size vs. familiar size in the perception of represented depth. *American Journal of Psychology,* 1955, *68,* 294–296.

Hochberg, J. E., and Silverstein, A. A quantitative index of stimulus similarity: Proximity vs. differences in brightness. *American Journal of Psychology,* 1956, *69,* 456–458.

Hochberg, J. E., Triebel, W., and Seaman, G. Color adaptation under conditions of homogeneous visual stimulation (*Ganzfeld*). *Journal of Experimental Psychology,* 1951, *41,* 153–159.

Hochhaus, L. A table for the calculation of d' and β. *Psychological Bulletin,* 1972, *77,* 375–376.

Hockey, R. Changes in information-selection patterns in multisource monitoring as a function of arousal shifts. *Journal of Experimental Psychology,* 1973, *101,* 35–42.

Hohle, R. H. Detection of a visual signal with low background noise: An experimental comparison of two theories. *Journal of Experimental Psychology,* 1965, *70,* 459–463.

Holding, D. H. A line illusion with irrelevant depth cues. *American Journal of Psychology,* 1970, *83,* 280–282.

Holubář, J. *The sense of time: An electrophysiological study of its mechanisms in man.* Cambridge, Mass.: M.I.T. Press, 1969.

Holway, A. H., and Boring, E. G. The moon illusion and the angle of regard. *American Journal of Psychology,* 1940, *53,* 109–116. (a)

Holway, A. H., and Boring, E. G. The apparent size of the moon as a function of the angle of regard: Further experiments. *American Journal of Psychology,* 1940, *53,* 537–553. (b)

Holway, A. H., and Boring, E. G. Determinants of apparent visual size with distance variant. *American Journal of Psychology,* 1941, *54,* 21–37.

Horeman, H. W. Relations between brightness and luminance under induction. *Vision Research,* 1965, *5,* 331–340.

Howard, I. P., and Templeton, W. B. *Human spatial orientation*. London: Wiley, 1966.

Howell, W. C., and Goldstein, I. L. *Engineering psychology: Current perspectives in research. New York: Appleton, 1971.*

Howes, D. H., and Solomon, R. L. A note on McGinnies' "Emotionality and perceptual defense." *Psychological Review*, 1950, *57*, 229–234.

Howes, D. H., and Solomon, R. L. Visual duration threshold as a function of word-probability. *Journal of Experimental Psychology*, 1951, *41*, 401–410.

Hubel, D. H. The visual cortex of the brain. *Scientific American*, 1963, *209*, 54–62.

Hubel, D. H., and Wiesel, T. N. Receptive fields of single neurons in the cat's striate cortex. *Journal of Physiology*, 1959, *148*, 574–591.

Hubel, D. H., and Wiesel, T. N. Receptive fields, binocular interaction and functional architecture in the cat's visual cortex. *Journal of Physiology*, 1962, *160*, 106–154.

Hubel, D. H., and Wiesel, T. N. Shape and arrangement of columns in cat's striate cortex. *Journal of Physiology*, 1963, *165*, 559–568.

Hubel, D. H., and Wiesel, T. N. Binocular interaction in striate cortex of kittens reared with artificial squint. *Journal of Neurophysiology*, 1965, *28*, 1041–1059.

Hubel, D. H., and Wiesel, T. N. Receptive fields and functional architecture of monkey striate cortex. *Journal of Physiology*, 1968, *195*, 215–243.

Hughes, R. N. Spontaneous alternation and response to stimulus change in the ferret. *Journal of Comparative and Physiological Psychology*, 1965, *60*, 149–150.

Hull, C. L. *Principles of behavior*. New York: Appleton, 1943.

Hurvich, L. M., and Jameson, D. *The perception of brightness and darkness*. Boston: Allyn and Bacon, 1966.

Hymovitch, B. The effects of experimental variations on problem solving in the rat. *Journal of Comparative and Physiological Psychology*, 1952, *45*, 313–321.

Indow, T., and Stevens, S. S. Scaling of saturation and hue. *Perception & Psychophysics*, 1966, *1*, 253–271.

Ittelson, W. H. Size as a cue to distance: Static localization. *American Journal of Psychology*, 1951, *64*, 54–67.

Ittelson, W. H., and Kilpatrick, F. P. Experiments in perception. *Scientific American*, 1951, *185*, 50–55.

Jackson, D. N. A further examination of the role of autism in a visual figure–ground relationship. *Journal of Psychology*, 1954, *38*, 338–357.

James, W. *Principles of psychology*. New York: Holt, 1890.

Jameson, D., and Hurvich, L. M. Complexities of perceived brightness. *Science*, 1961, *133*, 174–179.

Jasper, H., and Shagass, C. Conscious time judgments related to conditioned time intervals and voluntary control of alpha rhythm. *Journal of Experimental Psychology*, 1941, *28*, 503–508.

Jastrow, J. A critique of psycho-physic methods. *American Journal of Psychology*, 1888, *1*, 271–309.

Jenkin, N., and Hyman, R. Attitude and distance-estimation as variables in size matching. *American Journal of Psychology*, 1959, *72*, 68–76.

Jerison, H. J. Activation and long term performance. *Acta Psychologica*, 1967, *27*, 373–389.

Jerison, H. J. Vigilance, discrimination and attention. In D. I. Mostofsky (Ed.), *Attention: Contemporary theory and analysis*. New York: Appleton, 1970.

Jerison, H. J. Vigilance: Biology, psychology, theory, and practice. In R. R. Mackie (Ed.), *Vigilance: Theory, operational performance and physiological correlates.* New York: Plenum, 1977.

Jerison, H. J., and Pickett, R. M. Vigilance: A review and re-evaluation. *Human Factors,* 1963, *5,* 211–238.

Jerison, H. J., and Pickett, R. M. Vigilance: The importance of the elicited observing rate. *Science,* 1964, *143,* 970–971.

Jerome, E. A. Olfactory thresholds measured in terms of stimulus pressure and volume. *Archives of Psychology,* 1942, *274,* 1–44.

Johansson, G. Visual perception of biological motion and a model for its analysis. *Perception & Psychophysics,* 1973, *14,* 201–211.

Johansson, G. Visual motion perception. *Scientific American,* 1975, *232,* 76–88.

Johnson, C. A., and Leibowitz, H. W. Practice, refractive error and feedback as factors influencing peripheral motion thresholds. *Perception & Psychophysics,* 1974, *15,* 276–280.

Johnston, W. A., Howell, W. C., and Goldstein, I. L. Human vigilance as a function of signal frequency and stimulus density. *Journal of Experimental Psychology,* 1966, *72,* 736–743.

Jones, A., and MacLean, M. Perceived duration as a function of auditory stimulus frequency. *Journal of Experimental Psychology,* 1966, *71,* 358–364.

Jones, A., Wilkinson, H. J., and Braden, I. Information deprivation as a motivational variable. *Journal of Experimental Psychology,* 1961, *62,* 126–137.

Jones, F. L. Vigilance performance of normals and mental retardates: The effects of age and extraneous stimulation. Unpublished doctoral dissertation, University of Cincinnati, 1971.

Jones, P. D., and Holding, D. H. Extremely long-term persistence of the McCollough effect. *Journal of Experimental Psychology: Human Perception and Performance,* 1975, *1,* 323–327.

Jones, T. N., and Kirk, R. E. Monitoring performance on visual and auditory displays. *Perceptual and Motor Skills,* 1970, *30,* 235–238.

Julesz, B. Binocular depth perception without familiarity cues. *Science,* 1964, *145,* 356–362.

Julesz, B. *Foundations of cyclopean perception.* Chicago: University of Chicago Press, 1971.

Julesz, B., and Spivack, G. J. Stereopsis based on vernier acuity cues alone. *Science,* 1967, *157,* 563–565.

Jung, R., and Spillmann, L. Receptive-field estimation and perceptual integration in human vision. In F. A. Young and D. B. Lindsley (Eds.), *Early experience and visual information processing in perceptual and reading disorders.* Washington, D.C.: National Academy of Sciences, 1970.

Kahneman, D. Method, findings, and theory in studies of visual masking. *Psychological Bulletin,* 1968, *70,* 404–425.

Kahneman, D. *Attention and effort.* Englewood Cliffs, N.J.: Prentice-Hall, 1973.

Kahneman, D., and Wolman, R. E. Strobsoscopic motion: Effects of duration and interval. *Perception & Psychophysics,* 1970, *8,* 161–164.

Kammann, R. Verbal complexity and preferences in poetry. *Journal of Verbal Learning and Verbal Behavior,* 1966, *5,* 536–540.

Kanner, L. Autistic disturbances of affective contact. *Nervous Child*, 1943, *2*, 217–240.

Kaniza, G. Subjective contours. *Scientific American*, 1976, *234*, 48–52.

Kardos, L. Ding und Schatten: Eine experimentelle Untersuchung über die Grundlagen des Farbensehens. *Zeitschrift für Psychologie*, 1934, No. 23.

Karoly, A. J., and Isaacson, R. L. Scanning mechanisms in audition. Paper read at Michigan Academy of Sciences, Ann Arbor, Mich., 1956.

Katz, D. *The world of color*. Translated from the 2d German edition by R. B. MacLeod and C. W. Fox. London: Kegan Paul, 1935.

Kaufman, L. On the nature of binocular disparity. *American Journal of Psychology*, 1964, *77*, 393–402.

Kaufman, L. *Sight and mind: An introduction to visual perception*. New York: Oxford, 1974.

Kaufman, L., Cryulnick, I., Kaplowitz, J., Melnick, G., and Stof, D. The complementarity of apparent and real motion. *Psychologische Forschung*, 1971, *34*, 343–348.

Kaufman, L., and Pitblado, C. B. Further observations on the nature of effective binocular disparities. *American Journal of Psychology*, 1965, *78*, 379–391.

Kaufman, L., and Richards, W. Spontaneous fixation tendencies for visual forms. *Perception & Psychophysics*, 1969, *5*, 85–88.

Kaufman, L., and Rock, I. The moon illusion. *Science*, 1962, *136*, 953–961.

Keele, S. W. Attention demands of memory retrieval. *Journal of Experimental Psychology*, 1972, *93*, 245–248.

Keele, S. W. *Attention and human performance*. Pacific Palisades, Calif.: Goodyear, 1973.

Kelly, D. H. Flicker. In D. Jameson and L. M. Hurvich (Eds.), *Handbook of sensory physiology: Vol. VII/4. Visual psychophysics*. New York: Springer-Verlag, 1972.

Kennedy, J. L. The nature and physiological basis of visual movement discrimination in animals. *Psychological Review*, 1936, *43*, 494–521.

Kilpatrick, F. P., and Ittelson, W. H. The size-distance invariance hypothesis. *Psychological Review*, 1953, *60*, 223–231.

Kincaid, W. M., and Hamilton, C. E. An experimental study of the nature of forced-choice responses in visual detection. *Technical Report No. 2144-295-T*. Vision Research Laboratories, University of Michigan, 1959.

King, E. A. *Space Geology: An Introduction*. New York: Wiley, 1976.

King, W. L., and Gruber, H. E. Moon illusion and Emmert's law. *Science*, 1962, *135*, 1125–1126.

Kirk, R. E., and Hecht, E. Maintenance of vigilance by programmed noise. *Perceptual and Motor Skills*, 1963, *16*, 553–560.

Kish, G. B. Learning when the onset of illumination is used as reinforcing stimulus. *Journal of Comparative and Physiological Psychology*, 1955, *49*, 90–92.

Kivy, P. N., Earl, R. W., and Walker, E. L. Stimulus context and satiation. *Journal of Comparative and Physiological Psychology*, 1956, *49*, 90–92.

Klatzky, R. L. *Human memory: Structures and processes*. San Francisco: Freeman, 1975.

Kleber, R. J., Lhamon, W. T., and Goldstone, S. Hyperthermia, hyperthyroidism and time judgment, *Journal of Comparative and Physiological Psychology,* 1963, *56,* 362–365.

Klein, G. S., Spence, D. P., Holt, R. R., and Gourevitch, S. Cognition without awareness: Subliminal influences upon conscious thought. *Journal of Abnormal and Social Psychology,* 1958, *57,* 255–256.

Klemmer, E. T., and Frick, F. C. Assimilation of information from dot and matrix patterns. *Journal of Experimental Psychology,* 1953, *45,* 15–19.

Koffka, K. *Principles of Gestalt psychology.* New York: Harcourt, 1935.

Köhler, W. Die Farben der Sehdinge beim Schimpansen und beim Haushuhun. *Zeitschrift für Psychologie,* 1917, *77,* 248–255.

Kolers, P. A. Intensity and contour effects in visual masking. *Vision Research,* 1962, *2,* 277–294.

Kolers, P. A. Some differences between real and apparent visual movement. *Vision Research,* 1963, *3,* 191–206.

Kolers, P. A. The illusion of movement. *Scientific American,* 1964, *211,* 98–106.

Komoda, M. K., and Ono, H. Oculomotor adjustments and size-distance perception. *Perception & Psychophysics,* 1974, *15,* 353–360.

Kornblum, S. Serial-choice reaction time: Inadequacies of the information hypothesis. *Science,* 1968, *159,* 432–434.

Korte, A. Kinematoskopische Untersuchungen. *Zeitschrift für Psychologie,* 1915, *72,* 193–296.

Kraft, A. L. and Winnick, W. A. The effect of pattern and texture gradient on slant and shape judgments. *Perception & Psychophysics,* 1967, *2,* 141–147.

Krantz, D. H. Threshold theories of signal detection. *Psychological Review,* 1969, *76,* 308–324.

Krantz, D. H. Measurement structures and psychological laws. *Science,* 1972, *175,* 1427–1435.

Krauskopf, J. and Riggs, L. A. Interocular transfer in the disappearance of stabilized images. *American Journal of Psychology,* 1959, *72,* 248–252.

Krech, D., Crutchfield, R. S., and Livson, N. *Elements of psychology,* 2d ed. New York: Knopf, 1969.

Krechevsky, I. Brain mechanisms and variability: I. Variability within a means–end readiness. *Journal of Comparative Psychology,* 1937, *23,* 121–138. (a)

Krechevsky, I. Brain mechanisms and variability: II. Variability where no learning is involved. *Journal of Comparative Psychology,* 1937, *23,* 139–163. (b)

Krechevsky, I. Brain mechanisms and variability: III. Limitations of the effect of cortical injury upon variability. *Journal of Comparative Psychology,* 1937, *23,* 351–364. (c)

Kristofferson, A. B. Word recognition, meaningfulness, and familiarity. *Perceptual and Motor Skills,* 1957, *7,* 219–220.

Kristofferson, A. B. Successiveness discrimination as a two-state quantal process. *Science,* 1967, *158,* 1337–1339.

Kristofferson, A. B. Attention. In R. M. Patton and T. A. Tanner, Jr. (Eds.), *Applications of research on human decision making.* Washington, D.C.: National Aeronautics and Space Administration Report, NASA SP-209, 1968.

Kristofferson, A. B. A real-time criterion theory of duration discrimination. *Perception & Psychophysics,* 1977, *21,* 105–117.

Kruger, L. E. Gregory's theory of illusions: Some disconfirming evidence in the case of the Müller–Lyer illusion. *Psychological Review,* 1972, *79,* 538–539.

Krulewitz, J. E., and Warm, J. S. The event rate context in vigilance: Relation to signal probability and expectancy. *Bulletin of the Psychonomic Society*, 1977, *10*, 429–432.

Krulewitz, J. E., Warm, J. S., and Wohl, T. H. Effects of shifts in the rate of repetitive stimulation on sustained attention. *Perception & Psychophysics*, 1975, *18*, 245–249.

Kuffler, S. W. Discharge patterns and functional organization of mammalian retina. *Journal of Neurophysiology*, 1953, *16*, 37–68.

Kuhn, T. S. *The structure of scientific revolutions*. Chicago: University of Chicago Press, 1962.

Kulp, R. A., and Alluisi, E. A. Effects of stimulus–response uncertainty on watchkeeping performance and choice reactions. *Perception & Psychophysics*, 1967, *2*, 511–515.

Künnapas, T. Distance perception as a function of available visual cues. *Journal of Experimental Psychology*, 1968, 77, 523–529.

Lack, L. C. The effect of practice on binocular rivalry control. *Perception & Psychophysics*, 1969, *6*, 397–400.

Lack, L. C. The role of accommodation in the control of binocular rivalry. *Perception & Psychophysics*, 1971, *10*, 38–42.

Lack, L. C. Selective attention and the control of binocular rivalry. *Perception & Psychophysics*, 1974, *15*, 193–200.

Lambert, W. W., Solomon, R. L., and Watson, P. D. Reinforcement and extinction as factors in size estimation. *Journal of Experimental Psychology*, 1949, *39*, 637–641.

Landauer, A. A., and Epstein, W. Does retinal size have a unique correlate in perceived size? *Perception & Psychophysics*, 1969, *6*, 273–275.

Landauer, A. A., and Rodger, R. S. Effect of "apparent" instructions on brightness judgments. *Journal of Experimental Psychology*, 1964, *68*, 80–84.

Langer, J., Wapner, S., and Werner, H. The effect of danger upon the experience of time. *American Journal of Psychology*, 1961, *74*, 94–97.

Larkin, W. D., and Norman, D. A. An extension and experimental analysis of the neural quantum theory. In R. C. Atkinson (Ed.), *Studies in mathematical psychology*. Stanford, Calif.: Stanford University Press, 1964.

Lashley, K. S. The mechanism of vision: I. A method for rapid analysis of pattern vision in the rat. *Journal of Genetic Psychology*, 1930, *37*, 453–460.

Lashley, K. S., and Russell, J. T. The mechanism of vision: XI. A preliminary test of innate organization. *Journal of Genetic Psychology*, 1934, *45*, 136–144.

Lasko, W. J., and Lindauer, M. S. Experience with congruity in the perception of incongruity. *Psychonomic Science*, 1968, *12*, 59.

Lawrence, D. H., and Coles, G. R. Accuracy of recognition with alternatives before and after the stimulus. *Journal of Experimental Psychology*, 1954, 47, 208–214.

Lawson, R. B., Cowan, E., Gibbs, T. D., and Whitmore, C. G. Stereoscopic enhancement and erasure of subjective contours. *Journal of Experimental Psychology*, 1974, *103*, 1142–1146.

Lawson, R. B., and Gulick, W. L. Stereopsis and anomalous contour. *Vision Research*, 1967, *1*, 271–297.

Lawson, R. B., and Mount, D. C. Minimum conditions for stereopsis and anomalous contour. *Science*, 1967, *158*, 804–806.

Lawson, R. B., and Pandina, R. J. Effects of matrix elements on stereopsis and anomalous contour. *Journal of Experimental Psychology,* 1969, *81,* 322–325.

Lazarus, R. S., and McCleary, R. A. Autonomic discrimination without awareness: A study of subception. *Psychological Review,* 1951, *58,* 113–122.

Lecomte Du Nouy, P. *Biological time.* New York: Macmillan, 1937.

Lee, B. S. Effects of delayed speech feedback. *Journal of the Acoustical Society of America,* 1950, *22,* 824–826.

Leeper, R. W. A study of a neglected portion of the field of learning — the development of sensory organization. *Journal of Genetic Psychology,* 1935, *46,* 41–75.

Leeper, R. W. The structure and functional unity of psychological processes. *Annals of the New York Academy of Sciences,* 1972, *193,* 200–216.

Lefton, L. A. Metacontrast: A review. *Psychonomic Monograph Supplements,* 1972, *4,* 245–255, Whole No. 62.

Legge, G. E. Adaptation to a spatial impulse: Implications for Fourier transform models of visual processing. *Vision Research,* 1976, *16,* 1407–1418.

Lehman, R. S. Eye-movements and the autokinetic illusion. *American Journal of Psychology,* 1965, *78,* 490–492.

Leibowitz, H. W. Effect of reference lines on the discrimination of movement. *Journal of the Optical Society of America,* 1955, *45,* 829–830. (a)

Leibowitz, H. W. The relation between the rate threshold for the perception of movement and luminance for various durations of exposure. *Journal of Experimental Psychology,* 1955, *49,* 209–214. (b)

Leibowitz, H. W. Sensory, learned and cognitive mechanisms of size perception. *Annals of the New York Academy of Sciences,* 1971, *188,* 47–62.

Leibowitz, H. W., Brislin, R., Perlmutter, L., and Hennessy, R. Ponzo perspective illusion as a manifestation of space perception. *Science,* 1969, *166,* 1174–1176.

Leibowitz, H. W., and Chinetti, P. Effect of reduced exposure duration on brightness constancy. *Journal of Experimental Psychology,* 1957, *54,* 49–53.

Leibowitz, H. W., and Gwozdecki, J. The magnitude of the Poggendorff illusion as a function of age. *Child Development,* 1967, *38,* 573–580.

Leibowitz, H. W., Johnson, C. A., and Isabelle, E. Peripheral motion detection and refractive error. *Science,* 1972, *177,* 1207–1208.

Leibowitz, H. W., and Judisch, J. M. The relation between age and the magnitude of the Ponzo illusion. *American Journal of Psychology,* 1967, *80,* 105–109.

Leibowitz, H. W., and Moore, D. Role of changes in accommodation and convergence in the perception of size. *Journal of the Optical Society of America,* 1966, *8,* 1120–1123.

Leibowitz, H. W., Mote, F. A., and Thurlow, W. R. Simultaneous contrast as a function of separation between test and inducing fields. *Journal of Experimental Psychology,* 1953, *46,* 453–456.

Leibowitz, H. W., Myers, N. A., and Chinetti, P. The role of simultaneous contrast in brightness constancy. *Journal of Experimental Psychology,* 1955, *50,* 15–18.

Leibowitz, H. W., Pollard, S. W., and Dickson, D. Monocular and binocular size-matching as a function of distance at various age-levels. *American Journal of Psychology,* 1967, *80,* 263–268.

Leibowitz, H. W., Shiina, K., and Hennessy, R. T. Oculomotor adjustments and size constancy. *Perception & Psychophysics,* 1972, *12,* 497–500.

Leonard, J. A. Tactual choice reactions: I. *Quarterly Journal of Experimental Psychology,* 1959, *11,* 76–83.

Lettvin, J. Y., Maturana, H. R., McCulloch, W. S., and Pitts, W. H. What the frog's eye tells the frog's brain. *Proceedings of the Institute of Radio Engineers,* 1959, *47,* 1940–1951.

Levelt, W. J. H. *On binocular rivalry.* The Hague: Mouton, 1968.

Levine, J. M., Romashko, T., and Fleishman, E. A. Evaluation of an abilities classification system for integrating and generalizing human performance research findings: An application to vigilance tasks. *Journal of Applied Psychology,* 1973, *58,* 149–157.

Levy, J. Autokinetic illusion: A systematic review of theories, measures, and independent variables. *Psychological Bulletin,* 1972, *78,* 457–474.

Lewis, J. L. Semantic processing of unattended messages using dichotic listening. *Journal of Experimental Psychology,* 1970, *85,* 225–228.

Lewis, M. S. The determinants of visual attention: A psychophysical approach to saliency and ecological validity. Unpublished doctoral dissertation, University of Cincinnati, 1973.

Lewis, M. S., Honeck, R. P., and Fishbein, H. Does shadowing differentially unlock attention? *American Journal of Psychology,* 1975, *88,* 455–458.

Lichten, W., and Lurie, S. A new technique for the study of perceived size. *American Journal of Psychology,* 1950, *63,* 280–282.

Licklider, J. C. R. Three auditory theories. In S. Koch (Ed.), *Psychology: A study of a science,* Vol. 1. New York: McGraw-Hill, 1959.

Lifshitz, S. Two integral laws of sound perception relating loudness and apparent duration of sound impulses. *Journal of the Acoustical Society of America,* 1933, *5,* 31–33.

Lilly, J. C. Mental effects of reduction of ordinary levels of physical stimuli in intact, healthy persons. *Psychiatric Research Reports,* 1956, *5,* 1–28.

Lindsay, P. H., and Norman, D. A. *Human information processing: An introduction to psychology,* 2nd ed. New York: Academic Press, 1977.

Lisper, H. O., and Törnros, J. Effects of inter-signal interval regularity on increase in reaction time in a one hour auditory monitoring task. *Acta Psychologica,* 1974, *38,* 455–460.

Lit, A., and Finn, J. P. Variability of depth-discrimination thresholds as a function of observation distance. *Journal of the Optical Society of America,* 1976, *66,* 740–742.

Locke, J. *An essay concerning human understanding.* London, 1690.

Locke, N. M. Color constancy in the rhesus monkey and in man. *Archives of Psychology,* 1935, No. 193.

Lockhart, J. M. Ambient temperature and time estimation. *Journal of Experimental Psychology,* 1967, *73,* 286–291.

Lockhead, G. R. Effects of dimensional redundancy on visual discrimination. *Journal of Experimental Psychology,* 1966, *72,* 95–104.

Lodge, H., and Wist, E. R. The growth of the equidistance tendency over time. *Perception & Psychophysics,* 1968, *3,* 97–103.

Loeb, M., and Alluisi, E. A. Influence of display, task, and organismic variables on indices of monitoring behavior. *Acta Psychologica,* 1970, *33,* 343–366.

Loeb, M., and Alluisi, E. A. An update of findings regarding vigilance and a reconsideration of underlying mechanisms. In R. R. Mackie (Ed.), *Vigilance: Theory, operational performance, and physiological correlates.* New York: Plenum, 1977.

Loeb, M., Behar, I., and Warm, J. S. Cross-modal correlations of the perceived durations of auditory and visual stimuli. *Psychonomic Science,* 1966, *6,* 87.

Loeb, M., and Binford, J. R. Some factors influencing the effective auditory intensive difference limen. *Journal of the Acoustical Society of America,* 1963, *35,* 884–891.

Loeb, M., and Binford, J. R. Variation in performance on auditory and visual monitoring tasks as a function of signal and stimulus frequencies. *Perception & Psychophysics,* 1968, *4,* 361–367.

Loeb, M., Hawkes, G. R., Evans, W. O., and Alluisi, E. A. The influence of d-amphetamine, benactyzine, and chlorpromazine on performance in an auditory vigilance task. *Psychonomic Science,* 1965, *3,* 29–30.

Loeb, M., and Schmidt, E. A. A comparison of the effects of different kinds of information in maintaining efficiency on an auditory monitoring task. *Ergonomics,* 1963, *6,* 75–81.

Loehlin, J. C. The influence of different activities on the apparent length of time. *Psychological Monographs,* 1959, *73,* No. 4, Whole No. 474.

Lorenz, K. The companion in the bird's world. *Auk,* 1937, *54,* 245–273.

Luce, R. D. A threshold theory for simple detection experiments. *Psychological Review,* 1963, *70,* 61–79. (a)

Luce, R. D. Detection and recognition. In R. D. Luce, R. R. Bush, and E. Galanter (Eds.), *Handbook of mathematical psychology.* New York: Wiley, 1963. (b)

Luce, R. D. What sort of measurement is psychophysical measurement? *American Psychologist,* 1972, *27,* 96–106.

Luce, R. D., and Green, D. M. A neural timing theory for response times and the psychophysics of intensity. *Psychological Review,* 1972, *79,* 14–57.

Luce, R. D., and Mo, S. S. Magnitude estimation of heaviness and loudness by individual subjects: A test of a probabilistic response theory. *British Journal of Mathematical and Statistical Psychology,* 1965, *18,* 159–174.

Lynn, R. *Attention, arousal and the orientation reaction.* New York: Pergamon, 1966.

MacKay, D. M. Interactive processes in visual perception. In W. A. Rosenblith (Ed.), *Sensory communication.* Cambridge, Mass.: M.I.T. Press, 1961.

MacKay, D. M. Psychophysics of perceived intensity: A theoretical basis for Fechner's and Stevens' laws. *Science,* 1963, *139,* 1213–1216.

Mackworth, J. F. The effect of true and false knowledge of results on the detectability of signals in a vigilance task. *Canadian Journal of Psychology,* 1964, *18,* 106–117.

Mackworth, J. F. The effect of amphetamine on the detectability of signals in a vigilance task. *Canadian Journal of Psychology,* 1965, *19,* 104–110.

Mackworth, J. F. Vigilance, arousal, and habituation. *Psychological Review,* 1968, *75,* 308–322.

Mackworth, J. F. *Vigilance and habituation.* Baltimore: Penguin, 1969.

Mackworth, N. H. Researches on the measurement of human performance. Medical Research Council Special Report Series 268, H. M. Stationery Office, 1950. Reprinted in H. W. Sinaiko (Ed.), *Selected papers on human factors in the design and use of control systems.* New York: Dover, 1961.

Mackworth, N. H., Kaplan, I. T., and Matlay, W. Eye movements during vigilance. *Perceptual and Motor Skills,* 1964, *18,* 397–402.

Mackworth, N. H., and Morandi, A. J. The gaze selects informative details within pictures. *Perception & Psychophysics,* 1967, *2,* 547–552.

MacLeod, R. B. An experimental investigation of brightness constancy. *Archives of Psychology*, 1932, No. 135.

MacMillan, N. A., Moschetto, C. F., Bialostozky, F. M., and Engel, L. Size judgment: The presence of a standard increases the exponent of the power law. *Perception & Psychophysics*, 1974, *16*, 340–346.

MacRae, A. W. Channel capacity in absolute judgment tasks: An artifact of information bias? *Psychological Bulletin*, 1970, *73*, 112–121.

Malmo, R. B. Activation: A neuropsychological dimension. *Psychological Review*, 1959, *66*, 367–386.

Malmo, R. B. *On emotions, needs, and our archaic brain.* New York: Holt, Rinehart and Winston, 1975.

Marg, E. Recording from single cells in the human visual cortex. In R. Jung (Ed.), *Handbook of sensory physiology*, Vol. 7, Part 3B. New York: Springer-Verlag, 1973.

Marks, L. E. On scales of sensation: Prolegomena to any future psychophysics that will be able to come forth as science. *Perception & Psychophysics*, 1974, *16*, 358–376. (a)

Marks, L. E. *Sensory processes: The new psychophysics.* New York: Academic Press, 1974. (b)

Marks, L. E., and Stevens, J. C. Individual brightness functions. *Perception & Psychophysics*, 1966, *1*, 17–24.

Marshall, A. J., and Stanley, G. The apparent length of light and dark arcs seen peripherally in rotary motion. *Australian Journal of Psychology*, 1964, *16*, 120–128.

Mashour, M., and Hosman, J. On the new "psychophysical law": A validation study. *Perception & Psychophysics*, 1968, *3*, 367–375.

Massaro, D. W. *Experimental psychology and information processing.* Chicago: Rand-McNally, 1975.

Massaro, D. W., and Anderson, N. H. A test of a perspective theory of geometrical illusions. *American Journal of Psychology*, 1970, *83*, 567–575.

Massaro, D. W., and Idson, W. L. Temporal course of perceived auditory duration. *Perception & Psychophysics*, 1976, *20*, 331–352.

Mates, B. Effect of reference marks and luminance on discrimination of movement. *Journal of Psychology*, 1969, *73*, 209–221.

Matheny, W. G. Human operator performance under non-normal environmental operating conditions. In S. B. Sells and C. K. Berry (Eds.), *Human factors in jet and space travel.* New York: Ronald, 1961.

Matin, L., and MacKinnon, G. E. Autokinetic movement: Selective manipulation of directional components by image stabilization. *Science*, 1964, *143*, 147–148.

Matthews, B. H. The response of a muscle spindle during active contraction of a muscle. *Journal of Physiology*, 1931, *72*, 153–174.

Mattson, J. M., and Natsoulas, T. Emotional arousal and stimulus duration as determinants of stimulus selection. *Journal of Abnormal and Social Psychology*, 1962, *65*, 142–144.

Mavrides, C. M., and Brown, D. R. Discrimination and reproduction of patterns: Feature measures and constraint redundancy as predictors. *Perception & Psychophysics*, 1969, *6*, 276–280.

Mayhew, J. E. W. Movement aftereffects contingent on size: Evidence for movement detectors sensitive to direction of contrast. *Vision Research*, 1973, *13*, 1789–1795.

McClelland, D. C., and Liberman, A. M. The effect of need for achievement on recognition of need-related words. *Journal of Personality*, 1949, *18*, 236–251.

McCollough, C. Color adaptation of edge-detectors in the human visual system. *Science*, 1965, *149*, 1115–1116.

McCormack, P. D. A two-factor theory of vigilance in the light of recent studies. In A. F. Sanders (Ed.), *Attention and performance*. Amsterdam: North Holland Publishing Co., 1967.

McFarland, B. P., and Halcomb, C. G. Expectancy and stimulus generalization in vigilance. *Perceptual and Motor Skills*, 1970, *30*, 147–151.

McGinnies, E. Emotionality and perceptual defense. *Psychological Review*, 1949, *56*, 244–251.

McGrath, J. J. Irrelevant stimulation and vigilance performance. In D. N. Buckner and J. J. McGrath (Eds.), *Vigilance: A symposium*. New York: McGraw-Hill, 1963.

McGrath, J. J., and O'Hanlon, J. Temporal orientation and vigilance performance. In A. F. Sanders (Ed.), *Attention and performance*. Amsterdam: North Holland Publishing Co., 1967.

McKennel, A. C. Visual size and familiar size: Individual differences. *British Journal of Psychology*, 1960, *51*, 27–35.

McKinney, J. P. Disappearance of luminous designs. *Science*, 1963, *140*, 403–404.

McKinney, J. P. Luminous-design phenomena. *Science*, 1964, *144*, 1359.

Meredith, G. M., and Meredith, C. G. W. Effect of instructional conditions on rate of binocular rivalry. *Perceptual and Motor Skills*, 1962, *15*, 655–664.

Merkel, J. Die zeitlichen Verhältnisse der Willensthätigkeit. *Philosophische Studien*, 1885, *2*, 73–127.

Mershon, D. H., and Gogel, W. C. Effect of stereoscopic cues on perceived whiteness. *American Journal of Psychology*, 1970, *83*, 55–67.

Metelli, F. Achromatic color conditions in the perception of transparency. In R. B. Macleod and H. L. Pick (Eds.), *Perception: Essays in honor of James J. Gibson*. Ithaca, N.Y.: Cornell University Press, 1974. (a)

Metelli, F. The perception of transparency. *Scientific American*, 1974, *230*, 90–98. (b)

Metzger, K. R., Warm, J. S., and Senter, R. J. Effects of background event rate and critical signal amplitude on vigilance performance. *Perceptual and Motor Skills*, 1974, *38*, 1175–1181.

Metzger, W. Optische Untersuchungen am Ganzfeld: II. Zur Phänomenologie des homogenen Ganzfelds. *Psychologische Forschung*, 1930, *13*, 6–29.

Michael, C. R. Retinal processing of visual images. *Scientific American*, 1969, *220*, 105–114.

Michels, K. M., and Zusne, L. Metrics of visual form. *Psychological Bulletin*, 1965, *63*, 74–86.

Miles, R. C. Learning in kittens with manipulatory, exploratory, and food incentives. *Journal of Comparative and Physiological Psychology*, 1958, *51*, 39–42.

Miller, G. A. What is information measurement? *American Psychologist*, 1953, *8*, 3–11.

Miller, G. A. The magical number seven, plus or minus two: Some limits on our capacity for processing information. *Psychological Review*, 1956, *63*, 81–97.

Miller, G. A., and Frick, F. C. Statistical behavioristics and sequences of responses. *Psychological Review*, 1949, *56*, 311–324.

Miller, G. A., and Garner, W. R. Effect of random presentation on the psychometric function: Implications for a quantal theory of discrimination. *American Journal of Psychology,* 1944, *57,* 451–467.

Miller, G. A., Heise, G. A., and Lichten, W. The intelligibility of speech as a function of the context of the text materials. *Journal of Experimental Psychology,* 1951, *41,* 329–335.

Miller, G. W. Prospective temporal judgment of tachistoscopic flashes as a function of stimulus complexity and recognizability. Unpublished doctoral dissertation, State University of New York at Albany, 1977.

Miller, I. Perception of nonsense passages in relation to amount of information and speech-to-noise ratio. *Journal of Experimental Psychology,* 1957, *53,* 388–393.

Miller, N. E. Studies of fear as an acquirable drive: I. Fear as motivation and fear-reduction as reinforcement in the learning of new responses. *Journal of Experimental Psychology,* 1948, *38,* 89–101.

Milošević, S. Effect of time and space uncertainty on a vigilance task. *Perception & Psychophysics,* 1974, *15,* 331–334.

Milošević, S. Changes in detection measures and skin resistance during an auditory vigilance task. *Ergonomics,* 1975, *18,* 1–8.

Minard, J. G. Response-bias interpretation of "perceptual defense." *Psychological Review,* 1965, *72,* 74–88.

Mo, S. S. Temporal reproduction of duration as a function of numerosity. *Bulletin of the Psychonomic Society,* 1975, *5,* 165–167.

Moltz, H. Imprinting: Empirical basis and theoretical significance. *Psychological Bulletin,* 1960, *57,* 291–314.

Montgomery, H., and Eisler, H. Is an equal interval scale an equal discriminability scale? *Perception & Psychophysics,* 1974, *15,* 441–448.

Montgomery, K. C. A test of two explanations of spontaneous alternation. *Journal of Comparative and Physiological Psychology,* 1952, *45,* 287–293.

Montgomery, K. C. The role of the exploratory drive in learning. *Journal of Comparative and Physiological Psychology,* 1954, *47,* 60–64.

Montgomery, K. C., and Segall, M. Discrimination learning based upon the exploratory drive. *Journal of Comparative and Physiological Psychology,* 1955, *48,* 225–228.

Moon, L. E., and Lodahl, T. M. The reinforcing effect of changes in illumination on lever-pressing in the monkey. *American Journal of Psychology,* 1956, *69,* 288–290.

Moore, J. J., and Massaro, D. W. Attention and processing capacity in auditory recognition. *Journal of Experimental Psychology,* 1973, *99,* 49–54.

Moore, S. F., and Gross, S. J. Influence of critical signal regularity, stimulus event matrix and cognitive style on vigilance performance. *Journal of Experimental Psychology,* 1973, *99,* 137–139.

Morgan, B. B., Jr., and Alluisi, E. A. Effects of discriminability and irrelevant information on absolute judgments. *Perception & Psychophysics,* 1967, *2,* 54–58.

Moray, N. Attention in dichotic listening: Affective cues and the influence of instructions. *Quarterly Journal of Experimental Psychology,* 1959, *11,* 56–60.

Moray, N. *Attention: Selective processes in vision and hearing.* New York: Academic Press, 1969. (a)

Moray, N. *Listening and attention.* Baltimore: Penguin, 1969. (b)

Moray, N., and O'Brien, T. Signal-detection theory applied to selective listening. *Jour-*

nal of the Acoustical Society of America, 1967, *42,* 765–772.

Moruzzi, G., and Magoun, H. W. Brain stem reticular formation and activation of the EEG. *Electroencephalography and Clinical Neurophysiology Journal,* 1949, *1,* 455–473.

Moskowitz, H. R. Intensity scales for pure tastes and for taste mixtures. *Perception & Psychophysics,* 1971, *9,* 51–56.

Mote, F. A., Jr., and Finger, F. W. Exploratory drive and secondary reinforcement in the acquisition and extinction of a simple running response. *Journal of Experimental Psychology,* 1942, *31,* 57–68.

Mowbray, G. H. Choice reaction time for skilled responses. *Quarterly Journal of Experimental Psychology,* 1960, *12,* 193–202.

Mowbray, G. H., and Gebhard, J. W. Man's senses as informational channels. In H. W. Sinaiko (Ed.), *Selected papers on human factors in the design and use of control systems.* New York: Dover, 1961.

Mowbray, G. H. and Rhoades, M. V. On the reduction of choice reaction times with practice. *Quarterly Journal of Experimental Psychology,* 1959, *11,* 16–23.

Mueller, C. G. Frequency of seeing functions for intensity discrimination at various levels of adapting intensity. *Journal of General Physiology,* 1951, *34,* 463–474.

Muir, D. W., and Mitchell, D. E. Visual resolution and experience: Acuity deficits in cats following early selective visual deprivation. *Science,* 1973, *180,* 420–422.

Mulhern, T. J., Warm, J. S., and Clark, D. Intensity modulation and the reproduction of auditory duration by nonretarded and retarded children. *American Journal of Mental Deficiency,* 1974, *78,* 721–726.

Munsinger, H., and Kessen, W. Uncertainty, structure and preference. *Psychological Monographs,* 1964, *78,* No. 9, whole No. 586.

Murch, G. Binocular relationships in a size and color orientation specific aftereffect. *Journal of Experimental Psychology,* 1972, *93,* 30–34.

Murphy, L. E. Absolute judgments of duration. *Journal of Experimental Psychology,* 1966, *71,* 260–263.

Murray, E. L. Methodological considerations and dependent variables in research on stimulus complexity. Unpublished master's thesis, University of Cincinnati, 1975.

Musselman, D. R. Free choice behavior as a function of stimulus changes along three dimensions of complexity. Unpublished doctoral dissertation, Claremont Graduate School, 1963.

Myers, A. K., and Miller, N. E. Failure to find a learned drive based on hunger: Evidence for learning motivated by "exploration." *Journal of Comparative and Physiological Psychology,* 1954, *47,* 428–436.

Näätänen, R. Selective attention and evoked potentials in humans—a critical review. *Biological Psychology,* 1975, *2,* 237–307.

Natsoulas, T. Converging operations for perceptual defense. *Psychological Bulletin,* 1965, *64,* 393–401.

Natsoulas, T. What are perceptual reports about? *Psychological Bulletin,* 1967, *67,* 249–272.

Needham, J. The effect of the time interval upon the time error at different intensive levels. *Journal of Experimental Psychology,* 1935, *18,* 530–543.

Neff, W. S. A critical investigation of the visual apprehension of movement. *American Journal of Psychology,* 1936, *48,* 1–42.

Neisser, U. An experimental distinction between perceptual process and verbal response. *Journal of Experimental Psychology,* 1954, *47,* 399–402.

Neisser, U. *Cognitive psychology.* New York: Appleton, 1967.

Neisser, U. *Cognition and reality.* San Francisco: Freeman, 1976.

Neuhaus, W. Experimentelle Untersuchung der Scheinbewegung. *Archiv für Gesamte Psychologie,* 1930, *75,* 315–458.

Newman, C. V. The influence of texture density gradients on judgments of length. *Psychonomic Science,* 1970, *20,* 333–334.

Newman, C. V. Familiar and relative size cues and surface texture as determinants of relative distance judgments. *Journal of Experimental Psychology,* 1972, *96,* 37–42. (a)

Newman, C. V. The role of gradients of binocular disparity in Gibson's theory of space perception. *Perception & Psychophysics,* 1972, *12,* 237–238. (b)

Nicely, P. E., and Miller, G. A. Some effects of unequal spatial distribution on the detectability of radar targets. *Journal of Experimental Psychology,* 1957, *53,* 195–198.

Nilsson, T. H. Two-pulse interval vision thresholds. *Journal of the Optical Society of America,* 1969, *59,* 753–757.

Nisbett, R. E., and Wilson, T. D. Telling more than we can know: Verbal reports on mental processes. *Psychological Review,* 1977, *84,* 231–259.

Nissen, H. W., Chow, K. L., and Semmes, J. Effects of restricted opportunity for tactual, kinesthetic, and manipulative experience on the behavior of a chimpanzee. *American Journal of Psychology,* 1951, *64,* 485–507.

Noble, C. E. The meaning–familiarity relation. *Psychological Review,* 1953, *60,* 89–98.

Norman, D. A. Toward a theory of memory and attention. *Psychological Review,* 1968, *75,* 522–536.

Norman, D. A. Memory while shadowing. *Quarterly Journal of Experimental Psychology,* 1969, *21,* 85–93.

Norman, D. A. Neural quantum controversy in sensory psychology. *Science,* 1973, *181,* 467–469.

Norman, D. A. *Memory and attention,* 2d ed. New York: Wiley, 1976.

Noton, D., and Stark, L. Scanpaths in eye movements during pattern perception. *Science,* 1971, *171,* 308–311.

Nunnally, J. C., and Lemond, L. C. Exploratory behavior and human development. *Advances in Child Development and Behavior,* 1973, *8,* 59–109.

O'Connell, R. H. Comparison of alternation and response to stimulus change. *Journal of Comparative and Physiological Psychology,* 1964, *57,* 362–366.

Ogle, K. N. *Researches in binocular vision.* Philadelphia: Saunders, 1950.

Ogle, K. N. On the limits of stereoscopic vision. *Journal of Experimental Psychology,* 1952, *44,* 253–259.

Ogle, K. N. Precision and validity of stereoscopic depth perception from double images. *Journal of the Optical Society of America,* 1953, *43,* 906–913.

Ogle, K. N. Theory of stereoscopic vision. In S. Koch (Ed.), *Psychology: A study of a science: Vol. I: Sensory, perceptual and physiological formulations.* New York: McGraw-Hill, 1959.

O'Hanlon, J. F. Adrenaline and noradrenaline: Relation to performance in a visual vigilance task. *Science,* 1965, *150,* 507–509.

Oléron, G. Influence de l'intensité d'un son sur l'estimation de sa durée apparente. *Année Psychologique,* 1952, *52,* 383–392.

Olson, R. K., and Attneave, F. What variables produce similarity grouping? *American Journal of Psychology,* 1970, *83,* 1–21.

Ono, H. Apparent distance as a function of familiar size. *Journal of Experimental Psychology,* 1969, *79,* 109–115.

Ornstein, R. E. *On the experience of time.* Baltimore: Penguin, 1969.

Osgood, C. E. *Method and theory in experimental psychology.* New York: Oxford, 1953.

Oswald, I., Taylor, A. M., and Treisman, M. Discrimination responses to stimulation during human sleep. *Brain,* 1960, *83,* 440–453.

Over, R. A comparison of haptic and visual judgments of some illusions. *American Journal of Psychology,* 1966, *79,* 590–595.

Over, R. Intermanual transfer of practice decrements with a haptic illusion. *Quarterly Journal of Experimental Psychology,* 1967, *19,* 215–218.

Over, R. Explanations of geometrical illusions. *Psychological Bulletin,* 1968, *70,* 545–562.

Owen, D. H., and Brown, D. R. Physical correlates of pattern perception for the visual and tactual modalities. *Proceedings of the American Psychological Association,* 1966, 71–72.

Padilla, S. G. Further studies on the delayed pecking of chicks. *Journal of Comparative Psychology,* 1935, *20,* 413–443.

Palen, G. F. Focusing cues in the visual cliff behavior of day-old chicks. *Journal of Comparative and Physiological Psychology,* 1965, *59,* 452–454.

Pantle, A., and Picciano, L. A multistable movement display: Evidence for two separate motion systems in human vision. *Science,* 1976, *193,* 500–502.

Pantle, A., and Sekuler, R. W. Size detecting mechanisms in human vision. *Science,* 1968, *162,* 1146–1148.

Pantle, A., and Sekuler, R. W. Contrast response of human visual mechanisms sensitive to orientation and direction of motion. *Vision Research,* 1969, *9,* 397–406.

Parasuraman, R., and Davies, D. R. Response and evoked potential latencies associated with commission errors in visual monitoring. *Perception & Psychophysics,* 1975, *17,* 465–468.

Parasuraman, R., and Davies, D. R. A taxonomic analysis of vigilance performance. In R. R. Mackie (Ed.), *Vigilance: Theory, operational performance, and physiological correlates.* New York: Plenum, 1977.

Parducci, A., and Sandusky, A. J. Limits on the applicability of signal detection theories. *Perception & Psychophysics,* 1970, *7,* 63–64.

Park, J. N. and Michaelson, G. J. Distance judgments under different size-information conditions. *Perception & Psychophysics,* 1974, *15,* 57–60.

Pastore, N. *Selective history of theories of visual perception.* New York: Oxford, 1971.

Pastore, R. E., and Scheirer, C. J. Signal detection theory: Considerations for general application. *Psychological Bulletin,* 1974, *81,* 945–958.

Patterson, J., and Deffenbacher, K. Haptic perception of the Mueller–Lyer illusion by the blind. *Perceptual and Motor Skills,* 1972, *35,* 819–824.

Pearce, D., and Matin, L. Variation in the magnitude of the horizontal–vertical illusion with retinal eccentricity. *Perception & Psychophysics,* 1969, *6,* 241–243.

Pfaff, D. Effects of temperature and time of day on time judgments. *Journal of Experimental Psychology,* 1968, *76,* 419–422.

Piaget, J. *The mechanisms of perception.* Translated by G. N. Geagrin. New York: Basic Books, 1969.

Pierce, J. Determinants of threshold for form. *Psychological Bulletin,* 1963, *60,* 391–407.

Piéron, H. *The sensations, their functions, processes and mechanisms.* New Haven: Yale University Press, 1952.

Pillsbury, W. B. *Attention.* New York: Macmillan, 1908.

Plateau, J. A. Sur la mesure des sensations physiques, et sur la loi qui lie l'intensite de ces sensations à l'intensité de la cause excitante. *Bulletins de l'Académie Royale des Sciences, des Lettres, et des Beaux-Arts de Belgique,* 1872, *33,* 376–388.

Pola, J., and Matin, L. Eye movements following autokinesis. *Bulletin of the Psychonomic Society,* 1977, *10,* 397–398.

Pollack, I. The information of elementary auditory displays: II. *Journal of the Acoustical Society of America,* 1953, *25,* 765–769.

Pollack, I. Message uncertainty and message reception. *Journal of the Acoustical Society of America,* 1959, *31,* 1500–1508.

Pollack, I., and Ficks, L. Information of elementary multi-dimensional auditory displays. *Journal of the Acoustical Society of America,* 1954, *26,* 155–158.

Posner, M. I. Abstraction and the process of recognition. In G. H. Bower and J. T. Spence (Eds.), *Psychology of learning and motivation,* Vol. 3. New York: Academic Press, 1969.

Posner, M. I., and Boies, S. J. Components of attention. *Psychological Review,* 1971, *78,* 391–408.

Posner, M. I., and Keele, S. W. On the genesis of abstract ideas. *Journal of Experimental Psychology,* 1968, *77,* 353–363.

Postman, L., and Bruner, J. S. Multiplicity of set as a determinant of perceptual behavior. *Journal of Experimental Psychology,* 1949, *39,* 369–377.

Postman, L., Bruner, J. S., and McGinnies, E. Personal values as selective factors in perception. *Journal of Abnormal and Social Psychology,* 1948, *43,* 142–154.

Poulton, E. C. The new psychophysics: Six models for magnitude estimation. *Psychological Bulletin,* 1968, *69,* 1–19.

Poulton, E. C., Simmonds, D. C., and Warren, R. M. Response bias in very first judgments of the reflectance of grays: Numerical versus linear estimates. *Perception & Psychophysics,* 1968, *3,* 112–114.

Pradhan, P. L., and Hoffman, P. J. Effect of spacing and range of stimuli on magnitude estimation judgments. *Journal of Experimental Psychology,* 1963, *66,* 533–541.

Pressey, A. W. Age changes in the Ponzo and filled-space illusions. *Perception & Psychophysics,* 1974, *15,* 315–319.

Pressey, A. W., and Wilson, A. E. The Poggendorff illusion in imagination. *Bulletin of the Psychonomic Society,* 1974, *3,* 447–449.

Pribram, K. H. The limbic systems, efferent control of neural inhibition and behavior. *Progress in Brain Research,* 1967, *27,* 318–336.

Pribram, K. H. Editorial foreword. In Mackworth, J. F., *Vigilance and habituation.* Baltimore: Penguin, 1969.

Price-Williams, D. R. The kappa effect. *Nature,* 1954, *173,* 363–364.

Pritchard, R. M. Visual illusions viewed as stabilized retinal images. *Quarterly Journal of Experimental Psychology,* 1958, *10,* 77–81.

Pritchard, R. M. Stabilized images on the retina. *Scientific American*, 1961, *204*, 72–78.

Provence, S., and Lipton, R. C. *Infants in institutions*. New York: International Universities Press, 1962.

Rafales, L. S. Psychobiological and psychophysical factors in the discrimination of acoustic durations: The effects of input channel and signal intensity. Unpublished doctoral dissertation, University of Cincinnati, 1976.

Randel, J. M. Attenuation of the vigilance decrement through stimulation in a second modality. *Human Factors*, 1968, *10*, 505–512.

Ratliff, F. *Mach bands: Quantitative studies on neural networks in the retina*. San Francisco: Holden-Day, 1965.

Ratliff, F. Contour and contrast. *Scientific American*, 1972, *226*, 90–101.

Ratliff, F., and Hartline, H. K. The response of *Limulus* optic nerve fibers to patterns of illumination on the receptor mosaic. *Journal of General Physiology*, 1959, *42*, 1241–1255.

Reed, S. K. *Psychological processes in pattern recognition*. New York: Academic Press, 1973.

Reicher, G. M. Perceptual recognition as a function of meaningfulness of stimulus material. Technical Report No. 7, The University of Michigan, Human Performance Center, 1968.

Restle, F. Moon illusion explained on the basis of relative size. *Science*, 1970, *167*, 1092–1096.

Reynolds, A. G., and Flagg, P. W. *Cognitive psychology*. Cambridge, Mass.: Winthrop, 1977.

Richards, W., and Foley, J. M. Effect of luminance and contrast on processing large disparities. *Journal of the Optical Society of America*, 1974, *64*, 1703–1705.

Richards, W., and Miller, J. F., Jr. Convergence as a cue to depth. *Perception & Psychophysics*, 1969, *5*, 317–320.

Richards, W., and Miller, J. F., Jr. The corridor illusion. *Perception & Psychophysics*, 1971, *9*, 421–423.

Riesen, A. H. The development of visual perception in man and chimpanzee. *Science*, 1949, *106*, 107–108.

Riesen, A. H. Arrested vision. *Scientific American*, 1950, *183*, 16–19.

Riggs, L. A. Curvature as a feature of pattern vision. *Science*, 1973, *181*, 1070–1072.

Riggs, L. A., Cornsweet, J. C., and Lewis, W. G. Effects of light on electrical excitation of the human eye. *Psychological Monographs*, 1957, *71* (5), Whole No. 435.

Riggs, L. A., Ratliff, F., Cornsweet, J. C., and Cornsweet, T. N. The disappearance of steadily fixated visual test objects. *Journal of the Optical Society of America*, 1953, *43*, 495–501.

Ritter, M. Effect of disparity and viewing distance on perceived depth. *Perception & Psychophysics*, 1977, *22*, 400–407.

Robinson, D. N. Disinhibition of visually masked stimuli. *Science*, 1966, *154*, 157–158.

Robinson, J. O. Retinal inhibition in visual distortion. *British Journal of Psychology*, 1968, *58*, 29–36.

Robinson, J. O. *The psychology of visual illusion*. London: Hutchinson, 1972.

Rock, I. *Orientation and form.* New York: Academic Press, 1973.

Rock, I. The perception of disoriented figures. *Scientific American,* 1974, *230,* 78–85.

Rock, I. *An introduction to perception.* New York: Macmillan, 1975.

Rock, I., and Brosgole, L. Grouping based on phenomenal proximity. *Journal of Experimental Psychology,* 1964, *67,* 531–538.

Rock, I., and Ebenholtz, S. The relational determination of perceived size. *Psychological Review,* 1959, *66,* 387–401.

Rock, I., and Ebenholtz, S. Stroboscopic movement based on change of phenomenal location rather than retinal location. *American Journal of Psychology,* 1962, *75,* 193–207.

Rock, I., and Fleck, F. S. A re-examination of the effect of monetary reward and punishment in figure–ground perception. *Journal of Experimental Psychology,* 1950, *40,* 766–776.

Rock, I., and Heimer, W. The effect of retinal and phenomenal orientation on the perception of form. *American Journal of Psychology,* 1957, *70,* 493–511.

Rock, I., Hill, A. L., and Fineman, M. Speed constancy as a function of size constancy. *Perception & Psychophysics,* 1968, *4,* 37–40.

Rock, I., and Kaufman, L. The moon illusion: II. *Science,* 1962, *136,* 1023–1031.

Rock, I., and McDermott, W. The perception of visual angle. *Acta Psychologica,* 1964, *22,* 119–134.

Rock, I., Tauber, E. S., and Heller, D. P. Perception of stroboscopic movement: Evidence for its innate basis. *Science,* 1965, *147,* 1050–1052.

Rosch, E. Human categorization. In N. Warren (Ed.), *Studies in cross-cultural psychology,* Vol. 1. New York: Academic Press, 1977.

Rosenzweig, M. R., Bennett, E. L., and Diamond, M. C. Brain changes in response to experience. *Scientific American,* 1972, *226,* 22–30.

Rosner, B. S., and Goff, W. R. Electrical responses of the nervous system and subjective scales of intensity. In W. D. Neff (Ed.), *Contributions to sensory physiology,* Vol. 2. New York: Academic Press, 1967.

Ross, H. E., and Ross, G. M. Did Ptolemy understand the moon illusion? *Perception,* 1976, *5,* 377–385.

Ross, J. The resources of binocular perception. *Scientific American,* 1976, *234,* 80–86.

Ross, J., and DiLollo, V. Judgment and response in magnitude estimation. *Psychological Review,* 1971, *78,* 515–527.

Royer, F. L., and Garner, W. R. Response uncertainty and perceptual difficulty of auditory temporal patterns. *Perception & Psychophysics,* 1966, *1,* 41–47.

Rubin, E. *Synsoplevede figure.* Copenhagen: Gyldendalske, 1915.

Rubin, E. *Visuell wahrgenommene figuren.* Copenhagen: Gyldendalske, 1921.

Rudel, R. G., and Teuber, H. L. Decrement of visual and haptic Müller–Lyer illusion on repeated trials: A study of crossmodal transfer. *Quarterly Journal of Experimental Psychology,* 1963, *15,* 125–131.

Rule, S. J., Laye, R. C., and Curtis, D. W. Magnitude judgments and difference judgments of lightness and darkness: A two-stage analysis. *Journal of Experimental Psychology,* 1974, *103,* 1108–1114.

Rumelhart, D. E. *Introduction to human information processing.* New York: Wiley, 1977.

Saayman, G., Ames, E. W., and Moffett, A. Response to novelty as an indicator of visual discrimination in the human infant. *Journal of Experimental Child Psychology,* 1964, *1,* 189–198.

Samuels, I. Reticular mechanisms and behavior. *Psychological Bulletin,* 1959, *56,* 1–25.

Santa, J. L. Verbal coding and redintegrative memory for shapes. *Journal of Experimental Psychology: Human Learning and Memory,* 1975, *104,* 286–294.

Saugstad, P. Effect of food deprivation on perception–cognition. *Psychological Bulletin,* 1966, *65,* 80–90.

Schafer, R., and Murphy, G. The role of autism in a visual figure–ground relationship. *Journal of Experimental Psychology,* 1943, *32,* 335–343.

Scharf, B. The scope of sensory psychology. In B. Scharf (Ed.), *Experimental sensory psychology.* Glenview, Ill.: Scott, Foresman, 1975.

Schendel, J. D., and Shaw, P. A test of the word-context effect. *Perception & Psychophysics,* 1976, *19,* 383–393.

Schiff, W. The perception of impending collision: A study of visually directed avoidant behavior. *Psychological Monographs,* 1965, *79,* Whole No. 604.

Schiffman, H. R. Size-estimation of familiar objects under informative and reduced conditions of viewing. *American Journal of Psychology,* 1967, *80,* 229–235.

Schiffman, H. R. *Sensation and perception.* New York: Wiley, 1976.

Schiffman, H. R., and Bobko, D. J. Effects of stimulus complexity on the perception of brief temporal intervals. *Journal of Experimental Psychology,* 1974, *103,* 156–159.

Schiffman, H. R., and Bobko, D. J. The role of number and familiarity of stimuli in the perception of brief temporal intervals. *American Journal of Psychology,* 1977, *90,* 85–93.

Schiffman, H. R., and Thompson, J. The role of eye movements in the perception of the horizontal–vertical illusion. *Perception,* 1974, *3,* 49–52.

Schiffman, H. R., and Walk, R. D. Behavior on the visual cliff of monocular as compared to binocular chicks. *Journal of Comparative and Physiological Psychology,* 1963, *56,* 1064–1068.

Schiller, P., and Wiener, M. Binocular and stereoscopic viewing of geometric illusions. *Perceptual and Motor Skills,* 1962, *15,* 739–747.

Schlaer, R. Shift in binocular disparity causes compensatory change in the cortical structure of kittens. *Science,* 1971, *173,* 638–641.

Schmidt, M. W., and Kristofferson, A. B. Discrimination of successiveness: A test of a model of attention. *Science,* 1963, *139,* 112–113.

Schroeder, S. R., and Holland, J. G. Operant control of eye movement during human vigilance. *Science,* 1968, *161,* 292–293.

Schuck, J. R., Brock, T. C., and Becker, L. A. Luminous figures: Factors affecting the reporting of disappearances. *Science,* 1964, *146,* 1598–1599.

Schwartz, M. *Physiological psychology,* 2d ed. Englewood Cliffs, N.J.: Prentice-Hall, 1978.

Segall, M. H., Campbell, D. T., and Herskovits, M. J. *The influence of culture on visual perception.* Indianapolis: Bobbs-Merrill, 1966.

Sekuler, R. W., and Ganz, L. Aftereffect of seen motion with a stabilized retinal image. *Science,* 1963, *139,* 419–420.

Selfridge, O. G. Pandemonium: A paradigm for learning. In *The mechanisation of thought processes.* London: H. M. Stationary Office, 1959.

Senden, M. von. *Raum und Gestaltaffaussung bei operierten Blindgebornen vor und nach der Operation.* Leipzig: Barth, 1932. Translated by P. Heath, *Space and sight.* London: Methuen; and Glencoe, Ill.: Free Press, 1960.

Seroshevskii, V. R. *Iakuti.* St. Petersburg: Royal Geographical Society, 1896.

Sgro, F. J. Beta motion thresholds. *Journal of Experimental Psychology,* 1963, *66,* 281–285.

Shaffer, L. H., and Hardwick, J. Monitoring simultaneous auditory messages. *Perception & Psychophysics,* 1969, *6,* 401–404.

Shaffer, R. W., and Ellis, H. C. An analysis of intersensory transfer of form. *Journal of Experimental Psychology,* 1974, *102,* 948–953.

Shannon, C. E., and Weaver, W. *The mathematical theory of communication.* Urbana, Ill.: University of Illinois Press, 1949.

Sharma, S., and Moskowitz, H. Effects of two levels of attention demand on vigilance performance under marihuana. *Perceptual and Motor Skills,* 1974, *38,* 967–970.

Sharpless, S., and Jasper, H. H. Habituation of the arousal reaction. *Brain,* 1956, *79,* 655–680.

Shepard, R. N., and Metzler, J. Mental rotation of three-dimensional objects. *Science,* 1971, *171,* 701–703.

Sherrington, C. S. Observations on the sensual role of the proprioceptive nerve-supply of the extrinsic ocular muscles. *Brain,* 1918, *41,* 332–343.

Shevrin, H., and Fritzler, D. E. Visual evoked response correlates of unconscious mental processes. *Science,* 1968, *161,* 295–298.

Shevrin, H., and Luborsky, L. The measurement of preconscious perception in dreams and images: An investigation of the Poetzl phenomenon. *Journal of Abnormal and Social Psychology,* 1958, *56,* 285–294.

Shiffrin, R. M., Pisoni, D. B., and Castaneda-Mendez, K. Is attention shared between the ears? *Cognitive Psychology,* 1974, *6,* 190–215.

Shinar, D., and Owen, D. H. Effects of form rotation on the speed of classification: The development of shape constancy. *Perception & Psychophysics,* 1973, *14,* 149–154.

Shinkman, P. G. Visual depth discrimination in animals. *Psychological Bulletin,* 1962, *59,* 489–501.

Shinkman, P. G. Visual depth discrimination in day-old chicks. *Journal of Comparative and Physiological Psychology,* 1963, *56,* 410–414.

Shurley, J. T. Profound experimental sensory isolation. *American Journal of Psychiatry,* 1960, *117,* 539–545.

Siddle, D. A. T. Vigilance decrement and speed of habituation of the GSR component of the orienting response. *British Journal of Psychology,* 1972, *63,* 191–194.

Siegel, A. I. Deprivation of visual form definition in the ring dove: I. Discrimination learning. *Journal of Comparative and Physiological Psychology,* 1953, *46,* 115–119.

Siegel, J. A., and Siegel, W. Absolute judgment and paired-associate learning: Kissing cousins or identical twins? *Psychological Review,* 1972, *79,* 300–316.

Siegel, W. Memory effects in the method of absolute judgment. *Journal of Experimental Psychology,* 1972, *94,* 121–131.

Simner, M. L. Response to visual depth cues in the newly hatched chick. Unpublished doctoral dissertation, University of Cincinnati, 1967.

Simon, H. A. An information-processing explanation of some perceptual phenomena. *British Journal of Psychology,* 1967, *58,* 1–12.

Simon, H. A., and Barenfeld, M. Information-processing analysis of perceptual processing in problem solving. *Psychological Review*, 1969, *76*, 473–483.

Siqueland, E. R., and DeLucia, C. A. Visual reinforcement of nonnutritive sucking in human infants. *Science*, 1969, *165*, 1144–1146.

Skavenski, A. A., Haddad, G., and Steinman, R. M. The extraretinal signal for the visual perception of direction. *Perception & Psychophysics*, 1972, *11*, 287–290.

Skowbo, D., Timney, B. N., Gentry, T. A., and Morant, R. B. McCollough effects: Experimental findings and theoretical accounts. *Psychological Bulletin*, 1975, *82*, 497–510.

Slack, C. W. Familiar size as a cue to size in the presence of conflicting cues. *Journal of Experimental Psychology*, 1956, *52*, 194–198.

Sluckin, W. *Imprinting and early learning.* Chicago: Aldine, 1965.

Smith, A. T., and Over, R. Color-selective tilt aftereffects with subjective contours. *Perception & Psychophysics*, 1976, *20*, 305–308.

Smith, E. E. Choice reaction time: An analysis of the major theoretical positions. *Psychological Bulletin*, 1968, *69*, 77–110.

Smith, R. P., Warm, J. S., and Alluisi, E. A. Effects of temporal uncertainty on watchkeeping performance. *Perception & Psychophysics*, 1966, *1*, 293–299.

Snodgrass, J. G. Psychophysics. In B. Scharf (Ed.), *Experimental sensory psychology.* Glenview, Ill.: Scott, Foresman, 1975.

Snodgrass, J. G. Objective and subjective complexity measures for a new population of patterns. *Perception & Psychophysics*, 1971, *10*, 217–224.

Snyder, F. W., and Snyder, C. W. The effects of monetary reward and punishment on auditory perception. *Journal of Psychology*, 1956, *41*, 177–184.

Sokolov, Y. N. *Perception and the conditioned reflex.* Translated by S. W. Waydenfeld. New York: Macmillan, 1963.

Sokolov, Y. N. The modeling properties of the nervous system. In M. Cole and I. Maltzman (Eds.), *A handbook of contemporary Soviet psychology.* New York: Basic Books, 1969.

Solhkhah, N., and Orbach, J. Determinants of the magnitude of the moon illusion. *Perceptual and Motor Skills*, 1969, *29*, 87–98.

Solley, C. M., and Murphy, G. *Development of the perceptual world.* New York: Basic Books, 1960.

Solley, C. M., and Sommer, R. Perceptual autism in children. *Journal of General Psychology*, 1957, *56*, 3–11.

Solomon, P., and Mendelson, J. Hallucinations in sensory deprivation. In L. J. West (Ed.), *Hallucinations.* New York: Grune & Stratton, 1962.

Solomon, R. L., and Postman, L. Frequency of usage as a determinant of recognition threshold for words. *Journal of Experimental Psychology*, 1952, *43*, 195–201.

Sommer, R. The effects of rewards and punishments during perceptual organization. *Journal of Personality*, 1957, *25*, 550–558.

Spence, D. The multiple effects of subliminal stimuli. *Journal of Personality*, 1961, *29*, 40–53.

Sperling, G. The information available in brief visual presentations. *Psychological Monographs*, 1960, *74*(11), Whole No. 498.

Spigel, I. M. Problems in the study of visually perceived movement: An introduction. In I. M. Spigel (Ed.), *Readings in the study of visually perceived movement.* New York: Harper & Row, 1965.

Spitz, H. The channel capacity of educable mental retardates. In D. K. Routh (Ed.), *The experimental psychology of mental retardation.* Chicago: Aldine, 1973.

Spitz, R. A. Hospitalism: An inquiry into the genesis of psychiatric conditions in early childhood. *Psychoanalytic Study of the Child,* 1945, *1,* 53–74.

Spong, P., Haider, M., and Lindsley, D. B. Selective attentiveness and cortical evoked responses to visual and auditory stimuli. *Science,* 1965, *148,* 395–397.

Stacey, B. G., and Pike, A. R. Depth location of shafts filling half the space between Mueller–Lyer fins. *Perceptual and Motor Skills,* 1968, *27,* 1019–1022.

Stang, D. J. Six theories of repeated exposure and affect. *JSAS Catalog of Selected Documents in Psychology,* 1973, *3,* 126.

Stang, D. J. On the relationship between novelty and complexity. *The Journal of Psychology,* 1977, *95,* 317–323.

Stanley, G. Varying amount of static visual noise and the Ansbacher effect. *Psychonomic Science,* 1970, *12,* 343–344.

Staples, R. The responses of infants to color. *Journal of Experimental Psychology,* 1932, *15,* 119–141.

Stecher, S. Luminance-difference thresholds and simultaneous contrast. *American Journal of Psychology,* 1968, *81,* 27–35.

Stevens, J. C., and Guirao, M. Individual loudness functions. *Journal of the Acoustical Society of America,* 1964, *36,* 2210–2213.

Stevens, J. C., and Mack, J. D. Scales of apparent force. *Journal of Experimental Psychology,* 1959, *58,* 405–413.

Stevens, J. C., and Marks, L. E. Apparent warmth as a function of thermal irradiation. *Perception & Psychophysics,* 1967, *2,* 613–619.

Stevens, J. C., Marks, L. E., and Gagge, A. P. The quantitative assessment of thermal discomfort. *Environmental Research,* 1969, *2,* 149–165.

Stevens, S. S. A scale for the measurement of psychological magnitude: Loudness. *Psychological Review,* 1936, *43,* 405–416.

Stevens, S. S., Ed. *Handbook of experimental psychology.* New York: Wiley, 1951. (a).

Stevens, S. S. Mathematics, measurement, and psychophysics. In S. S. Stevens (Ed.), *Handbook of experimental psychology.* New York: Wiley, 1951. (b)

Stevens, S. S. The direct estimation of sensory magnitudes—loudness. *American Journal of Psychology,* 1956, *69,* 1–25.

Stevens, S. S. On the psychophysical law. *Psychological Review,* 1957, *64,* 153–181.

Stevens, S. S. Problems and methods of psychophysics. *Psychological Bulletin,* 1958, *55,* 177–196.

Stevens, S. S. Cross-modality validation of subjective scales for loudness, vibration, and electric shock. *Journal of Experimental Psychology,* 1959, *57,* 201–209.

Stevens, S. S. The psychophysics of sensory function. *American Scientist,* 1960, *48,* 226–254.

Stevens, S. S. Is there a quantal threshold? In W. A. Rosenblith (Ed), *Sensory communication.* Cambridge, Mass.: M.I.T. Press, 1961. (a)

Stevens, S. S. To honor Fechner and repeal his law. *Science,* 1961, *133,* 80–86. (b)

Stevens, S. S. The surprising simplicity of sensory metrics. *American Psychologist,* 1962, *17,* 29–39.

Stevens, S. S. Duration, luminance, and the brightness exponent. *Perception & Psychophysics,* 1966, *1,* 96–100. (a)

Stevens, S. S. On the operation known as judgment. *American Scientist,* 1966, *54,* 385–401. (b)

Stevens, S. S. Intensity functions in sensory systems. *International Journal of Neurology,* 1967, *6,* 202–209.

Stevens, S. S. Mathematics, statistics, and the schemapiric view. *Science,* 1968, *161,* 849–856. (a)

Stevens, S. S. Tactual vibration: Change of exponent with frequency. *Perception & Psychophysics,* 1968, *3,* 223–228. (b)

Stevens, S. S. On predicting exponents for cross-modality matches. *Perception & Psychophysics,* 1969, *6,* 251–256. (a)

Stevens, S. S. Sensory scales of taste intensity. *Perception & Psychophysics,* 1969, *6,* 302–308. (b)

Stevens, S. S. Neural events and the psychophysical law. *Science,* 1970, *170,* 1043–1050.

Stevens, S. S. Issues in psychophysical measurement. *Psychological Review,* 1971, *78,* 428–450.

Stevens, S. S. A neural quantum in sensory-discrimination. *Science,* 1972, *177,* 749–762.

Stevens, S. S. Perceptual magnitude and its measurement. In E. C. Carterette and M. P. Friedman (Eds.), *Handbook of perception,* Vol. 2. New York: Academic Press, 1974.

Stevens, S. S. *Psychophysics: Introduction to its perceptual, neural and social prospects.* New York: Wiley, 1975.

Stevens, S. S., and Galanter, E. H. Ratio scales and category scales for a dozen perceptual continua. *Journal of Experimental Psychology,* 1957, *54,* 377–409.

Stevens, S. S., and Greenbaum, H. B. Regression effect in psychophysical judgment. *Perception & Psychophysics,* 1966, *1,* 439–446.

Stevens, S. S., and Guirao, M. Loudness, reciprocality, and partition scales. *Journal of the Acoustical Society of America,* 1962, *34,* 1466–1471.

Stevens, S. S., and Guirao, M. Subjective scaling of length and area and the matching of length to loudness and brightness. *Journal of Experimental Psychology,* 1963, *66,* 177–186.

Stevens, S. S., and Guirao, M. Scaling of apparent viscosity. *Science,* 1964, *144,* 1157–1158.

Stevens, S. S., Guirao, M., and Slawson, A. W. Loudness: A product of volume times density. *Journal of Experimental Psychology,* 1965, *69,* 503–510.

Stevens, S. S., Morgan, C. T., and Volkmann, J. Theory of the neural quantum in the discrimination of loudness and pitch. *American Journal of Psychology,* 1941, *54,* 315–335.

Stevens, S. S., and Volkmann, J. The quantum of sensory discrimination. *Science,* 1940, *92,* 583–585.

Stewart, E. C. The Gelb effect. *Journal of Experimental Psychology,* 1959, *57,* 235–242.

Street, R. F. *A Gestalt completion test.* New York: Teachers College, Columbia University, 1931.

Stroh, C. M. *Vigilance: The problem of sustained attention.* New York: Pergamon, 1971.

Surwillo, W. W., and Quilter, R. E. The relation of frequency of spontaneous skin potential responses to vigilance and to age. *Psychophysiology,* 1965, *1,* 272–276.

Sutherland, N. S. Stimulus analyzing mechanisms. In *The mechanisation of thought processes*. London: H. M. Stationery Office, 1959.

Suto, Y. The effect of space on time estimation in tactual space. *Japanese Journal of Psychology,* 1952, *22,* 189–201.

Swets, J. A. Is there a sensory threshold? *Science,* 1961, *134,* 168–177.

Swets, J. A. The relative operating characteristic in psychology. *Science,* 1973, *182,* 990–1000.

Swets, J. A., and Kristofferson, A. B. Attention. In P. H. Mussen and M. R. Rosenzweig (Eds.), *Annual Review of Psychology.* Palo Alto, Calif.: Annual Reviews, Inc., 1970.

Swets, J. A., Tanner, W. P., Jr., and Birdsall, T. G. Decision processes in perception. *Psychological Review,* 1961, *68,* 301–340.

Tajfel, H. Value and the perceptual judgment of magnitude. *Psychological Review,* 1957, *64,* 192–204.

Tajfel, H. Quantitative judgment in social perception. *British Journal of Psychology,* 1959, *50,* 16–29.

Tallarico, R. B. Studies of visual depth perception: III. Choice behavior of newly-hatched chicks on a visual cliff. *Perceptual and Motor Skills,* 1961, *12,* 259–262.

Tanner, W. P., Jr., and Swets, J. A. A decision-making theory of visual detection. *Psychological Review,* 1954, *61,* 401–409.

Tanner, W. P., Jr., Swets, J. A., and Green, D. M. Some general properties of the hearing mechanism. Technical Report No. 30, University of Michigan, Electronic Defense Group, 1956.

Taub, H. A., and Osborne, F. H. Effects of signal and stimulus rates on vigilance performance. *Journal of Applied Psychology,* 1968, *52,* 133–138.

Tauber, E. S., and Koffler, S. Optomotor response in human infants to apparent motion: Evidence of innateness. *Science,* 1966, *152,* 382–383.

Taylor, D. W., and Boring, E. G. The moon illusion as a function of binocular regard. *American Journal of Psychology,* 1942, *55,* 189–201.

Taylor, W. "Cloze procedure": A new tool for measuring readability. *Journalism Quarterly,* 1953, *30,* 415–433.

Teghtsoonian, M., and Teghtsoonian, R. How repeatable are Stevens' power law exponents for individual subjects? *Perception & Psychophysics,* 1971, *10,* 147–152.

Teghtsoonian, R. On the exponents in Stevens' law and the constant in Ekman's law. *Psychological Review,* 1971, *78,* 71–80.

Teichner, W. H. Recent studies of simple reaction time. *Psychological Bulletin,* 1954, *51,* 128–149.

Teichner, W. H. The detection of a simple visual signal as a function of time of watch. *Human Factors,* 1974, *16,* 339–353.

Teichner, W. H., and Krebs, M. J. Laws of the simple visual reaction time. *Psychological Review,* 1972, *79,* 344–358.

Teichner, W. H., and Krebs, M. J. Laws of visual choice reaction time. *Psychological Review,* 1974, *81,* 75–98.

Teyler, T. J., Shaw, C., and Thompson, R. F. Unit responses to moving visual stimuli in the motor cortex of the cat. *Science,* 1972, *176,* 811–813.

Theodor, L. H. A neglected parameter: Some comments on "A table for the calculation of d' and β." *Psychological Bulletin,* 1972, *78,* 260–261.

Thiéry, A. Über geometrisch-optische Täuschungen. *Philosophische Studien,* 1896, *12,* 67–126.

Thomas, E. A. C., and Brown, I., Jr. Time perception and the filled-duration illusion. *Perception & Psychophysics,* 1974, *16,* 449–458.

Thomas, E. A. C., and Weaver, W. B. Cognitive processing and time perception. *Perception & Psychophysics,* 1975, *17,* 363–367.

Thomas, H. Unidirectional changes in preference for increasing visual complexity in the cat. *Journal of Comparative and Physiological Psychology,* 1969, *68,* 296–302.

Thomas, J. P. Model of the function of receptive fields in human vision. *Psychological Review,* 1970, *77,* 121–134.

Thompson, R. F. *Introduction to biopsychology.* San Francisco: Albion, 1973.

Thompson, R. F., and Spencer, W. A. Habituation: A model phenomenon for the study of neuronal substrates of behavior. *Psychological Review,* 1966, *73,* 16–43.

Thompson, W. R., and Solomon, L. M. Spontaneous pattern discrimination in the rat. *Journal of Comparative and Physiological Psychology,* 1954, *47,* 104–107.

Thor, D. H., Winters, J. J., Jr., and Hoats, D. L. Vertical eye movement and space perception: A developmental study. *Journal of Experimental Psychology,* 1969, *82,* 163–167.

Thor, D. H., Winters, J. J., Jr., and Hoats, D. L. Eye-elevation and visual space in monocular regard. *Journal of Experimental Psychology,* 1970, *86,* 246–249.

Thorndike, E. L., and Lorge, I. *The teacher's word book of 30,000 words.* New York: Teachers College, Columbia University, 1944.

Thouless, R. H. Phenomenal regression to the real object. *British Journal of Psychology,* 1931, *21,* 339–359.

Thurlow, W. R. Audition. In J. W. Kling and L. A. Riggs (Eds.), *Woodworth & Schlosberg's experimental psychology,* 3d ed. New York: Holt, Rinehart and Winston, 1971.

Tickner, A. H., Poulton, E. C., Copeman, A. K., and Simmonds, D. C. V. Monitoring 16 television screens showing little movement. *Ergonomics,* 1972, *15,* 279–291.

Titchener, E. B. *Experimental psychology: Vol. II. Instructor's manual, Part II.* New York: Macmillan, 1905.

Titchener, E. B. *Lectures on the elementary psychology of feeling and attention.* New York: Macmillan, 1908.

Tolin, P., and Fisher, P. G. Sex differences and effects of irrelevant auditory stimulation on performance of a visual vigilance task. *Perceptual and Motor Skills,* 1974, *39,* 1255–1262.

Torgerson, W. S. Distances and ratios in psychophysical scaling. *Acta Psychologica,* 1961, *19,* 201–205.

Treisman, A. M. Contextual cues in selective listening. *Quarterly Journal of Experimental Psychology,* 1960, *12,* 242–248.

Treisman, A. M. The effect of irrelevant material on the efficiency of selective listening. *American Journal of Psychology,* 1964, *77,* 533–546. (a)

Treisman, A. M. Verbal cues, language, and meaning in selective attention. *American Journal of Psychology,* 1964, *77,* 206–219. (b)

Treisman, A. M. Strategies and models of selective attention. *Psychological Reveiw,* 1969, *76,* 282–299.

Treisman, A. M., and Geffen, G. Selective attention: Perception or response? *Quarterly Journal of Experimental Psychology,* 1967, *19,* 1–17.

Treisman, A. M., and Riley, J. G. A. Is selective attention selective perception or selective response? *Journal of Experimental Psychology,* 1969, *79,* 27–34.

Treisman, M. Temporal discrimination and the indifference interval: Implications for a model of the "internal clock." *Psychological Monographs*, 1963, 77(13), Whole No. 576.

Treisman, M. Noise and Weber's law: The discrimination of brightness and other dimensions. *Psychological Review*, 1964, 71, 314–330.

Treisman, M. Relation between signal detectability theory and the traditional procedures for measuring thresholds: An addendum. *Psychological Bulletin*, 1973, 79, 45–47.

Treisman, M., and Leshowitz, B. The effects of duration, area, and background intensity on the visual intensity difference threshold given by the forced-choice procedure: Derivations from a statistical decision model for sensory discrimination. *Perception & Psychophysics*, 1969, 6, 281–296.

Treisman, M., and Watts, T. R. Relation between signal detectability theory and the traditional procedures for measuring sensory thresholds: Estimating d' from results given by the method of constant stimuli. *Psychological Bulletin*, 1966, 66, 438–454.

Tyler, D. M., Waag, W. L., and Halcomb, C. G. Monitoring performance across sense modes: An individual differences approach *Human Factors*, 1972, 14, 539–547.

Tynan, P., and Sekuler, R. W. Moving visual phantoms: A new contour completion effect. *Science*, 1975, 188, 951–952.

Uhr, L., Ed. *Pattern recognition.* New York: Wiley, 1966.

Underwood, B. J. *Experimental psychology*, 2d ed. New York: Appleton, 1966.

Underwood, B. J., and Shaughnessy, J. J. *Experimentation in psychology.* New York: Wiley, 1975.

Uttal, W. R. Masking of alphabetic character recognition by dynamic visual noise (DVN). *Perception & Psychophysics*, 1969, 6, 121–128.

Uttal, W. R. The psychobiological silly season, or what happens when neurophysiological data become psychological theories. *Journal of General Psychology*, 1971, 84, 151–166.

Uttal, W. R. *The psychobiology of sensory coding.* New York: Harper & Row, 1973.

Uttal, W. R. *An autocorrelation theory of form detection.* Hillsdale, N.J.: Erlbaum Associates, 1975.

Uttal, W. R., Bunnell, L. M., and Corwin, S. On the detectability of straight lines in visual noise: An extension of French's paradigm into the millisecond domain. *Perception & Psychophysics*, 1970, 8, 385–388.

Vanderplas, J. M., and Blake, R. R. Selective sensitization in auditory perception. *Journal of Personality*, 1949, 18, 252–266.

Vanderplas, J. M., and Garvin, E. A. The association value of random shapes. *Journal of Experimental Psychology*, 1959, 57, 147–154.

Van Eyl, F. P. Induced vestibular stimulation and the moon illusion. *Journal of Experimental Psychology*, 1972, 94, 326–328.

Vickers, D. Perceptual economy and the impression of visual depth. *Perception & Psychophysics*, 1971, 10, 23–27.

Viemeister, H. F. Intensity discrimination: Performance in three paradigms. *Perception & Psychophysics*, 1970, 8, 417–419.

Vincent, R. J., Brown, B. R., Markley, R. P., and Arnoult, M. D. Distance discrimination in a simulated space environment. *Perception & Psychophysics*, 1969, 5, 235–238.

Vitz, P. C., and Todd, T. C. A coded element model of the perceptual processing of sequential stimuli. *Psychological Review,* 1969, *76,* 433–449.

Vitz, P. O. Preference for different amounts of visual complexity. *Behavioral Science,* 1966, *11,* 105–114. (a)

Vitz, P. O. Affect as a function of stimulus variation. *Journal of Experimental Psychology,* 1966, *71,* 74–79. (b)

Vogel, J. M., and Teghtsoonian, M. The effects of perspective alterations on apparent size and distance scales. *Perception & Psychophysics,* 1972, *11,* 294–298.

von Holst, E., and Mittelstädt, H. Das Reafferenz-Prinzip. *Die Naturwissenschaften,* 1950, *20,* 464–476.

Von Wright, J. M., Anderson, K., and Stenman, U. Generalization of conditioned GSRs in dichotic listening. In P. M. Rabbitt and S. Dornic (Eds.), *Attention and performance: V.* London: Academic Press, 1975.

Vroon, P. A. Effects of presented and processed information on duration experience. *Acta Psychologica,* 1970, *34,* 115–121.

Wade, N. J. The effect of orientation in binocular contour rivalry of real images and afterimages. *Perception & Psychophysics,* 1974, *15,* 227–232.

Wales, R., and Fox, R. Increment detection thresholds during binocular rivalry suppression. *Perception & Psychophysics,* 1970, *8,* 90–94.

Walk, R. D. Response of dark- and light-reared rats to stimulus change. *Journal of Comparative and Physiological Psychology,* 1960, *53,* 609–611.

Walk, R. D. The study of visual depth and distance perception in animals. In D. S. Lehrman, R. A. Hinde, and E. Shaw (Eds.), *Advances in the study of behavior.* New York: Academic Press, 1965.

Walk, R. D., and Gibson, E. J. A comparative and analytical study of visual depth perception. *Psychological Monographs,* 1961, *75,* 15, Whole No. 519.

Walk, R. D., Gibson, E. J., Pick, H. L., Jr., and Tighe, T. J. Further experiments on prolonged exposure to visual forms: The effect of single stimuli and prior reinforcement. *Journal of Comparative and Physiological Psychology,* 1958, *51,* 483–487.

Walk, R. D., Gibson, E. J., and Tighe, T. J. Behavior of light- and dark-reared rats on a visual cliff. *Science,* 1957, *126,* 80–81.

Walker, E. L., Dember, W. N., Earl, R. W., and Karoly, A. J. Choice alternation: I. Stimulus vs. place vs. response. *Journal of Comparative and Physiological Psychology,* 1955, *48,* 19–23.

Wallace, M., and Rabin, A. I. Temporal experience. *Psychological Bulletin,* 1960, *57,* 214–236.

Wallach, H. On constancy of visual speed. *Psychological Review,* 1939, *46,* 541–552.

Wallach, H. Brightness constancy and the nature of achromatic colors. *Journal of Experimental Psychology,* 1948, *38,* 310–324.

Wallach, H. On the moon illusion (letters to the editor). *Science,* 1962, *137,* 900–902.

Wallach, H. The perception of neutral colors. *Scientific American,* 1963, *208,* 107–116.

Wallach, H., and Floor, L. The use of size matching to demonstrate the effectiveness of accommodation and convergence as cues for distance. *Perception & Psychophysics,* 1971, *10,* 423–428.

Wallach, H., and Norris, C. M. Accommodation as a distance-cue. *American Journal of Psychology,* 1963, *76,* 659–664.

Wallach, H., and O'Connell, D. N. The kinetic depth effect. *Journal of Experimental Psychology,* 1953, *45,* 205–217.

Wallach, H., O'Connell, D. N., and Neisser, U. The memory effect of visual perception of three-dimensional form. *Journal of Experimental Psychology,* 1953, *45,* 360–368.

Walsh, R. N., and Cummins, R. A. Mechanisms mediating the production of environmentally induced brain changes. *Psychological Bulletin,* 1975, *82,* 986–1000.

Walters, R. H., Banks, R. K., and Ryder, R. B. A test of the perceptual defense hypothesis. *Journal of Personality,* 1959, *27,* 47–55.

Wanschura, R. G., and Dawson, W. E. Regression effect and individual power functions over sessions. *Journal of Experimental Psychology,* 1974, *102,* 806–812.

Ward, A. J. Early infantile autism. *Psychological Bulletin,* 1970, *73,* 350–362.

Ward, L. M. Category judgments of loudness in the absence of an experimenter-induced identification function: Sequential effects and power-function fit. *Journal of Experimental Psychology,* 1972, *94,* 179–184.

Ward, L. M., and Coren, S. The effect of optically induced blur on the magnitude of the Mueller–Lyer illusion. *Bulletin of the Psychonomic Society,* 1976, 7, 483–484.

Ward, L. M., and Lockhead, G. R. Sequential effects and memory in category judgments. *Journal of Experimental Psychology,* 1970, *84,* 27–34.

Ward, L. M., and Lockhead, G. R. Response system processes in absolute judgment. *Perception & Psychophysics,* 1971, *9,* 73–78.

Wardlaw, K. A., and Kroll, N. E. A. Autonomic responses to shock-associated words in a non-attended message: A failure to replicate. *Journal of Experimental Psychology: Human Perception and Performance,* 1976, *2,* 357–360.

Warm, J. S. Psychological processes in sustained attention. In R. R. Mackie (Ed.), *Vigilance: Theory, operational performance, and physiological correlates.* New York: Plenum, 1977.

Warm, J. S., and Alluisi, E. A. Influence of temporal uncertainty and sensory modality of signals on watchkeeping performance. *Journal of Experimental Psychology,* 1971, *87,* 303–308.

Warm, J. S., Clark, J. L., and Foulke, E. Effects of differential spatial orientation on tactual pattern recognition. *Perceptual and Motor Skills,* 1970, *31,* 87–94.

Warm, J. S., Epps, B. D., and Ferguson, R. P. Effects of knowledge of results and signal regularity on vigilance performance. *Bulletin of the Psychonomic Society,* 1974, *4,* 272–274.

Warm, J. S., Greenberg, L. F., and Dube, C. S. Stimulus and motivational determinants in temporal perception. *Journal of Psychology,* 1964, *58,* 243–248.

Warm, J. S., Hagner, G. L., and Meyer, D. The partial reinforcement effect in a vigilance task. *Perceptual and Motor Skills,* 1971, *32,* 987–993.

Warm, J. S., Kanfer, F. H., Kuwada, S., and Clark, J. L. Motivation in vigilance: Effects of self-evaluation and experimenter controlled feedback. *Journal of Experimental Psychology,* 1972, *92,* 123–127.

Warm, J. S., Loeb, M., and Alluisi, E. A. Variations in watchkeeping performance as a function of the rate and duration of visual signals. *Perception & Psychophysics,* 1970, 7, 97–99.

Warm, J. S., and McCray, R. E. Influence of word frequency and length on the apparent duration of tachistoscopic presentations. *Journal of Experimental Psychology,* 1969, *79,* 56–58.

Warm, J. S., Riechmann, S. W., Grasha, A. F., and Seibel, B. Motivation in vigilance: A test of the goal-setting hypothesis of the effectiveness of knowledge of results. *Bulletin of the Psychonomic Society,* 1973, *1,* 291–292.

Warm, J. S., Smith, R. P., and Caldwell, L. S. Effects of induced muscle tension on judgment of time. *Perceptual and Motor Skills,* 1967, *25,* 153–160.

Warm, J. S., Stutz, R. M., and Vassolo, P. A. Intermodal transfer in temporal discrimination. *Perception & Psychophysics,* 1975, *18,* 281–286.

Warm, J. S., Wait, R. G., and Loeb, M. Head restraint enhances visual monitoring performance. *Perception & Psychophysics,* 1976, *20,* 299–304.

Warren, R. M. A basis for judgments of sensory intensity. *American Journal of Psychology,* 1958, *71,* 675–687.

Warren, R. M. Visual intensity judgments: An empirical rule and a theory. *Psychological Review,* 1969, *76,* 16–30.

Warren, R. M. Quantification of loudness. *American Journal of Psychology,* 1973, *86,* 807–825.

Warren, R. M., Serson, E. A., and Pores, E. A basis for loudness-judgments. *American Journal of Psychology,* 1958, *71,* 700–709.

Warren, R. M., and Warren, R. P. Basis for judgments of relative brightness. *Journal of the Optical Society of America,* 1958, *48,* 445–450.

Weintraub, D. J., and Gardner, G. T. Emmert's laws: Size constancy vs. optical geometry. *American Journal of Psychology,* 1970, *83,* 40–54.

Weintraub, D. J., and Hake, H. W. Visual discrimination, an interpretation in terms of detectability theory. *Journal of the Optical Society of America,* 1962, *52,* 1179–1184.

Weisstein, N. Neural symbolic activity: A psychophysical measure. *Science,* 1970, *168,* 1489–1491.

Weisstein, N. What the frog's eye tells the human brain: Single cell analyzers in the human visual system. *Psychological Bulletin,* 1969, *72,* 157–176.

Weisstein, N. Metacontrast. In D. Jameson and L. M. Hurvich (Eds.), *Handbook of sensory physiology,* Vol. 7, Part 4. New York: Springer-Verlag, 1972.

Weisstein, N. Beyond the yellow-Volkswagen detector and the grandmother cell: A general strategy for the exploration of operations in human pattern recognition. In R. L. Solso (Ed.), *Contemporary issues in cognitive psychology: The Loyola symposium.* Washington, D.C.: Winston, 1973.

Weisstein, N., and Bisaha, J. Gratings mask bars and bars mask gratings: Visual frequency response to aperiodic stimuli. *Science,* 1972, *176,* 1047–1049.

Weisstein, N., and Harris, C. S. Visual detection of line segments: An object-superiority effect. *Science,* 1974, *186,* 752–755.

Weisstein, N., Maguire, W., and Berbaum, K. A phantom-motion aftereffect. *Science,* 1977, *198,* 955–957.

Weisstein, N., Ozog, G., and Szoc, R. A comparison and elaboration of two models of metacontrast. *Psychological Review,* 1975, *82,* 325–343.

Welford, A. T. *Fundamentals of skill.* London: Methuen, 1968.

Welker, W. I. Some determinants of play and exploration in chimpanzees. *Journal of Comparative and Physiological Psychology,* 1956, *49,* 84–89.

Wenderoth, P., and Beh, H. Component analysis of orientation illusions. *Perception,* 1977, *6,* 57–75.

Werblin, F. S. Functional organization of a vertebrate retina: Sharpening up in space and intensity. *Annals of the New York Academy of Sciences,* 1972, *193,* 75–85.

Werner, H. Studies on contour: I. Qualitative analyses. *American Journal of Psychology,* 1935, *47,* 40–64.

Werner, H. *Comparative psychology of mental development.* Chicago: Follett, 1948.

Wertheimer, M. Experimentelle Studien über das Sehen von Bewegung. *Zeitschrift für Psychologie*, 1912, *61*, 161–265.

Wertheimer, M. Hebb and Senden on the role of learning in perception. *American Journal of Psychology*, 1951, *64*, 133–137.

Wheatstone, C. Contributions to the physiology of vision: Part the first. On some remarkable and hitherto unobserved phenomena of binocular vision. *Philosophical Transactions, Royal Society of London*, 1838, *128*, 371–394.

Wheeler, D. D. Processes in word recognition. *Cognitive Psychology*, 1970, *1*, 59–85.

White, B. L., and Held, R. Plasticity of sensorimotor development in the human infant. In J. F. Rosenblith, and W. Allinsmith (Eds.), *The causes of behavior: Readings in child development and educational psychology*. Boston: Allyn & Bacon, 1966.

White, M. J. Effect of response instructions on the perceived duration of briefly exposed words. *Journal of General Psychology*, 1973, *88*, 175–177.

Whitmore, C. L. G., Lawson, R. B., and Kozora, C. E. Subjective contours in stereoscopic space. *Perception & Psychophysics*, 1976, *19*, 211–213.

Whorf, B. L. *Four articles on metalinguistics*. Washington, D.C.: Foreign Service Institute, 1950.

Wiener, E. L. Knowledge of results and signal rate in monitoring: A transfer of training approach. *Journal of Applied Psychology*, 1963, *47*, 214–222.

Wiener, E. L. Transfer of training in monitoring: Signal amplitude. *Perceptual and Motor Skills*, 1964, *18*, 104.

Wiener, E. L. An adaptive vigilance task with knowledge of results. *Human Factors*, 1974, *16*, 333–338.

Wiener, N. *Cybernetics*. New York: Wiley, 1948.

Williges, R. C., and North, R. A. Knowledge of results and decision making performance in visual monitoring. *Organizational Behavior and Human Performance*, 1972, *8*, 44–57.

Wispé, L. G., and Drambarean, N. C. Physiological need, word frequency, and visual duration thresholds. *Journal of Experimental Psychology*, 1953, *46*, 25–31.

Witkin, H. A., Dyk, R. B., Faterson, H. F., Goodenough, D. G., and Karp, S. A. *Psychological differentiation*. New York: Wiley, 1962.

Witkin, H. A., Goodenough, D. R., and Karp, S. A. Stability of cognitive style from childhood to young adulthood. *Journal of Personality and Social Psychology*, 1967, *3*, 291–300.

Witkin, H. A., Lewis, H. B., Hertzman, M., Machover, K., Meissner, P., and Wapner, S., *Personality through perception*. New York: Harper & Row, 1954.

Wohlwill, J. F. Developmental studies of perception. *Psychological Bulletin*, 1960, *57*, 249–288.

Wong, T. S., Ho, R., and Ho, J. Influence of shape of receptor organ on the horizontal–vertical illusion in passive touch. *Journal of Experimental Psychology*, 1974, *103*, 414–419.

Wood, R. J., Zinkus, P. W., and Mountjoy, P. T. The vestibular hypothesis of the moon illusion. *Psychonomic Science*, 1968, *11*, 356.

Woodrow, H. Time perception. In S. S. Stevens (Ed.), *Handbook of experimental psychology*. New York: Wiley, 1951.

Woods, P. J., and Jennings, S. Response to environmental change: A further confirmation. *Psychological Reports*, 1959, *5*, 560.

Woodworth, R. S. *Experimental psychology*. New York: Holt, 1938.

Woodworth, R. S. *Dynamics of behavior.* New York: Holt, Rinehart and Winston, 1958.

Woodworth, R. S., and Schlosberg, H. *Experimental psychology,* rev. ed. New York: Holt, Rinehart and Winston, 1954.

Woodworth, R. S., and Sheehan, M. R. *Contemporary schools of psychology,* 3d ed. New York: Ronald, 1964.

Wright, A. A. Psychometric and psychophysical theory within a framework of response bias. *Psychological Review,* 1974, *81,* 322–347.

Yntema, D. B., and Trask, F. P. Recall as a search process. *Journal of Verbal Learning and Verbal Behavior,* 1963, *2,* 65–74.

Yost, W. A., and Nielsen, D. W. *Fundamentals of hearing: An introduction.* New York: Holt, Rinehart and Winston, 1977.

Zajonc, R. B. Attitudinal effects of mere exposure. *Journal of Personality and Social Psychology Monograph Supplement,* 1968, *9,* No. 2, Pt. 2, 2–27.

Zajonc, R. B., Swap, W. C., Harrison, A. A., and Roberts, P. Limiting conditions of the exposure effect: Satiation and relativity. *Journal of Personality and Social Psychology,* 1971, *18,* 386–391.

Zeigler, H. P., and Leibowitz, H. W. Apparent visual size as a function of distance for children and adults. *American Journal of Psychology,* 1957, *70,* 106–109.

Zelkind, I., and Ulehla, J. Estimated duration of an auditory signal as a function of its intensity. *Psychonomic Science,* 1968, *11,* 185–186.

Zinnes, J. L. Scaling. In P. H. Mussen and M. R. Rosenzweig (Eds.), *Annual Review of Psychology.* Palo Alto, Calif.: Annual Reviews, Inc., 1969.

Zipf, G. K. *The psycho-biology of language.* Boston: Houghton Mifflin, 1935.

Zubek, J. P. (Ed.), *Sensory deprivation: Fifteen years of research.* New York: Appleton-Century-Crofts, 1969.

Zuercher, J. D. The effects of extraneous stimulation on vigilance. *Human Factors,* 1965, *7,* 101–105.

Zusne, L. *Visual perception of form.* New York: Academic Press, 1970.

Acknowledgments (Continued)

Chapanis, A. "How we see: A summary of basic principles." Reproduced from *Human factors in undersea warfare,* page 10, with the permission of the National Academy of Sciences, Washington, D.C. and Corso, J.F. *The experimental psychology of sensory behavior.* Copyright © 1967 by Holt, Rinehart and Winston. Reprinted by permission of Holt, Rinehart and Winston. Figure 2.7 — Hecht, S., & Shlaer, S. "An adoptometer for measuring human dark adaptation." *Journal of the Optical Society of America, 28:*269–275, 1938. Figure 2.8 — Woodworth, R.S., & Schlosberg, H. *Experimental psychology. Copyright* © 1954 by Holt, Rinehart and Winston. Reprinted by permission of Holt, Rinehart and Winston. Figure 2.9 — Boring, E.G., Langfeld, H.S., & Weld, H.P. *Introduction to psychology.* Copyright © 1939 by John Wiley & Sons. Reprinted by permission. Boring, E.G. *Sensation and perception in the history of experimental psychology.* Copyright © 1942 by Appleton-Century-Crofts. Figure 2.10 — Vincent, R.J., Brown, B.R., Markley, R.P., & Amoult, M.D. "Distance discrimination in a simulated space environment." *Perception and Psychophysics, 5:*235–238. 1969.

Figure 3.1 — Mueller, C.G. "Frequency of seeing functions for intensity discrimination at various levels of adapting intensity." *Journal of General Physiology, 34:*463–474, 1951. Figure 3.2 — from *Experiments in hearing* by G. von Békésy (edited by E.G. Wever). Copyright © 1960 by McGraw-Hill. Used with permission of McGraw-Hill Book Company. Figure 3.4 — Stevens, S.S., & Volkmann, J. "The quantum of sensory discrimination." *Science, 92:*583–585, 1940. Figure 3.5 — Stevens, S.S., Morgan, C.T., & Volkmann, J. "Theory of the neural quantum in the discrimination of loudness and pitch." *American Journal of Psychology, 54:*315–335, 1941. Reprinted by permission of the University of Illinois Press. Figure 3.8 — Green, D.M., & Swets, J.A. *Signal detection theory and psychophysics.* Copyright © 1966 by John Wiley & Sons, Inc. Reprinted by permission. Figures 3.9 and 3.10 — Green, D.M., & Swets, J.A. *Signal detection theory and psychophysics* (reprint). Copyright © 1974 by Robert E. Krieger Publishing Co., Inc. Reprinted by permission. Figure 3.11 — Green, D.M., Birdsall, T.G., & Tanner, W. P. "Signal detection as a function of signal intensity and duration." *Journal of the Acoustical Society of America, 29:*523–531, 1957. Figures 3.12, 3.13, and 3.14 — Swets, J.A., Tanner, W. P., & Birdsall, T.G. "Decision processes in perception." *Psychological Review, 68:*301–340, 1961. Copyright © 1961 by the American Psychological Association. Reprinted by permission.

Table 4.1 — Stevens, S.S. "The psychophysics of sensory function." *American Scientist, 48:*226–254, 1960.

Figure 4.2 — Woodworth, R.S., & Schlosberg, H. *Experimental psychology.* Copyright © 1954 by Holt, Rinehart and Winston. Reprinted by permission of Holt, Rinehart and Winston. Figure 4.3 — Engen, T., "Psychophysics II. Scaling Methods. In J.W. Kling & L.A. Riggs, (Eds.) *Woodworth & Schlosberg's experimental psychology,* 3rd ed. Copyright © 1971 by Holt, Rinehart and Winston. Reprinted by permission of Holt, Rinehart and Winston. Figure 4.4 — Hanes, R.M. "A scale of subjective brightness." *Journal of Experimental Psychology, 39:*438–452, 1949. Copyright © 1949 by the American Psychological Association. Reprinted by permission. Figures 4.5, 4.6, and 4.7 — Stevens, S.S. "The surprising simplicity of sensory metrics." *American Psychologist, 17:*29–39, 1962. Copyright © 1962 by the American Psychological Association. Reprinted by permission. Figure 4.8 — Stevens, S.S. "Cross modality validation of subjective scales for loudness, vibration, and electric shock." *Journal of Experimental Psychology, 57:*201–209, 1959. Copyright © 1959 by the American Psychological Association. Reprinted by permission. Figure 4.9 — Stevens, S.S., "The surprising simplicity of sensory metrics." *American Psychologist, 17:*29–39, 1962. Copyright © 1962 by the American Psychological Association. Reprinted by permission. Figure 4.10 — Stevens, S.S. "On the operation known as judgment." *American Scientist, 54:*385–401, 1966. Reprinted by permission, American Scientist, Journal of Sigma Xi, the Scientific Research Society of North America. Figures 4.11 and 4.12 — Stevens, S.S., & Guirao, M. "Subjective scaling of length and area and the matching of length to loudness and brightness."

514   Acknowledgements

*Journal of Experimental Psychology, 66:*177–86, 1963. Copyright © 1963 by the American Psychological Association. Reprinted by permission. Figure 4.13—Stevens, J.C., & Guirao, M. "Individual loudness functions." *Journal of the Acoustical Society of America, 36:*2210–2213, 1964. Figure 4.14—Stevens, S.S., & Galanter, E.H. "Ratio scales and category scales for a dozen perceptual continua." *Journal of Experimental Psychology, 54:*377–409, 1957. Copyright © 1957 by the American Psychological Association. Reprinted by permission. Figure 4.15—Teghtsoonian, M. & Teghtsoonian, R. "How repeatable are Stevens's power law exponents for individual subjects?" *Perception and Psychophysics, 10:*147–152, 1971. Figure 4.16—Shannon, C.E., & Weaver, W. "The mathematical theory of communication." Copyright © 1949 by the University of Illinois Press. Reprinted by permission. Figure 4.18—Miller, G.A., Heise, G.A., & Lichten, W. "The intelligibility of speech as a function of the context of the text materials." *Journal of Experimental Psychology, 41:*329–335, 1951. Copyright © 1951 by the American Psychological Association. Reprinted by permission. Figure 4.19—Miller, I. "Perception of nonsense passages in relation to amount of information and speech-to-noise ratio." *Journal of Experimental Psychology, 53:*388–393, 1957. Copyright © 1957 by the American Psychological Association. Reprinted by permission. Figure 4.20—Pollack, I. "Message uncertainty and message reception." *Journal of the Acoustical Society of America, 31:*1500–1508, 1959, Figure 4.21—Miller, G.A. "What is information measurement?" *American Psychologist, 8:*3–11, 1953. Copyright © 1953 by the American Psychological Association. Reprinted by permission. Figure 4.23—Miller, G.A. "The magical number seven, plus or minus two: Some limits on our capacity for processing information." *Psychological Review, 63:*81–97, 1956. Copyright © 1956 by the American Psychological Association. Reprinted by permission. Figure 4.25—Alluisi, E.A., Strain, G.S., & Thurmond, J.B. "Stimulus-response compatibility and the rate of gain of information." *Psychonomic Science, 1:*111–112, 1964. Adopted with permission of the senior author from Alluisi, Strain, & Thurmond, 1964, p. 112.

Table 5.1—*From Introduction to Physiological Psychology: Information processing in the nervous system.* by J. Beatty. Copyright © 1975 by Wadsworth Publishing Company, Inc. Reprinted by permission of Brooks/Cole Publishing Company, Monterey, California. Figure 5.1—Hernández-Peón, R. "Physiological mechanisms in attention." In R.W. Russell (Ed.) *Frontiers in physiological psychology.* Copyright © 1966 by Academic Press. Reprinted by permission. Figures 5.2 and 5.3—Berlyne, D.E. "Curiosity and exploration." *Science, 153:*25–33, 1966. Copyright © 1966 by the American Association for the Advancement of Science. Figure 5.4—Noton, D., & Stark, L. "Scanpaths in eye movements during pattern perception." *Science, 171:*308–311, 1971. Copyright © 1971 by the American Association for the Advancement of Science. Figure 5.5—Reproduced from Broadbent, D. *Perception and communication. Pergamon Press* (1958) by permission of the author. Figure 5.6—Hernández-Peón, R., Scherrer, H., and Jouvet, M. "Modification of electric activity in a cochlear nucleus during 'attention' in unanesthetized cats." *Science, 123:*331–332, 1956. Copyright © 1956 by the American Association for the Advancement of Science. Figure 5.7—Moray, N. *Listening and attention.* (Penguin Science of Behavior, 1969, p. 26. Copyright © 1969 by Neville Moray. Reprinted by permission of the author and Penguin Books Ltd. Figure 5.8—Treisman, A.M. "Contextual cues in selective listening." *Quarterly Journal of Experimental Psychology, 12:*242–248, 1960. Reproduced by permission of Experimental Psychology Society. Figure 5.9—Kahneman, D. *Attention and effort.* Copyright © 1973, p. 6. Reprinted by permission of Prentice-Hall, Inc., Englewood Cliffs, New Jersey. Figure 5.10—Mackworth, N.H. Researches on the measurement of human performance. Medical Research Council Special Report Series 268, H.M. Stationary Office, 1950. Reprinted in H.W. Sinaiko (Ed.) *Selected papers on human factors in the design and use of control systems.* Copyright © 1961 by Dover Press. Reprinted by permission. Figure 5.11—Loeb, M., & Binford, J.R. "Some factors influencing the effective auditory intensive difference limen." *Journal of the Acoustical Society of America, 35:*884–891, 1963. Figure 5.12—Baker, C.H. "Signal duration as a factor in vigilance tasks." *Science, 141:*1196–1197, 1963. Copyright © 1963 by the American Association for the Advancement of Science. Figure 5.13—Jerison, H.J., & Pickett, R.M. "Vigilance: The importance of the elicited observing rate." *Science, 143*:970–971, 1964. Copyright © 1964 by the American Association for the Advancement of Science. Figure 5.14 – Reprinted with permission of author and publisher from: Metzger, K., Warm, J., & Senter, R. "Effects of background event rate and critical signal amplitude on vigilance performance." *Perceptual and Motor Skills, 38*:1175–1181, 1974. Figure 5.15 – Jerison, H.J., & Pickett, R.M. "Vigilance: A review and re-evaluation. *Human Factors, 5*:211–238, 1963. Figure 5.16 – Smith, R.P., Warm, J.S., & Alluisi, E.A. "Effects of temporal uncertainty on watchkeeping performance." *Perception & Psychophysics, 1*:293–299, 1966. Figure 5.17 – Moore, S.F., & Gross, S.J. "Influence of critical signal regularity, stimulus event matrix and cognitive style on vigilance performance." *Journal of Experimental Psychology, 99*:137–139, 1973. Copyright © 1973 by the American Psychological Association. Reprinted by permission. Figure 5.18 – Warm, J.S., Kanfer, F.H. Kuwada, S., & Clark, J.L. "Motivation in vigilance: Effects of self-evaluation and experimenter controlled feedback." *Journal of Experimental Psychology, 92*:123–127, 1972. Copyright © 1972 by the American Psychological Association. Reprinted by permission. Figure 5.19 – French, J.D. "The reticular formation." *Scientific American, 196*:54–60, 1957. Figure 5.20 – Davies, D.R., & Krkovic, A. "Skin-conductance, alpha-activity, and vigilance." *American Journal of Psychology, 78*:304–306, 1965. Reprinted by permission of the University of Illinois Press. Figure 5.21 – O'Hanlon. J.F. "Adrenaline and noradrenaline: Relation to performance in a visual vigilance task." *Science, 150*:507–509, 1965. Copyright © 1965 by the American Association for the Advancement of Science. Figure 5.22 – Krulewitz, J.E. Warm, J.S., & Wohl, T.H. "Effects of shifts in the rate of repetitive stimulation on sustained attention." *Perception & Psychophysics, 18*:245–249, 1975.

Figure 6.5 – Woodworth, R.S., & Schlosberg H., *Experimental psychology.* Copyright © 1954 by Holt, Rinehart and Winston. Reprinted by permission of Holt, Rinehart and Winston. Figure 6.6 – Beck, J. "The perception of surface color." *Scientific American, 233*:62–75, 1975. Figure 6.7 – Hurvich, L.M., [7] Jameson, D. "The perception of brightness and darkness." Copyright © 1966 by Allyn & Bacon. Reprinted by permission. Figures 6.9 and 6.10 – Ratliff, F.R. *Mach bands: Quantitative studies on neural networks in the retina.* Copyright © 1965 by Holden-Day. Reprinted by permission. Figure 6.11 – Jameson, D., & Hurvich, L.M. "Complexities of perceived brightness." *Science, 133*:174–179, 1961. Copyright © 1961 by the American Association for the Advancement of Science. Figure 6.12 – Hurvich, L.M., & Jameson, D. *The perception of brightness and darkness.* Copyright © 1966 by Allyn & Bacon. Reprinted by permission. Figure 6.13 – Gilchrist, A.L. "Perceived lightness depends on perceived spatial arrangement." *Science, 195*:185–187, 1977. Copyright © 1977 by the American Association for the Advancement of Science. Figure 6.18 – Leibowitz, H.W. "Sensory, learned, and cognitive mechanisms of size perception." *Annals of the New York Academy of Sciences, 188*:47–62, 1971. Figure 6.19 – Holway, A.H., & Boring, E.G. "Determinants of apparent visual size with distance variant." *American Journal of Psychology, 54*:21–37, 1941. Reprinted by permission of the University of Illinois Press. Figure 6.20 – Rock, I., & Ebenholtz, S. "The relational determination of perceived size." *Psychological Review, 66*:387–401, 1959. Copyright © 1959 by the American Psychological Association. Reprinted by permission. Figure 6.22 – Leibowitz, H.W. "Sensory, learned, and cognitive mechanisms of size perception." *Annals of the New York Academy of Sciences, 188*:47–62, 1971. Figure 6.24 – Boring, E.G. "The moon illusion." *American Journal of Physics, 11*:55–60, 1943. Figure 6.25 – Kaufman, L., & Rock, I. "The moon illusion." *Science, 136*:953–961, 1962. Copyright © 1962 by the American Association for the Advancement of Science. Figure 6.26 – Riggs, L.A., Ratliff, F., Cornsweet, U.C., & Cornsweet, T.N. "The disappearance of steadily fixalated visual test objects." *Journal of the Optical Society of America, 53*:495–501, 1953. Figure 6.27 – Pritchard, R.M. "Stabilized images on the retina." *Scientific American, 204*:72–78, 1961. Figure 6.28 – McKinney, J.P. "Disappearance of luminous designs." *Science, 140*:403–404, 1963. Copyright © 1963 by the American Association for the Advancement of Science.

Table 7.1 – Barlow, H.B., Narasimhan, R., & Rosenfeld, A. "Visual pattern analysis in machines and animals." *Science, 177*:567–575, 1972. Copyright © 1972 by the American Association for the Advancement of Science. Figure 7.1 – Escher, M.C. "Fish and fowl." By permission of the "Escher Foundation – Haags Gemeentemuseum – The Hague." Figure 7.2 – Attneave, F. "Some informational aspects of visual perception." *Psychological Review, 61*:183–193, 1954. Copyright © 1954 by the American Psychological Association. Reprinted by permission. Figure 7.3 – Woodworth, R.S., & Schlosberg, H. *Experimental psychology* (Revised edition) Copyright © 1954 by Holt, Rinehart and Winston. Reprinted by permission of Holt, Rinehart and Winston. Figure 7.4 – Dowling, J.E., & Boycott, B.B. "Organization of the primate retina: Electron microscopy." Proceedings of the Royal Society, London, 1966. Reprinted by permission. Figure 7.6 – Brown, J.L., & Mueller, C.G. "Brightness discrimination and brightness contrast" in C.H. Graham (Ed.) *Vision and visual perception.* Copyright © 1965 by John Wiley & Sons, Inc. Reprinted by permission. Figure 7.8 – Ratliff, F. "Mach bands and observed brightness curves." *Scientific American, 226*:10, 1972. Figure 7.11 – Ratliff, R., & Hartline, H.K. "The response of limulus optic nerve fibers to patterns of illumination on the receptor mosaic." *Journal of General Physiology, 42*:1241–1255, 1959. Figure 7.12 – MacKay, D.M. "Interactive processes in visual perception." In W.A. Rosenblith (Ed.) *Sensory communication.* Reprinted by permission of M.I.T. Press, Cambridge, Massachusetts. Figure 7.13 – Thompson, R.F. *Introduction to biopsychology.* Copyright © 1973 by Albion Publishing Co. Reprinted by permission. Figure 7.14 – Bruce, R.L. *Fundamentals of physiological psychology.* Copyright © 1977 by Holt, Rinehart and Winston. Reprinted by permission. Figures 7.15 and 7.16 – Hubel, D.H., & Wiesel, T.N. "Receptive fields, binocular interaction and functional architecture in the cat's visual cortex." *Journal of Physiology, 160*:106–154, 1962. Reprinted by permission of Cambridge University Press. Figure 7.17 – McCollough, C. "Color adaptation of edge-detectors in the human visual system." *Science, 149*:1115–1116, 1965. Copyright © 1965 by the American Association for the Advancement of Science. Figure 7.18 – Riggs, L.A. "Curvature as a feature of pattern vision." *Science, 181*:1070–1072, 1973. Copyright © 1973 by the American Association for the Advancement of Science. Figure 7.19 – Blakemore, C., & Sutton, P. "Size adaptation: A new aftereffect." *Science, 166*:245–247, 1969. Copyright © 1969 by the American Association for the Advancement of Science. Figure 7.20 – Uttal, W.R. "Masking of alphabetic character recognition by dynamic visual noise (DVN)." *Perception & Psychophysics, 6*:121–128, 1969. Figure 7.21 – Weisstein, N. "Neural symbolic activity: A psychophysical measure." *Science, 168*:1489–1491, 1970. Copyright © 1970 by the American Association for the Advancement of Science. Figure 7.22 – Coren, S. "Subjective contours and apparent depth." *Psychological Review, 79*:359–367, 1972. Copyright © 1972 by the American Psychological Association. Reprinted by permission. Figure 7.23 – Gregory, R.L. "Cognitive contours." *Nature, 238*:51–52, 1972. Figure 7.25 – Breitmeyer, B. G. & Ganz, L. "Implications of sustained and transient channels for theories of visual pattern-masking, saccadic suppression, and information processing." *Psychological Review, 83*:1–36, 1976. Copyright © 1976 by the American Psychological Association. Reprinted by permission. Figure 7.27 – Dember, W.N., & Purcell, D.G. "Recovery of masked visual targets by inhibition of the masking stimulus." *Science, 157*:1335–1336, 1967. Copyright © 1967 by the American Association for the Advancement of Science. Figure 7.34 – Reprinted by permission of the author. Figure 7.35 – Woodworth, R.S., & Schlosberg, H. *Experimental psychology* (Revised edition) Copyright © 1954 by Holt, Rinehart and Winston. Reprinted by permission of Holt, Rinehart and Winston. Figure 7.36 – From *Principles of gestalt psychology* by K. Koffka, Copyright © 1935 by Harcourt Brace Jovanovich, Inc.; renewed 1963 by Elizabeth Koffka. Reproduced by permission of the publishers. Figure 7.37 – Beck, J. "Effect of orientation, and of shape similarity on perceptual grouping." *Perception & Psychophysics, 1*:300–302, 1966. Figure 7.38 – Olson, R.K., & Attneave, F. "What variables produce similarity grouping?" *American Journal of Psychology, 83*:1–21, 1970. Reprinted by permission of the University of Illinois Press. Figure 7.39 – Hochberg, J.E., & McAlister, E. "A quantitative approach to figural 'goodness'" *Journal of Experimental Psychology, 46*:361–364, 1953. Copyright © 1953 by the American Psychological Association. Reprinted by permission. Figure 7.40 – Garner, W.R., & Clement, D.E. "Goodness of pattern and pattern uncertainty." *Journal of Verbal Learning and Verbal Behavior, 2*:446–452,

1963. Figure 7.41—Attneave, F., & Arnoult, M.D. "The quantitative study of shape and pattern perception." *Psychological Bulletin, 53:*452–471, 1956. Copyright © 1956 by the American Psychological Association. Reprinted by permission. Figure 7.42—Reprinted with permission of author and publisher from Brown. D.R., Hitchcock, L., Jr., & Michels, K.M. "Quantitative studies in form perception: An evaluation of the role of selected stimulus parameters in the visual discrimination performance of human subjects." *Perceptual and Motor Skills, 14:*519–529, 1962. Figure 7.43—Shepard, R.N., & Metzler, J. "Mental rotation of three-dimensional objects." *Science, 171:*701–703, 1971. Copyright © 1971 by the American Association for the Advancement of Science. Figure 7.44—Rock, I. *Orientation and form.* Reprinted by permission of Academic Press. Figure 7.45—Franks, J.J., & Bransford, J.D. "Abstraction of visual patterns." *Journal of Experimental Psychology, 90:*65–74, 1971. Copyright © 1971 by the American Psychological Association. Reprinted by permission.

Figure 8.1—Woodworth, R.S., & Schlosberg, H. *Experimental psychology* (Revised edition) Copyright © 1954 by Holt, Rinehart and Winston. Reprinted by permission of Holt, Rinehart and Winston. Figure 8.2—Woodworth, R.S. *Experimental psychology.* Copyright © 1938 by Holt, Rinehart and Winston. Reprinted by permission of Holt, Rinehart and Winston. Figures 8.3 and 8.4—From Burian, H.M., & von Noorden, G.K. *Binocular vision and ocular motility.* Copyright © 1974 the C.V. Mosby Co. Reprinted by permission. Figure 8.6—Geldard, F.A. *Fundamentals of psychology.* Copyright © 1962 by John Wiley & Sons, Inc. Reprinted by permission. Figure 8.7—Julesz, B. "Binocular depth perception without familiarity cues." *Science, 145:*356–362, 1964. Copyright © 1964 by the American Association for the Advancement of Science. Figures 8.8 and 8.9—Gibson, J.J. *The perception of the visual world.* Copyright © 1950 by James J. Gibson. Reprinted by permission of Houghton Mifflin Co. Figures 8.10 and 8.11—Photos by Leventhal. Figure 8.12—Gibson, J.J. *The perception of the visual world.* Copyright © 1950 by James J. Gibson. Reprinted by permission of Houghton Mifflin Co. Figure 8.13—Epstein, W. "Perceived depth as a function of relative height under three background conditions." *Journal of Experimental Psychology, 72:*335–338, 1966. Copyright © 1966 by the American Psychological Association. Reprinted by permission. Figure 8.15—King, E.A., 1976, *Space geology: An introduction.* Copyright © 1976 by John Wiley & Sons, Inc. Reprinted by permission. Figure 8.18—Dember, W.N., & Jenkins, J.J. *General psychology: Modeling behavior and experience.* Reprinted by permission of author. Figure 8.19—Reprinted by permission of the author. Figure 8.20—Behar, I., & Bevan, W. "The perceived duration of auditory and visual intervals: Cross-modal comparison and interaction." *American Journal of Psychology, 74:*17–26, 1961. Reprinted by permission of the University of Illinois Press. Figure 8.21—Hicks, R.E., Miller, G.W., Gaes, G. & Bierman, K. "Concurrent processing demands and the experience of time-in-passing." *American Journal of Psychology, 90:*431–446, 1977. Reprinted by permission of the University of Illinois Press. Figure 8.22—Leibowitz, H.W., Johnson, C.A., & Isabelle, E. "Peripheral motion detection and refractive error." *Science, 177:*1207–1208, 1972. Copyright © 1972 by the American Association for the Advancement of Science. Figure 8.24—Day, R.H. *Human perception.* Copyright © 1969 by John Wiley & Sons, Inc. Reprinted by permission. Figure 8.26—Harker, G.S. "A saccadic suppression explanation of the Pulfrich phenomenon." *Perception & Psychophysics, 2:*423–426, 1967. Figure 8.27—Matin, L., & MacKinnon, G.E. "Autokinetic movement: Selective manipulation of directional components by image stabilization." *Science, 143:*147–148, 1964. Copyright © 1964 by the American Association for the Advancement of Science. Figures 8.28 and 8.29—Reprinted with the permission of the author and publisher from Geldard, F.A., *Sensory saltation: Melastability in the perceptual world.* Hillsdale, N.J.: Lawrence Erlbaum Associates, 1975.

Figure 9.1—Reprinted by permission of the publisher from Street, R.F. A gestalt completion test. (New York: Teachers College Press, 1931). Figure 9.3—Boring, E.G. "A new ambiguous figure." *American Journal of Psychology, 42:*444–445, 1930. Reprinted by permission of the University of Illinois Press. Figure 9.4—Reicher, G.M. "Perceptual recognition as a function of meaningfulness of stimulus material." Technical Report No. 7, 1968. University of Michigan, Human Performance Center. Figure 9.5—Weisstein, N., & Harris, C.S. "Visual detection of line seg-

518   Acknowledgements

ments: An object-superiority effect." *Science, 186:*752–755, 1974.   Copyright © 1974 by the American Association for the Advancement of Science.

Figure 10.1—Fox, C. "Modification of perceptual and associative response by subthreshold stimuli," Reprinted by permission of the author. Figures 10.2 and 10.3—Schafer, R., & Murphy, G. role of autism in a visual figure-ground relationship." *Journal of Experimental Psychology, 32:*335–343, 1943. Copyright © 1943 by the American Psychological Association. Reprinted by permission.

Figure 11.2—Fantz, R., Ordy, J.M., & Udelf, M.S. "Maturation of pattern vision in infants during the first six months." *Journal of Comparative and Physiological Psychology, 55:*907–917, 1962. Copyright © 1962 by the American Psychological Association. Reprinted by permission. Figure 11.3—Berlyne, D.E., "The influence of albedo and complexity of stimuli on visual fixation in the human infant." *British Journal of Psychology, 49:*315–318, 1958. By permission of the author and the British Psychological Society. Figure 11.4—Berlyne, D.E. "The influence of complexity and change in visual figures on orienting responses." *Journal of Experimental Psychology, 55:*289–296, 1958. By permission of the author and the American Psychological Association.

Figures 11.5, 11.6, and 11.7—Munsinger, H., & Kessen, W. "Uncertainty, structure, and preference." *Psychological Monographs, 78:*7–16, 1964. Copyright © 1964 by the American Psychological Association. Reprinted by permission.

Figure 12.1—Lashley, K.S. "The mechanism of vision: I. A. method for rapid analysis of pattern vision in the rat." *Journal of Genetic Psychology, 37:*453–460, 1930. Figure 12.2—Fantz, R.L. "The origin of form perception." *Scientific American, 204:*66–72, 1961. Figure 12.5—Gibson, E., & Walk, R. "The visual cliff." Used by permission of William Vandivert and *Scientific American.* Figure 12.6—Held, R., & Hein, A. "Movement produced stimulation in the development of visually guided behavior." *Journal of Comparative and Physiological Psychology, 56:*872–876, 1963. Copyright © 1963 by the American Psychological Association. Reprinted by permission. Figure 12.7—Ames, A. "Visual perception and the rotating trapezoidal window." *Psychological Monographs, 65:*30, 1951. Copyright © 1951 by the American Psychological Association. Reprinted by permission. Figure 12.8—Ittelson, W.H., & Kilpatrick, F.P. "Experiments in perception." *Scientific American, 185:*50–55, 1951. Reproduced by permission of the authors and the *Scientific American.*

Name Index

Subject Index